LAWRENCE HENRY GIPSON

AUTHOR

JARED INGERSOLL: A STUDY OF AMERICAN LOYALISM
IN RELATION TO BRITISH COLONIAL GOVERNMENT

STUDIES IN CONNECTICUT COLONIAL TAXATION

THE MORAVIAN INDIAN MISSION ON WHITE RIVER

LEWIS EVANS

THE COMING OF THE REVOLUTION, 1763–1775

THE BRITISH EMPIRE BEFORE THE AMERICAN REVOLUTION

THE BRITISH EMPIRE
BEFORE THE AMERICAN REVOLUTION
VOLUME XIV

A BIBLIOGRAPHICAL GUIDE
TO THE HISTORY OF THE BRITISH EMPIRE
1748–1776

THE BRITISH EMPIRE
BEFORE THE AMERICAN REVOLUTION
VOLUME XIV

A
BIBLIOGRAPHICAL GUIDE

TO THE HISTORY OF
THE BRITISH EMPIRE, 1748-1776

BY

LAWRENCE HENRY GIPSON

MCMLXIX
ALFRED A. KNOPF
NEW YORK

THIS IS A BORZOI BOOK
PUBLISHED BY ALFRED A. KNOPF, INC.

FIRST EDITION

Library of Congress Catalog Card Number: 58-9670

This volume is dedicated to

LAWRENCE QUINCY MUMFORD,

*Librarian of Congress, and his
Efficient Staff.*

Preface

WHEN the bibliography for this series on the British Empire before the American Revolution was initially contemplated, it was my plan to restrict it to the primary and secondary works cited in the respective volumes. However, over forty years have lapsed between the time I drew up my prospectus in 1926 and the publication of Volume XIII in the late spring of 1967. During this extended period many valuable works have come from the press to which no reference could be made either in the text or footnotes of the series. It is certainly a matter of the first importance that the student, coming fresh to the study of the period covered by the series, 1748-1776, should be brought in touch not only with the original authorities and earlier secondary works concerned with these years but with the most recent studies bearing upon them. This is the purpose of the present volume and of a final volume (a guide to the manuscript sources) that is to follow. It rests upon the assumption that no historical work is definitive and that what has been presented in the preceding thirteen volumes of the series somewhat in detail is but one student's interpretation of the course of events within the British Empire during the quarter of a century preceding the Declaration of Independence by the Thirteen North American Colonies. Doubtless for many years to come there will be those who will be eagerly searching for still more light on the problems that faced the Old British Empire during this relatively brief but important period of time. It is my hope that these bibliographical guides will be of some assistance to that end.

The present volume does not claim to be an exhaustive listing of all printed works of importance bearing on the history of the British Empire between 1748 and 1776. For example, more attention is given to the

Empire beyond Great Britain rather than to the mother country. Nevertheless, it is doubtless the most complete bibliography specifically concerned with this brief epoch in the life of the Empire. Again, the chief emphasis has been placed on those works dealing with constitutional, political (including diplomatic and other foreign relations), and economic developments; in addition, sources covering those aspects of social history that illustrate broadly the way of life of people living within the Empire have been included. But the purely intellectual histories and studies, as well as those concerned with the great fields of the fine arts and aesthetics, are not stressed in this volume, as these approaches were not the focus of the series. To have attempted to be comprehensive would have made it impossible to keep the contents of the successive volumes of the text closely integrated or within manageable limits.

It is true that when the first three volumes of this series made their appearance in 1936, the prospectus listed among the future volumes one on cultural developments within the Empire. For many sound reasons I reluctantly decided to forgo the writing of such a volume. The purely cultural approach to the period, it now seems to me, should be treated as a distinct enterprise, indeed, as a major one. That it may be fittingly undertaken by some scholar prepared and with the leisure to do justice to the theme is my earnest hope.

Because the present volume, along with the one to follow, will, I trust, be of service not only to the advanced history scholar but also to others, I have provided the titles of a number of books, pamphlets, and articles that might not otherwise have been included. In doing so it was my thought that some of this material not only is more apt to be found in the college or public library of moderate size than are many of the works designed to meet the needs of the specialist, but better serves as an introduction to the field for the beginner.

While I am indebted to certain of my colleagues for preliminary advice and some of the groundwork during the earliest stages of planning these bibliographical volumes, I shall perhaps best acquit my debt to them by not including their names here, since I ultimately chose another direction for my plan of work. However, I must not fail to make the fullest acknowledgment to Mr. Neal T. Neamand, a graduate student who devoted his full-time energies as my assistant on this project for a period of over a year. His contribution to the work at hand has been of inestimable value. He was supported by the following graduate students who gave part-time assistance: Mr. Jerome J. Gillen, Mr. Lyle Rosenberger, Mr. Leslie Rudnyanszky, and Miss Jean M. Stauffer, as well as by Mrs. Evelyn J. Evans, my full-time secretary. When it became necessary for Mr. Neamand to relinquish his work on the project, Miss Stauffer took up the supervision of the completion of the volume. She has carried on with a high degree of efficiency and dedication to the task. I cannot praise too highly the work done by this small staff under the careful direction first of Mr. Neamand and thereafter of Miss Stauffer. Nor must I omit mention of the continuing support of Lehigh University, which has made the writing of the series possible in a number of ways, including the housing of the project within the walls of the University Library with its excellent resources and competent, always cooperative staff.

Finally, whatever defects may become apparent in the volume must rest on my own shoulders, since every detail of it has come under my final scrutiny. Although great care has been exercised at every stage of the work, it is too much to hope that no publication deserving recognition has been overlooked or that no errors will be detected. Indeed, I shall be grateful to my fellow historians for any information that may lead to corrections and addenda for use in future printings of the volume so as to make is at useful as possible to the inquiring student.

Lawrence Henry Gipson

The Library
Lehigh University
Bethlehem, Pennsylvania
February 13, 1968

Contents

CHAPTER III

IRELAND

CHAPTER IV

THE NORTH AMERICAN COLONIES

Part I: General

CHAPTER V

THE NORTH AMERICAN COLONIES

Part II: The Individual Colonies

CHAPTER VI

THE WEST INDIES
AND OTHER ATLANTIC POSSESSIONS

CHAPTER VII

INDIA

CHAPTER VIII

AFRICA, GIBRALTAR, AND MINORCA

CHAPTER IX

GEOGRAPHICAL AIDS

THE BRITISH EMPIRE
BEFORE THE AMERICAN REVOLUTION
VOLUME XIV

A BIBLIOGRAPHICAL GUIDE
TO THE HISTORY OF THE BRITISH EMPIRE
1748–1776

CHAPTER I

The Empire: General

A. BIBLIOGRAPHICAL AIDS

Since most of the bibliographical aids and bibliographies are listed under particular portions of the British Empire, 1748-1776, only certain works sufficiently comprehensive are placed in the list that immediately follows. Further, as a concluding volume of this series will be concerned with manuscript materials, guides to such collections are therefore not included here unless these contain specific information bearing upon the series.

AMERICAN HISTORICAL ASSOCIATION: *Guide to Historical Literature* (George Frederick Howe, *et al.*, eds., New York, 1961). Also available are the earlier editions of this work, appearing with the same title in 1931 and 1949, under the general editorship of George Matthew Dutcher.

ANDREWS, CHARLES M.: "List of Commissions, Instructions, and Additional Instructions Issued to the Royal Governors and Others in America," American Historical Association, *Annual Report, 1911* (2 vols., Washington, D.C., 1913), I: 393-528. Much useful data embodied in this report is made available to the student.

BESTERMAN, THEODORE: *A World Bibliography of Bibliographies* . . . (4th edn., 5 vols., Lausanne, Switzerland, c. 1965).

Bibliography in Economics for the Oxford Honour School of Philosophy, Politics and Economics (2nd edn., 2 vols., Oxford, 1960).

BROMLEY, JOHN SELWYN, and A. GOODWIN: *A Select List of Works on Europe and Europe Overseas, 1715-1815* . . . (Oxford, 1956).

CALLENDER, GEOFFREY A. R.: *A Bibliography of Naval History*, Historical Association, *Publications*, Nos. 58 and 61 (2 pts., London, 1924-5).

CHARLES, DOROTHY, and BEA JOSEPH, eds.: *The Bibliographic Index: A Cumulative Bibliography of Bibliographies, 1937-1942* (New York, 1945).

CRAVEN, WESLEY FRANK: "Historical Study of the British Empire," *Journal of Modern History*, VI (1934), 40-69.

[DAVENPORT, FRANCES GARDINER]: "Materials for English Diplomatic History, 1509-1783. Calendared in the Reports of the Historical Manuscripts Commission with Reference to Similar Materials in the British Museum," Historical Manuscripts Commission, *Eighteenth Report* (London, 1917), Appendix II, 357-402.

FREWER, LOUIS BENSON, ed.: *Bibliography of Historical Writings Published in Great Britain and the Empire, 1940-1945* (Oxford, 1947).

International Bibliography of Historical Sciences (32 vols.+, Paris, 1926-63+).

International Bibliography of Political Science (14 vols.+ [Paris], 1953-1965+).

KITSON CLARK, G., and G. R. ELTON: *Guide to Research Facilities in History in the Universities of Great Britain and Ireland* (Cambridge, Eng., 1963; 2nd edn., 1965).

LEWIN, PERCY E.: *Subject Catalogue of the Library of the Royal Empire Society . . .* (4 vols., London, 1930-7).

MORRELL, W. P.: *British Overseas Expansion and the History of the Commonwealth: A Select Bibliography. Helps for Students of History,* No. 63 (London, 1961). This was first published in 1929 as No. 46 of the Historical Association, *Publications,* and was revised by A. P. Newton and reissued as No. 130 in the same series in 1944.

PARGELLIS, STANLEY, and D. J. MEDLEY: *Bibliography of British History: The Eighteenth Century, 1714-1789* (Oxford, Eng., 1951).

PENSON, LILLIAN M., ed.: "Bibliography," *The Cambridge History of the British Empire, Volume I: The Old Empire from the Beginnings to 1783* (Cambridge, Eng. & New York, 1929), 823-88.

RAGATZ, LOWELL JOSEPH, comp.: *A List of Books and Articles on Colonial History and Overseas Expansion Published in the United States [1900-1930]* (London, 1939). The years 1931-1935 have also been covered in two publications (London [1934-6]).

ROYAL HISTORICAL SOCIETY: *Writings on British History, 1934 . . . A Bibliography of Books and Articles on the History of Great Britain from about 450 A.D. to 1914. Published During the Year . . . With an Appendix Containing a Select List of Publications . . . on British History since 1914 . . .* (Alexander T. Milne, ed., 8 vols.+, London, 1937-60).

WINKS, ROBIN W., ed.: *The Historiography of the British Empire-Commonwealth: Trends, Interpretations, and Resources* (Durham, N.C., 1966). Included in this collection are 21 historiographical essays and an up-to-date bibliography.

B. PRINTED SOURCE MATERIALS

1. Government and related documents

BELOFF, MAX, ed.: *The Debate on the American Revolution, 1761-1783* (London, 1949). This is volume I of *The British Political Tradition,* and it contains extracts from numerous important pamphlets and speeches of both British and American writers.

BRIGHAM, CLARENCE SAUNDERS, ed.: *British Royal Proclamations Relating to America, 1603-1783,* American Antiquarian Society, *Transactions,* XII (Worcester, Mass., 1911).

CHALMERS, GEORGE: *Opinions of Eminent Lawyers on Various Points of English Jurisprudence, Chiefly Concerning the Colonies, Fisheries, and Commerce of Great Britain* (2 vols., London, 1814).

GALLOWAY, JOSEPH. *Anglo-American Union: Joseph Galloway's Plans to Preserve the British Empire, 1774-1788* by Julian P. Boyd (Philadelphia, 1941). Includes the various plans of union proposed by Galloway. See also "Joseph Galloway to Charles Jenkinson on the British Constitution," Julian P. Boyd, ed., *Pennsylvania Magazine of History and Biography,* LXIV (1940), 516-44; and *The Examination of Joseph Galloway by a Committee of the House of Commons* (Thomas Balch, ed., Philadelphia, 1855).

GREENE, JACK P., ed.: "'A Dress of Horror': Henry McCulloh's Objections to the Stamp Act," *Huntington Library Quarterly,* XXVI (1963), 253-62.

KEITH, ARTHUR BERRIEDALE, ed.: *Selected Speeches and Documents on British Colonial Policy, 1763-1917* (2 vols., London & New York, 1933).

[KNOX, WILLIAM]: "A Project for Imperial Reform: 'Hints Respecting the Settlement for Our American Provinces,' 1763," Thomas C. Barrow, ed., *William and Mary Quarterly,* XXIV (1967), 108-26.

LABAREE, LEONARD WOODS, ed.: *Royal Instructions to British Colonial Governors, 1670-1776* (2 vols., London & New York, 1935).

LEE, WILLIAM: *Letters of William Lee, Sheriff and Alderman of London, Commercial Agent of the Continental Congress in France, and Minister to the Courts of Vienna and Berlin, 1766-1783* (W. C. Ford, ed., 3 vols., Brooklyn, N. Y., 1891).

LORDS COMMISSIONERS FOR TRADE AND PLANTATIONS: *Journal of the Commissioners for Trade and Plantations from April 1704 to May 1782: Preserved in the Public Record Office* (14 vols., London, 1920-38).

MC CULLOH, HENRY: *Miscellaneous Representations Relative to Our Concerns in America: Submitted in 1761 to the Earl of Bute . . . Now First Printed from the Original Ms. . . .* (London [1905]; rep. in W.K. Boyd's *Some Eighteenth Century Tracts . . . ,* pp. 141-56). A memorial of McCulloh to Bute providing an excellent example of the ideals of the new British imperialism.

PITT, WILLIAM: *Correspondence of William Pitt, when Secretary of State, with Colonial Governors and Military and Naval Commissioners in America* (Gertrude S. Kimball, ed., 2 vols., London & New York, 1906). See also "Chatham and the Representation of the Colonies in the Imperial Parliament," Basil Williams, ed., *English Historical Review,* XXII (1907), 756-8, which prints a plan for giving the colonies a voice in Parliament.

PRIVY COUNCIL: *Acts of the Privy Council of England: Colonial Series [1613-1783]* (William Lawson Grant and James Munro, eds., 6 vols., Hereford, Eng., 1908-12).

SECRETARY OF STATE: *Calendar of Home Office Papers of the Reign of George III, 1760-1775* (Joseph Redington and Richard Arthur Roberts, eds., 4 vols., London, 1878-99).

WIGHT, MARTIN, ed.: *British Colonial Constitutions, 1947* (Oxford, 1952).

2. *Published contemporary writings: Chronologically arranged*

[OLDMIXON, JOHN]: *The British Empire in America: Containing the History of the Discovery, Settlement, Progress, and State of the British Colonies on the Continent and Islands of America . . . [1710-1740]* (2nd edn., 2 vols., London, 1741 [1st edn., 1708]). Chiefly useful for background material.

BICKHAM, GEORGE: *The British Monarchy: Or a New Chorographical Description of All the Dominions Subject to the King of Great Britain, Comprehending the British Isles, the American Colonies . . .* (London, 1748).

[MC CULLOH, HENRY]: *A Miscellaneous Essay concerning the Course Pursued by Great Britain in the Affairs of Her Colonies: With Some Observations on the Great Importance of Our Settlements in America and the Trade Thereof* (London, 1755).

[MITCHELL, JOHN]: *The Contest in America between Great Britain and France with Its Consequences and Importance Giving an Account of the Views and Designs of the French, with the Interests of Great Britain and the Situation of the British and French Colonies in All Parts of America . . .* (London, 1757). The authorship of this pamphlet has also been attributed to Dr. Oliver Goldsmith.

RUTHERFORD, JOHN: *The Importance of the Colonies to Great Britain: With Some Hints towards Making Improvements to Their Mutual Advantage . . .* (London, 1761).

ENTICK, JOHN: *The General History of the Late War: Containing Its Rise, Progress, and Event in Europe, Asia, Africa, and America . . .* (5 vols., London, 1763).

The Operations of the Allied Army under the Command of . . . Ferdinand

Duke of Brunswic[k] and Lune[n]berg During the Greatest Part of the Six Campaigns . . . [1757-1762] By an Officer Who Served in the British Forces (London, 1764).

POWNALL, THOMAS: *The Administration of the Colonies . . .* (1st edn., London, 1764; 5th edn., 2 vols., 1774). The first edition was published anonymously.

HUSKE, JOHN: "John Huske's Proposals for Improving American Trade, 1765," William L. Sachse, ed., Colonial Society of Massachusetts, *Publications*, XLII (*Transactions, 1952-1956*), 474-87. This is the printing of a manuscript entitled "Observations on the Trade of Great Britain to Her American Colonies, & on Their Trade to Foreign Plantations: With a Plan for Retreiving, Extending & Securing thereof."

[BOLLAN, WILLIAM]: *A Succinct View of the Origin of Our Colonies: With Their Civil State . . . Whereby the Nature of the Empire Established in America and the Errors of Various Hypotheses Formed thereupon May be Clearly Understood . . .* (London, 1766).

[GOLDSMITH, J.]: *The Present State of the British Empire in Europe, Asia, Africa, and America: Containing a Concise Account of Our Possessions in Every Part of the Globe* (London, 1767).

[MITCHELL, JOHN]: *The Present State of Great Britain and North America with Regard to Agriculture, Population, Trade and Manufactures, Impartially Considered . . .* ([London, 1767]; rep., New York, 1965).

[MASÈRES, FRANCIS, and WILLIAM HEY]: *Considerations of the Expediency of Admitting Representatives from the American Colonies into the British House of Commons* (London, 1770).

WYNNE, JOHN HUDDLESTONE: *A General History of the British Empire in America: Containing an Historical, Political, and Commercial View of the English Settlements: Including all the Countries in North-America and the West-Indies Ceded by the Peace of Paris* (2 vols., London, 1770).

[LA TROBE, BENJAMIN]: *A Succinct View of the Missions Established among the Heathen by the Church of the Brethren, or Unitas Fratrum. In a Letter to a Friend* (London, 1771).

[CAMPBELL, JOHN]: *Political Essays Concerning the Present State of the British Empire . . .* (London, 1772). The pamphlet has also been attributed to Arthur Young.

MANTE, THOMAS: *The History of the Late War in North-America and the Islands of the West-Indies: Including the Campaigns of MDCCLXIII and MDCCLXIV against His Majesties Indian Enemies* (London, 1772).

BERNARD, FRANCIS: *Select Letters on the Trade and Government of America: and the Principles of Law and Polity Applied to the American Colonies . . .* (London, 1774).

ENTICK, JOHN, and JAMES WEBSTER: *An Historical and Geographical Description of the British Empire: Containing a State of the Kingdoms . . . Dependent upon the Crown of Great Britain in Every Part of the World . . .* (4 vols., London [1774]). The work is a manual of information about Britain and the Empire.

[GALLOWAY, JOSEPH]: *Political Reflections on the Late Colonial Governments in Which Their Original Constitutional Defects Are Pointed Out and Shewn to Have Naturally Produced the Rebellion Which . . . Terminated in the Dismemberment of the British Empire . . .* (London, 1783).

PINKERTON, JOHN: *A General Collection of the Best and Most Interesting Voyages and Travels in all Parts of the World . . .* (17 vols., London, 1808-14; 6 vols., Philadelphia, 1810-12).

C. SECONDARY WORKS

The following list contains the titles of studies which especially stress *imperial* relations between the units of the Old British Empire.

ADAMS, RANDOLPH G.: *Political Ideas of the American Revolution: Britannic-American Contributions to the Problem of Imperial Organization, 1765 to 1775* (1st edn., Durham, N.C., 1922; 3rd edn., w/commentary by Merrill Jensen, New York, 1958).

ANDERSON, JAMES S. M.: *The History of the Church of England in the Colonies and Foreign Dependencies of the British Empire* (3 vols., London, 1845-56).

ANDREWS, CHARLES MC LEAN: "Anglo-French Commercial Rivalry, 1700-1750: The Western Phase," *American Historical Review*, XX (1914-1915), 539-56, 761-80.

————: *The Colonial Background of the American Revolution: Four Essays in American Colonial History* (New Haven, Conn., 1924; rev. edn., 1931).

————: *The Colonial Period* (New York, 1912). A small but very important volume concerned with the imperial theme.

————: "The Royal Disallowance," American Antiquarian Society, *Proceedings*, n. ser., XXIV (1914), 342-62.

ARCHENHOLZ, JOHANN WILHELM VON: *Geschichte des Siebenjährigen Krieges in Deutschland von 1756 bis 1763* (Berlin, 1793; numerous other editions).

BARROW, THOMAS C.: *Trade and Empire: The British Customs Service in Colonial America, 1660-1775* (Cambridge, Mass., 1967).

BASYE, ARTHUR HERBERT: *The Lords Commissioners of Trade and Plantations . . . 1748-82, Yale Historical Publications: Miscellany*, XIV (New Haven, Conn., 1925).

———: "The Secretary of State for the Colonies, 1768-1782," *American Historical Review*, XXVIII (1922-3), 13-23.

BEER, GEORGE LOUIS: *British Colonial Policy, 1754-1765* (New York, 1907; reiss., 1922).

———: *The Commercial Policy of England toward the American Colonies*, Columbia University, *Studies in History, Economics, and Public Law*, No. 2 (New York, 1893; rep., 1948).

BINING, ARTHUR CECIL: *British Regulation of the Colonial Iron Industry* (London & Philadelphia, 1933).

BROWN, GERALD SAXON: *The American Secretary: The Colonial Policy of Lord George Germain, 1775-1778* (Ann Arbor, Mich., c. 1963).

BROWN, WELDON A.: *Empire or Independence: A Study in the Failure of Reconciliation, 1774-1783* ([Pineville], La., 1941).

BUCK, PHILIP W.: *The Politics of Mercantilism* (New York [1942]).

CHANNING, EDWARD: "The Navigation Laws," American Antiquarian Society, *Proceedings*, n. ser., VI (1889-90), 160-79.

CLARK, DORA MAE: "The American Board of Customs, 1767-1783," *American Historical Review*, XLV (1939-40), 777-806.

———: *British Opinion and the American Revolution, Yale Historical Publications: Miscellany*, XX (New Haven, Conn., 1930).

CLARKE, MARY PATTERSON: "The Board of Trade at Work," *American Historical Review*, XVII (1911-12), 17-43.

———: *Parliamentary Privilege in the American Colonies, Yale Historical Publications: Miscellany*, XLIV (New Haven, Conn., 1943).

CLIVE, JOHN, and BERNARD BAILYN: "England's Cultural Provinces: Scotland and America," *William and Mary Quarterly*, 3rd ser., XI (1954), 200-13.

CNATTINGIUS, HANS: *Bishops and Societies: A Study of Anglican Colonial and Missionary Expansion, 1698-1850* (London, 1952).

COUPLAND, REGINALD: *The American Revolution and the British Empire* (London, 1930).

DAVIDSON, PHILIP: *Propaganda and the American Revolution, 1763-1783* (Chapel Hill, N.C., 1941).

DICKERSON, OLIVER M.: *American Colonial Government, 1696-1765: A Study of the British Board of Trade in Its Relation to the American Colonies—Political, Industrial, Administrative* (Cleveland, O., 1912).

———: "The Attempt to Extend British Customs Controls over Intercolonial Commerce by Land," *South Atlantic Quarterly*, L (1951), 361-8.

———: *The Navigation Acts and the American Revolution* (Philadelphia, 1951).

———: "Use Made of the Revenue from the Tax on Tea," *New England Quarterly*, XXXI (1958), 232-43.

DORN, WALTER LOUIS: *Competition for Empire, 1740-1763* (London & New York, 1940).

DOTY, JOSEPH DAVID: *The British Admiralty Board as a Factor in Colonial Administration, 1689-1763* (Philadelphia, 1930).

DOW, GEORGE FRANCIS: *Slave Ships and Slaving*, Marine Research Society, Publications, No. 15 (Salem, Mass., 1927).

EAST, ROBERT A.: "The Business Entrepreneur in a Changing Colonial Economy, 1763-1795," *Journal of Economic History, Supplement*, VI (1946), 16-27.

EGERTON, HUGH E.: *The Causes and Character of the American Revolution* (Oxford, Eng., 1923).

——: *A Short History of British Colonial Policy* (London, 1897; 2nd edn., 1908; 9th edn., rev. by A.P. Newton, 1932).

EISENSTADT, SHMUEL NOAH: *The Political Systems of Empires* (London, c. 1963).

ERICSON, FREDERIC J.: *The British Colonial System and the Question of Change of Policy on the Eve of the American Revolution* (Chicago, Ill., 1943). See also: "British Motives for Expansion in 1763: Territory, Commerce, or Security?" Michigan Academy of Science, Arts, and Letters, *Papers*, XXVII (1942), 581-94.

ERNST, JOSEPH ALBERT: "Genesis of the Currency Act of 1764: Virginia Paper Money and the Protection of British Investments," *William and Mary Quarterly*, 3rd ser., XXII (1965), 33-74.

FARNIE, D. A.: "The Commercial Empire of the Atlantic, 1607-1783," *Economic History Review*, 2nd ser., XV (1962-3), 205-18.

FIELDHOUSE, DAVID K.: *The Colonial Empires: A Comparative Survey from the Eighteenth Century, Delacourt World History*, XXIX (New York, 1967).

FRIEDENWALD, HERBERT: *The Declaration of Independence: An Interpretation and an Analysis* (London & New York, 1904).

GIPSON, LAWRENCE HENRY: "The American Revolution as an Aftermath of the Great War for the Empire, 1754-1763," *Political Science Quarterly*, LXV (1950), 86-104.

——: *The Coming of the American Revolution, 1763-1775* (New York, 1954).

——: *Jared Ingersoll: A Study of American Loyalism in Relation to British Colonial Government, Yale Historical Publications: Miscellany*, VIII (New Haven, Conn., 1920).

GOODWIN, A., ed.: *The New Cambridge Modern History, Vol. VIII: The American and French Revolution, 1763-93* (Cambridge, Eng., 1965). See particularly the following chapters: Chapter II, "Populations, Commerce and Economic Ideas" by H. J. Habakkuk; Chapter VII, "Armed Forces and the Art of War, Part I: Navies" by Christopher Lloyd; Chapter VIII, "European Relations with Asia and Africa, Part I: Relations with India" by K. A. Ballhatchet and "Part II: Relations with Africa" by J. D. Hargreaves; Chapter XV, "Social and Psychological Foundations of the Revolutionary Era" by R. R. Palmer; Chapter XVI, "American Independence and Its Constitutional Aspects" by Max Beloff; Chapter XVIII, "American Independence in Its American Context: Social and Political Aspects: Western Expansion" by Esmond Wright; and Chapter XIX, "The Beginnings of Reform in Great Britain: Imperial Problems: Politics and Administration, Economic Growth" by W. R. Ward.

GRANT, ALASTAIR MAC PHERSON: *General James Grant of Ballindalloch, 1720-1806; Being an Account of His Long Services in Flanders, America and the West Indies: With Original Letters* (London [1930]).

GRANT, WILLIAM L.: "Canada versus Guadeloupe: An Episode of the Seven Years' War," *American Historical Review*, XVII (1911-12), 735-43.

GRAY, LEWIS CECIL: "The Market Surplus Problem of Colonial Tobacco," *Agricultural History*, II (1928), 1-34.

———: "Economic Efficiency and Competitive Advantages of Slavery under the Plantation System," *ibid.*, IV (1930), 31-47.

GREENE, EVARTS BOUTELL: *The Provincial Governor in the English Colonies of North America, Harvard Historical Studies*, VII (New York, 1898).

HALL, HUBERT: "Chatham's Colonial Policy," *American Historical Review*, V (1899-1900), 659-75.

HAMILTON, J. TAYLOR: *A History of the Church Known as the Moravian Church, or the Unitas Fratrum or the Unity of the Brethren, during the Eighteenth and Nineteenth Centuries*, Moravian Historical Society, *Transactions*, VI (Bethlehem, Pa., 1900). This work has been revised and up-dated by Bishop Hamilton and his son, Kenneth G. Hamilton (also now a bishop) with the title *History of the Moravian Church: The Renewed Unitas Fratrum, 1722-1957* (Bethlehem, Pa., 1967).

HARLOW, VINCENT TODD: *The Founding of the Second British Empire, 1763-1793* (2 vols., London, 1952-64; vol. II was completed by F. McC. Madden).

HARPER, LAWRENCE AVERELL: *The English Navigation Laws: A Seventeenth-Century Experiment in Social Engineering* (New York, 1939). An important work.

———: "Mercantilism and the American Revolution," *Canadian Historical Review*, XXIII (1942), 2-15; reprinted in Edward N. Saveth, ed.: *Understanding the American Past: American History and Its Interpretation* (Boston, 1954), pp. 101-14.

HAZELTINE, HAROLD DEXTER: "Appeals from Colonial Courts to the King in

Council: With Special Reference to Rhode Island," American Historical Association, *Annual Report,* (Washington, D.C., 1895), pp. 299-350.

HAZELTON, JOHN HAMPDEN: *The Declaration of Independence: Its History* (New York, 1906).

HEATON, HERBERT: *The Economics of Empire,* James Ford Bell Lectures, No. 3 ([Minneapolis, Minn.], 1966).

HECKSCHER, ELI FILIP: *Mercantilism . . .* (Mendel Shapiro, trans., 2 vols., London, 1935).

HERTZ, GERALD BERKELEY: *British Imperialism in the Eighteenth Century* (London, 1908).

————: *The Old Colonial System,* Victoria University, *Publications: Historical Series,* No. 3 (Manchester, Eng., 1905). Both of these works are dated but still useful.

HINKHOUSE, FRED J.: *The Preliminaries of the American Revolution as Seen in the English Press, 1763-1775,* Columbia University, *Studies in History, Economics, and Public Law,* No. 276 (New York, 1926).

HOLDSWORTH, WILLIAM: *A History of English Law* (16 vols., London, 1903-65). The student should consult volumes X and XI, concerned with the eighteenth century, especially the sections on the executive, Parliament, Ireland, the colonies, and India. It may be noted that after the death of Professor Holdsworth in 1945, two of his colleagues at Oxford, Professors A. L. Goodhart and H. G. Hanbury, brought out volumes XIII and XVI of this great series on the English law.

HOON, ELIZABETH E.: *The Organization of the English Customs System, 1696-1786* (London & New York, 1938).

HOTBLACK, KATE: *Chatham's Colonial Policy: A Study in the Fiscal and Economic Implications of the Colonial Policy of the Elder Pitt* (London & New York, 1917).

————: "The Peace of Paris, 1763," Royal Historical Society, *Transactions,* 3rd ser., II (1908), 235-67.

INNIS, HAROLD ADAMS: *The Cod Fisheries: The History of an International Economy* (New Haven, Conn. & Toronto, 1940).

JOHNSON, VICTOR L.: "Internal Financial Reform or External Taxation: Britain's Fiscal Choice, 1763," American Philosophical Society, *Proceedings,* XCVIII (1954), 31-7.

KELLER, HANS GUSTAV: "Pitts 'Provisional Act for Settling the Troubles in America': Das Problem der Einheit des Britischen Reiche," *Historische Zeitschrift,* No. 194 (1962), 599-645.

KEITH, ARTHUR BERRIEDALE: *Constitutional History of the First British Empire* (Oxford, Eng., 1930).

KNORR, KLAUS E.: *British Colonial Theories, 1570-1850* (Toronto, 1944, w/foreword by H. A. Innis).

KOEBNER, RICHARD: *Empire* (London, 1961).

LABAREE, LEONARD WOODS: "The Nature of American Loyalism," American Antiquarian Society, *Proceedings*, n. ser., LIV (1944), 15-58.

————: *Royal Government in America: A Study of the British Colonial System before 1783*, Yale Historical Publications: Miscellany, VI (London & New Haven, Conn., 1930).

————: "The Royal Governors of New England," Colonial Society of Massachusetts, *Publications*, XXXII (*Transactions*, 1933-1937), 120-31.

LANE, FREDERICK C.: "Oceanic Expansion: Force and Enterprise in the Creation of Oceanic Commerce," *Journal of Economic History, Supplement* X (1950), 19-31.

LAWSON, MURRAY G.: *Fur: A Study in English Mercantilism, 1700-1775*, University of Toronto, *Studies: History and Economic Series*, IX (Toronto, 1943).

LINDSAY, J. O., ed.: *The New Cambridge Modern History, Vol. VII: The Old Regime, 1713-63* (Cambridge, Eng., 1957). Among the important contributions directly concerned with British developments and expansion for the period under review are the following: Chapter II, "The Growth of Overseas Commerce and European Manufacture" by C. H. Wilson; Chapter V, "The Enlightenment" by A. Cobban; Chapter VII, "Monarchy and Administration" by J. O. Lindsay and W. R. Brock; Chapter VIII, "The Armed Forces and the Art of War" by Eric Robson; Chapter IX, "International Relations" by J. O. Lindsay; Chapter XI, "England" by W. R. Brock; Chapter XIX, "The Diplomatic Revolution" by D. B. Horn; Chapter XX, "The Seven Years' War" by Eric Robson; Chapter XXI, "The Development of the American Communities, Sec. 2: North America" by Frank Thistlethwaite; Chapter XXII, "Rivalries in America" by J. H. Parry and Frank Thistlethwaite; Chapter XXIII, "Rivalries in India" by C. C. Davies; and Chapter XXIV, "Economic Relations in Africa and the Far East" by J. Gallacher and Victor Purcell.

MC CORMAC, EUGENE IRVING: *Colonial Opposition to Imperial Authority during the French and Indian War*, University of California, *Publications in History*, I (Berkeley, Calif., 1911).

MC ILWAIN, CHARLES HOWARD: *The American Revolution: A Constitutional Interpretation* (New York, 1923).

MAC INNES, CHARLES MALCOLM: *The Early English Tobacco Trade* (London, 1926).

MACKENZIE-GRIEVE, AVERIL: *The Last Years of the English Slave Trade: Liverpool, 1750-1807* (London, 1941).

MACKESY, PIERS: *The War for America, 1775-1783* (Cambridge, Mass., 1964).

MARSHALL, PETER: "The First and Second British Empires: A Question of Demarcation," *History*, XLIX (1964), 13-23.

MAURO, F.: "Towards an 'Intercontinental Model': European Overseas Expansion between 1500 and 1800," *Economic History Review*, 2nd ser., XIV (1961-2), 1-17.

MILLER, GENEVIEVE: "Smallpox Inoculation in England and America: A Reappraisal," *William and Mary Quarterly*, 3rd ser., XIII (1956), 476-92.

MORTON, W. L.: "The Local Executive in the British Empire, 1763-1828," *English Historical Review*, LXXVIII (1963), 436-57.

MULLET, CHARLES F.: *Colonial Claims to Home Rule (1764-1775): An Essay in Imperial Politics* (Columbia, Mo., 1927; rep. from University of Missouri, *Studies: A Quarterly of Research*, II: No. 4).

——: "English Imperial Thinking, 1764-1783," *Political Science Quarterly*, XLV (1930), 548-79.

——: *Fundamental Law and the American Revolution, 1760-1776*, Columbia University, *Studies in History, Economics, and Public Law*, No. 385 (New York, 1933).

NETTELS, CURTIS P.: "The Place of Markets in the Old Colonial System," *New England Quarterly*, VI (1933), 491-512.

——: "British Mercantilism and the Economic Development of the Thirteen Colonies," *Journal of Economic History*, XII (1952), 105-114.

NEWTON, ARTHUR PERCIVAL: *The British Empire to 1783: Its Political, Social, and Economic Development* (London, 1935).

O'CONOR, NORREYS JEPHSON: *A Servant of the Crown in England and in North America, 1756-1761: Based upon the Papers of John Appy, Secretary and Judge Advocate of His Majesty's Forces* (London & New York, 1938).

OLSON, ALISON GILBERT: "The British Government and Colonial Union, 1754," *William and Mary Quarterly*, 3rd ser., XVII (1960), 22-34.

OSGOOD, HERBERT L.: "England and the Colonies," *Political Science Quarterly*, II (1887), 440-69.

PALMER, JOHN: *The Practice on Appeals from the Colonies to the Privy Council* (London, 1831).

PALMER, ROBERT R.: *The Age of the Democratic Revolution: A Political History of Europe and America, 1760-1800* (2 vols., Princeton, N. J., 1959-65).

PARES, RICHARD: "The Economic Factors in the History of the Empire," *Economic History Review*, 1st ser., VII (1936-7), 119-44.

PASCOE, CHARLES FREDERICK: *Two Hundred Years of the S.P.G.: An Historical Account of the Society for the Propagation of the Gospel in Foreign Parts, 1701-1900* (2 vols., London, 1901).

ROBBINS, CAROLINE: "'When It Is That Colonies May Turn Independent': An Analysis of the Environment and Politics of Francis Hutcheson (1694-1746)," *William and Mary Quarterly*, 3rd ser., XI (1954), 214-51.

ROBINSON, HOWARD: *The Development of the British Empire* (Boston & New York, 1922).

ROSE, J. HOLLAND, A. P. NEWTON, and E. A. BENIANS, eds.: *The Cambridge History of the British Empire, Vol. I: The Old Empire from the Beginnings to 1783* (Cambridge, Eng. & New York, 1929). Among the chapters by various historians, especial notice should be taken of the following: Charles McLean Andrews: "Chapter IX: The Acts of Trade," and "Chapter XIV: The Government of the Empire, 1660-1763"; J. Ewing: "Chapter XXI: The Constitution and the Empire: From Bacon to Blackstone"; Cecil Headlam: "Chapter XIII: The Development of the Colonies under the First Georges, 1714-1755," and "Chapter XXII: [Part] I: Imperial Reconstruction," and "[Part] II: The Constitutional Struggle with the American Colonies, 1765-1776"; A. Pearce Higgins: "Chapter XIX: The Growth of International Law: Maritime Rights and Colonial Titles, 1648-1763"; J. F. Rees: "Chapter XX: Mercantilism and the Colonies"; and J. Holland Rose: "Chapter XVIII: [British] Sea Power and Expansion, 1660-1763."

RUSSELL, ELMER BEECHER: *The Review of American Colonial Legislation by the King in Council,* Columbia University, *Studies in History, Economics, and Public Law,* No. 155 (New York, 1915).

RYERSON, EDGERTON: *Loyalists of America and Their Times: From 1620-1816* (2 vols., Toronto, 1880).

SAVELLE, MAX: *The Origins of American Diplomacy: The International History of Angloamerica, 1492-1763* (New York, c. 1967).

SCHAEFER, ARNOLD DIETRICH: *Geschichte des Siebenjährigen Kriegs* (2 vols., Berlin, 1867-74).

SCHLESINGER, ARTHUR MEIER: "Colonial Appeals to the Privy Council," *Political Science Quarterly,* XXVIII (1913), 279-97, 433-50.

————: *The Colonial Merchants and the American Revolution, 1763-1776,* Columbia University, *Studies in History, Economics, and Public Law,* No. 182 (London & New York, 1918).

————: *Prelude to Independence: The Newspaper War on Britain* (New York, 1958).

SCHLOTE, WERNER: *British Overseas Trade from 1700 to the 1930's* . . . (W. O. Henderson & W. H. Chaloner, trans., Oxford, Eng., 1952).

SCHUYLER, ROBERT LIVINGSTON: "British Imperial Theory and American Territorial Policy: A Suggested Relationship," American Philosophical Society, *Proceedings,* XCVII (1953), 317-31.

————: *The Fall of the Old Colonial System: A Study in British Free Trade, 1770-1870* (London & New York, 1945).

————: *Parliament and the British Empire: Some Constitutional Controversies Concerning Imperial Legislative Jurisdiction* (New York, 1929).

SEELEY, JOHN ROBERT: *The Expansion of England* (London, 1883).

SHERIDAN, RICHARD B.: "The British Credit Crisis of 1772 and the American Colonies," *Journal of Economic History*, XX (1960), 161-86.

———: "The Commercial and Financial Organization of the British Slave Trade, 1750-1807," *Economic History Review*, 2nd ser., XI (1958-9), 249-63.

SINCLAIR, J.: *The History of the Public Revenue of the British Empire . . . with a Review of the Financial Administration of . . . W. Pitt* (3rd edn., 3 vols., London, 1803-4).

SIOUSSAT, ST. GEORGE L.: "The Breakdown of the Royal Management of Lands in the Southern Provinces, 1773-1775," *Agricultural History*, III (1929), 67-98.

SMITH, HUBERT LLEWELLYN: *The Board of Trade* (London & New York, 1928); especially "William III's Board of Trade, 1698-1782," pp. 15-35, which provides a brief discussion of the Board's relations with the American colonies.

SMITH, JOSEPH HENRY: *Appeals to the Privy Council from the American Plantations* (New York, 1950).

SMITH, PAUL H.: *Loyalists and Redcoats: A Study in British Revolutionary Policy* (Chapel Hill, N. C., 1964). A study of British policy relating to the role of the loyalists in the colonies.

SOSIN, JACK M.: *Agents and Merchants: British Colonial Policy and the Origins of the American Revolution, 1763-1775* (Lincoln, Neb., 1965).

———: "Imperial Regulation of Colonial Paper Money, 1764-1773," *Pennsylvania Magazine of History and Biography*, LXXXVIII (1964), 174-98.

SPANGENBERG, AUGUSTUS GOTTLIEB: *An Account of the Manner in Which the . . . United Brethren Preach the Gospel and Carry on Their Missions among the Heathen* (London, 1788; Philadelphia, 1789).

SPECTOR, MARGARET MARION: *The American Department of the British Government, 1768-1782*, Columbia University, *Studies in History, Economics, and Public Law*, No. 466 (New York, 1940).

STOKES, ANTHONY: *A View of the Constitution of the British Colonies in North-America and the West Indies at the Time the Civil War Broke Out on the Continent of America . . .* (London, 1783).

TATHAM, WILLIAM: *An Historical and Practical Essay on the Culture and Commerce of Tobacco* (London, 1800).

TAUSSIG, CHARLES WILLIAM: *Rum, Romance, and Rebellion* (New York, 1928). Concerned with the triangular trade and the influence of rum on colonial New England.

THOMAS, ROBERT PAUL: "A Quantitative Approach to the Study of the Effects of British Imperial Policy upon Colonial Welfare: Some Preliminary Findings," *Journal of Economic History*, XXV (1965), 615-38.

THOMPSON, HENRY PAGET: *Into All Lands: The History of the Society for the Propagation of the Gospel in Foreign Parts, 1701-1950* (London, 1951).

THOMSON, MARK ALMÉRAS: *The Secretaries of State, 1681-1782* (Oxford, Eng., 1932).

TIELKE, JOHANN GOTTLIEB: *Beyträge zur Krieges-Kunst und Geschichte des Krieges von 1756 bis 1763* (2nd edn., 6 vols., Freyberg, 1776-86).

TYLER, MOSES COIT: "The Party of the Loyalists in the American Revolution," *American Historical Review*, I (1895-6), 24-45.

UBBELOHDE, CARL: *The Vice-Admiralty Courts and the American Revolution* (Chapel Hill, N.C., 1960).

VAN ALSTYNE, RICHARD W.: *Empire and Independence: The International History of the American Revolution* (New York, c. 1965).

VAN TYNE, CLAUDE HALSTEAD: *The Causes of the War of Independence: Being the First Volume of the Founding of the American Republic* (Boston & New York, 1922).

———: *The Loyalists in the American Revolution* (New York, 1902; rep. 1929 & 1959).

WADDINGTON, RICHARD: *La Guerre de Sept Ans: Histoire Diplomatique et Militaire* (5 vols., Paris, 1899-1914).

WALKER, ERIC ANDERSON: *The British Empire: Its Structure and Spirit, 1497-1953* (2nd edn., ext., Cambridge, Eng. & Cambridge, Mass., 1956).

WARD, A. W., G. W. PROTHERO, and STANLEY LEATHES, eds.: *The Cambridge Modern History, Vol. VI: The Eighteenth Century* (Cambridge, Eng., 1909). Among the important contributions directly concerned with British imperial expansion during the period under examination are the following: Chapter IX, "The Seven Years War" by Emil Daniels; Chapter XI, "The Reversal of Alliances and the Family Compact" by Jean Lemoine; Chapter XIII, "Great Britain (1756-93)" by Alfred Comyn Lyall and P. E. Roberts; and Chapter XXIII, "English Political Philosophy in the Seventeenth and Eighteenth Centuries" by Arthur Lionel Smith.

WASHBURNE, GEORGE ADRIAN: *Imperial Control of the Administration of Justice in the Thirteen American Colonies, 1684-1776*, Columbia University, *Studies in History, Economics, and Public Law*, No. 238 (New York, 1923).

WICKWIRE, FRANKLIN B.: *British Subministers and Colonial America, 1763-1783* (Princeton, N. J., 1966).

WIGHT, MARTIN: *The Development of the [Colonial] Legislative Council, 1606-1945*, Nuffield College, *Studies in Colonial Legislatures*, I (London, 1946). Only Chapter I, pp. 23-40, is relevant to the period.

WILLIAMSON, ARTHUR SHELBURN: "Credit Relations between Colonial and

English Merchants in the 18th Century," *Abstracts in History . . . 1922-1930*, University of Iowa: *Studies in the Social Sciences*, X (1932), 47-60.

WILLIAMSON, JAMES A.: *A Short History of British Expansion* (1st edn., London, 1922; rev. ed., 2 vols., 1943-5; 4th edn., 1953-4).

WILSON, CHARLES HENRY: *Mercantilism*, Historical Association, *General Series*, No. 37 (London, 1958). See also Wilson's articles: "The Other Face of Mercantilism," Royal Historical Society, *Transactions*, 5th ser., IX (1959), 81-100; "'Mercantilism': Some Vicissitudes of an Idea," *Economic History Review*, 2nd ser., X (1957-8), 181-8; and "Treasure and Trade Balances: The Mercantilist Problem," *ibid.*, 2nd ser., II (1949), 152-61.

WRONG, GEORGE M.: "The Background of the Loyalist Movement, 1763-1783," Ontario Historical Society, *Papers*, XXX (1934), 171-80.

WYNDHAM, HUGH ARCHIBALD: *The Problems of Imperial Trusteeship: The Atlantic and Slavery* (London, 1935).

D. MAPS AND CARTOGRAPHICAL AIDS

For maps pertaining to specific parts of the British Empire, 1748-1776, see the map section in each chapter.

BICKHAM, GEORGE: *British Monarchy: Or a New Chorographical Description of All the Dominions Subject to the King of Great Britain . . .* (2 vols., London, 1743; 1754). The first edition was done by the elder Bickham and subsequent editions were done by the younger Bickham.

BOWLES, CARINGTON: *North America and the West Indies: A New Map, wherein the British Empire and Its Limits According to the Definitive Treaty of Peace in 1763 Are Accurately Described* (London [1763]).

DUNN, SAMUEL: *A Map of the British Empire in North America* (London, 1774).

JEFFERYS, THOMAS: *Chart of the Atlantic Ocean, with the British, French & Spanish Settlements in North America, and the West Indies; as Also on the Coast of Africa.* In Jefferys: *A General Topography of North America and the West Indies*, No. 13.

LUCAS, C. P., HUGH E. EGERTON, and JOHN D. ROGERS: *A Historical Geography of the British Colonies* (7 vols. in 11, Oxford, Eng., 1900-11).

THE GREAT WAR FOR THE EMPIRE IN MAPS

The chronological arrangement of maps in the following sections is according to event rather than date of publication.

North America: Chronologically arranged

1 7 5 3

DRAPER, JOHN: *How Washington Rode to Fort Le Boeuf in 1753.* A modern map in Douglas Southall Freeman's *George Washington: A Biography,* I: 279.

A Map of the Western Parts of the Colony of Virginia [1753]. This interesting English map to be found in the Archives de la Marine in Paris lays down the route used by George Washington on his memorable trip to Fort Le Boeuf in 1753. In S. K. Stevens and D. H. Kent: *Wilderness Chronicles of Northwestern Pennsylvania,* p. 106.

Part of North America Shewing the British, French, & Spanish Possessions at the Opening of the War. In Corbett: *England in the Seven Years' War,* I: opp. p. 14.

1 7 5 4

DRAPER, JOHN: *The Region of Washington's "Campaign of 1754."* A modern map in Freeman: *George Washington: A Biography,* I: 364.

STOBO, ROBERT: *Fort Du Quesne, 1754.* In Jefferys: *A General Topography of North America and the West Indies,* No. 45.

1 7 5 5

Braddock's Route, A.D. 1755. Drawn by Middleton. In Sargent: *History of an Expedition against Fort Du Quesne, 1755 . . . ,* opp. p. 198.

GILLELAND, J. C.: *Plan of the Battle at Braddock's Defeat: At the Beginning of the Action, July 9th, 1755. The Form of the Ground Drawn on the Spot* [1830]. In *ibid.,* p. 354.

MACKELLAR, PATRICK: *Monongahela, July 8th, 1755.* In Fortescue: *A History of the British Army,* II: opp. p. 338.

[ORME, ROBERT]: *Six Plans of the Different Dispositions of the English Army under the Command of the Late Gen. Braddock, in North America.* In Jefferys: *A General Topography of North America and the West Indies,* Nos. 46-52. Among these plans is *A Plan of the Field of Battle and Distribution of the Troops as They Were on the March* [against Fort Du Quesne] *at the Time of the Attack on the 9th of July 1755.* These maps have been reproduced in Sargent: *The History of an Expedition against Fort Du Quesne, 1755 . . . ,* pp. 218, 282, 316, 336, 337, and 352.

Fort Beauséjour and Adjacent Country Taken Possession of by Colonel Monckton in June, 1755. In Mante: *History of the Late War in North America . . . ,* p. 17.

JEFFERYS, THOMAS, sculp.: *A Prospective View of the Battle Fought near Lake George on the 8th of Sept. 1755, between 2000 English with*

250 Mohawks under the Command of Genl. Johnson & 2500 French & Indians under the Command of Genl. Deskau in which the English were Victorious. In Jefferys: *A General Topography of North America and the West Indies,* No. 37; see also O'Callaghan: *Documentary History of the State of New York,* IV: opp. p. 169.

1 7 5 6

DRAPER, JOHN: *Washington's Tour of the Frontier, 1756.* A modern map in Freeman: *George Washington: A Biography,* II: 215.

ROCQUE, JOHN, sculp.: *Plan and Profile of Retrenched Work round Herkemer's House at ye German Flats, 1756.* In [John and] Ann Rocque: *A Set of Plans and Forts in America . . . ,* No. 27.

1 7 5 7

DRAPER, JOHN: *Approximate Locations of the Virginia Frontier Forts.* A modern map in Freeman: *George Washington: A Biography,* II: 229.

ROCQUE, JOHN, sculp.: *A Plan of Fort William Henry and the English Camps & Intrenchment, with the French Different Camps and Attacks thereon . . . .* In [John and] Ann Rocque: *A Set of Plans and Forts in America . . . ,* No. 21.

SEALE, R. W., sculp.: *A New and Accurate Map of the Present War in North America.* In the *Universal Magazine,* XX (1757), opp. p. 193.

1 7 5 8

Colonial Wars. Operations in New York, 1755-1769. This map contains an inset: *Capture of Louisbourg, 2 June-27 July 1758.* In Vincent J. Esposito: *The West Point Atlas of American Wars* (2 vols., New York, 1959), I: No. 2.

DRAPER, JOHN: *Forbes's Line of Advance, 1758.* A modern map of the campaign against Fort Duquesne in Freeman: *George Washington . . . ,* II: 325.

JEFFERYS, THOMAS: *The Landing on Cape Breton Island at Gabarus Bay and the Siege of Louisbourg, 1758.* In Jefferys: *The Natural and Civil History of the French Dominion in America . . . .*

———: *Plan of the Town and Fortifications of Montreal or Ville Marie in Canada* (London, 1758). In Jefferys: *A General Topography of North America and the West Indies,* No. 20.

KITCHIN, THOMAS: *Attack on Louisbourg, the Fleet Commanded by the Honb^{le} Adm^{l}. Boscawen, the Army by Major Genl. Amherst.* In Mante: *History of the Late War in North-America . . . ,* opp. p. 109.

Map of the Braddock and Forbes Roads [to Fort Duquesne]. In Sparks, ed.: *The Writings of George Washington,* II: opp. p. 38.

PHINN, T., sculp.: *A Plan of the Country from the Landing Place with the Encampments and Marches of the Troops under Major General Abercrombie at the Attack of Ticonderoga.* In the *Scots Magazine,* XX (1758), btwn. pp. 436-7.

Plan of Fort Frontenac. In [John and] Ann Rocque: *A Set of Plans and Forts in America . . . ,* No. 28.

Plan of the City and Fortress of Louisburg with the Attacks. In [John, and] Ann Rocque: *ibid.,* No. 24.

A Plan of the Fort and Bay of Frontenac, with the Adjacent Countries. In the *London Magazine,* XXVII (1758), 552.

A Plan of the Town and Fort of Carillon at Ticonderoga, with the Attack Made by the British Army . . . 1758. In Jefferys: *A General Topography of North America and the West Indies,* No. 36.

POUCHET, M.: *Plan of Fort Niagara.* In O'Callaghan: *Documents Relative to the Colonial History of the State of New York,* X: 976.

ROCQUE, JOHN, sculp.: *Plan of the New Fort & Redoubts at Crown Point [before 1759].* In [John and] Ann Rocque: *A Set of Plans and Forts in America . . . ,* Nos. 16-17.

1 7 5 9

Colonial Wars. Operations in Canada, 1759-1760. This map contains an inset: *Operations against Quebec. June-September 1759.* In Esposito: *The West Point Atlas of American Wars,* I: No. 3.

Plan of Fort Niagara, with Its Environ. In [John and] Ann Rocque: *A Set of Plans and Forts in America . . . ,* No. 10.

JEFFERYS, THOMAS, sculp.: *An Authentic Plan of the River St. Lawrence from Sillery to the Fall of Montmorenci with the Operations of the Siege of Quebec under the Command of Vice Adm. Saunders & Major Gen. Wolfe, down to the 5th of Sept. 1759 . . . .* In Jefferys: *A General Topography of North America and the West Indies,* No. 17.

SKINNER, H.: *Plan of Ticonderoga [&] A Perspective View of Lake George.* In the *Universal Magazine,* XXV (1759), opp. p. 266.

SMYTH, HERVEY: *A View of the Fall of Montmorenci and the Attack Made by General Wolfe on the French Entrenchment near Beauport with the Grenadiers of the Army, July 31, 1759 . . . .* (London, 1760). William Elliot was the engraver of this map which may be found among the Library of Congress maps.

A View of the Landing Places above the Town of Quebec, Describing the Assault of the Enemys Post on the Banks of the River St. Lawrence, with a Distant View of the Action between the British and French Armys on the Hauteurs d'Abraham Sept^br. 13, 1759. Cap. Her'y Smyth, delin; Francis Swain, pinxit; P. C. Canet, sculp't. (n.p., [1759]). Library of Congress maps.

1 7 6 0

KITCHIN, THOMAS: *A Plan of the Attack upon Fort Levi [1760].* In Mante: *History of the Late War in North America . . . ,* opp. p. 303.

Map to Illustrate the Montreal Campaign [1760]. In Corbett: *England in the Seven Years' War . . . ,* II: opp. p. 105. A modern map.

A Particular Map to Illustrate Gen. Amherst's Expedition to Montreal, with a Plan of the Town and Draught of ye Island. In the *Gentleman's Magazine,* XXX (1760), opp. p. 460.

1 7 6 1

SEALE, R. W.: *An Accurate Map of Canada with the Adjacent Countries, Exhibiting the Late Seat of War between the English & French in Those Parts.* In the *Universal Magazine,* XXVIII (1761), opp. p. 57.

1 7 6 2

KITCHIN, THOMAS: *Plan of the Retaking Newfoundland, The Squadron Commanded by Lord Colville, the Troops by Lieut. Col. Amherst.* In Mante: *History of the Late War in North America . . . ,* opp. p. 467.

The West Indies: Chronologically arranged

West Indies in 1756. In Corbett: *England in the Seven Years' War,* I: opp. p. 351.

1 7 5 9

Guadeloupe: The Army Commanded by Major General Barrington; the Fleet by Commodore Moore. In Mante: *History of the Late War in North America . . . ,* opp. p. 163.

Plan of the Attack against Fort Levis, now Fort George, at Point à Pitre on the Island of Guadeloupe: by a Squadron of His Majesty's Ships of War Detached from Com. Moore & Commanded by Capt. Wm. Harman; Feb. 14, 1759 . . . (London, 1760). In Jefferys: *A General Topography of North America and the West Indies,* No. 98.

Plan of the General Attack upon the Island of Guadeloupe, Jan. 23rd, 1759. ([London, 1759]). In the *London Magazine,* XXVIII (1759), opp. p. 287.

1 7 6 2

LODGE, JOHN: *Attack on the Havanna: The Army Commanded by the Right Hon*[ble]*. The Earl of Albemarle; the Fleet by Sir George*

Pococke, K. B. In Mante: *History of the Late War in North-Amer-ica* . . . , opp. p. 397.

A New & Accurate Map of the Seat of the Late War in the West Indies, with a Plan of the City and Harbour of Havannah. In Entick: *The History of the Late War* . . . , IV: opp. p. 142.

Plan of the City and Harbour of Havanna. In the *Gentleman's Magazine,* XXXII (1762), 416.

A Plan of the Straights of Bahama, through which the Expedition Fleet Was Conducted in the Year 1762 against the Havanna. In the *London Magazine,* XXXII (1763), opp. p. 40.

A Plan of the Town and Citadel of Fort Royal in Martinico, the Last Landing Place of Our Army and Country through which It Marched to the Attack. In the *London Magazine,* XXXI (1762), opp. p. 208.

Ireland

GIBSON, JOHN, sculp.: *A Correct Chart of the Irish Sea &c. Exhibiting a View of the Several Islands & Bays Lately Touched at by M. Thurot in His Attempt upon Ireland.* In the *Gentleman's Magazine,* XXX (1760), opp. p. 108.

Europe: General

Map of North Western Europe to Illustrate the Disturbance of Continental Strategy by British Action from the Sea. A modern map in Corbett: *England in the Seven Years' War* . . . , I: opp. p. 476.

A New and Correct Chart of the Late War on the Coasts of France, Spain, and Portugal with the Adjacent Coasts and Islands. In Entick: *The General History of the Late War* . . . , opp. p. 284.

A New and Correct Chart of the Seat of War on the Coasts of France, Spain, Portugal, and Italy. . . . In the *Annual Register* . . . *for the Year 1763* (London, 1764), at the end of the volume.

Europe: France

The Bombardment of Havre de Grace, July 5th, 1759, with an inset *Plan of Havre de Grace.* In the *Gentleman's Magazine,* XXIX (1759), opp. p. 343.

Carte de la Normandie et de la Bretagne. In Bellin: *Le Petit Atlas Maritime* . . . , V: No. 21.

Carte de l'Isle de Belle-Isle. In *ibid.,* V: No. 71.

Chart to Illustrate Hawke's Blockade, 1759 . . . . In Corbett: *England in the Seven Years' War* . . . , II: opp. p. 1.

The Coast of Brittany between St. Malo's and Cancale Bay where the

English Army Landed, June 1758. In the *Gentleman's Magazine*,
  XXVIII (1758), 288.
*A Map of the Coast of France from Rochelle & Rochfort with the Islands
  of Ree, Oleron & Aix*. In the *Gentleman's Magazine*, XXVII (1757),
  492.
Le Morbihan et Presqu'Isle de Quiberon. In Bellin: *Le Petit Atlas Mari-
  time . . .* , V: No. 69.
Plan of Dunkirk . . . in 1757. In the *Gentleman's Magazine*, XXXIII
  (1763), opp. p. 108.
Rade de Dunkerque et ses Bancs. In Bellin: *Le Petit Atlas Maritime . . .* ,
  V: No. 5.
Rochefort and the Basque Roads, 1757. In Corbett: *England in the Seven
  Years' War . . .* , opp. p. 197.
St. Malo et Environs. In Bellin: *Le Petit Atlas Maritime . . .* , V: No. 44.

Europe: Germany

1 7 5 6

BOWEN, EMANUEL: *An Accurate Map of the North West Part of Germany
  Indicating the Possessions of the Elector of Hanover in 1756*. Map
  Room, New York Public Library.

1 7 5 7

*Map of That Part of Hannover where the Battle between the Duke of
  Cumberland and Marshall D'Étrees Was Fought, July 25, 26, 27*.
  In the *Gentleman's Magazine*, XXVII (1757), 376.
*A Map of the Upper Saxony Comprehending That Part of Germany
  which is the Present Seat of War*. In the *Gentleman's Magazine*,
  XXVII (1757), 574.

1 7 5 8

*A Map of the Rhine between Wessel & Dusseldorp [sic] Shewing the
  Country round Crevelt Where the Battle Was Fought between the
  Allied & French Armies, June 23*. In *ibid.*, XXVIII (1758), 330.

1 7 5 9

*A Compleat Map of Germany, Comprehending in One View the Differ-
  ent Seats of the Present War [1759]*. In *ibid.*, XXIX (1759), opp.
  p. 1.
*A Map of the Seat of War on the Rhine and Parts Adjacent in Germany,
  1759*. In *ibid.*, p. 188.

A Map of that Part of Westphalia in Which the French Army where [sic] Defeated Aug. 1, 1759. In *ibid.*, p. 386.

Minden, Aug. 1st, 1750. The Action at the Moment of the Attack of the British Infantry. In Fortescue: *A History of the British Army,* II: opp. p. 494.

1 7 5 6 - 6 3

A Map of the Seat of War in Germany, Etc., Shewing the Places where and at what Times the Battles Were Fought . . . during the Late War. In Entick: *The General History of the Late War . . .* , II: opp. p. 72.

WALKER, EMERY, sculp.: *North West Germany, 1756-63.* This map shows, among other things, the possessions of the Electors of Hanover in relation to those of other German princes, and indicates places that were important in the history of this period. In Fortescue: *A History of the British Army,* II: at end of volume.

Mediterranean Sea

The Siege of Fort St. Philip in 1755 Indicating the Position of the French Artillery Brought to Bear on the Fortifications. In Waddington: *Louis XV et le Renversement des Alliances.*

The Three Phases of the Naval Battle off Minorca. In Mahan: *The Influence of Sea Power upon History, 1660-1783,* opp. p. 265. This is a diagram of three positions assumed by Admiral Byng in the battle.

India

A New & Accurate Map of the Seat of the Late War on the Coast of Coromandel, in the East Indies, 1763. In Entick: *The History of the Late War . . .* , I: opp. p. 347.

Plassey, June 23rd, 1757. In Fortescue: *A History of the British Army,* II: opp. p. 474.

Wandewash, 22nd Jan. 1760. In *ibid.*

WELLER, E.: *Map to Illustrate the Wars in Coromandel, 1744-1780.* In Beveridge: *A Comprehensive History of India . . .* , I: the 2nd of six maps at the beginning of the volume.

———: *Map to Illustrate the Wars in Mysore, 1767-1799.* In *ibid.*, the third map.

CHAPTER II

Great Britain

England, Scotland, and Wales:
General

A. BIBLIOGRAPHICAL AIDS

Annual Bulletin of Historical Literature (London, 1911-1964+). Also available is *A General Index to the Bulletins of Historical Literature, Nos. I-XII* (1911-22). A useful and critical survey in essay form of the best books and articles, chiefly in English and French, published during each year.

ASHTON, THOMAS SOUTHCLIFFE: *The Industrial Revolution: A Study in Bibliography*, Economic History Society, *Bibliographies and Pamphlets*, No. 3 (London, 1937); and "The Industrial Revolution, *Economic History Review*, V (1934-5), 104-19.

BATESON, FREDERICK W.: *The Cambridge Bibliography of English Literature* (5 vols., Cambridge, Eng. & New York, 1941-7). Volume II covers the period from 1660 to 1800.

BENT, WILLIAM: *A General Catalogue of Books in All Languages, Arts, and Sciences Printed in Great Britain and Published in London from . . . MDCC to MDCCLXXXVI* (London, 1786).

BRIGGS, GRACE M.: *The William W. Clary Oxford Collection: A Descriptive Catalogue* (Oxford, Eng., 1956).

BULTMANN, WILLIAM A.: "Early Hanoverian England (1714-60): Some Recent Writings," *Journal of Modern History*, XXXV (1963), 46-61.

CALLENDER, GEOFFREY A. R.: *Bibliography of Naval History, Historical Association Leaflets*, Nos. 58 & 61 (2 pts., London, 1924-5).

CONFERENCE ON BRITISH STUDIES: *Current Research in British Studies by American and Canadian Scholars* (5 edns., New York & Marquette, Mich., 1953, 1955, 1957, 1960, and 1964). The report for 1964 was prepared by Anthony M. Forbes and Marion Johnson and was published at Marquette, Wisconsin; a supplement to this report, prepared by William C. Wilbur, was published in New York in 1966.

COX, EDWARD GODFREY: *A Reference Guide to the Literature of Travel* . . . , University of Washington, *Publications in Language and Literature*, IX (2 vols., Seattle, Wash., 1935-8).

CUSHING, WILLIAM: *Anonyms: A Dictionary of Revealed Authorship* (Cambridge, Mass., 1889), and *Initials and Pseudonyms: A Dictionary of Literary Disguises* (New York, 1885; 2nd ser., 1888). Both works are useful in studying contemporary writings.

FREWER, LOUIS BENSON: *Bibliography of Historical Writings Published in Great Britain and the Empire, 1940-45* (Oxford, Eng., 1947).

GROSE, CLYDE L.: *A Select Bibliography of British History, 1660-1760* (Chicago, 1939). For a supplement to the above, see "Studies of 1931-40 on British History, 1660-1760," *Journal of Modern History*, XII (1940), 515-34.

———: "Thirty Years' Study of a Formerly Neglected Century of British History, 1660-1760," *Journal of Modern History*, II (1930), 448-71.

GROSS, CHARLES: *A Bibliography of British Municipal History Including Gilds and Parliamentary Representation* (Cambridge, Mass., 1897; *Harvard Historical Studies*, V, New York, 1915; reiss., Leicester, Eng., 1965).

GUTHRIE, DOROTHY A., and CLYDE L. GROSE: "Forty Years of Jacobite Bibliography," *Journal of Modern History*, XI (1939), 49-60.

HALKETT, SAMUEL, and JOHN LAING: *Dictionary of Anonymous and Pseudonymous English Literature* (n. edn., J. Kennedy, W. A. Smith, and A. F. Johnson, eds., 9 vols., Edinburgh, 1926-62). An indispensable work for the study of pamphlet literature.

HALL, A. C. S.: *Guide to the Reports of the Historical Manuscripts Commission, 1911-1957* (3 vols., London, 1966).

HECHT, J. JEAN: "The Reign of George III in Recent Historiography: A Bibliographical Essay," New York Public Library, *Bulletin*, LXX (1966), 279-304.

HIGGS, HENRY: *Bibliography of Economics* (Cambridge, Eng., 1935). The work covers the period 1751 through 1775.

HISTORICAL ASSOCIATION: *English Local History Handlist: A Short Bibliography and List of Sources for the Study of Local History and Antiquities* . . . (3rd edn., London, 1965).

HISTORICAL MANUSCRIPTS COMMISSION: *A Guide to the Reports on Collections of Manuscripts of Private Families, Corporations and Institutions in Great Britain and Ireland Issued by the Royal Commissioners for Historical Manuscripts* (2 vols. in 3, London, 1914-38).

———: *Reports*, Nos. 1-78 (162 vols., London, 1870-1962).

HORN, DAVID BAYNE: *British Diplomatic Representatives, 1689-1789*, Royal

Historical Society, *Publications, Camden Third Series*, XLVI (London, 1932).

—— and MARY RANSOME: "General Bibliography," *English Historical Documents, 1714-1783* (London & New York, 1957), pp. 68-88.

HUDDLESTON, FRANCIS JOSIAH, comp.: *Catalogue of the War Office Library* (3 pts., London, 1906-12). Annual supplements by W. Y. Baldry have been published since 1913. Part 3 is a subject index.

HUMPHREYS, ARTHUR LEE: *A Handbook to County Bibliography: Being a Bibliography of Bibliographies Relating to the Counties and Towns of Great Britain and Ireland* (London, 1917).

INSTITUTE OF HISTORICAL RESEARCH: *Guide to the Historical Publications of the Societies of England and Wales* (London, 1930+).

KUHLICKE, F. W., and F. G. EMMISON, eds.: *English Local History Handlist: A Short Bibliography and List of Sources for the Study of Local History and Antiquities, Helps for Students of History*, No. 69 (3rd edn., London, 1965).

LANCASTER, JOAN C.: *Bibliography of Historical Works Issued in the United Kingdom, 1946-1956* (comp. for the 6th Anglo-American Conference of Historians, London, 1957).

LAPRADE, W. T.: "The Present State of the History of England in the Eighteenth Century," *Journal of Modern History*, IV (1932), 581-603.

MANWARING, GEORGE ERNEST: *A Bibliography of British Naval History: A Biographical and Historical Guide to Printed and Manuscript Sources* (London, 1930).

MATTHEWS, WILLIAM: *British Autobiographies: An Annotated Bibliography of British Autobiographies Published or Written before 1951* (Berkeley, Calif., 1955).

NORTON, JANE E.: *Guide to the National and Provincial Directories of England and Wales, Excluding London, Published before 1856*, Royal Historical Society, *Guides and Handbooks*, No. 5 (London, 1950). Especially useful for the period after 1760.

PARGELLIS, STANLEY, and D. J. MEDLEY: *Bibliography of British History: The Eighteenth Century, 1714-1789* (Oxford, Eng., 1951). A new edition of this most important work is being prepared.

PARSLOE, GUY and ZIRPHIE, *et al.*: *Guide to the Historical Publications of the Societies of England and Wales*, Institute of Historical Research, *Bulletin*, Nos. 1-13+, (London, 1930-48+), annual supplement.

PEDDIE, ROBERT ALEXANDER: *Subject Index of Books Published up to and Including 1880* (4 vols., London, 1933-48). Many eighteenth-century titles are included in this listing.

POWER, EILEEN EDNA: *The Industrial Revolution, 1750-1850: A Select Bibliography Compiled for the Economic History Society*, Economic History Society, *Bibliographies*, No. 1 (London, 1927).

POWICKE, F. MAURICE, and E. B. FRYDE, eds.: *Handbook of British Chronology*, Royal Historical Society, *Guides and Handbooks*, No. 2 (1st edn., London, 1939; 2nd edn., 1962).

PUBLIC RECORD OFFICE: *Record Publications, Government Publications Sectional List No. 24, Revised to 31st July, 1965* (London, 1965).

REDINGTON, JOSEPH, and RICHARD ARTHUR ROBERTS: *Calendar of Home Office Papers of the Reign of George III, 1760-1775* (4 vols., London, 1878-99).

STEPHENS, FREDERIC GEORGE, and MARY DOROTHY GEORGE: *Catalogue of Prints and Drawings in the British Museum, Division I: Political and Personal Satires* (11 vols., London, 1870-1954).

TATE, W. E.: *The Parish Chest: A Study of the Records of Parochial Administration in England* (Cambridge, Eng., 1946).

TAYLOR, ARTHUR J.: "List of Publications on the Economic History of Great Britain and Ireland," *Economic History Review*, 2nd ser., IX (1957), 520-42.

THOMPSON, ALEXANDER HAMILTON: *A Short Bibliography of [English] Local History*, Historical Association Leaflet, No. 72 ([London], 1928). This sixteen-page pamphlet contains four pages of local histories.

Titles and Forms of Address: A Guide to Their Correct Use (9th edn., London, 1955).

WATT, ROBERT: *Bibliotheca Britannica: Or, a General Index to British and Foreign Literature* (4 vols., Edinburgh, 1824).

WILLIAMS, BASIL: "Bibliography," *The Whig Supremacy, 1714-70* (Oxford, Eng., 1939; 2nd edn., rev. by C. H. Stuart, 1962), pp. 434-68.

WILLIAMS, JUDITH B.: *A Guide to the Printed Materials for English Social and Economic History, 1750-1850* (2 vols., New York, 1926).

B. SELECTION OF PRINTED SOURCE MATERIALS

1. Government and related documents

A. THE CONSTITUTION AND LAWS

Special collections of documents

DYKES, DAVID OSWALD, ed.: *Source Book of Constitutional History from 1660* (London, 1930).

HORN, DAVID BAYNE, and MARY RANSOME, eds.: *English Historical Documents, Vol. X: 1714-1783* (New York, 1957).

ROBERTSON, CHARLES GRANT, ed.: *Select Statutes, Cases, and Documents to Illustrate English Constitutional History, 1660-1832: With a Supplement from 1832-1894* (London, 1904; n. issue, 1935).

WATSON, J. STEVEN, and W. C. COSTIN, eds.: *The Law and Working of the Constitution: Documents, 1660-1914* (2 vols., London, 1952).

The common law

BLACKSTONE, WILLIAM: *Commentaries on the Laws of England* (4 vols., Oxford, Eng., 1765-9; 9th edn., 1783).

The statutory law

CUNNINGHAM, TIMOTHY, ed.: *The Merchant's Lawyer or the Law of Trade in General: Containing an Abridgement of All the Statutes Relative to the East-India Company, and All the Public Annuities . . .* (2 vols., London, 1762).

The Statutes at Large from Magna Charta to the Twenty-Fifth Year of the Reign of King George the Third . . . (Owen Ruffhead and Charles Runnington, eds., n. edn., rev., 10 vols., London, 1786).

The Statutes at Large from Magna Charta to . . . 1761 (Danby Pickering, ed., 24 vols., cont. to 1806, vols. 25-46, Cambridge, Eng., 1762-1807).

The courts of law

COWPER, HENRY, ed.: *Reports of Cases Adjudged in the Courts of King's Bench from Hilary Term, the 14th of George III to Trinity Term, the 18th of George III . . .* (London, 1783; Dublin, 1784; 2nd edn., London, 1800).

HOWELL, THOMAS BAYLEY, and T. J. HOWELL, eds.: *[Cobbett's] Complete Collection of State Trials and Proceedings for High Treason and Other Crimes and Misdemeanors: From the Earliest Period to the Present Time* (34 vols., London, 1809-28).

VESEY, FRANCIS, ed.: *Cases Argued and Determined in the High Court of Chancery in the Times of Lord Chancellor Hardwicke . . .* (2 vols., London, 1771; 3rd edn., 1788).

B. PARLIAMENT

Parliamentary history

Abstracts of the Principal Regulations Contained in the Acts of Parliament Relative to the Trade of the British Plantations (Charleston, S. C., 1774).

"Debates on the Declaratory Act and the Repeal of the Stamp Act, 1766," C. H. Hull and H. W. V. Temperley, eds., *American His-*

torical *Review*, XVII (1911-12), 563-86. Based on Grey Cooper's Parliamentary Notes.

The Parliamentary History of England from the Earliest Period to 1803 (William Cobbett and T. C. Hansard, eds., 36 vols., London, 1806-20). Hansard took over the editing with Volume XIII in 1812. Under Cobbett's editorship, the title had been *Cobbett's Parliamentary History of England from the Norman Conquest in 1066 to the Year 1803*. The Johnson Reprint Corporation now has available reprints of the 36 volumes.

The History, Debates and Proceedings of Both Houses of Parliament . . . [1743-1774] ([John Debrett], ed., 7 vols., London, 1792). Debrett also edited *Parliamentary Papers, Consisting of a Complete . . . Collection of King's Speeches, Messages to Parliament . . . Lords Protests . . . Standing Orders of the House of Lords [and] Commons Relative to [Private Bills], List of the Speakers of the House of Commons* (3 vols., London, 1797).

Proceedings and Debates of the British Parliaments Respecting North America [to 1754+] (Leo Francis Stock, ed., 5 vols.+, Washington, D.C., 1924-41+).

The House of Commons

British House of Commons Sessional Papers of the 18th and 19th Centuries: The Sessional Papers: Last Phase. These papers have been reproduced by the Readex Microprint Corporation (Edgar L. Erickson, ed., New York, 1960). Included are the famous *Reports* of both the Select Committee and the Committee of Secrecy concerned with the United East India Company and the East Indies. These were printed in the years 1772 and 1773 but not published. Both reports contain mines of information. There are four *Reports* of the Select Committee and eight *Reports* of the Committee of Secrecy.

The Debates and Proceedings of the British House of Commons . . . 1743-1774 ([John Almon, *et al.*, eds.], 11 vols., London, 1766-75).

Hansard's Catalogue and Breviate of Parliamentary Papers, 1696-1834 (rep. in facsimile, Oxford, Eng., 1953). Also available in Readex Microprints of *British Sessional Papers: House of Commons Reports, 1731-1800*, edited by Edgar L. Erickson.

Journals of the House of Commons. Volumes XVII-XLIV cover the years 1714-89; see also Edward Moore: *A General Index . . . Vols. XVIII to XXXIV . . . 1714-1774* (London, 1778).

The Parliamentary Register: Or, History of the Proceedings and Debates of the House of Commons . . . (John Almon, ed., 17 vols., London, 1775-80).

Report from the Committee Appointed to Examine and State to the House of Commons the Matter of Fact in the Several Petitions of the Manufacturers of, and Dealers and Traders in the Linen Manufactory (London, 1751).

Reports from Committees of the House of Commons . . . Not Inserted in the Journals, 1715-1801 (16 vols., London, 1803-6). Volume XVI is a general index.

The Speeches in the Last Session of the Present Parliament Delivered by Several of the Principal Advocates in the House of Commons in Favour of the Rights of America . . . (New York, 1775).

Sir Henry Cavendish's Debates of the House of Commons during the Thirteenth Parliament . . . 1768-71 (John Wright, ed., 2 vols., London, 1841-3). See also under Canada: Cavendish's debates relating to the Quebec Bill of 1774.

The House of Lords

The Humble Address of the Right Honourable the Lords Spiritual and Temporal in Parliament Assembled Presented to His Majesty, October 27, 1775: With His Majesty's Most Gracious Answer (London, 1775). Deals with the disaffection of the American colonies.

Journals of the House of Lords. Volumes XX-XXXVIII cover the years 1714-89. See also Thomas Brodie: *General Index to the Journals [of the House of Lords] . . . 1714-1779* (London, 1817).

The Parliamentary Register: Or, History of the Proceedings and Debates of the [House of Lords] . . . 1774-1780 (John Almon, ed., 17 vols., London, 1775-80).

PITT, WILLIAM, EARL OF CHATHAM: *The Speeches of the Right Honourable the Earl of Chatham in the House of Lords and Commons . . .* (W. S. Hathaway, ed., London, 1806; n. edn., 1848).

Protest against the Bill to Repeal the American Stamp Act of Last Session (Paris [i.e. London], 1766). See also *Second Protest with a List of the Voters against the Bill to Repeal the American Stamp Act of Last Session* (Paris [i.e. London], 1766), and *A Comlete Collection of the Protests of the Lords with Historical Introductions: Edited from the Journals of the Lords* (James Edwin Thorold Rogers, ed., 3 vols., Oxford, Eng., 1875).

The Report of the Lords Committees, Appointed by the House of Lords to Enquire into the Several Proceedings in the Colony of Massachuset's [sic] Bay, in Opposition to the Sovereignty of His Majesty, in His Parliament of Great Britain over that Province . . . (London, 1774).

Reports of Cases upon Appeals and Writs of Error in the High Court of Parliament from 1701 to 1779 (7 vols., London, 1779-83; cont. to 1800, with notes by J. E. Jomelius, 8 vols., 1803).

Diplomatic relations

All the Memorials of Great Britain and France Since the Peace of Aix la Chapelle (3 vols., London & The Hague, 1755-6); also published in French as *Mémoires des Commissaires du Roi et de Ceux de Sa Majesté Britannique, Sur les Possessions* . . . (4 vols., Paris, 1755-7).

ALMON, JOHN, ed.: *A Collection of All the Treaties of Peace, Alliance, and Commerce, between Great-Britain and Other Powers from the Revolution of 1688 to the Present Time* (2 vols., London, 1772).

British Diplomatic Instructions, 1689-1789, Royal Historical Society (7 vols., London, 1922-34); Vol. VII: *France, Part IV, 1745-1789* (Leopold George Wickham Legg, ed.).

CHALMERS, GEORGE, ed.: *A Collection of Treaties between Great Britain and Other Powers* (2 vols., London, 1790).

DAVENPORT, FRANCES GARDINER, ed.: *European Treaties Bearing on the History of the United States and Its Dependencies* (4 vols., Vol. IV edited by Charles Oscar Paullin, Washington, D.C., 1917-37).

JENKINSON, CHARLES, ed.: *A Collection of All the Treaties of Peace, Alliance, and Commerce between Great Britain and Other Powers from* . . . *[1648-1783]* (3 vols., London, 1785).

Papers Relative to the Rupture with Spain Laid Before Both Houses of Parliament . . . (London, 1762).

SANDWICH, JOHN MONTAGU, 4TH EARL OF: *Diplomatic Correspondence, 1763-1765* (Frank Spencer, ed., Manchester, Eng., c. 1961).

Foreign documents

The following is a select list of contemporary writings by foreigners having to do with the political relations of the powers of Europe with Great Britain and with one another during the period 1748-1776.

ARGENSON, RENÉ LOUIS DE VOYER, MARQUIS DE: *Journal et Mémoires, publiés pour la première fois d'apres les manuscrits autographes de la bibliothèque du Louvre* . . . , Société de l'Histoire de France, *Publications*, I (E. J. B. Rathery, ed., 9 vols., Paris, 1859-67).

BARBIER, EDMOND-JEAN-FRANÇOIS: *Journal historique et anecdotique du règne de Louis XV* . . . , Société de l'Histoire de France, *Publications*, II (A. de La Villegille, ed., 4 vols., Paris, 1847-56).

BERNIS, FRANÇOIS JOACHIM DE PIERRE, DE: *Correspondance du Cardinal de Bernis avec M. Pâris-Du-Verney* . . . *depuis 1752, jusqu'en 1769* . . . (2 vols., Paris, 1790), and also *Mémoires et Lettres de F. J. de Pierre, Cardinal de Bernis, 1715-1758* (2 vols., Paris, 1825).

BROGLIE, CHARLES-FRANÇOIS, COUNT DE: *Correspondance Inédite* . . . *avec le Prince Xavier de Saxe* . . . *pour servir à l'Histoire de la Guerre de Sept Ans, Compagnes de 1759 à 1761* (4 vols., Paris, 1903-5) and *Le Secret du Roi . . . Correspondance secrète de Louis XV avec ses agents diplomatiques, 1752-1774* (Jacques Victor Albert, Duke de Broglie, ed., 2 vols., Paris, 1878).

BRÜHL, HEINRICH, GRAF VON: *Correspondenz des . . . Grafen von Brühl mit dem . . . Freiherrn von Riedesel . . . als ein Beitrag zur Geschichte des 7-jährigen Krieges, 1760-1761* (Max von Eelking, ed., Leipzig, 1854).

CHOISEUL, ÉTIENNE-FRANÇOIS, DUC DE CHOISEUL and D'AMBOISE: *Mémoire historique sur la negociation de la France et de l'Angleterre depuis le 26 Mars 1761 jusqu'au 20 Septembre de la même année, avec les pièces justificatives* (Paris, London, & Leipzig, 1761), and *Mémoires de M. le duc de Choiseul . . . écrits par lui-même et imprimés sous ses yeux . . . en 1778* (J. L. G. Soulavie, ed., 2 vols., Canteloup, 1790).

DUCLOS, CHARLES PINOT (PINEAU-DUCLOS, CHARLES): *Mémoires Secrets sur les Règnes de Louis XIV et de Louis XV* (C. S. Sautreau de Marsy, ed., 2 vols., Paris, 1791).

ESTERHÁZY, VALENTIN LADISLAV, COUNT: *Mémoires du Comte Valentin Esterházy . . .* (E. Daudet, ed., Paris, 1905).

FREDERICK II of PRUSSIA: *Œuvres de Frédéric le Grand, Vols. IV and V: Histoire de la Guerre de Sept Ans* (J. D. E. Preuss, ed., 31 vols., Berlin, 1846-56), and *Politische Correspondenz Friedrichs des Grossen* (Johann Gustav Droysen, Maximilian Wolfgang Duncker, and G. B. Volz, eds., 46 vols.+, Berlin, 1879-1939+).

HERTZBERG, COUNT E. F. VON: *Recueil des Déductions, Manifestes, Déclarations, Traités, et autres actes et écrits publics, qui ont été rédigés et publiés pour la cour de Prusse, depuis l'Année 1756 jusq'a l'Année 1790* (2nd edn., 3 vols., Berlin, 1790-5).

Histoire de la dernière Guerre, commencée l'an 1756 & finie par la Paix d'Hubertsbourg, le 15 fevrier 1763 (Berlin, 1767; Cologne, 1770).

KAUNITZ-RIETBERG, WENZEL ANTON VON: *Correspondance Secrète Entre le Comte W. A. Kaunitz-Rietberg, Ambassadeur Impérial à Paris, et le Baron Ignaz de Koch, Secrétaire de l'Impératrice Marie-Thérèse, 1750-1752* (Paris, 1899).

LAFUENTE Y ZAMALLON (MODESTO): *Historia General de España . . .* (30 vols., Madrid, 1840-67). Volumes XIX-XXI contain numerous documents bearing upon the period.

LOUIS XV: *Correspondance Secrète Inédite de Louis XV sur la Politique Étrangère, Avec le Comte de Broglie, Tercier, Etc., et Autres Documents . . .* (E. Boutarie [ed.], 2 vols., Paris, 1866).

MARTENS, GEORG FRIEDRICH VON, ed.: *Recueil de Traités d'Alliance, de Paix, de Trêve, de Neutralité, de Commerce, . . .* [by the states of Europe since 1761] (2nd edn., rev. & enl., 8 vols., Göttingen, Germany, 1817-35).

MAUREPAS, JEAN-FRÉDÉRIC PHELYPEAUX, COMTE DE: *Mémoires du Comte de Maurepas* (J. L. G. Soulavie, ed., 4 vols., Paris, 1792).

MIREPOIX, CHARLES PIERRE GASTON FRANÇOIS DE LÉVIS, DUC DE: "Intercepted Letters to the Duke de Mirepoix, 1756," American Historical Association, *Annual Report, 1896* (2 vols., Washington, D.C., 1897), I: 660-703.

NIVERNOIS, DUC DE: *Œuvres Posthumes du Duc de Nivernois . . .* (N. François de Neufchâteau, ed., 2 vols., Paris, 1807).

Commercial relations

JARVIS, RUPERT C., ed.: *Customs Letter Books of the Port of Liverpool, 1711-1813* (Manchester, Eng., 1956).

MOORE, JOHN BASSETT, ed.: *International Adjudications, Ancient and Modern: History and Documents Together with Mediatorial Reports, Advisory Opinions, and the Decisions of Domestic Commissions on International Claims* (6 vols., New York, 1929-33).

The armed forces

CORBETT, JULIAN STAFFORD, ed.: *Fighting Instructions, 1530-1816,* Navy Records Society, *Publications,* XXIX (London, 1905).

HODGES, HAROLD WINTER, and EDWARD ARTHUR HUGHES, eds.: *Select Naval Documents* (Cambridge, Eng., 1922).

JAMESON, JOHN FRANKLIN, ed.: *Privateering and Piracy in the Colonial Period: Illustrative Documents* (New York, 1923).

MARSDEN, REGINALD GODFREY, ed.: *Documents Relating to Law and Custom of the Sea, Vol. II: 1649-1767,* Navy Records Society, *Publications,* L (London, 1916).

2. Non-official contemporary writings

Although it is obvious that some of the writings embodied in collections here listed are of an official character, in that they speak in the name of the government, most of them are not. It therefore has appeared best to bring them together as a group.

[ALMON, JOHN], ed.: *A Collection of Interesting, Authentic Papers Relative to the Dispute between Great Britain and America: Shewing the Causes and Progress of that Misunderstanding from 1764 to 1775* (London, 1777). Generally known by the running title: *Prior Documents.*

[————]: *Memoirs of John Almon, Bookseller of Picadilly* (London, 1790). Contains numerous political anecdotes.

ANDERSON, ADAM: *Anderson's Historical and Chronological Deduction of the Origin of Commerce from the Earliest Accounts: Containing an History of the Great Commercial Interests of the British Empire* . . . (2 vols., London, 1764; rev. by William Combe, 4 vols., 1787-1789; 6 vols., Dublin, 1790).

ANSON, GEORGE, LORD: *A Voyage Round the World in the Years 1740, 1, 2, 3, 4: Compiled from the Papers and other Materials of the Right Honourable George Lord Anson* (Richard Walter, comp., London, 1748; 16th edn., 1781; n. edn., G. S. Laird Clowes, ed., Boston, 1928).

ATTICUS, LUCIUS, and JUNIUS, pseuds.: *A Collection of the Letters of Atticus, Lucius, Junius, and Others: With Observations and Notes, A New Edition* . . . (London, 1769).

BEATSON, ROBERT, ed.: *Naval and Military Memoirs of Great Britain from 1727 to 1783* (3 vols., London, 1790; 6 vols., 1804).

BEAWES, WYNDHAM: *Lex Mercatoria Rediviva or the Merchant's Directory: Being a Compleat Guide to All Men in Business* . . . (London, 1752; 2nd edn., 1761). A law book and merchant's guide.

BEDFORD, JOHN RUSSELL, 4TH DUKE OF: *Correspondence of John, Fourth Duke of Bedford* . . . (Lord John Russell, ed., 3 vols., London, 1842-6).

BELSHAM, WILLIAM: *Memoirs of the Kings of Great Britain of the House of Brunswic[k]-Lune[n]burg* (2 vols., London, 1793; 2nd edn., 1796).

————: *Memoirs of the Reign of George III to the Session of Parliament Ending A.D. 1793* (4 vols., London, 1795; 3rd edn., continued to 1799, 6 vols., 1796-1801).

BERKELEY, GEORGE: *The Works of George Berkeley, D.D.* (Alexander Campbell Fraser, ed., 3 vols., Oxford, Eng., 1871).

BLAND, A. E., P. A. BROWN, and R. H. TAWNEY, eds.: *English Economic History: Select Documents, Part III: 1660-1846* (London, 1919). Includes documents on industry, agriculture, trade, social conditions, finances, etc.

BOLINGBROKE, HENRY ST. JOHN, 1ST VISCOUNT: *The Miscellaneous Works of* . . . (4 vols., Edinburgh, 1768). Of an earlier period but pertinent.

BOSWELL, JAMES: *Life of Johnson, together with Boswell's Journal of a Tour to the Hebrides and Johnson's Diary of a Journey into North Wales* (George Birkbeck Hill, ed., 6 vols., Oxford, Eng., 1934-50). This classic biography was also edited by Mowbray Morris (2 vols. in 1, New York [1914]). See also *Letters of James Boswell* (Chauncey Brewster Tinker, ed., 2 vols., Oxford, Eng., 1924) and *Private Papers of James Boswell from Malahide Castle* . . . (Geoffrey Scott and Frederick Albert Pottle, eds., 18 vols., Mount Vernon, N. Y., 1928-34; index, 1937). Recently, three more volumes of material have become available: *London Journal, 1762-1763* . . .

(Frederick A. Pottle, ed., preface by Christopher Morley, New York, 1950; London, 1951); *Boswell for the Defence, 1760-1774* (William K. Wimsatt and Frederick A. Pottle, eds., New York, 1959); and *Boswell: The Ominous Years, 1774-1776* (Charles Ryskamp and Frederick A. Pottle, eds., New York, 1963).

BURKE, EDMUND: In view of the fact that the British Museum Catalogue requires thirty-six columns to cover the various editions of Burke's writings, it is neither possible nor desirable to list more than a few of the more significant ones here. Two important editions of *The Works of the Right Honourable Edmund Burke* were published, one edited by Walker King and French Lawrence (8 vols., London, 1792-1827; 12 vols., Boston, 1865-7), and a twelve-volume edition (London, 1899). Collections of correspondence worthy of special mention include *Correspondence of the Right Honourable Edmund Burke* . . . (Charles William, Earl Fitzwilliam and Sir Richard Bourke, eds., 4 vols., London, 1844; a new edn. under the title *Works and Correspondence*, 8 vols., 1852); a one-volume collection, *The Early Life, Correspondence and Writings of the Rt. Hon. Edmund Burke* . . . (Arthur P. I. Samuels, ed., Cambridge, Eng., 1923); the best and most recent collection is *The Correspondence of Edmund Burke* (Thomas W. Copeland, *et al.*, eds., 6 vols.+, Cambridge, Eng. & Chicago, 1958-67+); and the single volume, *Edmund Burke, New York Agent: With His Letters to the New York Assembly and Intimate Correspondence with Charles O'Hara, 1761-1776*, American Philosophical Society, *Memoirs*, XLI (Ross J. S. Hoffman, ed., Philadelphia, 1956).

BURN, RICHARD: *The History of the Poor Laws: With Observations* (London, 1764).

BUTLER, JOHN: *Stanhope Memorials of Bishop Butler [Bishop of Durham]* (William Morley Egglestone, ed., London, 1878).

[BYRON, JOHN]: *A Voyage Round the World in His Majesty's Ship the Dolphin* . . . (London & Dublin, 1767). Also included in Volume I of John Hawkesworth's *An Account of the Voyages Undertaken* . . . *for Making Discoveries in the Southern Hemisphere.* . . .

CAMPBELL, JOHN: *A Political Survey of Britain: Being a Series of Reflections on the Situation, Lands, Inhabitants, Revenues, Colonies, and Commerce of This Island* . . . (2 vols., London, 1774).

CHESTERFIELD, PHILIP DORMER STANHOPE, 4TH EARL OF: *The Letters of Philip Dormer Stanhope, 4th Earl of Chesterfield* (Bonamy Dobrée, ed., 6 vols., London, 1932). See also *Letters Written by the Late Right Honourable Philip Dormer Stanhope, Earl of Chesterfield, to His Son Philip Stanhope, Esq.* . . . *Together with Several Other Pieces on Various Subjects* (Eugenia Stanhope, ed., 2 vols., London, 1774). The letters to his son have been reprinted several times.

CLARKE, E.: *Letters Concerning the Spanish Nation Written at Madrid during the years 1760 and 1761* (London, 1763).

CLERK, JOHN: *An Essay on Naval Tactics, Systematical and Historical: With Explanatory Notes* (4 pts., Edinburgh, 1790-7; 2nd edn., 1804).

COLLINS, ARTHUR: *The Peerage of England: Containing a Genealogical and Historical Account of All the Peers of That Kingdom* (4th edn., 7 vols., London, 1768).

COOK, JAMES: *A Journal of a Voyage Round the World in His Majesty's Ship Endeavour in the Years 1768, 1769, 1770 and 1771 . . .* (London, 1771; Dublin, 1772). See also the account of his second expedition: *A Voyage Towards the South Pole and Round the World Performed in His Majesty's Ships the Resolution and Adventure in the Years 1772, 1773, 1774, and 1775 . . .* (2 vols., London, 1777).

CREED, JOHN MARTIN, and JOHN S. B. SMITH, eds.: *Religious Thought in the 18th Century: Illustrated from Writers of the Period* (Cambridge, Eng., 1934). A selection of extracts on theological and ecclesiastical subjects.

DALRYMPLE, ALEXANDER, comp.: *An Historical Collection of the Several Voyages and Discoveries in the South Pacific Ocean* (2 vols., London, 1770-1).

DODINGTON, GEORGE BUBB: *The Diary of the Late George Bubb Dodington, Baron of Melcombe Regis: From March 8, 1749 to February 6, 1761 . . .* (Henry Penruddocke Wyndham, ed., 1st edn., Salisbury, Eng., 1784; 4th edn., London, 1809). See also *The Political Journal of George Bubb Dodington* (John Carswell and Lewis Arnold Dralle, eds., Oxford, Eng., 1965).

EDEN, WILLIAM (LORD AUCKLAND): *Principles of Penal Law* (London, 1771).

FOX, CHARLES JAMES: *Memorials and Correspondence of Charles James Fox* (Lord John Russell, ed., 2 vols., London, 1853).

FRANCIS, PHILIP. *Memoirs of Sir Philip Francis, K. C. B.: With Correspondence and Journals* by Joseph Parkes (completed & ed. by Herman Merivale, 2 vols., London, 1867).

GARRICK, DAVID: *The Private Correspondence of David Garrick . . .* (James Boaden, ed., 2 vols., London, 1831-2).

GEORGE III: *The Correspondence of King George the Third from 1760 to December 1783: Printed from the Original Papers in the Royal Archives at Windsor Castle* (Sir John Fortescue, ed., 6 vols., London, 1927-8). See in connection with this work: Lewis B. Namier's *Additions and Corrections to Sir John Fortescue's Edition of the Correspondence of King George the Third* (Manchester, Eng., 1937). Also available are *The Correspondence of King George the Third with Lord North from 1768 to 1783* (William Bodham Donne, ed., 2 vols., London, 1867); *Letters from George III to Lord Bute,*

1756-1766 (Romney Sedgwick, ed., London, 1939); and *The Letters of King George III* (Bonamy Dobrée, ed., London, 1935). Of limited value is Robert Huish's *The Public and Private Life of His Late Excellent and Most Gracious Majesty George the Third* . . . (London, 1821), and John Heneage Jesse's *The Memoirs of the Life and Reign of George the Third* (2nd edn., 3 vols., 1867).

GEORGE, PRINCE of WALES: *The Correspondence of George, Prince of Wales, 1770-1812, Vol. I: 1770-1789* (A. Aspinall, ed., London & New York, 1963).

GIBBON, EDWARD: *The Autobiographies of Edward Gibbon: Printed Verbatim from Hitherto Unpublished MSS* (J. Murray, ed., London, 1896).

[GLOVER, RICHARD]: *Memoirs by a Celebrated Literary and Political Character from* . . . *[1742-1757] Containing Strictures on Some of the Most Distinguished Men of That Time* (London, 1813).

GOUGH, JOHN: *A History of the People Called Quakers from Their First Rise to the Present Time [1764]* . . . (4 vols., Dublin, 1789-90).

GRAFTON, AUGUSTUS HENRY FITZROY, 3RD DUKE OF: *Autobiography and Political Correspondence of Augustus Henry, Third Duke of Grafton* . . . (Sir William Reynell Anson, ed., London, 1898).

GRENVILLE, RICHARD, EARL TEMPLE, and GEORGE GRENVILLE: *The Grenville Papers: Being the Correspondence of Richard Grenville, Earl Temple, and the Right Hon. George Grenville, Their Friends and Contemporaries* (William James Smith, ed., 4 vols., London, 1852-3). See also *Additional Grenville Papers, 1763-1765* (John R. G. Tomlinson, ed., Manchester, Eng., 1962).

HAMPDEN, JOHN, comp.: *An Eighteenth Century Journal: Being a Record of the Years 1774-1776* (London, 1940). An unusual source book concerned with the period of three years.

HARDWICKE, PHILIP YORKE, 1ST EARL OF: *The Life and Correspondence of Philip Yorke, Earl of Hardwicke, Lord High Chancellor of Great Britain* by Philip Chesney Yorke (3 vols., Cambridge, Eng., 1913). See also the earlier work by George Harris: *The Life of Chancellor Hardwicke: With Selections from His Correspondence, Diaries, Speeches, and Judgments* (3 vols., London, 1847).

HAWKESWORTH, JOHN, comp.: *An Account of the Voyages Undertaken by the Order of His Present Majesty for Making Discoveries in the Southern Hemisphere* . . . (3 vols., London, 1773). This work was questioned by Alexander Dalrymple in *A Letter from Mr. Dalrymple to Dr. Hawkesworth Occasioned by Some Groundless and Illiberal Imputations in His Account of the Late Voyages to the South* (London, 1773).

[HENRY, DAVID], ed.: *An Historical Account of All the Voyages Round the World Performed by English Navigators* . . . (London, 1774).

HERVEY, JOHN, LORD: *Memoirs of the Reign of George the Second, from*

His Accession to the Death of Queen Caroline (John W. Croker, ed., 2 vols., London, 1848; rep., 3 vols., New York, 1884). A more complete manuscript was located and published as *Lord Hervey's Memoirs: Edited from a Copy of the Original MS in the Royal Archives at Windsor Castle* (Romney Sedgewick, ed., London, 1952).

HERVEY, WILLIAM: *Journals of the Hon. William Hervey, in North America and Europe from 1755 to 1814* . . . (Bury St. Edmonds, 1906).

HISTORICAL MANUSCRIPTS COMMISSION: *Reports.* Many of the *Reports* print whole documents or portions of them. Among the more important collections of manuscripts having to do with Great Britain for the period under examination and described in the *Reports* are the following: (1) Bedford, John Russell, 4th Duke of, diary, 1751-3, and papers, 1766-70, in the *Second Report, The Bedford Manuscripts;* (2) Bristol, George Williamson Hervey, Earl of, letters, 1756-8, in the *Sixth Report, Leconfield Manuscripts;* (3) Carlisle, Frederick Howard, 5th Earl of, letters and papers, 1767-81, in the *Fifteenth Report, Carlisle Manuscripts,* Vol. 6; (4) Dartmouth, William Legge, 2nd Earl of, letters, in the *Second, Eleventh, Thirteenth, Fourteenth and Fifteenth Reports, Dartmouth Manuscripts;* (5) Dodington, George Bubb, letters, 1717-62, in the "Eyre-Matcham Manuscripts," in *Various Collections,* VI (1909); (6) Egremont, Charles Wyndham, 2nd Earl of, letters and papers, in the *Sixth Report, Leconfield Manuscripts;* (7) Germain, Viscount George Sackville, Lord, letters and papers, in the *Ninth Report, Stopford-Sackville Manuscripts,* Vol. III; (8) Gower-Granville Leveson-Gower, Earl, letters, 1771-92, in the *Fifth Report, Sutherland Manuscripts;* (9) Granby, John Manners, Marquis of, letter books, 1759-70, in the *Twelfth Report, Rutland Manuscripts;* (10) Holdernesse, Robert D'Arcy, 4th Earl of, letters and papers, 1749-76, in the *Eleventh Report, Leeds Manuscripts,* Vol. 7; (11) Huntingdon, Selina Hastings, Countess of, letters, 1774-84, in the *Sixth Report, T. S. Raffles Manuscripts;* (12) Knox, William, letters, 1757-1808, in "H. V. Knox Manuscripts" in *Various Collections,* Vol. VI; (13) Lyttelton, William Henry, letters, 1756-65, in the *Second Report, Lyttelton Manuscripts;* (14) Manchester, George Montagu, 2nd Duke of, papers, 1707-58, in the *Eighth Report, Manchester Manuscripts,* Vol. 11; (15) Newcastle, Thomas Pelham-Holles, Duke of, letters, 1724-68, in the *Third Report, Chichester Manuscripts;* (16) Pitt, William, letters, 1757-60, in the *Sixth Report, Leconfield Manuscripts;* (17) Savile, Sir George, letters, 1763-82, in the *Fifteenth Report, the F. J. Savile Foljambe Manuscripts,* Vol. V; (18) Shelburne, William Petty, Earl of, papers, 1754-83, in the *Third, Fifth,* and *Sixth Reports, Landsdowne Manuscripts;* (19) Temple, Richard Grenville, Earl, papers, 1761-8, in the *Second Report, the Countess Cowper and Baroness Lucas Manuscripts;* (20) Townshend Family, letters and papers, 1714-71, in the *Eleventh Report, Townshend Manuscripts,* Vol. IV, and also the *Eighth Report, Ashburnham Manuscripts,* Vol. III; (21) Weston, Edward, letters and papers, 1722-70, in the *Tenth Report, C. Fleetwood Weston Underwood Manuscripts,* Vol. I; (22) White-field, George, letters, 1736-69, in the *Sixth Report, T. S. Raffles Manuscripts;* (23) Wilkes, John, letters and papers, 1750-90, in the *Fourth Report, Macaulay Manuscripts.*

The above list is given simply as an aid to printed sources. The student should, however, be warned that since the Historical Manuscript Commission issued its various *Reports* some of the collections in private hands have shifted location and ownership. In the *Twenty-Second Report* issued by the Commission in 1946, the then location of papers is recorded; the *Bulletin* of the Institute of Historical Research from time to time also supplies information respecting the movement of collections. To illustrate, reference above is made to Holdernesse Papers embodied in the Leeds Papers. These papers at the time the *Eleventh Report* was issued were in Hornby Castle; today they are a part of the Egerton Collection of Manuscripts in the British Museum. Again, the great-est portion of the Shelburne Papers in the possession of the Marquis of Landsdowne at the time the *Reports* were prepared are now in the Clements Library of American History, University of Michigan. *A Guide to Manuscripts Relating to America in Great Britain and Ireland* (H. L. Beales, B. R. Crick, and Miriam Alman, eds., London, 1961) will aid in the present location of many collections.

HOADLY, BENJAMIN: *The Works of B. Hoadly . . .* (J. Hoadly, ed., 3 vols., London, 1773). Hoadly was bishop of Winchester.

HOLLIS, THOMAS: *Memoirs of T[homas] H[ollis]* (F. Blackburne, comp., 2 vols., London, 1780). For Hollis's correspondence with Jonathan Mayhew, see Mayhew, under Chapter V, Massachusetts Bay, B2.

HORNE, JOHN (later JOHN HORNE TOOKE): *Controversial Letters of John Wilkes . . . , the Rev. J. Horne and Their Principal Adherents . . .* (London, 1771). See also Alexander Stephens's *Memoirs of J. Horne Tooke . . .* (2 vols., London, 1813) and John Andrew Graham's *Memoirs of John Horne Tooke together with His . . . Speeches and Writings . . .* (New York, 1828).

HUME, DAVID: There were two contemporary collections, *Essays and Treatises on Several Subjects* (London, 1758; other edns., 4 vols., 1770, 1777; 2 vols., Dublin, 1779), and *Essays: Literary, Moral, and Political* (London, n.d.), and also the later collection, *The Philosophical Works of David Hume* (Thomas Hill Green and Thomas Hodge Grose, eds., 4 vols., London, 1878). For Hume's correspondence, see John Hill Burton's *Life and Correspondence of*

David Hume . . . (2 vols., Edinburgh, 1846), also *Letters of David Hume to William Strahan* . . . (G. Birkbeck Hill, ed., Oxford, Eng., 1888); *The Letters of David Hume* (J. Y. T. Greig, ed., 2 vols., Oxford, Eng., 1932); and *New Letters of David Hume* (Raymond Klibansky and Ernest C. Mossner, eds., Oxford, Eng., 1954).

HUTTON, JAMES. *Memoirs of James Hutton: Comprising the Annals of His Life, and Connection with the United Brethren* by Daniel Benham (London, 1856). Hutton was the founder of the Moravian Church in England.

INDFIELD, WILLIAM: *An Essay towards a History of Liverpool Drawn from Papers Left by the Late Mr. George Perry* . . . ([Liverpool, Eng.], 1773).

JENKINSON, CHARLES (later 1ST EARL of LIVERPOOL): *The Jenkinson Papers, 1760-1766* (Ninetta S. Jucker, ed., London, 1949).

JOHNSON, SAMUEL: *The Works of Samuel Johnson, LL.D.: Together with His Life* . . . (Sir John Hawkins and John Stockdale, eds., 13 vols., London, 1787). The best edition of Johnson's writings is that edited by Francis Pearson Walesby: *The Works of Samuel Johnson* (11 vols., Oxford, Eng., 1825).

JUNIUS, pseud.: The stir made by his letters to the press was such that at least fifty-three people have been identified with their composition. The most complete holding of the various editions of the writings of "Junius" published in the eighteenth and early part of the nineteenth centuries is to be found in the British Museum. The student should consult the printed catalogue. There were a number of editions published contemporaneously, including: *A Complete Collection of Junius' Letters with Those of Sir W. Draper* (London, 1770), and four London editions entitled *The Letters of Junius*: one appeared in 1770, another in two volumes in 1770-4, and a third in two volumes in 1774, the fourth, Robert Heron's edition in three volumes in 1801, in which Junius is identified as Dimring. Then there is an edition entitled *The Genuine Letters of Junius* . . . (London, 1771) in which Junius was identified as Edmund Burke; also an edition entitled simply *Junius* (2 vols., London, 1772); and *The Letters of the Celebrated Junius* . . . (2 vols., London, 1783). J. M. Good edited *Junius: Including Letters by the Same Writer under Other Signatures* . . . (3 vols., London, 1812; 2nd edn., 1814), and another edition of two volumes appeared under the same title in London in 1850. The most recent edition is that edited by Charles Warren Everett: *The Letters of Junius* (London, 1927) in which Shelburne is given credit for the letters. For material relating to the identity of Junius, see Frederick Griffin's *Junius Discovered* (Boston, 1854), David Hannay's sketch in the 1911 edition of the *Encyclopedia Britannica*, XV: 557-9, and the articles which appeared in the *Journal of Modern History*, Volume IV for 1932, one by Frank Monaghan: "A New Document on the Identity of 'Junius,'" pp. 68-71, and one by Helen B. Bates: "Some Notes on Thomas Mante (alias 'Junius')," pp. 232-4. The most recent work on the subject is by Alvar Ellegård: *Who Was Junius?* (Stockholm, 1962) and *A Statistical Method for Determining Authorship: The Junius Letters, 1769-1772, Gothenburg Studies in English,* No. 13 (Gothenburg, Sweden, 1962). For additional material about the authorship of the letters, see John Edwards's "A Junius Bibliography," Mercantile Library of Philadelphia, *Bulletin,* II (1890-7), *passim,* as well as the printed catalogue of the British Museum. The conclusion now generally accepted is that Sir Philip Francis was "Junius."

KALM, PETER: *Kalm's Account of His Visit to England on His Way to America in 1748* (Joseph Lucas, trans., London, 1892).

KEENE, BENJAMIN: *The Private Correspondence of Sir Benjamin Keene, K. B.* (Sir Richard Lodge, ed., Cambridge, Eng., 1933).

KEITH, ROBERT MURRAY: *Memoirs and Correspondence (Official and Familiar) of Sir Robert Murray Keith . . .* by Amelia Gillespie Smyth (2 vols., London, 1849).

LEEDS, FRANCIS OSBORNE, 5TH DUKE OF: *The Political Memoranda of Francis, Fifth Duke of Leeds . . .,* Camden Society, *Publications,* n. ser., XXXIV (Oscar Browning, ed., London, 1884).

LENNOX, SARAH: *The Life and Letters of Lady Sarah Lennox, 1745-1826 . . . Also a Short Political Sketch of the Years 1760 to 1763 by Henry Fox, 1st Lord Holland* (Countess of Ilchester and Lord Stavordale, eds., 2 vols., London, 1901-2; 1 vol. edn., 1902).

LOLME, JEAN LOUIS DE: *Constitution de l'Angleterre* (Amsterdam, 1771), and in translation, *The Constitution of England: Or, an Account of the English Government . . .* (London, 1775; other edns., 1777, 1781, & 1784). Reprinted as *The Rise and Progress of the English Constitution: The Treatise of J. L. Lolme . . .* (Archibald John Stevens, ed., 2 vols., London, 1838).

"London Merchants on the Stamp Act Repeal," Massachusetts Historical Society, *Proceedings,* LV (1921-2), 215-23.

LYTTELTON, GEORGE, LORD: *Memoirs and Correspondence of George, Lord Lyttelton: From 1734 to 1773* (Robert J. Phillimore, ed., 2 vols., London, 1845).

MAC FARLANE, ROBERT: *The History of the Reign of George III* (4 vols. [London], 1770, 1782, 1794, and 1796).

[MAGENS, NICOLAS]: *The Universal Merchant: Containing the Rationale of Commerce, in Theory and Practice . . . Exemplified by Remarks Historical, Critical, and Political . . .* (London, 1753), and *Farther Explanations of Some Particular Subjects Relating to Trade, Coin, and Exchanges Contained in "The Universal Merchant"* (London, 1756).

MAITLAND, WILLIAM: *The History of London from Its Foundation by the Romans to the Present Time* . . . (London, 1739; 2 vols., 1756; 3rd edn., 2 vols., 1760).

MINCHINTON, W. E., ed.: *Politics and the Port of Bristol in the Eighteenth Century: The Petitions of the Society of Merchant Venturers, 1698-1803*, Bristol Record Society, *Publications*, XXIII (Bristol, Eng., 1963).

———: *The Trade of Bristol in the Eighteenth Century*, Bristol Record Society, *Publications*, XX (Bristol, Eng., 1957).

MITCHELL, ANDREW. *Memoirs and Papers of Sir Andrew Mitchell* . . . by Andrew Bisset (2 vols., London, 1850).

MORTIMER, THOMAS: *A New and Complete Dictionary of Trade and Commerce* (2 vols., London, 1766-7). This work is an expansion and reorganization of Postlethwayt.

Museum Rusticum et Commerciale: Or, Select Papers on Agriculture, Commerce, Arts, and Manufactures . . . (6 vols., London, 1764-6).

NEWCASTLE, THOMAS PELHAM-HOLLES, DUKE OF: *A Narrative of the Changes in the Ministry, 1765-1767: Told by the Duke of Newcastle in a Series of Letters to John White, M. P.*, Royal Historical Society, *Publications, Camden Second Series*, LIX (Mary Bateson, ed., London & New York, 1898).

NICHOLLS, JOHN: *Recollections and Reflections, Personal and Political: As Connected with Public Affairs during the Reign of George III* (2 vols., London, 1820-22).

NORTH, FREDERICK, LORD: "Lord North's Correspondence, 1766-83," Edward Hughes, ed., *English Historical Review*, LXII (1947), 218-38.

PARKINSON, SYDNEY: *A Journal of a Voyage to the South Seas in His Majesty's Ship the Endeavour: Faithfully Transcribed from the Papers of the late Sydney Parkinson* . . . (London, 1773).

PELHAM, HENRY. *Memoirs of the Administration of the Right Honourable Henry Pelham: Collected from the Family Papers and Other Authentic Documents* by William Coxe (2 vols., London, 1829).

PETTY, WILLIAM: *The Economic Writings of Sir William Petty* . . . (Charles Henry Hull, ed., Cambridge, Eng., 1899).

PITT, WILLIAM, EARL OF CHATHAM: *Correspondence of William Pitt, Earl of Chatham* (William Stanhope Taylor and John Henry Pringle, eds., 4 vols., London, 1838-40). Also available are *The Speeches of the Right Honourable the Earl of Chatham in the Houses of Lords and Commons* . . . (W. S. Hathaway, ed., 4 vols., London, 1806); *The Speeches of the Right Hon. the Earl of Chatham with a Biographical Memoir* . . . (London, 1848); and a small collection in the Old South Leaflet series, Volume 8, No. 199, *Speeches on the American Revolution* (Boston, 1908). Also of some use is Francis S. Thackeray's *A History of the Right Honourable William Pitt, Earl of Chatham: Containing His Speeches in Parliament* . . . (2 vols., London, 1827), and the contemporary *Authentic Memoirs of the Right Honourable, the Late Earl of Chatham* (London, 1778). Finally, see "Letters from William Pitt to Lord Bute, 1755-1758," Romney Sedgwick, ed., *Essays Presented to Sir Lewis Namier* (Richard Pares and A. J. P. Taylor, eds., London & New York, 1956), 108-66; and "Pitt's Retirement from Office, 5 Oct. 1761," H. W. V. Temperley, ed., *English Historical Review*, XXI (1906), 327-30.

POSTLETHWAYT, JAMES: *The History of the Public Revenue from the Revolution in 1688 . . . to Christmas 1758: Containing a Comprehensive View of All Our Public Transactions Relative to Money and Trade . . .* (London, 1759).

POSTLETHWAYT, MALACHY: *The Universal Dictionary of Trade and Commerce. Translated from the French of . . . Monsieur Savary . . . with Large Additions . . .* (2 vols., London, 1751-55; 4th edn., 1774).

RICHMOND, CHARLES LENNOX, 3RD DUKE OF: "The Duke of Richmond's Memorandum, 1-7 July, 1766," Alison Gilbert Olson, ed., *English Historical Review*, LXXV (1960), 475-82.

RIGBY, RICHARD: *Authentic Memoirs and a Sketch of the Real Character of the Late Right Honourable Richard Rigby* (London, 1788).

ROBINSON, JOHN: *Parliamentary Papers of John Robinson, 1774-1784*, Royal Historical Society, *Publications, Camden Third Series*, XXXIII (William T. Laprade, ed., London, 1922).

ROCKINGHAM, CHARLES WATSON-WENTWORTH, 2ND MARQUESS OF: *Memoirs, of the Marquis of Rockingham and His Contemporaries . . .* by George Thomas Keppel, Earl of Albemarle (2 vols., London, 1852).

RODNEY, GEORGE BRYDGES RODNEY, 1ST BARON. *The Life and Correspondence of the Late Admiral Lord Rodney* by Godfrey Basil Mundy (2 vols., London, 1830).

ROLT, RICHARD: *A New Dictionary of Trade and Commerce Compiled from the Information of the Most Eminent Merchants and from the Works of the Best Writers on Commercial Subjects . . .* (London, 1756; 2nd edn., 1761).

SANDWICH, JOHN MONTAGU, 4TH EARL OF: *The Private Papers of John, Earl of Sandwich, First Lord of the Admiralty, 1771-1782*, Navy Records Society, *Publications*, LXIX, LXXI, LXXV, LXXVIII (G. R. Barnes and J. H. Owen, eds., 4 vols., London, 1932-8).

SAUSSURE, CESARE DE: *A Foreign View of England in the Reigns of George I and George II: The Letters of Monsieur Cesare de Saussure to His Family* (B. Van Muyden, trans., London & N. Y., 1902).

SAXBY, HENRY: *The British Customs: Containing an Historical and Practical Account of Each Branch of That Revenue . . .* (London, 1757).

SECKER, THOMAS: *The Works of Thomas Secker . . . Published from the Original Manuscripts . . .* (Beilby Porteus and George Stinton, eds., n. edn., 6 vols., London, 1825). Secker was Archbishop of Canterbury.

SELWYN, GEORGE AUGUSTUS: *George Selwyn: His Letters and Life* (E. S. Roscoe and H. Clergue, eds., London, 1899).

SHARP, GRANVILLE. *Memoirs of Granville Sharp, Esq.: Composed from His Own Manuscripts . . .* by Prince Hoare (London, 1820; 2nd edn., 2 vols., 1828).

SHELBURNE, WILLIAM PETTY, 2ND EARL OF. *Life of William, Earl of Shelburne, Afterwards First Marquess of Landsdowne: With Extracts from His Papers and Correspondence* by Lord Edmond Fitzmaurice (3 vols., London, 1875-6).

SHERLOCK, THOMAS: *The Works of Bishop Sherlock: With Some Account of His Life . . .* (Thomas Smart Hughes, ed., 5 vols., London, 1830).

SOCIETY FOR THE PROPAGATION OF THE GOSPEL: *Classified Digest of the Records of the Society . . . 1701-1892: With Much Supplementary Information* (C. F. Roscoe and H. W. Tucker, eds., London, 1893).

STONE, GEORGE: "Correspondence of Archbishop Stone and the Duke of Newcastle," C. Litton Falkiner, ed., *English Historical Review,* XX (1905), 508-42, 735-63.

STRAHAN, WILLIAM: "Correspondence between William Strahan and David Hall, 1763-1777," *Pennsylvania Magazine of History and Biography,* X (1886)–XII (1888), *passim.* Also, "Some Further Letters of William Strahan, Printer [1750-1778]," J. E. Pomfret, ed., *ibid.,* LX (1936), 455-89. These letters deal primarily with British-American issues.

SULLIVAN, FRANCIS STOUGHTON: *An Historical Treatise on the Feudal Law and the Constitution and Laws of England: With Commentary on Magna Charta and . . . Illustrations of Many of the English Statutes . . .* (1st edn., London, 1772; 2nd edn., 1776).

TUCKER, JOSIAH: *Josiah Tucker: A Selection from His Economic and Political Writings* (Robert Livingston Schuyler, ed., New York, 1931).

The Under-Sheriff: Containing the Office and Duty of High Sheriffs, Under-Sheriffs, and Bailiffs: With an Appendix of Precedents Never before Published. By a Gentleman of the Inner-Temple (London, 1766).

VAN ALSTYNE, RICHARD W., ed.: "Europe, the Rockingham Whigs, and the War for American Independence: Some Documents," *Huntington Library Quarterly,* XXV (1961-2), 1-28; and "Parliamentary Supremacy versus Independence: Notes and Documents," *ibid.,* XXVI (1962-3), 201-33.

WALDEGRAVE, JAMES WALDEGRAVE, 2ND EARL: *Memoirs from 1754 to 1758 . . .* (H. R. V. Fox, ed., London, 1821).

WALPOLE, HORACE, 4TH EARL OF ORFORD: *Memoires of the Last Ten Years of the Reign of George the Second* ([Henry R. V. Fox, 3rd Lord Holland], ed., 2 vols., London, 1822; 2nd edn., 3 vols., 1846). There are also Walpole's writings from George III's reign, *Jour-*

nal of the Reign of King George the Third from the Year 1771 to 1783 ... (Dr. Doran, ed., 2 vols., London, 1859); reissued as *The Last Journals of Horace Walpole* ... (Archibald Francis Steuart, ed., 2 vols., London, 1910), and *Memoirs of the Reign of King George the Third* (Sir Denis Le Marchant, ed., 4 vols., London, 2 vols., Philadelphia, 1845; re-ed. by George F. Russell Barker, 4 vols., London, 1894). See in conjunction with this last work, Carl L. Becker's "Horace Walpole's Memoirs of the Reign of George the Third," *American Historical Review*, XVI (1910-11), 255-77, 496-507. Walpole's letters have appeared in numerous editions. Since they have had a great influence on historical writing, the following extensive listing is included. Two early collections were *The Works of Horace Walpole, Earl of Orford* (Mary Berry, ed., 5 vols., London, 1798), and *The Private Correspondence of Horace Walpole, Earl of Orford* ... (4 vols., London, 1820), followed by *Correspondence of H. W. with G. Montagu, Esq., Hon. H. S. Conway, Rev. W. Cole, Lady Hervey* ... (3 vols., London, 1837), and *Letters of Horace Walpole, Earl of Orford, to Sir Horace Mann, His Britannic Majesty's Resident at the Courts of Florence from 1760 to 1785* ... (4 vols., London, 1843-4). These general collections of correspondence are available: Peter Cunningham's edition, *Letters of H. W.* .... (9 vols., London, 1857-9); Mrs. Paget Toynbee's edition of great merit: *The Letters of Horace Walpole, 4th Earl of Orford* ... (16 vols., Oxford, Eng., 1903-5; supplements, 3 vols., 1918-25); and, finally, the superb *The Yale Edition of Horace Walpole's Correspondence* (Wilmarth S. Lewis, et al., eds., 34 vols.+, New Haven, Conn., 1937-65+) which takes precedence over all other editions of Walpole's letters.

WARBURTON, WILLIAM: *The Works of* ... *William Warburton* (14 vols., London, 1811-41). Warburton was Bishop of Gloucester.

WESLEY, CHARLES: *The Journal of the Rev. Charles Wesley* ... *To Which Are Appended Selections from His Correspondence and Poetry* (Thomas Jackson, ed., 2 vols., London, 1849).

WESLEY, JOHN: *The Works of the Rev. J. W.* .... (32 vols., Bristol, 1771-4; 2nd edn., Joseph Benson, ed., London, 1809-13; 3rd edn., Thomas Jackson, ed., 14 vols., 1829-31; 1st Am. edn., 10 vols., New York & Philadelphia, 1826-8; 11th edn., John Beacham, ed., London, 1856). See also *The Journal of the Rev. John Wesley* ... (Nehemiah Curnock, ed., 8 vols., London, 1909-16).

WHITEFIELD, GEORGE. A *Narrative of the Life of the Reverend Mr. George Whitefield* ... *with Extracts from Several Sermons* ... by T. Robert (London [1770]). In addition, there are several editions of his collected writings: *The Works of the Rev. George Whitefield* ... *With a Select Collection of Letters* ... (6 vols., London, 1771-2); *A Select Collection of the Letters of the Late Reverend*

George Whitefield . . . [1734-1770] (3 vols., London, 1772); and the more recent *Whitefield's Journals to which is Prefixed His "Short Account" and "Farther Account"* . . . (W. Wale, ed., London, 1905).

[WHITWORTH, CHARLES]: *A Collection of the Supplies and Ways and Means from the Revolution to the Present Time: By a Member of Parliament* (London, 1763; 2nd edn., 1765), and *State of the Trade of Great Britain in Its Imports and Exports* . . . [1697-1773] (2 pts., London, 1776).

WILKES, JOHN: *A Collection of All Mr. Wilkes's Addresses to the Gentlemen, Clergy, and Freeholders of . . . Middlesex* ([London], 1769), and *Speeches of J. Wilkes . . . in the Parliament . . . [1774-1777]* . . . (3 vols., London, 1777). Other collected materials available are: *The Controversial Letters of J. W. . . . , the Rev. John Horne, and Their Principal Adherents* . . . (London, 1771), and *The Correspondence of the Late John Wilkes with His Friends: Printed from the Original Manuscripts* . . . (5 vols., London, 1805). See also "John Wilkes and Boston," Worthington Chauncey Ford, ed., Massachusetts Historical Society, *Proceedings*, XLVII (1913-14), 190-215, and "John Wilkes and William Palfrey," George M. Elsey, ed., Colonial Society of Massachusetts, *Publications*, XXXIV (*Transactions, 1937-1942*), 411-28.

WILLARD, MARGARET WHEELER, ed.: *Letters on the American Revolution, 1774-1776* (Boston & New York, 1925). This work is comprised of selections from the *Bristol Journal*, the *Bristol Gazette*, and various London newspapers.

WRAXALL, NATHANIEL WILLIAM: *Historical Memoirs of My Own Time: From 1772 to 1784* (2 vols., London, 1815; 3rd edn., rev. & cor., 3 vols., 1818; 4th edn., 4 vols., 1836).

YOUNG, ARTHUR: *The Autobiography of Arthur Young: With Selections from His Correspondence* (M. Batham-Edwards, ed., London, 1898). Three other useful writings by Young are: *The Farmer's Letters to the People of England: Containing the Sentiments of a Practical Husbandman on Various Subjects* . . . (London, 1768); *A Six Months Tour through the North of England* . . . (1st edn., 4 vols., London, 1770; 2nd edn., 1770-1); and *A Six Weeks Tour through the Southern Counties of England and Wales* . . . (London, 1768).

3. *Contemporary pamphlets, tracts, and related materials: Chronologically arranged*

It is hardly necessary to call attention to the importance of the following works, mostly pamphlets, in revealing the state of mind of the people of eighteenth-century Britain.

Sir Lewis Namier in his writings has left the impression that the leaders in Great Britain were interested in little other than personal or family promotion or advantage; other historians have stressed the point that it was the so-called King's Friends who plunged Great Britain into war with her colonies—the public simply followed on behind. In no country or in no part of the British Empire, however, were public issues so openly and vigorously debated in the press as in Great Britain; this is particularly true from 1763 to the end of 1776. In order to emphasize the growing attention of British writers to public affairs and the demand for their output the following list begins with the year 1744 and is presented in some fullness.

Pre - 1 7 4 8

DECKER, MATTHEW: *An Essay on the Causes of the Decline of the Foreign Trade, Consequently of the Value of the Lands of Britain, and on the Means to Restore Both* . . . (London, 1744; 2nd edn., w/add., London, 1750).

The Present State of British and French Trade to Africa and America Considered and Compared . . . (London, 1745).

BURGH, JAMES: *Britain's Remembrancer or the Danger Not Over: Being Some Thoughts on the Proper Improvement of the Present Juncture* . . . *A Brief View from History of the Effects of the Vices Which Now Prevail in Britain* . . . (London, 1746; 5th edn., 1748).

Interest of Great Britain in Supplying Herself with Iron Impartially Considered ([London, 1746]).

CAMPBELL, R.: *The London Tradesman: Being a Compendious View of All the Trades, Professions, Arts, Both Liberal and Mechanic, now Practised in the Cities of London and Westminster* (London, 1747; 3rd edn., 1757). Provides a wealth of data regarding conditions, profits, and wages in various trades.

DEVEIL, THOMAS: *Observations on the Practice of a Justice of the Peace: Intended for Such Gentlemen as Design to Act for Middlesex or Westminster* (London, 1747).

1 7 4 8

The Conduct of the Government with Regard to Peace and War Stated (London, 1748).

Considerations on the Definitive Treaty Signed at Aix-la-Chapelle, October 7/18, 1748 . . . (London, 1748).

[SQUIRE, SAMUEL]: *An Historical Essay upon the Ballance [sic] of Civil Power in England* . . . (London, 1748). The author was bishop of St. David's.

1 7 4 9

[BOLINGBROKE, HENRY ST. JOHN, VISCOUNT]: *The Idea of a Patriot King* ([London, 1749]). This was written much earlier by Bolingbroke and periodically reprinted after 1749.

A Free Apology in Behalf of the Smugglers so Far as Their Case Affects the Constitution . . . (London, 1749).

[NUGENT, ROBERT CRAGGS]: *Considerations upon a Reduction of the Land-Tax* (London, 1749).

POSTLETHWAYT, MALACHY: *Considerations on the Revival of the Royal-British-Asiento between His Catholick-Majesty and the Honourable the South-Sea Company* . . . (London, 1749).

The Present Taxes Compared to the Payments Made to the Publick within the Memory of Man with Some Thoughts on the Possible Consequences That May Ensue from the National Debts: In a Letter . . . (London, 1749).

[TOZER, AARON]: *A Blow at the Root: or an Attempt to Prove that No Time Ever Was* . . . *so Proper and Convenient as the Present for Introducing a Further Reformation into Our National Church, Universities and Schools* . . . (London, 1749).

[TUCKER, JOSIAH]: *A Brief Essay on the Advantages and Disadvantages which Respectively Attend France and Great Britain with Regard to Trade* . . . (London, 1749). There were several editions of this work printed between 1749 and 1787.

The Wealth of Great Britain in the Ocean: Exemplified from Materials Laid before the Committee of the House of Commons Appointed . . . *to Examine into the State of the British Fisheries* . . . (London, 1749).

1 7 5 0

HOOKE, ANDREW: *An Essay on the National Debt and National Capital: Or the Account Truly Stated, Debtor and Creditor* . . . (London, 1750; 2nd edn. w/add., 1751). The pamphlet gives tables on money, stock, and land in England in order to estimate the capital of the country between 1600 and 1749.

The State of the Trade and Manufactory of Iron in Great Britain Considered ([London], 1750).

1 7 5 1

[GRAY, CHARLES]: *Considerations on the Several Proposals Lately Made for the Better Maintenance of the Poor* (London, 1751; 2nd edn. w/appendix, 1752). This essay, calling for the supervision of the poor, was answered by an anonymous pamphlet, presumably authored by James Creed, *An Impartial Examination of A Pamphlet Intitled "Considerations . . ."* (London, 1752); and also by the anonymous *A Letter to the Author of "Considerations . . ."* (London, 1752).

[HAY, WILLIAM]: *Remarks on the Laws Relating to the Poor: With Proposals for Their Better Relief and Employment . . .* (London, 1751). This work was first published in 1735, and its reissue stimulated much discussion.

The Present State of the Tobacco Trade as the Late Act Affects the London Manufacturers Considered: In a Letter to a Friend (London, 1751).

[TUCKER, JOSIAH]: *An Impartial Inquiry into the Benefits and Damages Arising to the Nation from the Present Very Great Use of Low-Priced Spirituous Liquors . . .* (London, 1751).

1 7 5 2 - 3

ALCOCK, THOMAS: *Observations on the Defects of the Poor Laws and on the Causes and Consequences of the Great Increase and Burden of the Poor With a Proposal for Redressing These Grievances . . .* (London, 1752).

HUME, DAVID: *Political Discourses* (Edinburgh, 1752). Despite the title, this work is primarily a discussion of economic matters, including trade, exchange, manufacturing, and finance.

POWNALL, THOMAS: *Principles of Polity: Being the Grounds and Reasons of Civil Empire* (London, 1752). Pownall herein presented the viewpoint that individual rights could only be sanctioned by the united will or "public conscience." Part of this pamphlet was published anonymously in 1750 as *A Treatise on Government . . .*

FIELDING, HENRY: *A Proposal for Making an Effectual Provision for the Poor, for Amending Their Morals, and for Rendering Them Useful Members of the Society . . .* (London, 1753).

1 7 5 4

[PLUMARD DE DANGUEL] JOHN NICKOLLS: *Remarks on the Advantages and Disadvantages of France and of Great Britain with Respect to Commerce and to the Other Means of Increasing the Wealth and Power of the State . . .* (London, 1754).

Select Essays on Commerce, Agriculture, Mines, Fisheries, and Other Useful Subjects (London, 1754). This pamphlet is a translated selection from the *Journal Œconomique . . .*, published at Paris from 1751 to 1757.

WELCH, SAUNDERS: *Observations on the Office of Constable: With Cautions for the More Safe Execution of that Duty . . .* (London, 1754).

1 7 5 5

BURN, RICHARD: *The Justice of the Peace and Parish Officer* (2 vols. [London], 1755; numerous editions; 20th edn., cont'd by W. Woodfall, 4 vols., 1805; 23rd edn., 6 vols., 1820-3). This was a very popular work explaining the function and duties of the justice of the peace.

CLARKE, WILLIAM: *Observations on the Late and Present Conduct of the French With Regard to Their Encroachments Upon the British Colonies . . . To Which is Added Observations Concerning the Increase of Mankind . . .* (London, 1755). Benjamin Franklin wrote the latter "Observations . . ."

[MC CULLOCH, ————]: *A Miscellaneous Essay Concerning the Courses Pursued by Great Britain in the Affairs of Her Colonies . . .* (London, 1755). The author suggested in the pamphlet that colonial affairs be brought under more direct control of the Crown for the benefit of both. See also: *The Wisdom and Policy of the French in the Construction of Their Great Offices so as Best to Answer the Purpose of Extending Their Trade and Commerce and Enlarging Their Foreign Settlements . . .* (London, 1755), which was written as an introductory essay to the first pamphlet.

[SHEBBEARE, JOHN]: *A Letter to the People of England on the Present Situation and Conduct of National Affairs: Letter I* (1st & 2nd edns., London, 1755; 3rd edn., 1756).

[TUCKER, JOSIAH]: *The Elements of Commerce and Theory of Taxes* ([Bristol, 1755]). A discussion of population, manufacturing, agriculture, and the enclosures.

[————]: *The Important Question Concerning Invasions, a Sea-War, Raising the Militia, and Paying Subsidies for Foreign Troops . . .* (London, 1755).

1 7 5 6

Case of the Importation of Bar-Iron from Our Own Colonies of North America: Humbly Recommended to the Consideration of the Present Parliament by the Iron Manufacturers of Great Britain (London, 1756). For a reply, see *Reflections on the Importation of Bar-Iron . . . In Answer to a Late Pamphlet on That Subject . . .* ([London, 1757]).

CLEEVE, BOURCHIER: *A Scheme for Preventing a Further Increase of the National Debt and for Reducing the Same . . .* (London, 1756; 2nd & 3rd edns., 1767). The pamphlet contains a proposal for a single general tax.

[EGMONT, JOHN PERCEVAL, 2ND EARL OF]: *Thoughts on the Pernicious Consequences of Borrowing Money with a Proposal for Raising a Supply for the Current Service . . .* (London, 1756; 2nd edn., 1759). The pamphlet presented a proposal for an "equal land tax."

[FAUQUIER, FRANCIS]: *An Essay on Ways and Means for Raising Money for the Support of the Present War Without Increasing the Public Debts* (London, 1756; rep., Baltimore, Md., 1915). The author, who signed himself F.F., suggested that a tax be placed on houses.

[MASSIE, JOSEPH]: *Calculations on the Present Taxes Yearly Paid by a Family of Each Rank, Degree, or Class for One Year* (London, 1756; 2nd edn., 1761). The pamphlet illustrated the inequalities of existing taxes.

[SHEBBEARE, JOHN]: *A Fourth Letter to the People of England on the Conduct of the M——rs in Alliances, Fleets, and Armies since the First Differences on the Ohio to the Taking of Minorca by the French* (London, 1756).

1 7 5 7

A Letter from a Merchant of the City of London to the R——t H——ble W—— P——, Esq., upon the Affairs and Commerce of North America, and the West Indies: Our African Trade . . . (London, 1757).

POSTLETHWAYT, MALACHY: *Britain's Commercial Interest Explained and Improved in a Series of Dissertations on Several Important Branches of Her Trade and Police . . .* (London, 2 vols., 1757; 2nd edn., 2 vols., 1759). A discussion of government policy aimed at promoting the encouragement of agriculture and commerce.

——: *Great Britain's True System . . .* (London, 1757). In this work, a source of various commercial information, it is suggested that supplies be raised by taxation rather than by loans.

Proposals for Carrying on the War with Vigour, Raising the Supplies within the Years, and Forming a National Militia: To Which Are Added Considerations in Respect to Manufacturers and Labourers and the Taxes Paid by Them (London, 1757). The pamphlet contains suggestions for shifting taxes to the consumers and taxing luxuries and houses.

1 7 5 8

FIELDING, JOHN: *An Account of the Origin and Effects of a Police Set on Foot by His Grace the Duke of Newcastle in the Year 1753 . . . With a Plan for Preserving Those Deserted Girls in This Town Who Become Prostitutes of Necessity* (London, 1758; 1770).

MASSIE, JOSEPH: *A Plan for the Establishment of Charity-Houses for Exposed or Deserted Women and Girls; Observations Concerning the Foundling Hospital . . . , Considerations Relating to the Poor and Poor's Laws . . .* (London, 1758).

[TEMPLE, WILLIAM]: *Vindication of Commerce and the Arts, Proving that*

They Are the Source of the Greatness, Power, Riches, and Populousness of a State (London, 1758). The pamphlet is an argument for the expansion of commerce.

WALLACE, ROBERT: *Characteristics of the Present Political State of Great Britain* (London, 1758). An optimistic discussion of matters of national finance and wealth.

1 7 5 9

SMITH, ADAM: *The Theory of Moral Sentiments* . . . (London, 1759). For a reply, published anonymously, see Arthur Lee's *An Essay in Vindication of the Continental Colonies of America from the Censure of Mr. Adam Smith in His Theory of Moral Sentiments* . . . (London, 1764).

[YOUNG, ARTHUR]: *Reflections on the Present State of Affairs at Home and Abroad* . . . (London, 1759).

1 7 6 0

Conjectures on the Present State of Affairs in Germany: Containing Remarks on the Conduct of His Prussian Majesty and the Probability of His Concluding a Safe and Honourable Peace. By an Impartial Hand (London, 1760).

[DOUGLAS, JOHN]: *A Letter Addressed to Two Great Men [Pitt and Newcastle] on the Prospect of Peace and on the Terms Necessary to Be Insisted upon in the Negociation* (2nd edn., London, 1760). This pamphlet, urging the retention of Canada in any treaty with France, sparked the following reply attributed to William Burke: *Remarks on the Letter Address'd to Two Great Men: In a Letter to the Author of that Piece* (London, 1760); this pamphlet may also have been written by Charles Townshend.

[FRANKLIN, BENJAMIN]: *The Interest of Great Britain Considered with Regard to Her Colonies and the Acquisitions of Canada and Guadeloupe* . . . (London, 1760). This pamphlet, usually attributed to Richard Jackson, has been identified as being written by Franklin by V. W. Crane in American Bibliographical Society, *Papers*, XXVIII (1934), 5ff. A reply to the pamphlet may be found in *An Examination into the Value of Canada and Guadeloupe* . . . *In Answer to a Late Pamphlet Entitled "The Interest of Great Britain* . . ." (London, 1761).

HEATHCOTE, GEORGE: *A Letter to the Right Honourable the Lord Mayor, the Worshipful Aldermen, and Common Council, the Merchants, Citizens, and Inhabitants of the City of London: From an Old Servant* (London, 1760). This pamphlet was an attack on the preliminary terms of peace.

A Letter to the People of England on the Necessity of Putting an Imme-

diate End to the War and the Means of Obtaining an Advantageous Peace (London, 1760).

MASSIE, JOSEPH: *A Computation of the Money . . . Raised Upon the People of Great Britain by the Sugar Planters in One Year . . .* ([London, 1760]). A broadside.

————: *A Representation Concerning the Knowledge of Commerce as a National Concern . . .* (London, 1760).

[MAUDUIT, ISRAEL]: *Considerations on the Present German War* (1st-3rd edns., London, 1760). This pamphlet provoked the following replies: *The Conduct of the Ministry Impartially Examined and the Pamphlet Entitled "Considerations . . ." Refuted from Its Own Principles* (London, 1760), which in turn brought a reply, published anonymously, from John Shebbeare: *An Answer to a Pamphlet Call'd "The Conduct . . ." in Which It Is Proved that neither Imbecillity nor Ignorance in the M——r Have Been the Causes of the Present Unhappy Situation of This Nation . . .* (London [1760]). See also: *A Full and Candid Answer to a Pamphlet Entitled "Considerations . . ."* (London, 1760); and *A Letter from a British Officer now in Germany: Containing Many Interesting Particulars Relative to the "Considerations . . ."* (London, 1761).

PHILMORE, J.: *Two Dialogues on the Man-Trade* (London, 1760). The pamphlet presents a long argument against the slave trade.

The Trial of the Right Honourable Lord George Sackville at a Court-Martial Held at the Horse Guards . . . With His Lordship's Defence (2 vols., London [1760]).

TUCKER, JOSIAH: *The Manifold Causes of the Increase of the Poor Distinctly Set Forth Together with a Set of Proposals . . .* ([Gloucester, Eng., 1760]). The pamphlet presented a detailed plan for the care of the poor.

WALLIN, BENJAMIN: *The Joyful Sacrifice of a Prosperous Nation: A Sermon Preached . . . on Account of the Repeated Success against Our Enemies the French . . .* (London, 1760).

1761

The Case of the British Troops Serving in Germany Submitted to the Consideration of Parliament . . . (London, 1761).

[DOUGLAS, JOHN]: *Seasonable Hints from an Honest Man on the Present Important Crisis of a New Reign and a New Parliament* (London, 1761). Douglas was Bishop of Carlisle.

A Letter to a Great M——r on the Prospect of Peace Wherein the Demolition of the Fortifications of Louisbourg Is Shewn to Be Absurd, the Importance of Canada Fully Refuted, the Proper Barrier Pointed Out in North America, and the Reasonableness and Necessity of Retaining the French Sugar Islands . . . (London, 1761).

[MAUDUIT, ISRAEL]: *Occasional Thoughts on the Present German War* . . . (London, 1761).

Reasons for Keeping Guadeloupe at a Peace, Preferable to Canada: Explained in Five Letters from a Gentleman in Guadeloupe to His Friend in London (London, 1761). The author suggested that it would be more advantageous for Britain to retain Guadeloupe than Canada since the former could supply many raw materials and markets while the latter was limited to fur trade. Also, by allowing France to retain Canada, the British Colonies would be discouraged from revolting.

1 7 6 2

[ALMON, JOHN]: *A Review of Mr. Pitt's Administration* (1st edn., London, 1762; 4th edn., 1764). The third edition, 1763, contained "An Appendix to the Review . . . ."

————: *A Review of the Reign of George the Second: In Which a New Light Is Thrown on Transactions and the Effects of Ministerial Influence Are Traced and Laid Open* (London, 1762).

Comparative Importance of Our Acquisitions from France in America . . . (London, 1762).

An Examination of the Commercial Principles of the Late Negotiations between Great Britain and France in 1761: In Which the System of that Negotiation with Regard to Our Colonies and Commerce Is Considered (1st & 2nd edns., London, 1762). The pamphlet, favoring the retention of Guadeloupe, argued that trade with the West Indies was more important than that with North America.

A General View of England Respecting Its Policy, Trade, Commerce, Taxes, Debts, Produce of Lands, Colonies, Manners, Etc. . . . [1600-1762] ([London, 1762]). Signed M.V.D.M., i.e. M. Vivant de Mezague. The pamphlet aimed at disproving the theory of England's economic superiority.

1 7 6 3

[ALMON, JOHN]: *A Letter to the Right Hon. George Grenville [on his political conduct]* (London, 1763; 3rd edn. w/add., 1763); signed "An Independent Whig." See also the anonymous reply *A Letter to the Author of a Letter to the Right Hon. G. G.* (London, 1763).

————: *A Review of Lord Bute's Administration* (London, 1763).

An Appeal to the Public in Behalf of G[eorge] J[ohnstone], Esq., Governor of West Florida. In Answer to the North Briton . . . (London, 1763).

BATH, WILLIAM PULTENEY, EARL OF: *Reflections on the Domestic Policy Proper to Be Observed on the Conclusion of Peace* . . . (London, 1763).

[BUTLER, JOHN]: *Serious Considerations on the Measures of the Present Administration* (London, 1763). Butler was Bishop of Hereford.

The Constitution Asserted and Vindicated (London, 1763).

DALRYMPLE, JOHN (later 5th Earl of Stair): *An Appeal of Reason to the People of England on the Present State of Parties in the Nation* (London, 1763). A defence of John Stuart, Earl of Bute; see also his *An Appeal to Facts: In a Letter to the Right Hon. Earl Temple* (London, 1763).

DOUGLAS, JOHN: *Reflections on the Domestic Policy* (London, 1763). A sympathetic review of trade and colonial and economic affairs under George III.

[DOWDESWELL, WILLIAM]: *An Address to Such of the Electors of Great Britain as Are Not Makers of Cyder and Perry . . .* (London, 1763).

Expediency of Securing Our American Colonies by Settling the Country Adjoining the River Mississippi and the Country upon the Ohio Considered (Edinburgh, 1763).

IGNATUS, pseud.: *Thoughts on Trade in General, Our West-Indian in Particular, Our Continental Colonies, Canada, Guadeloupe, and the Preliminary Articles of Peace . . .* (London, 1763).

A Letter to the Right Hon. the Earl of Temple on the Subject of the Forty-Fifth Number of the North-Briton . . . (London, 1763).

Letter to the Right Hon. the Earls of Egremont and Halifax on the Seizure of Papers (London, 1763).

Reflections on the Terms of Peace (2nd edn., London, 1763).

[ROBERTS, JOHN]: *Considerations on the Present Peace as Far as It Is Relative to the Colonies and the African Trade* (London, 1763).

[RUFFHEAD, OWEN]: *Considerations on the Present Dangerous Crisis* (London, 1763). See also, the anonymous rebuttal: *The Opposition to the Late Minister [Lord Bute] Vindicated from the Aspersions of a Pamphlet Intitled "Considerations . . ."* (London, 1763).

Some Hints to People in Power on the Present Melancholy Situation of Our Colonies in North America . . . (London, 1763).

[TUCKER, JOSIAH]: *The Case of Going to War for the Sake of Preserving, Enlarging, or Securing of Trade Considered in a New Light . . .* (London, 1763).

WILKES, JOHN: *An Authentick Account of the Proceedings against J[ohn] W[ilkes], Esq., Member of Parliament . . . Containing All the Papers Relative to This Interesting Affair . . .* (London [1763]).

———: *[An Essay on Woman]* ([London, 1763]). Wilkes's famous or infamous poem was printed but not published and prompted John Kidgell's pamphlet, *A Genuine and Succinct Narrative of a Scandalous, Obscene, and Exceedingly Profane Libel Entitled "An Essay on Woman"* (London [1763]), which was in turn answered by John Almon in *A Letter to J. Kidgell Containing a Full Answer to His Narrative* (London, 1763). See also: Thomas Farmer's *The Plain Truth: Being a Genuine Narrative of the Methods Made Use of to Procur a Copy of the "Essay on Woman . . ."* (London, 1763); and two anonymous pamphlets *A Full and Candid Answer to a Pamphlet Called "A Genuine and Succinct Narrative . . ." By a Friend of Truth* (London, 1763), and *An Expostulatory Letter to Mr. Kidgell Occasioned by His Late Extraordinary Publication . . . By a Layman* (3rd edn., w/additions, London, 1763).

1 7 6 4

[BRECKNOCK, TIMOTHY]: *Droit le Roy: Or a Digest of the Rights and Prerogatives of the Imperial Crown of Great Britain . . .* (London, 1764).

BUTLER, JOHN: *Some Account of the Character of the Late Rt. Hon. H[enry] B[ilson] Legge* (London, 1764). Butler was the Bishop of Hereford; his pamphlet was answered by the anonymous *Observations on a Pamphlet Published by J. Almon Intitled "Some Account . . ."* (London [1764]).

CANDOR, pseud.: *A Letter from Candor to the Public Advertiser: Containing a Series of Constitutional Remarks on Some Late Interesting Trials and Other Points of the Most Essential Consequence to Civil Liberty . . .* (2nd edn., London, 1764). This pamphlet has been attributed to Charles Pratt, Lord Camden.

[CUNNINGHAM, J.]: *Considerations on Taxes as They Are Supposed to Affect the Price of Labour in Our Manufactories: Also Some Reflections on the General Behaviour and Disposition of the Manufacturing Populace of This Kingdom . . .* (London, 1764; 2nd edn., 1765). The author presented the opinion that rising costs of production were caused by the idleness of the poor.

An Essay on the Trade of the Northern Colonies of Great Britain in North America . . . (London, 1764). Presents a British view.

[GILBERT, THOMAS]: *A Scheme for the Better Relief and Employment of the Poor . . .* (London, 1764).

[HARTLEY, DAVID]: *The Budget: Inscribed to the Man Who Thinks Himself Minister . . .* (1st edn., London, 1764; 11th edn., 1766). For a reply to this pamphlet see that published anonymously by Thomas Whately: *Remarks on "The Budget": Or a Candid Examination of the Facts and Arguments Offered to the Public in That Pamphlet . . .* (London, 1765), to which Hartley responded with *The State of the Nation (with Regard to Its Income, Expenditure and Unfunded Debts): With a Preliminary Defence of the Budget* (London, 1765).

An Enquiry into the Doctrine, Lately Propagated, Concerning Libels, Warrants, and the Seizure of Papers . . . In a Letter to Mr. Almon from the Father of Candor (London, 1764). There were several other editions of this tract, some entitled *A Letter Concerning Libels, Warrants, and the Seizure of Papers. . . .* This pamphlet, prompted a reply from John Almon: *A Postscript to the Letter on Libels, Warrants, Etc.* ([London], 1765).

An Impartial Examination of the Conduct of the Whigs and Tories (London, 1764).

A Letter to the Common Council of the City of London [respecting certain of their late votes, etc.] . . . (London, 1764). See also, *A Second Letter to the Common Council of the City of London* . . . (London, 1764).

A Letter to the Right Hon. G[eorge] G[renville] upon the Conduct of the Late Opposition (London, 1764). The British Museum Catalog suggests that John Almon was the author.

Remarks on the Present State of the National Debt: Together with Some Strictures upon the General Modes of Taxation in England (London, 1764).

[TEMPLE, RICHARD TEMPLE GRENVILLE-TEMPLE, EARL]: *The Principles of the Late Changes Impartially Examined: In a Letter from a Son of Candor to the Public Advertiser* (London, 1764). For a reply, see: *Secret Springs of the Late Changes in the Ministry Fairly Explained: In Answer to a Pretended 'Son of Candor'* (London, 1766).

[TOWNSHEND, CHARLES]: *A Defence of the Minority in the House of Commons on the Question Relating to General Warrants* (London, 1764). The pamphlet was answered by the anonymous *A Letter to the Right Honourable Charles Townshend* (London, 1764), and also by a pamphlet written by Charles Lloyd and published anonymously: *Defense of the Majority in the House of Commons on the Question Relating to General Warrants: In Answer to the Defence of the Minority* (London, 1764), the latter of which was in turn answered by the anonymous *Reply to the Defence of the Majority on the Question Relating to General Warrants* (London, 1765).

[WALLACE, ROBERT]: *A View of the Internal Policy of Great Britain* . . . (London, 1764).

WILKES, JOHN: *A Letter to the Worthy Electors of . . . Aylesbury . . . [22 October 1764]* (London, 1764).

1 7 6 5

[ALMON, JOHN, and HUMPHREY COTES]: *The History of the Late Minority: Exhibiting the Conduct, Principles, and Views of That Party during the Years 1762, 1763, 1764, and 1765.* (London, 1765).

[BOLLAN, WILLIAM]: *The Mutual Interest of Great Britain and the*

American Colonies Considered: With Respect to an Act Passed Last Sessions of Parliament for Laying a Duty on Merchandise . . . (London, 1765).

[BROWN, JOHN]: *Thoughts on Civil Liberty, on Licentiousness, and Faction . . .* (1st edn., Newcastle-upon-Tyne, 1765; 2nd edn., London, 1765).

CATO, pseud.: *Thoughts on a Question of Importance Proposed to the Public: Whether It Is Probable that the Immense Extent of Territory Acquired by This Nation at the Late Peace Will Operate Towards the Prosperity or the Ruin of the Island of Great Britain?* (London, 1765).

Considerations on the Legality of General Warrants and the Propriety of a Parliamentary Regulation of the Same . . . (London, 1765).

Considerations on Taxes as They Are Supposed to Affect the Price of Labour in Our Manufacturies: Also Some Reflections on the General Behaviour and Disposition of the Manufacturing Populace of This Kingdom . . . (2nd edn., London, 1765).

[COOPER, GREY]: *The Merits of the New Administration Duly Stated* (London, 1765).

CUNNINGHAM, TIMOTHY: *A New Treatise on the Laws Concerning Tithes . . .* (London, 1765).

DUMMER, JEREMIAH: *A Defence of the New-England Charters* (London [1765]). This powerful pamphlet was penned in 1715 and first printed in 1721. Dummer was the London agent for Massachusetts Bay from 1710 to 1721. Its republication in 1765 is significant.

[FOTHERGILL, JOHN]: *Considerations Relative to the North American Colonies* (London, 1765).

[JENYNS, SOAME]: *The Objections to the Taxation of Our American Colonies, by the Legislature of Great Britain, Briefly Consider'd* (London, 1765). This pamphlet was reprinted in the *Newport Mercury* and the *Massachusetts Gazette and Weekly News-Letter* and prompted the following anonymously-published reply by James Otis: *Considerations on Behalf of the Colonists: In a Letter to a Noble Lord* (1st & 2nd edns., London, 1765). This pamphlet, signed F.A., is reprinted in Charles F. Mullett's "Some Political Writings of James Otis," University of Missouri, *Studies: A Quarterly of Research, IV* (1929), 361-81. For a more weighty reply see: Daniel Dulany's *Considerations on the Propriety of Imposing Taxes in the British Colonies for the Purpose of Raising Revenue, by Act of Parliament* (Annapolis, Md., 1765).

[KNOX, WILLIAM]: *The Claim of the Colonies to an Exemption from Internal Taxes Imposed by Authority of Parliament Examined . . .* (London, 1765). The author supports the Stamp Act on legal grounds. For an anonymously-published American reply see Ebenezer Devotion's *The Examiner Examined: A Letter from a*

Gentleman in Connecticut to His Friend in London in Answer to a Letter . . . Intitled "The Claim of the Colonies . . ." (New London, Conn., 1766).

A Letter to a Member of Parliament: Wherein the Power of the British Legislature and the Case of the Colonists Are Briefly and Impartially Considered (London, 1765). While the author opposed the Stamp Act, he took a legalistic position, asserting that the colonists had to obey the acts of Parliament. It has been suggested that the pamphlet was the product of William Knox.

A Letter to the Common Council of London on Their Late Very Extraordinary Address to His Majesty (1st & 2nd edns., London, 1765).

A Letter to the Public Containing Some Important Hints Relating to the Revenue (London, 1765).

[LLOYD, CHARLES]: *An Honest Man's Reasons for Declining to Take Any Part in the New Administration . . .* (London, 1765).

[MAUDUIT, ISRAEL]: *Some Thoughts on the Method of Improving and Securing the Advantages Which Accrue to Great-Britain from the Northern Colonies* (London, 1765).

MILDMAY, WILLIAM: *The Laws and Policy of England Relating to Trade Examined by the Maxims and Principles of Trade in General and by the Laws and Policy of Other Trading Nations . . .* (London, 1765). The author presented in this pamphlet a theoretical discussion of commercial policy.

The Political Balance: In Which the Principles and Conduct of the Two Parties Are Weighed (London, 1765).

The Regulations Lately Made Concerning the Colonies and the Taxes Imposed upon Them Considered (London, 1765).

The Rights of the British Colonies Considered: The Administration and Regulation of the Colonies Exploded and the Best Means Recommended to Make the Colonies Most Useful to the Mother Country (London [1765]).

A Second Letter to the Rt. Hon. Charles Townshend Occasioned by His Commendations of the Budget: In Which the Merits of that Pamphlet Are Examined (London, 1765).

A Vindication of the Whigs against the Clamours of a Tory Mob . . . (London, 1765).

[WHATELY, THOMAS]: *The Regulations Lately Made Concerning the Colonies and Taxes Imposed upon Them Considered* (London, 1765). This pamphlet, which was published anonymously, was attributed to George Grenville, but was really the work of Whately. Richard Bland replied to the pamphlet with *An Inquiry into the Rights of the British Colonies Intended as an Answer to the "Regulations Lately Made . . ."* (Williamsburg, Va., 1766; London, 1769).

YONGE, PHILIP: *A Sermon Preached before the Incorporated Society for the Propagation of the Gospel in Foreign Parts: At Their Anniversary Meeting . . . February 15, 1765* (London, 1765). Yonge was Bishop of Norwich.

1 7 6 6

An Application of Some General Political Rules to the Present State of Great-Britain, Ireland, and America: In a Letter to the Right Honourable Earl Temple (London, 1766).

[BACON, ANTHONY]: *The True Interest of Great Britain with Respect to Her American Colonies Stated and Impartially Considered . . .* (London, 1766).

BENEZET, ANTHONY: *A Caution and Warning to Great-Britain and Her Colonies in a Short Representation of the Calamitous State of the Enslaved Negroes in the British Dominions: Collected from Various Authors . . .* (Philadelphia, 1766; London, 1767).

BOLLAN, WILLIAM: *The Freedom of Speech and Writing upon Public Affairs Considered* (London, 1766).

BURKE, EDMUND: *A Short Account of a Late Short Administration* (London, 1766).

The Celebrated Speech of a Celebrated Commoner [WILLIAM PITT] (London, 1766). See the reply, probably by Richard Pennant: *The Answer at Large to Mr. P—tt's Speech . . .* (London, 1766), which refers to the repeal of the Stamp Act.

Considerations on the American Stamp Act and on the Conduct of the Minister Who Planned It (London, 1766). Repeal of the Stamp Act is this author's suggestion for restoring good relations between the colonies and England.

Constitutional Considerations on the Power of Parliament to Levy Taxes on the North American Colonies (London, 1766).

[COTES, HUMPHREY]: *An Enquiry into the Conduct of a Late Right Honourable Commoner* (London, 1766). The Commoner was William Pitt. Earl Temple assisted in the preparation of this work which was answered by the anonymous *A Short View of the Political Life and Transactions of a Late Right Honourable Commoner . . .* (London, 1766).

An Examination of the Rights of the Colonies upon Principles of Law. By a Gentleman of the Bar (London, 1766).

Free and Candid Remarks on a Late Celebrated Oration: With Some Few Occasional Thoughts on the Late Commotions in America . . . (London, 1766). This pamphlet is a censure of Pitt's speech against the Stamp Act.

The General Opposition of the Colonies to the Payment of the Stamp Duty and the Consequence of Enforcing Obedience by Military

Measures Impartially Considered . . . (London, 1766). The author discouraged the use of force to make the colonists comply with the Stamp Act.

Good Humour or Away with the Colonies wherein Is Occasionally Enquired into Mr. P—t's Claim to Popularity, and the Principles of Virtuous Liberty as Taught in the School of Mr. Wilkes and Other Peripatetics (London, 1766). An attempt to vindicate Parliament from the implication of unconstitutional severity regarding the Stamp Act.

[HOMER, HENRY]: *An Essay on the Nature and Method of Ascertaining the Specifick Shares of Proprietors upon the Inclosure of Common Fields* . . . (Oxford, Eng., 1766).

The Justice and Necessity of Taxing the American Colonies Demonstrated: Together with a Vindication of the Authority of Parliament (London, 1766). This "fiery politician" felt that there was a definite need for a standing army in the colonies because of the crude and undisciplined colonists.

The Late Occurrences in North America and Policy of Great Britain Considered (London, 1766). The author of the pamphlet called for Britain to try all means to reconcile her differences with the American colonies in order to avoid war.

The Legislative Authority of the British Parliament with Respect to North America and the Privileges of the Assemblies There Briefly Considered. By J. M. of the Inner-Temple (London, 1766). This pamphlet has been ascribed to Jasper Mauduit, but research has shown that he was never a member of the Inner Temple.

A Letter to the Gentlemen of the Committee of London Merchants Trading to North America Shewing . . . That the Trade and Manufactures of Britain May Be affected by Some Late Restrictions on the American Commerce . . . (London, 1766). The pamphlet presents the argument that the colonists should be represented in Parliament.

List of the Minority in the House of Commons Who Voted against the Bill to Repeal the American Stamp Act (Paris [i.e., London], 1766).

[LLOYD, CHARLES]: *An Examination of the Principles and Boasted Disinterestedness of a Late Right Honourable Gentleman [W. Pitt]* . . . (London, 1766).

[————]: *A True Story of a Late Short Administration* (London, 1766).

The Necessity of Repealing the American Stamp Act Demonstrated: Or a Proof that Great-Britain Must Be Injured by that Act . . . (London, 1766). In a sympathetic approach to the American colonials, the author offered various reasons why they should not be taxed.

A Plain and Seasonable Address to the Freeholders of Great-Britain on the Present Posture of Affairs in America (London, 1766). This pamphlet ridiculed Pitt and opposed the actions of the Americans.

RAY, NICHOLAS: *The Importance of the Colonies of North America and the Interest of Great Britain with Regard to Them Considered: Together with Remarks on the Stamp-Duty* . . . (London & New York, 1766).

Reflexions on Representation in Parliament: Being an Attempt to Shew the Equity and Practicability not only of Establishing a More Equal Representation throughout Great Britain but also of Admitting the Americans to a Share in the Legislature . . . (London, 1766).

The Rights of Parliament Vindicated on Occasion of the Late Stamp-Act: In Which Is Exposed the Conduct of the American Colonists . . . (London, 1766).

A Short and Friendly Caution to the Good People of England (London, 1766), presenting the argument that a repeal of the Stamp Act would ruin England.

A Short History of the Conduct of the Present Ministry with Regard to the American Stamp Act (London, 1766). An attack on the actions of the Ministry.

SMITH, CHARLES: *Three Tracts on the Corn-Trade and Corn Laws* . . . (London, 1766).

The Speech of Mr. P[itt] and Several Others in a Certain August Assembly on a Late Important Debate . . . ([London, 1766]). Pertaining to the Stamp Act.

[STEELE, JOSHUA]: *An Account of a Late [Imaginary] Conference on the Occurrences in America: In a Letter to a Friend* (London, 1766). This pamphlet was viewed at the time as a fair presentation but favourable to America.

[TUCKER, JOSIAH]: *A Letter from a Merchant in London to His Nephew in North America Relative to the Present Posture of Affairs in the Colonies* . . . *and the Consequences of an Attempt towards Independency Set in a True Light* (London, 1766). This letter was reprinted as Tract III in Tucker's *Four Tracts, together with Two Sermons, on Political and Commercial Subjects* (Gloucester, Eng., 1774), which elicited the following replies: *A Letter to Doctor Tucker on his Proposal of a Separation between Great Britain and Her American Colonies* (London, 1774), and *Some Reasons for Approving of the Dean of Gloucester's Plan of Separating from the Colonies* (London, 1775).

A Vindication of the Conduct of the Late Great C———r: Addressed to Every Impartial Englishman . . . (London, 1766).

WARBURTON, WILLIAM: *A Sermon Preached before the Incorporated Society for the Propagation of the Gospel in Foreign Parts at Their Anniversary Meeting* . . . *February 21, 1766* (London, 1766). For a reply, see Andrew Croswell's *Observations on Several Passages*

in a Sermon by William Warburton . . . Wherein Our Colonies
Are Defended against His Most Injurious and Abusive Reflections
(Boston, 1768).

[WHATELY, THOMAS]: *Considerations on the Trade and Finances of This*
Kingdom and on the Measures of Administration with Respect to
Those Great National Objects since the Conclusion of the Peace
(London, 1766). A criticism of the Rockingham government's
financial and commercial policy, considering the national debt,
customs, colonial trade regulations, and American taxation.

1 7 6 7

[ADDINGTON, STEPHEN]: *An Enquiry into the Reasons for and Against*
Inclosing Open-Fields (Coventry, Eng., 1767; 2nd edn., 1772).
The author was an opponent of indiscriminate enclosures and in
this pamphlet recommended policies for helping the poor.

EWER, JOHN: *A Sermon Preached before the Incorporated Society for*
the Propagation of the Gospel in Foreign Parts at Their Anni-
versary Meeting . . . February 20, 1767 (London, 1767; rep., New
York, 1768). This sermon, in which the Bishop of Llandaff referred to Americans as "infidels and barbarians," drew responses
from Charles Chauncy: *A Letter to a Friend, Containing Remarks*
on Certain Passages in a Sermon . . . in which the Highest Re-
proach Is Undeservedly Cast Upon the American Colonies (Boston, 1767; London, 1768), and from William Livingston: *A Letter*
to the Right Reverend Father in God, John, Lord Bishop of
L[l]andaff . . . (Boston & New York, 1768). Charles Inglis replied
to these pamphlets with *A Vindication of the Bishop of L[l]andaff's*
Sermon from the Gross Misrepresentations and Abusive Reflec-
tions . . . (New York, 1768).

FERGUSON, ADAM: *An Essay on the History of Civil Society* (Edinburgh,
1767). This pamphlet went through seven editions, the last appearing in 1814.

A Free Appeal to the People of Great Britain on the Conduct of the
Present Administration since the Thirtieth of July, 1766 (1st &
2nd edns., London, 1767).

GEE, JOSHUA: *The Trade and Navigation of Great-Britain Considered . . .*
A New Edition with Interesting Additions (London, 1767); the
1st edition of this work appeared in 1729.

HANWAY, JONAS: *Letters on the Importance of the Rising Generation*
of the Labouring Part of Our Fellow Subjects (2 vols., London,
1767).

An Impartial History of the Late Glorious War in Europe, Asia, Africa,
and America: With an Account of the Places Ceded to Great
Britain (Manchester, Eng., 1767).

KING, EDWARD: *An Essay on the English Constitution and Government* (London, 1767).

A Letter to G[eorge] G[renville]: "Stiff in Opinions, Always in the Wrong" (London, 1767). A well-written discussion meant as an answer to some of the pamphlets published defending Grenville's ministerial measures.

[LEWIS, JOHN]: *Uniting and Monopolizing Farms Plainly Proved Disadvantageous to the Land-Owners and Highly Prejudicial to the Public: By a Gentleman in the Country* (London, 1767; 2nd edn., 1772). The author argued that the results of enclosures were a reduction in produce and depopulation.

LLOYD, CHARLES: *The Conduct of the Late Administration Examined . . .* (London & Boston, 1767).

MACAULAY, CATHERINE: *Loose Remarks on Certain Positions to Be Found in Mr. Hobbes's Philosophical Rudiments of Government and Society: With a Short Sketch of a Democratic Form of Government . . .* (London, 1767). A second edition, published in London, 1769, contained two letters on democratic government written to the author by "An American."

[MANSFIELD, WILLIAM MURRAY, LORD]: *A Speech against the Suspending and Dispensing Prerogative . . .* (London, 1767). While the British Museum credits George Grenville with this speech, Grenville, in his "Diary" (*Grenville Papers,* III: 397) declared that on this issue Mansfield "made the most eloquent speech . . . that ever was heard" against the suspending and dispensing powers of the Crown.

A New and Impartial Collection of Interesting Letters from the Public Papers, Many of Them Written by Persons of Eminence on a Great Variety of Important Subjects . . . (2 vols., London, 1767).

Political Speculations: Or an Attempt to Discover the Causes of the Dearness of Provisions and High Price of Labour in England . . . (London, 1767).

[RAWLINSON, CHRISTOPHER]: *An Inquiry into the Management of the Poor and Our Usual Polity Respecting the Common People . . .* (London, 1767).

SHORT, THOMAS: *A Comparative History of the Increase and Decrease of Mankind in England and Several Countries Abroad . . .* (London, 1767).

STEUART, JAMES: *An Inquiry into the Principles of Political Œconomy: Being an Essay on the Science of Domestic Policy in Free Nations . . .* (2 vols., London, 1767; 3 vols., Philadelphia, 1771).

Two Papers on the Subject of Taxing the British Colonies in America . . . (London, 1767).

WILKES, JOHN: *A Letter to His Grace the Duke of Grafton . . .* (London, 1767). This pamphlet relates to the outlawry of Wilkes.

1 7 6 8

An Address to the Electors of Great Britain on the Choice of Members to Serve Them in Parliament . . . (London, 1768).

The Battle of the Quills: Or Wilkes Attacked and Defended: An Impartial Selection of . . . Prose and Verse Relative to J.W. . . . (London, 1768).

[BOLLAN, WILLIAM]: *Continued Corruption, Standing Armies, and Popular Discontents Considered, and the Establishment of the English Colonies in America . . . Examined* . . . (London, 1768).

[CANNING, GEORGE]: *A Letter to the Right Honourable Wills, Earl of Hillsborough, on the Connection between Great Britain and Her American Colonies* (London & Dublin, 1768).

[CAREY, GEORGE SAVILLE]: *Liberty Chastised or Patriotism in Chains: A Tragi, Comi, Political Farce* . . . (London, 1768).

A Cautionary Address to the Electors of England: Being a Touchstone between the Constituents and Candidates, with a Word Touching John Wilkes, Esq. (London, 1768).

A Celebrated Letter Sent from John Wilkes, Esq., at Paris to the Electors of Aylesbury in the Year 1764 (London, 1768).

A Comparative View of the Conduct of J. W. [John Wilkes] as Contrasted with the Opposite Measures during the Last Six Years (London, 1768).

The Constitutional Right of the Legislature of Great Britain to Tax the British Colonies in America Impartially Stated (London, 1768).

Essay on Patriotism and on the Character and Conduct of Some Late Famous Pretenders to That Virtue, Particularly of the Present Popular Gentleman [Chatham] (London, 1768).

The First Measures Necessary to Be Taken in the American Department (London, 1768).

The Foundation of British Liberty . . . (London, 1768). Signed W. P., this pamphlet discusses the rights of the individual and the common law.

An Infallible Remedy for the High Prices of Provisions: Together with a Scheme for Laying Open the Trade to the East-Indies . . . (London, 1768).

An Inquiry into the Nature and Causes of the Present Disputes between the British Colonies in America and Their Mother-Country and Their Reciprocal Claims and Just Rights Impartially Examined and Fairly Stated (London, 1768; 2nd edn., 1769).

[KNOX, WILLIAM, and GEORGE GRENVILLE]: *The Present State of the Nation: Particularly with Respect to Its Trade, Finances, Etc.* . . . (London, 1768). This is a criticism of the Chatham government, particularly in regard to the management of finances, and was answered for the government by Edmund Burke with *Observations on a*

Late Publication Entitled "The Present State of the Nation" (London, 1769), which was followed by William Knox's *An Appendix to the Present State of the Nation Containing a Reply to the Observations on That Pamphlet* (London & Dublin, 1769); there also appeared the anonymous *Remarks on the Appendix to the Present State of the Nation* (London, 1769).

A Letter to the Right Hon. T[homas] H[arley] Esq., Lord Mayor of . . . London: To Which Is Added a Serious Expostulation with the Livery on Their Late Conduct to J. Wilkes, Esq., during the Election of City Members . . . (London, 1768). Signed "By an Alderman of London."

[MORTIMER, THOMAS]: *The National Debt no National Grievance: Or the Real State of the Nation with Respect to Its Civil and Religious Liberty, Commerce, Public Credit and Finance . . . By a Financier* (London, 1768).

PRIESTLEY, JOSEPH: *An Essay on the First Principles of Government and on the Nature of Political, Civil, and Religious Liberty* (London, 1768). This pamphlet is a strong argument for complete toleration, civil as well as religious; it is reprinted in *Joseph Priestley: Selections from His Writings* (Ira V. Brown, ed., University Park, Pa., 1962), pp. 150-64.

Reflections on the Case of Mr. Wilkes and on the Right of the People to Elect Their Own Representatives . . . (London, 1768).

[SAYRE, STEPHEN]: *The Englishman Deceived: A Political Piece Wherein Some Very Important Secrets of State Are Briefly Recited and Offered to the Consideration of the Public* (London, 1768).

A State of the Public Revenues and Expence: From the Year 1751 to 1767 (n.p. [1768]).

[TEMPLE, RICHARD GRENVILLE-TEMPLE, EARL]: *A Letter to His Grace the Duke of Grafton on the Present Situation of Public Affairs . . .* (London [1768]).

WILKES, JOHN: *English Liberty Established: Or a Mirrour for Posterity . . .* (London [1768]). The book is comprised of a series of extracts from addresses and letters of Wilkes.

——: *The History of England from the Revolution to the Accession of the Brunswick Line* (1 vol. only pub., London, 1768).

[——]: *A Narrative of the Proceedings against J. W., Esq. from His Commitment in April 1763 to His Outlawry: With a Full View of the Arguments Used . . .* (London, 1768).

——: *Mr. Wilkes's Speech to the Court of the King's Bench on Wednesday the 20th of April, 1768* ([London, 1768]).

——: *To the Gentlemen, Clergy and Freeholders of the County of Middlesex . . .* ([London, 1768]). There are eight letters under this basic title informing the people of Middlesex of Wilkes's activities and asking for their continued support and subsequently thanking them for their support.

1 7 6 9

[ALMON, JOHN]: *A Letter to the Rt. Hon. George Grenville Occasioned by His Speech on the Motion Expelling Mr. Wilkes, 3 Feb. 1769: With a Letter on the Public Conduct of Mr. Wilkes* (London, 1769). Grenville defended Wilkes's right to a seat in Parliament.

[BLACKSTONE, WILLIAM]: *The Case of the Late Election [of John Wilkes] for the County of Middlesex Considered on the Principles of the Constitution . . .* (London, 1769). This tract has also been attributed to Jeremiah Dyson.

[BOLLAN, WILLIAM]: *The Free Briton's Memorial to All the Freeholders, Citizens and Burgesses who Elect the Members of the British Parliament Presented in Order to the Effectual Defence of Their Injured Right of Election* (London, 1769).

Britannica's Intercessions for the Deliverance of John Wilkes, Esq., from Persecution and Banishment: To which Is Added a Political and Constitutional Sermon and a Dedication to L** B*** (London [1769]; 6th edn., Boston, 1769; 9th edn., London, 1769).

[BUTLER, GEORGE B.]: *The Case of Great-Britain and America: Addressed to the King and Both Houses of Parliament* (1st & 2nd edns., London, 1769). Various writers have also attributed this pamphlet to Gervase Parker Bushe.

A Description of a Parliament in no Instance Similar to the Present . . . (London, 1769).

[ERSKINE, JOHN]: *Shall I go to War with My American Brethren? A Discourse from Judges the XXth and 28th . . .* (London, 1769; another edn., Edinburgh, 1776).

[GRENVILLE, GEORGE]: *The Speech of a Right Honourable Gentleman on [opposing] the Motion of Expelling Mr. Wilkes, Friday, February 3, 1769* (1st–4th edns., London, 1769). The following anonymous response was published: *Letter to the Right Hon. G. Grenville Occasioned by His Speech in the House of Commons . . . To which is Added a Letter on the Public Conduct of Mr. Wilkes* (London, 1769), which has been attributed to John Almon, but was probably the work of Wilkes himself.

JUNIUS, pseud.: *The Political Contest; Containing, a Series of Letters, between Junius and Sir William Draper: Also the Whole of Junius's Letters to His Grace the D[uke] of G[rafton] Brought into One Point of View* (London [1769]). See also the anonymous reply: *A Vindication of the D[uke] of G[rafton] in Answer to a Letter Signed Junius . . .* (London, 1769).

[KNOX, WILLIAM]: *The Controversy between Great-Britain and Her Colonies Reviewed: The Several Pleas of the Colonies . . . Stated and Considered* . . . (London, Dublin & Boston, 1769). Replies to this pamphlet include Edward Bancroft's *Remarks on the Review of the Controversy between Great Britain and Her Colonies: In which the Errors of Its Author Are Exposed and the Colonies Vindicated* . . . (London, 1769), and Arthur Lee's *Observations on the Review of the Controversy between Great-Britain and Her Colonies* (London, 1769). Both of these replies were published anonymously.

A Letter to the Right Honourable the Earl of Hillsborough on the Present Situation in America: In Which the Arguments in Favour of the Colonies Are . . . Incontestably Demonstrated on Constitutional Principles . . . (London & Boston, 1769).

[MEREDITH, WILLIAM]: *The Question Stated whether the Freeholders of Middlesex Lost Their Right by Voting for Mr. Wilkes at the Last Election?* . . . (London [1769]). See also the anonymous reply by William Blackstone: *A Letter to the Author of "The Question Stated"* . . . (London, 1770), which was answered in William Meredith's *Letter to Dr. Blackstone, by the author of The Question Stated. To which Is Prefixed Dr. Blackstone's Letter to Sir William Meredith* (London, 1770), also published anonymously.

[MULGRAVE, CONSTANTINE JOHN PHIPPS, 2ND BARON]: *A Letter from a Member of Parliament . . . on the Late Proceedings of the House of Commons in the Middlesex Elections* . . . (London, 1769).

PENNINGTON, W.: *Reflections on the Various Advantages Resulting from the Draining, Inclosing, and Allotting of Large Commons and Common Fields* (London, 1769). The author favored enclosures in a manufacturing country.

[PHELPS, RICHARD]: *The Rights of the Colonies and the Extent of the Legislative Authority of Great-Britain Briefly Stated and Considered* (London, 1769). The author's position was that the colonies had no right to demand representation and a voice in taxation.

The Political Conduct of the Earl of Chatham [on the Stamp Act, etc.] (London, 1769).

[PRIESTLEY, JOSEPH]: *The Present State of Liberty in Great Britain and Her Colonies. By an Englishman* (London, 1769).

Private Letters from an American in England to His Friends in America (London, 1769).

[RAMSAY, ALLEN]: *Thoughts on the Origin and Nature of Government: Occasioned by the Late Disputes between Great Britain and Her American Colonies, Written in the Year 1766* (London, 1769).

SECKER, THOMAS: *A Letter to the Right Honourable Horatio Walpole, Esq.: Written Jan. 9, 1750-1 . . . Concerning Bishops in America*

(London, 1769). For a reply see the anonymous publication by Francis Blackburne: *A Critical Commentary on Archbishop Secker's Letter* . . . (London, 1770; Philadelphia, 1771). A much later reply in support of Secker is that of Thomas Bradbury Chandler: *A Free Examination of the Critical Commentary on Archbishop Secker's Letter* . . . (New York, 1774).

SHARP, GRANVILLE: *A Representation of the Injustice and Dangerous Tendency of Tolerating Slavery or of Admitting the Least Claim of Private Property in the Persons of Men in England* . . . (London, 1769; another edn., 1772). See also Sharp's *An Appendix to a Representation of the Injustice* . . . (London, 1772).

[SMOLLETT, TOBIAS GEORGE]: *The History and Adventures of an Atom* (2 vols., London, 1749 [i.e., 1769]). This work was a satirical attack on nearly everyone prominent in political life between 1754 and 1768. Smollett used the name "Nathaniel Peacock."

[————]: *A North Briton Extraordinary: Containing a Curious and Comprehensive Review of English and Scottish History* . . . (London & Philadelphia, 1769). This pamphlet supported the Scots against John Wilkes's attacks in the *North Briton*.

The True Constitutional Means for Putting an End to the Disputes between Great Britain and the American Colonies . . . (London, 1769). The author proposed a tax upon all lands possessed by British subjects in America.

WILKES, JOHN: *English Liberty: Being a Collection of Interesting Tracts* . . . *[1762-1769] Containing the Private Correspondence, Public Letters, and Addresses of J. W.* . . . (2 vols., London [1769]).

1 7 7 0

ALMON, JOHN: *The Trial of John Almon, Bookseller* . . . *for Selling Junius's Letter to the K————* . . . (London, 1770).

The American Gazette: Being a Collection of All the Authentic Addresses, Memorials, Letters . . . *Which Relate to the Present Disputes between Great Britain and Her Colonies* . . . (Nos. 1-6 & Appendix, London, 1768-70).

Another Letter to Mr. Almon in the Matter of Libel (London, 1770).

BEDFORD, THOMAS: *The Origin of Our Grievances: A Sermon* (London, 1770). Bedford was the Rector of Wike St. Mary, Cornwall.

The Beginning, Progress, and Conclusion of the Late War: With Other Interesting Matters Considered . . . (London, 1770).

[BOLLAN, WILLIAM]: *The Free Briton's Supplemental Memorial to the Electors of the Members of the British Parliament: Wherein the Origin of Parliaments in Europe and Other Interesting Matters Are Considered* . . . (London, 1770).

BURKE, EDMUND: *Thoughts on the Cause of the Present Discontents* (London, 1770; 5th edn., 1775). For a reply, see Catherine Macaulay's *Observations on a Pamphlet Entitled "Thoughts . . ."* (London, 1770).

[CUNNINGHAM, J]: *An Essay on Trade and Commerce: Containing Observations on Taxes as They Are Supposed to Affect the Price of Labour in Our Manufactories: Together with Some Reflections on the Importance of Our Trade to America . . .* (London, 1770). Presents basically the same views as his 1764 pamphlet, blaming the poor for rising production costs. It is a good example of the views of a manufacturer of the time.

An Enquiry Whether the Absolute Independence of America Is Not to Be Preferr'd to Her Partial Dependence as Most Agreeable to the Real Interests of Great Britain . . . (London [1770]).

A First Letter to the Duke of Grafton . . . (London, 1770).

[JOHNSON, SAMUEL]: *The False Alarm* (1st & 2nd edns., London, 1770). Anonymous replies were published, one by John Scott: *The Constitution Defended and the Pensioner Exposed: In Remarks on "The False Alarm"* (London, 1770), and another by John Wilkes: *A Letter to Sam. Johnson, LL. D.* ([London], 1770).

[LEE, ARTHUR]: *The Political Detection: Or the Treachery and Tyranny of Administration Both at Home and Abroad Displayed in a Series of Letters Signed Junius Americanus* (London, 1770).

MORRIS, ROBERT: *A Letter to Sir R. Aston [Judge on the Court of King's Bench] . . . Containing a Reply to His Scandalous Abuse [of R. Morris in Almon's libel prosecution] and Some Thoughts on the Modern Doctrine of Libels* (London, 1770).

[PITT, WILLIAM]: *Authentic Copy of Lord Ch—m's Speech in the H—se of L—ds in Eng—nd in the D——e on the Present State of the Nation, Nov. 22, 1770* (London [1770]).

[WESLEY, JOHN]: *Free Thoughts on the Present State of Public Affairs: In a Letter to a Friend . . .* (London, 1770). See Joseph Towers's anonymous reply: *A Letter to the Rev. Mr. J. Wesley in Answer to His Late Pamphlet Entitled "Free Thoughts . . ."* (London, 1771).

[WHEELOCK, MATTHEW]: *Reflections, Moral and Political, on Great Britain and Her Colonies* (London, 1770).

WILKES, JOHN. *Wilkes's Jest Book, or the Merry Patriot: Being a Collection of All the Choicest Bon-Mots . . . Songs and Other Witticisms Said or Written . . . Respecting J. W. [1764-1770]* (London, 1770).

1 7 7 1

Considerations on the Policy, Commerce and Circumstances of the Kingdom (London, 1771). An attack on the government giving a gloomy view of economic conditions.

[POWNALL, THOMAS]: *Two Speeches of an Honourable Gentleman on the Late Negotiation and Convention with Spain* (London, 1771).

PRICE, RICHARD: *Observations on Reversionary Payments, on Schemes for Providing Annuities for Widows, and for Persons in Old Age . . . and on the National Debt* . . . (London, 1771; 2nd edn., 1772). The pamphlet went through seven editions, the last appearing in 1812.

[RAMSAY, ALLAN]: *An Historical Essay on the English Constitution: Or an Impartial Inquiry into the Elective Power of the People . . . wherein the Right of Parliament to Tax Our Distant Provinces Is Explained* . . . (London, 1771).

RIGGE, AMBROSE: *Brief and Serious Warning to Such as Are Concerned in Commerce and Trading* . . . (London, 1771). Originally published in 1678.

1 7 7 2

[BLACKSTONE, WILLIAM]. *An Interesting Appendix to Sir W. Blackstone's Commentaries on the Laws of England* . . . (Philadelphia, 1772).

Candid Reflections upon the Judgement Lately Awarded by the Court of King's Bench in Westminster-Hall on What Is Commonly Called the Negroe-Cause. By a Planter (London, 1772). The author quoted numerous authorities to prove that Negroes were property.

[DAGGE, HENRY]: *Considerations on Criminal Law* (London, 1772; 2nd edn., 3 vols., 1774).

An Essay on the Right of Every Man in a Free State to Speak and Write Freely in Order to Defend the Public Rights and Promote the Public Welfare . . . (London, 1772).

GROSLEY, PIERRE JEAN: *A Tour to London: Or New Observations on England and Its Inhabitants* . . . (Thomas Nugent, trans., 2 vols., London, 1772). Originally published in French as *Londres* . . . (3 vols., Lausanne, 1770; n. edn., 1774).

HARGRAVE, FRANCIS: *An Argument in the Case of James Somersett, a Negro, Lately Determined by the Court of King's Bench: Wherein It is Attempted to Demonstrate the Present Unlawfulness of Domestic Slavery in England* . . . (London, 1772; rep., Boston, 1774). Hargrave was one of Somersett's counsellors; he argued that villeinage was extinct in England and that there could be no new slavery.

[JENYNS, SOAME]: *A Scheme for the Coalition of Parties Humbly Submitted to the Publick* (London, 1772).

A Letter to the Right Honourable Lord North: Attempting to Shew the Causes and the Remedies of the High Price of Provisions upon a New Plan (London, 1772). Signed "Amicus Patriae."

Letters Concerning the Present State of England: Particularly Respecting the Politics, Arts, Manners, and Literature of the Times (London, 1772).

[LONG, EDWARD]: *Candid Reflections upon the Judgement Lately Awarded by the Court of King's Bench . . . on What is Commonly called "The Negro Cause"* . . . (London, 1772).

MORTIMER, THOMAS: *The Elements of Commerce, Politics, and Finances: In Three Treatises* . . . (London, 1772).

[PAINE, THOMAS]: *The Case of the Officers of Excise: With Remarks on the Qualifications of Officers and on the Numerous Evils Arising to the Revenue from the Insufficiency of the Present Salary* ([Lewes, Eng., 1772]).

PRICE, RICHARD: *An Appeal to the Public on the Subject of the National Debt* (1st edn., London, 1772; 2nd edn. w/appendix, 1772). For a reply, see the anonymous critique of Price's theories: *Remarks upon Dr. Price's "Appeal . . . "* (London, 1772), and Joseph Wimpey's *The Challenge: Or Patriotism Put to the Test: In a Letter to the Rev. Dr. Price* . . . (London, 1772).

THOMPSON, THOMAS: *The African Trade for Negro Slaves Shewn to Be Consistent with Principles of Humanity and with the Laws of Revealed Religion* (Canterbury, Eng. [1772]).

TUCKER, JOSIAH: *An Apology for the Present Church of England as by Law Established: Occasioned by a Petition . . . for Abolishing Subscriptions* . . . (Gloucester, Eng., 1772).

1 7 7 3

[ARBUTHNOT, JOHN]: *An Inquiry into the Connection Between the Present Price of Provisions and the Size of Farms: With Remarks on Population* . . . (London, 1773). The author argues for enclosures and the cultivation of waste lands to enhance food production.

ESTWICK, SAMUEL: *Considerations on the Negro Cause Commonly so Called: Addressed to the Right Honourable Lord Mansfield . . . By a West Indian* (London, 1773). An attack on Mansfield's decision relating to the Negro Somersett.

FURNEAUX, PHILIP: *An Essay on Toleration: With a Particular View to the Late Application of the Protestant Dissenting Ministers to Parliament for Amending and Rendering Effectual . . . the Act of Toleration* (London, 1773).

[SCOTT, JOHN]: *Observations on the Present State of the Parochial and Vagrant Poor* (London, 1773).

SHARP, GRANVILLE: *An Essay on Slavery Proving from Scripture Its Inconsistency with Humanity and Religion* (Burlington, N.J., 1773; rep., London, 1776).

SHIPLEY, JONATHAN: *A Sermon Preached before the Incorporated Society*

*for the Propagation of the Gospel in Foreign Parts at Their An-
niversary Meeting . . . February 19, 1773* (London, 1773). Shipley
was Bishop of St. Asaph's.

[YOUNG, ARTHUR]: *Observations on the Present State of the Wastelands
of Great Britain . . .* (London, 1773). The pamphlet contains suggestions for the settlement of the waste lands in order to lessen
immigration to America.

<h2 style="text-align:center">1 7 7 4</h2>

ALLEN, WILLIAM: *The American Crisis: A Letter . . . on the Present
Alarming Disturbances in the Colonies . . . and an Idea Is Offered
towards a Complete Plan for Restoring the Dependence of America upon Great Britain to a State of Perfection* (London, 1774).

*America Vindicated from the High Charges of Ingratitude and Rebellion:
With a Plan . . . for Establishing a Permanent and Solid Foundation
for a Just Constitutional Union between Great Britain and Her
Colonies . . .* ([London], 1774). The pamphlet, sympathetic to the
American colonies, suggested that they be given a constitution such
as Ireland's.

*An Argument in Defence of the Exclusive Right Claimed by the Colonies
to Tax Themselves . . .* (London, 1774). The writer was sympathetic to the position taken by the American colonists.

[BERNARD, THOMAS]: *An Appeal to the Public: Stating and Considering
the Objections to the Quebec Bill* (n. p., 1774).

*A Brief Review of the Rise and Progress, Services and Sufferings of New
England, Especially the Province of Massachusetts-Bay: Humbly
Submitted to the Consideration of Both Houses of Parliament*
(London, 1774).

BURGH, JAMES: *Political Disquisitions: Or an Enquiry into Public Errors, Defects, Abuses . . .* (3 vols., London, 1774, Philadelphia,
1775).

BURKE, EDMUND: *Mr. Burke's Speeches on His Arrival at Bristol and at
the Conclusion of the Poll* (London, 1774).

———: *The Speech of Edmund Burke, Esq., on American Taxation,
April 19, 1774* (London, 1774; 2nd edn., 1775). See also the
anonymously published replies by John Cartwright: *A Letter to
Edmund Burke, Esq., Controverting the Principles of American
Government Laid down in His Lately Published Speech . . .* (Lon-
don, 1775), and John Shebbeare: *An Answer to the Printed
Speech of Edmund Burke, Esq. . . . In Which His Knowledge in
Polity, Legislature, Humankind, History, Commerce and Finance,
Is Candidly Examined; His Arguments Are Fairly Refuted . . .*
(London, 1775).

CARTWRIGHT, JOHN: *American Independence, the Interest and Glory of*

*Great Britain: Or Arguments to Prove that not only in Taxation,
but in Trade, Manufactures, and Government, the Colonies are
Entitled to an Entire Independency on the British Legislature . . .*
(London, 1774; 2nd edn., 1775; Am. edn., Philadelphia, 1776).
The author declared in this pamphlet that it would be impossible
to govern the colonies by Parliamentary legislation and suggested
a union of Britain with the colonies, each having a separate legislature.

COSMOPOLITE, pseud.: *A Plan to Reconcile Great Britain and Her Colonies
and Preserve the Dependency of America* (London, 1774). Suggested that the Colonies, under their own taxation and representation, be allowed to manufacture goods and carry on foreign trade
in British ships.

[CROWLEY, THOMAS]: *Dissertations on the Grand Dispute between Great
Britain and America* ([London, 1774]; New York, n.d.).

[DAY, JOHN]: *Remarks on American Affairs* (London, 1774).

[DRAPER, WILLIAM]: *The Thoughts of a Traveller, upon Our American
Disputes* (London, 1774).

[GREAVES, WILLIAM]: *Reasons Humbly Submitted . . . for Introducing a
Law to Prevent Unnecessary and Vexatious Removals of the
Poor . . .* (Cambridge, Eng., 1774).

*The Interests of the Merchants and Manufacturers of Great Britain in
the Present Contest with the Colonies Stated and Considered*
(London, 1774). The pamphlet presents the argument that the
authority of Parliament must be maintained in the colonies.

[JOHNSON, SAMUEL]: *The Patriot: Addressed to the Electors of Great
Britain* (London, 1774; 2nd & 3rd edns., 1775). For comment, see
[John Scott's] *Remarks on The Patriot: Including some Hints
respecting the Americans: With an Address to the Electors of
Great Britain* (London, 1775).

[KNOX, WILLIAM]: *The Interest of the Merchants and Manufacturers of
Great Britain in the Present Contest with the Colonies Stated and
Considered* (London, 1774).

[LEE, ARTHUR]: *An Appeal to the Justice and Interests of the People of
Great Britain in the Present Disputes with America: By an Old
Member of Parliament* (London, 1774). The author, a Virginian
who was never a member of Parliament, took the position that
Parliament had no right to tax the colonists.

*A Letter to a Member of Parliament on the Present Unhappy Dispute
between Great-Britain and Her Colonies: Wherein the Supremacy
of the Former is Asserted and Proved . . .* (London, 1774). The
government, it argued, should never give in to the colonies on any
point, even if its validity was dubious.

[MARAT, JEAN PAUL]: *The Chains of Slavery: A Work wherein the Clan-
destine and Villianous Attempts of Princes to Ruin Liberty are*

Pointed out and the Dreadful Scenes of Despotism Disclosed . . . (London, 1774).

[MEREDITH, WILLIAM]: *A Letter to the Earl of Chatham on the Quebec Bill* (London & Boston, 1774). While this letter has been attributed to Thomas, Lord Lyttelton, the weight of evidence seems to favor Meredith. There is the following reply: *A Letter to Sir William Meredith, Bart.: In Answer to His Late Letter to the Earl of Chatham* (London, 1774).

[PRIESTLEY, JOSEPH]: *An Address to Protestant Dissenters of All Denominations on the Approaching Election of Members of Parliament: With Respect to the State of Public Liberty in General and of American Affairs in Particular* (London, 1774). This pamphlet is reprinted in *Joseph Priestley: Selections from His Writings* (Ira V. Brown, ed., University Park, Pa., 1962), pp. 165-73.

The Right of the British Legislature to Tax the [American] Colonies' Considered in a Letter to the Right Hon. Frederick Lord North . . . (London [1774]).

The Right of the British Legislature to Tax the American Colonies' Vindicated and the Means of Asserting that Right Proposed . . . (London, 1774; 2nd edn., 1775). The author contended that the freedom of the American colonists had not been curtailed and that Parliament was not acting unconstitutionally by passing legislation to govern them; if anything, Parliament was too lenient.

The Rights of the English Colonies Established in America Stated and Defended: Their Merits and Importance to Great Britain Displayed . . . (London, 1774). The author used histories of colonial America and source materials of the period to write his account.

[ROKEBY, MATHEW ROBINSON-MORRIS, 2ND BARON]: *Considerations on the Measures Carrying on with Respect to the British Colonies in North-America . . .* (London, 1774). The pamphlet constitutes an arraignment of the American policy of Lord North.

SHARP, GRANVILLE: *A Declaration of the People's Natural Right to a Share in the Legislature which Is the Fundamental Principle of the British Constitution of State* (London, 1774).

[SHIPLEY, JONATHAN]: *A Speech Intended to Have Been Spoken on the Bill for Altering the Charters of Massachusetts Bay* (London, 1774). In this "speech," Shipley, the Bishop of St. Asaph, wrote: "My Lords, I look upon North America as the only [real] nursery of freemen now left upon the face of the earth." Two anonymous replies were published: *A Speech Never Intended to Be Spoken: In Answer to "A Speech . . . " Dedicated to the Right Reverend the Lord Bishop of St. A——* (London, 1774), and *A Complaint to the —— of —— against a Pamphlet Intitled "A Speech . . ."* (London, 1775).

TUCKER, JOSIAH: *Four Tracts, together with Two Sermons: On Political and Commercial Subjects* (Gloucester, Eng., 1774; 3rd edn., 1776).

———: *The True Interest of Great Britain Set Forth in Regard to the Colonies and the Only Means of Living in Peace and Harmony with Them* (Norfolk, Eng., 1774; Philadelphia, 1776). In this pamphlet which was also published as Tract IV in *Four Tracts . . .* , the author pointed out that radical steps must be taken to solve the problem between the American colonies and the mother country. After discussing various attitudes on Parliament's actions and the seating of colonists in Parliament, Tucker suggested giving them independence.

Two Chapters of the Lost Book of Chronicles, Six Letters to the Good People of England, and Several Other Pieces Relative to the Dispute between Englishmen in Europe and America . . . (London, 1774).

WALLIN, BENJAMIN: *The Popular Concern in the Choice of Representatives: A Sermon . . .* (London, 1774).

WESLEY, JOHN: *Thoughts upon Slavery* (London, 1774).

[WHATELY, GEORGE]: *Principles of Trade: Fredom [sic] and Protection Are Its Best Suport [sic]; Industry, the Only Means to Render Manufactures Cheap . . .* (2nd edn., cor. & enl., London, 1774).

YOUNG, ARTHUR: *Political Arithmetic: Containing Observations on the Present State of Great Britain and the Principles of Her Policy in the Encouragement of Agriculture . . .* (London, 1774).

[ZUBLY, JOHN JOACHIM]: *Great Britain's Right to Tax Her Colonies: Placed in the Clearest Light by a Swiss* (London, 1774). This first appeared in America in 1769 under title *An Humble Enquiry into . . . The Right of Parliament to lay Taxes on the said Colonies . . . .* A pamphlet sympathetic to the colonists but opposed to a break with Great Britain.

1 7 7 5

An Address to the Right Honourable L——d M——sf ——d: In Which the Measures of Government Respecting America Are Considered in a New Light With a View to His Interpretation Therein (London, 1775).

The Annals of Administration . . . Inscribed . . . to Edmund Burke (London, 1775). This is an allegorical explanation of the causes of the issues between England and her American colonies.

Arguments in Support of the Supremacy of the British Legislature and Their Right to Tax the Americans: Addressed to the Citizens of London . . . (London, 1775).

Authentic Papers from America: Submitted to the Dispassionate Con-

sideration of the Public (London, 1775). The pamphlet, signed "Impartial" and dated 10 January 1775, is a comparison of American petitions against the Stamp Act and the petitions of the First Continental Congress.

[BACON, ANTHONY]: *A Short Address to the Government, the Merchants, Manufacturers, and the Colonists in America and the Sugar Islands on the Present State of Affairs* (London, 1775).

[BAILLIE, HUGH]: *An Appendix to a Letter to Dr. Shebbeare: To which Are Added Some Observations on a Pamphlet Intitled "Taxation no Tyranny"* . . . *By a Doctor of Law* (London, 1775).

A Brief Extract or Summary of Important Arguments Advanced by Some Late Distinguished Writers In Support of the Supremacy of the British Legislature and Their Right to Tax the Americans . . . (London, 1775).

[BURGOYNE, JOHN]: *The Speech of a General Officer in the House of Commons, February 20, 1775* ([London, 1775]).

BURKE, EDMUND: *Speech of Edmund Burke, Esq., on Moving His Resolutions for Conciliation with the Colonies, March 22nd, 1775* (London, 1775). Josiah Tucker wrote the reply: *A Letter to Edmund Burke, Esq.* . . . *in Answer to His Printed Speech Said to Be Spoken in the House of Commons on the Twenty-Second of March, 1775* (1st edn., Gloucester, Eng., 1775; 2nd edn., Dublin, 1775).

Common Sense: In Nine Conferences between a British Merchant and a Candid Merchant of America . . . (London, 1775).

Conciliatory Address to the People of Great Britain and of the Colonies on the Present Important Crisis (London, 1775).

The Conduct of Administration with Regard to Colonies (London [1775]). A condemnation of the Ministry's attitude toward the American colonial problems.

A Crisis Extraordinary, Wednesday, August 9, 1775 ([London], 1775). This pamphlet written by Thomas Paine was later bound with his *The Crisis* (Philadelphia, 1780).

[DAWES, MANASSEH]: *A Letter to Lord Chatham Concerning the Present War of Great Britain against America: Reviewing Candidly and Impartially Its Unhappy Cause and Consequences* . . . (London [1775]).

Extracts from Resolutions of Assemblies, Petitions, Letters, Addresses, from the Colonies to His Majesty, to the Parliament and to Persons in Administration . . . *[1765-1775]* ([London, 1775]).

HARTLEY, DAVID: *Speech and Motions Made in the House of Commons on Monday, March 27th, 1775: Together with a Draught of a Letter of Requisition to the Colonies* (1st & 2nd edns., London, 1775).

[JOHNSON, SAMUEL]: *Taxation no Tyranny: An Answer to the Resolutions and Address of the American Congress* (1st-4th edns., London, 1775). This is one of those pamphlets that provoked a flurry of replies among them the following: *An Answer to a Pamphlet Entitled Taxation no Tyranny: Addressed to the Author and to the Persons in Power* (London, 1775); *A Defence of the Resolutions and Address of the American Congress, in Reply to Taxation no Tyranny* . . . (London [1775]). *A Letter to Dr. Samuel Johnson: Occasioned by His Late Political Publications* . . . (London, 1775); *The Pamphlet Entitled "Taxation no Tyranny" Candidly Considered and It's [sic] Arguments and Pernicious Doctrines Exposed and Refuted* (London, 1775); *Resistance no Rebellion: In Answer to Doctor Johnson's "Taxation no Tyranny"* (London, 1775); *Taxation, Tyranny: Addressed to Samuel Johnson, LL.D.* (London, 1775); and *Tyranny Unmasked: An Answer to a Late Pamphlet Entitled "Taxation no Tyranny"* (London, 1775).

KENT, NATHANIEL: *Hints to Gentlemen of Landed Property* (London, 1775).

[LEE, ARTHUR]: *A Second Appeal to the Justice and Interests of the People on the Measures Respecting America* . . . (London, 1775).

[———]: *A Speech Intended to Have Been Delivered in the House of Commons in Support of the Petition from the General Congress at Philadelphia* (London, 1775). The author, again under guise as a member of Parliament, discussed colonial grievances and defended the measures which the colonists had been taking. The wording of this pamphlet is after the manner of the title of the Bishop of St. Asaph's pamphlet printed in 1774.

A Letter to the People of Great-Britain in Answer to that Published by the American Congress (London, 1775). This pamphlet contradicted every argument used by Congress against Parliament.

A Letter to the Right Honourable Lord Camden on the Bill for Restraining the Trade and Fishery of the Four Provinces of New England (London, 1775).

A Letter to the Right Honourable Lord M***** on the Affairs of America. From a Member of Parliament (London, 1775).

A Letter to Those Ladies Whose Husbands Possess a Seat in Either House of Parliament (London, 1775).

[LIND, JOHN]: *An Englishman's Answer to the Address from the Delegates [of the Continental Colonies] to the People of Great-Britain: In a Letter to the Several Colonies* . . . (New York, 1775; London, 1776).

[———]: *Remarks on the Principal Acts of the Thirteenth Parliament of Great Britain* . . . (London, 1775).

LYTTELTON, THOMAS LYTTELTON, 2ND BARON: *The Speech of Lord Lyttelton on a Motion Made in the House of Lords for a Repeal of the Canada Bill, May 17, 1775* (London, 1775).

MACAULAY, CATHERINE: *An Address to the People of England, Scotland,*

and Ireland, on the Present Important Crisis of Affairs (Bath, Eng., & New York, 1775).

PITT, WILLIAM: *Plan Offered by the Earl of Chatham to the House of Lords: Entitled a Provisional Act for Settling the Troubles in America and for Asserting the Supreme Legislative Authority and Superintending Power of Great Britain over the Colonies . . .* (London, 1775).

A Plain State of the Argument between Great-Britain and Her Colonies (London, 1775). The author, whom Sabin indicates may have been Samuel Johnson, uses the standard arguments for Parliamentary control of the American colonies.

A Plan for Conciliating the Jarring Political Interests of Great Britain and Her North American Colonies and for Promoting a General Re-Union throughout the Whole of the British Empire (London, 1775).

The Present Crisis with Respect to America Considered (London, 1775). A defence of Parliament's right to tax the colonies.

A Proposition for the Present Peace and Future Government of the British Colonies in North America (London [1775]).

Resistance no Rebellion: In which the Right of a British Parliament to Tax the American Colonies Is Fully Considered and Found Unconstitutional . . . ([London], 1775).

[SERLE, AMBROSE]: *Americans against Liberty: Or an Essay on the Nature and Principles of True Freedom Shewing that the Designs and Conduct of the Americans Tend only to Tyranny and Slavery* (London, 1775). A defence of the British position.

Seasonable Advice to the Members of the British Parliament: Concerning Conciliatory Measures with America . . . (London, 1775).

A Short View of the Lord High Admiral's Jurisdiction and of the Several Acts for Regulating and Restraining the Trade of the British Plantations and the Commissions of Vice-Admiralty Courts there: Together with the Heads of a Bill for Better Regulating the Same (London, 1775).

Some Candid Suggestions towards Accommodation of Differences with America Offered to Consideration of the Public (London, 1775).

Speech on the 20th of January, 1775: Taken by a Member (London, 1775). This speech by William Pitt was on the motion for removing English troops from Boston. It was republished in London and Philadelphia under various titles. Pitt denied having made the speech.

[STAIR, JOHN DALRYMPLE, 5TH EARL OF]: *The Address of the People of Great Britain to the Inhabitants of America* (London, 1775). As Stair had been sympathetic to the American position this pamphlet was printed at public expense for American distribution.

The Supremacy of the British Legislature over the Colonies Candidly Discussed (London, 1775).

Thoughts upon the Present Contest between Administration and the British Colonies in America: Addressed to Merchants . . . (London, 1775).

Three Letters to a Member of Parliament on the Subject of the Present Dispute with Our American Colonies . . . (London, 1775).

TUCKER, JOSIAH: *An Humble Address and Earnest Appeal to those Respectable Personages in Great-Britain and Ireland . . . the Ablest to Judge and Fittest to Decide whether a Connection with or a Separation from the Continental Colonies of America Be Most for the National Advantage and the Lasting Benefit of These Kingdoms* (Gloucester, Eng., 1775). For a reply, see Samuel Estwick's *A Letter to Reverend Josiah Tucker, D.D., Dean of Gloucester: In Answer to His Humble Address and Earnest Appeal . . .* (London, 1776).

————: *The Respective Pleas and Arguments of the Mother Country and of the Colonies Distinctly Set Forth, and the Impossibility of a Compromise of Differences or a Mutual Concession of Rights Plainly Demonstrated . . .* (Gloucester, Eng., 1775).

The Voice of God: Being Serious Thoughts on the Present Alarming Crisis with an Appeal to the Nation . . . Respecting the Unhappy Situation of Affairs between England and the American Colonies . . . (London, 1775). Signed "Christianus."

WESLEY, JOHN: *A Calm Address to the Americans on the Subject of Their Present War* (London, Bristol, & Salisbury, Eng., 1775). This pamphlet leans heavily upon Dr. Johnson's *Taxation No Tyranny,* and just as that pamphlet did, provoked a deluge of replies and defences; among them are the following: *A Constitutional Answer to the Rev. Mr. John Wesley's Calm Address . . .* (London, 1775); W.D.: *A Second Answer to Mr. John Wesley: Being a Supplement to the Letter of Americanus in which the Idea of Supreme Power and the Nature of Royal Charters are Briefly Considered* (London, 1775); [Caleb Evans] signed "Americanus": *A Letter to the Rev. Mr. John Wesley: Occasioned by His Calm Address . . .* (London & Bristol, Eng., 1775). A reply to this work came from John William Fletcher: *A Vindication of the Rev. Mr. Wesley's "Calm Address . . ."* (London, [1776]), which was in turn answered by Evans: *A Reply to the Rev. Mr. Fletcher's Vindication . . .* (Bristol, Eng. [1775]), and also by the anonymous pamphlet: *The Rev. John Fletcher's Arguments Contained in His "Vindication . . ." in Defence of the Assured Right of the British Parliament to Tax America Considered . . .* (London, 1776), and by Thomas Oliver: *A Full Defence of the Rev. John Wesley in Answer to the Several Personal Reflections Cast on that Gentleman by the Rev. Caleb Evans* . . . (London, 1776). Additional replies include: *Fallacy Detected: In a Letter to the Rev. Mr. Wesley . . .* (n.p., 1775); *A Full and Impartial Examination of the Rev. Mr. John Wesley's Address to the Americans: In which That Gentleman's Inconsistencies are Remarked . . . and His Principles in General Demonstrated to Be Subversive of the British Constitution* . . . ([Manchester, Eng., 1776]); *A Letter to the Rev. Mr. John Wesley on His "Calm Address . . ." Wherein Is Shewn that His Arguments Are Inconclusive, His Principles Arbitrary, and That His Assertions Are Without Foundation* . . . ([Manchester, Eng., 1775]); [James Murray]: *A Grave Answer to Mr. Wesley's Calm Address* . . . (n.p., 1775); *Political Empiricism: A Letter to the Rev. Mr. John Wesley* (London, 1776); Thomas Stanley: *A Cool Reply to a Calm Address Lately Published by Mr. John Wesley* . . . (London, 1775); [Augustus Montague Toplady]: *An Old Fox Tarr'd and Feather'd: Occasioned by What is Called Mr. John Wesley's Calm Address* . . . (London, 1775); and finally W.Y.: *A Serious Answer to Mr. Wesley's Calm Address* . . . (Bristol, Eng., 1775).

[WILLIAMSON, HUGH]: *The Plea of the Colonies on the Charges Brought against them by Lord M———d, and Others* . . . (London, 1775). Other editions with varying titles were published in London, 1776, and Philadelphia, 1777.

1 7 7 6

An Address to the People of Great-Britain in General, the Members of Parliament, and the Leading Gentlemen of Opposition in Particular: On the Present Crisis of American Politics (Bristol, Eng., 1776).

[BENTHAM, EDWARD]: *The Honor of the University of Oxford Defended against the Illiberal Aspersions of E———d B———e, Esq.: With Pertinent Observations on the Present Rebellion in America* . . . (London [1776]).

BLACKLOCK, THOMAS: *Remarks on the Nature and Extent of Liberty as Compatible with the Genius of Civil Societies: In the Principles of Government and the Proper Limits of Its Powers in Free States* (Edinburgh, 1776).

[CARTWRIGHT, JOHN]: *Take Your Choice! Representation and Respect— Imposition and Contempt: Annual Parliaments and Liberty—Long Parliaments and Slavery* (London, 1776).

[CHAMPION, J.]: *Reflections on the State of Parties on the National Debt and the Necessity and Expediency of the Present War with America* (London, 1776). A second edition with a slightly different title was also published in London, 1776.

Considerations on the American War: Addressed to the People of England (London, 1776). This pamphlet gives a derogatory description of Americans.

The Constitutional Advocate: By which . . . Every Reader May Form His Own Judgement Concerning the Justice and Policy of the Present War with America . . . (London, 1776). Defends the colonies on the basis of "ancient charters, statutes, and law authorities."

[DALRYMPLE, SIR JOHN]: *The Rights of Great Britain Asserted against the Claims of America . . .* (London, 1776). Numerous editions were published in 1776 in Great Britain and America. Sir John is not to be confused with John Dalrymple, 5th Earl of Stair.

Declaration of Those Rights of the Commonality of Great Britain without which They Cannot Be Free ([London, 1776]). Broadside.

DE PINTO, ISAAC: *Letters on the American Troubles: Translated from the French of M. de Pinto* (London, 1776). Although the author defends Great Britain's war against the American colonies, he forsees the colonists as being ultimately victorious in winning their freedom.

Dialogue on the Principles of the Constitution and Legal Liberty Compared with Despotism: Applied to the American Question . . . (London, 1776). The author provides a serious and reasonable defence of the American colonists.

[ERSKINE, JOHN]: *The Equity and Wisdom of Administration in Measures that Have Unhappily Occasioned the American Revolt . . .* (Edinburgh, 1776).

[———]: *Reflections on the Rise, Progress, and Probable Consequences of the Present Contentions with the Colonies . . .* (Edinburgh, 1776). Erskine claims English resentment was kindled by colonial pamphlets; he examines these pamphlets to determine what concessions the colonists were willing to make.

FLETCHER, JOHN WILLIAM: *American Patriotism Farther Confronted with Reason, Scripture, and the Constitution: Being Observations on the Dangerous Politicks Taught by the Rev. Mr. Evans, M.A., and the Rev. Dr. Price . . .* (Shrewsbury, Eng., 1776). Caleb Evans replied to this pamphlet, which was a defence of Great Britain's right to tax her colonies, with *Political Sophistry Detected: Or Brief Remarks on the Rev. Mr. Fletcher's Late Tract . . .* (Bristol, Eng., 1776).

GLASCOTT, CRADOCK: *The Best Method of Putting an End to the American War: Being the Substance of a Sermon Preached on the 13th of December, 1776 . . .* (London, 1776).

[HAMPSON, JOHN]: *Reflections on the Present State of the American War* (London, 1776).

HARTLEY, DAVID: *Substance of a Speech in Parliament upon the State of*

*the Nation and the Present Civil War with America: Upon Mon-
day, April 1, 1776* (London, 1776).

HEY, RICHARD: *Observations on the Nature of Civil Liberty and the Principles of Government* (London, 1776).

H-ISTORICUS, POPLICOLA, pseud.: *America Pois'd in the Balance of Justice
. . . In this Research the Present Dissention between the Mother
Country and Her Colonies Is Considered in a New Light . . .*
(London [1776]).

[HOME, M. J.]: *A Letter from an Officer Retired: To His Son in Parliament* (n. edn., Edinburgh, 1776). An argument based upon the
necessity to subdue the colonies in order to ensure the safety of
Britain.

*Independency the Object of the Congress in America: Or an Appeal to
Facts* (London, 1776).

JOHNSON, SAMUEL: *Hypocrisy Unmasked: Or a Short Inquiry into the
Religious Complaints of Our American Colonies . . .* (London,
1776). Johnson defended the religious freedom granted by the
Quebec Act to Canadian Roman Catholics, claiming that the American colonists should not criticize it because it granted no more
than they themselves gave to colonial Roman Catholics.

————: *Political Tracts: Containing the False Alarm, Falkland's Islands,
The Patriot, and Taxation no Tyranny* (London, 1776).

[————]: *A Short Appeal to the People of Great-Britain: Upon the Un-
avoidable Necessity of the Present War with Our Disaffected
Colonies . . .* (London, 1776).

JOHNSTONE, GEORGE: *Gov. Johnstone's Speech [in Parliament] on America
Affairs: On the Address in Answer to the King's Speech . . .* (Edinburgh, 1776). Johnstone's complaint was that the British government obtained all its information about the colonies from Governor
Hutchinson and followed his policies.

JULIAN, pseud.: *A Letter to Lord G[eorge] G[ermain] on the American
Question* (London, 1776).

A Letter to Lord George Germain (London, 1776). Contended that
British forces would be unable to subdue the colonies.

[LIND, JOHN]: *An Answer to the Declaration of the American Congress*
(London, 1776). This pamphlet was commissioned by the Treasury
and is, therefore, to be viewed as a quasi-official work.

[MACPHERSON, JAMES]: *The Rights of Great Britain Asserted against the
Claims of America: Being an Answer to the Declaration of the
General Congress* (London, 1776). This pamphlet, which went
through many editions and was published "at the instance of the
British government," has also been attributed to Sir John Dal-
rymple and Lord George Germain.

MARRIOTT, G.: *Judgement Begun in the House of God to Be Finished on*

Its Enemies: A Sermon Preached . . . On Occasion of the War with the American Colonies (London [1776]).

MARTIN, JOHN: *Familiar Dialogues between Americus and Britannicus: In which the Right of Private Judgement, the Exploded Doctrines of Infallibility, Passive Obedience, Non-Resistance [etc.] . . . Are Particularly Considered* (London, 1776). The author seems to have had little knowledge of the American colonies.

PENROSE, THOMAS: *Public Tranquility the Object of Every Individual's Concern: A Sermon Preached in the Parish Church of Newbery, Berks, December 13, 1776 . . .* (London, 1776).

The Plain Question upon the Present Dispute with Our American Colonies (2nd edn., London, 1776).

PRICE, RICHARD: *Observations on the Nature of Civil Liberty, the Principles of Government, and the Justice and Policy of the War with America . . .* (London, 1776). Price's pamphlet was one of the few which prompted numerous replies, most of which were in opposition to Price's statements. This was an extreme example of pamphleteering. Replies came from John Shebbeare: *An Essay on the Origin, Progress, and Establishment of National Society: In which the Principles . . . Contained in Dr. Price's Observations &c. are Fairly Examined and Fully Refuted . . .* (London, 1776); James Stewart: *The Total Refutation and Political Overthrow of Doctor Price: Or Great Britain Successfully Vindicated against All American Rebels and Their Advocates . . .* (London, 1776); and John Wesley: *Some Observations on Liberty: Occasioned by a Late Tract* (Edinburgh & London, 1776). Most of the replies were published anonymously and the authors of many of these have now been identified. Adam Ferguson wrote *Remarks on a Pamphlet Lately Published by Dr. Price . . .* (London, 1776); Henry Goodricke wrote *Observations on Dr. Price's Theory and Principles of Civil Liberty and Government . . .* (York, Eng., 1776); Jonathan Lind produced *Three Letters to Dr. Price: Containing Remarks on His Observations . . .* (London, 1776). *Obedience the Best Charter or Law the Only Sanction of Liberty . . .* (London, 1776) was presumably written by John Moir, and James Stewart wrote *A Letter to the Rev. Dr. Price, F.R.S.: Wherein His Observations . . . Are Candidly Examined . . .* (London, 1776). A Mr. Nourse wrote *A Letter to the Rev. Dr. Price . . .* (London, 1776) in which he praised Price's work although he did take exception to certain points. Perhaps the best and most decent reply was *Experience Preferable to Theory: An Answer to Dr. Price's Observations . . .* (London, 1776) which apparently was written by Thomas Hutchinson. In addition, see *A Letter to the Rev. Dr. Price on His Observations on the Nature of Civil Liberty* (London, 1776), signed T.D., and other anonymous and unidentified pamphlets: *Cursory*

Observations upon Dr. Price's Essay on Civil Liberty, Particularly Relating to Specie and Paper Currency . . . (London, 1776); *Cursory Remarks on Dr. Price's Observations on the Nature of Civil Liberty: In a Letter to a Friend. By a Merchant* (London, 1776); and *The Honour of Parliament and the Justice of the Nation Vindicated* . . . (London, 1776).

A Prospect of the Consequences of the Present Conduct of Great Britain towards America (London, 1776).

[RAMSAY, ALLAN]: *A Plan of Reconciliation between Great Britain and Her Colonies* . . . *By which the Rights of Englishmen in Matters of Taxation Are Preserved to the Inhabitants of America and the Islands Beyond the Atlantic* . . . (London, 1776).

Reflections on the American Contest: In Which the Consequences of a Forced Submission and the Means of a Lasting Reconciliation Are Pointed Out . . . (London, 1776). Signed "A.M." Sabin suggests that this pamphlet was written in 1769 upon the author's return from America; it points out the consequences of using force to rule the colonies.

Reflections on the Most Proper Means of Reducing the Rebels and What Ought to Be the Consequences of Our Success: By an Officer who Served in the Last War (London, 1776). The author saw no cause for revolution save the acts of a few self-interested and designing men.

[ROEBUCK, JOHN]: *An Enquiry whether the Guilt of the Present Civil War in America Ought to Be Imputed to Great Britain or America* (London, 1776). Places blame for the American Revolution directly on the colonies.

[ROKEBY, MATTHEW ROBINSON MORRIS, 2ND BARON]: *A Further Examination of Our Present American Measures and of the Reasons and the Principles on Which They are Founded* . . . (Bath, Eng., 1776).

SHARP, GRANVILLE: *The Just Limitation of Slavery in the Laws of God Compared with the Unbounded Claims of the African Slave' Traders and British American Slaveholders* (London, 1776).

————: *The Law of Liberty or Royal Law by Which All Mankind Will Certainly Be Judged: Earnestly Recommended to the Serious Consideration of All Slaveholders and Slavedealers* (London, 1776).

————: *The Law of Passive Obedience or Christian Submission to Personal Injuries* . . . ([London, 1776]).

————: *The Law of Retribution: Or a Serious Warning to Great Britain and Her Colonies* . . . (London, 1776).

The Simple Cobbler of Clerkenwell Willing to Help to Mend His Native Country . . . *with All the Honest Stitches He Can Take* ([London], 1776). A useful and valuable pamphlet.

SMITH, ADAM: *An Inquiry into the Nature and Causes of the Wealth of Nations* (2 vols., London, 1776). There have been numerous editions of this exceedingly valuable work which provides both economic theory and a view of contemporary conditions. Thomas Pownall wrote a criticism entitled: *A Letter from Governor Pownall to Adam Smith, LL.D. F.R.S.: Being an Examination of Several Points of Doctrine Laid down in His "Inquiry . . . "* (London, 1776).

STAIR, JOHN DALRYMPLE, 5TH EARL OF: *The State of the National Debt, the National Income and the National Expenditure: With Some Short Inferences and Reflections Applicable to the Present Dangerous Crisis* (London, 1776).

The Tears of the Foot Guards upon Their Departure for America: Written by an Ensign of the Army . . . (1st & 2nd edn., London, 1776).

TOULMIN, JOSHUA: *The American War Lamented: A Sermon Preached at Taunton, February the 18th and 25th, 1776* . . . (London, 1776).

TUCKER, JOSIAH: *A Series of Answers to Certain Popular Objections against Separating from the Rebellious Colonies and Discarding Them Entirely* . . . (Gloucester, Eng., 1776).

4. Newspapers and periodicals published in Great Britain

The following items are bibliographical materials which would be of aid in the study and use of contemporary British periodical publications:

BARWICK, GEORGE FREDERICK: "Some Magazines of the Eighteenth Century," Bibliographical Society, *Transactions*, X (1908-9), 109-40.

CRANE, RONALD SALMON, FREDERICK BENJAMIN KAYE, and M. E. PRIOR: *A Census of British Newspapers and Periodicals, 1620-1800* (London, Chapel Hill, N.C., 1927).

CRANFIELD, G. A., comp.: *A Hand-List of English Provincial Newspapers and Periodicals, 1700-1760*, Cambridge Bibliographical Society, *Monograph*, No. 2 (Cambridge, Eng., 1952). See also R. M. Wiles: "Further Additions and Corrections to G. A. Cranfield's *Hand-List of English Provincial Newspapers and Periodicals, 1700-1760*," Cambridge Bibliographical Society, *Transactions*, II (1958), 385-9.

GABLER, ANTHONY J., comp.: "Check List of English Newspapers and Periodicals before 1801 in the Huntington Library," Huntington Library, *Bulletin*, II (1931), 1-66.

GRAHAM, W. J.: *English Literary Periodicals* (New York, 1930).

HEWITT, A. R., comp.: *Union List of Commonwealth Newspapers in London, Oxford, and Cambridge* (London & New York, 1960).

MARR, GEORGE SIMPSON: *Periodical Essayists of the Eighteenth Century: With Illustrative Extracts from the Rarer Periodicals* (London [1923]).

MILFORD, ROBERT T., and DONALD M. SUTHERLAND: *A Catalogue of English Newspapers and Periodicals in the Bodleian Library, 1622-1800*

(Oxford, Eng., 1936; 1st printed in Oxford Bibliographical Society, *Proceedings and Papers*, IV).

MUDDIMAN, JOSEPH GEORGE: *Tercentenary Handlist of English and Welsh Newspapers, Magazines, and Reviews . . .* (London, 1920).

WEED, KATHERINE K., and RICHMOND P. BOND: *Studies of British Newspapers and Periodicals from Their Beginning to 1800: A Bibliography, Studies in Philology,* Extra Series, No. 2 (Chapel Hill, N. C. [1946]).

The following entries are given with title they carried within the period 1748-1776; the beginning or ending dates or both are also given when these dates fall within the period, the preface letters b and e indicating beginning and ending respectively. A single date not prefaced by a letter indicates the periodical's existence for one year only, while brackets indicate a change in title or uncertainty as to the date of origin or of termination of the specific publications.

Aberdeen's Journal [The Aberdeen Journal and North-British Magazine], b. 1748, Aberdeen, Scot.

Adams's Weekly Courant, Chester, Eng.

The American Gazette. Being a Collection of All the Authentic Addresses . . . Published from . . . February 1768 to the Present Time, 1768-1770, London.

The Annual Register: Or a View of the History, Politicks and Literature of the Year . . . , b. 1758, London. See William B. Todd's article: "A Bibliographical Account of the *Annual Register,* 1758-1825," *Library,* 5th ser., XVI (1961), 104-20.

Aris's Birmingham Gazette, Birmingham, Eng.

The Auditor, 1762-1763, London.

The Bath Chronicle [The Bath Advertiser, The Bath Chronicle or Universal Register, Martin's Bath Chronicle, Pope's Bath Chronicle, and Archer's Bath Chronicle], b. 1755, Bath, Eng.

Bingley's Journal or the Universal Gazette [Bingley's Journal; Bingley's London Journal], b. 1770, London.

Boddley's Bath Journal [The Bath Journal], Bath, Eng.

Bonner & Middleton's British Journal, b. 1774, Bristol, Eng.

The Bristol Gazette and Public Advertiser, b. 1767, Bristol, Eng.

Bristol Weekly Intelligencer, 1749-1750, Bristol, Eng.

The British Chronicle, or Pugh's Hereford Journal, b. 1770, Hereford, Eng.

The British Magazine: Or Monthly Repository for Gentlemen and Ladies, 1760-1767, London.

The Briton, 1762-1763, London.

Caledonia Mercury and Daily Express, Edinburgh, Scot.

The Cambridge Chronicle and Journal [The Cambridge Chronicle], Cambridge, Eng.

The Chester Chronicle; or, Commercial Intelligencer, b. 1775, Chester, Eng.

Court and City Kalendar: Or Gentleman's Register, e. 1769, London.

The Critical Review: Or, Annals of Literature, b. 1756, London.

The Daily Advertiser, London.

The Derby Mercury [Drewry's Derby Mercury], b. 1753, Derby, Eng.

The Gazetteer and New Daily Advertiser [The London Gazetteer; Gazetteer and London Daily Advertiser; Daily Gazetteer or London Advertiser], London.

The General Evening Post, London.

The Gentleman's Magazine, and Historical Chronicle [Gentleman's Magazine or Monthly Intelligencer], London.

The Glasgow Courant [1760 merged in *The Glasgow Journal*], Glasgow, Scot.

The Glasgow Journal, Glasgow, Scot.

The Gloucester Journal, 1749-53, 1756-57, 1762-68, 1770-, Gloucester, Eng.

Harrop's Manchester Mercury [The Manchester Mercury and Harrop's General Advertiser], b. 1752, Manchester, Eng.

The Ipswich Journal [The Original Ipswich Journal], Ipswich, Eng.

Jopson's Coventry and Northampton; and Warwick Mercury or the Weekly Country Journal, Coventry, Eng.

The Kentish Gazette, 1768-1774, Canterbury, Eng.

The Leeds Mercury, published for the entire period except the years 1755, 1756, and 1757, Leeds, Eng.

The Leicester and Nottingham Journal, b. 1753, Leicester, Eng.

Lloyd's Evening Post and British Chronicle, b. 1757, London.

London Chronicle or Universal Evening Post, b. 1757, London.

London Daily Post and General Advertiser [The General Advertiser; The Public Advertiser], London.

The London Evening Post, London.

The London Gazette, London.

The London Gazette Extraordinary, London.

The London Magazine or Gentleman's Monthly Intelligencer, London.

The London Packet [New Lloyd's Evening Post], b. 1769, London.

The Middlesex Journal or Chronicle of Liberty [Universal Evening Post; Evening Advertiser; London Evening Post], b. 1769, London.

The Monitor or British Freeholder, 1755-1765, London.

The Monthly Review or New Literary Journal [The Monthly Review or Journal; The Monthly Review or Literary Journal Enlarged], b. 1749, London.

The Morning Chronicle, and London Advertiser, b. 1769, London.

The Morning Post, and Daily Advertiser [The New Morning Post or General Advertiser], 1776, London.

The Morning Post, and Daily Advertising Pamphlet, b. 1772, London.

New Weekly Chronicle or Universal Journal [Owen's Weekly Chronicle], 1758-1770, London.

New Weekly Miscellany [The Westminster Journal or New Weekly Miscellany; Royal Westminster Journal and London Political Miscellany], Westminster, Eng.

The Newcastle Chronicle, or Weekly Advertiser, and Register of News, Commerce & Entertainment [Newcastle Weekly Chronicle], b. 1764, Newcastle, Eng.

Newcastle Courant: With News, Foreign and Domestick, Newcastle, Eng.

The Newcastle Journal, Newcastle, Eng.

News, Boys, News! or the Electioneering Journal [News, Boys, News! Election News. Jackson's Oxford Journal; Jackson's Oxford Journal], b. 1753, Oxford, Eng.

The Norfolk Chronicle or Norwich Gazette, b. 1761, Norfolk, Eng.

The North Briton, 1762-1763, London.

The Northampton Mercury or the Monday's Post, Northampton, Eng.

The Political Register; and Impartial Review of New Books . . . [The Political Register and List of New Books; and the Political Register and London Museum], 1767-1772, London.

Prescott's Manchester Journal, b. 1771, Manchester, Eng.

The Public Advertiser [The General Advertiser], London.

The Public Ledger, b. 1760, London.

The Reading Mercury and Oxford Gazette [The Oxford Gazette and Reading Mercury], Reading, Eng.

The Remembrancer: Or Impartial Repository of Public Events, b. 1775, London.

St. James's Chronicle or the British Evening Post, b. 1761, London.

The Scots Magazine, or General Repository of Literature, History, and Politics, Edinburgh, Scot.

The Stamford Mercury, Stamford, Eng.

The Town and Country Magazine, or Universal Repository of Knowledge, Instruction and Entertainment, b. 1769, London.

The Traveller's Magazine, or Gentleman and Lady's Agreeable Companion, 1749, London.

The True Briton . . ., 1751-1753, London.

The Universal Magazine, of Knowledge and Pleasure, London.

The Westminister Journal [The Royal Westminister Journal and London Political Miscellany], London.

The Westminister Magazine, or the Pantheon of Taste, b. 1772, London.

The Whisperer, 1770-1772, London.

The Whitehall Evening Post: Or London Intelligencer, London.

Williamson's Liverpool Advertiser [Liverpool Advertiser], b. 1756, Liverpool, Eng.

The York Courant, York, Eng.

C. SECONDARY WORKS

1. General

ADOLPHUS, JOHN: *The History of England: From the Accession of King George the Third* . . . (1st edn., 3 vols., London, 1802; cont'd. to 1804, 7 vols., London, 1840-5).

BELSHAM, WILLIAM: *History of Great Britain: From the Revolution, 1688, to the Conclusion of the Treaty of Amiens, 1802* (1st edn., 12 vols., London, 1798; reiss. 1805-6).

BISSET, ROBERT: *The History of the Reign of George III: To the Termination of the Late War* . . . (6 vols., London, 1803).

BUCKLE, HENRY THOMAS: *History of Civilization in England* (2 vols., London, 1857; n. edn., 3 vols., 1869).

HARRIS, RONALD W.: *A Short History of Eighteenth-Century England* (New York, 1963).

HUNT, WILLIAM: *The History of England From the Accession of George III to the Close of Pitt's First Administration, 1760-1801. Political History of England,* X (London, 1905).

JOHNSTON, EDITH M.: *Great Britain and Ireland, 1760-1800: A Study in Political Administration* (Pittsburgh, Pa., 1963).

LEADAM, ISAAC SAUNDERS: *The History of England: From the Accession of Anne to the Death of George II. Political History of England,* IX (London, 1909).

LECKY, WILLIAM EDWARD HARTPOLE: *A History of England in the Eighteenth Century* (8 vols., London, 1878-90).

MAHON, PHILIP HENRY STANHOPE, VISCOUNT: *History of England: From the Peace of Utrecht to the Peace of Versailles, 1713-1783* (1st edn., 7 vols., London, 1836-54; 5th edn., rev., 7 vols., 1858).

MARSHALL, DOROTHY: *Eighteenth Century England, A History of England,* VII (London, 1962).

MASSEY, WILLIAM NATHANIEL: *A History of England during the Reign of George III* (4 vols., London, 1855-63).

MOWAT, R. B.: *England in the Eighteenth Century* (London & New York, 1932).

ROBERTSON, CHARLES GRANT: *England under the Hanoverians, A History of England,* VI (London, 1911; 16th edn., London, 1949).

SMOLLETT, TOBIAS G.: *The History of England from the Revolution to the Death of George II* . . . (5 vols., London, 1790).

VAN ALSTYNE, RICHARD W.: "Great Britain, the War for Independence, and the 'Gathering Storm' in Europe, 1775-1778," *Huntington Library Quarterly,* XXVII (1963-4), 311-46.

WATSON, JOHN STEVEN: *The Reign of George III, 1760-1815, The Oxford History of England,* XII (Oxford, Eng., 1960).

2. Local

Students should consult *The Victoria History of the Counties of England*. Publication of this work began in 1900 with William Page, H. Arthur Doubleday, and many others involved in this great enterprise which is still in progress and doubtless will be for many years to come. The following list is limited to works concerned with towns, boroughs, and cities that have a special relation to the developing British Empire, 1748-1776.

BARRETT, WILLIAM: *The History and Antiquities of the City of Bristol . . .* (Bristol, Eng. [1789]).

BESANT, WALTER: *London in the Eighteenth Century* (London, 1902).

BRAND, JOHN: *The History and Antiquities of . . . Newcastle upon Tyne . . .* (2 vols., London, 1789).

BROOKE, RICHARD: *Liverpool as It Was during the Last Quarter of the Eighteenth Century, 1775-1800* (London & Liverpool, Eng., 1853).

COATES, CHARLES: *The History and Antiquities of Reading* (London, 1802).

[COMBE, WILLIAM]: *The History and Antiquities of the City of York . . . to the present time* (3 vols. [York, Eng.], 1785).

DODSLEY, R. and J., publishers: *London and Its Environs* (6 vols., London, 1761).

ENTICK, JOHN: *A New and Accurate History and Survey of London, Westminster, Southwark, and Places Adjacent . . .* (4 vols., London, 1766).

FASNACHT, RUTH: *A History of the City of Oxford* (Oxford, Eng., 1954).

GATTY, ALFRED: *Sheffield: Past and Present . . .* (London, 1873).

GILL, CONRAD: *History of Birmingham, Vol. I: Manor and Borough to 1865* (London & New York, 1952).

GILMAN, ARTHUR, ed.: *The Cambridge of Eighteen Hundred and Ninety-Six . . .* (Cambridge, Eng., 1896).

GREEN, JOHN RICHARD: *Oxford Studies* (Mrs. J. R. Green and Kate Norgate, eds., London & New York, 1901). Stresses eighteenth-century Oxford.

GRINLING, CHARLES HERBERT, THOMAS ALLAN INGRAM, and BENNETT CORCYA POLKINGHORNE, eds.: *A Survey and Record of Woolwich and West Kent . . .* (London, 1909).

HUTTON, WILLIAM: *An History of Birmingham . . .* (Birmingham, Eng., 1781; 2nd edn., 1783).

————: *The History of Derby . . . [to 1791]* (London, 1791; 2nd edn., 1817).

LANGFORD, JOHN A.: *A Century of Birmingham Life: Or a Chronicle of Local Events from 1741 to 1841* (Birmingham, Eng., 1868).

LATIMER, JOHN: *Annals of Bristol in the Eighteenth Century* (London & Frome, Eng., 1893).

LEADER, ROBERT EADON: *Sheffield in the Eighteenth Century* (Sheffield, Eng., 1901).

MAC INNES, CHARLES MALCOLM: *A Gateway to Empire* (Bristol, Eng., 1939). Deals with the port of Bristol.

MINCHINTON, W. E.: "Bristol: Metropolis of the West in the Eighteenth Century," Royal Historical Society, *Transactions,* 5th ser., IV (1954), 69-89.

NASH, TREADWAY RUSSELL: *Collections for the History and Antiquities of Worcestershire* (2 vols., London, 1781-99).

PARKINSON, CYRIL NORTHCOTE: *The Rise of the Port of Liverpool* (Liverpool, Eng., 1952).

PROCTER, RICHARD W.: *Memorials of Bygone Manchester* (Manchester, Eng., 1880).

ROWE, JOHN: *Cornwall in the Age of the Industrial Revolution* (Liverpool, Eng., 1953).

SEYER, SAMUEL: *Memoirs, Historical and Topographical, of Bristol and Its Neighborhood* . . . (2 vols., Bristol, Eng., 1821-3).

SHARPE, REGINALD ROBINSON: *London and the Kingdom* . . . (London, 1894).

SHEAHAN, JAMES JOSEPH: *General and Concise History and Description of the Town and Port of Kingston-upon-Hull* (London, 1864).

SIMPSON, ROBERT: *A Collection of Fragments Illustrative of the History and Antiquities of Derby* . . . (2 vols., Derby, Eng., 1826).

TOULNIN, JOSHUA: *The History of Taunton in the County of Somerset* . . . (1st edn., London, 1791; enl. edn., James Savage, ed., 1822).

[WALLACE, JAMES]: *A General and Descriptive History of the Ancient and Present State of Liverpool* . . . (Liverpool, Eng., 1795).

WALTON, MARY: *Sheffield: Its Story and Its Achievements* (1st edn., Sheffield, Eng., 1948; 3rd edn., 1952).

WARDELL, JAMES: *The Municipal History of the Borough of Leeds* . . . (London, 1846).

WHEATLEY, H. B., and PETER CUNNINGHAM: *London, Past and Present* . . . (3 vols., London, 1891; n. edn., 1930).

WILLIAMS, J. E.: "Whitehaven in the Eighteenth Century," *Economic History Review,* 2nd ser., VIII (1955-6), 393-404.

3. Political

In listing political works it seems desirable to include the writings of certain foreigners which have a bearing upon British external relations.

ANSON, WILLIAM REYNELL: *The Law and Custom of the Constitution* . . . (1st edn., 2 vols., London, 1886-92; 5th edn., Maurice L. Gwyer, ed., 1922).

ARIBAU, B. C.: "Obras origanales del Conde de Floridablanca, y escritos referentes à su persona," *Biblioteca de autores Españoles,* LIX (Madrid, 1867). These writings are important in throwing light on British-Spanish relations.

ASPINALL, A.: "The Reporting and Publishing of the House of Commons' Debates, 1771-1834," *Essays Presented to Sir Lewis Namier* (Richard Pares and A. J. P. Taylor, eds., London & New York, 1956), pp. 227-57.

BARGAR, B. D.: "Lord Dartmouth's Patronage, 1772-1775," *William and Mary Quarterly,* 3rd ser., XV (1958), 191-200.

BARROW, THOMAS C.: "Background to the Grenville Program, 1757-1763," *ibid.,* XXII (1965), 93-104.

BARTHÉLEMY, COMTE ÉDOUARD DE: "Le Traité de Paris entre la France et l'Angleterre (1763)," *Revue des Questions Historiques,* XLIII (Paris, 1888), 420-88.

BEER, SAMUEL H.: "The Representation of Interests in British Government: Historical Background," *American Political Science Review,* LI (1957), 613-50.

BELLOT, H. HALE: "Parliamentary Printing, 1660-1837," Institute of Historical Research, *Bulletin,* XI (1933-4), 85-98.

BINNEY, JOHN EDWARD DOUGLAS: *British Public Finance and Administration, 1774-92* (Oxford, Eng. & New York, 1958).

BLACK, EUGENE CHARLTON: *The Association: British Extraparliamentary Political Organization, 1769-1793, Harvard Historical Monographs,* No. 54 (Cambridge, Mass., 1963).

BLAUVELT, MARY TAYLOR: *The Development of Cabinet Government in England* (New York, 1902).

BOULTON, JAMES T.: *The Language of Politics in the Age of Wilkes and Burke* (London & Toronto, 1963).

BOURGUET, ALFRED: *Études sur la Politique étrangère du Duc de Choiseul* (Paris, 1900), and *Le Duc de Choiseul et l'alliance espagnole* (Paris, 1906). See also "Le Duc de Choiseul et l'Angleterre," *Revue Historique,* LXXXI (1899), 1-32, and another article with the same title in *Revue d'Histoire Diplomatique,* XVII (1903), 456-68, 541-56.

BROGLIE, JACQUES VICTOR ALBERT, DUC DE: *La Paix d'Aix-la-Chapelle, 1748* (Paris, 1892).

BROOKE, JOHN: *The Chatham Administration, 1766-1768* (London & New York, 1956).

BROUGHAM, HENRY PETER, LORD: *An Inquiry into the Colonial Policy of the European Powers* (2 vols., Edinburgh, 1803).

BUTTERFIELD, HERBERT: *The Englishman and His History, Current Problems Series, No. 19* (Cambridge, Eng., 1944).

————: *The Whig Interpretation of History* (London, 1931; New York, 1951).

CARTER, ALICE: "Analysis of Public Indebtedness in Eighteenth-Century

England," Institute of Historical Research, *Bulletin*, XXIV (1951), 173-81.

CHRISTIE, IAN R.: *Wilkes, Wyvill, and Reform: The Parliamentary Movement in British Politics, 1760-1785* (London & New York, 1962). See also his articles: "Was There a 'New Toryism' in the Earlier Part of George III's Reign?" *Journal of British Studies*, V (1965), 60-76; "The Cabinet during the Grenville Administration, 1763-1765," *English Historical Review*, LXXIII (1958), 86-92; and "The Political Allegiance of John Robinson, 1770-1784," Institute of Historical Research, *Bulletin*, XXIX (1956), 108-22.

CLARK, DORA MAE: *British Opinion and the American Revolution, Yale Historical Publications: Miscellany*, XX (New Haven, Conn., 1930).

————: *The Rise of the British Treasury: Colonial Administration in the Eighteenth Century, Yale Historical Publications, Studies*, No. 20 (New Haven, Conn., 1960).

COATS, A. W.: "Economic Thought and Poor Law Policy in the Eighteenth Century," *Economic History Review*, 2nd ser., XIII (1960-1), 39-51.

COQUELLE, P.: *L'Alliance franco-hollandaise contre l'Angleterre 1735-1788* (Paris, 1902).

COXE, WILLIAM: *Memoirs of the Kings of Spain of the House of Bourbon from the Accession of Philip the Fifth to the Death of Charles the Third: 1700 . . . to . . . 1788* (3 vols., London, 1813; 2nd edn., 5 vols., London, 1815).

DANVILA Y COLLADO, MANUEL: *Reinado de Carlos III* (6 vols., Madrid, 1893+). These scholarly volumes form part of the *Historia General de España* by members of the Real Acad. de Historia.

DAVIES, ALFRED MERVYN: *The Influence of George III on the Development of the Constitution* (London, 1921).

DICKERSON, OLIVER M.: "England's Most Fateful Decision," *New England Quarterly*, XXII (1949), 388-94.

DONOUGHUE, BERNARD: *British Politics and the American Revolution: The Path to War, 1773-75* (London & New York, 1964).

DOWDELL, ERIC GEORGE: *A Hundred Years of Quarter Sessions: The Government of Middlesex from 1660 to 1760* (London, 1932).

DOWELL, STEPHEN: *A History and Explanation of Stamp Duties: Containing Remarks on the Origin of Stamp Duties . . .* (London, 1873), and *A History of Taxation and Taxes in England . . .* (4 vols., London, 1884).

DUNCKER, MAX: "Die Bildung der Koalition des Jahres 1756," *Preussische Jahrbücher*, XLIX (1882), 191-211.

ELDON, CARL WILLIAM: *England's Subsidy Policy Towards the Continent during the Seven Years' War* (Philadelphia, 1938).

ELLIS, KENNETH L.: *The Post Office in the Eighteenth Century: A Study in Administrative History* (London & New York, 1958), and his article "British Communications and Diplomacy in the Eighteenth

Century," Institute of Historical Research, *Bulletin,* XXXI (1958), 159-67.

ERICSON, FREDERIC J.: "The Contemporary British Opposition to the Stamp Act, 1764-65," Michigan Academy of Science, Arts and Letters, *Papers,* XXIX (1943), 489-505.

FEILING, KEITH GRAHAME: *The Second Tory Party, 1714-1832* (London, 1938).

FOORD, ARCHIBALD S.: *His Majesty's Opposition, 1714-1830* (Oxford, Eng., 1964).

GIPSON, LAWRENCE HENRY: "British Diplomacy in the Light of Anglo-Spanish New World Issues, 1750-1757," *American Historical Review,* LI (1946), 627-48; "A French Project for Victory Short of a Declaration of War, 1755," *Canadian Historical Review,* XXVI (1945), 361-71; and "The Great Debates in the Committee of the Whole House of Commons on the Stamp Act, 1766: As Reported by Nathaniel Ryder," *Pennsylvania Magazine of History and Biography,* LXXXVI (1962), 10-41.

GOUGH, JOHN WIEDHOFFT: *Fundamental Law in English Constitutional History* (Oxford, Eng., 1955).

GRAHAM, WILLIAM: *English Political Philosophy from Hobbes to Maine* (London, 1899).

GREEN, V. H. H.: *The Hanoverians, 1714-1815* (London, 1948; rep., 1951).

GUTTRIDGE, G. H.: *English Whiggism and the American Revolution,* University of California, *Publications in History,* XXVIII (Berkeley, Calif., & Los Angeles, 1942).

HANSON, LAURENCE: *Government and the Press, 1695-1763* (Oxford, Eng., 1936).

HEMMEON, JOSEPH CLARENCE: *The History of the British Post Office* (Cambridge, Mass., 1912).

HODGE, HELEN HENRY: "The Repeal of the Stamp Act," *Political Science Quarterly,* XIX (1904), 252-76.

HOLDSWORTH, WILLIAM: *A History of English Law* (16 vols., London, 1903-66), X.

HOOVER, BENJAMIN BEARD: *Samuel Johnson's Parliamentary Reporting: Debates in the Senate of Lilliput,* University of California, *Publications: English Studies,* No. 7 (Berkeley, Calif., & Los Angeles, 1953).

HORN, D. B.: *The British Diplomatic Service: 1689-1789* (Oxford, Eng., 1941).

HUGHES, EDWARD: "The English Stamp Duties, 1664-1764," *English Historical Review,* LVI (1941), 234-64.

INNES, ARTHUR DONALD: *Britain and Her Rivals in the Eighteenth Century, 1713-89* (London, 1895).

JANY, CURT: *Geschichte der Koeniglich Preussischen Armee bis zum Jahre 1807 . . .* (5 vols., Berlin, 1928-37).

JENKS, EDWARD: *A Short History of English Law* . . . (5th edn., London, 1938).

JOHNSON, ALLEN S.: "British Politics and the Repeal of the Stamp Act," *South Atlantic Quarterly*, LXII (1963), 169-88, and "The Passage of the Sugar Act," *William and Mary Quarterly*, 3rd ser., XVI (1959), 507-14.

JOYCE, HERBERT: *The History of the Post Office* . . . *to 1836* (London, 1893).

KEMP, BETTY: *King and Commons, 1660-1832* (London & New York, 1957).

LACRETELLE, CHARLES DE: *Histoire de France pendant le dix-huitième Siècle* (4th edn., 6 vols., Paris, 1819).

LAPRADE, WILLIAM T.: "The Stamp Act in British Politics," *American Historical Review*, XXXV (1929-30), 735-57.

LODGE, RICHARD: *Great Britain and Prussia in the Eighteenth Century* . . . (Oxford, Eng., 1923).

MACCOBY, SIMON: *The English Radical Tradition, 1763-1914* (London, 1952), and *English Radicalism, Vol. I: 1762-1785: The Origins* (London, 1955).

MC LACHLAN, JEAN: "The Uneasy Neutrality: A Study of Anglo-Spanish Disputes over Ships Prized, 1756-1759," *Cambridge Historical Journal*, VI (1938-40), 55-77.

MAC KINTOSH, JOHN P.: *The British Cabinet* (London & Toronto, 1962).

MAITLAND, FREDERIC WILLIAM: *The Constitutional History of England: A Course of Lectures* . . . (Cambridge, Eng., 1908).

MARCHAM, FREDERICK GEORGE: *A Constitutional History of Modern England, 1485 to the Present* (New York, 1960).

MARSHALL, CHAPMAN F. D.: *The British Post Office* . . . *[to] 1925* (London, 1926).

MARTIN, HENRI: *Histoire de France depuis les temps les plus reculés jusqu'en 1789* (19 vols., Paris, 1839-54).

MASSLOWSKI, DMITRY THEDOROVICH: *Der Siebenjährige Krieg nach russicher Darstellung* (3 vols., Berlin, 1888-93).

MAY, THOMAS ERSKINE: *The Constitutional History of England since the Accession of George the Third, 1760-1860* (1st edn., London, 1861-1863; n. edn., edited and continued to 1911 by Francis Holland, 1912).

MENG, JOHN JOSEPH: *The Comte de Vergennes; European Phases of His American Diplomacy (1774-1780)* (Washington, D.C., 1932).

MORGAN, EDMUND S.: "The Postponement of the Stamp Act," *William and Mary Quarterly*, 3rd ser., VII (1950), 353-92.

NAMIER, SIR LEWIS: *Crossroads of Power: Essays on Eighteenth-Century England* (London, 1962).

——: *England in the Age of the American Revolution* (London, 1930; 2nd edn., 1963).

————: *Personalities and Power* (London, 1955).

————: *The Structure of Politics at the Accession of George III* (2 vols., London, 1929; 2nd edn., London & New York, 1957).

————, and JOHN BROOKE: *The History of Parliament: The House of Commons 1754-1790* (3 vols., London & New York, 1957).

NOBBE, GEORGE: *The North Briton: A Study in Political Propaganda, Columbia University, Studies in English and Comparative Literature,* No. 140 (New York, 1939).

PARES, RICHARD: *Limited Monarchy in Great Britain in the Eighteenth Century,* Historical Association, General Series, No. 35 (London, 1957).

PERRY, THOMAS W.: *Public Opinion, Propaganda, and Politics in Eighteenth-Century England: A Study of the Jewish Naturalization Act of 1753, Harvard Historical Monographs,* No. 51 (Cambridge, Mass., 1962).

PLUCKNETT, THEODORE F. T.: *A Concise History of the Common Law* (3rd edn., rev., London, 1940).

POCOCK, J. G. A.: "Machiavelli, Harrington, and English Political Idealogies in the Eighteenth Century," *William and Mary Quarterly,* 3rd ser., XXII (1965), 549-83.

PORRITT, EDWARD and ANNIE G.: *The Unreformed House of Commons: Parliamentary Representation before 1832* (2 vols., Cambridge, Eng., 1903; London, 1912; rep., New York, 1963).

RADZINOWICZ, LEON: *A History of English Criminal Law and Its Administration from 1750, Vol. I: The Movement for Reform [1750-1833]* (London & New York, 1948).

RAE, W. FRASER: *Wilkes, Sheridan, Fox: The Opposition under George the Third* (London, 1874).

RASHED, ZENAB ESMOT: *The Peace of Paris, 1763* (Liverpool, Eng., 1951).

REA, ROBERT R.: *The English Press in Politics, 1760-1774* (Lincoln, Neb., 1963).

RITCHESON, CHARLES R.: *British Politics and the American Revolution* (Norman, Okla., 1954), and his article: "The Preparation of the Stamp Act," *William and Mary Quarterly,* 3rd ser., X (1953), 543-559.

ROBBINS, CAROLINE: *The Eighteenth-Century Commonwealthman: Studies in the Transmission, Development and Circumstance of English Thought from the Restoration of Charles II until the War with the Thirteen Colonies* (Cambridge, Mass., 1959), and her articles: "Algernon Sidney's *Discourse Concerning Government* [1698]: Textbook of Revolution," *William and Mary Quarterly,* 3rd ser., IV (1947), 267-96, including its influence on eighteenth-century thought; and "Discordant Parties: A Study of the Acceptance of Party by Englishmen," *Political Science Quarterly,* LXXIII (1958), 505-29.

ROBINSON, HOWARD: *The British Post Office: A History* (Princeton, N. J., 1948).

RODRIGUEZ VILLA, ANTONIO: *Don C. de Somodevilla, Marqués de la Ensenada. Ensayo biográfica formado con documentos . . . originales . . .* (Madrid, 1878).

ROUSSEAU, FRANÇOIS: *Règne de Charles III d'Espagne, 1759-1788* (2 vols., Paris, 1907). Deals specifically with Franco-Spanish relations.

RUDÉ, GEORGE F.: *Wilkes and Liberty; a Social Study of 1763 to 1774* (Oxford, Eng., 1962), and "The Middlesex Electors of 1768-1769," *English Historical Review*, LXXV (1960), 601-17.

SMITH, GEORGE BARNETT: *History of the English Parliament: Together with an Account of the Parliaments of Scotland and Ireland* (2 vols., London, 1892).

SMITH, PAUL H.: *Loyalists and Redcoats: A Study in British Revolutionary Policy* (Chapel Hill, N. C., 1964).

SOSIN, JACK M.: "A Postscript to the Stamp Act: George Grenville's Revenue Measures: A Drain on Colonial Specie?" *American Historical Review*, LXIII (1957-8), 918-23.

SOUTHWICK, ALBERT B.: "The Molasses Act: Source of Precedents," *William and Mary Quarterly*, 3rd ser., VIII (1951), 389-405.

SPENCER, FRANK: "The Anglo-Prussian Breach of 1762: An Historical Revision," *History*, n. ser., XLI (1956), 100-12.

SUTHERLAND, LUCY S.: *The City of London and the Opposition to Government, 1768-1774: A Study in the Rise of Metropolitan Radicalism* (London, 1959); *The City of London and the Devonshire-Pitt Administration, 1756-7* (London, 1961); and "The City of London in Eighteenth-Century Politics," *Essays Presented to Sir Lewis Namier* (Richard Pares and A. J. P. Taylor, eds., London & New York, 1956), pp. 49-74.

TASWELL-LANGMEAD, THOMAS PITT: *English Constitutional History . . .* (8th edn., Boston, 1919).

TEMPERLEY, HAROLD W. V.: "Inner and Outer Cabinet and Privy Council, 1679-1783," *English Historical Review*, XXVII (1912), 682-99.

THOMAS, PETER D. G.: "The Beginning of Parliamentary Reporting in Newspapers, 1768-1774," *English Historical Review*, LXXIV (1959), 623-36.

THOMSON, MARK ALMÉRAS: *A Constitutional History of England, Vol. IV: 1642-1801* (London, 1938).

TODD, ALPHEUS: *On Parliamentary Government in England* (S. Walpole, ed., 2 vols., London, 1892).

TORRENS, W. M.: *History of Cabinets: From the Union with Scotland to the Acquisition of Canada and Bengal* (2 vols., London, 1894).

TURBERVILLE, ARTHUR STANLEY: *The House of Lords in the XVIIIth Century* (Oxford, Eng., 1927).

TURNER, EDWARD RAYMOND: *The Cabinet Council of England in the*

Seventeenth and Eighteenth Centuries, 1622-1784 (2 vols., Baltimore, Md., 1930-2), and *The Privy Council of England in the Seventeenth and Eighteenth Centuries, 1603-1784* (2 vols., Baltimore, Md., 1927-8).

———, and GAUDENS MEGARO: "The King's Closet in the Eighteenth Century," *American Historical Review*, XLV (1939-40), 761-76.

VINER, JACOB: "Power versus Plenty as Objectives of Foreign Policy in the Seventeenth and Eighteenth Centuries," *World Politics*, I (1948), 1-29.

WADDINGTON, RICHARD: *Louis XV et le Renversement des Alliances: Préliminaires de la guerre de Sept Ans, 1754-1756* (Paris, 1896).

WARD, ADOLPHUS WILLIAM: *Great Britain and Hanover: Some Aspects of the Personal Union* (Oxford, Eng., 1899).

WARD, WILLIAM REGINALD: *The English Land Tax in the Eighteenth Century* (London, 1953).

———: "Some Eighteenth Century Civil Servants: The English Revenue Commissioners, 1754-98," *English Historical Review*, LXX (1955), 25-54.

WATSON, J. STEVEN: "Parliamentary Procedure as a Key to the Understanding of Eighteenth Century Politics," *Burke Newsletter*, III (1962), 107-29.

WEBB, SIDNEY and BEATRICE: *English Local Government . . .* (9 vols., London, 1906-29). A comprehensive and authoritative account of the complexities of British local government in the eighteenth century and following.

WESTON, CORINNE C.: *English Constitutional Theory and the House of Lords, 1556-1832*, Columbia University, *Studies in History, Economics, and Public Law*, No. 607 (London & New York, 1965).

WICKWIRE, FRANKLIN B.: "Admiralty Secretaries and the British Civil Service," *Huntington Library Quarterly*, XXVIII (1964-5), 235-54; and "King's Friends, Civil Servants, or Politicians," *American Historical Review*, LXXI (1965-6), 18-42.

WILKES, JOHN W.: "British Politics Preceding the American Revolution," *Huntington Library Quarterly*, XX (1956-7), 301-19.

WILLIAMS, BASIL: *The Whig Supremacy, 1714-1760* (Oxford, Eng., 1939; 2nd edn., rev. by C. H. Stuart, 1962), and his earlier article "The Eclipse of the Yorkes," Royal Historical Society, *Transactions*, 3rd ser., II (1908), 129-51.

WILLIAMS, E. TREVOR: "The Cabinet in the Eighteenth Century," *The Making of English History* (R. L. Schuyler and H. Ausubel, eds., New York, 1952), 378-92.

WINSTANLEY, DENYS ARTHUR: *Personal and Party Government: A Chapter in the Political History of the Early Years of the Reign of George III, 1760-1766* (Cambridge, Eng., 1910).

WOLKINS, GEORGE G.: "Writs of Assistance in England," Massachusetts Historical Society, *Proceedings*, LXVI (1936-41), 357-64.

4. Economic

ARMITAGE, GODFREY W.: *The Lancashire Cotton Trade from the Great Inventions to the Great Disaster* ([Manchester, Eng., 1951]).

ASHTON, THOMAS S.: *An Economic History of England: The 18th Century* (London, 1955). See also his more specialized works: *Economic Fluctuations in England, 1700-1800* (Oxford, Eng., 1959); *The Industrial Revolution, 1760-1830* (London, 1948); *Iron and Steel in the Industrial Revolution* (London, 1924; 2nd edn., Manchester, Eng., 1951); and the volume written in collaboration with Joseph Sykes: *The Coal Industry of the Eighteenth Century*, University of Manchester, *Publications: Economic History Series, No. 5* (Manchester, Eng., 1929).

BARNES, DONALD GROVE: *A History of the English Corn Laws from 1660-1846* (London, 1930).

BIRCH, ALAN: "Foreign Observers of the British Iron Industry during the Eighteenth Century," *Journal of Economic History*, XV (1955), 23-33.

BIRNIE, ARTHUR: *An Economic History of the British Isles* (8th edn., London, 1961).

CANE, CHARLES HENRY: *A History of Banking in Bristol from 1750 to 1899* (Bristol, Eng., 1899).

CHALMERS, GEORGE: *An Estimate of the Comparative Strength of Britain During the Present and Four Preceding Reigns and of the Losses of Her Trade from Every War since the Revolution* . . . (London, 1782).

CHAMBERS, JONATHAN DAVID: *The Vale of Trent, 1670-1800: A Regional Study of Economic Change, Economic Review: Supplements*, No. 3 (London & New York, 1957).

CLAPHAM, JOHN HAROLD: *A Concise Economic History of Britain from the Earliest Times to 1750* (Cambridge, Eng., 1949).

CLARK, COLIN GRANT: *The Conditions of Economic Progress* (London, 1940; 3rd edn., London & New York, 1957).

CLARK, GEORGE NORMAN: *The Wealth of England from 1496-1760* (London & New York, 1946).

COATS, A. W.: "Economic Thought and Poor Law Policy in the Eighteenth Century," *Economic History Review*, 2nd ser., XIII (1960-1), 39-51.

COURT, WILLIAM H. B.: *The Rise of the Midland Industries, 1600-1838* (London, 1938; n. edn., 1958).

CUNNINGHAM, WILLIAM: *The Growth of English Industry and Commerce* (3rd edn., 3 vols., London, 1896-1903).

CURTLER, WILLIAM H. R.: *The Enclosure and Redistribution of Our Land* (Oxford, Eng., 1920).

DANIELS, GEORGE WILLIAM: *The Early English Cotton Industry: With Some Unpublished Letters of Samuel Crompton*, University of Manchester, *Publications: Historical Series*, No. 36 (Manchester, Eng., 1920).

DAVIS, RALPH: *The Rise of the English Shipping Industry in the Seventeenth and Eighteenth Centuries* (London & New York, 1962). See also his "English Foreign Trade, 1700-1774," *Economic History Review*, 2nd ser., XV (1962-3), 285-303.

DEANE, PHYLLIS: "The Output of the British Woollen Industry in the 18th Century," *Journal of Economic History*, XVII (1957), 207-23.

DIETZ, FREDERICK C.: *An Economic History of England* (New York, 1942).

DOUBLEDAY, THOMAS: *A Financial, Monetary, and Statistical History of England from the Revolution to the Present Time* . . . (London, 1847).

DUBOIS, ARMAND BUBINGTON: *The English Business Company after the Bubble Act, 1720-1800* (London & New York, 1938).

FISHER, H. E. J.: "Anglo-Portuguese Trade, 1700-1770," *Economic History Review*, 2nd ser., XVI (1963-4), 219-33.

FITTON, R. S., and A. P. WADSWORTH: *The Strutts and the Arkwrights, 1758-1830* (Manchester, Eng., 1958).

FLINN, M. W.: "Revision in Economic History, XVII: The Growth of the English Iron Industry, 1660-1760," *Economic History Review*, 2nd ser., XI (1958-9), 144-53.

———: "Agricultural Productivity and Economic Growth in England, 1700-1760: A Comment," *Journal of Economic History*, XXVI (1966), 93-8.

FUSSEL, G. W.: "Population and Wheat Production in the Eighteenth-Century," *History Teachers Miscellany*, VII (1929), 65-8.

GIBBINS, HENRY DE B.: *The Industrial History of England* (London, 1890; 19th edn., 1913; 28th edn., 1926).

GILBOY, ELIZABETH WATERMAN: *Wages in Eighteenth Century England*, *Harvard Economic Studies*, XLV (Cambridge, Mass., 1934). See also her article with the same title in the *Journal of Economic and Business History*, II (1929-30), 603-29.

GOULD, J. D.: "Agricultural Fluctuations and the English Economy in the Eighteenth Century," *Journal of Economic History*, XXII (1962), 313-33.

GRAMPP, WILLIAM D.: "The Liberal Elements in English Mercantilism," *Quarterly Journal of Economics*, LXVI (1952), 465-501.

GRAY, HOWARD LEVI: *English Field Systems* (Cambridge, Mass., 1915).

HABAKKUK, H. J.: "Economic Functions of English Landowners in the Seventeenth and Eighteenth Centuries," *Explorations in Entrepreneurial History*, VI (1953), 92-102, and "Essays in Bibliography and Criticism, XXXII: The Eighteenth Century," *Economic History Review*, 2nd ser., VIII (1955-6), 434-8.

HAMILTON, CHARLES JOSEPH: *The Trade Relations between England and India, 1600-1896* (Calcutta, 1919).

HAMILTON, HENRY: *The English Brass and Copper Industries to 1800 . . .* (London, 1926).

HEATON, HERBERT: *The Yorkshire Woolen and Worsted Industries from the Earliest Times to the Industrial Revolution* (Oxford, Eng., 1920; 2nd edn., 1965).

HENDERSON, WILLIAM OTTO: *Britain and Industrial Europe, 1750-1870: Studies in British Influence on the Industrial Revolution in Western Europe* (1st edn., Liverpool, Eng., 1954; 2nd edn., Leicester, Eng., 1966).

HOFFMANN, WALTHER GUSTAV: *British Industry, 1700-1950* (W. O. Henderson and W. H. Chaloner, trans., Oxford, Eng., 1955).

HUGHES, EDWARD: "The Eighteenth-Century Estate Agent," *Essays in British and Irish History in Honour of James Eadis Todd* (H. A. Cronne, T. W. Moody, and D. B. Quinn, eds., London, 1949), pp. 185-99.

HUNT, H. G.: "Landownership and Enclosure, 1750-1830," *Economic History Review*, 2nd ser., XI (1958-9), 497-505.

HYDE, FRANCIS E., BRADBURY B. PARKINSON, and SHEILA MARRINER: "The Nature and Profitability of the Liverpool Slave Trade," *ibid.*, 2nd ser., V (1952-3), 368-77.

JOHN, A. H.: "Agricultural Productivity and Economic Growth in England, 1700-1760," *Journal of Economic History*, XXV (1965), 19-34; and "War and the English Economy, 1700-1763," *Economic History Review*, 2nd ser., VII (1954-5), 329-44.

JOHNSON, ARTHUR HENRY: *The Disappearance of the Small Landowner* (Oxford, Eng., 1909).

LEVI, LEONE: *History of British Commerce and of the Economic Progress of the British Nation, 1763-1870* (London, 1872).

LIPSON, EPHRAIM: *The Economic History of England* (3 vols., London, 1937-43), and *The History of the Woolen and Worsted Industries* (London, 1921).

LOW, J. M.: "An Eighteenth Century Controversy in the Theory of Economic Progress," *Manchester School of Economic and Social Studies*, XX (1952), 311-30.

MACPHERSON, DAVID: *Annals of Commerce, Manufactures, Fisheries and Navigation . . .* (4 vols., London, 1805).

MANTOUX, PAUL JOSEPH: *The Industrial Revolution in the Eighteenth Century* (rev. edn., London, 1947).

MARTIN, FREDERICK: *The History of Lloyd's and of Marine Insurance in Great Britain: With an Appendix Containing Statistics Relating to Marine Insurance* (London, 1876).

MATHIAS, PETER: *The Brewing Industry in England, 1700-1830* (London, 1959).

MINCHINTON, WALTER E.: "The Merchants in England in the Eighteenth Century," *The Entrepreneur: Papers Presented at the Annual Conference of the Economic History Society at Cambridge, England, April 1957* (Cambridge, Mass., 1957), pp. 22-31.

MURRAY, ALICE EFFIE: *A History of the Commercial and Financial Relations between England and Ireland from the Period of the Restoration* (n. edn., London, 1907).

NEF, JOHN ULRIC: *The Rise of the British Coal Industry* (2 vols., London, 1932).

PARES, RICHARD: "The London Sugar Market, 1740-1769," *Economic History Review*, 2nd ser., IX (1956-7), 254-70.

PARKER, R. A. C.: "Coke of Norfolk and the Agrarian Revolution," *ibid.*, 2nd ser., VIII (1955-6), 156-66.

———: *Enclosures in the Eighteenth Century, Aids for Teachers Service*, No. 7 (London, 1960).

PELHAM, R. A.: "The West Midland Iron Industry and the American Market in the Eighteenth Century," University of Birmingham, *Historical Journal*, II (1949-50), 141-62.

PENSON, LILLIAN M.: "The London West India Interest in the Eighteenth Century," *English Historical Review*, XXXVI (1921), 373-92.

PLUMB, J. H.: "The Mercantile Interest: The Rise of the British Merchant after 1689," *History Today*, V (1955), 762-7.

PRICE, JACOB M.: "Who Was John Norton? A Note on the Historical Character of Some Eighteenth-Century London Virginia Firms," *William and Mary Quarterly*, 3rd ser., XIX (1962), 400-7.

PROTHERO, ROWLAND EDMUND: *English Farming: Past and Present* (London, 1912).

RAISTRICK, ARTHUR: "The South Yorkshire Iron Industry," Newcomen Society, *Transactions*, XIX (1938-9), 51-86.

RAMSAY, GEORGE D.: *English Overseas Trade During the Centuries of Emergence* . . . (London & New York, 1957), and his article "The Smugglers' Trade: A Neglected Aspect of English Commercial Development," Royal Historical Society, *Transactions*, 5th ser., II (1952), 131-57.

RIVE, ALFRED: "A Brief History of the Regulation and Taxation of Tobacco in England," *William and Mary Quarterly*, 2nd ser., IX (1929), 1-12, 73-87, and his two other articles on tobacco: "The Consumption of Tobacco since 1600," *Economic History*, I (1926-9), 57-75; and "A Short History of Tobacco Smuggling," *ibid.*, (1926-9), 554-69.

ROEPKE, HOWARD G.: *Movements of the British Iron and Steel Industry, 1720-1951, Illinois Studies in the Social Sciences*, XXXVI (Urbana, Ill., 1956).

ROGERS, JAMES E. T.: *A History of Agriculture and Prices in England . . . [1259-1793]* (7 vols., Oxford, Eng., 1866-1902); see volumes VI and VII. See also Rogers's *Industrial and Commercial History of England: Lectures Delivered to the University of Oxford . . .* (1st edn., London, 1892; n. edn., 2 vols., 1902), and *Six Centuries of Work and Wages: The History of English Labour* (2 vols., London, 1884).

ROSE, ROBERT B.: "Eighteenth Century Price Riots and Public Policy in England," *International Review of Social History*, VI (1961), 277-92.

SCHUBERT, JOHN R. T.: *History of the British Iron and Steel Industry . . . to A.D. 1775* (London, 1957).

SCHUMPETER, ELIZABETH B.: *English Overseas Trade Statistics, 1697-1808* (Oxford, Eng. & New York, 1960).

SCRIVENOR, HARRY: *History of the Iron Trade from the Earliest Records to the Present Period* (n. edn., London, 1854).

SLATER, GILBERT: *The English Peasantry and the Enclosure of Common Fields* (London, 1907).

WADSWORTH, ALFRED POWELL, and JULIA DE LACY MANN: *The Cotton Trade and Industrial Lancashire, 1600-1780*, University of Manchester, Publications: Economic History Series, No. 7 (Manchester, Eng., 1931).

WILLIAM, E. N.: "'Our Merchants Are Princes': The English Middle Classes in the Eighteenth Century," *History Today*, XII (1962), 548-57.

WILLIAMS, GOMER: *History of the Liverpool Privateers and Letters of Marque: With an Account of the Liverpool Slave Trade* (London, 1897).

5. Social

ABBEY, CHARLES JOHN: *The English Church and Its Bishops, 1700-1800* (2 vols., London, 1887).

——, and JOHN HENRY OVERTON: *The English Church in the Eighteenth Century* (2 vols., London, 1878; n. edn., 1887).

ACKERMANN, RUDOLPH, and WILLIAM COMBE: *The History of the Colleges of Winchester, Eton, and Westminster: With the Charterhouse, and Schools of St. Paul's, Merchant Taylors', Harrow and Rugby and the Free-School of Christ's Hospital* (London, 1816).

ADAMS, HENRY C.: *Wykehamica: A History of Winchester College and Commoners from the Foundation to the Present Day* (London, 1878).

ADAMSON, JOHN WILLIAM: *A Short History of Education* (Cambridge, Eng., 1919).

ALLEN, WILLIAM OSBORN BIRD, and EDMUND MAC CLURE: *Two Hundred*

Years: The History of the Society for Promoting Christian Knowl-edge, 1698-1898 (London, 1898).

ANDREWS, ALEXANDER: *The History of British Journalism from the Founda-tion of the Newspaper Press in England to . . . [1855]* (2 vols., London, 1859).

ASHTON, JOHN: *The Fleet: Its River, Prison, and Marriages* (London, 1888).

BARLOW, RICHARD B.: *Citizenship and Conscience: A Study in the Theory and Practice of Religious Toleration in England during the Eight-eenth Century* (Philadelphia, 1963).

BAYNE-POWELL, ROSAMOND: *The English Child in the Eighteenth Century* (London & New York, 1939).

BOTSFORD, JAY BARRETT: *English Society in the Eighteenth Century As Influenced from Overseas* (New York, 1924).

BOURNE, HENRY RICHARD FOX: *English Newspapers: Chapters in the His-tory of Journalism* (2 vols., London, 1887).

BRODRICK, GEORGE CHARLES: *A History of the University of Oxford* (Lon-don, 1886).

CAMPBELL, MILDRED: "English Emigration on the Eve of the American Revolution," *American Historical Review*, LXI (1955-6), 1-20.

CARPENTER, S. C.: *Eighteenth-Century Church and People* (London, 1959).

CHALMERS, ALEXANDER: *A History of the Colleges, Halls, and Public Buildings Attached to the University of Oxford . . .* (Oxford, 1810).

CHAMBERS, JONATHAN DAVID: *Nottinghamshire in the Eighteenth Century: A Study of Life and Labour under the Squirearchy* (London, 1932).

CLARKSON, THOMAS: *History of the Rise, Progress, and Accomplishment of the Abolition of the African Slave-Trade by the British Parlia-ment* (2 vols., London & Philadelphia, 1808).

———: *A Portraiture of Quakerism: As Taken from a View of . . . the Society of Friends* (3 vols., London, 1806).

COATS, A. W.: "Changing Attitudes to Labour in the Mid-Eighteenth Century," *Economic History Review*, 2nd ser., XI (1958-9), 35-51.

COLE, GEORGE DOUGLAS HOWARD, and RAYMOND POSTGATE: *The Common People, 1746-1946* (2nd edn., London, 1956).

COLE, W. A.: "Trends in Eighteenth-Century Smuggling," *Economic His-tory Review*, 2nd ser., X (1957-8), 395-410. Deals primarily with tea.

[COMBE, WILLIAM]: *A History of the University of Cambridge . . .* (2 vols., London, 1815).

———: *A History of the University of Oxford . . .* (2 vols., London, 1814).

COOPER, WILLIAM DURRANT: "Smuggling in Sussex," *Sussex Archeological Collections*, X (1858), 69-94.

CRAGG, GERALD R.: *Reason and Authority in the Eighteenth Century* (Cam-bridge, Eng. & New York, 1964). A study of English thought.

CRANFIELD, G. A.: *The Development of the Provincial Newspaper, 1700-1760* (London, 1962).

CRANZ, DAVID: *The Ancient and Modern History of the Brethren . . .* (Benjamin LaTrobe, trans., London, 1780).

DALE, ROBERT WILLIAM: *History of English Congregationalism* (completed & ed. by Alfred W. W. Dale; 2nd edn., London, 1907).

DAVIES, GERALD S.: *Charterhouse in London: Monastery, Mansion, Hospital, School* (London, 1921).

DITCHFIELD, PETER HAMPSON: *The History of the City Companies of London and Their Good Works* (London, 1904).

DRYSDALE, ALEXANDER HUTTON: *History of the Presbyterians in England: Their Rise, Decline, and Revival* (London, 1889).

ELLIOTT-BINNS, LEONARD ELLIOT: *The Early Evangelicals: A Religious and Social Study* (London, 1953).

GEORGE, MARY DOROTHY: *England in Transition: Life and Work in the Eighteenth Century* (London, 1931; n. edn., 1953); *English Social Life in the Eighteenth Century . . .* (London, 1923); *London Life in the Eighteenth Century* (London & New York, 1925); and *England in Johnson's Day* [1709-1784] (London [1928]).

———: *English Political Caricature: A Study of Opinion and Propaganda* (2 vols., Oxford, Eng., 1959).

GLASS, D. V.: "The Population Controversy in the Eighteenth Century, Part I: The Background," *Population Studies*, VI (1952-3), 69-91.

GODLEY, ALFRED DENIS: *Oxford in the Eighteenth Century* (London, 1908).

GONNER, EDWARD C. K.: "The Population of England in the Eighteenth Century," Royal Statistical Society, *Journal*, LXXVI (1912-13), 261-303.

GORDON, STRATHEARN, and T. G. B. COCKS: *A People's Conscience* (London, 1952).

GRAY, BENJAMIN KIRKMAN: *A History of English Philanthropy from the Dissolution of the Monasteries to the Taking of the Census* (London, 1905).

GREENWOOD, ALICE DRAYTON: *Horace Walpole's World: A Sketch of Whig Society under George III* (London, 1913).

GRIFFITHS, OLIVE MERIVEL: *Religion and Learning: A Study in English Presbyterian Thought . . .* (Cambridge, Eng., 1935).

HABAKKUK, H. J.: "English Population in the Eighteenth Century," *Economic History Review*, 2nd ser., VI (1953-4), 117-33.

HAIG, ROBERT L.: *The Gazetteer, 1735-1797: A Study in the Eighteenth Century English Newspaper* (Carbondale, Ill., c. 1960).

HART, A. TINDAL: *The Eighteenth-Century Country Parson* (Shrewsbury, Eng., 1955).

HECHT, J. JEAN: *The Domestic Servant Class in Eighteenth Century England* (London, 1956).

HERD, HAROLD: *The March of Journalism: The Story of the British Press from 1622 to the Present Day* (London, 1952).

HUGHES, EDWARD WILLIAM: *North Country Life in the Eighteenth Century* (2 vols., New York, 1952-65). See also his article of the same title in *History*, n. ser., XXV (1940), 113-31.

HUNT, JOHN: *Religious Thought in England from the Reformation to the End of the Last Century* . . . (3 vols., London, 1870-3).

IVIMEY, JOSEPH: *A History of the English Baptists: Including an Investigation of the History of Baptism in England* . . . (4 vols., London, 1811-30).

JONES, MARY GWLADYS: *The Charity School Movement: A Study of Eighteenth Century Puritanism in Action* (Cambridge, Eng., 1938).

JONES, ROBERT TUDUR: *Congregationalism in England, 1662-1962* (London, 1962).

KEPPERSON, WILBUR S.: *British Emigration to North America* (Oxford, Eng., 1957).

KLINGBERG, FRANK J.: *The Anti-Slavery Movement in England: A Study in English Humanitarianism, Yale Historical Publications: Miscellany*, XVII (New Haven, Conn., 1926), and "The Evolution of the Humanitarian Spirit in Eighteenth-Century England," *Pennsylvania Magazine of History and Biography*, LXVI (1942), 260-78.

KLINGENDER, F. D., ed.: *Hogarth and English Caricature* (London & New York, 1944). This book is comprised of reprints of Hogarth's prints and cartoons. Other graphic material of the same nature may be found in Douglass Adair: "The Stamp Act in Contemporary English Cartoons," *William and Mary Quarterly*, 3rd ser., X (1953), 538-42; in M. D. George: "America in English Satirical Prints," *ibid.*, 511-37; and in Richard T. H. Halsey: *The Boston Port Bill as Pictured by a Contemporary London Cartoonist* (New York, 1904). These all have social as well as political implications.

KRONENBERGER, LOUIS: *Kings and Desperate Men: Life in Eighteenth Century England* (New York, 1942).

LAPRADE, WILLIAM T.: "The Power of the English Press in the Eighteenth Century," *South Atlantic Quarterly*, XXVII (1928), 426-34.

LEE, UMPHREY: *The Historical Backgrounds of Early Methodist Enthusiasm* (New York, 1931).

LEWIS, WILMARTH S., RALPH M. WILLIAMS, and JOHN M. WEBB: *Private Charity in England, 1747-1757* (New Haven, Conn., 1938).

LYLES, ALBERT M.: *Methodism Mocked* (London, 1960).

LYTE, HENRY CHURCHILL MAXWELL: *A History of Eton College, 1440-1910* (4th edn., London, 1911).

MAC DONAGH, MICHAEL: *The Reporters' Gallery* (London & New York, 1913).

MC DONNELL, MICHAEL F. J.: *A History of St. Paul's School* . . . (London, 1909).

MAC INNES, CHARLES M.: *England and Slavery* (Bristol, Eng., 1934).

MC LACHLAN, HERBERT: *The Unitarian Movement in the Religious Life of England* . . . (London, 1934).

MALLET, CHARLES EDWARD: *A History of the University of Oxford* (3 vols., London, 1924-7).

MARGOLIOUTH, MOSES: *The History of the Jews in Great Britain* (3 vols., London, 1851).

MARSHALL, DOROTHY: *English People in the Eighteenth Century* (London & New York, 1956), and the more specialized *The English Poor in the Eighteenth Century: A Study in Social and Administrative History* (London, 1926).

MATHIAS, PETER: "The Social Structure in the Eighteenth Century: A Calculation by Joseph Massie," *Economic History Review,* 2nd ser., X (1957-8), 30-45.

MELLOR, GEORGE R.: "Emigration from the British Isles to the New World, 1765-1775," *History,* XL (1955), 68-83.

MINGAY, G. E.: *English Landed Society in the Eighteenth Century* (London & Toronto, 1963).

MORISON, STANLEY: *The English Newspaper: Some Account of the Physical Development of Journals in London* . . . *[1662-1932]* (Cambridge, Eng., 1932). This work is considered the authoritative one with regard to early English periodicals.

OWEN, DAVID E.: *English Philanthropy, 1660-1960* (Cambridge, Mass., 1964).

PARKER, IRENE: *Dissenting Academies in England: Their Rise and Progress and Their Place among the Education Systems of the Country* (Cambridge, Eng., 1914).

PEARCE, ERNEST H.: *Annals of Christ's Hospital* (London, 1901).

PICCIOTTO, JAMES: *Sketches of Anglo-Jewish History* (London, 1875).

PINE, LESLIE GILBERT: *The Story of the Peerage* (Edinburgh, 1956).

RAZZELL, P. E.: "Population Change in Eighteenth Century England: A Reinterpretation," *Economic History Review,* 2nd ser., XVIII (1965), 312-32.

RICHARDSON, ALBERT EDWARD: *Georgian England: A Survey of Social Life, Trades, Industries, and Art from 1700 to 1820* (London & New York, 1931).

ROBSON, ROBERT: *The Attorney in Eighteenth-Century England* (Cambridge, Eng., 1959).

ROGERS, BETSY: *Cloak of Charity: Studies in Eighteenth Century Philanthropy* (London, 1949).

RUDÉ, GEORGE: "The London 'Mob' of the Eighteenth Century," *Historical Journal,* II (1959), 1-18.

SARGEAUNT, JOHN: *Annals of Westminister School* (London, 1898).

SIEBERT, FREDERICK SEATON: *Freedom of the Press in England, 1476-1776: The Rise and Decline of Government Control* (Urbana, Ill., 1952).

SMITH, GEORGE: *History of Wesleyan Methodism* (3 vols., London, 1857-1861).

STEPHEN, LESLIE: *History of English Thought in the Eighteenth Century* (2 vols., London, 1876; 3rd edn., 1902; rep., New York, 1949).

———: *English Literature and Society in the Eighteenth Century* (London, 1904; rep., New York, 1967).

STEVENS, ABEL: *The History of the Religious Movement of the Eighteenth Century Called Methodism . . .* (3 vols., London & New York, 1858-61).

STOUGHTON, JOHN: *History of Religion in England: From the Opening of the Long Parliament to 1850* (6 vols., London, 1881; reiss., 8 vols., London, 1901).

STROMBERG, ROLAND N.: *Religious Liberalism in Eighteenth Century England* (Oxford, Eng., 1954).

SUMMERSON, JOHN NEWENHAM: *Georgian London* (London, 1945).

SYDNEY, WILLIAM CONNOR: *England and the English in the Eighteenth Century: Chapters in the Social History of the Times* (2 vols., London, 1891).

SYKES, NORMAN: *From Sheldon to Secker: Aspects of English Church History, 1660-1768* (Cambridge, Eng., 1959).

THOMPSON, EDWARD PALMER: *The Making of the English Working Class* (London, c. 1963).

TOWNSEND, W. J., H. B. WORKMAN, and G. FAYES, eds.: *A New History of Methodism* (2 vols., London, 1909).

TRAILL, HENRY DUFF, ed.: *Social England . . .* (6 vols., London, 1893-7). Volume V pertains to the eighteenth century.

TURBERVILLE, ARTHUR STANLEY, ed.: *Johnson's England: An Account of the Life and Manners of His Age* (2 vols., Oxford, Eng., 1933).

VINTER, DOROTHY: "The Acadian Exiles in England, 1756-1763," *Dalhousie Review*, XXXVI (1956-7), 344-53.

WADDINGTON, JOHN: *Congregational History, 1700-1800: In Relation to Contemporaneous Events* (London, 1876).

WALLACE, ROBERT: *Antitrinitarian Biography . . . to which is Prefixed a History of Unitarianism in England [to 1800]* (3 vols., London, 1850).

WARD, WILLIAM REGINALD: *Georgian Oxford: University Politics in the Eighteenth Century* (Oxford, Eng., 1958).

WEARMOUTH, ROBERT FEATHERSTONE: *Methodism and the Common People of the Eighteenth Century* (London, 1945).

WHITELEY, JOHN HAROLD: *Wesley's England: A Survey of XVIIIth Century Social and Cultural Conditions* (London, 1938).

WHITLEY, WILLIAM THOMAS: *A History of British Baptists* (London, 1923; 2nd edn., 1932).

WILLEY, BASIL: *The Eighteenth Century Background: Studies on the Idea of Nature in the Thought of the Period* (London, 1940).

WILLIAMS, ERIC: "The Golden Age of the Slave System in Britain," *Journal of Negro History*, XXV (1940), 60-106.

WILLIAMS, J. FISCHER: *Harrow . . .* (London, 1901).

WINSTANLEY, DENYS ARTHUR: *The University of Cambridge in the Eighteenth Century* (Cambridge, Eng., 1922), and *Unreformed Cambridge: A Study of Certain Aspects of the University in the Eighteenth Century* (Cambridge, Eng., 1935).

WORDSWORTH, CHRISTOPHER, comp.: *Social Life at the English Universities in the Eighteenth Century* (Cambridge, Eng., 1874).

6. Biographical

COLLECTED BIOGRAPHIES

BROUGHAM, HENRY PETER, BARON BROUGHAM and VAUX: *Historical Sketches of Statesmen Who Flourished in the Time of George III . . .* (1st-3rd ser., 3 vols., London, 1839-43; n. edn., 1st-3rd ser., Philadelphia, 1840-44). Included in this work are biographical sketches of George III, Pitt, Lords North, Loughborough, Thurlow and Mansfield, Burke and Fox.

BURKE, JOHN: *A Genealogical and Heraldic History of the Commoners of Great Britain and Ireland . . .* (4 vols., London, 1835-8).

CAMPBELL, JOHN: *Lives of the British Admirals and Other Eminent British Seamen . . .* (4 vols., London, 1742-4; later edn., 8 vols., 1812-17).

CAMPBELL, JOHN CAMPBELL, 1ST BARON: *The Lives of the Chief Justices of England: From the Norman Conquest till the Death of Lord Mansfield* (3 vols., London, 1849-57; 3rd edn., 4 vols., London, 1874).

———: *The Lives of the Lords Chancellors and Keepers of the Great Seal of England . . .* (8 vols., London, 1845-9; 5th edn., 10 vols., London, 1868).

Chambers's Biographical Dictionary . . . (London & New York, 1897; rev. edn., William Geddie and J. Liddell Geddie, eds., New York, 1956; n. edn., J. O. Thorne, ed., 1962).

The Concise Dictionary of National Biography (London, 1939). The Institute of Historical Research *Bulletin* periodically prints additions and corrections to this useful work which is an epitome to the D.N.B.

Dictionary of National Biography (Leslie Stephen, Sidney Lee, et al., eds., 66 vols., London, 1885-1901, with supplements).

EWALD, ALEXANDER CHARLES: *Studies Re-Studied: Historical Sketches from Original Sources* (London, 1885).

GILLOW, JOSEPH: *A Literary and Biographical History or Bibliographical*

Dictionary of the English Catholics from . . . *[1534]* (5 vols., London & New York, 1885-1902).

KIRK, JOHN: *Biographies of English Catholics in the Eighteenth Century* . . . (John H. Pollen & Edwin Burton, eds., London, 1909).

LUCAS, FRANK L.: *The Search for Good Sense: Four Eighteenth-Century Characters; Johnson, Chesterfield, Boswell, Goldsmith* (London, 1958); and *The Art of Living: Four Eighteenth Century Minds: Hume, Horace Walpole, Burke, Benjamin Franklin* (London & New York, 1959).

MC CARTHY, JUSTIN: *History of the Four Georges* (4 vols., London, 1884-1901).

NAMIER, LEWIS, and JOHN BROOKE: *The House of Commons, 1754-1790* (3 vols., London & New York, 1964). Volume I contains sketches of members.

PLUMB, J. H.: *The First Four Georges* (London, 1956; New York, 1957).

INDIVIDUAL BIOGRAPHICAL WORKS

BARRINGTON, WILLIAM WILDMAN, VISCOUNT. *The Political Life of William Wildman, Viscount Barrington: Compiled from Original Papers* . . . by Shute Barrington (London, 1815).

BERKELEY, GEORGE. *George Berkeley: A Study of His Life and Philosophy* by John Wild (Cambridge, Mass., 1936).

BLACKSTONE, WILLIAM. "Blackstone and the Reform of the Legal Profession" by Paul Lucas, *English Historical Review*, LXXVII (1962), 456-89. See also Walter H. Zeydel's "Sir William Blackstone and His Commentaries," Library of Congress, *Quarterly Journal*, XXIII (1966), 302-12.

BOTETOURT, NORBORNE BERKELEY, LORD. "Norborne Berkeley: Gloucestershire Magnate" by Bryan Little, *Virginia Magazine of History and Biography*, LXIII (1955), 379-409.

BOSWELL, JAMES. Among the numerous studies relating to Boswell the following may be mentioned: *Boswell's Political Career* by Frank Brady, Yale University, *Studies in English*, No. 155 (New Haven, Conn., 1965); *The Hooded Hawk: Or the Case of Mr. Boswell* by Dominic Bevan Wyndham Lewis (New York, 1947); *James Boswell: The Earlier Years, 1740-1769* by Frederick Albert Pottle (New York [1966]); *Young Boswell: Chapters on James Boswell* . . . by Chauncy Brewster Tinker (Boston, 1922). For a bibliographical study see Pottle's *The Literary Career of James Boswell* (Oxford, Eng., 1929).

BOULTON, MATTHEW. "Matthew Boulton and the Birmingham Petition of 1775" by B. D. Bargar, *William and Mary Quarterly*, 3rd ser., XIII (1956), 26-39.

BRAUND, WILLIAM. *A London Merchant, 1695-1774* by Lucy S. Sutherland (London, 1933).

BURGH, JAMES. "James Burgh and American Revolutionary Theory" by Oscar and Mary Handlin, Massachusetts Historical Society, *Proceedings*, LXXIII (1961), 38-57.

BURKE, EDMUND. Of the mass of materials relating to Burke, a few of the items pertinent to the period under consideration have been selected. General biographies available include the contemporary work by Robert Bisset: *The Life of Edmund Burke: Comprehending an Impartial Account of His Literary and Poetical Efforts . . .* (London, 1798; 2nd edn., 2 vols., 1800). See also Viscount John Morley's *Burke, English Men of Letters,* V (New York, 1879; London, 1904). Recent worthwhile volumes are Robert Henry Murray's *Edmund Burke: A Biography* (Oxford, Eng., 1931); Philip Montefiore Magnus's *Edmund Burke: A Life* (London, 1939); and Thomas W. Copeland's *Our Eminent Friend Edmund Burke: Six Essays* (New Haven, Conn., 1949). In recent years, a great amount of energy has gone into the study of Burke's thought. These works include Charles W. Parkin's *The Moral Basis of Burke's Political Thought* (Cambridge, Eng., 1956); Peter J. Stanlis's *Edmund Burke and the Natural Law* (Ann Arbor, Mich., 1958); Francis P. Canavan's *The Political Reason of Edmund Burke* (Durham, N.C., 1960); and Carl B. Cone's *Burke and the Nature of Politics, Vol. I: The Age of the American Revolution* (Lexington, Ky., c. 1957). C. P. Courtney's *Montesquieu and Burke* (Oxford, Eng., 1963) is a study of the influence of Montesquieu's work on Burke's thought and Harvey C. Mansfield, Jr.'s *Statesmanship and Party Government: A Study of Burke and Bolingbroke* (Chicago, 1965) considers the relationship of the ideas of Burke and Bolingbroke. There are also other articles treating Burke's thought, most of which deal with his views on politics. See, for example, Francis P. Canavan's "Edmund Burke's Conception of the Role of Reason in Politics," *Journal of Politics,* XXI (1959), 60-79; Goldwin Smith's "Burke on Party," *American Historical Review,* XI (1905-6), 36-41; and Peter J. Stanlis's "The Basis of Burke's Political Conservatism," *Modern Age,* V (1960-1), 263-74. Two aspects of Burke's thought are also treated in J. G. A. Pocock's "Burke and the Ancient Constitution: A Problem in the History of Ideas," *Historical Journal,* III (1960), 125-43, and in John C. Weston, Jr.'s "Edmund Burke's View of History," *Review of Politics,* XXIII (1961), 203-29. Other articles include W. T. Laprade's "Edmund Burke: An Adventure in Reputation," *Journal of Modern History,* XXXII (1960), 321-32; John Brooke's "Burke in the 1760's," *South Atlantic Quarterly,* LXIII (1959), 548-55; Thomas H. D. Mahoney's "Edmund Burke and the American Revolution: The Repeal of the Stamp Act," *Burke Newsletter*, VIII (1965-6), 503-21; and Lucy Sutherland's "Edmund Burke and the First Rockingham Ministry," *English Historical Review*, XLVIII (1932), 46-72. Two articles by P. T. Underdown dealing with Burke's political activities relating to Bristol are: "Henry Cruger and Edmund Burke: Colleagues and Rivals at the Bristol Election of 1774," *William and Mary Quarterly*, 3rd ser., XV (1958), 14-34, and "Edmund Burke, the Commissary of Bristol Constituents, 1774-1780," *English Historical Review*, LXXIII (1958), 252-69. For a historiographical essay on the writings on Burke and how he has been viewed by authors in various periods, see Thomas W. Copeland's "The Reputation of Edmund Burke," *Journal of British Studies*, I (1961-2), 78-90; and for a general bibliographical discussion of the work that has been done on Burke, see Donald C. Bryant's "Edmund Burke: A Generation of Scholarship and Discovery," *ibid.*, II (1962-3), 91-114.

BUTE, JOHN STUART, 3RD EARL OF. "Frederick the Great and Lord Bute" by Walter L. Dorn, *Journal of Modern History*, I (1929), 529-60.

BUTLER, JOSEPH. *Bishop Butler and the Age of Reason: A Study in the History of Thought* by Ernest Campbell Mossner (New York, 1936), and *Bishop Butler, Moralist and Divine* by William Joseph Norton (New Brunswick, N.J., 1938; rep., Rutgers University, *Studies in Philosophy*, No. 1, 1940).

CARTERET, JOHN, EARL GRANVILLE. *Lord Carteret: A Political Biography, 1690-1763* by Archibald Ballantyne (London, 1887); *Carteret, The Brilliant Failure of the Eighteenth Century* by Noel William Baring Pemberton (London, 1936); and *Carteret and Newcastle: A Contrast in Contemporaries* by Basil Williams (Cambridge, Eng., 1943).

CHALMERS, GEORGE. *The Public Life of George Chalmers* by Grace Amelia Cockcroft (London & New York, 1939).

CHESTERFIELD, PHILIP DORMER STANHOPE, 4TH EARL OF. *Life of Lord Chesterfield: An Account of the Ancestry, Personal Character, and Public Services* . . . by William Henry Craig (London & New York, 1907), and *Lord Chesterfield and His World* by Samuel Shellabarger (Boston, 1951).

CRUGER, HENRY, *see* Burke, Edmund

CUMBERLAND, AUGUSTUS WILLIAM, DUKE OF. *The Conqueror of Culloden: Being the Life and Times of William Augustus, Duke of Cumberland, 1721-1765* by B. W. Kelly (London, 1903), and *William Augustus, Duke of Cumberland and the Seven Years' War* . . . by Evan Edward Charteris (London [1925]).

DARTMOUTH, WILLIAM LEGGE, 2ND EARL OF. *Lord Dartmouth and the American Revolution* by B. D. Bargar (Columbia, S.C., 1965).

DRUMMOND, THOMAS, LORD. "Lord Drummond and Reconciliation [1775]" by Herbert A. Meistrich, New Jersey Historical Society, *Proceedings*, n. ser., LXXXI (1963), 256-77.

FOTHERGILL, JOHN. *Dr. John Fothergill and His Friends: Chapters in Eighteenth Century Life* by Richard Hingston Fox (London, 1919), and "Dr. John Fothergill, Peacemaker" by Betsy C. Corner and Dorothea W. Singer, American Philosophical Society, *Proceedings*, XCVIII (1954), 11-22.

FOX, CHARLES JAMES. *The Early History of Charles James Fox* by George Otto Trevelyan (New York, 1880; London, 1881, 1908) and *Fox* by Christopher Hobhouse (London, 1934; n. edn., 1947). See also the sketch "Charles James Fox" by Ian R. Christie, *History Today*, VIII (1958), 110-18.

FOX, HENRY, 1ST LORD HOLLAND. *Henry Fox, First Lord Holland: A Study of the Career of an Eighteenth Century Politician* by Thad Weede Riker (2 vols., Oxford, Eng., 1911), and *Henry Fox, First Lord Holland: His Family and Relations* by the Earl of Ilchester (2 vols., London, 1920). See also the article by Lucy Sutherland and J. Binney: "Henry Fox as Paymaster General of the Forces," *English Historical Review*, LXX (1955), 229-57.

FREDERICK, PRINCE OF WALES. *A Forgotten Prince of Wales* by Henry Cartier (London [1912]), and *Poor Fred: The People's Prince* by George Young (London & New York, 1937).

GARRICK, DAVID. *Garrick* by Margaret Burton (London, 1948; New York, 1949), and *Life of David Garrick: From Original Family Papers and Numerous Published and Unpublished Sources* by Percy Hetherington Fitzgerald (2 vols., London, 1868).

GEORGE II. *George II and His Ministers* by Reginald J. Lucas (London, 1910), and *A King in Toils* by John D. G. Davis (London, 1938).

GEORGE III. For general biographies of George III, see the early work of Edward Holt: *The Public and Domestic Life of His late Gracious Majesty, George the Third . . .* (2 vols., London, 1820); *George III: As Man, Monarch, and Statesman* by Beckles Willson (London, 1907); *Royal George: A Study of King George III, His Experiment in Monarchy, His Decline and Retirement . . .* by Colwyn Edward Vulliamy (London & New York, 1937); and the recent work by John C. Long: *George III; The Story of a Complex Man* (Boston, 1961). For a worthwhile sketch see William Hunt's "George III" in the *Dictionary of National Biography* (1908 edn.); XXI: 172-92. See also: Herbert Butterfield's *George III and the Historians* (London, 1957); and his articles: "George III and the Constitution," *History*, XLVII (1958), 14-33, and "Some Reflections on the Early Years of George III's Reign," *Journal of British Studies*, IV (1965), 78-101. Other articles of value include S. D. Kennedy's brief sketch: "The Accession and Early Years of George

III," *Quarterly Review*, 298 (1960), 435-42, and the following studies of the king and politics: W. R. Fryer's "King George III: His Political Character and Conduct, 1760-1784: A New Whig Interpretation," *Renaissance and Modern Studies*, VI (1962), 68-101; Richard Pares's article: "George III and the Politicians," Royal Historical Society, *Transactions*, 5th ser., I (1951), 127-51 and still more important, his volume of Ford Lectures delivered at Oxford, in 1951 and 1952 published under the same title (Oxford, Eng., 1953); see also D. A. Winstanley's "George III and His First Cabinet," *English Historical Review*, XVII (1902), 678-691. For discussions of the King's illness, see Manfred S. Guttmacher's *America's Last King: An Interpretation of the Madness of George III* (New York, 1941), and Charles Chenevix-Trench's *The Royal Malady* (London & New York, 1965). Finally, see Gerda Richards Crosby: "George III: Historians and a Royal Reputation," *Essays in Modern English History: In Honor of Wilbur Cortez Abbott* (Cambridge, Mass., 1941), pp. 295-313.

GERMAIN, LORD GEORGE. *Lord George Germain* by Alan C. Valentine (Oxford, Eng., 1962), and "The Court Martial of Lord George Sackville, Whipping Boy of the Revolutionary War" by Gerald S. Brown, *William and Mary Quarterly*, 3rd ser., IX (1952), 317-37.

GIBBON, EDWARD. *Edward Gibbon, 1736-1794* by David M. Low (London, 1937).

GRAHAM, ROBERT. *Doughty Deeds: An Account of the Life of Robert Graham of Gartmore, Poet and Politician, 1735-1797* . . . by R. B. Cunninghame Graham (London, 1925).

GRENVILLE, GEORGE. "George Grenville as First Lord of the Treasury and Chancellor of the Exchequer, 1763-65" by Dora Mae Clark, *Huntington Library Quarterly*, XIII (1949-50), 383-97; see also Lewis M. Wiggin's work: *The Faction of Cousins: A Political Account of the Grenvilles, 1733-1763* (New Haven, Conn., 1958).

HANBURY-WILLIAMS, CHARLES. *Sir Charles Hanbury-Williams and European Diplomacy, 1747-1758* by David Bayne Horn (London, 1930).

HANWAY, JONAS. *Jonas Hanway, 1712-1786* by John Harold Hutchins (London, 1940).

HARTLEY, DAVID. *David Hartley M.P.: An Advocate of Conciliation, 1774-1783* by G. H. Guttridge, University of California, *Publications in History*, XIV (Berkeley, Calif., 1926).

HAWKE, EDWARD. *The Life of Edward, Lord Hawke* . . . by Montagu Burrows (London, 1883; rev. edn., 1896), and *Admiral Hawke* by Ruddock F. Mackay (New York & Oxford, Eng., 1965).

HOLLIS, THOMAS. "The Strenuous Whig: Thomas Hollis of Lincoln's Inn" by Caroline Robbins, *William and Mary Quarterly*, 3rd ser., VII (1950), 406-53.

HORNE, JOHN (later John Horne Tooke). *John Horne Tooke* by Minnie Clare Yarborough (New York, 1926).

HOWE, RICHARD HOWE, EARL. *Life of Richard, Earl Howe, K.G., Admiral of the Fleet and General of Marines* by Sir John Barrow (London, 1838).

HOWE, WILLIAM. *Sir Billy Howe* by Bellamy Partridge (London & New York, 1932), and "Lord Howe and Lord George Germain: British Politics and the Winning of American Independence" by Ira D. Gruber, *William and Mary Quarterly*, 3rd ser., XXII (1965), 225-243. For an account of the military activities of William and Richard, see: *The Command of the Howe Brothers During the American Revolution* by Troyer Steele Anderson (London & New York, 1936).

JOHNSON, SAMUEL. *The Life of Samuel Johnson LL.D.: Comprehending an Account of His Studies and Numerous Works*... by James Boswell (2 vols., London, 1791), a masterpiece; see also *Samuel Johnson* by Joseph Wood Krutch (New York, 1944); *Young Sam Johnson* by James L. Clifford (New York, 1955); and Lord Macaulay's "Samuel Johnson" in the *Encylopaedia Britannica*, a brilliant essay that first appeared in the 7th edition and was repeated in subsequent editions with minor corrections.

KEPPEL, AUGUSTUS KEPPEL, 1ST VISCOUNT. *Life of Augustus, Viscount Keppel, Admiral of the White and First Lord of the Admiralty in 1782-3* by Thomas Keppel (2 vols., London, 1842).

LIGONIER, JOHN LIGONIER, VISCOUNT. *Field Marshall Lord Ligonier: A Story of the British Army, 1720-1770* by Rex Whitworth (Oxford, Eng., 1958).

LOWTHER, JAMES. *Sir James Lowther and Cumberland and Westmorland Elections, 1754-1775* by Brian Bonsall (Manchester, Eng., 1960).

LYTTELTON, GEORGE LYTTELTON, 1ST BARON. *The Good Lord Lyttelton: A Study in Eighteenth Century Politics and Culture* by Rose Mary Davis (Bethlehem, Pa., 1939).

MACLEANE, LAUCHLIN. *Reward Is Secondary: The Life of a Political Adventurer and an Inquiry into the Mystery of "Junius"* by J. N. Mackensie Maclean (London, 1963).

MANNERS, JOHN, MARQUIS OF GRANBY. *Some Account of the Military, Political, and Social Life of the Right Hon. John Manners, Marquis of Granby* by Walter Evelyn Manners (London, 1899).

MANSFIELD, WILLIAM MURRAY, EARL OF. *The Life of William Murray, Late Earl of Mansfield* by John Holliday (London, 1797).

MELCOMBE, GEORGE BUBB DODINGTON, LORD. *Patron and Place-Hunter: A Study of George Bubb Dodington, Lord Melcombe* by Lloyd Charles Sanders (London & New York, 1919).

NORTH, FREDERICK, LORD. *Lord North, Second Earl of Guilford, K.G., 1732-1792* by Reginald Lucas (2 vols., London, 1913), and "Lord North's

Posture of Defense" by Charles Daniel Smith, *Quarterly Journal of Speech*, XLV (1959), 29-38.

OGLETHORPE, JAMES EDWARD. *Oglethorpe: A Study of Philanthropy in England and Georgia* by Leslie Frederick Church (London, 1932), and *James Edward Oglethorpe: Imperial Idealist* by Amos Aschbach Ettinger (Oxford, Eng., 1936).

PELHAM, HENRY, and THOMAS PELHAM-HOLLIS. *The Rise of the Pelhams* by John Beresford Owen (London, 1957). See also "Henry Pelham and the Duke of Newcastle" by Donald Grove Barnes, *Journal of British Studies*, I (1961-2), 62-77.

PITT, WILLIAM, EARL OF CHATHAM. There are a number of general biographies of Pitt that are valuable, including Frederic Harrison's *Chatham* (London & New York, 1905); the two studies by Albert von Ruville: *William Pitt (Chatham) und Graf Bute . . .* (Berlin, 1895), and *William Pitt, Graf von Chatham* (3 vols., Stuttgart, 1905; H. J. Chaytor and M. Morrison, trans., 3 vols., London & New York, 1907); *Lord Chatham: His Early Life and Connections* by Archibald Philip Primrose, 5th Lord of Rosebery (London & New York, 1910); and especially Basil Williams's *The Life of William Pitt, Earl of Chatham* (2 vols., London, 1913). More recent studies include Brian Tunstall's *William Pitt, Earl of Chatham* (London, 1938); John Cuthbert Long's *Mr. Pitt and America's Birthright: A Biography of William Pitt, the Earl of Chatham, 1708-1778* (New York, 1940); Erich Eyck's *Pitt versus Fox: Father and Son, 1735-1806* (Eric Northcott, trans., London, 1950); and J. H. Plumb's *Chatham* (London, 1953). Also worth consulting for original material is Francis Thackeray's *A History of the Right Honorable William Pitt . . .* (2 vols., London, 1827), and the work compiled by John Almon: *Anecdotes of the Life of the Right Honourable William Pitt, Earl of Chatham . . .* (3rd edn., 3 vols., London, 1793). More specialized studies on Pitt include Denys Arthur Winstanley's *Lord Chatham and the Whig Opposition* (Cambridge, Eng., 1912), and Sir Charles Grant Robertson's *Chatham and the British Empire* (London, 1946; New York, 1962). For work on Pitt's relationship to America see O. A. Sherrard's *Lord Chatham and America* (London, 1958), and Henry King Siebeneck's "William Pitt, Earl of Chatham, and the Taxation of America," *Western Pennsylvania Historical Magazine*, XXVI (1943), 1-20. For Pitt's role in the Great War for the Empire, see O. A. Sherrard's *Lord Chatham: A War Minister in the Making* (London, 1952), and the articles by Henry King Siebeneck: "William Pitt and John Forbes," *Western Pennsylvania Historical Magazine*, XXIV (1941), 69-92, and by Eric McDermott: "The Elder Pitt and His Admirals and Generals," *Military Affairs*, XX (1956), 65-71.

POWNALL, JOHN. "John Pownall and British Colonial Policy" by Franklin B. Wickwire, *William and Mary Quarterly*, 3rd ser., XX (1963), 543-54.

PRICE, RICHARD. *Torchbearer of Freedom: The Influence of Richard Price on Eighteenth-Century Thought* by Carl B. Cone (Lexington, Ky., 1952).

RICHMOND, CHARLES LENNOX, 3RD DUKE OF. *The Radical Duke: Career and Correspondence of Charles Lennox, Third Duke of Richmond* by Alison G. Olson (Oxford, Eng., 1961).

ROBERTS, JOHN. "John Roberts, M.P., and the First Rockingham Administration" by J. E. Tyler, *English Historical Review*, LXVII (1952), 547-60.

ROCKINGHAM, CHARLES WATSON-WENTWORTH, MARQUESS OF. *The Early Career of Lord Rockingham, 1730-1765* by George Herbert Guttridge, University of California, *Publications in History*, XLIV (Berkeley, Calif., & Los Angeles, 1952), and *Memoirs of the Marquis of Rockingham and his Contemporaries . . .* by George Thomas Keppel, Earl of Albemarle (2 vols., London, 1852).

RUMFORD, BENJAMIN THOMPSON, COUNT. *Count Rumford of Massachusetts* by James Alden Thompson (New York, 1935).

SANDWICH, JOHN MONTAGU, 4TH EARL OF. *Jemmy Twitcher: A Life of the Fourth Earl of Sandwich, 1718-1792* by George Martelli (London, 1962); see also the article by J. H. Broomfield: "Lord Sandwich at the Admiralty Board: Politics and the British Navy, 1771-1778," *Mariner's Mirror*, LI (1965), 7-17.

SHARP, GRANVILLE. *Granville Sharp and the Freedom of Slaves in England* by E. C. Ponsonby Lascelles (London, 1928).

SHELBURNE, WILLIAM PETTY, 2ND EARL OF. *Shelburne and Reform* by John M. Norris (London & New York, 1963). In addition, there are several worthwhile articles which the student should consult: W. O. Simpson's "Lord Shelburne and North America," *History Today*, X (1960), 52-63; two articles by R. A. Humphreys: "Lord Shelburne and British Colonial Policy, 1766-1768," *ibid.*, L. (1935), 257-77; and "Lord Shelburne and a Projected Recall of Colonial Governors in 1767," *American Historical Review*, XXXVII (1931-1932), 269-72. Finally, there is Lucy S. Sutherland's "Lord Shelburne and East India Company Politics, 1766-9," *English Historical Review*, XLIX (1934), 450-86.

SMITH, ADAM. *Adam Smith (1723-1790)* by James A. Farrer (London, 1881); *Life of Adam Smith* by Viscount Richard Burdon Haldane (London, 1887); *Life of Adam Smith* by John Rae (London & New York, 1895; rep., New York, 1965). The 1965 edition contains an introduction by Jacob Viner which was published as *Guide to John Rae's Life of Adam Smith* (New York, 1965). See also:

"Adam Smith and the Industrial Revolution" by Richard Koebner, Economic History Review, 2nd ser., XI (1935-9), 381-91.

SMOLLETT, TOBIAS. *Tobias Smollett: Doctor of Men and Manners* by Lewis Mansfield Knapp (Princeton, N. J., 1949).

STRAHAN, WILLIAM. *Dr. Johnson's Printer: The Life of William Strahan* by James A. Cochrane (London & Cambridge, Mass., 1964).

THURLOW, EDWARD. *Chancellor Thurlow: The Life and Times of an XVIIIth Century Lawyer* by Robert Gore-Browne (London, 1953).

TOWNSHEND, CHARLES. *Charles Townshend: Wit and Statesman* by Percy Hetherington Fitzgerald (London, 1866); *Charles Townshend* by Lewis Namier and John Brooke (London & New York, 1964), and Namier's brief volume, *Charles Townshend: His Character and Career* (Cambridge, Eng., 1959).

TOWNSHEND, GEORGE TOWNSHEND, 4TH VISCOUNT and 1ST MARQUIS. *The Military Life of Field-Marshall George, First Marquess Townshend, 1724-1807* ... by Charles V. F. Townshend (London, 1901).

TOWNSHEND, JAMES. "James Townshend, M.P." by W. P. Courtney, *Notes and Queries: A Medium of Inter-Communication for Literary Men*, 11th ser., V (1912), 2-4.

TRECOTHICK, BARLOW. "Barlow Trecothick" by Theodore D. Jervey, *South Carolina Historical and Genealogical Magazine*, XXXII (1931-2), 157-69.

TULL, JETHRO. "Jethro Tull and the 'New Husbandry' of the Eighteenth-Century" by T. H. Marshall, *Economic History Review*, II (1929-1930), 41-60, and "A Note on Jethro Tull: Innovator or Crank" by E. R. Wicker, *Agricultural History*, XXXI (1957), 46-8.

WALPOLE, HORACE. *Horace Walpole: A Memoir...* by Austin Dobson (New York, 1890; 4th edn., rev. by Paget Toynbee, London, 1927). Among several other older works are Paul Yvon's *La Vie d'un Dilettante: Horace Walpole, 1717-1797: Essai de Biographie Psychologique et Litteraire...* (London & Paris, 1924); Dorothy Margaret Stuart's *Horace Walpole* (London & New York, 1927); and Stephen Gwynn's *Life of Horace Walpole* (London, c. 1932). Two more recent studies are *Horace Walpole: A Biography* by Robert Wyndham Ketton-Cremer (London, 1940; 1st Am. edn., Ithaca, N.Y., 1966), and Wilmarth Sheldon Lewis's *Horace Walpole* (London, 1961); see also James William Johnson's article: "Horace Walpole and W. S. Lewis," *Journal of British Studies*, VI (1966-7), 64-75.

WESLEY, CHARLES. *The Life of the Rev. Charles Wesley... Comprising a Review of His Poetry, Sketches of the Rise and Progress of Methodism: With Notices of Contemporary Events and Characters* by Thomas Jackson (2 vols., London, 1841).

WESLEY, JOHN. *Three Eighteenth Century Figures... John Wesley...*

by Bonamy Dobrée (London & New York, 1962); two works by John Smith Simon: *John Wesley: The Master Builder* (London, 1927), and *John Wesley and the Methodist Societies* (London, 1923); *John Wesley* by J. Telford (n. edn., London, 1906), and *John Wesley* by John Donald Wade (New York, 1930). See also Lynwood M. Holland's article: "John Wesley and the American Revolution," *Journal of Church and State,* V (1963), 199-213.

WHITEFIELD, GEORGE. *The Life of the Rev. George Whitefield* by Luke Tyerman (London, 1876-7); *George Whitefield, M.A.: Field Preacher* by James Paterson Gledstone (London, 1900); and *George Whitefield, the Awakener: A Modern Study of the Evangelical Revival . . .* by Albert David Belden (London, 1930).

WILKES, JOHN. Wilkes has been a fairly popular subject for biographers. For older works, see Horace Bleackley's *Life of John Wilkes* (London & New York, 1917); William P. Treloar's *Wilkes and the City . . .* (London, 1917); Raymond Postgate's *"That Devil Wilkes"* (London, 1930); and O. A. Sherrard's *A Life of John Wilkes* (London, 1930). Two recent studies are *Wilkes and Liberty: A Social Study of 1763-1774* by George Rudé (Oxford, Eng., 1960), and the work by Charles Chenevix-Trench, *Portrait of a Patriot: A Biography of John Wilkes* (Edinburgh, 1962). Also worth consulting are the following articles: P. D. G. Thomas's "John Wilkes and the Freedom of the Press (1771)," Institute of Historical Research, *Bulletin,* XXXIII (1960), 86-98; George Rudé's "John Wilkes and the Middlesex Elections," *History Today,* XI (1961), 128-35; and Pauline Maier's "John Wilkes and American Disillusionment with Britain," *William and Mary Quarterly,* 3rd ser., XX (1963), 373-95. See also under Political: I. R. Christie.

7. Military and naval

ALBION, ROBERT GREENHALGH: *Forests and Sea Power: The Timber Problem of the Royal Navy, 1652-1862* (Cambridge, Mass., 1926; rep., Hamden, Conn., 1965).

ALLEN, JOSEPH: *Battles of the British Navy from A.D. 1000 to 1840* (2 vols., London, 1842).

ANDERSON, OLIVE: "The Establishment of British Supremacy at Sea and the Exchange of Naval Prisoners of War, 1689-1783," *English Historical Review,* LXXV (1960), 77-89.

ATKINSON, CHRISTOPHER THOMAS: "British Strategy and Battles in the Westphalian Campaign of 1758-62," *Journal of the Royal United Service Institute,* LXXIX (1934), 733-40.

BAMFORD, PAUL WALDEN: *Forests and French Sea Power, 1660-1789* (London & Toronto, 1956).

CARLTON, WILLIAM R.: "New England Masts and the King's Navy," *New England Quarterly*, XII (1939), 4-18.

CASTEX, RAOUL VICTOR PATRICE: *Les Idées Militaire de la Marine du XVIIIme Siècle. Du Ruyter à Suffren* (Paris, 1911).

CLOWES, WILLIAM LAIRD, *et al.*: *The Royal Navy: A History from the Earliest Times to the Present* (7 vols., London, 1897-1903).

COLOMB, PHILIP HOWARD: *Naval Warfare, Its Ruling Principles and Practice, Historically Treated* (London, 1891; 3rd edn., 1899).

CORBETT, JULIAN STAFFORD: *England in the Seven Years' War: A Study in Combined Strategy* (2 vols., London, 1907).

CURTIS, EDWARD E.: *Organization of the British Army in the American Revolution, Yale Historical Publications: Miscellany*, No. 19 (London & New Haven, Conn., 1926).

CUST, EDWARD: *Annals of the Wars of the Eighteenth Century: Compiled from the Most Authentic Histories of the Period* (5 vols., London, 1857-60).

EKINS, CHARLES: *Naval Battles from 1744 to the Peace in 1814* (London, 1824; 2nd edn., 1828).

FORTESCUE, JOHN W.: *A History of the British Army* (13 vols. & 6 atlases, London & New York, 1899-1920).

FULLER, JOHN F. C.: *British Light Infantry in the Eighteenth Century* (London [1925]).

GRAHAM, GERALD S.: "Fisheries and Sea Power," Canadian Historical Association, *Report, 1941* (Toronto, 1941), 24-31.

GRENIER, JACQUES RAIMOND DE: *The Art of War at Sea: Or Naval Tactics Reduced to New Principles* . . . (J. N. Jouin de Saudeuil, trans., London, 1788).

GROSE, FRANCIS: *Military Antiquities, Respecting a History of the English Army from the Conquest to the Present Time* (2 vols., London, 1786-8).

HAYES, JAMES: "The Royal House of Hanover and the British Army, 1714-1760," John Rylands Library, *Bulletin*, XL (1957-8), 328-57.

LACOUR-GAYET, GEORGES: *Le Marine Militaire de la France sous le Regne de Louis XV* (Paris, 1902; 2nd edn., Paris, 1910).

LEWIS, MICHAEL: *The History of the British Navy* (Hammondsworth, Eng., 1957).

LLOYD, ERNEST MARSH: *A Review of the History of Infantry* (London & New York, 1908), and "The Raising of the Highland Regiments in 1757," *English Historical Review*, XVII (1902), 466-9.

MAHAN, ALFRED THAYER: *The Influence of Sea Power on History, 1660-1783* (Boston, 1890; 17th edn., 1903).

MARCUS, GEOFFREY J.: *A Naval History of England, Vol. I: The Formative Centuries* (London, 1961). This volume ends with the War for American Independence.

124   A BIBLIOGRAPHICAL GUIDE

————: *Quiberon Bay* (London, 1960). A general study of British naval activities against the French.

RAMSAY, DAVID: *Military Memoirs of Great Britain: Or a History of the War, 1755-1763* ... (Edinburgh, 1779).

RICHMOND, HERBERT: *Statesmen and Sea Power* ... (Oxford, Eng., 1946).

RITTMEYER, RUDOLPH: *Seekriege und Seekriegswesen in Ihrer Weltgeschichtlichen Entwicklung* (2 vols., Berlin, 1907-11).

STEEL, DAVID: *A System of Naval Tactics* (London, 1797).

TROUDE, O.: *Batailles Navales de la France* (4 vols., Paris, 1867-8).

WESTERN, JOHN R.: *The English Militia in the Eighteenth Century: The Story of a Political Issue, 1660-1802* (London & Toronto, 1965).

YONGE, CHARLES DUKE: *The History of the British Navy from the Earliest Period to the Present Time* (2 vols., London, 1863).

D. MAPS

For information on the availability of pertinent maps of England, see the *Catalogue of the Printed Maps, Plans, and Charts in the British Museum* (2 vols., London, 1885). In the words of W. W. Ristow, this is "undoubtedly the most comprehensive map catalog ever published." Supplemental lists, each entitled *Catalog of Maps: Accessions*, have been published since 1884. See also Thomas Chubb's *The Printed Maps in the Atlases of Great Britain and Ireland: A Bibliography, 1579-1870* (London [1927]), which contains a wealth of information, and Sir Herbert George Fordham's *Hand-List of Catalogues and Works of Reference Relating to Carto-Bibliography and Kindred Subjects for Great Britain and Ireland, 1720-1927* (Cambridge, Eng., 1928). The most recent guide, an excellent book with extensive bibliographies, is R. V. Tooley's *Maps and Map-Makers* (London, 1949; rev. edns., 1952, 1962); see especially Chapter VII, "English Map-Makers," Chapter VIII, "The County Maps of England and Wales," and Chapter IX, "Scotland and Ireland."

BOWEN, EMANUEL and THOMAS: *Atlas Anglicanus* (London, 1767; another edn., 1777). This atlas contains 45 maps.

BOWEN, EMANUEL, and THOMAS KITCHIN: *The Large English Atlas: Or a New Set of Maps of All the Counties in England and Wales* (London [1755]; other edns., 1760, 1763, 1787). There are 45 maps in the first edition and 47 maps in subsequent editions. This important series of maps contains the most attractive and the best county maps done in the eighteenth century.

————: *The Royal English Atlas: Being a New and Accurate Set of Maps of All the Counties of South Britain* (London, 1762; another edn., 1778). This atlas contains 44 maps; it was reissued in 1794 as *The English Atlas*.

CARY, JOHN: *Cary's New Map of England and Wales: With Part of Scotland* (London, 1794).

ELLIS, J.: *Ellis's English Atlas* (London, 1766; other edns., 1768, 1773, 1777). There were 48 maps in the first edition and 54 maps in the subsequent editions.

GIBSON, JOHN: *New and Accurate Maps of the Counties of England and Wales* (London, 1759; other edns., 1770, 1779). The atlas contains 53 maps.

KITCHIN, THOMAS: *England Illustrated* (London, 1764). There are 54 maps in this book; see also: *Kitchin's English Atlas* (London, 1770), with 54 maps.

LEWIS, SAMUEL: *Topographical Dictionary of England* ... (London, 1831). There are 43 maps in this work. Lewis also published *Topographical Dictionary of Wales* (London, 1773), which has 13 maps.

ROBINSON, A. H. W.: *Marine Cartography in Britain: A History of the Sea Chart to 1855* (Leicester, Eng., 1962).

ROCQUE, JOHN: *England and Wales Drawn from the Most Accurate Surveys Containing All the Cities, Boroughs, Market Towns, and Villages.* . . . In Kitchin: *A General Atlas* . . . , Nos. 6-7.

————: *The Small British Atlas* (London, 1753; other edns., 1762, 1764, 1769). The first edition had 54 maps: later editions had 29 maps and were published under the title *England Displayed.*

SCOTLAND

Although both Scotland and Wales are a part of Great Britain, each has had its identity and many writings relate so specifically to one or the other that it has seemed desirable to list them separately.

A. BIBLIOGRAPHICAL AIDS

HORN, DAVID BAYNE: "Some Scottish Writers of History in the Eighteenth Century," *Scottish Historical Review*, XL (1961), 1-18.

MARWICK, W. H.: "Bibliography of Scottish Economic History," *Economic History Review*, III (1931-2), 117-37. See also his supplementary article in *ibid.*, 2nd ser., IV (1951-2), 376-82.

MEIKLE, HENRY WILLIAM: *A Brief Bibliography of Scottish History for the Use of Teachers*, Historical Association, *Pamphlet*, No. 109 (London, 1937).

TERRY, CHARLES SANFORD: *A Catalogue of the Publications of Scottish Historical and Kindred Clubs and Societies and of the Volumes Relative to Scottish History Issued by His Majesty's Stationary Office, 1780-1908* ... (Glasgow, 1909, cont'd to 1927 by C. Matheson).

B. PRINTED SOURCE MATERIALS

ADAM, CHARLES ELPHINSTONE, ed: *View of the Political State of Scotland in the Last Century: A Confidential Report of the Political Opinions ... of the 2662 County Voters in 1788* (Edinburgh, 1887).

ANDERSON, JAMES: *Observations on the Means of Exciting a Spirit of National Industry ... to Promote the Agriculture, Commerce, Manufactures, and Fisheries of Scotland* (Edinburgh, 1777).

ARNOT, HUGO: *The History of Edinburgh from the Earliest Accounts to the Present Time ...* (1st edn., London, 1779; another edn., Edinburgh, 1788).

BURT, EDWARD: *Letters from a Gentleman in the North of Scotland to His Friend in London: Containing ... An Account of the Highlands with the Customs and Manners of the Highlanders* (1st edn., 2 vols., London, 1754; 5th edn., 1818).

CARLYLE, ALEXANDER: *The Autobiography of the Rev. Dr. Alexander Carlyle, Minister of Inveresk: Containing Memorials of the Men and Events of His Time* (John H. Burton, ed., Edinburgh & London, 1860; n. edn., 1910).

CREGEEN, ERIC R., ed.: *Argyll Estate Instructions: Mull, Morvern, Tiree, 1771-1805*, Scottish History Society, *Publications*, 4th ser., I (Edinburgh, 1964).

DEMPSTER, GEORGE: *Letters of George Dempster to Sir Adam Fergusson, 1756-1813: With Some Account of His Life* (James Fergusson, ed., London, 1934).

ERSKINE, JOHN: *An Institute of the Law of Scotland in the Order of Sir G. MacKenzie's Institutions of That Law* (2 vols., Edinburgh, 1773; James B. Nicolson, ed., 2 vols., Edinburgh, 1871).

GIBSON, JOHN: *The History of Glasgow ... with an Account of the Rise, Progress, and Present State of ... the Commerce and Manufactures now Carried on in the City* (Glasgow, 1777).

HUME, DAVID: *Commentaries on the Law of Scotland, Respecting the Description and Punishment of Crimes* (Benjamin Robert Bell, ed., 2 vols., Edinburgh, 1797). Hume was Baron of the Exchequer.

[JOHNSON, SAMUEL]: *A Journey to the Western Isles of Scotland* (London, 1775).

LANG, ANDREW, ed.: *The Highlands of Scotland in 1750: From Manuscript 104 in the King's Library, British Museum* (Edinburgh, 1898).

LOCH, DAVID: *Essays on the Trade, Commerce, and Manufactures of Scotland ...* (Edinburgh, 1775).

MAITLAND, WILLIAM: *History of Edinburgh from Its Foundation to the Present Time ...* (Edinburgh, 1753).

MARWICK, JAMES DAVID, ed.: *Extracts from the Records of the Convention of the Royal Burghs of Scotland* (5 vols., Edinburgh, 1880-1918). Vols. III and IV cover the years 1738-1779.

————, and ROBERT RENWICK, eds.: *Extracts from the Records of the Burgh of Glasgow* (6 vols., Glasgow, 1908-14).

MILL, JOHN: *The Diary of the Reverend John Mill, Minister... in Shetland, 1740-1803: With Selections from Local Records and Original Documents Relating to the District,* Scottish History Society, *Publications,* V (Gilbert Goudie, ed., Edinburgh, 1889).

[MORREN, NATHANIEL], ed.: *Annals of the General Assembly of the Church of Scotland... [1739-1766]* (2 vols., Edinburgh, 1838-40).

MUNRO, ALEXANDER MAC DONALD, ed.: *Records of Old Aberdeen* (2 vols., Aberdeen, 1899-1909).

MURE, WILLIAM, ed.: *Selections from the Family Papers Preserved at Caldwell,* Maitland Club, *Publications,* No. 71 (2 vols., Glasgow, 1854).

[MURRAY, PATRICK, 5TH BARON ELIBANK]: *Considerations on the Present State of the Peerage of Scotland... By a Peer of Scotland* (London, 1771).

PENNANT, THOMAS: *A Tour in Scotland, 1769, and a Tour in Scotland and Voyage to the Hebrides, 1772* (3 vols., London, 1776). The 1769 tour was first published at Chester, Eng., in 1771 and the 1772 tour was published in two volumes at Chester and London in 1774-5.

POCOCKE, RICHARD: *Tours in Scotland, 1747, 1750, 1760 . . . ,* Scottish History Society, *Publications,* I (Daniel William Kemp, ed., Edinburgh, 1887).

RAMSAY, JOHN: *Scotland and Scotsmen in the Eighteenth Century: From the Mss. of John Ramsay, Esq., of Ochertyre* (Alexander Allardyre, ed., 2 vols., Edinburgh & London, 1888).

RIDPATH, GEORGE: *Diary of George Ridpath, Minister of Stitchel, 1755-1761,* Scottish History Society, *Publications,* 3rd ser., II (James Balfour Paul, ed., Edinburgh, 1922).

SINCLAIR, JOHN, ed.: *Statistical Account of Scotland: Drawn up from the Communications of the Ministers of the Different Parishes* (21 vols., Edinburgh, 1791-9; reiss. under title *New Statistical Account ...,* 15 vols., 1845).

SOMERVILLE, THOMAS: *My Own Life and Times, 1741-1814* ([William Lee], ed., Edinburgh [1861]).

The Statutes at Large Concerning Election of Members of Parliament for Scotland . . . (Edinburgh, 1744).

STEUART, JOHN: *The Letter-Book of Bailie John Steuart of Inverness, 1715-1752,* Scottish Historical Society, *Publications,* 2nd ser., IX (William Mackay, ed., Edinburgh, 1915).

[TOPHAM, EDWARD]: *Letters from Edinburgh Written in the Years 1774 and 1775: Containing Observations on the Diversions, Customs, Manners, and Laws of the Scotch Nation . . .* (Edinburgh & London, 1776).

WARDEN, ALEXANDER JOHNSTON: *Burgh Laws of Dundee with the History, Statutes and Proceedings of the Guild of Merchants and Fraternities of Craftsmen* (Dundee, 1872).

C. SECONDARY WORKS

1. *General*

ARGYLL, GEORGE DOUGLAS CAMPBELL, 8TH DUKE OF: *Scotland as It Was and as It Is* (New York, 1887).

BROWN, PETER HUME: *History of Scotland, Vol. III: From . . . 1689 to 1843* (Cambridge, Eng., 1909).

BROWNE, JAMES: *History of the Highlands and of the Highland Clans; With an Extensive Selection from the Hitherto Inedited Stuart Papers* (4 vols., Glasgow, 1838-45).

CRAIK, HENRY: *A Century of Scottish History from the Days before the '45 to Those within Living Memory* (2 vols., Edinburgh & London, 1901).

FAY, C. R.: *Adam Smith and the Scotland of His Day* (Cambridge, Eng., 1956).

KELTIE, JOHN SCOTT, ed.: *A History of the Scottish Highlands, Highland Clans, and Highland Regiments . . .* (2 vols., Edinburgh & London, 1885).

KERMACK, W. R.: *The Scottish Highlands: A Short History* (Edinburgh & London, 1957).

MACKENZIE, AGNES MURE: *A History of Scotland . . . , Vol. IV: Scotland in Modern Times, 1720-1939* (Edinburgh & London, 1941).

MATHIESON, WILLIAM LAW: *The Awakening of Scotland: A History from 1747-1797* (Glasgow, 1910).

2. *Local*

BROWN, ANDREW: *History of Glasgow and of Paisley, Greenock, and Port-Glasgow . . .* (2 vols., Edinburgh & Glasgow, 1795-7).

CHAMBERS, ROBERT: *Traditions of Edinburgh* (n. edn., rev., Edinburgh & London, 1869).

GRANT, JAMES: *Cassell's Old and New Edinburgh* (3 vols., London, 1884-7).

JOYCE, MICHAEL: *Edinburgh: The Golden Age, 1769-1832* (London & New York, 1951).

PAGAN, JAMES: *Sketch of the History of Glasgow* (Glasgow, 1847).

SMEATON, OLIPHANT: *Edinburgh and Its Story* (London & New York, 1904).

TODD, GEORGE EYRE: *The Story of Glasgow from the Earliest Times to the Present Day* (Glasgow, 1911).

3. Political

FERGUSSON, JAMES: *The Sixteen Peers of Scotland: An Account of the Elections of the Representative Peers of Scotland, 1707-1959* (Oxford, Eng. & New York, 1960).

INSH, GEORGE PRATT: *The Scottish Jacobite Movement: A Study in Economic and Social Forces* (Edinburgh, 1952).

RIDDELL, JOHN: *Inquiry into the Law and Practice in Scottish Peerages before and after the Union . . .* (2 vols., Edinburgh, 1842).

WARD, W. R.: "The Land Tax in Scotland, 1707-98," John Rylands Library, *Bulletin*, XXXVII (1954-5), 288-308.

4. Economic

BARKER, T. C.: "Smuggling in the Eighteenth Century: The Evidence of the Scottish Tobacco Trade," *Virginia Magazine of History and Biography*, LXII (1954), 387-99.

CAMPBELL, R. H.: *Scotland since 1707: The Rise of an Industrial Society* (New York, 1965).

GRAY, MALCOLM: *The Highland Economy, 1750-1850* (Edinburgh, 1956).

HAMILTON, HENRY: *An Economic History of Scotland in the Eighteenth Century* (Oxford, Eng., 1963), and *The Industrial Revolution in Scotland* (Oxford, Eng., 1932).

HANDLEY, JAMES: *Scottish Farming in the 18th Century* (London, 1953).

PRICE, JACOB M.: "The Rise of Glasgow in the Chesapeake Tobacco Trade, 1707-1775," *William and Mary Quarterly*, 3rd ser., XI (1954), 179-99.

ROBERTSON, M. L.: "Scottish Commerce and the American War of Independence," *Economic History Review*, 2nd ser., IX (1956), 123-31.

THOMSON, GEORGE: "The Dalnotter Iron Co.: An Eighteenth Century Scottish Industrial Undertaking," *Scottish Historical Review*, XXXV (1956), 10-20.

5. Social

ADAMS, MARGARET I.: "Eighteenth Century Highland Landlords and the Poverty Problem," *Scottish Historical Review*, XIX (1921-2), 1-20, 161-79, and "The Highland Emigration of 1770," *ibid.*, XVI (1918-19), 280-93.

[ALEXANDER, WILLIAM]: *Notes and Sketches Illustrative of Northern Rural Life in the Eighteenth Century . . .* (Edinburgh, 1877).

BELLESHEIM, ALPHONS: *History of the Catholic Church in Scotland . . .* (D. Oswald Hunter Blair, trans., 4 vols., Edinburgh, 1887-90).

CUNNINGHAM, AUDREY: *The Loyal Clans* (Cambridge, Eng., 1932).

CUNNINGHAM, JOHN: *The Church History of Scotland from the Com-*

mencement of the Christian Era to the Present Century (2 vols., Edinburgh, 1859; 2nd edn., 2 vols., 1882).

DAICHES, DAVID: *The Paradox of Scottish Culture: The Eighteenth-Century Experience* (London & New York, 1964).

FAGERSTROM, DALPHY I.: "Scottish Opinion and the American Revolution," *William and Mary Quarterly,* 3rd ser., XI (1954), 252-75.

GRAHAM, HENRY GREY: *The Social Life of Scotland in the Eighteenth Century* (1st edn., London, 1899; another edn., 2 vols., 1937).

GRANT, ALEXANDER: *The Story of the University of Edinburgh during Its First Three Hundred Years* (2 vols., London, 1884).

GRUB, GEORGE: *An Ecclesiastical History of Scotland from the Introduction of Christianity to the Present Time* (4 vols., Edinburgh, 1861).

KERR, JOHN: *Scottish Education: School and University from Early Times to 1908* (Cambridge, Eng., 1910).

MAC KERROW, JOHN: *History of the Secession Church* (rev. edn., Edinburgh, 1841).

PLANT, MARJORIE: *Domestic Life of Scotland in the Eighteenth Century* (Edinburgh, 1952).

PRYDE, GEORGE SMITH: *The Scottish Universities and the Colleges of Colonial America* (Glasgow, 1957).

D. MAPS

DORRET, JAMES: *Scotland* (London, 1750; numerous edns.). Was long the standard map of the country.

INGLIS, HARRY R. G., JOHN MATHIESON, and CHARLES BRODIE BOOG WATSON: *The Early Maps of Scotland: With an Account of the Ordnance Survey* (Edinburgh, 1934; 2nd edn., 1936).

KITCHEN, THOMAS: *Geographia Scotiae* (London, 1749; 1756), a pocket atlas with 33 maps. See also: *Scotland . . . Improved from the Large Map of Mr. Dorret* (London, 1777).

WALES

A. BIBLIOGRAPHICAL AIDS

JENKINS, R. I., and WILLIAM REES, eds.: *A Bibliography of the History of Wales . . .* (Cardiff, Wales, 1931).

LLOYD, JOHN EDWARD, ed.: *A Brief Bibliography of Welsh History . . . , Historical Association Leaflet,* No. 49 (London, 1921).

B. PRINTED SOURCE MATERIALS

BOWEN, IVOR, ed.: *The Statutes of Wales* (London, 1908). A listing of the statutes of Parliament relating to Wales.

[EDWARDS, OWEN], ed.: "The Diocese of Bangor in the Eighteenth Century," *Wales*, No. 11 (1895), 121-3. Continued in Nos. 13 (1895), 20 (1895), and 21 (1896).

GILPIN, WILLIAM: *Observations on the River Wye and Several Parts of South Wales . . . Made the Summer of the Year 1770* (London, 1782).

HARRIS, HOWELL: *The Trevecka Letters: Or the Unpublished Mss. Correspondence of Howell Harris and His Contemporaries: An Inventory of the Letters with a Digest of Their Contents* (Morgan Hugh Jones, ed., Caernarvon, Wales, 1932).

JOHNSON, SAMUEL: *A Diary of a Journey into North Wales in 1774* (R. Duppa, ed., London, 1816).

JONES, GRIFFITH: *Welch Piety: Or A Farther Account of the Circulating Welch Charity Schools . . .* (London, 1758).

LIPSCOMB, GEORGE: *Journey into South Wales . . . in the Year 1799* (London, 1802).

PENNANT, THOMAS: *A Tour in Wales, 1770* [1773] (2 vols., London, 1778-1781; n. edn., John Rhys, ed., 3 vols., Caernarvon, Wales, 1883).

ROBERTS, PETER: *The Cambrian Popular Antiquities: Or an Account of Some Traditions, Customs, and Superstitions of Wales . . .* (4 vols., Dublin, 1779; London, 1815).

WYNDHAM, HENRY PENRUDDOCKE: *A Tour through Monmouthshire and Wales Made in . . . 1774 and in . . . 1777* (2nd edn., Salisbury, Eng., 1781).

C. SECONDARY WORKS

ADDIS, JOHN P.: *The Crawshay Dynasty: A Study in Industrial Organization and Development, 1765-1867* (Cardiff, Wales, 1957). Relating to the iron industry in Wales.

BALLINGER, JOHN: *The Bible in Wales: A Study in the History of the Welsh People* (London, 1906).

BOWEN, IVOR: *The Great Enclosures of Common Lands in Wales* (London, 1914).

BRADNEY, JOSEPH ALFRED: *A History of Monmouthshire from the Coming of the Normans into Wales down to the Present Time* (4 vols., London, 1904-32).

CATHRALL, WILLIAM: *The History of North Wales Comprising a Top-ographical Description of the Several Counties* . . . (Manchester, Eng., 1828).

CAVENAGH, F. A.: *The Life and Work of Griffith Jones of Llanddowror* (Cardiff, Wales, 1930).

DAVIES, DAVID J.: *The Economic History of South Wales Prior to 1800* (Cardiff, Wales, 1935).

DAVIES, LEONARD, and A. EDWARDS: *Welsh Life in the Eighteenth Century* (London, 1939).

DAVIES, WALTER: *General View of the Agriculture and Domestic Economy of North Wales* . . . (London, 1810). See also his *General View of the Agriculture and Domestic Economy of South Wales* . . . (2 vols., London, 1814). In 1794, John Clark issued his surveys of agriculture in the county of Brecknock and in the county of Rad-nor. Several other agricultural surveys were published in the same year: Charles Hassall's surveys of the county of Carmarthen and the county of Pembroke; and the independent surveys by Thomas Lloyd and the Rev. Mr. Thomas of the county of Cardigan; John Fry published a survey of Glamorgan in 1796; and in 1812 came Hassall's *General View of the Agriculture of the County of Mon-mouth.*

DODD, ARTHUR HERBERT: "The Enclosure Movement in North Wales," Board of Celtic Studies, *Bulletin,* III (1926), pt. 2.

EVANS, GWENLLIAN N.: *Social Life in Mid-Eighteenth Century Anglesey* (Cardiff, Wales, 1936).

FRANCIS, GEORGE GRANT: *The Smelting of Copper in the Swansea District from the Time of Elizabeth to the Present Day* (Swansea, 1867; 2nd edn., London, 1881).

HUGHES, HUGH J.: *Life of Howell Harris, the Welsh Reformer* (London, 1892).

JENKINS, DAVID E.: *Calvinistic Methodist Holy Orders* (Carnarvon, Wales, 1911).

JOHN, ARTHUR HENRY: *The Industrial Development of South Wales, 1750-1850: An Essay* (Cardiff, Wales, 1950).

JONES, ELIZABETH INGLIS: *The Story of Wales* (London, 1955).

JONES, THEOPHILUS: *A History of the County of Brecknock* . . . (2 vols., Brecknock, Wales, 1805-9; rep., 2 vols. in 1, 1898; n. edn., enl., 4 vols., 1909-30).

LEWIS, EILUNED and PETER: *The Land of Wales* . . . (3rd edn., London & New York, 1949).

MALKIN, BENJAMIN HEATH: *The Scenery, Antiquities, and Biography of South Wales from Materials Collected during Two Excursions in the Year 1803* (London, 1804)

MEYRICK, SAMUEL RUSH: *The History and Antiquities of the County of Cardigan* . . . (Brecon, Wales, 1907)

PEATE, IORWERTH C.: *The Welsh House: A Study in Folk Culture* (2nd edn., London, 1944).

PHILLIPS, ELIZABETH: *A History of the Pioneers of the Welsh Coalfield* (Cardiff, Wales, 1925).

REES, FREDERICK: *Of Welsh Nationality and Historians* (London, 1951), *The Story of Milford-Milford Haven* (Cardiff, Wales, 1954), and *Studies in Welsh History: Collected Papers, Lectures, and Reviews* (Cardiff, Wales, 1947).

REES, THOMAS: *History of Protestant Nonconformity in Wales: From Its Rise to the Present Time* (London, 1861), and *A History of the Quakers in Wales and Their Emigration to North America* (Carmarthen, Wales, 1925).

RIDER, SYDNEY W., and ARTHUR E. TRUEMAN: *South Wales: A Physical and Economic Geography* . . . (London, 1929).

SKEEL, CAROLINE: "The Cattle Trade between Wales and England from the Fifteenth to the Nineteenth Centuries," Royal Historical Society, *Transactions*, 4th ser., IX (1926), 135-58.

WILKINS, CHARLES: *The History of Merthyr Tydfil* (Merthyr Tydfil, Wales, 1867); *Tales and Sketches of Wales* (Cardiff, Wales, 1879); and *Wales: Past and Present* (Merthyr Tydfil, Wales, 1870). See also Wilkins's economic studies: *The History of the Iron, Steel, Tin-Plate, and Other Trades of Wales* . . . (Merthyr Tydfil, Wales, 1903), and *The South Wales Coal Trade and Its Allied Industries from the Earliest Days to the Present Time* (Cardiff, Wales, 1888).

WILLIAMS, JONATHAN: *A General History of the County of Radnor* . . . (Edwin Davies, ed., Brecknock, Wales, 1905).

WILLIAMS, L. J.: "The Welsh Tinplate Trade in the Mid-Eighteenth Century," *Economic History Review*, 2nd ser., XIII (1960-1), 440-9.

WILLIAMS, MITA: "Ancient Marriage Customs," *Wales*, No. 12 (1895), 156-63.

WILLIAMS, R.: "Quakerism in Montgomeryshire," *Wales*, No. 21 (1896), 7-12.

WILLIAMS, WILLIAM: *Welsh Calvinistic Methodism: A Historic Sketch of the Presbyterian Church of Wales* (2nd edn., enl., London, 1884).

WILLIAMS, WILLIAM RETLAW: *The Parliamentary History of the Principality of Wales* . . . *1541-1895* (Brecknock, Wales, 1895).

YOUNG, DAVID: *The Origin and History of Methodism in Wales and the Borders* . . . (London, 1893).

CHAPTER III

Ireland

A. BIBLIOGRAPHICAL AIDS

Bibliography of Irish History (Dublin, 1936).

Catalogue of the Books in the Irish Section [of the Linen Hall Library, Belfast] (Belfast, 1917).

A Catalogue of the Bradshaw Collection of Irish Books in the University Library, Cambridge (3 vols., Cambridge, Eng., 1916).

GROSE, C. L.: *Select Bibliography of British History, 1660-1760* (Chicago, 1939), section XIV.

HORN, DAVID BAYNE, and MARY RANSOME, eds.: "Ireland: Bibliography," *English Historical Documents, Vol. X: 1714-1783* (New York, 1957), 679-81.

HUGHES, J. L. J.: "The Chief Secretaries in Ireland, 1566-1921," *Irish Historical Studies,* VIII (1952), 59-72. A listing.

Irish Historical Studies publishes annual lists of "Writings on Irish History," among these are "Research on Irish History in Irish Universities," and "Research on Irish History in Irish, British and American Universities" (Dublin, 1938+).

IRISH MANUSCRIPTS COMMISSION: *Catalogue of Publications Issued or in Preparation, 1928-1957* (Dublin, 1957).

MAXWELL, CONSTANTIA ELIZABETH: *Short Bibliography of Irish History (Revised), Historical Association Leaflet,* No. 23 (London, 1921). This is an excellent brief bibliography.

MURRAY, R. H.: *Ireland . . . [1494-1829], Helps for Students of History Series,* Nos. 33-5 (3 pts., London, 1920). Part 3, No. 35, deals with the period 1714-1829.

PARGELLIS, STANLEY, and D. J. MEDLEY: "Ireland," *Bibliography of British History* (Oxford, 1951), pp. 422-41.

PRENDEVILLE, P. L.: "A Select Bibliography of Irish Economic History, Part 2: The Seventeenth and Eighteenth Centuries," *Economic History Review*, III (1931-2), 402-16.

See also the full but dated bibliography containing an extensive selection of older books for the period: "Bibliographies, Part XIV: Ireland from 1700-89" in *The Cambridge Modern History, Vol. VI: The Eighteenth Century*, pp. 913-24.

B. PRINTED SOURCE MATERIALS

1. Government and related documents

[CALDWELL, JAMES], ed.: *Debates Relative to the Affairs of Ireland in the Years 1763 and 1764: Taken by a Military Officer, to Which Are Added His Remarks on the Trade of Ireland* . . . (2 vols., London, 1766).

The Journals of the House of Commons of the Kingdom of Ireland, 18th May 1613-2nd August 1800 . . . (20 vols., Dublin, 1779-1800).

Journals of the House of Lords of the Kingdom of Ireland . . . *[1634-1800]* (8 vols., Dublin, 1779-1800).

Report from the Committee Appointed to Enquire into the Present State of the Linen Trade in Great Britain and Ireland (London, 1773).

The Statutes at Large, Passed in the Parliaments Held in Ireland: From the Third Year of Edward the Second, A.D. 1310, to the [Fortieth Year of George the Third, A.D. 1800] (20 vols., Dublin, 1786-1801).

2. Non-official contemporary writings

BERESFORD, JOHN: *The Correspondence of the Right Hon. John Beresford, Illustrative of the Last Thirty Years of the Irish Parliament* [1770-1804] (William Beresford, ed., 2 vols., London, 1854).

BODKIN, M., ed.: "Notes on the Irish Parliament in 1773," *Royal Irish Academy, Proceedings*, XLVIII-XLIX, section C (1942-4), 145-232.

BURKE, EDMUND: *Letters, Speeches, and Tracts on Irish Affairs* . . . [1765-97] (Matthew Arnold, ed., London, 1881). For additional Burke material on Ireland, see R. J. S. Hoffman's edition of *Edmund Burke, New York Agent . . . and Intimate Correspondence with Charles O'Hara, 1761-1776* (Philadelphia, 1956).

CHARLEMONT, JAMES CAULFIELD, 1ST EARL OF. *Memoirs of the Political and Private Life of James Caulfield, Earl of Charlemont* by Francis Hardy (London, 1810; 2nd edn., 2 vols., 1812); and *The Manu-*

scripts and Correspondence of James, First Earl of Charlemont, Vol. I: 1745-1783, Historical Manuscripts Commission, Twelfth Report, Appendix, Part X (John T. Gilbert, ed., London, 1891).

CLARENDON, R. V.: A Sketch of the Revenue and Finances of Ireland and of the Appropriated Funds, Loans, and Debt of the Nation from Their Commencement . . . (London, 1791).

[ELSTOB, MARK]: A Trip to Kilkenny from Durham by Way of White-haven and Dublin in the Year 1776 (Stockton, Eng., 1778; Dublin, 1779).

FLOOD, HENRY: Memoirs of the Life and Correspondence of the Right Hon. Henry Flood . . . Containing Reminiscences of the Irish Commons . . . (Dublin, 1838).

GRATTAN, HENRY. Memoirs of the Life and Times of the Rt. Hon. Henry Grattan by Henry Grattan (the younger) (5 vols., London, 1839-46; n. edn., 1849).

HARCOURT, EDWARD WILLIAM, ed.: The Harcourt Papers (13 vols., Oxford, Eng. [1876-1903]). A memoir of Simon, Earl of Harcourt, comprises vols. 3 and 4, and his correspondence while Lord-Lieutenant of Ireland, 1771-6, is to be found in vols. 9-10.

HOWARD, GORGES EDMOND: A Treatise on the Exchequer and Revenue of Ireland (2 vols., Dublin, 1776).

HUNT, WILLIAM, ed.: The Irish Parliament, 1775: From an Official and Contemporary Manuscript (London, 1907). A list of the members of the Irish Parliament and their connections.

LARGE, DAVID, ed.: "The Irish House of Commons in 1769," Irish Historical Studies, XI (1958-9), 18-45.

LASCELLES, ROWLEY: Liber Munerum Publicorum Hiberniae, 1152-1827: Or, the Establishments of Ireland (2 vols., London, 1824-30). Contains lists of officials, members of Parliament, and clergy, and excerpts from various pertinent source materials.

LEINSTER, EMILY, DUCHESS OF: Correspondence of Emily, Duchess of Leinster, Irish Manuscripts Commission (Brian Fitzgerald, ed., 3 vols., Dublin, 1949-57).

LODGE, JOHN: The Peerage of Ireland: Or a Genealogical History of the Present Nobility of that Kingdom . . . (4 vols., London, 1754; rev. & enl. by M. Archdall, 7 vols., Dublin & London, 1789). Records family histories and connections.

[LUCKOMBE, PHILIP]: A Tour through Ireland . . . to Which Is Prefixed a General Description of the Kingdom . . . (London, 1780).

[MACARTNEY, GEORGE, LORD]: An Account of Ireland in 1773: By a Late Chief Secretary of That Kingdom (London, 1773).

———. Some Account of the Public Life and a Selection from the Unpublished Writings of the Earl of Macartney . . . by John Barrow (2 vols., London, 1807).

MORAN, PATRICK FRANCIS, ed.: *Spicilegium Ossoriense: Being a Collection of Original Letters and Papers Illustrative of the History of the Irish Church from the Reformation to the Year 1800* (3 vols., Dublin, 1874-84).

The Orrery Papers (Emily Charlotte De Burgh Canning, Countess of Cork and Orrery, ed., 2 vols., London, 1903). The final sections of volume II have some materials relevant to this period.

The Patriot Miscellany: Or a Collection of Essays Relative to the Political Contest in Ireland during the Administration of His Grace the Duke of Dorset (2 vols., Dublin, 1756). There are forty-two pamphlets reprinted in these volumes, each of which was published separately.

The Peerage of Ireland: A Genealogical and Historical Account of All the Peers of that Kingdom . . . (2 vols., London, 1768).

POCOCKE, RICHARD: *A Tour in Ireland in 1752* (G. T. Stokes, ed., Dublin, 1891). Illustrates social conditions in Ireland.

PRIOR, THOMAS: *A List of the Absentees of Ireland and the Yearly Value of Their Estates and Incomes Spent Abroad: With Observations on . . . [Ireland]* (2nd edn., Dublin, 1729; 3rd edn., w/add., 1769; 6th edn., 1783).

ROCKINGHAM, CHARLES WATSON-WENTWORTH, MARQUESS OF: "A Letter from the Marquis of Rockingham to Sir William Mayne on the Proposed Absentee Tax," J. E. Tyler, ed., *Irish Historical Studies*, VIII (1952-3), 362-9.

SEWARD, WILLIAM WENMAN: *Collectanea Politica: Or the Political Transactions of Ireland from the Accession of George III to the Present Time . . .* (3 vols., Dublin, 1801-4). Vol. I contains material relevant to this period.

SHACKLETON, RICHARD and ELIZABETH: *Memoirs and Letters of Richard and Elizabeth Shackleton, Late of Ballitore, Ireland . . .* (Mary Leadbeater, ed., London, 1822; New York, 1823). The letters cover the years 1752-92.

SHELBURNE, WILLIAM PETTY, 2ND EARL OF. *Life of William, Earl of Shelburne, afterwards First Marquess of Lansdowne: With Extracts from His Papers and Correspondence* by Edmond George Petty, Baron Fitzmaurice (3 vols., London, 1875; 2nd edn., rev., 2 vols., 1912).

SMITH, CHARLES: Smith wrote four books dealing with the counties in Ireland, the first of which, published anonymously, was *The Ancient and Present State of the County Down . . .* (Dublin, 1744). It was followed by *The Ancient and Present State of the County of Waterford . . .* (Dublin, 1746; 2nd edn., 1774); *The Ancient and Present State of the County and City of Cork . . .* (2 vols., Dublin, 1760; Robert Day and W. A. Copinger, eds., Cork, 1893-4); and

The Ancient and Present State of the County of Kerry . . . (Dublin, 1765).

STONE, GEORGE, ARCHBISHOP OF ARMAGH: "Correspondence of Archbishop Stone and the Duke of Newcastle," C. Litton Falkiner, ed., *English Historical Review,* XX (1905), 508-42, 735-63. Prints manuscript letters of the Archbishop of Armagh for the years 1752-5 which may be found in the British Museum, *Additional Mss.*

SWIFT, JONATHAN: *The Drapier's Letters to the People of Ireland against Receiving Woods' Halfpence* (Herbert Davis, ed., Oxford, Eng., 1935). While the letters were first published in 1724, they provide a revealing background view of Ireland; furthermore, the issues raised by the letters were still alive in the period 1748-1776.

THOM, ALEXANDER, & SONS, eds.: *A Collection of Tracts and Treatises Illustrative of the Natural History, Antiquities, and the Political and Social State of Ireland* (2 vols., Dublin, 1860-1). This literature relates to absenteeism in Ireland in the eighteenth century.

A Tour Through Ireland: In Several Entertaining Letters Wherein the Present State of that Kingdom Is Consider'd and the Most Noted Cities, Towns, Seats, Rivers, Buildings, &c. Are Described . . . *By Two English Gentlemen* (London, 1748). The British Museum indicates that this may be the work of W. R. Chatwood.

[TWISS, RICHARD]: *A Tour in Ireland in 1775* (London, 1776). A detailed book which became very unpopular in Ireland.

YOUNG, ARTHUR: *A Tour in Ireland with General Observations on the Present State of That Kingdom: Made in the Years 1776, 1777, and 1778 and Brought down to the End of 1779* (Dublin & London, 1780; 2nd edn., 2 vols., 1780; A. W. Hutton, ed., 2 vols., London, 1892). This work is an important source for Irish economic conditions during the period.

3. Contemporary pamphlets, tracts, and related materials: Chronologically arranged

1 7 4 9

BERKELEY, GEORGE: *A Word to the Wise: Or the Bishop of Cloyne's Exhortation to the Roman Catholic Clergy of Ireland* . . . (Dublin, 1749; 4th edn., Boston, 1750).

PRIOR, THOMAS: *An Essay to Encourage and Extend the Linen Manufacture in Ireland by Praemiums and Other Means* (Dublin, 1749). See also Richard Cox: *A Letter* . . . *to Thomas Prior, Esq. Shewing from Experience a Sure Method to Establish the Linen-Manufacture and the Beneficial Effects It will Immediately Produce* (Dublin, 1749).

1 7 5 0

A Representation of the State of Trade of Ireland Laid before the House of Lords of England . . . on Occasion of a Bill before that House for Laying a Duty on Irish Sail Cloth Imported into Great Britain (Dublin, 1750).

Some Consideration on the British Fisheries: With a Proposal for Establishing a General Fishery on the Coasts of Ireland . . . (Dublin, 1750).

1 7 5 1

LUCAS, CHARLES: *The Political Constitution of Great Britain and Ireland Asserted and Vindicated: The Connection and Common Interest of Both Kingdoms Demonstrated . . .* (2 vols., London, 1751).

A Proposal for Uniting the Kingdoms of Great Britain and Ireland (London, 1571). This pamphlet was answered by the anonymous *An Answer to the Late Proposal . . .* (Dublin & London, 1751) and by N. Archdall's *An Alarm to the People of Great-Britain and Ireland: In Answer to a Late Proposal . . .* (Dublin, 1751).

1 7 5 2

BERKELEY, GEORGE: *A Miscellany: Containing Several Tracts on Various Subjects* (Dublin, 1752).

1 7 5 3

An Attempt to Prove That a Free and Open Trade between the Kingdom of Ireland and All the Ports of the Southern Coasts of England Would Be Highly Advantageous to Both Kingdoms . . . (Exon [Exeter], Eng., 1753).

HENRY, WILLIAM: *An Earnest Address to the People of Ireland against the Drinking of Spirituous Liquors* (Dublin, 1753).

[HOWARD, GORGES EDMOND]: *A Short Account of His Majesty's Hereditary Revenue and Private Estate in the Kingdom of Ireland* (Dublin, 1753; 2nd edn., w/add., 1754).

1 7 5 4

An Account of the Life, Character, and Parliamentary Conduct of the Right Honourable Henry Boyle, Esq. [later Earl of Shannon] . . . (Dublin [1754]). The dedication is signed C. Philo-Patriae.

[COX, RICHARD]: *The Proceeding of the Honourable House of Commons of Ireland in Rejecting the Altered Money-Bill on December 17, 1753:*

Vindicated by Authorities Taken from the Law and Usage of Parliament . . . (Dublin, 1754). For a reply see the pamphlet published anonymously by E. Robinson: *An Answer to a Pamphlet Intitled, "The Proceedings . . ."* (Dublin, 1754), and also the anonymous *An Answer to Part of a Pamphlet Intitled "The Proceedings . . ."* (Dublin, 1754).

The History of the Ministerial Conduct of the Chief Governors of Ireland . . . [1688-1753] With a General Review of the Most Remarkable Proceedings in Parliament during That Period . . . (London, 1754).

HOWARD, GORGES EDMOND: *A Letter to the Publick on the Present Posture of Affairs* . . . (Dublin, 1754).

[LELAND, JOHN]: *The Case Fairly Stated: Or, an Inquiry How Far the Clause lately Rejected by the . . . House of Commons Would . . . Have Affected the Liberties of the People of Ireland* (Dublin, 1754). For a reply, see *Truth against Craft or Sophistry and Falsehood Detected: In Answer to a Pamphlet Intitled "The Case Fairly Stated"* . . . (Dublin, 1754).

ROBINSON, CHRISTOPHER: *Considerations on the Late Bill for Payment of the Remainder of the National Debt in which the Occasion of Inserting the Clause Relative to His Majesty's Consent and the Arguments in Support of . . . [are] Stated* (Dublin, 1754). The text of the bill was included in this pamphlet.

Some Observations Relative to the Late Bill for Paying off the Residue of the National Debt of Ireland: Humbly Submitted to the Consideration of the True Friends of the Country (Dublin, 1754).

The State of Ireland Laid Open to His Majesty's Subjects . . . (London, 1754).

To His Grace, Lionel, Duke of Dorset, Lord Lieutenant General and General Governour of the Kingdom of Ireland: The Humble Petition of Trust, Virtue, and Liberty (Dublin, 1754).

Tyranny Display'd: In a Letter from a Looker-on, Earnestly Recommended to the Serious Perusal of All True Lovers of Their Country (Dublin, 1754).

1 7 5 5

The Conduct of a Certain Member of Parliament during the Last Session and the Motives on Which He Acted: Explained in a Letter to a Friend (Dublin, 1755).

A Few Words More of Advice to the Friends of Ireland on the Present Crisis (Dublin, 1755).

[GAST, JOHN]: *Faction's Overthrow: Or More Fair Warning and Good Advice to the Nobility, Gentry, and Commonalty of Ireland . . .* (Dublin, 1755).

A Letter to a Member of Parliament in Dublin from His Friend in the Country on the Present Posture of Affairs in the North (Dublin, 1755).

A Letter to the Right Hon. J. P. Esq.: In Relation to a National Affair in the House of Commons on the 1st of November, 1755 (Dublin, 1755).

The Libeller Lashed: Or Fair Warning to the Nobility and Gentry of Ireland ([Dublin], 1755).

[O'Conor, Charles]: *The Case of the Roman Catholics of Ireland wherein the Principles and Conduct of That Party Are Fully Explained and Vindicated* (Dublin, 1755). This work can also be found reprinted in the *Eighth Report* of the Historical Manuscripts Commission, Appendix, Part I, Section II (London, 1908), 445[b]-7[b]. For a reply see: *A Vindication of a Pamphlet Lately Intitled Policy and Justice: An Essay Being a Proposal for Augmenting the Power and "The Case ..."* (Dublin, 1755).

Policy and Justice: An Essay Being a Proposal for Augmenting the Power and Wealth of Great Britain by Uniting Ireland (Dublin, 1755).

Seasonable Advice to the Friends of Ireland on the Present Crisis of Affairs (Dublin, 1755).

WHYTE, MICHAEL: *An Inquiry into the Causes of Our Want of Tillage in Ireland: With Some Hints for Establishing a Yeomanry* (Dublin, 1755).

1 7 5 6

Advice to the Patriot Club of the County of Antrim: On the Present State of Affairs in Ireland and some Late Changes in the Administration of That Kingdom (Dublin, 1756).

Advice to the Speaker Elect: Or a Letter to the Right Honourable John Ponsonby, Esq. (Dublin, 1756).

An Epistle to the Citizens of Dublin. By —— —— (Dublin, 1756).

A Few Thoughts on the Times: In a Letter from a Free-Citizen of Dublin to His Friend in the North: Humbly Offered to the Consideration of Every Lover of Truth and Justice (Dublin, 1756).

Heads of a Bill for a Register of Popish Priests (Dublin, 1756).

The Last Speech, Confession, and Dying Words of the Old Traytor who Sold His Country for the Lucre of Gain, Who Was Executed ... March, 1756 (Dublin, 1756).

LUCAS, CHARLES: *An Appeal to the Commons and Citizens of London* (London, 1756).

A New Scheme for Increasing the Protestant Religion and Improving the Kingdom of Ireland ... (Dublin, 1756).

The Question of Previous Consent Discussed: By a Gentleman of the Bar (Dublin, 1756).

Some Queries Relative to the Present State of Popery in Ireland (Dublin, 1756).

The Touchstone of Patriotism: In a Series of Interesting Queries to the Public (Dublin, 1756).

1 7 5 7

Consideration on the Revenues of Ireland Shewing the Right . . . of now Applying the Duties . . . to Naval Services . . . (London, 1757).

A Letter from a Gentleman in the City to a Member of Parliament in the North of Ireland ([Dublin], 1757).

A Letter to His Gr——e the D——e of B——d, L——d, L——t of Ir——d (2nd edn., London, 1757).

[PERY, EDMUND SEXTON]: *Letters from an Armenian in Ireland to His Friends at Trebisond, &c: Translated in the Year 1756* (London, 1757). This pamphlet has also been attributed to Robert Hellen.

The Protestant Interest Considered Relatively to the Operation of Popery Acts in Ireland (Dublin, 1757). Contains data on various subjects, including the penal laws, industry, and agriculture.

STEPHENSON, ROBERT: *An Inquiry into the State and Progress of the Linen Manufacture of Ireland . . .* (3 numbers, Dublin, 1757).

1 7 5 8

[GRATTAN, JAMES]: *A Letter to the Gentry, Clergy, Freemen and Free-holders of the City of Dublin* (Dublin, 1758), and *The Recorder's Second Letter to the Gentry, Clergy, Freemen, and Freeholders of the City of London* (Dublin, 1758).

Remarks upon Poynings' Law and the Manner of Passing Bills in the P———t of I———d: By a Gentleman of Ireland (Dublin, 1758).

Some Thoughts on the General Improvement of Ireland . . . (Dublin, 1758).

1 7 6 0

Considerations on the Present Calamities of This Kingdom and the Causes of the Decay of Public Credit with the Means of Restoring It (Dublin, 1760).

An Essay on the Antient and Modern State of Ireland: With the Various Important Advantages thereunto Derived under . . . George the Second . . . (Dublin, 1760).

1 7 6 1

BROOKE, HENRY: *The Tryal of the Cause of the Roman Catholics on a Special Commission Directed to Lord Chief Justice Reason, Lord*

Chief Baron Interest, and Mr. Justice Clemency, Wednesday, August 5th, 1761 (Dublin, 1761).

HOWARD, GORGES EDMOND: *Queries Relative to Several Defects and Grievances in Some of the Present Laws of Ireland* . . . (2nd edn., Dublin, 1761; 3rd edn., 1763).

Impartial Reflections upon the Present State of Affairs; With Incidental Remarks upon Certain Transactions (Dublin, 1761).

1 7 6 2

An Alarm to the Unprejudiced and Well-Minded Protestants . . . *[on] the White Boys* (Cork, 1762).

COX, RICHARD: *The Present State of His Majesty's Revenue Compared with That of Some Late Years* (Dublin, 1762).

1 7 6 3

An Account of the Progress of Charles Coote, Esq. . . . *[against the Oakboys]* (Dublin, 1763).

MAC AULAY, ALEXANDER: *Enquiry into the Legality of Pensions on the Irish Establishment* (London, 1763).

1 7 6 4

CALDWELL, JAMES: *A Brief Examination of the Question Whether It Is Expedient* . . . *to Pass an Act to Enable Papists to Take Real Securities for Money which They May Lend* . . . (Dublin, 1764).

Some Arguments for Limiting the Duration of Parliaments . . . (Dublin, 1764).

1 7 6 6

BULLINGBROOKE, EDWARD: *The Duty and Authority of the Peace and Parish-Officers for Ireland* (Dublin, 1766).

Considerations on the Expediency . . . *of Frequent New Parliaments in Ireland* (Dublin, 1766).

[CURRY, JOHN]: *An Inquiry into the Causes of the Late Riots in Munster* (Dublin, 1766).

MAC AULAY, ALEXANDER: *Septennial Parliaments Vindicated* . . . (2nd edn. w/add., Dublin, 1766).

Some Hints for the Better Promoting of the Laws in This Kingdom . . . (Dublin, 1766).

TAAFFE, NICHOLAS: *Observations on Affairs in Ireland from the Settlement in 1691 to the Present Time* (London, 1766). A temperate plea for the toleration of Irish Catholics.

1 7 6 7

[BUSH, JOHN]: *Hibernia Curiosa: A Letter from a Gentleman in Dublin to His Friend at Dover in Kent Giving a General View of . . . the Inhabitants of Ireland . . .* (London [1767]).

A Candid Enquiry into the Causes and Motives of the Late Riots in the Province of Munster in Ireland by the People Called White-Boys or Levellers . . . (London, 1767). This pamphlet is signed L. T. and has been attributed to John Curry.

TOWNSHEND, GEORGE, 1st Marquess: *Meditations upon a Late Excursion in Ireland* (n.p., 1767).

1 7 6 8

[JACKSON, GEORGE; afterwards SIR GEORGE DUCKETT]: *Reasons for an Augmentation of the Army on the Irish Establishment Offered to the Consideration of the Public* (Dublin & London, 1768).

LUCAS, CHARLES: *To the Right Honorable the Lord Mayor, the Worshipful the Board of Aldermen, the Sherifs, Commons, Citizens, and Free-holders of Dublin: The Address of C. Lucas . . . upon the Proposed Augmentation of the Military Establishment* (Dublin, 1768).

WOODWARD, RICHARD. *An Argument in Support of the Right of the Poor in the Kingdom of Ireland to a National Provision . . .* (Dublin, 1768), and *A Scheme for Establishing County Poor-Houses in the Kingdom of Ireland . . .* (2nd edn., Dublin, 1768). The latter pamphlet was published anonymously.

1 7 6 9

[LANGRISHE, HERCULES]: *Considerations on the Dependencies of Great Britain: With Observations on a Pamphlet Intitled "The Present State of the Nation"* (London, 1769).

Some Arguments for Limiting the Duration of Parliaments . . . Submitted to the Consideration of the Public (Dublin, 1769).

Some Observations on the Circumstances of Ireland ([Dublin, 1769]).

A State of the Publick Revenues and Expence from the Year 1751 to 1767 ([Dublin, 1769]).

1 7 7 0

An Address from a Noble Lord to the People of Ireland on the Present State of Affairs ([Dublin], 1770).

BOULTER, HUGH: *Letters Written to . . . Several Ministers of State and Some Others . . .* (Ambrose Philips, ed., 2 vols., Dublin, 1770).

These letters of Boulter, the Archbishop of Dublin, concern the period prior to 1748, but are nevertheless valuable.

[FRENCH, ROBERT]: *The Constitution of Ireland and Poynings' Laws Explained: By a Friend to His Country* (Dublin & London, 1770).

HELLEN, ROBERT: *Observations on a Speech [by Lord Townshend, on the Rejection of a Money Bill by the Irish Commons] Delivered the 26th Day of December, 1769, in the House of Lords in Ireland* (Dublin, 1770).

HOWARD, GORGES EDMOND: *Some Questions upon the Legislative Constitution of Ireland* (Dublin, 1770).

Letter to the People of Ireland (3rd edn., London, 1770); on the commercial situation.

[LODGE, JOHN]: *The Usage of Holding Parliaments and of preparing and Passing Bills of Supply in Ireland Stated from Record . . .* (Dublin, 1770).

LUCAS, CHARLES: *The Rights and Privileges of Parliaments Asserted upon Constitutional Principles . . . Humbly Addressed to His Excellency George, Lord Visc. Townshend, Lord Lieutenant General and General Governor of Ireland* (Dublin, 1770).

MOLYNEUX, WILLIAM: *The Case of Ireland's Being Bound by Acts of Parliament in England Stated . . .* ([6th edn.], London, 1770). This was first published in Dublin in 1698 to indicate the independence of the Irish Parliament.

MORAL, FRANCES: *An Address to the K**** (Dublin, 1770).

[POWER, RICHARD]: *A Comparative State of the Two Rejected Money Bills, in 1692 and 1769: With Some Observations on Poynings' Act and the Explanatory Statute of Philip and Mary. By a Barrister* (Dublin, 1770).

Thoughts, English and Irish, on the Pension List of Ireland (London, 1770).

1 7 7 1

CALDWELL, JAMES: *An Address to the House of Commons of Ireland: By a Freeholder . . .* (3rd edn. [Dublin], 1771).

[————]: *An Essay on the Character and Conduct of His Excellency Lord Visc. Townshend . . .* ([London], 1771).

[CURRY, JOHN, and CHARLES O'CONOR]: *Observations on the Popery Laws* (Dublin, 1771; 2nd edn., 1774).

[HOWARD, GORGES EDMOND]: *A Candid Appeal to the Public on the Subject of a Late Epistle* (Dublin, 1771), and *Postscript to the Candid Appeal to the Public . . .* (Dublin [1771]). These are concerned with the revenue of Ireland.

The Protest of the Lords, Dec. 18, 1771 (Dublin, 1771).

1 7 7 2

A Comparative View of the Public Burdens of Great Britain and Ireland: With a Proposal for . . . Equality in . . . Freedom of Foreign Trade (London, 1772).

1 7 7 3

BARATARIANA, pseud.: *A Select Collection of Fugitive Political Pieces Published during the Administration of Lord Townshend in Ireland* (Dublin, 1773). Most of the pieces were written by Sir Hercules Langrishe, Henry Grattan, and Henry Flood. For a reply to this work, see *The Batchelor: Or Speculations of Jeoffry Wagstaffe, Esq.* (Dublin, 1773).

CAVENDISH, W.: *Letters Which Passed in Great Britain [between the Duke of Devonshire and others and Lord North] Relative to the Absentee Tax* (Dublin, 1773).

A Letter upon the Subject of Taxing the Estates of Absentees (Dublin, 1773).

1 7 7 4

BRUTUS, and HUMPHREY SEARCH, pseuds.: *Essays, Historical, Political, and Moral: Being a Proper Supplement to Baratariana* (2 vols., Dublin [1774]).

1 7 7 5

GILBERT, THOMAS: *Observations upon the Orders and Regulations of the House of Commons with Respect to the Poor, Vagrants and Houses of Correction* (London, 1775).

An Inquiry into the Laws Affecting the Popish Inhabitants of Ireland Preceded by a Short Political Analysis of the History and Constitution of Ireland (Dublin & London, 1775). This pamphlet was also issued as *An Inquiry into the Policy of the Penal Laws. . . .*

A Letter to the People of Ireland on the . . . Fisheries (Dublin, 1775).

1 7 7 6

BRUTUS, pseud.: *Brutus's Third Letter on the Present Situation of Affairs . . .* (Dublin, 1776).

Letters Addressed to the Electors of the County of Antrim by a Freeholder: Published Previous to the General Election (Belfast, 1776).

PHILLIPS, CATHARINE: *An Epistle to Friends in Ireland [on vital religion]* (Dublin, 1776).

Post - 1 7 7 6

[CAMPBELL, THOMAS]: *A Philosophical Survey of the South of Ireland in a Series of Letters to John Watkinson* (London, 1777).

[KNOX, WILLIAM]: *Considerations on the State of Ireland* (Dublin, 1778).

A Letter . . . on the Subject of Tythes (Dublin, 1778). There were also second and third letters published.

CALDWELL, JAMES: *An Inquiry How Far the Restrictions Laid upon the Trade in Ireland by British Acts of Parliament Are a Benefit or Disadvantage to the British Dominions in General and to England in Particular* (Dublin, 1779).

[HELY-HUTCHINSON, JOHN]: *The Commercial Restraints of Ireland Considered: In a Series of Letters to a Noble Lord . . .* (Dublin, 1779; reiss., William George Carroll, ed., Dublin, 1882). Hely-Hutchinson was the provost of Trinity College and in this pamphlet he advocated free trade, home rule, parliamentary reform, and Catholic emancipation.

Observations on the Finances and Trade of Ireland Humbly Addressed to the Immediate Consideration of Gentlemen of Landed Interest, More Particularly to Members of the House of Commons (Dublin [1779]).

HOWARD, GORGES EDMOND: *An Abstract and Common Place of All the Irish, British, and English Statutes Relative to the Revenue of Ireland and the Trade Connected Therewith . . .* (2 vols., Dublin, 1780-1).

A Congratulatory Address to His Majesty from the Peasantry of Ireland, Vulgarly Denominated White Boys or Right Boys (Dublin, 1786). Relates to the poor conditions of agricultural workers.

An Impartial Discussion of the Subject of Tithes: Addressed to Members of Both Houses of Parliament (Dublin, 1786).

Considerations on the Political and Commercial Circumstances of Great Britain and Ireland as They Are Connected with Each Other . . . (London, 1787).

TRANT, DOMINICK: *Considerations on the Present Disturbances in the Province of Munster* (3rd edn., Dublin, 1787).

A Vindication of the [Church of Ireland] Clergy by a Southern Clergyman (Dublin, 1788).

[SCOTT, JOHN ROBERT]: *Parliamentary Representation: Being a Political and Critical Review of All the Counties, Cities, and Boroughs of the Kingdom of Ireland, with regard to their Representation: By Falkland* (Dublin, 1790).

4. Newspapers and periodicals

For information on Irish newspapers, see Ernest McClintock Dix: *Tables Relating to Some Dublin Newspapers of the Eighteenth Century . . .*

(Dublin, 1910). Dix wrote numerous brief works on the printing of books, newspapers, etc., not only those published in Dublin in the eighteenth century, but also in Belfast, Cork, Waterford, and other Irish towns. See also Richard Robert Madden's *The History of Irish Periodical Literature from the End of the Seventeenth to the Middle of the Nineteenth Century* . . . (2 vols., London, 1867).

Belfast Newsletter, Belfast.
The Cork Evening Post, b. ca. 1754, Cork.
Dublin Mercury [Hoey's Dublin Mercury], 1766-1773, Dublin.
The Dublin Spy, 1753-1754, Dublin.
The Dublin Weekly Journal, Dublin.
Faulkner's Dublin Journal [The Dublin Journal], Dublin.
Finn's Leinster Journal, b. 1766, Kilkenny.
The Hibernian Chronicle, b. 1768, Cork.
The Hibernian Journal or Chronicle of Liberty, b. 1771, Dublin.
Public Register or the Freeman's Journal [Freeman's Journal], b. 1763, Dublin.
Pue's Occurrences [John Roe's Pue's Occurrences], b. 1763, Dublin.
The Universal Advertiser, 1752-1766, Dublin.

C. SECONDARY WORKS

1. General

BARLOW, STEPHEN: *The History of Ireland . . . to the Present Time: Embracing also a Statistical and Geographical Account of That Kingdom* . . . (2 vols., London, 1814).

BEAUMONT, GUSTAVE AUGUSTE DE LA BONNINIERE: *L'Irlande: Sociale, Politique, et Religieuse* (2 vols., Paris, 1839; William Cooke Taylor, trans. & ed., London, 1839).

BECKETT, JAMES CAMLIN: *The Making of Modern Ireland, 1603-1923* (New York, 1966). See especially chapters IX through XI.

CRAWFORD, WILLIAM: *A History of Ireland . . . in a Series of Letters Addressed to William Hamilton, Esq.* (2 vols., Strabane, Ireland, 1783). Vol. II has relevant material.

CURTIS, EDMUND: *A History of Ireland* (London, 1936; 6th edn., rev., 1950).

D'ALTON, EDWARD ALFRED: *History of Ireland from the Earliest Times . . . [to 1908]* (3 vols., Dublin, 1903-10; 3rd edn., 4 vols., Dublin & Belfast [1920]-5).

DUNLOP, ROBERT: *Ireland from the Earliest Times . . .* ([London], 1922); and "Ireland in the Eighteenth Century," *The Cambridge Modern History, Vol. VI: The Eighteenth Century,* 479-505.

FALKINER, C. LITTON: *Studies in Irish History and Biography: Mainly of the Eighteenth Century* (London, 1902).

FROUDE, JAMES ANTHONY: *The English in Ireland in the Eighteenth Century* (3 vols., London, 1872-4; 1st Am. edn., 3 vols., New York, 1873-4). This work brought forth a number of replies, including two books by Thomas N. Burke: *English Misrule in Ireland: A Course of Lectures . . .* , *Irish-American Library*, I (New York, 1873) and *Froude's Crusade . . .* (New York, 1872); Warden Hatton Flood's *Notes and Historical Criticisms on Mr. A. Froude's English in Ireland in the 18th Century* (Torquay, Eng., 1874); John Mitchel's *The Crusade of the Period and Last Conquest of Ireland (perhaps), Irish-American Library*, IV (New York, 1872); and the anonymous *"Thumping English Lies": Froude's Slanders on Ireland and Irishmen . . .* (New York, 1872).

GLASGOW, MAUDE: *The Scotch-Irish in Northern Ireland and in the American Colonies* (New York, 1936).

HASSENCAMP, ROBERT: *The History of Ireland from the Reformation to the Union* (E. A. Robinson, trans. & ed., London, 1888).

INGRAM, THOMAS DUNBAR: *A Critical Examination of Irish History . . . [to 1800]* (2 vols., London, 1900; reiss., 1904).

JOHNSTON, EDITH MARY: *Great Britain and Ireland, 1760-1800* (Edinburgh, 1963).

KRAUS, MICHAEL: "America and the Irish Revolutionary Movement in the Eighteenth Century," *Era of the American Revolution: Studies Inscribed to Evarts Boutell Greene* (Richard B. Morris, ed., New York, 1937), pp. 332-48.

LECKY, WILLIAM EDWARD HARTPOLE: *A History of Ireland in the Eighteenth Century* (5 vols., London, 1892). This work is quite critical of Froude's *The English in Ireland. . . .*

MARTIN, ROBERT M.: *Ireland before and after the Union with Great Britain* (London, 1843; 3rd edn., w/add., 1848).

MAXWELL, CONSTANTIA: *Country and Town in Ireland under the Georges* (London, 1940; rev. edn., Dundalk, Eire, 1949).

PLOWDEN, FRANCIS PETER: *An Historical Review of the State of Ireland . . . [to] 1801* (2 vols., London, 1803). See also [Richard Musgrave's] *Strictures upon "An Historical Review . . ." by Francis Plowden . . .* (London, 1804) which was published anonymously. Plowden replied with *An Historical Letter from F. Plowden, Esq., to Sir R. Musgrave* (London, 1805).

SMYTH, GEORGE LEWIS: *Ireland: Historical and Statistical* (3 vols., London, 1844-9).

2. Local

BALL, FRANCIS ELRINGTON: *A History of the County of Dublin: The People, Parishes, and Antiquities . . . to the Close of the Eighteenth Century* (6 vols., Dublin, 1902-20).

BENN, GEORGE: *A History of the Town of Belfast . . . to the Close of the Eighteenth Century* (Belfast, 1823; 2 vols., Vol. II ed. by John Carlisle, London, 1877).

CHART, DAVID A.: *The Story of Dublin* (London, 1907).

CORKERY, DANIEL: *The Hidden Ireland: A Study of Gaelic Munster in the Eighteenth Century* (Dublin, 1925; n. edn., 1956).

CRAIG, MAURICE JAMES: *Dublin, 1660-1860* (London, 1952).

FALKINER, C. LITTON: "The Counties of Ireland: An Historical Sketch of Their Origin, Constitution, and Gradual Delimitation," Royal Irish Academy, *Proceedings*, XXIV, Sec. C (1903), 169-94.

GILBERT, JOHN THOMAS: *A History of the City of Dublin* (3 vols., Dublin, 1854-9).

[JOY, HENRY]: *Historical Collections Relative to the Town of Belfast . . . to the Union with Great Britain* (Belfast, 1817).

MAXWELL, CONSTANTIA: *Dublin under the Georges, 1714-1830* (1st edn., London, 1936; 2nd edn., rev., 1956).

STUART, JAMES: *Historical Memoirs of the City of Armagh for a Period of 1373 Years . . .* (Newry, Ireland, 1819; rev. edn., Ambrose Coleman, ed., Dublin, 1890). The Coleman edition is virtually a new work.

3. Political

BALL, F. ELRINGTON: *The Judges of Ireland, 1221-1921* (2 vols., London, 1926; New York, 1927); contains biographical information and observations on the organization of the judiciary, as well as succession lists.

BALL, JOHN THOMAS: *Historical Review of the Legislative Systems Operative in Ireland . . . [1172-1800]* (London & New York, 1889).

BECKETT, J. C.: "Anglo-Irish Constitutional Relations in the Later Eighteenth Century," *Irish Historical Studies*, XIV (1964), 20-38.

BURNS, R. E.: "Ireland and British Military Preparations for War in America in 1775," *Cithara*, II (1963), 42-61.

DADSON, ARTHUR J.: *A Short Sketch of English Misrule in Ireland, 1171-1887* (London, 1887).

FLOOD, WARDEN HATTON: *Historical Review of the Irish Parliaments from the Epoch of Henry II to the Union . . .* (2 pts., London, 1863).

KIERNAN, THOMAS JOSEPH: *History of the Financial Administration of Ireland to 1817*, London School of Economics and Political Science, *Monographs*, No. 15 (London, 1930).

MC CRACKEN, J. L.: "The Conflict between the Irish Administration and Parliament, 1753-6," *Irish Historical Studies*, III (1942-3), 159-79, and "Irish Parliamentary Elections, 1727-68," *ibid.*, V (1947), 209-30. See also McCracken's article: "The Irish Viceroyalty, 1760-1773," *Essays in British and Irish History in Honour of James Eadis*

Todd (H. A. Cronne, T. W. Moody, and D. B. Quinn, eds., London, 1949), pp. 152-68.

MAC NEIL, JOHN GORDON SWIFT: *The Constitutional and Parliamentary History of Ireland till the Union* (Dublin & London, 1917).

NICHOLLS, GEORGE: *A History of the Irish Poor Law in Connexion with the Condition of the People* (2 vols., London, 1854; n. edn., rev. & enl., 3 vols., 1898-9).

O'FLANAGAN, JAMES R.: *Annals, Anecdotes, Traits, and Traditions of the Irish Parliaments, 1172 to 1800* (Dublin [1893]).

O'MAHONY, CHARLES: *The Viceroys of Ireland: The Story of the Long Line of Noblemen and Their Wives who Have Ruled Ireland and Irish Society . . .* (London, 1912).

PARNELL, HENRY BROOKE: *A History of the Penal Laws against the Irish Catholics from the Treaty of Limerick to the Union* (4th edn., London, 1825).

SMYTH, CONSTANTINE JOSEPH: *Chronicle of the Law Officers of Ireland: Containing Lists of the Lord Chancellors and Keepers of the Great Seal, Masters of the Rolls . . .* (Dublin & London, 1839).

WAKEFIELD, EDWARD: *An Account of Ireland: Statistical and Political* (2 vols., London, 1812).

WALL, MAUREEN: *The Penal Laws, 1691-1760: Church and State from the Treaty of Limerick to the Accession of George III, Irish History Series,* I (Dundalk, Eire, 1961).

4. Economic

ALGER, J. G.: "An Irish Absentee and His Tenants, 1786-92," *English Historical Review,* X (1895), 663-74. Discusses the estate of Francis Thomas Fitzmaurice, 3rd Earl of Kerry.

BIGGER, FRANCIS JOSEPH: *The Ulster Land War in 1770: The Hearts of Steel* (Dublin, 1910).

CHART, DAVID ALFRED: *An Economic History of Ireland* (Dublin, 1920).

CULLEN, L. M.: "Problems in the Interpretation and Revisions of Eighteenth-Century Irish Economic History," Royal Historical Society, *Transactions,* 5th ser., XVII (1967), 1-22.

————: "The Value of Contemporary Printed Sources for Irish Economic History in the Eighteenth Century," *Irish Historical Studies,* XIV (1964), 142-55; deals primarily with the early eighteenth century.

GILL, CONRAD: *The Rise of the Irish Linen Industry* (Oxford, Eng., 1925).

HUGHES, EDWARD: See under II: C:4.

JAMES, FRANCIS G.: "Irish Colonial Trade in the Eighteenth Century," *William and Mary Quarterly,* 3rd ser., XX (1963), 574-85. See also his "Irish Smuggling in the Eighteenth Century," *Irish Historical Studies,* XII (1961), 299-317.

JOHNSTON, J.: "Commercial Restriction and Monetary Deflation in Eighteenth Century Ireland," *Hermathena*, LIII (1939), 79-87.

LARGE, DAVID: "The Wealth of Greater Irish Landowners, 1750-1815," *Irish Historical Studies*, XV (1966), 21-47.

LYNCH, PATRICK, and JOHN VAIZEY: *Guinness's Brewery in the Irish Economy, 1759-1876* (Cambridge, Eng., 1960).

MURRAY, ALICE EFFIE: See under II: C:4.

O'BRIEN, GEORGE: *The Economic History of Ireland in the Eighteenth Century* (Dublin & London, 1918).

O'DONOVAN, JOHN: *The Economic History of Livestock in Ireland* (Cork & Dublin, 1940).

O'SULLIVAN, WILLIAM: *The Economic History of Cork City from the Earliest Times to the Act of Union* (Dublin & Cork, 1937).

WEBB, JOHN JOSEPH: *Industrial Dublin since 1698 [and] The Silk Industry in Dublin: Two Essays* (Dublin, 1913).

5. *Social*

BARKLEY, JOHN M.: *A Short History of the Presbyterian Church in Ireland* . . . (Belfast, 1959).

BECKETT, JAMES C.: *Protestant Dissent in Ireland, 1687-1780, Studies in Irish History*, II (London, 1948).

BRENAN, M. J.: *An Ecclesiastical History of Ireland . . . to the Year 1829* (2 vols., Dublin, 1840; new edn., rev., 1864).

BURKE, WILLIAM P.: *The Irish Priests in the Penal Times, 1660-1760 . . .* (Waterford, Ireland, 1914).

CALKIN, HOMER L.: "American Influence in Ireland, 1760 to 1800," *Pennsylvania Magazine of History and Biography*, LXXI (1947), 103-20. This article dealing primarily with the post-1776 period contains a discussion of the effect of the American Revolution on Ireland.

CONNELL, KENNETH H.: *The Population of Ireland, 1750-1845* (Oxford, Eng., 1950). See also his article "Some Unsettled Problems in English and Irish Population History, 1750-1845," *Irish Historical Studies*, VII (1950-1), 225-34.

DOWLING, P. J.: "Illegal Education [in the Eighteenth Century]: A Study in Irish History," *Dublin Review*, CLXXXIV (1929), 206-17. A study of Catholic education.

HANNA, CHARLES A.: *The Scotch-Irish or the Scot in North Briton, North Ireland, and North America* (London & New York, 1902).

KILLEN, WILLIAM DOOL: *The Ecclesiastical History of Ireland . . .* (2 vols., London, 1875).

LATIMER, WILLIAM THOMAS: *A History of Irish Presbyterians* (Belfast [1893]; 2nd edn., 1902).

LEYBURN, JAMES: *The Scotch-Irish: A Social History* (Chapel Hill, N. C., 1962).

MCDOWELL, ROBERT BRENDAN: *Irish Public Opinion, 1750-1800* (London, 1944).

MAC NEILL, JOHN GORDON SWIFT: *Titled Corruption: The Sordid Origin of Some Irish Peerages* (London, 1894).

MANT, RICHARD: *History of the Church of Ireland from the Reformation . . . [to 1801]* (2 vols., London, 1840).

MORAN, PATRICK FRANCIS: *The Catholics of Ireland under the Penal Laws in the Eighteenth Century* (London, 1899).

MUNTER, ROBERT L.: *The History of the Irish Newspaper, 1685-1760* (London & New York, 1966).

PHILLIPS, WALTER ALISON, ed.: *History of the Church of Ireland from the Earliest Times to the Present Day* (3 vols., London, 1933-4).

POLLARD, HUGH B. C.: *The Secret Societies of Ireland: Their Rise and Progress* (London, 1922).

REID, JAMES SEATON: *History of the Presbyterian Church in Ireland: Comprising the Civil History of the Province of Ulster . . .* (3 vols., Edinburgh, 1834-53; n. edn., W. D. Killen, ed., Belfast, 1867).

STRAIN, ROBERT WILLIAM MAGILL: *Belfast and Its Charitable Society: A Story of Urban Social Development* (London & New York, 1961). Relevant material in most chapters.

WALL, MAUREEN: "The Rise of a Catholic Middle Class in Eighteenth-Century Ireland," *Irish Historical Studies*, XI (1958), 91-115. A reassessment of the part played by Roman Catholics in commercial life.

WITHEROW, THOMAS: *Historical and Literary Memorials of Presbyterianism in Ireland* (2 vols., Belfast & London, 1879-80), Vol. II: 1731-1800.

6. Biographical

ALLEN, THOMAS. "The Career and Correspondence of Thomas Allen, c. 1725-1798" by Edith M. Johnston, *Irish Historical Studies*, X (1957), 298-324.

BURKE, EDMUND. *Edmund Burke and Ireland* by Thomas H. D. Mahoney (Cambridge, Mass., 1960).

CHARLEMONT, JAMES CAULFIELD, 1ST EARL OF. *The Volunteer Earl: Being the Life and Times of James Caulfield, First Earl of Charlemont* by Maurice James Craig (London, 1948).

CRONE, JOHN S.: *A Concise Dictionary of Irish Biography* (Dublin, 1928; rev. edn., 1937). The *Dictionary of National Biography* also contains biographical sketches of prominent Irishmen.

FLOOD, HENRY. "Henry Flood" by William E. H. Lecky in *Leaders of Public Opinion in Ireland* (2 vols., new edn., London & New York, 1912), I: 35-93.

GRATTAN, HENRY. *Henry Grattan and His Times* by Stephen L. Gwynn (London, 1939), *Henry Grattan: A Historical Study* by John G.

MacCarthy (3rd. edn., Dublin, 1886), and "Henry Grattan" by William E. H. Lecky in *Leaders of Public Opinion in Ireland* (2 vols., new edn., London & New York, 1912), I: 94-321.

KEOGH, JOHN. *John Keogh: The Pioneer of Catholic Emancipation* by Denis Rolleston Gwynn (Dublin & Cork, 1930).

D. MAPS

LEWIS, SAMUEL: *Lewis's Atlas Comprising the Counties of Ireland and a General Map of the Kingdom* (London, 1837).

————: *Topographical Dictionary of Ireland . . . with Engravings . . .* (2 vols., London, 1837).

ROCQUE, JOHN: *A Map of the Kingdom of Ireland Divided into Provinces, Counties, and Baronies . . . .* In Kitchin: *A General Atlas . . .* , Nos. 10-11.

SCALE, BERNARD: *An Hibernian Atlas: Or General Description of the Kingdom of Ireland, Divided into Provinces with Its Sub-Divisions of Counties, Baronies, Etc. . . .* (London, 1776; another edn., 1809). The 1776 edition contained 41 maps, the 1809 edition, 37 maps. For further aids on the cartography of Ireland, see T. Chubb: *The Printed Maps in the Atlases of Great Britain and Ireland: A Bibliography, 1579-1870* (London, 1927), and R. V. Tooley: *Maps and Map-Makers* (London, 1949; rev. edn., 1952, 1962).

CHAPTER IV

The British
North American Colonies

Part I: General

A. BIBLIOGRAPHICAL AIDS

ADAMS, THOMAS R., ed.: *American Independence: The Growth of an Idea. A Bibliographic Study of the American Political Pamphlets Printed between 1764 and 1776 Dealing with the Dispute between Great Britain and Her Colonies* (Providence, R. I., 1965). This is an exceedingly important and useful work for the study of contemporary literature. The author is presently working on a companion volume of British political pamphlets.

ALBION, ROBERT GREENHALGH: *Naval and Maritime History: An Annotated Bibliography* (3rd edn., rev. & exp., Mystic, Conn., 1963).

AMERICAN HISTORICAL ASSOCIATION: *A Guide to Historical Literature* (New York, 1931; n. edn., 1961).

BEALER, ROY P., DONALD H. MUGRIDGE, and BLANCHE P. MC CRUM, comps.: *A Guide to the Study of the United States of America: Representative Books Reflecting the Development of American Life and Thought* (Washington, D. C., 1960).

BEERS, HENRY PUTNEY: *Bibliographies in American History: Guide to Materials for Research* (rev. edn., New York, 1942).

BOLANDER, LOUIS H., comp.: *Bibliography of Naval Literature in the United States Naval Academy Library* ([Annapolis, Md.], 1929).

BROWN, C. R., P. A. MAXWELL, and L. F. MAXWELL, comps.: *A Legal Bibliography of the British Commonwealth of Nations, Vol. III: Canadian and British-American Colonial Law from the Earliest Times to December 1956* (London & Toronto, 1957).

BURCHFIELD, LAVERNE, ed.: *Students' Guide to Materials in Political Science* (New York, c. 1935).

CHANNING, EDWARD, ALBERT BUSHNELL HART, and FREDERICK JACKSON TURNER, eds.: *Guide to the Study and Reading of American History* (rev. edn., London & Boston, 1912). The original edition was edited by Channing and Hart under the title *Guide to the Study of American History* (1896).

CLARK, THOMAS D.: *Travels in the Old South: A Bibliography, American Exploration and Travel Series,* No. 19 (2 vols., Norman, Okla., 1956).

The Colonial Scene, 1602-1800 . . . (intro. by Edmund S. Morgan, Worcester, Mass., 1950). Reprinted from the American Antiquarian Society, *Proceedings,* LX (1950), 53-160. This listing is based on a catalogue of books exhibited by the John Carter Brown Library in 1949 and supplemented with titles from the library of the American Antiquarian Society.

COULTER, E. MARGARET, and MELANIE GERSTENFELD, eds.: *Historical Bibliographies: A Systematic and Annotated Guide* (Berkeley, Calif., 1935).

EDWARDS, EVERETT E.: *A List of American Economic Histories,* U. S. Dept. of Agriculture: Library, *Bibliographical Contributions,* No. 27 (Washington, D. C., 1935; 2nd edn., 1939).

——: *References on American Colonial Agriculture,* U. S. Dept. of Agriculture: Library, *Bibliographical Contributions,* No. 33 (Washington, D. C., 1938).

——: *References on Economic History as a Field of Research and Study,* U. S. Dept. of Agriculture: Library, *Bibliographical Contributions,* No 31 (Washington, D. C., 1936).

EVANS, CHARLES, ed.: *American Bibliography: A Chronological Dictionary of all Books, Pamphlets, and Periodical Publications Printed in the United States of America . . . [1639-1820]* (12 vols., Chicago, 1903-1934; rep., 14 vols., New York, 1941-59). This is one of the two major reference works for contemporary literature and is most useful when used in connection with the microprint publications series, *Early American Imprints, 1639-1800,* carried out under the direction of Clifford K. Shipton at the American Antiquarian Society, Worcester, Mass. The Evans numbers are retained, but where necessary, corrections are made and additions introduced. See also the mimeographed *American Imprints before 1801 in the Libraries of Williams College not in Evans* (Williamstown, Mass., 1957).

FORBES, HARRIETTE M., comp.: *New England Diaries, 1602-1800: A Descriptive Catalogue of Diaries, Orderly Books, and Sea Journals* ([Topsfield, Mass.], 1923).

FORD, PAUL LEICESTER: *Some Materials for a Bibliography of the Official Publications of the Continental Congress* (Boston, 1890). This was first published in the Boston Public Library, *Bulletin,* for 1888.

GRIFFIN, APPLETON P. C.: *Bibliography of the Historical Publications Issued by the New England States* (Cambridge, Mass., 1895). This was reprinted from the Colonial Society of Massachusetts, *Publications, III.*

GRIFFIN, GRACE GARDNER, *et al.*: *Writings in American History* (45 vols. + index, Washington, D. C., 1904-64). This is undoubtedly the most useful and complete compilation of materials, listing virtually all items that were printed between 1906 and 1940 and then, after a lapse of seven years, from 1948 through 1957. A recent addition is the index which covers the years 1902 through 1940. The two volumes for 1902 and 1903 were issued prior to the beginning of the annual publications with the volume for 1906.

HANDLIN, OSCAR, *et al.*: *Harvard Guide to American History* (Cambridge, Mass., 1954). Parts nine and ten of section III are most relevant for the period 1748-1776, although other sections must also be consulted for additional material. The *Harvard Guide* is probably the most prominent of the guides now in use, concerned with the British American colonies although much pertinent material has appeared since 1954.

HARPER, LAWRENCE A.: "Recent Contributions to Economic History: American History to 1789," *Journal of Economic History*, XIX (1959), 1-24.

———, *et al.*: "Colonial Statistics," *Historical Statistics of the United States: Colonial Times to 1957* (Washington, D. C., 1960), 743-74.

HASSE, ADELAIDE R.: "Materials for a Bibliography of the Public Archives of the Thirteen Original States Covering the Colonial Period and the State Period to 1789," American Historical Association, *Annual Report, 1906* (2 vols., Washington, D. C., 1908), II: 239-572.

HOWES, WRIGHT, comp.: *U. S.-iana (1700-1950): A Descriptive Check-List of 11,450 Printed Sources Relating to Those Parts of Continental North America now Comprising the United States* (New York, 1954).

INSTITUTE OF EARLY AMERICAN HISTORY AND CULTURE: *Readable Books about Early American History: A Selective Reading List* (Williamsburg, Va., 1960).

JAMESON, J. FRANKLIN: "Guide to the Items Relating to American History in the Reports of the English Historical Manuscripts Commission and Their Appendixes," American Historical Association, *Annual Report, 1898* (Washington, D. C., 1899), pp. 611-700.

JEFFREY, WILLIAM, JR.: "Early New England Court Records [1620-1800]: A Bibliography of Published Materials," Boston Public Library, *Quarterly*, VI (1954), 160-84.

JENKINS, WILLIAM SUMNER: *A Guide to the Microfilm Collection of Early State Records* (Washington, D. C., 1950).

KUEHL, WARREN F.: *Dissertations in History: An Index to Dissertations Completed in History Departments of United States and Canadian Universities, 1873-1960* ([Lexington, Ky.], 1965).

LAPHAM, RUTH, ed.: *Check List of American Revolutionary War Pamphlets in the Newberry Library* (Chicago, 1922).

LARNED, JOSEPHUS N., ed.: *The Literature of American History: A Bibliographic Guide in which the Scope, Character, and Comparative Worth of Books in Selected Lists Are Set Forth in Brief Notes by Critics of Authority* (Boston, 1902). Charles M. Andrews was one of the contributors.

LARSON, HENRIETTA MELIA, ed.: *Guide to Business History: Materials for the Study of American Business History and Suggestions for Their Use, Harvard Studies in Business History*, XII (Cambridge, Mass., 1948).

List of Doctoral Dissertations in History in Progress or Completed at Universities in the U.S. since 1955 (4th edn., Washington, D.C., 1964).

MAC DONALD, GRACE E., comp.: *Check-List of Statutes of States of the United States of America: Including Revisions, Compilations, Digests, Codes, and Indexes* (Providence, R.I., 1937).

———, ed.: *Check List of Session Laws* (New York, 1936; supplement by F. H. Pollock, Boston, 1941).

MATTHEWS, WILLIAM, and ROY HARVEY PEARCE, comps.: *American Diaries: An Annotated Bibliography of American Diaries Written Prior to the Year 1861*, University of California, *Publications in English*, XVI (Berkeley, Calif., & Los Angles, 1945).

MEYNEN, EMIL: *Bibliographie des deutschtums der kolonialzeitlichen einwanderung in Nordamerika, insbesondere der Pennsylvanien-Deutschen und ihrer nachkommen, 1683-1933*, or in English: *Bibliography on German Settlements in Colonial North America: Especially on the Pennsylvania Germans and Their Descendants, 1683-1933* (Leipzig, 1937).

MYERS, DENYS PETER: *Manual of Collections of Treaties and of Collections Relating to Treaties, Harvard Bibliographies, Library Series*, II (Cambridge, Mass., & London, 1922).

NELSON, WILLIAM: *The Controversy Over the Proposition for an American Episcopate, 1767-1774: A Bibliography of the Subject* (Paterson, N.J., 1909). This listing covers only those works of American origin.

O'NEILL, EDWARD H., ed.: *Biography by Americans, 1658-1936: A Subject Bibliography* (Philadelphia, 1939).

PARGELLIS, STANLEY, and D. J. MEDLEY: *Bibliography of British History: The Eighteenth Century, 1714-1789* . . . (Oxford, Eng., 1951), Section XV, pp. 452-94.

POWELL, JOHN HARVEY: *The Books of a New Nation: United States Government Publications, 1774-1814* (Philadelphia [1952]).

PRAGER, HERTA, and WILLIAM W. PRICE: "A Bibliography on the History of the Courts of the Thirteen Original States, [and] Maine, Ohio, and Vermont," *American Journal of Legal History*, I (1957), 336-362; II (1958), 35-52, 148-54.

RAGATZ, LOWELL JOSEPH: *Colonial Studies in the United States during the Twentieth Century* (London, 1932; Washington, D.C., 1934).

SABIN, JOSEPH, ed.: *Bibliotheca Americana: A Dictionary of Books Relating to America from Its Discovery* . . . (29 vols., New York, 1868-1936). Sabin's work was taken up upon his death by Wilberforce Eames and brought to completion by Robert W. G. Vail. The Sabin bibliography remains today one of the two major reference works for contemporary literature, encompassing most titles relevant to American history published before 1860.

STILLWELL, MARGARET BINGHAM: *Incunabula and Americana, 1450-1800: A Key to Bibliographical Study* (New York, 1931). A comprehensive listing of bibliographies of Americana.

THOMPSON, EDGAR T., comp.: *The Plantation: A Bibliography, Social Science Monographs*, IV (Washington, D.C., 1957).

VAIL, ROBERT W. G.: "A Check List of New England Election Sermons," American Antiquarian Society, *Proceedings*, n. ser., XLV (1935), 233-66.

——: *The Voice of the Old Frontier* (Philadelphia, 1949). This is an exceedingly important bibliographical guide to frontier history.

WINSOR, JUSTIN, ed.: *The Narrative and Critical History of America* (8 vols., Boston & New York, 1884-9). The chief importance of this series lies in its extensive bibliographical comments. See especially Winsor's article: "Authorities on the French and Indian Wars of New England and Acadia, 1688-1763," V: 420-71.

——: *The Reader's Handbook to the American Revolution, 1761-1783* (Boston, 1880). Gives comments and views on selected source and secondary materials.

WINTERICH, JOHN T.: *Early American Books & Printing* (Boston & New York, 1935). This is primarily a bibliographic discussion of printting in early America, giving a brief view of the books printed; it can be useful as a partial guide to sources.

WORK, MONROE N., ed.: *Bibliography of the Negro in Africa and America* (New York, 1928).

There are a number of worth-while bibliographies contained in secondary works. A dated but nevertheless excellent bibliography edited by Lillian M. Penson is to be found in *The Cambridge History of the British Empire, Vol. I: The Old Empire* . . . (Cambridge, Eng., & New York, 1929), pp. 823-88, while a very good and much more recent bibliography may be found in Merrill Jensen's *English Historical Documents, Vol. IX: American Colonial Documents to 1776* (New York, 1955), which includes a "Select Bibliography" as well as individual bibliographical sections preceding each of the major portions of the book. Many of the secondary works published in the past few years also contain valuable bibliographies. See, for instance, Dickerson's *Navigation Acts* . . . , Knollenberg's

Origin of the American Revolution . . . , Sosin's *Whitehall and the Wilderness* . . . , and Donoughue's *British Politics and the American Revolution.* Two reference items of use to students are Arthur H. Cole's *Wholesale Commodity Prices in the United States, 1700-1861* (Cambridge, Mass., 1938) and the work of Evarts B. Greene and Virginia D. Harrington: *American Population before the Federal Census of 1790* (New York, 1932).

B. PRINTED SOURCE MATERIALS

1. Government and related documents

BOYD, JULIAN P.: *The Declaration of Independence: The Evolution of the Text as Shown in Facsimiles of Various Drafts by Its Author, Thomas Jefferson* (Washington, D.C., 1943; Princeton, N.J., 1945). See in conjunction, Boyd's "New Light on Jefferson and His Great Task," *New York Times Magazine*, 13 April, 1947, pp. 17, 64-70.

BURNETT, EDMUND C., ed.: *Letters of Members of the Continental Congress* (8 vols., Washington, D.C., 1921-36).

CLARK, WILLIAM BELL, ed.: *Naval Documents of the American Revolution* . . . (2 vols.+, Washington, D.C., 1964-6+).

CONTINENTAL CONGRESS: *Journals of the Continental Congress, 1774-1789* (Worthington C. Ford, ed., 34 vols., Washington, D.C., 1904-37). Volumes I thru VI cover the period to December 31, 1776. The *Journals* were also published in 13 vols., at Philadelphia from 1777 to 1801, of which the first two volumes are germane to this period. There are also available the various published *Journals of the Proceedings* and *Extracts from the Votes and Proceedings* of individual sessions of the Congress; most of this material is easily obtained on the Readex microprint cards. Also available are numerous published petitions, resolves and notices of the Congress, again most of them available on Readex cards. A few of the more significant of these items include *The Address of the Twelve United Colonies, by Their Delegates in Congress, to the Inhabitants of Great-Britain . . . [and] Ireland . . .* (New York, 1775) and the *Articles of Confederation and Perpetual Union between the Colonies . . .* ([Philadelphia, 1776]). The latter was a printing of the first draft of the Articles as presented to Congress on July 12, 1776; the second draft was likewise published. A printing of the first copy of the association is available as *The Association, &c.: We His Majesty's Most Loyal Subjects, the Delegates of the Several Colonies . . .* ([Philadelphia, 1774]). For the declaration of the Congress, see *A Declaration by the Representatives of the*

United Colonies of North-America, . . . Seting [sic] forth the Causes and Necessity of Their Taking up Arms (Philadelphia, 1775). There were numerous reprints of this publication, some of them as broadsides. For more information, see J. P. Boyd's article, "The Disputed Authorship of the Declaration on the Causes and Necessity of Taking up Arms, 1775," *Pennsylvania Magazine of History and Biography,* LXXIV (1950), 51-73. Other materials include *A Letter to the Inhabitants of the Province of Quebec* . . . (Philadelphia, 1774), which was bound with the *Extracts* . . . and was published separately in French, and *The Petition of the Grand American Continental Congress to the King's Most Excellent Majesty* (Boston [1774]). For additional information on this petition, see Edwin Wolf, II: "The Authorship of the 1774 Address to the King Restudied," *William and Mary Quarterly,* 3rd ser., XXII (1965), 189-224, which prints three mss. drafts of the address. Also separately published were *The Petition of the American Continental Congress to the King; Worthy the Perusal of His Majesty and Every Subject in His Dominions* (Boston, 1775); *To the People of Great-Britain from the Delegates Appointed by the Several English Colonies* . . . ([Philadelphia, 1774]; London, 1775); and *The Twelve United Colonies, by Their Delegates in Congress, to the Inhabitants of Great-Britain: Friends, Countrymen, and Brethren* . . . (New York & Philadelphia [1775]). Finally, see the reprinted materials "Draft of an Address of the Continental Congress to the People of the United States, 1776," Herbert Friedenwald, ed., *American Historical Review,* I (1895-6), 684-96, and the writings of Silas Deane which deal primarily with the Congress: *The Deane Papers, 1774-1790,* New York Historical Society, *Collections,* XIX-XXIII (5 vols., New York, 1887-90), I: 1774-1777 and "Silas Deane Reports on the Continental Congress: A Diary Fragment, October 1-6, 1774," Christopher Collier, ed., Connecticut Historical Society, *Bulletin,* XXIX (1964), 1-8, which is an account of debates in Congress.

FINLAY, HUGH: *Journal Kept by Hugh Finlay, Surveyor of the Post Roads of North America* . . . *[1773-4]* (Frank H. Norton, ed., Brooklyn, N.Y., 1867).

FORBES, JOHN: *The Writings of General John Forbes Relating to His Service in North America* (Alfred Procter James, ed., Menasha, Wis., 1938).

FORCE, PETER, comp.: *American Archives: Consisting of a Collection of Authentick Records, State Papers, Debates, and Letters and Other Notices of Publick Affairs* . . . (9 vols., Washington, D.C., 1837-53). This collection was to have run to 6 series covering the period 1493 to 1789, but only 6 volumes of the fourth series, covering the period of March 1774 thru 4 July 1776, and 3 volumes of the fifth series, covering the period 4 July 1776 thru 31 December 1776, were published. The fourth series is at this writing "the most complete set of printed source material available" (Pargellis).

GAGE, THOMAS: *The Correspondence of General Thomas Gage with the Secretaries of State and with the War Office and the Treasury, 1763-1775, Yale Historical Publications: Manuscripts and Edited Texts,* XI-XII (Clarence E. Carter, ed., 2 vols., New Haven, Conn., 1931-3).

HALDIMAND, FREDERICK: "The Haldimand Papers: Copies of Papers on File in the Dominion Archives at Ottawa, Canada," Michigan Pioneer and Historical Society, *Collections,* IX (1886)-X (1887), *passim.*

HAZARD, EBENEZER, comp.: *Historical Collections Consisting of State Papers, and Other Authentic Documents: Intended as Materials for an History of the United States of America* (2 vols., Philadelphia, 1792-4).

JENSEN, MERRILL, ed.: *English Historical Documents, Vol. IX: American Colonial Documents to 1776* (New York, 1955).

JOHNSON, WILLIAM: *Letter dated: Camp at Lake George, Sept. 9, 1755, To the Governours of the Several Colonies Who Raised the Troops on the Present Expedition; Giving an Account of the Action of the Preceding Day* (n.p., 1755). For *The Sir William Johnson Papers* see Chapter V, "Indian Relations."

KEMBLE, STEPHEN: *The Kemble Papers,* New York Historical Society, *Collections,* XVI-XVII (2 vols., New York, 1883-4), I: 1773-1779. Vol. I contains Col. Kemble's Journal (1773-79) and the Order Books of General Howe (1775-78) and General Clinton (1778), giving an official account of the activities of the British army in America from 1773 to 1778.

KIMBALL, GERTRUDE SELWYN, ed.: *Correspondence of William Pitt, When Secretary of State, With Colonial Governors and Naval Commissioners in America* (2 vols., London & New York, 1966).

KNOX, JOHN: *An Historical Journal of the Campaigns in North America for the Years 1757, 1758, 1759 and 1760* (A. G. Doughty, ed., 2 vols., Toronto, 1814-16).

MAC DONALD, WILLIAM, ed.: *Select Charters and Other Documents Illustrative of American History, 1606-1775* (London & New York, 1906).

MANTE, THOMAS: *The History of the Late War in North-America and the West Indies, Including the Campaigns of MDCCLXIII and MDCCLXIV Against His Majesty's Indian Enemies* (London, 1772). A contemporary account of great value.

PARGELLIS, STANLEY, ed.: *Military Affairs in North America, 1748-1765:*

Selected Documents from the Cumberland Papers in Windsor Castle (London & New York, 1936).

SHULDHAM, MOLYNEUX: *The Despatches of Molyneux Shuldham . . . January-July, 1776*, Robert W. Neeser, ed., Naval History Society, III (New York, 1913).

STAMP ACT CONGRESS: *Proceedings of the Congress at New York* (Annapolis, Md., 1766). This was reprinted in London the next year as *Authentic Account of the Proceedings* . . . See also "Journal of the Stamp Act Congress Held at New-York, 1765," *Niles Weekly Register*, II (1812), 337-42, and *Journal of the First Congress of the American Colonies* . . . (Lewis Cruger, ed., New York, 1845).

STONE, FREDERICK D., comp.: "Plans for the Union of the British Colonies of North America, 1643-1776," *History of the Celebration of the One Hundredth Anniversary of the Promulgation of the Constitution of the United States* (Hampton L. Carson, ed., 2 vols., Philadelphia, 1889), II: 439-503.

TANSILL, CHARLES C., ed.: *Documents Illustrative of the Formation of the Union of the American States*, House Document, No. 398 (Washington, D.C., 1927).

THORPE, FRANCIS NEWTON, ed.: *The Federal and State Constitutions, Colonial Charters, and Other Organic Laws of the States, Territories, and Colonies now or heretofore Forming the United States of America* (7 vols., Washington, D.C., 1909).

2. Non-official contemporary writings relating to more than one colony

ADAMS, AMOS: *A Concise, Historical View of the Perils, Hardships, Difficulties, and Discouragements which Attended the Planting and Progressive Improvements of New-England . . . in Two Discourses . . .* (Boston, 1769; London, 1770).

ALMON, JOHN, comp.: *A Collection of Tracts on the Subjects of Taxing the British Colonies in America and Regulating Their Trade* (4 vols., London, 1773). A collection of 19 pamphlets printed between 1765 and 1770.

American Husbandry Containing an Account of the Soil, Climate, Production and Agriculture of the British Colonies in North America and the West Indies . . . By an American (2 vols., London, 1775; Harry J. Carman, ed., New York, 1939). This work has been attributed to John Mitchell as well as to a number of other writers, such as Arthur Young.

AMHERST, JEFFERY AMHERST, LORD: *The Journal of Jeffery Amherst, Recording the Military Career of General Amherst in America from*

1758 to 1763 (John Clarence Webster, ed., Chicago & Toronto, c. 1931).

ANDREWS, CHARLES MC LEAN, ed.: " 'State of Trade,' 1763," Colonial Society of Massachusetts, *Publications*, XIX (*Transactions, 1916-1917*), 379-90.

APTHEKER, HERBERT, ed.: *A Documentary History of the Negro People in the United States [1661-1910]* (New York, 1951).

ARMSTRONG, MAURICE W., LEFFERTS A. LOETSCHER, and CHARLES A. ANDERSON, eds.: *The Presbyterian Enterprise: Sources of American Presbyterian History* (Philadelphia, 1956). Pages 11-95 contain relevant source materials with good introductions.

BACKUS, ISAAC: *A History of New-England: With Particular Reference to the Denomination of Christians Called Baptists* . . . (3 vols., Boston & Providence, R.I., 1777-96).

BAILYN, BERNARD, and JANE N. GARRETT, eds.: *Pamphlets of the American Revolution, 1750-1776* (1 vol.+, Cambridge, Mass., 1965+). When completed, this work will reprint 72 of the most important contemporary pamphlets of the period.

BARTRAM, JOHN: *Observations on the Inhabitants . . . and Other Matters Worthy of Notice: Made by Mr. John Bartram in His Travels from Pennsilvania to Onondago, Oswego and Lake Ontario in Canada* . . . (London, 1751; rep., London, 1951).

BARTRAM, WILLIAM: *Travels through North and South Carolina, Georgia, East & West Florida* . . . (Philadelphia, 1791; London, 1792; rep., New York, 1940).

BIRKET, JAMES: *Some Cursory Remarks Made by James Birket in His Voyage to North America, 1750-1751, Yale Historical Publications: Manuscripts and Edited Texts*, IV (New Haven, Conn., 1916).

BOLTON, ETHEL STANWOOD, comp.: *Immigrants to New England, 1700-1775* (Salem, Mass., 1931; rep. from Essex Institute, *Historical Collections*, LXIII-LXVII).

BOLZIUS, JOHANN MARTIN: "Johann Martin Bolzius Answers a Questionnaire on Carolina and Georgia," Klaus G. Loewald, Beverly Starlika, and Paul S. Taylor, trans. and eds., *William and Mary Quarterly*, 3rd ser., XIV (1957), 218-61, and XV (1958), 228-252.

[BURKE, EDMUND and WILLIAM]: *An Account of the European Settlements in America* . . . (1st edn., 2 vols., London, 1757; 6th edn., 1777).

BURNABY, ANDREW: *Travels through the Middle Settlements in North America in the Years 1759 and 1760: With Observations upon the State of the Colonies* (London, 1775; 3rd edn., rev. and enl., 1798; rep., Ithaca, N.Y., 1961).

CALDER, ISABEL M., ed.: *Colonial Captivities, Marches, and Journeys* (New York, 1935).

CALLENDER, GUY STEVENS, ed.: *Selections from the Economic History of the United States, 1765-1860* (Boston [1909]).

CARVER, JONATHAN: *Travels through the Interior Parts of North America in the Years, 1766, 1767, and 1768* . . . (London, 1778). In using Carver the student should realize the extent of his dependence upon other travelers' accounts. See Edward Gaylord Bourne: "The Travels of Jonathan Carver," *American Historical Review*, XI (1906-7), 287-302.

CATESBY, MARK: *The Natural History of Carolina, Florida, and the Bahama Islands* . . . (2 vols., London, 1771; 1st edn., pub., 1731-3).

CHALMERS, GEORGE: *An Introduction to the History of the Revolt of the American Colonies: Being a Comprehensive View of Its Origin* . . . (1 vol. only pub., London, 1782; 2 vols., Boston, 1845).

———: *Political Annals of the Present United Colonies* . . . *to the Peace of 1763* . . . (London, 1780). This was Book I of a projected series, but no more appeared until Book II was published in the New York Historical Society, *Collections*, I (1868), 1-176.

CHAMPION, RICHARD: *The American Correspondence of a Bristol Merchant, 1766-1776: Letters of Richard Champion*, G. H. Guttridge, ed., University of California, *Publications in History*, XXII (1934), 1-72. These letters relate chiefly to American matters.

CLINTON, HENRY: *The American Rebellion: Sir Henry Clinton's Narrative of His Campaigns, 1775-1782* . . . , *Yale Historical Publications: Manuscripts and Edited Texts*, XXI (William B. Willcox, ed., New Haven, Conn., 1954).

[CLUNY (or CLUNIE), ALEXANDER]: *The American Traveller: Or, Observations on the Present State, Culture, and Commerce of the British Colonies in America* . . . (London, 1769; [Philadelphia], 1770).

CRESSWELL, NICHOLAS: *The Journal of Nicholas Cresswell, 1774-1777* (New York, 1924). Cresswell was an Englishman who travelled in Virginia and the Ohio and Illinois countries.

CRÈVECOEUR, J. HECTOR ST. JOHN: *Letters from an American Farmer* . . . *Conveying Some Idea of the Late and Present Interior Circumstances of the British Colonies in North America* . . . (London, 1782). The letters cover the years 1770-1781 and have been frequently reprinted, in full and in part, most recently in New York in 1961.

DEARBORN, HENRY: *Revolutionary War Journals of Henry Dearborn, 1775-1783* (Lloyd A. Brown and Howard H. Peckham, eds., Chicago, 1939). Presenting a generally broad view of the revolution from the American side.

"Diary of a Journey of Moravians from Bethlehem, Pennsylvania, to Bethabara in Wachovia, North Carolina, 1753," *Travels in the American Colonies* (Newton D. Mereness, ed., New York, 1916), pp. 323-56. Nowhere else can be found a better account of the difficulties of travel in the mountainous backcountry of North America in the eighteenth century.

DONNAN, ELIZABETH, ed.: *Documents Illustrative of the History of the Slave Trade to America,* Carnegie Institute of Washington, *Publication,* No. 409 (4 vols., Washington, D.C., 1930-5).

DOW, GEORGE FRANCIS, comp.: *Arts and Crafts in New England, 1704-75: Gleanings from Boston Newspapers . . .* (Topsfield, Mass., 1927).

DRAKE, FRANCIS S., ed.: *Tea Leaves: Being a Collection of Letters and Documents Relating to the Shipment of Tea to the American Colonies in the Year 1773 by the East India Tea Company . . .* (Boston, 1884). A volume of great value containing copies of many documents for the year 1773 that have since disappeared.

EVELYN, W. GLANVILLE: *Memoir and Letters of Captain W. Glanville Evelyn of the 4th Regt. (King's Own) from North America, 1774-1776* (G. D. Scull, ed., Oxford, Eng., 1879).

FORCE, PETER, comp.: *Tracts and Other Papers Relating Principally to the Origin, Settlement, and Progress of the Colonies in North America . . . to the Year 1776* (4 vols., Washington, D.C., 1836-46; rep., 1947).

GALLOWAY, JOSEPH: *Historical and Political Reflections on the Rise and Progress of the American Rebellion . . .* (London, 1780).

GORDON, ADAM, LORD: "A Manuscript by Lord Adam Gordon," Keith W. Murray, ed., *Genealogist,* n. ser., XIV (1897-8), *passim.* Gordon's 'Journal' of his travels in North America and the West Indies during the years 1764-5 is also printed in Newton D. Mereness, *Travels in the American Colonies,* pp. 365-453.

GORDON, WILLIAM: *The History of the Rise, Progress, and Establishment of the Independence of the United States of America . . .* (4 vols., London, 1788). In conjunction with this work, see Orin Grant Libby's "A Critical Examination of Gordon's History of the American Revolution," American Historical Association, *Annual Report, 1899* (2 vols., Washington, D.C., 1900), I: 367-88.

HAMBURGH, ———: "Minutes from the Journal of Mr. Hamburgh's Travels in America and the West Indies, 1764-5," *Travels in the American Colonies* (Newton D. Mereness, ed., New York, 1916), pp. 357-64.

HAMILTON, ALEXANDER: *Gentleman's Progress: The "Itinerarium" of Dr. Alexander Hamilton, 1744* (Carl Bridenbaugh, ed., Chapel Hill, N.C., 1948). The diary of Hamilton's journey from Annapolis into and through New York and Maine.

HART, ALBERT BUSHNELL, ed.: *American History Told by Contemporaries, Vol. II: Building of the Republic, 1689-1783* (London & New York, 1910).

JARVIS, STEPHEN: "An American's Experience in the British Army: Manuscript of Colonel Stephen Jarvis . . . ," *Connecticut Magazine,* XI (1907), 191-215; also in *Journal of American History,* I (1907), 441-64, 727-40.

"Journal of a French Traveler in the Colonies, 1765," *American Historical Review*, XXVI (1920-1), 726-47; XXVII (1921-2), 70-89.

KALM, PETER: *The America of 1750; Peter Kalm's Travels in North America [1748-9]: The English Version of 1770, Revised from the Original Swedish and Edited by Adolph B. Benson . . . with a Translation of New Material from Kalm's Diary Notes* (2 vols., New York, 1937). The edition of 1770-1, published in London and edited by John Reinhold Forster, carried the title, *Travels in North America; Containing Its Natural History, and a Circumstantial Account of its Plantations and Agriculture in General, with the Civil, Ecclesiastical and Commercial State of the Country, the Manners of its Inhabitants, and Several Curious and Important Remarks on Various Subjects.* See also: "Peter Kalm's America: The Benefits which England Could Derive from Her Colonies in North America . . . [1763]," Esther Louise Larson, trans. & ed., *Pennsylvania History,* XXII (1955), 216-28.

KAMINKOW, JACK and MARION: *A List of Emigrants from England to America, 1718-1759* (Baltimore, Md., 1964).

KIRKLAND, FREDERICK RICHARDSON, ed.: *Letters on the American Revolution in the Library at "Karolfred"* (2 vols., Philadelphia, 1941-52). These manuscripts are now in the library of the Historical Society of Pennsylvania.

KNOX, JOHN: *An Historical Journal of the Campaigns in North-America, for the Years 1757, 1758, 1759, and 1760 . . . ,* Champlain Society, *Publications,* VIII-X (Arthur G. Doughty, ed., 3 vols., Toronto, 1914-16). This *Journal* was originally published in two volumes, London, 1769.

KREBS, FRIEDRICH, comp.: *Emigrants from the Palatinate to the American Colonies in the 18th Century* [1732-68], Pennsylvania German Society, *Special Study,* No. 1 (Norristown, Pa., 1953).

LEE, CHARLES: *The Lee Papers, 1754-1811,* New York Historical Society, *Collections,* IV-VII (4 vols., New York, 1872-5), I: 1754-1776. These papers throw light on General Lee, both before and after he came to America.

LIVINGSTON, ROBERT R.: "Robert R. Livingston and the Non-Exportation Policy: Notes for a Speech in the Continental Congress, October 27, 1775," Bernard Mason, ed., New York Historical Society, *Quarterly,* XLIV (1960), 296-307.

M'ROBERT, PATRICK: *A Tour through Part of the North Provinces of America: Being a Series of Letters Wrote on the Spot in the Years 1774 & 1775 . . .* (Edinburgh, 1776). This work, edited by Carl Bridenbaugh, was printed in the *Pennsylvania Magazine of History and Biography,* LIX (1935), 134-80 and later appeared as an offprint as No. 1 in the Historical Society of Pennsylvania, *Pamphlet Series: Narratives and Documents.*

MARCUS, JACOB RADER, ed.: *American Jewry, Documents: Eighteenth Century . . .* , American Jewish Archives, *Publication,* No. 3 (Cincinnati, O., 1959).

MARGRY, PIERRE: *Decouvertes et Établissements des Français dans l'ouest et dans le sud de l'Amérique Septentrionale (1614-1754), Mémoires et Documents originaux recueiles et publies* (6 vols., Paris, 1876-1886).

MERENESS, NEWTON D., ed.: *Travels in the American Colonies* (New York, 1916).

MONTRÉSOR, JOHN: *The Montrésor Journals,* G. D. Scull, ed., New York Historical Society, *Collections,* XIV (New York, 1882). The journals of Montrésor, who was a British army engineer, cover the period 1757 through 1779. A section of his journals not contained in the above work is printed as "Life of John Montrésor," J. Clarence Webster, ed., Royal Society of Canada, *Proceedings,* 3rd ser., XXII (1928), 1-31; this section of the journal covers his expedition of 1763 to relieve Major Gladwin who was beseiged at Fort Detroit by Pontiac and his followers.

MORGAN, EDMUND S., ed.: *Prologue to Revolution: Sources and Documents on the Stamp Act Crisis, 1764-1766* (Chapel Hill, N.C., 1959).

MORISON, SAMUEL E., ed.: *Sources and Documents Illustrating the American Revolution, 1764-1788, and the Formation of the Federal Constitution* (Oxford, Eng., 1923).

MOULTRIE, WILLIAM: *Memoirs of the American Revolution so Far as It Is Related to the States of North and South Carolina and Georgia: Compiled from the Most Authentic Materials . . .* (2 vols., New York, 1802).

MURRAY, JAMES: *An Impartial History of the Present War in America: Containing an Account of Its Rise and Progress, the Political Springs thereof, with Its Various Successes and Disappointments on Both Sides* (3 vols., Newcastle upon Tyne, 1778-80).

————: *Letters from America, 1773 to 1780: Being the Letters of a Scots Officer, Sir James Murray, to His Home during the War of American Independence* (Eric Robson, ed. [Manchester, Eng.], 1951).

NILES, HEZEKIAH, ed.: *Principles and Acts of the Revolution in America* . . . (Baltimore, Md., 1822; rev. by Alden T. Vaughan under the title *Chronicles of the American Revolution,* 1st edn., New York, 1965).

OLIVER, PETER: *Peter Oliver's Origin & Progress of the American Rebellion: A Tory View* (Douglass Adair and John A. Schutz, eds., San Marino, Calif., 1961).

PEMBERTON, THOMAS: *An Historical Journal of the American War, 1765-1784* (Boston, 1793). Extracted from the Massachusetts Historical Society, *Collections,* II (1st edn., Boston, 1793).

PERRY, WILLIAM S., ed.: *Historical Collections Relating to the American*

Colonial Church (5 vols., Hartford, Conn., 1870-8). The individual volumes deal with a specific colony in the following order: Virginia, Pennsylvania, Massachusetts, Maryland, Delaware.

PHILLIPS, ULRICH B., ed.: *Plantation and Frontier Documents, 1649-1863, Illustrative of Industrial History in the Colonial and Ante-Bellum South* . . . (2 vols., Cleveland, O., 1909); separate publication of Volumes I and II of *Documentary History of American Industrial Society,* edited by John R. Commons, *et al.*

POUCHOT, PIERRE: *Memoir upon the Late War in North America between the French and the English, 1755-60* . . . (Franklin B. Hough, trans. & ed., 2 vols., Roxbury, Mass., 1866).

POWNALL, THOMAS: *Considerations Towards a General Plan of Measures for the English Provinces Laid Before the Board of Commissioners at Albany* . . . (New York, 1756; rep., Edinburgh).

———: *A Topographical Description of Such Parts of North America as are Contained in the (Annexed) Map of the Middle Colonies, Etc. in North America* . . . (London, 1776).

RAMSAY, DAVID: *The History of the American Revolution* (Philadelphia, 1789; London, 1791). See in conjunction with this work, Page Smith's "David Ramsay and the Causes of the American Revolution," *William and Mary Quarterly,* 3rd. ser., XVII (1960), 51-77.

———: *History of the United States from their First Settlement as English Colonies in 1607 to the Year 1808* . . . (3 vols., Philadelphia, 1816-17).

ROBERTSON, ARCHIBALD: *Archibald Robertson, Lieutenant-General, Royal Engineers: His Diaries and Sketches in America, 1762-1780* (Harry Miller Lydenberg, ed., New York, 1930).

ROBERTSON, WILLIAM: *The History of America* (2 vols., London, 1777).

ROGERS, ROBERT: *A Concise Account of North America: Containing a Description of the Several British Colonies on that Continent* . . . (London, 1765; rep., New York, 1966). Good contemporary account of the territory added by the Treaty of Paris.

RUSSELL, WILLIAM: *The History of America . . . to the Conclusion of the Late War . . . Containing an Account of the Rise and Progress of the Present Unhappy Contest between Great Britain and Her Colonies* (2 vols., London, 1778).

SARGENT, WINTHROP, ed.: *The Loyalist Poetry of the Revolution* (Philadelphia, 1857).

SCHAW, JANET: *Journal of a Lady of Quality: Being the Narrative of a Journey from Scotland to the West Indies, North Carolina, and Portugal in the Years 1774 to 1776* (Evangeline Walker Andrews, ed., in collaboration with Charles McLean Andrews, New Haven, Conn., 1934).

SMITH, JOHN JAY, and JOHN F. WATSON, eds.: *American Historical and Literary Curiosities: Consisting of Fac-similes of Original Docu-*

ments Relating to the Events of the Revolution . . . (2 vols. in 1, Philadelphia, 1847).

SMITH, RICHARD: "Diary of Richard Smith in the Continental Congress, 1775-1776," *American Historical Review*, I (1895-6), 288-310, 493-516.

[SMITH, WILLIAM]: *Information to Emigrants: Being the Copy of a Letter from a Gentleman in North America, Containing* . . . *the Terms on which Settlers May Procure Lands in North America Particularly in the Provinces of New-York and Pensylvania [sic]* . . . *To Which is Added Observations on the Causes of Emigration* (Glasgow [1773]).

STILES, EZRA: *Extracts from the Itineraries and Other Miscellanies of Ezra Stiles, D.D., LL.D., 1755-1794: With a Selection from His Correspondence* (Franklin B. Dexter, ed., New Haven, Conn., 1916), and *The Literary Diary of Ezra Stiles* (Franklin B. Dexter, ed., 3 vols., New York, 1901). Although Stiles's name is usually connected with Connecticut, he spent the years 1755-1776 in Rhode Island. The material presented here deals with several colonies.

WARREN, MERCY OTIS: *History of the Rise, Progress, and Termination of the American Revolution* . . . (3 vols., Boston, 1805).

[WEIN, PAUL]: *A Concise Historical Account of All the British Colonies in North America; Comprehending Their Rise, Progress and Modern State, Particularly Massachusetts-Bay with Other Provinces of New England* . . . (London, 1775; Dublin, 1776).

WOOLMAN, JOHN: *The Works of John Woolman: In two Parts* (Philadelphia, 1774).

3. Contemporary pamphlets, tracts, and related materials relating to more than one colony: Chronologically arranged

1 7 4 8

ELIOT, JARED: *An Essay upon Field-Husbandry in New England as It Is or May Be Ordered* . . . (New London, Conn., 1748). Eliot also published eight other essays on "field-husbandry" between 1753 and 1762. These were for many years the most prized agricultural essays in America. They were brought together and published by Professors Harry J. Carman and Rexford G. Tugwell in 1934 as volume I of the Columbia University, *Studies in the History of American Agriculture.*

[LITTLE, OTIS]: *State of Trade in the Northern Colonies Considered* . . . (London, 1748; Boston, 1749).

1 7 4 9

A Brief Account of the Rise, Progress and Present State of the Paper Currency of New England . . . (Boston, 1749).

DOUGLASS, WILLIAM: A Summary, Historical and Political, of the First Planting, Progressive Improvements, and Present State of British Settlements in North America . . . (2 vols., Boston, 1749; London, 1760).

1 7 5 0

[KENNEDY, ARCHIBALD]: Obesrvations on the Importance of the Northern Colonies under Proper Regulations (New York, 1750).

MAYHEW, JONATHAN: A Discourse Concerning Unlimited Submission and Non-Resistance to the Higher Powers . . . (Boston, 1750); reprinted in J. W. Thornton: The Pulpit of the American Revolution, pp. 39-104 and as No. 1 in Bailyn's Pamphlets of the American Revolution. Mayhew contends that obedience to God demands resistance to the tyranny of both Church and State.

1 7 5 3

[APLIN, JOHN]: An Address to the People of New England: Occasioned by the Preaching . . . of Certain Doctrines, Destructive of Their Rights and Liberties . . . (Newport, R.I., 1753).

[MACSPARRAN, JAMES]: America Dissected: Being a Full and True Account of All the American Colonies . . . Published as a Caution to Unsteady People Who May be Tempted to Leave Their Native Country (Dublin, 1753). These letters, addressed to the Hon. Col. Henry Cary, Esq., were written by a missionary who served for thirty years in the Narragansett area.

1 7 5 4

[KENNEDY, ARCHIBALD]: Serious Considerations on the Present State of the Affairs of the Northern Colonies (New York, 1754). The author was Receiver-General of the Colony of New York.

1 7 5 5

Advice to the Inhabitants of the Northern Colonies on the Present Situation of Affairs (New York, 1755).

[BUTEL-DUMONT, GEORGE MARIE]: Histoire et Commerce des Colonies Angloises dans l'Amérique Septentrionale . . . ([Paris], 1755).

CHAUNCY, CHARLES: *A Letter to a Friend, Giving a Concise but Just Account . . . of the Ohio-Defeat . . . To Which is Added Some General Account of the New-England Forces with What They Have Already Done, Counter-Ballancing the Above Loss* (Boston, 1755). See also: *A Second Letter to a Friend, Giving a More Particular Narrative of the Defeat of the French Army at Lake-George . . .* (Boston, 1755). Both letters were published together as *Two Letters to a Friend on the Present Critical Conjuncture of Affairs in North America . . .* (Boston 1755).

CLARKE, WILLIAM: *Observations on the Late and Present Conduct of the French with Regard to the Encroachments upon the British Colonies in North America . . .* (Boston, 1755). The author contends that English exploration in the fifteenth century, especially by Cabot, gave England claim to this vast territory and that French activity south of the St. Lawrence was illegal.

EVANS, LEWIS: *Geographical, Historical, Political, Philosophical, and Mechanical Essays: The First, Containing an Analysis of a General Map of the Middle British Colonies in America . . .* (Philadelphia, 1755). This pamphlet is reprinted in L. H. Gipson's *Lewis Evans* (Philadelphia, 1939), pp. 141-76.

HOPKINS, STEPHEN: *A True Representation of the Plan Formed at Albany for Uniting All the British Northern Colonies in Order to [Insure] Their Common Safety and Defence . . .* ([Newport, R.I.], 1755). This pamphlet was answered by one from Philolethes: *A Short Reply to Mr. Stephen Hopkins's Vindication and False Reflections against the Governor and Council of the Colony of Rhode-Island, &c.* (n.p., 1755). Both of these pamphlets are reprinted in *Rhode Island Historical Tracts,* No. 9 (Providence, R.I., 1880).

State of the British and French Colonies in North America with Respect to Number of People, Forces, Forts, Indians, Trade, and Other Advantages . . . (London, 1755; rep., New York, 1966). The antagonism between English and French colonists was caused by mismanagement on both sides of the Atlantic. The author emphasizes the significance of the Ohio Valley and of strong Indian alliances.

1 7 5 6

EVANS, LEWIS: *Geographical, Historical, Political, Philosophical and Mechanical Essays: Number II . . .* (Philadelphia, 1756); reprinted in L. H. Gipson's *Lewis Evans* (Philadelphia, 1939), pp. 177-218.

[LIVINGSTON, WILLIAM]: *A Review of the Military Operations in North-America: From the Commencement of the French Hostilities . . . [1753-1756]* (London, 1757). This pamphlet was reprinted in the Massachusetts Historical Society, *Collections,* 1st ser., VII (1800),

67-163. A defence of Gov. William Shirley's conduct in the Great War for the Empire; sometimes also attributed to William Smith and J. M. Scott, his close associates.

1 7 5 7

A Memorial Containing a Summary View of Facts with their Authorities: In Answer to the Observations by the English Ministry to the Courts of Europe . . . (New York & Philadelphia, 1757). This pamphlet, originally published in French, is an attempt to vindicate French policy in North America.

[MITCHELL, JOHN]: *The Contest in America between Great Britain and France with Its Consequences and Importance* . . . (London, 1757; rep., New York, 1965). Written by a botanist who resided in Virginia from c. 1721 to 1746, this discussion of the causes and likely outcome of the Great War for the Empire was requested by the Lords of Trade and Plantations.

1 7 5 8

DAVIES, SAMUEL: *The Crisis of the Uncertain Doom of Kingdoms at Particular Times Consider'd with Reference to Great-Britain and Her Colonies in Their Present Circumstances: A Sermon Preached in Hanover, Virginia, October 28, 1756* . . . (London, 1758).

[YOUNG, ARTHUR]: *The Theatre of the Present War in North America: With Candid Reflections on the Great Importance of the War in That Part of the World* (London, 1758).

1 7 5 9

[BENEZET, ANTHONY]: *Observations on the Inslaving, Importing, and Purchasing of Negroes with Some Advice thereon* . . . (Germantown, Pa., 1759).

SMITH, THE REV. WILLIAM: *Discourses on Several Public Occasions during the War in America: Preached Chiefly with a View to the Explaining the Importance of the Protestant Cause in the British Colonies* . . . (London, 1759).

1 7 6 0

[FRANKLIN, BENJAMIN, and RICHARD JACKSON]: *The Interest of Great Britain Considered with Regard to Her Colonies and the Acquisitions of Canada and Guadeloupe* . . . (London & Philadelphia, 1760). This pamphlet, frequently attributed to Franklin, was reputedly written by Richard Jackson with Franklin's assistance.

JEFFERYS, THOMAS: *The Natural and Civil History of the French Dominions in North and South America . . .* (London, 1760).

1 7 6 1

MC CULLOH, HENRY: *Miscellaneous Representations Relative to Our Concerns in America . . .* (London [1761]; reprinted in W. K. Boyd: *Some Eighteenth Century Tracts . . .*, pp. 141-56).

WRIGHT, JOHN: *The American Negotiator: Or the Various Currencies of the British Colonies in America as well the Islands as the Continent . . .* (London, 1761). Contains various tables concerning finance and money.

1 7 6 2

[WELLES, NOAH]: *The Real Advantages which Ministers and People May Enjoy, Especially in the Colonies, by Conforming to the Church of England . . .* ([New York], 1762). For a reply, see John Beach: *A Friendly Expostulation with All Persons Concern'd in the Publishing a Late Pamphlet Entitled "The Real Advantages . . ."* (New York, 1763); also the answer by Noah Welles, signed A. Z., *Animadversions, Critical and Candid on Some Parts of Mr. Beach's Late "Friendly Expostulation" . . .* (New York, 1763).

1 7 6 3

APTHORP, EAST: *Considerations on the Institution and Conduct of the Society for the Propagation of the Gospel in Foreign Parts* (Boston, 1763). The pamphlet prompted the following one by Jonathan Mayhew.

MAYHEW, JONATHAN: *Observations on the Charter and Conduct of the Society for the Propagation of the Gospel in Foreign Parts . . .* (Boston, 1763). This pamphlet brought forth several replies, including John Aplin's anonymously published *Verses on Dr. Mayhew's Book of Observations . . .* (Providence, R.I., 1763; rep. in Bailyn: *Pamphlets . . .*, No. 3). Another reply, probably by Henry Caner: *A Candid Examination of Dr. Mayhew's Observations . . .* (Boston, 1763), was answered by Mayhew with *A Defence of the Observations . . . against an Anonymous Pamphlet, Falsely Intitled, A Candid Examination . . .* (Boston, 1763; London, 1764). Another reply, although published anonymously, probably came from the Archbishop of Canterbury, Thomas Secker: *An Answer to Dr. Mayhew's Observations . . .* (London, 1764; rep., Boston). Mayhew replied to this tract with *Remarks on an Anonymous*

Tract Entitled an Answer . . . (Boston, 1764), and was answered by East Apthorp's *A Review of Dr. Mayhew's Remarks on the Answer to His Observations* . . . (London, 1765).

MENZIES, ARCHIBALD: *Proposal for Peopling His Majesty's Southern Colonies on the Continent of America* (Perthshire, Scot., 1763). This rare tract may be found in the John Carter Brown Library.

1 7 6 4

Considerations upon the Act of Parliament, whereby a Duty Is Laid of Six Pence Sterling per Gallon on Molasses and Five Shillings per Hundred on Sugar of Foreign Growth Imported into any of the British Colonies . . . (Boston, 1764).

[FITCH, THOMAS, *et al.*]: *Reasons Why the British Colonies in America Should not Be Charged with Internal Taxes* . . . (New Haven, Conn., 1764); reprinted in *Colonial Records of Connecticut*, XII. This pamphlet was drawn up by a committee appointed by the Connecticut Assembly and chaired by Governor Fitch. It is usually filed under his name, although the Connecticut lawyer, Jared Ingersoll, seems to have played a leading part in its composition as a member of the Committee.

[FRANKLIN, BENJAMIN]: *Cool Thoughts on the Present Situation of Our Public Affairs* . . . (Philadelphia, 1764). Signed A. B.

[HOPKINS, STEPHEN]: *An Essay on the Trade of the Northern Colonies of Great Britain in North America* (London & Philadelphia, 1764). The author deals competently with the subject.

OTIS, JAMES: *The Rights of the British Colonies Asserted and Proved* (Boston, 1764; rep., London [1765]). This pamphlet is reprinted in Charles F. Mullett's "Some Political Writings of James Otis," University of Missouri, Studies: *A Quarterly of Research*, IV (1929), 301-57, and as No. 7 in Bailyn's *Pamphlets* . . . .

[POWNALL, THOMAS]: *Reasons against the Renewal of the Sugar Act, as It Will Be Prejudicial to the Trade* . . . (Boston, 1764).

[THACHER, OXENBRIDGE]: *The Sentiments of a British American* (Boston, 1764). This pamphlet concerns an "Act to lay Certain Duties in the British Colonies and Plantations." It is reprinted as No. 8 in Bailyn's *Pamphlets* . . . .

1 7 6 5

The Constitutional Courant: Containing Matters Interesting to Liberty— but no Wise Repugnant to Loyalty . . . ([Woodbridge, N.J., 1765]). A single issue of the *Courant* written against the Stamp Act and reprinted in New York, Boston, and Philadelphia.

[DICKINSON, JOHN]: *The Late Regulations Respecting the British Colo-*

nies on the Continent of America Considered . . . (London & Philadelphia, 1765). This pamphlet is reprinted as No. 14 in Bailyn's *Pamphlets* . . . .

———: *Friends and Countrymen* ([Philadelphia, 1765]). A broadside urging opposition to the Stamp Act.

DULANY, DANIEL: *Considerations on the Propriety of Imposing Taxes in the British Colonies for the Purpose of Raising a Revenue, by Act of Parliament* (Annapolis, Md., 1765). In this reply to several English pamphlets, the author challenges Parliament's right to levy an internal tax on the colonies. It has been suggested that his ideas influenced the thought of William Pitt. This pamphlet has been reprinted as No. 13 in Bailyn's *Pamphlets* . . . .

[HOPKINS, STEPHEN]: *The Rights of the Colonies Examined* . . . (Providence, R.I., 1765; rep., Bailyn: *Pamphlets* . . . , No. 9). This pamphlet was answered by Martin Howard's anonymous publication: *A Letter from a Gentleman at Halifax to His Friend in Rhode-Island Containing Remarks upon a Pamphlet Entitled the Rights* . . . (Newport, R.I., 1765; rep., Bailyn: *Pamphlets* . . . , No. 10). James Otis replied anonymously to Howard's pamphlet with *A Vindication of the British Colonies Against the Aspersions of the Halifax Gentleman* . . . (Boston, 1765; rep., Bailyn: *Pamphlets* . . . No. 11), to which Howard wrote *A Defence of the Letter from a Gentleman at Halifax* . . . (Newport, R.I., 1765). An anonymous reply to Howard's pamphlet, possibly by Hopkins, was published as *A Letter to the Author of the Halifax Letter: Occasioned by His Book Entitled A Defence* . . . ([Newport, R.I.], 1765). Otis finished the interchange with his *Brief Remarks on the Defence of the Halifax Libel on the British-American Colonies* (Boston, 1765), also published anonymously. Both of the Otis pamphlets are reprinted in Charles F. Mullett's "Some Political Writings of James Otis," University of Missouri, *Studies: A Quarterly of Research*, IV (1929), 382-407 and 409-32.

A Letter to His Most Excellent Majesty, George the Third, King of Great-Britain . . . ([New York, 1765]). Signed C.P., this pamphlet contends that Parliament had lessened the King's power by taxing the Colonies.

MAYHEW, JONATHAN: *Popish Idolatry: A Discourse Delivered in the Chapel of Harvard-College in Cambridge, New England, May 8, 1765* . . . (Boston, 1765).

MOORE, MAURICE: *The Justice and Policy of Taxing the American Colonies in Great-Britain Considered: Wherein Is Shewed that the Colonies Are Not a Conquered People* . . . (Wilmington, N.C., 1765). This pamphlet is reprinted in W. K. Boyd's *Some Eighteenth Century Tracts* . . . , pp. 157-74, and is to be reprinted in Bailyn's *Pamphlets* . . . , No. 16. Moore, prominent in North Carolina politics, declared that Parliament's taxation of the Colonies was illegal and the virtual representation existed only in theory. The solution as he saw it was equality between Britain and her colonies.

Oppression: A Poem By an American: With Notes by a North Briton (Boston & New York, 1765).

1 7 6 6

APPLETON, NATHANIEL: *A Thanksgiving Sermon on the Total Repeal of the Stamp-Act: Preached in Cambridge, New-England, May 20th* . . . (Boston, 1766).

BUCHANAN, GEORGE: *De Juri Regni: Or the Due Right of Government, by Way of a Dialogue betwixt George Buchanan and Thomas Maitland* (Philadelphia, 1766).

CHAUNCY, CHARLES: *A Discourse on the "The Good News from a Far Country"* . . . *on Occasion of the Repeal of the Stamp Act* . . . (Boston, 1766); reprinted in Thornton's *The Pulpit of the American Revolution* . . . (Boston, 1860), 105-46.

[COOPER, SAMUEL]: *The Crisis: Or a Full Defence of the Colonies in Which It Is Incontestibly Proved that the British Constitution Has Been Flagrantly Violated in the Late Stamp Act* . . . (London, 1766). A champion of the colonists, the author denies that the colonies were virtually represented in Parliament.

EMERSON, JOSEPH: *A Thanksgiving Sermon Preach'd at Pepperrell, July 24th, 1766* . . . *on the Account of the Repeal of the Stamp Act* (Boston, 1766). To be reprinted as No. 21 in Bailyn's *Pamphlets.* . . .

Four Dissertations on the Reciprocal Advantages of a Perpetual Union between Great Britain and Her American Colonies . . . (Philadelphia, 1766). The dissertations were written by John Morgan, Stephen Watts, Joseph Reed, and Francis Hopkinson at the College of Philadelphia.

FRANKLIN, BENJAMIN: *The Examination of Doctor Benjamin Franklin before an August Assembly Relating to the Repeal of the Stamp Act* . . . ([Philadelphia, 1766]; Boston & London, 1767).

Glorious News. Boston, Friday 11 o'clock, 16th May, 1766: This Instant Arrived Here the Brig Harrison . . . *with Important News* . . . ([Boston, 1766]). This is the Boston broadside announcing the repeal of the Stamp Act.

Good News for America: To the Sons of Liberty ([Philadelphia, 1766]). A broadside on the repeal of the Stamp Act.

[HICKS, WILLIAM]: *Considerations upon the Rights of the Colonists to the Privileges of British Subjects* . . . (New York, 1766). To be reprinted as No. 18 in Bailyn's *Pamphlets.* . . .

[HOPKINS, STEPHEN]: *The Grievances of the American Colonies Candidly Examined* (Providence, R.I., 1766); reprinted in *Colonial Records of Rhode Island*, VI: 416-27.

INGERSOLL, JARED: *Mr. Ingersoll's Letters Relating to the Stamp Act* (New Haven, Conn., 1766). These letters are included in *The Jared Ingersoll Papers*, New Haven Colony Historical Society, *Papers*, IX (Franklin B. Dexter, ed., New Haven, Conn., 1918).

[JOHNSON, STEPHEN]: *Some Important Observations Occasioned by and Adapted to the Publick Fast Ordered by Authority, December 18th, A.D. 1765: On Account of the Peculiar Circumstances of the Present Day* . . . (Newport, R.I., 1766). To be reprinted as No. 19 in Bailyn's *Pamphlets*. . . .

LEAMING, JEREMIAH: *A Defence of the Episcopal Government of the Church* . . . (New York, 1766). Leaming also wrote *A Second Defence of the Episcopal Government* . . . (New York, 1770).

MAYHEW, JONATHAN: *The Snare Broken: A Thanksgiving Discourse* . . . *Occasioned by the Repeal of the Stamp Act* (Boston, 1766).

[POWNALL, THOMAS]: *Considerations on the Points Lately Brought into Question as to the Parliament's Right of Taxing the Colonies and of the Measures Necessary to Be Taken at this Crisis* . . . (London, 1766). This was published separately as an appendix to *The Administration of the Colonies* and included in the third edition of that work.

STILLMAN, SAMUEL: *Good News from a Far Country: A Sermon Preached* . . . *Upon the Arrival of the Important News of the Repeal of the Stamp Act* . . . (Boston, 1766).

THROOP, BENJAMIN: *A Thanksgiving Sermon upon the Occasion of the Glorious News of the Repeal of the Stamp Act* . . . (New London, Conn., 1766).

ZUBLY, JOHN JOACHIM: *The Stamp Act Repealed: A Sermon Preached in the Meeting at Savannah in Georgia, June 25th, 1766* (Savannah, Ga., 1766).

1 7 6 7

CHANDLER, THOMAS BRADBURY: *Appeal to the Public in Behalf of the Church of England in America* (New York, 1767). Dr. Charles Chauncy replied to Chandler's pamphlet with *The Appeal to the Public Answered in Behalf of the Non-Episcopal Churches in America* . . . (Boston, 1768), and an anonymous reply, signed "An Antiepiscopalian," appeared in *A Letter Concerning an American Bishop, &c. to Dr. Bradbury Chandler* . . . ([Philadelphia], 1768). Chandler answered Chauncy with *The Appeal Defended: Or the Proposed American Episcopate Vindicated* . . . (New York, 1769), and Chauncy replied again with *A Reply to Dr. Chandler's 'Ap-*

peal Defended' . . . (Boston, 1770). Chandler got in the last word, however, with his *The Appeal Farther Defended in Answer to the Farther Misrepresentations of Dr. Chauncy* (New York, 1771).

FISH, ELISHA: *Joy and Gladness: A Thanksgiving Discourse . . . Occasioned by the Repeal of the Stamp Act* (Providence, R.I., 1767).

1 7 6 8

ADAMS, AMOS: *Religious Liberty an Invaluable Blessing: Illustrated in Two Discourses Preached at Roxbury, Dec. 3, 1767* . . . (Boston, 1768).

ADAMS, JOHN: *A Dissertation on the Canon and Feudal Law* ([London], 1768). This series of essays first appeared in *The Boston Gazette* in 1765.

CLARK, JONAS: *The Importance of Military Skill, Measures for Defence, and a Martial Spirit in a Time of Peace: A Sermon* . . . (Boston, 1768).

[DICKINSON, JOHN]: *Letters from a Farmer in Pennsylvania to the Inhabitants of the British Colonies* (Philadelphia, 1768). The *Letters*, first published almost simultaneously in the *Pennsylvania Chronicle, Pennsylvania Gazette,* and *Pennsylvania Journal,* were reprinted in nearly every colonial newspaper. One exception was the *Boston Evening Post* which ran a series of replies. A new reprint with an introduction by Richard T. H. Halsey was issued in New York in 1903. The most recent edition is that edited by Forrest McDonald: *Empire and Nation: Letters from a Farmer in Pennsylvania—John Dickinson. Letters from a Federal Farmer—Richard Henry Lee* (Englewood Cliffs, N.J., 1962).

For the Information of the Publick as It Has been Asserted, in Defiance of Truth, that no Application Was Ever Made for an American Bishop . . . ([New York, 1768]). Broadside.

[HICKS, WILLIAM]: *The Nature and Extent of Parliamentary Power Considered: In Some Remarks upon Mr. Pitt's Speech in the House of Commons Previous to the Repeal of the Stamp Act* . . . (Philadelphia, 1768). This is a reply to William Pitt's *Political Debates* (London, 1766).

Plain Truths in a Few Words to Freeholders and Freemen: That the Members of the Church . . . Have Been Desirous of Obtaining a Bishop Is True . . . ([New York, 1768]). Broadside.

The Power and Grandeur of Great-Britain Founded on the Liberty of the Colonies and the Mischiefs Attending the Taxing Them by Act of Parliament Demonstrated (New York & Philadelphia, 1768).

Some Observations of Consequence . . . Occasioned by the Stamp-Tax Lately Imposed on the British Colonies ([Philadelphia], 1768); signed "Loyal Patriot."

1 7 6 9

*A Collection of Tracts from the Late News Papers, &c. Containing Parti-
cularly the American Whig, a Whip for the American Whig . . .*
(2 vols., New York, 1768-9). A collection of essays from various
colonial newspapers dealing with current political questions.

CORNWELL, GEORGE: *Boston, 25 January 1769: A Dialogue between Sir
George Cornwell, A Gentleman Lately Arrived from England . . .
and Mr. Flint, an Independent Gentleman . . .* (London & Boston,
1769). An abusive pamphlet referring to some of the leading citizens of Boston.

[DICKINSON, JOHN, and ARTHUR LEE]: *The Farmer's and Monitor's Letters
to the Inhabitants of the British Colonies* (Williamsburg, Va.,
1769).

MARTIN, ALEXANDER: *America: A Poem . . . To which Is Added, Liberty:
A Poem by Rusticus . . .* ([Philadelphia, 1769]). *Liberty* was published separately at Philadelphia in 1768 and Charleston, S.C., in
1770.

*Observations on Several Acts of Parliament . . . and also on the Conduct
of the Officers of the Customs . . . and the Board of Commissioners
Appointed to Reside in America. Published by the Merchants of
Boston* ([Boston], 1769; London, 1770). Discusses the injustices
perpetrated by the customs officials.

[POWNALL, THOMAS]: *The Speech of Th-m-s P-wn-ll Esq., Late G-v-rn-r
of This Province in the H—se of C-m—ns in Favor of America*
([Boston, 1769]).

[ZUBLY, JOHN JOACHIM]: *An Humble Enquiry into the Nature of the De-
pendency of the American Colonies upon the Parliament of Great-
Britain and the Right of Parliament to Lay Taxes on the Said
Colonies . . .* ([Charleston, S.C.], 1769).

1 7 7 0

[ALLEN, JOHN]: *The Spirit of Liberty, or Junius' Loyal Address: Being a
Key to the English Cabinet, or a Humble Dissertation upon the
Rights and Liberties of the Ancient Britons . . .* (n. p., 1770; rep.,
Boston, 1772). Signed Junius Junior and attributed to J. Parkes
by Evans.

CHAMPION, JUDAH: *A Brief View of the Distresses, Hardships and Dangers
Our Ancestors Encounter'd in Settling New-England . . . In Two
Sermons . . .* (Hartford, Conn., 1770).

DOYLE, WILLIAM: *Some Account of the British Dominions beyond the
Atlantic: Containing Chiefly What Is Most Interesting and Least
Known with Respect to Those Parts . . .* (London [1770]).

LIVINGSTON, WILLIAM: *America: Or a Poem on the Settlement of the British Colonies* . . . (New Haven, Conn. [1770]).

Proposals for Erecting and Encouraging a New Manufactory: Wealth and Honorary Rewards Are Never Bestowed with Greater Propriety than on Those Who Expose Their Fortunes or Lives for the Salvation of Their Country . . . ([New York, 1770]). Broadside satirizing the non-importation agreements, signed A****** B*******.

1 7 7 1

[COOPER, MYLES]: *An Address from the Clergy of New-York and New-Jersey to the Episcopalians in Virginia: Occasioned by Some Late Transactions in That Colony Relative to an American Episcopate* (New York, 1771). Also attributed to Thomas Bradbury Chandler and Thomas Gwatkin.

TAYLOR, GEORGE: *A Voyage to North America Perform'd by G. Taylor of Sheffield in the Years 1768 and 1769* . . . (Nottingham Eng., 1771).

TOBLER, JOHN: *The Georgia Almanack for the Year of Our Lord 1771* (Charleston, S.C. [1771]). The significance of this publication is that it contains "An Essay by a Freeholder of South Carolina on the Very Important Subjects now in Debate between Great Britain and Her Colonies."

1 7 7 2

[COOPER, DAVID]: *A Mite Cast into the Treasury: Or Observations on Slave-Keeping* . . . (Philadelphia, 1772). This pamphlet has been credited to Anthony Benezet by both Sabin and Evans. See, however, Friends Historical Association, *Bulletin*, XXVI (1937), 45: "The author . . . is David Cooper . . . who in a manuscript diary speaks at length about writing it."

GWATKIN, THOMAS: *A Letter to the Clergy of New York and New Jersey Occasioned by An Address to the Episcopalians in Virginia* (Williamsburg, Va., 1772).

WISE, JOHN: *A Vindication of the Government of New England Churches* . . . (Boston, 1772). First published in 1717.

[ZUBLY, JOHN JOACHIM]: *Calm and Respectful Thoughts on the Negative of the Crown* . . . ([Savannah, Ga., 1772]). "By a Freeman."

1 7 7 3

[ALLEN, JOHN]: *The American Alarm: Or the Bostonian Plea for the Rights and Liberties of the People* . . . (Boston, 1773). Signed by the "British Bostonian," Evans attributes this work and the following one to Isaac Skillman.

[———]: *An Oration on the Beauties of Liberty: Or the Essential Rights of the Americans* . . . (Boston, 1773).

CHAPLIN, EBENEZER: *The Civil State Compared to Rivers, All under God's Controul and What People Have to Do when Administration Is Grievous: In a Discourse* . . . (Boston, 1773).

A Dissertation on the Rise, Progress, Views, Strength, Interests, and Characters of the Two Parties of the Whigs and Tories (Boston, 1773).

[MATHER, SAMUEL]: *An Attempt to Shew that America Must Be Known to the Ancients . . . [with] an Appendix Concerning the American Colonies and Some Modern Managements against Them . . .* (Boston, 1773).

MUCIUS, pseud.: *To the Freemen of America* ([Philadelphia, 1773]). Broadside on the tea tax.

Personal Slavery Established by the Suffrages of Custom and Right Reason: Being a Full Answer to the Gloomy and Visionary Reveries of All the Fanatical and Enthusiastical Writers on that Subject (Philadelphia, 1773).

[RUSH, BENJAMIN]: *An Address to the Inhabitants of the British Settlements in America upon Slave-Keeping: By a Pennsylvanian* (Philadelphia, 1773). A New York edition contains the "Address of the House of Burgesses of Virginia to the King of April 1, 1772, opposing the Slave-trade." An anonymously-published answer was forthcoming from Richard Nisbet: *Slavery not Forbidden by Scripture: Or a Defense of the West-India Planters from the Aspersions Thrown Out against Them by the author of a Pamphlet Entitled "An Address to the Inhabitants . . ."* (Philadelphia, 1773). When Rush's pamphlet was put into a second edition, he added a section entitled *A Vindication of the Address: In Answer to a Pamphlet Entitled "Slavery not Forbidden in Scripture. . . ."* (Philadelphia, 1773). A number of editions of the pamphlet were printed.

The Storm, or the American Syren: Being a Collection of the Newest and Most Approved Songs (Williamsburg, Va., 1773).

[WARREN, MERCY OTIS]: *The Adulateur: A Tragedy as It is now Acted in Upper Servia* (Boston, 1773). A satire on Governor Hutchinson.

1 7 7 4

ADAMS, JOHN: *History of the Dispute with America, from Its Origin in 1754: Written in the Year 1774* (London, 1774). This is the London edition of the letters of "Novanglus" which were originally published in the *Boston Gazette*, 1774. These letters were also collected in *Novanglus and Massachusettensis: Or, Political Essays, Published in the Years 1774 and 1775, on the Principal Points of*

Controversy between Great Britain and Her Colonies . . . (Boston, 1819).

[ALLEN, JOHN]: *The Patriotic Whisper in the Ears of the King . . . Being a Political Liberty Oration upon the Branches of the American Charters, Proving Them to Be as Sacred as the British Constitution* . . . ([Boston, 1774]).

[————]: *The Watchman's Alarm to Lord N—th, or the British Parliamentary Boston Port-Bill Uuwraped: Being An Oration on the Meridian of Liberty* . . . (Salem, Mass., 1774). This is another pamphlet signed by the "British Bostonian."

BENEZET, ANTHONY, ed.: *The Potent Enemies of America Laid Open: Being Some Account of the Baneful Effects Attending the Use of Distilled Spirituous Liquors, and the Slavery of the Negroes* (Philadelphia [1774]). Contains an original tract by a "Lover of Mankind," i.e. Benezet; a reprint of Wesley's *Thoughts on Slavery;* a sketch and letter of David Brainerd; and reprints of several religious tracts.

BERNARD, FRANCIS: *Select Letters on the Trade and Government of America and the Principles of Law and Polity Applied to the American Colonies* . . . (1st edn., London, 1769; 2nd edn., 1774). This work also contains the petition of the Massachusetts Assembly against Bernard, his reply, and the order of the King in Council regarding the issue.

[BOUCHER, JONATHAN]: *A Letter from a Virginian to the Members of the Congress to be held at Philadelphia on the First of September 1774* (Boston & London, 1774). This letter attempted "to dissuade Congress from adopting the non-importation and non-exportation agreements."

[CHANDLER, THOMAS BRADBURY]: *The American Querist: Or Some Questions Proposed Relative to the Present Disputes Between Great Britain and Her American Colonies* . . . ([New York], 1774). It contains "100 rhetorical questions aimed at the pretensions of the first Continental Congress." The confusion of the authorship of this pamphlet and other pamphlets is clarified by C. H. Vance: "Myles Cooper," *Columbia University Quarterly,* XXII (1930), 275-6.

[————]: *A Friendly Address to all Reasonable Americans on the Subject of Our Political Confusions: In Which the Necessary Consequences of Violently Opposing the King's Troops and of a General Non-Importation Are Fairly Stated* (New York, 1774). For an anonymously-published reply see: Charles Lee's *Strictures on a pamphlet, entitled, "A Friendly Address . . ." Addressed to the People of America* (Philadelphia, 1774) which was answered by a pamphlet attributed to Henry Barry: *The Strictures on the Friendly Address Examined, and a Refutation of the Principles Attempted: Addressed* to the People of America (Philadelphia & New London, Conn., 1775); see also another edition: *The General Attacked by a Subaltern: or the Strictures on the Friendly Address Examined and a Refutation of its Principles Attempted* . . . (Boston [1775]), which also contains Lee's *Strictures*. . . . For an explanation of authorship, see Thomas R. Adams: *American Independence* . . . p. 151 a and b. For another reply, see the anonymous pamphlet probably by Phillip Livingston: *The Other Side of the Question, Or A Defence of the Liberties of North-America: In Answer to the Late "Friendly Address* . . ." (New York, 1774).

A *Dialogue between a Southern Delegate and His Spouse, on His Return from the Grand Continental Congress* . . . (Boston & [New York], 1774). Signed Mary V. V., this verse pamphlet has been attributed to Jefferson.

[DICKINSON, JOHN]: *An Essay on the Constitutional Power of Great-Britain over the Colonies in America: With the Resolves of the Committee for the Province of Pennsylvania, and Their Instructions to Their Representatives in Assembly* (Philadelphia, 1774). Reprinted in the *Pennsylvania Archives*, 2nd ser., III: 565ff. Another edition had the slightly revised title: *A New Essay by the Pennsylvanian Farmer on the Constitutional Power*. . . . A reply was published the following year: *Remarks on the New Essay of the Pennsylvanian Farmer* . . . (London, 1775).

[DRAYTON, WILLIAM HENRY]: *A Letter from Freeman of South-Carolina to the Deputies of North-America Assembled in the High Court of Congress at Philadelphia* (Charleston, S.C., 1774). For a reply, see the pamphlet by "A Back Settler": *Some Fugitive Thoughts on a Letter Signed Freeman* . . . ([Charleston, S.C.], 1774).

[DUCHÉ, JACOB]: *Observations on a Variety of Subjects, Literary, Moral, and Religious: In a Series of Original Letters* . . . (Philadelphia, 1774).

The First Book of the American Chronicles of the Times (Norwich, Conn., 1774; other edns., Boston & Philadelphia, 1775). Written in a scriptural style, this work is primarily concerned with events of 1774.

[FISHER, JABEZ]: *Americanus Examined and His Principles Compared with Those of the Approved Advocates for America: By a Pennsylvanian* (Philadelphia, 1774). This is a reprinting, with a critical commentary in the form of footnotes and a brief essay, of a letter acknowledged by Joseph Galloway, first printed in the *New-York Gazette* for the 15th of August 1765 and subsequently appearing in both the *Pennsylvania Gazette* and the *Pennsylvania Journal* for the 25th of September 1766.

[FRANKLIN, BENJAMIN]: *The Causes of the Present Distractions in America*

Explained: In Two Letters to a Merchant in London (New York, 1774). This pamphlet, signed F—— B——, had consistently been attributed to Sir Francis Bernard, but V. W. Crane has shown it to be a product of Franklin's pen. See Crane's article in Bibliographical Society of America, *Papers*, XXVIII (1934), 12-15.

[GALLOWAY, JOSEPH]: *Arguments on Both Sides in the Dispute between Great-Britain and Her Colonies: In which Those in Favor of the Power of Parliament to Bind the Colonies are Stated and Answered and the Rights of the Colonists Explained and Asserted on New and Just Principles. By a Sincere Friend to Both Countries* ([Philadelphia], 1774; rep., New Jersey *Archives*, 1st ser., X: 478-94).

[HOPKINSON, FRANCIS]: *A Pretty Story: Written in the Year of Our Lord 1774 By Peter Grievous, Esq. A.B.C.D.E.* (Philadelphia & Williamsburg, Va., 1774). This pamphlet was reprinted under the title *The Old Farm and the New Farm: A Political Allegory* (New York, 1857).

JEFFERSON, THOMAS: *A Summary View of the Rights of British America: Set forth in Some Resolutions Intended for the Inspection of the Present Delegates of the People of Virginia . . .* (Williamsburg, Va., 1774). This is a straighforward political policy statement. For comment on this pamphlet see Anthony M. Lewis's "Jefferson's *Summary View* as a Chart of Political Union," *William and Mary Quarterly*, 3rd ser., V (1948), 35-41.

JINGLE, BOB, pseud.: *The Association, &c. of the Delegates of the Colonies at the Grand Congress, Held at Philadelphia, September 1, 1774, Versified and Adapted to Music . . .* ([Philadelphia], 1774). A Tory publication aimed at ridiculing the Continental Congress.

Letter to the People of Great Britain from the Delegates of the American Congress in Philadelphia ([Philadelphia, 1774]).

NILES, NATHANIEL: *Two Discourses on Liberty: Delivered at the North Church, in Newbury-Port, on Lord's Day June 5th, 1774 . . .* (Newbury-Port, Mass., 1774).

[PRESCOTT, BENJAMIN]: *A Free and Calm Consideration of the Unhappy Misunderstandings and Debates . . . between the Parliament of Great-Britain, and these American Colonies . . .* (Salem, Mass., 1774). This pamphlet is comprised of a series of eight letters signed "Philopolites" and dated from August 16, 1768 to July 30, 1770.

[SEABURY, SAMUEL]: *Free Thoughts on the Proceedings of the Continental Congress Held at Philadelphia, September 5, 1774: Wherein their Errors Are Exhibited, Their Reasonings Confuted, and the Fatal Tendency of Their Non-Importation, Non-Exportation, and Non-Consumption Measures Are Laid Open . . .* ([New York], 1774). Signed "A. W. Farmer." Reprinted in C. H. Vance's *Letters of a*

Westchester Farmer . . . , Westchester County Historical Society, *Publications*, VIII (White Plains, N.Y., 1930). For a reply, see Alexander Hamilton's pamphlet, published anonymously, *A Full Vindication of the Measures of the Congress from the Calumnies of Their Enemies: In Answer to a Letter under the Signature A. W. Farmer . . .* (New York, 1774). This pamphlet is reprinted in the *Papers of Alexander Hamilton*, Harold C. Syrett, ed., I: 45-78. Seabury replied to Hamilton with *The Congress Canvassed: Or an Examination into the Conduct of the Delegates at Their Grand Convention Held in Philadelphia September 1, 1774 . . .* ([New York], 1774), signed, A. W. Farmer, 28 Nov. 1774; and *A View of the Controversy between Great-Britain and Her Colonies: Including a Mode of Determining Their Present Disputes Finally and Effecually [sic] and of Preventing All Future Contentions . . .* (New York, 1774), both of which have been reprinted in Vance. These in turn evoked the following reply from Hamilton: *The Farmer Refuted: Or, a More Impartial and Comprehensive View of the Dispute between Great-Britain and the Colonies, Intended as a Further Vindication of the Congress . . .* (New York, 1775), which has been reprinted in *The Papers of Alexander Hamilton* I: 81-165; and was subsequently answered by Isaac Wilkins's *The Republican Dissected: Or the Anatomy of an American Whig* (New York, 1775).

SHERWOOD, SAMUEL: *A Sermon Containing Scriptural Instructions to Civil Rulers and All Freeborn Subjects: In which the Principles of Sound Policy and Good Government Are Established and Vindi- cated . . .* (New Haven, Conn. [1774]). This pamphlet also con- tains an appendix by Ebenezer Baldwin.

TENNENT, WILLIAM: *An Address, Occasioned by the Late Invasion of the Liberties of the American Colonies by the British Parliament, Delivered in Charlestown, South Carolina* (Philadelphia, 1774).

To the Public: Affidavit of Thomas Mesnard and Statement of Citizens on Importation of Arms . . . (New York, 1774). A broadside dated 30 Dec., 1774.

WEBSTER, SAMUEL: *The Misery and Duty of an Oppress'd and Enslav'd People: Represented in a Sermon Delivered at Salisbury July 14, 1774 . . .* (Boston, 1774).

[WELLS, RICHARD]: *A Few Political Reflections submitted to the Consider- ation of the British Colonies . . .* (Philadelphia, 1774). Reprint of six letters from the *Pennsylvania Packet*, originally published be- tween June 20 and August 8, 1774.

WHITNEY, PETER: *The Transgression of a Land Punished by a Multitude of Rulers: Considered in Two Discourses, Delivered July 14, 1774 . . .* (Boston, 1774).

[WILSON, JAMES]: *Considerations on the Nature and Extent of the Legislative Authority of the British Parliament* (Philadelphia, 1774). This pamphlet has been reprinted in Randolph G. Adams: *Selected Political Essays of James Wilson* (New York, 1930), 43-82.

1775

[BARRY, HENRY]: *The Advantages which America Derives from Her Commerce, Connexion, and Dependence on Britain: Addressed to the People of America* . . . ([Boston], 1775).

CARMICHAEL, JOHN: *A Self-Defensive War Lawful: Proved in a Sermon Preached at Lancaster* . . . *June 4th, 1775* . . . (Lancaster, Mass., 1775; another edn., Philadelphia). The title of the pamphlet, although a traditional phrase, was in 1775 of itself provocative.

[CHANDLER, THOMAS BRADBURY]: *What Think Ye of the Congress Now? Or, An Enquiry How Far the Americans Are Bound to Abide by, and Execute the Decisions of, the Late Congress?* . . . (New York, 1775). This pamphlet also contains Galloway's plan of union as an appendix. An attempt was made by Chandler to dissuade New York from supporting the activities of the Continental Congress.

[COOPER, MYLES]: *The Patriots of North America: A Sketch with Explanatory Notes* (New York, 1775). A Tory denunciation in verse of the Whigs.

DUCHÉ, JACOB: *The American Vine: A Sermon Preached in Christ-Church, Philadelphia, Before the Honourable Continental Congress, July 20th, 1775* . . . (Philadelphia, 1775).

———: *The Duty of Standing Fast in Our Spiritual and Temporal Liberties: A Sermon Preached in Christ-Church July 7th, 1775* . . . (Philadelphia, 1775).

An Essay upon Government, Adopted by the Americans: Wherein the Lawfulness of Revolutions Are Demonstrated . . . (Philadelphia, 1775).

FOSTER, DAN: *A Short Essay on Civil Government: The Substance of Six Sermons Preached in Windsor* . . . (Hartford, Conn., 1775).

[GALLOWAY, JOSEPH]: *A Candid Examination of the Mutual Claims of Great Britain and the Colonies: With a Plan of Accommodation on Constitutional Principles* (New York, 1775). This pamphlet states fully the position held by many American Loyalists. The pamphlet was answered by a letter authored by John Dickinson and Charles Thomson: "To the Author of a Pamphlet Entitled 'A Candid Examination . . .'" which appeared in the 8th March 1775 issue of the *Pennsylvania Journal*. Galloway answered the letter with *A Reply to an Address to the Author of a Pamphlet Entitled*

"*A Candid Examination. . . .*" A full discussion of the pamphlet-letter interchange can be found in J. P. Boyd's *Anglo-American Union* . . . (Philadelphia, 1941), pp. 45-50.

[————]: *A Plan of a Proposed Union Between Great Britain and the Colonies* . . . (n.p., 1775). The Plan was also published with Chandler's *What Think Ye of the Congress Now?* with its own special title page.

[GRAY, HARRISON]: *A Few Remarks upon Some of the Votes and Resolutions of the Continental Congress Held at Philadelphia in September, and the Provincial Congress Held at Cambridge in November 1774* . . . ([Boston], 1775). The author, a Loyalist, criticized the colonists for opposing the tea tax.

GROTIUS, pseud.: *Pills for the Delegates or the Chairman Chastised: In a Series of Letters Addressed to Peyton Randolph, Esq., on his Conduct as President of the General Congress* . . . (New York, 1775). The letters were originally published in the *Massachusetts Gazette*.

HEWES, JOSEPH: *A Collection of Occurrences and Facts Known by Living Evidences and also Recorded in a Public Manner* . . . *Concerning the Present Commotions in the Kingdom of Great-Britain* ([Providence, R.I.], 1775).

HUNT, ISAAC: *The Political Family: Or a Discourse Pointing Out the Reciprocal Advantages which Flow from an Uninterrupted Union between Great Britain and Her American Colonies* (Philadelphia, 1775).

JONES, DAVID: *Defensive War in a Just Cause Sinless: A Sermon Preached on the Day of the Continental Fast* . . . (Philadelphia, 1775).

LEE, CHARLES: *Letters of Major-General Lee to the Right Honourable Earl Percy and Major-General John Burgoyne. With The Answers* (New York, 1775).

[LEONARD, DANIEL]: *The Origin of the American Contest with Great-Britain: Or the Present Political State of the Massachusetts-Bay in General, and the Town of Boston, in Particular* . . . (New York, 1775). This pamphlet contains the collected letters of "Massachusettensis" and was also published as *Massachusettensis: Or a Series of Letters* . . . (Boston & London, 1776), and simply as *Massachusettensis* [Letters I-XVII: "To the Inhabitants of the Province of Massachusetts Bay, 12 Dec. 1774 to 3 April 1775"] ([Boston, 1775]). John Adams' replies to these letters, signed "Novanglus," were printed in London in an abridged version under the title *History of the Dispute with America from Its Origin in 1754*. The two groups of letters were reprinted in *Novanglus and Massachusettensis* . . . (Boston, 1819), but "Massachusettensis" was incorrectly identified as Jonathan Sewell, the Loyalist.

[MATHER, MOSES]: *America's Appeal to the Impartial World: Wherein the Rights of the Americans . . . Are Stated and Considered and the Opposition Made by the Colonies . . . Vindicated* (Hartford, Conn., 1775).

[MEIN, JOHN]: *Sagittarius's Letters and Political Speculations: Extracted from the Public Ledger . . .* (Boston, 1775). A Tory blast against the Puritans and their descendants with interesting personal anecdotes.

PICKERING, TIMOTHY: *An Easy Plan of Discipline for a Militia* (Salem, Mass., 1775).

RAYNAL, GUILLAUME THOMAS FRANÇOIS: *The Sentiments of a Foreigner on the Disputes of Great-Britain with America . . .* (Philadelphia, 1775). This was translated from the French.

SEWALL, JONATHAN: *The Americans Roused in a Cure for the Spleen or Amusement for a Winter's Evening: Being the Substance of a Conversation on the Times . . .* (New York [1775]). An amusing presentation of colonial grievances. Sewall later changed his name to Sewell.

SMITH, WILLIAM: *A Sermon on the Present Situation of American Affairs: Preached in Christ-Church, June 23, 1775 . . .* (Philadelphia, 1775).

Some Seasonable Observations and Remarks upon the State of Our Controversy with Great Britain and on the Proceedings of the Continental Congress . . . ([Boston], 1775).

STEARNS, WILLIAM: *A View of the Controversy Subsisting between Great-Britain and the American Colonies: A Sermon . . .* (Watertown, Mass., 1775).

STORY, ISAAC: *The Love of Our Country Recommended and Enforced: In a Sermon . . .* (Boston, 1775).

The Triumph of the Whigs: Or T'Other Congress Convened (New York, 1775). Although this pamphlet is sometimes attributed to Daniel Leonard, Thomas R. Adams in his *American Independence* claims there is no evidence to corroborate this.

[WARREN, MERCY OTIS]: *The Group: A Farce as Lately Acted and to Be Re-Acted to the Wonder of All Superior Intelligences . . .* (Boston, 1775). This play is an anti-Tory drama.

[WELLS, RICHARD]: *The Middle Line: Or an Attempt to Furnish Some Hints for Ending the Differences Subsisting between Great-Britain and the Colonies* (Philadelphia, 1775).

WILLIAMS, SAMUEL: *A Discourse on the Love of Our Country; Delivered . . . December 15, 1774* (Salem, Mass., 1775). A speech delivered on the fast day appointed by Congress, it is based on constitutional and theological arguments.

ZUBLY, JOHN JOACHIM: *The Law of Liberty: A Sermon on American Affairs Preached at the Opening of the Provincial Congress of Georgia . . .* (Philadelphia & London, 1775). The sermon was addressed to the Earl of Dartmouth.

1 7 7 6

[ADAMS, JOHN]: *Thoughts on Government: Applicable to the Present State of the American Colonies* . . . (Philadelphia, 1776). A treatise on government, partly in reply to Thomas Paine's proposals for American government in *Common Sense*. . . .

Civil Prudence, Recommended to the Thirteen United Colonies of North-America: A Discourse Shewing That It Is in the Power of Civil Prudence to Prevent or Cure State Distempers . . . (Norwich, Conn., 1776). Originally written shortly after the repeal of the Stamp Act, the author claims he was moved to publish his discourse by Paine's *Common Sense*. . . .

DEMOPHILUS, pseud.: *The Genuine Principles of the Ancient Saxon or English Constitution: Carefully Collected from the Best Authorities with Some Observations on Their Peculiar Fitness for the United Colonies in General and Pennsylvania in Particular* . . . (Philadelphia, 1776). "Pages 41-46 contain the Declaration of Independence. As the advertisement at the end is dated, Philadelphia, July 8, 1776, this is probably the first publication of the Declaration in book form made" (Evans, ‡14734).

A Discourse on the Times (Norwich, Conn., 1776). The pamphlet is signed: "A Hearty Friend to all the Colonies," possibly Jabez Huntington.

Four Letters on Interesting Subjects (Philadelphia, 1776). The letters deal with political and constitutional issues and with the relationship between the King and the Colonies.

[GREEN, JACOB]: *Observations on the Reconciliation of Great-Britain and the Colonies: In Which Are Exhibited Arguments for and against That Measure* . . . (Philadelphia, 1776).

HUNTINGTON, ENOCH: *The Happy Effects of Union, and the Fatal Tendency of Divisions: Shewn in a Sermon* . . . (Hartford, Conn., 1776).

HUTCHINSON, THOMAS: *Strictures upon the Declaration of the Congress at Philadelphia: In a Letter to a Noble Lord, &c.* (London, 1776). This pamphlet has been edited by Malcolm Freiburg and issued as No. 227 of the *Old South Leaflets* series (Boston, 1958).

[JENINGS, LAYCOCK]: *A Plan for Settling the Unhappy Dispute between Great Britain and Her Colonies* (n.p., 1776).

[LEACOCK (LAYCOCK), JOHN]: *The Fall of British Tyranny: Or American Liberty Triumphant* . . . (Philadelphia, 1776).

MAUDUIT, ISRAEL: *A Short View of the History of the New England Colonies, With Respect to Their Charters and Constitution* (4th edn., w/add., London, 1776).

[PAINE, THOMAS]: *Common Sense* . . . (Philadelphia, 1776). The most famous of all pamphlets published before the Declaration of Independence. For criticism, see: Candidus: *Plain Truth: Addressed to the Inhabitants of America, Containing Remarks on a Late Pamphlet, Entitled "Common Sense." Wherein Are Shewn that the Scheme of Independence is Ruinous, Delusive and Impracticable* . . . (Philadelphia, 1776). Candidus has been identified variously as James Chalmers and as Provost William Smith of Philadelphia. Bernard Bailyn and Thomas R. Adams, in the most recent studies, give James Chalmers the credit. Comment on this pamphlet was also made by Rusticus: *Remarks on a Late Pamphlet Entitled "Plain Truth"* (Philadelphia, 1776). Further criticism of Paine's pamphlet came from Candidus with his *Additions to Plain Truth: Addressed to the Inhabitants of America, Containing Further Remarks on a Late Pamphlet Entitled "Common Sense"* . . . (Philadelphia, 1776). Two pamphlets of reply likewise came from Charles Inglis: *The Deceiver Unmasked or Loyalty and Interest United: In Answer to a Pamphlet Entitled "Common Sense"* . . . (New York, 1776), and *The True Interest of America Impartially Stated: In Certain Strictures on a Pamphlet Entitled "Common Sense"* . . . (1st & 2nd edns., Philadelphia, 1776). An anonymous reply also appeared in Ireland: *Reason: In Answer to a Pamphlet Entitled "Common Sense"* (Dublin, 1776). A defense was offered in *The True Merits of a Late Treatise Printed in America Intitled "Common Sense" clearly Pointed out: Addressed to the Inhabitants of America* . . . (London, 1776). Paine elaborated on his argument in *Additions to "Common Sense": Addressed to the Inhabitants of America* (London & Philadelphia, 1776), and in *Large Additions to "Common Sense"* . . . (Philadelphia, 1776). See Richard Gimbel's *Thomas Paine: A Bibliographical Check List of Common Sense with an Account of Its Publication* (London & New Haven, Conn., 1956).

[————]: *A Dialogue between the Ghost of General Montgomery, Just Arrived from the Elysian Fields, and an American Delegate in a Wood near Philadelphia* ([Philadelphia], 1776). This pamphlet was printed on the end pages of one edition of *Common Sense,* but was also printed separately.

The People the Best Governors: Or a Plan of Government Founded on the Just Principles of Natural Freedom ([Hartford, Conn.], 1776).

ROSS, ROBERT: *A Sermon in Which the Union of the Colonies Is Considered and Recommended and the Bad Consequences of Divisions Are Represented: Delivered . . . November sixteenth, 1775* . . . (New York, 1776). Ross was pastor of the Church of Christ in Stratfield.

SHERWOOD, SAMUEL: *The Church's Flight into the Wilderness: An Address on the Times Containing Some . . . Observations on Scripture Prophecies* . . . (New York, 1776). The dedication honours John Hancock and the members of the Continental Congress.

WITHERSPOON, JOHN: *The Dominion of Providence over the Passions of Men: A Sermon* . . . (Philadelphia, 1776). This pamphlet went through numerous editions in Britain and America.

4. Newspapers and periodicals

The key reference work relating to American newspapers is Clarence S. Brigham's *History and Bibliography of American Newspapers, 1690-1820* (2 vols., Worcester, Mass., 1947; rev. edn., London, 1962). The work gives full data on newspapers including names of publishers, title variations, and listings of what issues are available in various libraries. Brigham has recently published "Additions and Corrections to History and Bibliography of American Newspapers, 1690-1820," American Antiquarian Society, *Proceedings*, n. ser., LXXI (1961), 15-62. See also William Beer's "Checklist of American Periodicals 1741-1800," American Antiquarian Society, *Proceedings*, n. ser., XXXII (1922), 330-45 and Winifred Gregory's *Union List of Serials in Libraries of the United States and Canada* (2nd edn., New York, 1943; supplements, 1945-1951). For a bibliography of American magazines, see Lyon N. Richardson's *A History of Early American Magazines, 1741-1789* (New York, 1931), pp. 362-75. See also, C. L. Cannon, ed.: *Journalism: A Bibliography* (New York, 1924) and E. H. Ford, ed.: *History of Journalism in the United States: A Bibliography of Books and Annotated Articles* (Minneapolis, Minn., c. 1938). All extant periodicals for the years 1741 through 1825 in the United States have been made available on microfilm through the efforts of the University of Michigan and the Clements Library. Newspapers are listed under the colony where they were published.

C. SECONDARY WORKS

1. General

While most of the histories listed below have a political approach, especially those relating to the American Revolution, it has seemed best to separate them from the more specialized studies that follow them.

ADAMS, JAMES TRUSLOW: *Revolutionary New England, 1691-1776* (Boston, c. 1923).

ALDEN, JOHN RICHARD: *The American Revolution, 1775-1783,* (New York, 1954).

——: *A History of the South, Vol. III: The South in the Revolution, 1763-1789* ([Baton Rouge, La.], 1957).

"The American Revolution: A Symposium," *Canadian Historical Review*, XXIII (1942), 1-41. This consists of an article by Lawrence A. Harper, "Mercantilism and the American Revolution," (pp. 1-15), with a critique by O. M. Dickerson (pp. 29-34), and an article by Winfred Trexler Root, "The American Revolution Reconsidered" (pp. 16-29), with a critique by L. H. Gipson (pp. 34-41).

ANDREWS, CHARLES MC LEAN: "The American Revolution: An Interpretation," *American Historical Review*, XXXI (1925-6), 219-32.

————: *The Colonial Period of American History* (4 vols., New Haven, Conn., 1934-8). Vol. IV has pertinent material.

APTHEKER, HERBERT: *The American Revolution, 1763-1783: A History of the American People: An Interpretation* (New York, 1960).

BANCROFT, GEORGE: *History of the United States of America: From the Discovery of the Continent* (10 vols., Boston, 1834-74; rev. edn., 6 vols., Boston, 1876 [Centenary Edition]).

BARCK, OSCAR THEODORE, JR., and HUGH TALMADGE LEFLER: *Colonial America* (New York, 1958).

BECKER, CARL L.: *Beginnings of the American People* (Boston, c. 1915).

————: *The Eve of the Revolution: A Chronicle of the Breach with England, The Chronicles of America Series*, XI (New Haven, Conn., 1918).

————, J. M. CLARK, and W. E. DODD: *The Spirit of '76 and Other Essays* (Washington, D.C., 1927). In addition to the title essay by Becker, the book also contains "Adam Smith and the Spirit of '76" by Clark and "Virginia Takes the Road to Revolution" by Dodd.

BILLINGTON, RAY ALLEN, ed.: *The Reinterpretation of Early American History: Essays in Honor of John Edwin Pomfret* (San Marino, Calif., 1966). This work contains the following essays relevant to the period under consideration: Frederick B. Tolles's "The Historians of the Middle Colonies," pp. 65-79; Clarence L. Ver Steeg's "Historians and the Southern Colonies," pp. 81-99; Merrill Jensen's "Historians and the Nature of the American Revolution," pp. 101-127; Jack P. Greene's "Changing Interpretations of Early American Politics," pp. 151-84; and L. H. Gipson's "The Imperial Approach to Early American History," pp. 185-99.

BOORSTIN, DANIEL J.: *The Americans: The Colonial Experience* (New York, c. 1958).

BRAEMAN, JOHN: *The Road to Independence: A Documentary History of the Causes of the American Revolution, 1763-1776* (New York, 1963).

BREWSTER, WILLIAM: *The Fourteenth Commonwealths: Vermont and the States That Failed* (Philadelphia, 1960).

CARMAN, HARRY J., and HAROLD C. SYRETT: *A History of the American People* (2nd edn., rev., 2 vols., New York, 1960-1).

CHAMBERLAIN, MELLEN: "The Revolution Impending," *Narrative and Critical History of America* (Justin Winsor, ed., 8 vols., Boston & New York, 1884-9), VI: 1-112.

CHANNING, EDWARD: *A History of the United States* (6 vols., New York, 1905-25; index, 1932); Volumes II and III relate to the period 1748-1776.

CHITWOOD, OLIVER PERRY: *A History of Colonial America* (3rd edn., New York, c. 1961).

COLBOURN, H. TREVOR, ed.: *The Colonial Experience: Readings in Early American History* (Boston, 1966). This collection is composed of ten major sections dealing with various aspects of the American colonies, each section containing several important articles by prominent historians with occasional original materials included.

DAVIS, WILLIAM T., ed.: *The New England States: Their Constitutional, Judicial, Educational, Commercial, Professional, and Industrial History* (4 vols., Boston, 1897).

DOYLE, JOHN ANDREW: *English Colonies in America* (5 vols., New York, 1882-1907).

EATON, CLEMENT: *A History of the Old South* (New York, 1949).

ELLIS, GEORGE E.: "The Sentiment of Independence, Its Growth and Consummation," *Narrative and Critical History of America*, VI: 231-74.

Essays in Colonial History Presented to Charles McLean Andrews by His Students (London & New Haven, Conn., 1931). Contains the following pertinent essays: "The Four Independent Companies of New York," pp. 96-123, by Stanley M. Pargellis; "Parliamentary Privilege in the American Colonies," pp. 124-43, by Mary Patterson Clarke; "The Early Careers of the Royal Governors," pp. 145-68, by Leonard W. Labaree; "Jonathan Belcher, Junior, Chief Justice and Lieutenant Governor of Nova Scotia," pp. 169-97, by Ralph Greenlee Lounsbury; "The Impressment of Seamen in the American Colonies," pp. 198-224, by Dora Mae Clark; "The Economic Causes of the Rise of Baltimore," pp. 225-51, by Clarence P. Gould; "The Settlement and Financing of British West India Plantations in the Eighteenth Century," pp. 252-83, by Frank Wesley Pitman; and "The Taxation of Connecticut Towns, 1750-1775," pp. 284-98, by Lawrence Henry Gipson.

FARRAND, LIVINGSTON: *Basis of American History, 1500-1900, The American Nation: A History*, II (London & New York, 1904).

FERNOW, BERTHOLD: "The Middle Colonies," *Narrative and Critical History of America*, V: 189-258.

FISHER, SYDNEY GEORGE: *The Struggle for American Independence* (London & Philadelphia, 1908).

———: *The True History of the American Revolution* (London & Philadelphia, 1903).

FISKE, JOHN: *The American Revolution* (2 vols., Boston & New York, 1891).

FROTHINGHAM, RICHARD: *Rise of the Republic of the United States* (Boston, 1872).

GIPSON, LAWRENCE HENRY: "A View of the Thirteen Colonies at the Close of the Great War for the Empire, 1763," *New York History*, XL (1959), 327-57.

GRAHAME, JAMES: *The History of the United States of North America: From the Plantation of the British Colonies till Their Assumption of National Independence* (London, 1827-29; rev. edn., 1836; 2nd edn., enl., 4 vols., Boston, 1845).

GREENE, JACK P.: *The Reappraisal of the American Revolution in Recent Historical Literature*, Service Center for Teachers of History, *Publications*, No. 68 (Washington, D.C., c. 1967).

GUTMAN, JUDITH MARA: *The Colonial Venture: An Autobiography of the American Colonies from Their Beginnings to 1763* (New York, c. 1966).

HAWKE, DAVID: *The Colonial Experience* (New York, 1966).

HAWKS, FRANCIS L. (using pseud. Lambert Lilly): *The Early History of the Southern States: Virginia, North and South Carolina, and Georgia . . .* (Philadelphia, 1832; Boston, 1833); *History of the Middle States . . .* (Boston, 1844); *History of New England . . .* (Boston, 1839).

HILDRETH, RICHARD: *The History of the United States of America . . .* (3 vols., New York, 1849; rev. edn., 6 vols., 1880).

HOLMES, ABIEL: *American Annals; Or a Chronological History of America from Its Discovery in MCCCCXCII to MDCCCVI* (2 vols., Cambridge, Mass., 1805; 2nd edn., under altered title, 1829).

HOWARD, GEORGE ELLIOT: *Preliminaries of the Revolution, 1763-1775, The American Nation: A History*, VIII (London & New York, 1905).

KERR, WILFRED B.: *The Maritime Provinces of British North America and the American Revolution* (Sackville, N.B. [1941]).

KNOLLENBERG, BERNHARD: *Origin of the American Revolution, 1759-1766* (New York, 1960).

LACY, DAN: *The Meaning of the American Revolution* ([New York], 1964).

LECKY, WILLIAM EDWARD HARTPOLE: *The American Revolution, 1763-1783: Being the Chapters and Passages Relating to America from the Author's History of England in the Eighteenth Century* (James Albert Woodburn, ed., Boston & New York, 1898; London & New York, 1913).

MAC NUTT, WALTER SCOTT: *The Making of the Maritime Provinces, 1713-1784*, Canadian Historical Association, *Booklet*, No. 4 (Ottawa, 1955).

MARSHALL, JOHN: *A History of the Colonies Planted by the English on the Continent of North America: From Their Settlement to the Commencement of the War Which Terminated in Their Independence* (Philadelphia, 1824).

MILLER, JOHN C.: *Origins of the American Revolution* (Boston, 1943; reiss., London & Stanford, Calif., c. 1959).

――――: *Triumph of Freedom, 1775-1783* (Boston, 1948).

MORGAN, EDMUND S.: *The Birth of the Republic, 1763-89* (Chicago, c. 1956).

MORRIS, RICHARD B.: *The American Revolution Reconsidered* (New York, c. 1967).

――――, ed.: *The Era of the American Revolution: Studies Inscribed to Evarts Boutell Greene* (New York, 1939). Among the essays the following should be listed: "The Effect of the Navigation Acts on the Thirteen Colonies," pp. 3-39, by Lawrence A. Harper; "Writs of Assistance as a Cause of the Revolution," pp. 40-75, by O. M. Dickerson; "Labor and Mercantilism in the Revolutionary Era," pp. 76-139, by Richard B. Morris; "The American Balance of Power and European Diplomacy, 1712-78," pp. 140-69, by Max Savelle; "The Office of Commander in Chief: A Phase of Imperial Unity on the Eve of the Revolution," pp. 170-213, by Clarence E. Carter; "The Royal Governors in the Middle and Southern Colonies on the Eve of the Revolution: A Study in Imperial Personnel," pp. 214-68, by Louise B. Dunbar; "The Sons of Liberty in New York," pp. 269-89, by Herbert M. Morais; "Eliphalet Dyer: Connecticut Revolutionist," pp. 290-304; by George C. Groce, Jr.; and "The Patriot Newspaper and the American Revolution," pp. 305-31, by Sidney I. Pomerantz.

MULLETT, CHARLES F.: "Classical Influences on the American Revolution," *Classical Journal*, XXXV (1939-40), 92-104. See also his study of the connection between Sir Edmund Coke and the advocates of the American Revolution: "Coke and the American Revolution," *Economica*, XII (1932), 457-71.

NELSON, WILLIAM H.: "The Revolutionary Character of the American Revolution," *American Historical Review*, LXX (1965), 998-1014.

NEVINS, ALLAN: *The American States During and After the Revolution, 1775-1789* (New York, 1924).

OSGOOD, HERBERT LEVI: *The American Colonies in the Eighteenth Century* (4 vols., New York, 1924-5).

――――: "The American Revolution," *Political Science Quarterly*, XIII (1898), 41-59.

PALFREY, JOHN GORHAM: *A Compendious History of New England* . . [1492-1765] (4 vols., Boston, 1873, 1884).

RANKIN, HUGH F.: *The American Revolution* (London, 1964).

RIVERS, WILLIAM J.: "The Carolinas," *Narrative and Critical History of America,* V: 285-356.

ROBSON, ERIC: "Prelude to Independence: The American Colonies in the Eighteenth Century," *History Today,* IV (1954), 121-8.

———: "The War of American Independence Reconsidered," *ibid.,* II (1952), 314-22.

SAVELLE, MAX: *The Foundations of American Civilization: A History of Colonial America* (New York, c. 1942; rev. edn. by Robert Middlekauff issued under the title *A History of Colonial America,* 1964).

STEDMAN, CHARLES: *The History of the Origin, Progress and Termination of the American War* (2 vols., Dublin & London, 1794). See also the article by R. Kent Newmyer, "Charles Stedman's *History of the American War,*" *American Historical Review,* LXIII (1957-8), 924-34.

THWAITES, REUBEN G.: *France in America, 1497-1763, The American Nation: A History,* VII (New York, 1905).

TREVELYAN, GEORGE OTTO: *The American Revolution* (4 vols., London & New York, 1899-1907; n. edn., 1905-12; a condensed version, Richard B. Morris, ed., New York, c. 1964).

TRUMBULL, BENJAMIN: *A General History of the United States of America from the Discovery in 1492, to 1792 . . .* (3 vols. planned, only 1 pub., Boston & New York, 1810).

VAN TYNE, CLAUDE HALSTEAD: *The American Revolution, 1776-1783, The American Nation: A History,* IX (London & New York, 1905).

———: *The War of Independence, American Phase: Being the Second Volume of a History of the Founding of the American Republic* (Boston & New York, 1929). See section C under The Empire for citation of the first volume.

VER STEEG, CLARENCE L.: *The Formative Years, 1607-1763* (New York, 1964).

WARD, CHRISTOPHER: *The War of the Revolution* (John Richard Alden, ed., New York, 1952).

WERTENBAKER, THOMAS J.: *The Founding of American Civilization: The Middle Colonies* (London & New York, 1938) and the companion volume: *The Old South: The Founding of American Civilization* (New York, c. 1942; n. edn., 1963).

WINSOR, JUSTIN: "New England, 1689-1763," *Narrative and Critical History of America,* V: 87-188; "Maryland and Virginia," *ibid.,* V: 259-84; and "The Conflict Precipitated," *ibid.,* VI: 113-230.

WOOD, GORDON: "Rhetoric and Reality in the American Revolution," *William and Mary Quarterly,* 3rd ser., XXIII (1966), 3-32.

WOOD, WILLIAM, and RALPH HENRY GABRIEL: *The Winning of Freedom, The Pageant of America Series,* VI (New Haven, Conn., 1927).

WRIGHT, LOUIS B.: *The Atlantic Frontier: Colonial American Civilization, 1607-1763* (New York, 1947).

2. Political

AKAGI, ROY HIDEMICHI: *The Town Proprietors of the New England Colonies . . . 1620-1770* (Philadelphia, 1924).

APPLETON, MARGUERITE: "The Agents of the New England Colonies in the Revolutionary Period," *New England Quarterly,* VI (1933), 371-87.

BAILYN, BERNARD: *The Ideological Origins of the American Revolution* (Cambridge, Mass., 1967). This represents an expansion of the book-length "Introduction" to *Pamphlets of the American Revolution* (Cambridge, Mass., 1965), I.

———: "Political Experience and Enlightenment Ideas in Eighteenth-Century America," *American Historical Review,* LXVII (1961-2), 339-51.

BECKER, CARL L.: *The Declaration of Independence: A Study in the History of Political Ideas* (New York, 1942; 1956).

BEIRNE, FRANCIS F.: "Mission to Canada, 1776," *Maryland Historical Magazine,* LX (1965), 404-20; with regard to the political mission sent by Congress.

BEMIS, SAMUEL FLAGG: *The Diplomacy of the American Revolution* (Bloomington, Ind., 1957).

BENTON, JOSIAH HENRY: *Warning Out in New England, 1656-1817* (Boston, 1911).

BERGER, CARL: *Broadsides and Bayonets: The Propaganda War of the American Revolution* (Philadelphia, c. 1961). A discussion of the efforts of public officials and agencies to win support from various groups (e.g. the Canadians, Hessians, and Indians) dealing primarily with official documents of propaganda.

BILLIAS, GEORGE ATHAN, ed.: *Law and Authority in Colonial America: Selected Essays* (Barre, Mass., 1965).

BISHOP, CORTLAND FIELD: *History of Elections in the American Colonies* (New York, 1893).

BOND, BEVERLEY WAUGH, JR.: "The Colonial Agent as a Popular Representative," *Political Science Quarterly,* XXXV (1920), 372-92.

———: *The Quit-Rent System in the American Colonies, Yale Historical Publications: Miscellany,* VI (London & New Haven, Conn., 1919).

BOORSTIN, DANIEL J.: *The Genius of American Politics* (Chicago, 1953).

BUEL, RICHARD, JR.: "Democracy and the American Revolution: A Frame of Reference," *William and Mary Quarterly,* 3rd ser., XXI (1964), 165-90.

BURNETT, EDMUND C.: *The Continental Congress* (New York, 1941).

BURNS, JAMES JOSEPH: *The Colonial Agents of New England* (Washington, D.C., 1935).

BURNS, JOHN FRANCIS: *Controversies Between Royal Governors and Their Assemblies in the Northern American Colonies . . .* (Boston, 1923).

CALKIN, HOMER L.: "Pamphlets and Public Opinion during the American Revolution," *Pennsylvania Magazine of History and Biography,* LXIV (1940), 22-42.

CALLAHAN, NORTH: *Royal Raiders: The Tories of the American Revolution* (Indianapolis, Ind., 1963).

CARPENTER, WILLIAM SEAL: *The Development of American Political Thought* (Princeton, N.J., 1930).

CECIL, ROBERT: "Oligarchy and Mob-Rule in the American Revolution," *History Today,* XIII (1963), 197-204.

CHAFEE, ZECHARIAH, JR.: "Colonial Courts and the Common Law," Massachusetts Historical Society, *Proceedings,* LXVIII (1944-7), 132-59. Contains material on the English common law in North American courts.

CHANNING, EDWARD: "Town and County Government in the English Colonies of North America," Johns Hopkins University, *Studies in Historical and Political Science,* 2nd ser. (1884), 433-89.

CHAPIN, BRADLEY: "The American Revolution as Lese Majesty," *Pennsylvania Magazine of History and Biography,* LXXIX (1955), 310-30.

CHROUST, ANTON-HERMANN: *The Rise of the Legal Profession in America: The Colonial Experience* (Norman, Okla., 1954), Vol. I.

COLEGROVE, KENNETH: "New England Town Mandates: Instructions to the Deputies in Colonial Legislatures," Colonial Society of Massachusetts, *Publications,* XXI (*Transactions, 1919*), 411-49. A discussion of voting instructions to deputies in popular assemblies and the use of the initiative, referendum, and recall.

COLEMAN, ROY V.: *Liberty and Property* (New York, 1951).

COLLINS, EDWARD D.: "Committees of Correspondence of the American Revolution," American Historical Association, *Annual Report, 1901,* (2 vols., Washington, D.C., 1902), I: 243-71.

CORWIN, EDWARD S.: "The 'Higher Law' Background of American Constitutional Law," *Harvard Law Review,* XLII (1928-9), 149-85, 365-409.

DANA, W. F.: "The Declaration of Independence as Justification for Revolution," *ibid.,* XIII (1899-1900), 319-43.

DAVIDSON, PHILIP G.: *Propaganda and the American Revolution, 1763-1783* (Chapel Hill, N.C., 1941).

———: "Sons of Liberty and Stamp Men," *North Carolina Historical Review,* IX (1932), 38-56.

DOUGLASS, E. P.: *Rebels and Democrats: The Struggle for Equal Political Rights and Majority Rule during the American Revolution* (Chapel Hill, N.C., c. 1955).

DUMBAULD, EDWARD: *The Declaration of Independence and What It Means Today* (Norman, Okla., 1950).

FORD, AMELIA CLEWLEY: *Colonial Precedents of Our National Land System as It Existed in 1800,* University of Wisconsin, *Bulletin,* No. 352; *History Series,* II (Madison, Wis., 1910).

GERLACH, DON R.: "A Note on the Quartering Act of 1774," *New England Quarterly,* XXXIX (1966), 80-8. A study of the provisions of the act, indicating that it was not so coercive as has been suggested by many writers.

GILBERT, FELIX: "The English Background of American Isolationism in the Eighteenth Century," *William and Mary Quarterly,* 3rd ser., I (1944), 138-60.

GIPSON, L. H.: "The Drafting of the Albany Plan of Union: A Problem in Semantics," *Pennsylvania History,* XXVI (1959), 291-316.

GOODMAN, LEONARD S.: "Mandamus in the Colonies: The Rise of the Superintending Power of American Courts," *American Journal of Legal History,* I (1957), 308-35, II (1958), 1-35, 129-47.

GRANGER, BRUCE I.: *Political Satire in the American Revolution, 1763-1783* (Ithaca, N.Y., 1960); see also his "The Stamp Act in Satire," *American Quarterly,* VIII (1956), 368-84.

GREENE, EVARTS BOUTELL: *The Revolutionary Generation, 1763-1790, A History of American Life,* IV (New York, 1943).

GREENE, JACK P.: *The Quest for Power: The Lower Houses of Assembly in the Southern Royal Colonies, 1689-1776* (Chapel Hill, N.C., 1963). See also his "The Role of the Lower Houses of Assembly in Eighteenth-Century Politics," *Journal of Southern History,* XXVII (1961), 451-74.

——, and RICHARD M. JELLISON: "The Currency Act of 1764 in Imperial-Colonial Relations, 1764-1776," *William and Mary Quarterly,* 3rd ser., XVIII (1961), 485-518.

GRIFFITH, ERNEST S.: *History of American City Government: The Colonial Period* (New York, 1938).

HAMILTON, J. G. DE ROULHAC: "Southern Members of the Inns of Court," *North Carolina Historical Review,* X (1933), 273-86.

HASKINS, GEORGE L.: "Law and Colonial Society," *American Quarterly,* IX (1957), 354-64.

HAWKE, DAVID: *A Transaction of Free Men: The Birth and Cause of the Declaration of Independence* (New York, 1964).

HENDERSON, ARCHIBALD: "A Pre-Revolutionary Revolt in the Old South-West," *Mississippi Valley Historical Review,* XVII (1930), 191-212. A consideration of why the West supported the Revolutionary forces.

HICKMAN, EMILY: "Colonial Writs of Assistance," *New England Quarterly,* V (1932), 83-104.

HOWARD, GEORGE E.: *An Introduction to the Local Constitutional History of the United States,* Johns Hopkins University, *Studies in Historical and Political Science, Extra Vol.,* IV (Baltimore, Md., 1889).

HOWELL, WILBUR SAMUEL: "The Declaration of Independence and Eighteenth-Century Logic," *William and Mary Quarterly*, 3rd ser., XVIII (1961), 463-84.

JENSEN, MERRILL: *The Articles of Confederation: An Interpretation of the Social-Constitutional History of the American Revolution, 1774-1781* (Madison, Wis., 1948).

———: "Democracy and the American Revolution," *Huntington Library Quarterly*, XX (1956-7), 321-41.

KAMMEN, MICHAEL G.: "The Colonial Agents, English Politics, and the American Revolution," *William and Mary Quarterly*, 3rd ser., XXII (1965), 244-63. See also Kammen's unpublished doctoral dissertation, "The Colonial Agents: English Politics and the American Revolution," Harvard, 1964.

KETCHAM, RALPH L.: "France and American Politics, 1763-1793," *Political Science Quarterly*, LXXVIII (1963), 198-223.

KOEPPEL, ADOLPH, ed.: *New Discovery from British Archives on the 1765 Tax Stamps for America* (Boyerstown, Pa., 1962). A catalog of the known stamps, with illustrations and additional narrative.

KYTE, GEORGE W.: "Some Plans for a Loyalist Stronghold in the Middle Colonies," *Pennsylvania History*, XVI (1949), 177-90.

LABAREE, BENJAMIN W.: "New England Town Meeting," *American Archivist*, XXV (1962), 165-72. A brief discussion of governmental practices in New England towns.

LABAREE, LEONARD W.: *Conservatism in Early American History* (New York, 1948).

———: "The Early Careers of the Royal Governors," *Essays in Colonial History Presented to Charles McLean Andrews . . .* (New York, 1931), pp. 145-68.

LEVY, LEONARD W.: *Legacy of Suppression: Freedom of Speech and Press in Early American History* (Cambridge, Mass., 1960).

LOKKEN, ROY N.: "The Concept of Democracy in Colonial Political Thought," *William and Mary Quarterly*, 3rd ser., XVI (1959), 568-80.

LONN, ELLA: *The Colonial Agents of the Southern Colonies* (Chapel Hill, N.C., 1945).

LOVEJOY, DAVID S.: "Rights Imply Equality: The Case Against the Admiralty Jurisdiction in America, 1764-1776," *William and Mary Quarterly*, 3rd ser., XVI (1959), 459-84.

MC KINLEY, ALBERT EDWARD: *The Suffrage Franchise in the Thirteen English Colonies in America*, University of Pennsylvania, *Publications: Series in History*, No. 2 (Philadelphia, 1905).

MC LAUGHLIN, ANDREW C.: "The Background of American Federalism," *American Political Science Review*, XII (1918), 215-40.

MACMILLAN, MARGARET BURNHAM: *The War Governors in the American Revolution*, Columbia University, *Studies in History, Economics, and Public Law*, No. 503 (New York, 1943).

MAIN, JACKSON TURNER: "Government by the People: The American Revolution and Democratization of the Legislatures," *William and Mary Quarterly*, 3rd ser., XXIII (1966), 391-407.

MALONE, JOSEPH J.: *Pine Trees and Politics: The Naval Stores and Forest Policy in Colonial New England, 1691-1775* (London & Seattle, Wash., 1964).

MEIGS, CORNELIA LYNDE: *The Violent Men: A Study of Human Relations in the First American Congress [1774-76]* (New York, 1949).

MERRIAM, CHARLES E.: *A History of American Political Theories* (New York, 1903; rep., 1924).

METZGER, CHARLES HENRY: *The Quebec Act: A Primary Cause of the American Revolution*, United States Catholic Historical Society, *Monograph Series*, XVI (New York, 1936).

MILLER, HELEN HILL: *The Case for Liberty* (Chapel Hill, N.C., 1965).

MILLER, RALPH N.: "American Nationalism as a Theory of Nature," *William and Mary Quarterly*, 3rd ser., XII (1955), 74-95.

MONTROSS, LYNN: *The Reluctant Rebels: The Story of the Continental Congress, 1774-1789* (New York, 1950).

MORGAN, EDMUND S.: "Colonial Ideas of Parliamentary Power, 1764-1766," *William and Mary Quarterly*, 3rd ser., V (1948), 311-41.

———, and HELEN M. MORGAN: *The Stamp Act Crisis: Prologue to Revolution* (Chapel Hill, N.C., 1953).

MORRIS, RICHARD B: *Government and Labor in Early America* (New York, 1946).

———: "Judicial Supremacy and the Inferior Courts in the American Colonies," *Political Science Quarterly*, LV (1940), 429-34.

———: "Legalism versus Revolutionary Doctrine in New England," *New England Quarterly*, IV (1931), 195-215.

———: *Studies in the History of American Law: With Special Reference to the Seventeenth and Eighteenth Centuries*, Columbia University, *Studies in History, Economics, and Public Law*, No. 316 (London & New York, 1930).

NELSON, HAROLD L.: "Seditious Libel in Colonial America," *American Journal of Legal History*, III (1959), 160-72.

NELSON, WILLIAM H.: *The American Tory* (Oxford, Eng., 1961).

NEWBOLD, ROBERT CLIFFORD: *The Albany Congress and Plan of Union of 1754* (New York, 1955).

OSTRANDER, GILMAN M. *The Rights of Man in America, 1606-1861* (Columbia, Mo., 1960).

PARES, RICHARD: *Colonial Blockade and Neutral Rights, 1739-1763* (Oxford, Eng., 1938).

PHILLIPS, HUBERT: *The Development of a Residential Qualification for Representatives in Colonial Legislatures* (Cincinnati, O., 1921).

PORTER, NOAH: *The New England Meeting House*, Connecticut Tercentenary Commission, *Pamphlet Series*, XVIII (New Haven, Conn., 1933).

RANNEY, JOHN C.: "The Bases of American Federalism," *William and Mary Quarterly*, 3rd ser., III (1946), 1-35.

RATCHFORD, BENJAMIN ULYSSES: *American State Debts* (Durham, N.C., 1941).

RICH, WESLEY EVERETT: *The History of the United States Post Office to the Year 1829, Harvard Economic Studies*, XXVII (Cambridge, Mass., 1924).

ROBSON, ERIC: *The American Revolution in Its Political and Military Aspects, 1763-1783* (London & New York, 1955).

ROSSITER, CLINTON L.: "The Political Theory of the American Revolution," *Review of Politics*, XV (1953), 97-108.

———: *Seedtime of the Republic: The Origin of the American Tradition of Political Liberty* (New York, c. 1953).

———: *The First American Revolution: The American Colonies on the Eve of Independence* (New York, c. 1956).

SANDERS, JENNINGS BRYAN: *Evolution of Executive Departments of the Continental Congress, 1774-1789* (Chapel Hill, N.C., 1935), and *The Presidency of the Continental Congress, 1774-89: A Study in American Institutional History* (Decatur, Ga., c. 1930).

SAVELLE, MAX: "Nationalism and Other Loyalties in the American Revolution," *American Historical Review*, LXVII (1961-2), 901-23.

SCHLESINGER, ARTHUR M.: "Political Mobs and the American Revolution, 1765-1776," American Philosophical Society, *Proceedings*, XCIX (1955), 244-50.

SCOTT, KENNETH: *Counterfeiting in Colonial America* [1650-1788] (New York, 1957).

SMITH, GLENN CURTIS: "An Era of Non-Importation Associations, 1768-73," *William and Mary Quarterly*, 2nd ser., XX (1940), 84-98.

SMITH, WILLIAM: "The Colonial Post-Office," *American Historical Review*, XXI (1915-16), 258-75.

SURRENCY, ERWIN C.: "The Lawyer and the Revolution," *American Journal of Legal History*, VIII (1964), 125-35. A discussion of the leadership roles of lawyers in events leading to the revolution. See also: "Revision of Colonial Laws," *ibid.*, IX (1965), 189-202.

TANNER, EDWIN PLATT: "Colonial Agencies in England during the Eighteenth Century," *Political Science Quarterly*, XVI, (1901), 24-49.

TATE, THAD W.: "The Social Contract in America, 1774-1787: Revolutionary Theory as a Conservative Instrument," *William and Mary Quarterly*, 3rd ser., XXII (1965), 375-91.

VAN TYNE, CLAUDE HALSTEAD: "Sovereignty in the American Revolution: An Historical Study," *American Historical Review*, XII (1906-7), 529-45.

VARG, PAUL A.: "The Advent of Nationalism, 1758-1776," *American Quarterly*, XVI (1964), 169-82.

WALSH, ROBERT, JR.: *An Appeal from the Judgments of Great Britain Respecting the United States: Containing an Historical Outline of Their Merits and Wrongs as Colonies* . . . (2nd edn., Philadelphia, 1819).

WELSH, EDWARD BURGETT: "Some Presbyterian Backgrounds of the Declaration of Independence," *Western Pennsylvania Historical Magazine*, XXIV (1941), 261-7.

WILLIAMSON, CHILTON: *American Suffrage: From Property to Democracy, 1760-1860* (Princeton, N.J., 1960).

WOOLLEY, MARY EMMA: *The Early History of the Colonial Post Office*, Rhode Island Historical Society, *Publications*, n. ser. I (Providence, R.I., 1894; also printed as volume III of the Rhode Island Historical Society, *Studies in Colonial History*, Providence, 1894).

WRIGHT, ESMOND: *Fabric of Freedom, 1763-1800* (London, 1965).

3. Economic

ACKERMAN, EDWARD AUGUSTUS: *New England's Fishing Industry* (Chicago, c. 1941).

ANDREWS, CHARLES MC LEAN: "Colonial Commerce," *American Historical Review*, XX (1914-15), 43-63.

BARROW, THOMAS C.: *Trade and Empire: The British Customs Service in Colonial America, 1660-1775* (Cambridge, Mass., 1967). A discussion of attempts to enforce the Navigation Acts in the American colonies.

BEAN, WALTON E.: "War and the British Colonial Farmer: A Re-evaluation in the Light of New Statistical Records," *Pacific Historical Review*, XI (1942), 439-47.

BIDWELL, PERCY WELLS, and JOHN I. FALCONER: *History of Agriculture in the Northern United States, 1620-1860* Carnegie Institution of Washington, *Publication*, No. 358. (Washington, D.C., 1925).

BINING, ARTHUR CECIL: *British Regulation of the Colonial Iron Industry* (Philadelphia, 1933), and *The Rise of American Economic Life* (New York, c. 1943; 3rd edn., 1955).

BISHOP, JAMES LEANDER: *A History of American Manufactures from 1608 to 1860* (3rd edn., 3 vols., Philadelphia, 1868).

BJORK, GORDON C.: "The Weaning of the American Economy: Independence, Market Changes, and Economic Development," *Journal of Economic History*, XXIV (1964), 541-60; this article is followed by a discussion by Albert Fishlow, pp. 561-6.

BLACK, JOHN DONALD: *The Rural Economy of New England: A Regional Study* (Cambridge, Mass., 1950).

BOWDEN, WITT: *The Industrial History of the United States* (New York, c. 1930).

BREBNER, JOHN BARTLET: *The North Atlantic Triangle: The Interplay of Canada, the United States, and Great Britain* (New Haven, Conn., 1945), the earlier portion.

BRUCHEY, STUART: *The Roots of American Economic Growth, 1607-1861: An Essay in Social Causation* (London & New York, 1965). See also his article "Success and Failure Factors: American Merchants in Foreign Trade in the Eighteenth and Early Nineteenth Centuries," *Business History Review*, XXXII (1958), 272-92.

BURSTEIN, M. L.: "Colonial Currency and Contemporary Monetary Theory: A Review Article," *Explorations in Entrepreneurial History*, 2nd ser., III (1966), 220-33.

CARRIER, LYMAN: *The Beginnings of Agriculture in America* (New York, 1923).

CLARK, VICTOR S.: *History of Manufactures in the United States, 1607-1860* (3 vols., London & Washington, D.C., 1929).

COLE, ARTHUR H.: "The Tempo of Mercantile Life in Colonial America," *Business History Review*, XXXIII (1959), 277-99.

DAVIS, ANDREW MC FARLAND: "Provincial Banks: Land and Silver," Colonial Society of Massachusetts, *Publications*, III (*Transactions, 1895-1897*), 2-40.

DEL MAR, ALEXANDER: *The History of Money in America . . .* [to 1789] (New York, 1899).

EAST, ROBERT A.: *Business Enterprise in the American Revolutionary Era*, Columbia University, *Studies in History, Economics, and Public Law*, No. 439 (London & New York, 1938).

EAVENSON, HOWARD N.: *The First Century and a Quarter of American Coal Industry* (Baltimore, Md., & Pittsburgh, Pa., 1942).

EGLESTON, MELVILLE: "The Land System of the New England Colonies," Johns Hopkins University, *Studies in Historical and Political Science*, 4th ser. (1886), 545-600.

FAIRBURN, WILLIAM ARMSTRONG: *Merchant Sail* (6 vols., Center Lovell, Me., 1945-55). Vol. I, pp. 269-388 are relevant.

FERGUSON, E. JAMES: "Currency Finance: An Interpretation of Colonial Monetary Practices," *William and Mary Quarterly*, 3rd ser., X (1953), 153-80.

FORSYTH, DAVID P.: *The Business Press in America* [1750-1865] (Philadelphia, 1964).

FRENCH, BENJAMIN FRANKLIN: *History of the Rise and Progress of the Iron Trade of the United States . . .* [1621-1857] (New York, 1858).

FREUND, MIRIAM K.: *Jewish Merchants in Colonial America: Their Achievements and Their Contributions to the Development of America* (New York, 1939).

GOEBEL, DOROTHY BURNE: "The 'New England Trade' and the French West Indies, 1763-1774: A Study in Trade Policies," *William and Mary Quarterly*, 3rd ser., XX (1963), 331-72.

GRAY, LEWIS CECIL: *History of Agriculture in the Southern United States to 1860*, Carnegie Institution of Washington, *Publication*, No. 430 (2 vols., Washington, D.C., 1933).

HACKER, LOUIS M.: *The Triumph of American Capitalism: The Development of Forces in American History to the End of the Nineteenth Century* (New York, 1940). See also: "The American Revolution: Economic Aspects," *Marxist Quarterly*, I (1937), 46-68; and "The First American Revolution," *Columbia University Quarterly*, XXVII (1935), 259-95, which deals briefly with the economic unrest preceding the revolution.

HARRIS, MARSHALL D.: *Origin of the Land Tenure System in the United States* (Ames, Iowa, 1953).

HAYWOOD, C. ROBERT: "Economic Sanctions: Use of the Threat of Manufacturing by the Southern Colonies," *Journal of Southern History*, XXV (1959), 207-19; and "Mercantilism and Colonial Slave Labor, 1700-1763," *ibid.*, XXIII (1957), 454-64.

HIDY, RALPH WILLARD: *The House of Baring in American Trade and Finance: English Merchant Bankers at Work, 1763-1861*, Harvard Studies in Business History, XIV (Cambridge, Mass., 1949).

HOULETTE, WILLIAM D.: "Rum-Trading in the American Colonies before 1763," *Journal of American History*, XXVIII (1934), 129-52.

HULBERT, ARCHER BUTLER: *Historic Highways of America* . . . (16 vols., Cleveland, O., 1902-5). Volumes II-V contain pertinent information.

HUNTER, DARD: *Papermaking in Pioneer America* (Philadelphia, 1952).

INNIS, HAROLD ADAMS: "An Introduction to the Economic History of the Maritimes (Including Newfoundland and New England)," Canadian Historical Association, *Report*, 1931, pp. 85-95.

JERNEGAN, MARCUS WILSON: "Slavery and the Beginnings of Industrialism in the American Colonies," *American Historical Review*, XXV (1919-20), 220-40.

LEONARD, EUGENIE ANDRUSS: "Paper as a Critical Commodity during the American Revolution," *Pennsylvania Magazine of History and Biography*, LXXIV (1950), 488-99.

LESTER, RICHARD A.: *Monetary Experiments: Early American and Recent Scandinavian* (Princeton, N.J., 1939).

LIVERSAGE, VINCENT: *Land Tenure in the Colonies* (Cambridge, Eng., 1945).

LORD, ELEANOR LOUISA: *Industrial Experiments in the British Colonies of North America*, Johns Hopkins University, *Studies in Historical and Political Science*, Extra Vol., XVII (Baltimore, Md., 1898).

LYDON, JAMES G.: "Fish and Flour for Gold: Southern Europe and the

Colonial American Balance of Payments," *Business History Review,* XXXIX (1965), 171-83.

MC FARLAND, RAYMOND: *A History of the New England Fisheries* (New York, 1911).

MAYO, LAWRENCE SHAW: "The King's Woods," Massachusetts Historical Society, *Proceedings,* LIV (1920-1), 50-61. Pages 55-61 discuss Governor John Wentworth's attempts to enforce the Crown's rules on cutting timber.

NEWMAN, ERIC P.: *Early Paper Money of America* (Racine, Wis., 1967). An exhaustive study covering colonial and continental currency.

OSTRANDER, GILMAN M.: "The Colonial Molasses Trade," *Agricultural History,* XXX (1956), 77-84.

PARES, RICHARD: *Yankees and Creoles: The Trade between North America and the West Indies before the American Revolution* (London & New York, 1956).

PEARSE, JOHN BARNARD: *A Concise History of the Iron Manufacture of the American Colonies [up to the Revolution] and of Pennsylvania until the Present Time* (Philadelphia, 1876).

PERRY, REGINALD: *Apprenticeship, Past and Present: A Story of Apprenticeship Training in the Skilled Trades since Colonial Days [1640-1949],* United States Bureau of Apprenticeship (Washington, D.C., 1950).

PHILLIPS, HENRY: *Historical Sketches of the Paper Currency of the American Colonies . . .* (2 vols. in 1, Roxbury, Mass., 1865).

ROBERT, JOSEPH CLARKE: *The Story of Tobacco in America* (New York, 1949).

SHEPHERD, JAMES: "A Balance of Payments for the Thirteen Colonies, 1768-1772: A Summary," *Journal of Economic History,* XXV (1965), 691-5.

SITTERSON, JOSEPH CARLYLE: *Sugar Country: The Cane Sugar Industry in the South, 1753-1950* ([Lexington, Ky., 1953]).

SOULE, GEORGE, and VINCENT P. CAROSSO: *American Economic History* (rev. edn., New York, 1957).

STACKPOLE, EDOUARD A.: *The Sea-Hunters: The New England Whalemen during Two Centuries, 1635-1835* (Philadelphia, 1953).

TAYLOR, GEORGE ROGERS: "American Economic Growth before 1840: An Exploratory Essay," *Journal of Economic History,* XXIV (1964), 427-44.

THAYER, THEODORE: "The Land Bank System in the American Colonies," *Journal of Economic History,* XIII (1953), 145-59.

TOWER, WALTER S.: *A History of the American Whale Fishery,* University of Pennsylvania, *Publications: Series in Political Economy and Public Law,* No. 20 (Philadelphia, 1907).

TRYON, ROLLA MILTON: *Household Manufactures in the United States, 1640-1860: A Study in Industrial History* (Chicago, 1917).

VER STEEG, CLARENCE L.: "The American Revolution Considered as an Economic Movement," *Huntington Library Quarterly*, XX (1957), 361-72.

WEEDEN, WILLIAM B.: *Economic and Social History of New England, 1620-1789* (2 vols., Boston & New York, 1890).

WHITRIDGE, ARNOLD: "The American Slave Trade," *History Today*, VIII (1958), 462-72.

WILLIAMS, WILLIAM APPLEMAN: "The Age of Mercantilism: An Interpretation of the American Political Economy, 1763 to 1828," *William and Mary Quarterly*, 3rd ser., XV (1958), 419-37.

4. Social

ADAMS, JAMES TRUSLOW: *Provincial Society, 1690-1763, A History of American Life*, III (New York, 1927).

ALBRIGHT, RAYMOND WOLF: *History of the Evangelical Church* (Harrisburg, Pa., 1942).

ANDREWS, CHARLES MC LEAN: *Colonial Folkways: A Chronicle of American Life in the Reign of the Georges, Chronicles of America Series*, IX (New Haven, Conn., 1921).

ANGOFF, CHARLES: *A Literary History of the American People* (2 vols. in 1, New York, 1935).

ARMSTRONG, MAURICE W., "The Dissenting Deputies and the American Colonies," *Church History*, XXIX (1960), 298-320.

ASBURY, HERBERT: *The Great Illusion: An Informal History of Prohibition [1735-1933]* (Garden City, N.Y., 1950).

ATKINS, GAIUS GLENN, and FREDERICK L. FAGLEY: *History of American Congregationalism* (Boston & Chicago, c. 1942).

BAILYN, BERNARD: *Education in the Forming of American Society: Needs and Opportunities for Study* (Chapel Hill, N.C., c. 1960).

BALDWIN, ALICE M.: *The New England Clergy and the American Revolution* (Durham, N. C., 1928).

BALDWIN, SIMEON EBEN: "The American Jurisdiction of the Bishop of London in Colonial Times," American Antiquarian Society, *Proceedings*, n. ser., XIII (1901), 179-221.

BARKER, HOWARD F.: "National Stocks in the Population of the United States as Indicated by Surnames in the Census of 1790," American Historical Association, *Annual Report, 1931* (3 vols., Washington, D. C., 1937), I: 126-359. This is part of the American Council of Learned Societies' "Report of the Committee on Linguistic and National Stocks in the Population of the United States."

BELL, WHITFIELD J., JR.: *Early American Science: Needs and Opportunities for Study* (Williamsburg, Va., 1955).

BENSON, MARY SUMNER: *Women in Eighteenth Century America: A Study of Opinion and Social Usage*, Columbia University, *Studies in*

History, Economics, and Public Law, No. 405 (London & New York, 1935).

BILLINGS, THOMAS HENRY: "The Great Awakening," *Essex Institute Historical Collections*, LXV (1929), 89-104.

BITTINGER, LUCY FORNEY: *The Germans in Colonial Times* (London & Philadelphia, 1901), and *German Religious Life in Colonial Times* (London & Philadelphia, 1906).

BRIDENBAUGH, CARL: *Cities in Revolt: Urban Life in America, 1743-1776* (New York, 1955). See also Bridenbaugh's *Cities in the Wilderness: The First Century of Urban Life in America, 1625-1742* (New York, c. 1938, 1955), the latter part of which is pertinent to the period under review.

————: *The Colonial Craftsman* (New York, 1950).

————: *Mitre and Sceptre: Transatlantic Faiths, Ideas, Personalities, and Politics, 1689-1775* (New York, 1962).

————: *Myths and Realities: Societies of the Colonial South* (Baton Rouge, La., c. 1952).

————: "The New England Town: A Way of Life," American Antiquarian Society, *Proceedings*, n. ser., LVI (1946), 19-48.

————: "Baths and Watering Places of Colonial America," *William and Mary Quarterly*, 3rd ser., III (1946), 151-81.

BRIGGS, CHARLES AUGUSTUS: *American Presbyterianism: Its Origin and Early History . . . with Letters and Documents . . .* (New York, 1885).

BRIGHAM, CLARENCE S.: *Journals and Journeymen: A Contribution to the History of Early American Newspapers* (Philadelphia, 1950).

BRINTON, HOWARD HAINES: *Friends for 300 Years: The History and Beliefs of the Society of Friends since George Fox Started the Quaker Movement* (New York, 1952).

BROCHES, SAMUEL: *Jews in New England* (2 vols., New York, 1942). Deals with Jews in Massachusetts and Rhode Island.

BROWN, INA CORINNE: *The Story of the American Negro* [1619-1950] (rev. edn., New York, 1950).

BROWN, WALLACE: "Negroes and the American Revolution," *History Today*, XIV (1964), 556-63.

BULTMANN, WILLIAM A.: "The S. P. G. and the Foreign Settler in the American Colonies," *British Humanitarianism: Essays Honoring Frank J. Klingberg . . .* (Samuel Clyde McCulloch, ed., Philadelphia, c. 1950), pp. 51-65.

BURANELLI, VINCENT: "Colonial Philosophy," *William and Mary Quarterly*, 3rd ser., XVI (1959), 343-62.

CALHOUN, DANIEL H.: *Professional Lives in America: Structure and Aspiration, 1750-1850* (Cambridge, Mass., 1965).

CATHCART, WILLIAM: *The Baptists and the American Revolution* (Philadelphia, 1876).

COBB, SANFORD HOADLEY: *The Rise of Religious Liberty in America: A History* (London & New York, 1902).

COLBOURN, H. TREVOR: *The Lamp of Experience: Whig History and the Intellectual Origins of American Revolution* (Chapel Hill, N. C., 1965).

COMETTI, ELIZABETH: "Women in the Revolution," *New England Quarterly*, XX (1947), 329-46. A brief survey of the activities of women during the war.

CONNELY, WILLARD: "Colonial Americans in Oxford and Cambridge," *American Oxonian*, XXIX (1942), 6-17.

CRARY, CATHARINE S.: "The Humble Immigrant and the American Dream: Some Case Histories, 1746-1776," *Mississippi Valley Historical Review*, XLVI (1959-60), 46-66.

CROSS, ARTHUR LYON: *The Anglican Episcopate and the American Colonies*, Harvard Historical Studies, IX (New York, 1902).

CURTI, MERLE: *Growth of American Thought* (London & New York, 1943). Part I (Chapters I-V) is pertinent.

DAVIDSON, ELIZABETH: *The Establishment of the English Church in Continental American Colonies*, Trinity College Historical Society, *Historical Papers*, XX (Durham, N. C., 1936).

DEXTER, FRANKLIN B.: "The Influences of English Universities in the Development of New England," Massachusetts Historical Society, *Proceedings*, XVII (1879-80), 340-52.

DEXTER, HENRY MARTIN: *The Congregationalism of the Last Three Hundred Years: As Seen in Its Literature* (New York, 1880).

DOUGLAS, DONALD: *The Huguenot: The Story of the Huguenot Emigrations, Particularly to New England* . . . (New York, 1954).

DRAKE, THOMAS EDWARD: *Quakers and Slavery in America*, Yale Historical Publications: Miscellany, LI (New Haven, Conn., 1950).

DRUMMOND, ANDREW L.: *Story of American Protestantism* (2nd edn., Boston, 1951).

DUFFY, JOHN: *Epidemics in Colonial America* (Baton Rouge, La., 1953).
———: "The Passage to the Colonies," *Mississippi Valley Historical Review*, XXXVIII (1951-2), 21-38.

ELLIS, JOHN TRACY: *Catholics in Colonial America*, Benedictine Studies, No. 8 (Baltimore, Md., 1965); see also his "Catholics in Colonial America [1526-1790]," *American Ecclesiastical Review*, CXXXVI (1957), *passim*.

EZELL, JOHN SAMUEL: *Fortune's Merry Wheel: The Lottery in America* (Cambridge, Mass., 1960); see also "The Lottery in Colonial America, 1612-1776," *William and Mary Quarterly*, 3rd ser., V (1948), 185-200.

FALKENSTEIN, GEORGE N.: "The German Baptist Brethren or Dunkers," Pennsylvania German Society, *Proceedings*, X (Lancaster, Pa., 1900). This article is Part VIII of the series of articles collectively entitled "Pennsylvania: The German Influence in Its Settlement and Development: A Narrative and Critical History."

FAUST, ALBERT BERNHARDT: *The German Element in the United States: With Special Reference to Its Political, Moral, Social, and Educational Influences* (2 vols., Boston, c. 1909; New York, 1927).

FISHER, SYDNEY GEORGE: *Men, Women and Manners in Colonial Times* (London & Philadelphia, 1898).

FORD, HENRY JONES: *The Scotch-Irish in America* (Princeton, N. J., 1915).

FORTENBAUGH, ROBERT: *The Development of the Synodical Polity of the Lutheran Church in America to 1829* . . . (Philadelphia, 1926).

FRANKLIN, JOHN HOPE: *From Slavery to Freedom: A History of American Negroes* (2nd edn., rev. & enl., New York, 1956).

GAUSTAD, EDWIN SCOTT: *The Great Awakening in New England* (New York, 1957).

GOEN, C. C.: *Revivalism and Separatism in New England, 1740-1800: Strict Congregationalists and Separate Baptists in the Great Awakening, Yale Publications in Religion, No. 2* (New Haven, Conn., 1962).

GOLDEN, HARRY LEWIS, and MARTIN RYWELL: *Jews in American History: Their Contribution to the United States of America* [1492-1950] (Charlotte, N. C., 1950).

GOODMAN, ABRAM VOSSEN: *American Overture: Jewish Rights in Colonial Times* (Philadelphia, 1947).

GRAHAM, IAN C. C.: *Colonists from Scotland: Emigration to North America, 1707-1783* (Ithaca, N. Y., 1956).

GREEN, EDWARD R. R.: "Scotch-Irish Emigration: An Imperial Problem," *Western Pennsylvania Historical Magazine*, XXXV (1952), 193-209.

GREENE, LORENZO J.: *The Negro in Colonial New England, 1620-1776*, Columbia University, *Studies in History, Economics, and Public Law*, No. 494 (London & New York, 1942).

GRIZZELL, EMIT DUNCAN: *Origin and Development of the High School in New England before 1865* (New York, 1923).

GUMMERE, RICHARD M.: *The American Colonial Mind and the Classical Tradition: Essays in Comparative Culture* (Cambridge, Mass., 1963).

HÄBERLE, DANIEL: *Auswanderung und Koloniergründungen der Pfälzer im 18 Jahrhundert* . . . (Kaiserlautern, Germany, 1909).

HACKER, LOUIS M.: *The Shaping of American Tradition* (New York, 1947). Part II, 123-230, is relevant.

HANDLIN, OSCAR and MARY F.: "Origins of the Southern Labor System," *William and Mary Quarterly*, 3rd ser., VII (1950), 199-222.

HANLEY, THOMAS O'BRIEN: "Colonial Protestantism and the Rise of Democracy," *American Ecclesiastical Review*, CXLI (1959), 24-32.

HANSEN, MARCUS LEE: *The Atlantic Migration, 1607-1860: A History of the Continuing Settlement of the United States* (Cambridge, Mass., 1940).

HAROUTUNIAN, JOSEPH: *Piety versus Moralism: The Passing of the New England Theology, Studies in Religion and Culture: American Religion Series,* IV (New York, 1932).

HARKNESS, REUBEN E. E.: "Early Relations of Baptists and Quakers," *Church History,* II (1933), 227-42.

HAWKINS, ERNEST: *Historical Notices of Missions of the Church of England in the North American Colonies . . .* (London, 1845).

HAWKS, FRANCIS LISTER: *Contributions to the Ecclesiastical History of the United States of America* (2 vols., New York, 1836-9).

HAYWOOD, C. ROBERT: "The Influence of Mercantilism on Social Attitudes in the South, 1700-1763," *Journal of the History of Ideas,* XX (1959), 577-86. Indicating the affect which English socio-economic concepts had on colonial ideas.

HEIMERT, ALAN: *Religion and the American Mind: From the Great Awakening to the Revolution* (Cambridge, Mass., 1966). An intellectual analysis and reinterpretation of the Revolution as a religious movement, dealing only with the Puritan mind.

HINDLE, BROOKE: *The Pursuit of Science in Revolutionary America, 1735-1789* (Chapel Hill, N. C., 1956).

HOLBROOK, STEWART H.: *The Yankee Exodus: An Account of Migration from New England* (New York, 1950).

HOLLIDAY, CARL: *The Wit and Humor of Colonial Days, 1607-1800* (reiss., New York, 1960).

HOYT, EDWARD A.: "Naturalization under the American Colonies: Signs of a New Community, 1658-1776," *Political Science Quarterly,* LXVII (1952), 248-66.

JAMES, SIDNEY V.: *A People Among Peoples: Quaker Benevolence in Eighteenth-Century America* (Cambridge, Mass., 1963). See also James's articles: "Quaker 'Charity' before the American Revolution," Friends Historical Association, *Bulletin,* L (1961), 82-95, and "Quaker Meetings and Education in the Eighteenth Century," *Quaker History,* LI (1962), 87-102.

JAMESON, J. FRANKLIN: *The American Revolution Considered as a Social Movement* (Princeton, N. J., 1926).

JERNEGAN, MARCUS W.: *Laboring and Dependent Classes in Colonial America 1607-1783 . . . , Social Service Monograph,* No. 17 (Chicago, 1931; reiss., New York, 1960). See also his "Slavery and Conversion in the American Colonies," *American Historical Review,* XXI (1915-16), 504-27.

JONES, MALDWYN ALLEN: *American Immigration* (Chicago, 1960). The first two chapters are applicable to the period under consideration.

JONES, RUFUS MATTHEW, ISAAC SHARPLESS, and AMELIA MOTT GUMMERE: *The Quakers in the American Colonies* (London, 1911).

KERR, HARRY P.: "Politics and Religion in Colonial Fast and Thanksgiving

Sermons, 1763-1783," *Quarterly Journal of Speech*, XLVI (1960), 372-82.

KLEIN, HARRY M. J.: *History of the Eastern Synod of the Reformed Church in the United States* (Lancaster, Pa., 1943).

KNIGHT, EDGAR W.: *Public Education in the South* (Boston, 1922).

KOBRE, SIDNEY: *The Development of the Colonial Newspaper* (Pittsburgh, Pa., 1944).

KOCH, ADRIENNE: *The American Enlightenment: The Shaping of the American Experiment and a Free Society [1765-1815]* (New York, 1965). See also Koch's somewhat earlier writings: *Power, Morals, and the Founding Fathers: Essays in the Interpretation of the American Enlightenment* (Ithaca, N. Y., 1961), and his "Pragmatic Wisdom and the American Enlightenment," *William and Mary Quarterly*, 3rd ser., XVIII (1961), 313-29.

KRAUS, MICHAEL: *The Atlantic Civilization: Eighteenth Century Origins* (Ithaca, N. Y., 1949), and *Inter-Colonial Aspects of American Culture on the Eve of the Revolution: With Special Reference to the Northern Towns*, Columbia University, *Studies in History, Economics, and Public Law*, No. 302 (London & New York, 1928).

LABAREE, LEONARD W.: "The Conservative Attitude toward the Great Awakening," *William and Mary Quarterly*, 3rd ser., I (1944), 331-352.

LEBESON, ANITA LIBMAN: *Jewish Pioneers in America, 1492-1848* (New York, c. 1931), and *Pilgrim People* (New York, 1950).

LEONARD, EUGENIE ANDRUSS, *et al.*: *The American Woman in Colonial and Revolutionary Times, 1565-1800: A Syllabus with Bibliography* (Philadelphia, 1962).

LOVE, WILLIAM DELOSS: *The Fast and Thanksgiving Days of New England* (Boston & New York, 1895).

LUTNICK, SOLOMON: *The American Revolution and the British Press, 1775-1783* (Columbia, Mo., 1967).

MC ANEAR, BEVERLY: "College Founding in the American Colonies, 1745-1775," *Mississippi Valley Historical Review*, XLII (1955-6), 24-44.

MAC LEAR, ANNE BUSH: *Early New England Towns: A Comparative Study of Their Development*, Columbia University, *Studies in History, Economics, and Public Law*, No. 78 (New York, 1908).

MC LOUGHLIN, WILLIAM G.: *Isaac Backus and the American Pietistic Tradition* (Boston, 1967).

MC MURTRIE, DOUGLAS C.: *A History of Printing in the United States: The Story of the Introduction of the Press and of Its History and Influence* . . . (4 vols., New York, 1936).

MAIN, JACKSON TURNER: *The Social Structure of Revolutionary America* (Princeton, N. J., 1965).

MANROSS, WILLIAM WILSON: *A History of the American Episcopal Church* (Milwaukee, Wis. & New York, 1935).

MASON, GEORGE C.: "The African Slave Trade in Colonial Times," *American Historical Record*, I (1872), 311-19, 338-45.

MAXON, CHARLES HARTSHORN: *The Great Awakening in the Middle Colonies* (Chicago, 1920).

MELLOR, GEORGE R.: "Emigration from the British Isles to the New World, 1765-1775," *History*, n. ser., XL (1955), 68-83.

MERRITT, RICHARD L.: *Symbols of American Community, 1735-1775, Yale Studies in Political Science*, XVI (London & New Haven, Conn., 1966), and "The Colonists Discover America: Attention Patterns in the Colonial Press, 1735-1775," *William and Mary Quarterly*, 3rd ser., XXI (1964), 270-87.

METZGER, CHARLES H.: *Catholics and the American Revolution: A Study in Religious Climate* (Chicago, 1962).

MIDDLEKAUFF, ROBERT: *Ancients and Axioms: Secondary Education in Eighteenth-Century New England* (New Haven, Conn., 1963). See also his articles, "Education in Colonial America," *Current History*, 2nd ser., XLI (1961), 5-9, and "A Persistent Tradition: The Classical Curriculum in Eighteenth-Century New England," *William and Mary Quarterly*, 3rd ser., XVIII (1961), 54-67.

MIDWINTER, EDWARD: "The Society for the Propagation of the Gospel and the Church in the American Colonies," *Historical Magazine of the Protestant Episcopal Church*, IV (1935), 67-115. The article deals with New York, New Jersey, and Massachusetts.

MILLER, DANIEL: "Early German American Newspapers," Pennsylvania German Society, *Proceedings*, XIX (Lancaster, Pa., 1911). This article is Part XXII of the series of articles collectively entitled "Pennsylvania: The German Influence in Its Settlement and Development: A Narrative and Critical History."

MOLLER, HERBERT: "Sex Composition and Correlated Cultural Patterns of Colonial America," *William and Mary Quarterly*, 3rd ser., II (1945), 113-53.

MORAIS, HERBERT M.: *Deism in Eighteenth Century America*, Columbia University, *Studies in History, Economics, and Public Law*, No. 397 (London & New York, 1934).

MORGAN, EDMUND S.: "The Puritan Ethic and the American Revolution," *William and Mary Quarterly*, 3rd ser., XXIV (1967), 3-43.

MORRIS, RICHARD B.: "Class Struggle and the American Revolution," *William and Mary Quarterly*, 3rd ser., XIX (1962), 3-29.

MOTT, FRANK LUTHER: *A History of American Magazines, 1741-1850* (London & New York, 1930).

NEWMAN, ALBERT HENRY: *A History of the Baptist Churches in the United States, American Church History Series*, II (New York, 1894).

NICHOLS, ROY F.: *Religion and American Democracy* (Baton Rouge, La., 1959).

O'GORMAN, THOMAS: *A History of the Roman Catholic Church in the*

United States, American Church History Series, IX (New York, 1895).

PARRINGTON, VERNON LOUIS: *Main Currents in American Thought: An Interpretation of American Literature . . .* (2 vols., New York, 1927; 3 vols. in 1, 1930), Vol. I: *The Colonial Mind, 1620-1800.*

PENNINGTON, EDGAR LEGARE: "Colonial Clergy Conventions," *Historical Magazine of the Protestant Episcopal Church,* VIII (1939), 178-218, and "Some Observations Regarding the Colonial Clergy," *ibid.,* X (1941), 45-56.

PERRY, WILLIAM STEVENS: *The History of the American Episcopal Church, 1587-1883* (2 vols., Boston, 1885).

PERSONS, STOW: *American Minds: A History of Ideas* (New York, c. 1958). See also his article, "The Cyclical Theory of History in Eighteenth-Century America," *American Quarterly,* VI (1954), 147-63.

PHILLIPS, ULRICH BONNELL: *American Negro Slavery: A Survey of the Supply, Employment, and Control of Negro Labor as Determined by the Plantation Regime* (London & New York, 1918).

PINE, LESLIE G.: *American Origins* (Garden City, N. Y., 1960). Genealogical sources for Americans.

POOL, DAVID DE SOLA: *Portraits Etched in Stone: Early Jewish Settlers, 1682-1831* (New York, 1952).

PROPER, EMERSON EDWARD: *Colonial Immigration Laws: A Study of the Regulation of Immigration by the English Colonies in America,* Columbia University, *Studies in History, Economics, and Public Law,* No. 31 (London & New York, 1900).

QUARLES, BENJAMIN: *The Negro in the American Revolution* (Chapel Hill, N. C., 1961).

REDDING, JAY SANDERS: *They Came in Chains: Americans from Africa* (Philadelphia, 1950).

The Religious History of New England: King's Chapel Lectures (Cambridge, Mass., & London, 1917). Contains historical sketches of Episcopalians, Methodists, Congregationalists, Baptists, and Quakers.

RICHARDSON, LYON N.: *A History of Early American Magazines, 1741-1789* (New York, 1931).

ROTHMAN, DAVID J.: "A Note on the Study of the Colonial Family," *William and Mary Quarterly,* 3rd ser., XXIII (1966), 627-34.

SACHS, WILLIAM S., and ARI HOOGENBOOM: *The Enterprising Colonials: Society on the Eve of the Revolution* (Chicago, 1965).

SACHSE, WILLIAM LEWIS: *The Colonial American in Britain* (Madison, Wis., 1956). Concerning the activities and attitudes of Americans who went to Britain in the years prior to the Revolution.

SAVELLE, MAX: *The Colonial Origins of American Thought* (Princeton, N. J., 1964) and *Seeds of Liberty: The Genesis of the American Mind* (New York, 1948; rep., Seattle, Wash., 1965).

SCHLESINGER, ARTHUR M.: "The Aristocracy in Colonial America," Massachusetts Historical Society, *Proceedings*, LXXIV (1962), 3-21.

———: "The Colonial Newspapers and the Stamp Act," *New England Quarterly*, VIII (1935), 68-83.

———: "The Liberty Tree: A Geneology," *New England Quarterly*, XXV (1952), 435-58. Traces the symbolic use of the Liberty Tree in the pre-Revolutionary period.

SCHUYLER, LIVINGSTON R.: *The Liberty of the Press in the American Colonies before the Revolutionary War* . . . (New York, 1905).

SHIPTON, CLIFFORD K.: "Secondary Education in the Puritan Colonies," *New England Quarterly*, VII (1934), 646-61.

SMITH, ABBOTT EMERSON: *Colonists in Bondage: White Servitude and Convict Labor in America, 1607-1776* (Chapel Hill, N. C., 1947).

SOSIN, JACK M.: "The Proposal in the Pre-Revolutionary Decade for Establishing Anglican Bishops in the Colonies," *Journal of Ecclesiastical History*, XIII (1962), 76-84.

SPRUILL, JULIA CHERRY: *Women's Life and Work in the Southern Colonies* (Chapel Hill, N. C., 1938).

STEPHENSON, GEORGE MALCOLM: *The Puritan Heritage* (New York, 1952).

SUTHERLAND, STELLA H.: *Population Distribution in Colonial America* (New York, 1936).

SYME, RONALD: *Colonial Elites: Rome, Spain, and the Americas* (London & New York, 1958).

THOMAS, ISAIAH: *The History of Printing in America: With a Biography of Printers and an Account of Newspapers* . . . (2 vols., Worcester, Mass., 1810).

THOMPSON, ROBERT ELLIS: *A History of the Presbyterian Churches in the United States, American Church History Series*, VI (New York, 1895).

TOLLES, FREDERICK B.: "The American Revolution Considered as a Social Movement: A Re-evaluation," *American Historical Review*, LX (1954-5), 1-12.

———: *Quakers and the Atlantic Culture* (New York, 1960).

TRACY, JOSEPH: *The Great Awakening: A History of the Revival of Religion in the Time of Edwards and Whitefield* (Boston, 1842).

TRINTERUD, LEONARD J.: *The Forming of an American Tradition: A Reexamination of Colonial Presbyterianism [1706-88]* (Philadelphia, 1949), and "Presbyterianism in Colonial New England [1718-1793]," Presbyterian Historical Society, *Journal*, XXVII (1949), 1-20.

TYLER, MOSES COIT: *The Literary History of the American Revolution, 1763-1783* (2 vols. in 1, London & New York, c. 1897).

VAN TYNE, CLAUDE HALSTEAD: "Influence of the Clergy, and Religious and Sectarian Forces on the American Revolution," *American Historical Review*, XIX (1913-14), 44-64.

VER STEEG, CLARENCE L.: *The Formative Years, 1607-1763* (New York, 1964).

WEAVER, GLENN: "The Germans of British North America during the French and Indian War," *Social Studies*, XLVIII (1957), 227-35, and "The German Reformed Church during the French and Indian War," Presbyterian Historical Society, *Journal*, XXXV (1957), 265-77. The latter is a discussion of the breakdown of interdenominational conflicts as a result of the war.

WEEKS, STEPHEN B.: *Southern Quakers and Slavery: A Study in Institutional History*, Johns Hopkins University, *Studies in Historical and Political Science, Extra Vol.* XV (Baltimore, Md., 1896).

WEIS, FREDERICK LEWIS: *The Colonial Clergy and the Colonial Churches of New England* (Lancaster, Mass., 1936).

WERTENBAKER, THOMAS J.: *The Golden Age of Colonial Culture* (London & New York, 1942).

WILLIAMS, GEORGE WASHINGTON: *History of the Negro Race in America from 1619 to 1880* . . . (2 vols., London & New York, c. 1882).

WISH, HARVEY: *Society and Thought in Early America: A Social and Intellectual History of the American People through 1865* (New York, 1950).

WITTKE, CARL: *We Who Built America: The Saga of the Immigrant* (New York, 1939; rev. edn., Cleveland, O., 1964). See "Part I: The Colonial Period," pp. 3-98 of this standard work on immigration.

WOOD, GORDON S.: "A Note on Mobs in the American Revolution," *William and Mary Quarterly*, 3rd ser., XXIII (1966), 635-42.

WRIGHT, LOUIS B.: *The Cultural Life of the American Colonies, 1607-1763* (New York, 1957). See also Wright, *et al.*: *The Arts in America: The Colonial Period* (New York, 1966).

WROTH, LAWRENCE C.: *An American Bookshelf, 1755* (London & Philadelphia, 1934). An examination of selected works published circa 1755. See also his *The Colonial Printer* (Portland, Me., 1938; 2nd edn., rev. & enl., Charlottesville, Va., 1964).

———: "Some American Contributions to the Art of Navigation, 1519-1802," Massachusetts Historical Society, *Proceedings*, LXVIII (1952), 72-112.

5. Biographical collections

DELAPLAINE, JOSEPH: *Delaplaine's Repository of the Lives and Portraits of Distinguished American Characters* (Philadelphia, 1815).

DEXTER, FRANKLIN BOWDITCH: *Biographical Sketches of the Graduates of Yale College* . . . (6 vols., New York, 1885-1919).

JOHNSON, ALLEN, and DUMAS MALONE, eds.: *Dictionary of American Biography* (22 vols., New York, 1928-44).

SABINE, LORENZO: *Biographical Sketches of Loyalists of the American Revolution: With an Historical Essay* (2 vols., Boston, 1864).

SHIPTON, CLIFFORD K.: *Sibley's Harvard Graduates: Biographical Sketches of Those Who Attended Harvard College* . . . (begun by John Langdon Sibley, 13 vols. +, Boston, 1933-1965 +).

WEIS, FREDERICK, LEWIS: "The Colonial Clergy of the Middle Colonies: New York, New Jersey and Pennsylvania, 1628-1776," American Antiquarian Society, *Proceedings*, n. ser., LXVI (1956), 167-351.

6. Military and naval

AMHERST, JEFFREY, LORD. *Lord Jeffrey Amherst: A Soldier of the King* by John Cuthbert Long (New York, 1933).

ANDERSON, NILES: "The General Chooses a Road: The Forbes Campaign of 1758 to Capture Fort Du Quesne," *Western Pennsylvania Historical Magazine*, XLII (1959), 109-38, 241-58, 383-401.

ATKINSON, C. T.: "British Forces in North America, 1774-1781: Their Distribution and Strength," Society for Army Historical Research, *Journal*, XVI (1937), 3-23.

BELCHER, HENRY: *The First American Civil War: First Period, 1775-78: With Chapters on the Continental or Revolutionary Army and on the Forces of the Crown* (2 vols., London, 1911).

BUTTERFIELD, LYMAN H.: "Psychological Warfare in 1776: The Jefferson-Franklin Plan to Cause Hessian Desertions," American Philosophical Society, *Proceedings*, XCIV (1950), 233-41.

CARTER, CLARENCE E.: "The Significance of the Military Office in America, 1763-1775," *American Historical Review*, XXVIII (1923), 475-88.

FRÉGAULT, GUY: *La Guerre de la Conquete* (Montreal [1955]). On the causes, events, and results of the Great War for the Empire, 1754-1763.

FRENCH, ALLEN: *The First Year of the American Revolution* (Boston & New York, 1934).

GAGE, THOMAS. *General Gage in America: Being Principally a History of His Role in the American Revolution* by John R. Alden (Baton Rouge, La., 1948).

GRAHAM, GERALD S.: *Empire of the North Atlantic: The Maritime Struggle for North America* (Toronto, 1950). See also his article "The Naval Defence of British North America, 1739-1763," Royal Historical Society, *Transactions*, 4th ser., XXX (1948), 95-110.

HATCH, LOUIS CLINTON: *The Administration of the American Revolutionary Army*, Harvard Historical Studies, X (New York, 1904).

HUSTON, JOHN W.: "The British Evacuation of Fort Pitt, 1772," *Western Pennsylvania Historical Magazine*, XLVIII (1965), 317-29.

LEE, CHARLES. *General Charles Lee: Traitor or Patriot?* by John R. Alden (Baton Rouge, La. [1951]).

LOUDOUN, JOHN CAMPBELL, 4TH EARL OF. *Lord Loudoun in North America* by Stanley M. Pargellis, Yale Historical Publications, *Studies*, No. 7 (New Haven & London, 1933).

LOWELL, E. J.: *The Hessians and Other German Auxiliaries of Great Britain in the Revolutionary War* (New York, 1884).

MOWAT, CHARLES L.: "The Southern Brigade: A Sidelight on the British Military Establishment in America, 1763-1775," *Journal of Southern History*, X (1944), 59-77.

NICHOLS, FRANKLIN THAYER: "The Organization of Braddock's Army," *William and Mary Quarterly*, 3rd ser., IV (1947), 125-47.

PARES, RICHARD: "American versus Continental Warfare, 1739-63," *English Historical Review*, LI (1936), 429-65.

PARKMAN, FRANCIS: *A Half Century of Conflict, Part VI: France and England in North America* . . . (2 vols., Boston, 1892).

PECKHAM, HOWARD H.: *The Colonial Wars, 1689-1762* (Chicago, 1964). See also his article "Speculations on the Colonial Wars," *William and Mary Quarterly*, 3rd ser., XVII (1960), 463-72.

———: *The War for Independence: A Military History* (Chicago, 1958).

QUARLES, BENJAMIN: "The Colonial Militia and Negro Manpower," *Mississippi Valley Historical Review*, XLV (1958-9), 643-52.

RUTLEDGE, JOSEPH LISTER: *Century of Conflict: The Struggle between the French and British in Colonial America*, Canadian History Series, No. 2 (Garden City, N. Y., 1956).

SHY, JOHN: *Toward Lexington: The Role of the British Army in the Coming of the American Revolution* (Princeton, N. J., 1965), and "A New Look at Colonial Militia," *William and Mary Quarterly*, 3rd ser., XX (1963), 175-85.

SIEBERT, WILBUR H.: "Loyalist Troops of New England," *New England Quarterly*, IV (1931), 108-47. This article is a discussion of the various Loyalist units during the years 1774-1784.

STEPHENSON, ORLANDO W.: "The Supply of Gunpowder in 1776," *American Historical Review*, XXX (1925-6), 271-81.

STOUT, NEIL R.: "Manning the Royal Navy in North America, 1763-1775," *American Neptune*, XXIII (1963), 174-85.

SWANSON, NEIL H.: *The First Rebel: Being . . . a True Narrative of America's First Uprising against English Military Authority and an Account of the First Fighting between Armed Colonists and British Regulars* . . . (New York & Toronto, c. 1937).

WALLACE, WILLARD MOSHER: *Appeal to Arms: A Military History of the American Revolution* (New York, 1951).

WINSOR, JUSTIN: "The Struggle for the Great Valleys of North America," *Narrative and Critical History of America*, V: 483-622.

WOOD, WILLIAM: "Canada and the American Revolution," *Canada and Its Provinces* . . . (Adam Shortt and Arthur G. Doughty, eds., 23 vols., Toronto, 1914-17), III: 73-103.

D. MAPS

Among the works concerned with the cartography of North America which will be helpful to the student are two by P. L. Phillips: *A List of Maps of America in the Library of Congress* (Washington, D. C., 1901), and *A List of Geographical Atlases in the Library of Congress* (4 vols., Washington, D. C., 1909-20). C. O. Paullin's *Atlas of the Historical Geography of the United States* (Washington, D. C., 1932), and W. R. Shepherd's *Historical Atlas* (New York, 1911) should also be mentioned. There are three series of facsimile maps relating to North America that should be consulted by the student. They are A. B. Hulbert's *Crown Collection of Photographs of American Maps* (5 vols., Cleveland, O., 1904-08); and his series of maps relating to Canada (3 vols., Cleveland, O., 1901); and L. C. Karpinski's *Manuscript Maps, Prior to 1800, Relating to America* (n.p., 1927).

An Accurate Map of the English Colonies in North America Bordering on the River Ohio. In the *Universal Magazine*, XV (1754), 241.

ANVILLE, JEAN BAPTISTE BOURGUINON D': *Canada, Louisiane et Terres Angloises* ([Paris, 1755]). In his *Atlas Général*, Nos. 32-3.

BELLIN, JACQUES NICOLAS: *Remarques sur la Carte de l'Amérique Septentrionale . . . avec une Description Géographique de ces Parties* (Paris, 1755). Library of Congress Maps.

BOWEN, EMANUEL: *A Map of the British American Plantations, Extending from Boston in New England to Georgia Including All the Back Settlements in the Respective Provinces as Far as the Mississippi.* In the *London Magazine*, XVIII (1749), opp. p. 308.

———: *A New and Accurate Map of New Jersey, Pensilvania, New York, and New England. . . .* In Bowen: *A Complete or Distinct View of the Known World*, No. 60.

———: *A New General Map of America.* In *ibid.*, No. 51.

———, and JOHN GIBSON: *An Accurate Map of North America, Describing and Distinguishing the British, Spanish, and French Dominions on This Great Continent According to a Definitive Treaty Concluded at Paris, 10th Feb., 1763: Also All the West India Islands* (London, 1772). In *American Maps*, II, Nos. 26-7; and in Thomas Jefferys: *General Topography . . .* , Nos. 8-11.

BOWEN, T., sculp.: *A Map of the British and French Settlements in North America.* In *A General Magazine of Arts and Sciences*, I (1755), 69.

BOWLES, CARINGTON: *A New and Accurate Map of North America Drawn from the Famous Mr. d'Anville with Improvements from the Best English Maps and Engraved by R. W. Seale. Also the New Divisions According to the Late Treaty of Peace* [by Peter Bell]

(London, 1771). Library of Congress maps. It was first issued in 1768.

————: *Bowles's New Pocket Map of the Most Inhabited Part of New England, Comprehending the Provinces of Massachusetts Bay and New Hampshire with the Colonies of Connecticut & Rhode Island; Divided into Their Counties, Townships, &c* . . . (London [1775]).

Cantonment of Forces in North America, 11th Oct. 1765. The original is in the British Museum and printed in Milton W. Hamilton, et al., eds: *The Papers of Sir William Johnson,* XI: opp. p. 958.

A Chorographical Map of the Northern Department of North America: Drawn from the Latest and Most Accurate Observations . . . (New Haven, Conn. [1749]). In E. B. O'Callaghan, ed.: *The Documentary History of the State of New York,* IV: 331.

A Correct Map of the Coast of New England (London, 1758). In *The English Pilot* (London, 1758), 4th Book, p. 18.

DOUGLAS, WILLIAM [R. W. SEALE, engr.]: *Plan of the British Dominions of New England in North America. Composed from Actual Surveys* ([London, 1753]).

DRAPER, JOHN: *Cape Ann to Baltimore: Principal Towns and Some of the Highways, 1759-1778;* a modern map in Douglas Southall Freeman: *George Washington: A Biography,* III: end-piece map.

DUNN, SAMUEL: *A Map of the British Empire in North America: Improved from the Surveys of Capt. Carver.* In Thomas Jefferys: *The American Atlas* . . . , No. 8.

EVANS, LEWIS: *A General Map of the Middle British Colonies in America* . . . *and of Part of New-France wherein Is also Shewn the Antient and Present Seats of the Indian Nations* . . . (London & Philadelphia, 1755). Reprinted in facsimile in *Pennsylvania Archives,* 3rd series, Appendix, which is a volume of maps, and in L. H. Gipson: *Lewis Evans* . . . , Pt. III, p. 222.

The Seat of War in the Northern Colonies: A General Map of the Northern British Colonies in America which Comprehends the Province of Quebec, the Governments of Newfoundland, Nova Scotia, New England & New York . . . (London, 1776). In Robert Sayer and John Bennett: *The American Military Pocket Atlas* . . . (London [1776]), No. 3.

GIBSON, JOHN, sculp.: *A New and Accurate Map of America.* In the *American Gazetteer* (London, 1762), I: frontispiece.

————: *A New and Accurate Map of Part of North America Comprehending the Provinces of New England, New York, Pensilvania, New Jersey, Connecticut, Rhode Island, & Part of Virginia, Canada and Halifax* ([London], 1771). In Peter Kalm: *Travels in North America.* . . .

GREEN, JOHN: *A Chart of North and South America: Including the Atlantic* and Pacific Oceans and with the Nearest Coasts of Europe, Africa and Asia (London, 1775). In Thomas Jefferys: *The American Atlas* . . . , Nos. 1-3.

[————]: *A Map of the Most Inhabited Part of New England Containing the Provinces of Massachuset[t]s Bay and New Hampshire with the Colonies of Con[n]ecticut and Rhode Island.* . . . In Jefferys: *A General Topography of North America and the West Indies* . . . , Nos. 26-9; also in Jefferys: *The American Atlas* . . . , Nos. 15-16.

HOLLAND, SAMUEL: *The Provinces of New York, and New-Jersey; with Part of Pensilvania and the Governments of Trois Rivières and Montreal.* . . . In Jefferys: *A General Topography of North America and the West Indies* . . . , No. 34. This was engraved by Thomas Jefferys.

JEFFERYS, THOMAS: *A Chorographical Map of the Country between Albany, Oswego, Fort Frontenac, and Les Trois Rivières; Exhibiting All the Grants Made by the French Governors on Lake Champlain and between That Lake and Montreal.* . . . *Drawn by Capt. Holland.* In Jefferys: *A General Topography of North America and the West Indies* . . . , No. 33.

————: *A General Map of the Middle British Colonies in America* . . . *By Lewis Evans, Corrected and Improved with the Addition of the Line of Forts on the Back Settlements* (London, 1758). In Jefferys: *A General Topography of North America and the West Indies* . . . , No. 32.

KITCHIN, THOMAS, sculp.: *A Map of the British and French Dominions in North America with the Roads, Distances, Limits, and Extent of the Settlement & Forts as They Are now. By I. Palairet, Revised and improved by J. Rocque* . . . (London, 1759). In *American Maps,* II: No. 23.

————: *A Map of New England and Nova Scotia, with Part of New York, Canada, and New Britain & the Adjacent Islands of Newfoundland, Cape Breton, &c.* ([London, 1758]). In the *London Magazine,* XXVII (1758), opp. p. 440.

————: *A New and Correct Map of North America: With the West India Islands.* . . . In Kitchin: *A General Atlas* . . . , Nos. 30-1.

————: *A New Map of North & South Carolina & Georgia.* In the *London Magazine,* XXXIV (1763), opp. p. 168.

LODGE, JOHN, sculp.: *A Chart of the Coast of New England from Beverly to Scituate Harbour Including the Ports of Boston and Salem.* In the *London Magazine,* XLIII (1774), opp. p. 165.

LOTTER, MATTHEW ALBERT: *A Map of the Provinces of New-York and New-Jersey, with a Part of Pennsylvania and the Province of Quebec: From the Topographical Observations of C. J. Sauthier* (Augsburg, Germany, 1777). In *Pennsylvania Archives,* 3rd series, Appendix, I-X.

A Map of the Five Great Lakes with Part of Pensilvania, New York,

Canada and Hudson Bay Territories, Etc. In the *London Magazine,* XXIV (1755), opp. p. 432.

A Map of the Whole Continent of America Divided into North and South and West Indies: With a Copious Table Fully Shewing the Several Possessions of Each European Prince and State as Settled by the Definite Treaty Concluded at Paris, Feb. 10, 1763 . . . (London, 1772). In *American Maps,* II, Nos. 31-2.

MITCHELL, JOHN [Thomas Kitchin, sculp]: *A Map of the British and French Dominions in North America with the Roads, Distances, Limits, and Extent of the Settlements. Humbly Inscribed to the Right Honourable the Earl of Halifax and Other Right Honourable the Lords Commissioners for Trade and Plantations* (London, 1755). This may be called the British official map of North America.

MOLL, HERMANN: *New England, New York, New Jersey and Pensilvania* ([London, 1736]). In Moll: *Atlas Minor* (1736).

A New and Correct Map of North America with the West India Islands. Which Compose the British Empire: Laid Down According to the Latest Surveys and Corrected from the Original Materials of Governor Pownall, 1777. In Jefferys: *The American Atlas* . . . , Nos. 5-6. It will be noted that the map carries the date 1777, although the index to the maps gives it the date 1776.

North American Colonies, 1755 to 1763. A modern map found in J. G. Bartholomew: *A Literary and Historical Atlas of America* (rev. by Samuel McKee, Jr., London, 1930), pp. 8-9. The map shows the English and French land holdings, the treaty settlement of 1763, approximate location of Indian tribes, and other details.

POWNALL, THOMAS: *A Map of the Middle British Colonies in North America: First Published by Mr. Lewis Evans of Philadelphia in 1755 and since Corrected and Improved, as also Extended* . . . (London, 1776).

ROBERT, SIEUR: *L'Amérique Septentrionale et Méridionale Divisée en ses Principales Parties par les Ms. Sansom; Rectifiée suivant les Nouvelles Découvertes et Assujettie aux Observations Astronomiques* . . . ([Paris, 1749]). In *American Maps,* II: No. 19. Library of Congress.

CHAPTER V

The
North American Colonies

Part II: The Individual Colonies

CANADA (*the Province of Quebec*)

A. BIBLIOGRAPHICAL AIDS

The printed sources here listed relate particularly to the period 1763-1776, with Canada as part of the British Empire.

BROWN, CHARLES RAYNOR: "Bibliography of Quebec or Lower Canada Laws," *Law Library Journal*, XIX (1927), 90-109. This article was reprinted in Toronto in 1927.

CASEY, MAGDALEN: *Catalogue of Pamphlets in the Public Archives of Canada, 1493-1931: With Index,* Public Archives of Canada, *Publications,* No. 13 (2 vols., Ottawa, 1931-2), Vol. I, 1493-1931. Many of the pamphlets listed do not deal directly with Canada.

FARIBAULT, GEORGES BARTHÉLEMI: *Catalogue d'Ouvrages sur l'Histoire de l'Amérique, et en Particulier sur celle du Canada* . . . (Quebec, 1837).

GARIGUE, PHILIP: *A Bibliographical Introduction to the Study of French Canada* (Montreal, 1956).

"Graduate Theses in Canadian History and Related Subjects," *Canadian Historical Review.* This section appeared annually in the September issue from 1927 until 1966 when it was replaced by *Register of Post-Graduate Dissertations in Progress in History and Related Subjects* to be published annually.

HIGGINS, MARION V., ed.: *Bibliography of Canadian Bibliographies* . . . , McGill University, *Publications Series,* VII, No. 20. (Montreal, 1930).

LANCTOT, GUSTAVE, comp.: *L'Oeuvre de la France en Amérique du Nord: Bibliographie Sélective et Critique* . . . (Montreal, 1951).

———: "Past Historians and Present History in Canada," *Canadian Historical Review*, XXII (1941), 241-53. A bibliographical introduction to the history of French Canada.

PUBLIC ARCHIVES OF CANADA: *Catalogue of Pamphlets, Journals, and Reports in the Public Archives of Canada, 1611-1867* (Norman Fee, ed., 2nd edn., Ottawa, 1916).

Rapport de l'Archiviste de la Province de Québec (43 vols.+, Quebec, 1921+).

Review of Historical Publications Relating to Canada, Vols. I-XXII (Toronto, 1896-1918). This publication was succeeded by the *Canadian Historical Review*.

SHORTT, ADAM, and ARTHUR G. DOUGHTY, eds.: *Canada and Its Provinces* . . . (23 vols., Toronto, 1914-17), XXIII: "Manuscript Sources," pp. 224-32; "Bibliography," pp. 233-83: "Chronological Outline," pp. 284-326; "Historical Tables," pp. 327-64.

STATON, FRANCES MARIA, and MARIE TREMAINE, eds.: *A Bibliography of Canadiana: Being Items in the Public Library of Toronto, Canada, Relating to the Early History and Development of Canada* (Toronto, 1934). A supplement with the same title, edited by Gertrude Boyle and Marjorie Colbeck, was published in Toronto in 1959.

STEWART, SHEILA J., and D. C. HARVEY: *A Catalogue of the [Thomas Beamish] Akins Collection of Books and Pamphlets*, Public Archives of Nova Scotia, *Publications*, No. 1 (Halifax, N.S., 1933).

TANGHE, RAYMOND: *Bibliography of Canadian Bibliographies* (Toronto, 1960).

TREMAINE, MARIE: *A Bibliography of Canadian Imprints, 1750-1800* (Toronto, 1952).

TROTTER, REGINALD GEORGE: "Bibliography: Printed Works," *The Cambridge History of the British Empire, Volume VI: Canada and Newfoundland* (Cambridge, Eng., 1930), pp. 832-79.

———: *Canadian History: A Syllabus and Guide to Reading* (New York, 1926; enl. edn., Toronto, 1934).

WINKS, ROBIN: *Recent Trends and New Literature in Canadian History*, Service Center for Teachers of History, *Publications*, No. 19 (Washington, D.C., c. 1959).

B. PRINTED SOURCE MATERIALS

1. Government and related documents

"Abstracts of the Actes de Foy et Hommage" [Vols. II, III, IV (1723-81)], Canadian Archives, *Report, 1884* (Ottawa, 1885), 1-29. For abstracts from Vols. I, V-VIII (1667-1854) of the Actes de Foy et Hommage, see *Report*, 1885 (Ottawa, 1886), 31-76.

An Abstract of those Parts of the Custom of the Viscounty and Provostship of Paris Which Were Received and Practised in the Province of Quebec in the Time of the French Government . . . (London, 1772).

CAVENDISH, HENRY: *Debates of the House of Commons in the Year 1774 on the Bill for Making More Effective Provision for the Government of the Province of Quebec* . . . (J. Wright, ed., London, 1839).

Convention for the Liquidation of the Canada Paper Money Belonging to the Subjects of Great Britain . . . (London, 1766).

CUGNET, FRANÇOIS JOSEPH, ed.: *Abstracts of the Several Royal Edicts and Declarations, and Provincial Regulations and Ordinances That Were in Force in the Province of Quebec in the Time of the French Government* . . . (London, 1772). A French edition was also prepared by Cugnet: *Extraits des Édits, Declarations, Ordonnances et Reglemens, de sa Majesté Très Chretienne* . . . (Quebec, 1775).

Edits, Ordonnances, Royaux, Declarations, et Arrêts du Conseil d'État du roi concernant le Canada (3 vols., Quebec, 1854-6).

KENNEDY, W. P. M., and GUSTAVE LANCTOT, eds.: *Reports on the Laws of Quebec, 1767-1770*, Public Archives of Canada, *Publications*, No. 12 (Ottawa, 1931).

MARRIOTT, JAMES: *Plan of a Code of Laws for the Province of Quebec; Reported by the Advocate General* (London, 1774).

MASÈRES, FRANCIS, ed.: *A Collection of Several Commissions and Other Public Instruments . . . and Other Papers Relating to the State of the Province in Quebec in North America since the Conquest of It by British Arms in 1760* (London, 1772; rep., New York, 1966).

[——]: "A View of the Civil Government [of Canada] while It Was Subject to the Crown of France [1768]" and "A Plan for Settling the Laws and the Administration of Justice in the Province of Quebec [1768]," *Lower Canada Jurist*, I (1857), Appendices. See in conjunction with this, S. Morley Scott's "The Authorship of Certain Papers in *The Lower Canada Jurist*," *Canadian Historical Review*, X (1929), 335-42.

MURRAY, JAMES: *Report of the State of the Government of Quebec in Canada, by General Murray, June 5, 1762* . . . (Quebec, 1902). Also printed in *Documents Relating to the Constitutional History of Canada* (A. Shortt and A. G. Doughty, eds., 2nd edn., Ottawa, 1918), 47-81.

"Ordinances Made for the Province of Quebec by the Governor and Council of the Said Province, since the Establishment of the Civil Government [1764-1791]," *Report of the Public Archives, 1913* (Arthur G. Doughty, ed., Ottawa, 1914), Appendix E; cont'd in *Report . . . 1915* (1916), Appendix C.

"Ordinances and Proclamations of the Règne Militaire [Sept. 18, 1759-Aug. 10, 1764]," *Report of the Public Archives, 1918* (Arthur G. Doughty, ed., Ottawa, 1919), Appendix B.

"Proclamations Issued by the Governor-in-Chief, 1764-1791," *ibid.,* Appendix C.

ROY, PIERRE-GEORGES, ed.: *Inventaire des Concessions en fief et seigneurie, fois et hommages et aveux et dénombrements conservés aux archives de la province de Québec* (6 vols., Beauceville, 1927-9). Deals with Canadian land grants.

SHORTT, ADAM, and ARTHUR G. DOUGHTY, eds.: *Documents Relating to the Constitutional History of Canada, 1759-1791,* Canadian Archives, *Report, 1905,* III (Ottawa, 1907; 2nd edn., rev., 2 pts., 1918).

2. Non-official contemporary writings

BIGOT, FRANÇOIS. *Mémoire pour Messire François Bigot . . . accusé contre Monsieur le Procureur-Général du Roi . . .* by [M. Dupont, *et al.*] (2 pts. in 1, Paris, 1763).

BOUGAINVILLE, LOUIS ANTOINE DE: *Mémoire d'Antoine de Bougainville sur l'État de la Nouvelle-France [à l'époque de la Guerre de Sept Ans]* ([Paris], 1757); reprinted in Pierre Margry: *Relations et Mémoirs inédits pour Servir à l'histoire de France dans les Pays d'outre-mer . . .* (Paris, 1867).

CASGRAIN, HENRI RAYMOND, ed.: *Guerre du Canada: Relations et Journaux de Différents Expéditions Durant des années 1756 . . . 1760, Collection des Manuscrits du Marechal du Lévis,* XI (Quebec, 1891), and *Lettres et Pièces Militaires; Instructions, Ordres, Mémoires, Plans de Campagne et de défense 1756 to 1760, ibid.,* IV (Quebec, 1891).

CHABERT, JOSEPH-BERNARD, MARQUIS DE: *Voyage fait par Ordre du Roi en 1750 et 1751 dans l'Amérique Septentrionale . . .* (Paris, 1753; rep., New York, 1966).

CHARLEVOIX, PIERRE FRANÇOIS-XAVIER DE: *Histoire et Description Générale de la Nouvelle France avec le Journal Historique d'un Voyage fait par Ordre du Roi dans l'Amérique Septentrionnale* (3 vols., Paris, 1744). In the same year the work was reprinted in six volumes, also in Paris, with a slightly different title. A six-volume translation prepared by John Gilmary Shea was published in New York, 1866-70. While early, it throws important light on the period.

Collection de Manuscrits Contenant Lettres, Mémoires, et Autres Documents Historiques Relatifs à la Nouvelle-France (4 vols., Quebec, 1883-5).

DOUGHTY, ARTHUR GEORGE, and GEORGE PARMELEE, eds.: *The Siege of Quebec and the Battle of the Plains of Abraham* (6 vols., Quebec,

1901). These volumes contain contemporary accounts of events in and about Quebec in 1759.

DUSSIEUX, LOUIS: *Le Canada sous la Domination Française d'après les Archives de la Marine et de la Guerre* (Paris, 1855).

[GALBREATH, C. B.] ed.: "La Mission de M. de Bougainville," Archiviste de Quebec, *Rapport* (1923-4), 1-70.

HENRY, JOHN JOSEPH: *An Accurate and Interesting Account of the Hardships and Sufferings of That Band of Heroes who Traversed the Wilderness in the Campaign against Quebec in 1775* (Lancaster, Pa., 1812; rep., New York [1967]). This is an account of Arnold's campaign in which Henry participated.

INNIS, HAROLD A., ed.: *Select Documents in Canadian Economic History, 1497-1783* (Toronto, 1929).

LÉVIS, FRANÇOIS GASTON, DUC DE: *Collection des Manuscrits du Maréchal de Lévis* (Henri Raymond Casgrain and L. Lecestre, eds., 12 vols., Montreal & Quebec, 1889-95). The collection contains letters and journals of Lévis, Montcalm, Vaudreuil, and others.

MARGRY, PIERRE, ed.: *Rélations et Mémoires Inédits pour Servir à l'Histoire de la France dans les Pays d'Outre-mer . . .* (Paris, 1867).

MASÈRES, FRANCIS: *The Masères Letters, 1766-68*, University of Toronto, *Studies: History and Economics*, III, No. 2 (William Stewart Wallace, ed., Toronto, 1919). These letters were written during Masères's service as attorney general of Quebec and are addressed primarily to Fowler Walker, the London agent of the Quebec merchants; they shed helpful light on the early British administration in Canada.

Mémoires sur le Canada, depuis 1749 jusqu'à 1760 . . . Literary and Historical Society of Quebec, *Historical Documents*, Ser. 1, No. 1 Quebec, 1838).

MUNRO, WILLIAM BENNETT, ed.: *Documents Relating to the Seigneurial Tenure in Canada, 1598-1854 . . .*, Champlain Society, *Publications*, No. 3 (Toronto, 1907).

MURRAY, JAMES: *Journal of the Siege of Quebec, 1760*, Literary and Historical Society of Quebec, *Historical Documents*, Ser. 3, No. 5 (Quebec, 1871); and *Governor Murray's Journal of Quebec: From 18th September, 1759 to 25th May, 1760, ibid.*, No. 6 (Quebec, 1871).

SAMUEL, SIGMUND, comp.: *Seven Years' War in Canada, 1756-1763: Being a Volume of Records and Illustrations . . .* (Toronto, 1934).

STEVENS, PHINEAS: "Journal of Captain Phineas Stevens' Journey from Charlestown, N.H., to Canada, 1752," *Travels in the American Colonies* (Newton D. Mereness, ed., New York, 1916), pp. 299-322.

STEVENS, SYLVESTER K., DONALD H. KENT, and EMMA EDITH WOODS, eds.: *Travels in New France by J. C. B.* (Harrisburg, Pa., 1941).

STONE, EDWIN MARTIN, ed.: *The Invasion of Canada in 1775: Including the "Journal of Captain Simeon Thayer"* . . . , Rhode Island Historical Society, *Collections,* VI (Providence, R.I., 1867).

[TREMAIS, QUERDISIEN]: *Considérations sur l'État présent du Canada [1758] d'apres un Manuscrit aux Archives du Bureau de la Marine à Paris* (Quebec, 1840).

WOLFE, JAMES. *The Life and Letters of James Wolfe* by Beckles Willson (London & New York, 1909). See also the *Life of Major-General James Wolfe: Founded on Original Documents and Illustrated by His Correspondence* . . . by Robert Wright (London, 1864).

WOOD, WILLIAM CHARLES HENRY, ed.: *Logs of the Conquest of Canada,* Champlain Society, *Publication,* IV (Toronto, 1909). Contains material relating to naval activities at Louisbourg, Quebec, and Montreal.

3. *Contemporary pamphlets, tracts, and related documents*

CUGNET, FRANÇOIS JOSEPH: *Traité de la Loi des Fiefs. Qui a Toujours été Suivie en Canada depuis son Établissement, Tirée de Celle Contenue en la Coutume* . . . (Quebec, 1775).

————: *Traité Abrégé des Ancienes Loix, Coutumes et Usages de la Colonie du Canada, Aujourd'huy Province de Québec* . . . (Quebec, 1774).

[KNOX, WILLIAM]: *The Justice and Policy of the Late Act of Parliament for Making More Effectual Provision for the Government of the Province of Quebec Asserted and Proved* . . . (London, 1774).

[LEE, CHARLES]: *The Importance of Canada Considered: In Two Letters to a Noble Lord* (London, 1761).

MASÈRES, FRANCIS: *An Account of the Proceedings of the British, and Other Protestant Inhabitants, of the Province of Quebeck in North-America* . . . (London, 1775). See also Masères's *Additional Papers Concerning the Province of Quebeck: Being an Appendix to the Book Entitled "An Account . . ."* (London, 1776). Both of these works deal with efforts of Canadians to obtain an assembly.

[————]: *The Canadian Freeholder: In Two Dialogues . . . Shewing the Sentiments of the Bulk of the Freeholders of Canada Concerning the late Quebeck-Act* . . . (3 vols., London, 1776-9).

[————]: *Considerations on the Expediency of Procuring an Act of Parliament for the Settlement of the Province of Quebec* (London, 1766).

Thoughts on the Act for Making More Effectual Provision for the Government of the Province of Quebec (London, 1774).

4. *Newspapers*

The Quebec Gazette [La Gazette de Québec], b. 1764, Quebec.

C. SECONDARY WORKS

1. General

BIBAUD, MICHEL: *Histoire du Canada, Sous la Domination Française* (Montreal, 1837; rep., New York [1967]). This was the first history of Canada written by a French-Canadian; it covers the period from 1492 to 1760. A second volume: *Histoire du Canada et des Canadiens, Sous la Domination Anglaise* (Montreal, 1844; rep., New York [1967]) covers the years 1760-1837. Bibaud's viewpoint is definitely Tory.

BOURINOT, JOHN GEORGE: *Canada Under British Rule, 1760-1900* (Cambridge, Eng., 1900).

BRASSEUR DE BOURBOURG, CHARLES ETIENNE: *Histoire du Canada de son Église et de Ses Missions, Depuis la Découverte de l'Amérique jusqu'a nos jours . . .* (2 vols., Paris & Plancy, 1852; reprint in preparation, New York).

BURT, ALFRED LEROY: *The Old Province of Quebec* (Minneapolis, Minn. & Toronto, 1933). This work of great merit covers the period 1760 through 1791.

COFFIN, VICTOR: "The Province of Quebec and the Early American Revolution: A Study in English-American Colonial History," University of Wisconsin, *Bulletin: Economics, Political Science, and History Series*, I (1896), 275-562.

CREIGHTON, DONALD: *Dominion of the North: A History of Canada* (n. edn., Toronto, 1957).

FERLAND, JEAN BAPTISTE ANTOINE: *Cours d'Histoire du Canada* (2 vols., Quebec, 1861-5; rep., New York [1967]), Vol. II: 1663-1759.

GARNEAU, FRANÇOIS XAVIER: *Histoire du Canada depuis sa Découverte jusqu'à nos jour* (1st edn., 3 vols., Quebec, 1845-8; 4th edn., 4 vols., Montreal, 1882-3; 6th edn., rev. & annotated by Hector Garneau, 2 vols., Paris, 1920; 1st English language edn., 3 vols., Montreal, 1860).

GOSSELIN, AUGUSTE: *L'Église du Canada après le Conquête . . .* (Quebec, 1916).

LOWER, A. R. M.: *Colony to Nation: A History of Canada* (New York & Toronto, 1946).

———: "Geographical Determinants in Canadian History," *Essays in Canadian History Presented to George MacKinnon Wrong . . .* (R. Flenley, ed., Toronto, 1939), pp. 229-52.

LUCAS, C. P.: *History of Canada, 1763-1812* (London, 1909).

MUNRO, WILLIAM BENNETT: *Crusaders of New France: A Chronicle of the Fleur-de-Lis in the Wilderness, Chronicles of America Series,*

IV (New Haven, Conn., 1918). Includes the settlement of Canada, to 1763.

PARKMAN, FRANCIS: *The Old Régime in Canada* (Boston, 1874; rev., w/add., 1896).

ROBINSON, PERCY J.: *Toronto during the French Régime: A History of the Toronto Region from Brûlé to Simcoe, 1615-1793* (2nd edn., Toronto, 1965).

SHORTT, ADAM, and ARTHUR G. DOUGHTY, eds.: *Canada and Its Provinces: A History of the Canadian People and Their Institutions* (23 vols., Toronto, 1914-17). A co-operative enterprise. Volumes I-IV, XI-XVIII, XXI, and XXIII contain very important material relevant to the period under consideration.

SMITH, WILLIAM: *History of Canada: From Its First Discovery . . .* (2 vols., Quebec, 1815; London, 1826).

WARKENTIN, JOHN, ed.: *The Western Interior of Canada: A Record of Geographical Discovery, 1612-1912* (Toronto, 1964). Explorers' reports with comments on them.

WRONG, GEORGE M.: *The Rise and Fall of New France* (2 vols., New York, 1928), and *Canada and the American Revolution: The Disruption of the First British Empire* (New York, 1935).

2. Political

BALLS, H. R.: "Quebec, 1763-1774: The Financial Administration," *Canadian Historical Review*, XLI (1960), 203-14.

COUPLAND, REGINALD: *The Quebec Act: A Study in Statesmanship* (Oxford, Eng., 1925).

KELLOGG, LOUISE PHELPS: "A Footnote to the Quebec Act," *Canadian Historical Review*, XIII (1932), 147-56. A discussion of the fears of the French in Illinois before the passing of the Quebec Act in 1774 which embodied this area in the Province of Quebec.

KENNEDY, WILLIAM PAUL MC CLURE: *The Constitution of Canada . . . [1534-1937]* (Toronto, 1938).

KERR, WILFRED B.: "The Stamp Act in Quebec," *English Historical Review*, XLVII (1932), 648-51.

MC ARTHUR, DUNCAN: "The New Régime," [1760-1774], *Canada and Its Provinces . . .* , III, 21-49; "Canada under the Quebec Act," *ibid.*, III, 107-38; "Constitutional History, 1763-1846," *ibid.*, IV, 421-88; and "History of Public Finances, 1763-1840," *ibid.*, IV, 491-518.

MARTIN, CHESTER B.: *Empire and Commonwealth: Studies in Governance and Self-Government in Canada* (Oxford, Eng., 1929).

NEATBY, HILDA M.: *The Administration of Justice under the Quebec Act* (London & Minneapolis, Minn., 1937); deals primarily with the post-1776 period.

SAVELLE, MAX: *The Diplomatic History of the Canadian Boundary, 1749-1763* (New Haven, Conn., & Toronto, 1940).

SCOTT, S. MORLEY: "Civil and Military Authority in Canada, 1764-1766," *Canadian Historical Review*, IX (1928), 117-36.

TRUDEL, MARCEL: *L'Église Canadienne sous le Régime Militaire, 1750-1764* . . . (2 vols. [Montreal], 1956-7).

WALLACE, W. S.: "The Beginnings of British Rule in Canada," *Canadian Historical Review*, VI (1925), 208-21.

3. Economic

CREIGHTON, DONALD G.: *The Commercial Empire of the St. Lawrence, 1760-1850* (New Haven, Conn. & Toronto, 1937). The work relates the development of the commercial system of the St. Lawrence to Canada's political development.

GRAHAM, GERALD SANFORD: *British Policy and Canada, 1774-1791: A Study in 18th Century Trade Policy*, Royal Commonwealth Society, *Imperial Studies*, No. 4 (London & New York, 1930).

INNIS, HAROLD A.: *The Fur Trade in Canada: An Introduction to Canadian Economic History* (London & New Haven, Conn., 1930), and *The Fur Trade of Canada*, University of Toronto, *Studies: History and Economics*, V (Toronto, 1927).

MUNRO, WILLIAM BENNETT: *The Seigniorial System in Canada: A Study in French Colonial Policy*, *Harvard Historical Studies*, XIII (London & New York, 1907). See also his "The Seigneurial System and the Colony," *Canada and Its Provinces* . . . , II: 531-93.

RICH, EDWIN E.: *Montreal and the Fur Trade* (Montreal, 1966).

SHORTT, ADAM: "The Colony in Its Economic Relations," *Canada and Its Provinces* . . . , II: 489-528; "General Economic History, 1763-1841," *ibid.*, IV: 521-96; and "Currency and Banking, 1760-1841," *ibid.*, IV: 596-636.

TACHÉ, JOSEPH CHARLES: *The Seigniorial Tenure in Canada and Plan of Commutation* (Quebec, 1854).

WALLACE, WILLIAM S.: *The Pedlars from Quebec and Other Papers on the Nor'westers* (Toronto, 1954). See also his article "The Pedlars from Quebec," *Canadian Historical Review*, XIII (1932), 387-402.

4. Social

BRADLEY, ARTHUR GRANVILLE: *The United Empire Loyalists: Founders of British Canada* (London, 1932). The New York edition (c. 1932) is entitled *Colonial Americans in Exile*.

DICKIE, GORDON: "Cultural Origins in [Canadian] Colonial Life," *Dalhousie Review*, XXXVII (1957-8), 41-51, 165-74.

FAUTEUX, AEGIDIUS: *The Introduction of Printing into Canada: A Brief History* (Montreal, 1930).

ROCHEMONTEIX, CAMILLE DE: *Les Jésuites et la Nouvelle-France au XVIIIᵉ Siécle d'après des Documents Inédits* (2 vols., Paris, 1906).

SAUNDERS, RICHARD M.: "The Cultural Development of New France before 1760," *Essays in Canadian History Presented to George Mac-Kinnon Wrong* . . . (R. Flenley, ed., Toronto, 1939), pp. 321-345.

WADE, MASON: *The French Canadians, 1760-1945* (New York, 1955). The first two chapters are relevant to the period.

5. Biographical

CARLETON, GUY (later Lord Dorchester). *Lord Dorchester* by Arthur Granville Bradley, *Makers of Canada Series*, III (London & Toronto, 1926). See also the older biography by William Wood: *The Father of British Canada: A Chronicle of Carleton, Chronicles of Canada Series*, XII (Glasgow & Toronto, 1916), and the recent one by A. L. Burt: *Guy Carleton, Lord Dorchester, 1724-1818: Revised Version*, Canadian Historical Association *Booklets*, V (Ottawa, 1955). Finally, see Burt's article: "Sir Guy Carleton and His First Council," *Canadian Historical Review*, IV (1923), 320-32.

GALISSONIÈRE, ROLAND MICHEL BARRIN, COMTE DE LA. *La Galissonière et le Canada* by Roland Lamontagne (Montreal, 1962).

MONTCALM, LOUIS JOSEPH GORSON DE SAINT-VERAN, MARQUIS DE. *Le Marquis de Montcalm (1712-1759)* by Thomas Chapais (Quebec, 1911). See also Parkman under Military.

MURRAY, JAMES. *Life of General the Hon. James Murray: A Builder of Canada* . . . by Reginald Henry Mahon (London, 1921).

NORTHINGTON, ROBERT HENLEY, 1ST EARL OF. "Lord Northington and the Laws of Canada" by R. A. Humphreys and S. Morley Scott, *Canadian Historical Review*, XIV (1933), 42-61.

WOLFE, JAMES. *The Rest to Fortune: The Life of Major-General James Wolfe* by Robin Reilly (London, 1960), and the older work by Robert Wright: *The Life of Major-General James Wolfe: Founded on Original Documents and Illustrated by His Correspondence* . . . (London, 1864). See also the articles by B. H. Liddell Hart: "General Wolfe: Grandsire of the United States," *Blackwood's Magazine*, CCXXI (1927), 336-66, and by S. D. Kennedy: "General James Wolfe," *Quarterly Review*, 298 (1960), 32-44. See under Military: Parkman's *Montcalm and Wolfe*.

6. Military

CASGRAIN, HENRI RAYMOND: *Guerre du Canada, 1756-1760: Montcalm et Lévis* (2 vols., Quebec, 1891).

LLOYD, CHRISTOPHER: *The Capture of Quebec* (New York, 1959).

PARKMAN, FRANCIS: *Montcalm and Wolfe, France and England in North America: A Series of Historical Narratives*, Pt. 7 (2 vols., Boston, 1884).

SMITH, JUSTIN H.: *Our Struggle for the Fourteenth Colony: Canada and the American Revolution* (2 vols., London & New York, 1907).

STACEY, CHARLES P.: *Quebec, 1759: The Siege and the Battle* (New York, 1959).

WOOD, WILLIAM: *The Fight for Canada: A Naval and Military Sketch from the History of the Great Imperial War* (Westminster, Eng., 1904; Boston, 1906).

WRONG, GEORGE M.: *The Fall of Canada: A Chapter in the History of the Seven Years' War* (Oxford, Eng., 1914).

D. MAPS

Catalogue of Maps, Plans, and Charts in the Map Room of the Dominion Archives, Canadian Archives, *Publications*, No. 8 (H. R. Holmden, ed., Ottawa, 1912).

ANVILLE, JEAN BAPTISTE BOUGUINON D': *Le Fleuve Saint-Laurent . . . [From Lake Ontario to the Gulf of St. Lawrence]*. This is No. 35 of a collection of 48 d'Anville maps bound together without title, Paris, 1771; Map Division, New York Public Library.

An Authentic Plan of the River St. Lawrence, from Sillery to the Falls of Montmorency. In the *Gentleman's Magazine*, XXIX (1759), 536.

BELLIN, JACQUES NICOLAS: *Cartes des Lacs du Canada, 1744*. In P. F. X. Charlevoix: *Histoire et Description de la Nouvelle France*, III, opp. p. 277.

———: *La Rivière du Détroit Depuis le Lac Sainte Claire jusqu'au Lac Erié*. In Bellin: *Le Petit Atlas Maritime . . .* , I: No. 12. *Plan du Fort du Detroit* is an inset on this map.

———: *Partie Occidentale de la Nouvelle France ou Canada* ([Paris, 1755]).

Canada by the Proclamation of 1763. In Hugh E. Egerton: *Historical Geography of the British Colonies, Vol. V: Canada: Part II: Historical* (Oxford, 1908), p. 5.

Canada under the Quebec Act of 1774. In *ibid.*, p. 14.

Carte des Cinq Grands Lacs du Canada. In Bellin: *Le Petit Atlas Maritime . . .* , I: No. 6.

CARVER, JONATHAN, *et al.*: *Plan of Montreal or Ville Marie, 1777*. In Faden: *The North American Atlas*, as an inset to map No. 3.

FADEN, WILLIAM: *A New Map of the Province of Quebec, According to the Royal Proclamation of the 7th of Oct. 1763. From the French*

Surveys Connected with Those Made after the War. By Capt. Carver and Other Officers in His Majesty's Service (London, 1776). In Faden: *The North American Atlas . . .* , No. 3.

The Isles of Montreal as They Have Been Survey'd by the French Engineers. In the *London Magazine,* XXX (1761), opp. p. 8.

JEFFERYS, THOMAS: *A Chart of the Gulf of St. Lawrence Composed from a Great Number of Actual Surveys and Other Materials.* In Jefferys: *The American Atlas . . .* , No. 10.

———: *An Exact Chart of the River St. Lawrence from Fort Frontenac to the Island of Anticosti, Shewing the Soundings, Rocks, Shoals, &c. with Views of the Lands and All Necessary Instructions for Navigating That River to Quebec* (London, 1757). In Jefferys: *A General Topography of North America and the West Indies,* No. 15-16.

———: *A Map of Canada and the Northern Part of Louisiana with the Adjacent Countrys* (London, 1762). In Jefferys: *The Natural and Civil History of the French Dominions in North and South America,* Part I: p. 1.

KITCHIN, THOMAS: *A New Map of the Province of Quebec in North America.* In the *London Magazine,* XXXIII (1764), opp. p. 496.

———: *River St. Lawrence from Montreal to the Island of Barnaby on the South Side and the Islands of Jeremy on the North Side.* In Mante: *History of the Late War in North America . . .* , opp. p. 333.

———: *Lake Ontario to the Mouth of the River St. Lawrence.* In *ibid.,* opp. p. 30.

A Map of the Island of Orleans with the Environs of Quebec. In the *Gentleman's Magazine,* XXIX (1759), 452.

OAKLEY, E.: *A Plan of Quebec* ([London], 1759). Library of Congress collection of maps.

POWNALL, THOMAS: *A Sketch of the Upper Parts of Canada,* 1770. In Robert Sayer and John Bennett: *The American Military Pocket Atlas . . .* , No. 4, inset.

SAUTHIER, CLAUDE JOSEPH: *A Map of the Inhabited Part of Canada from the French Surveys with the Frontiers of New York and New England. . . .* This map was engraved by William Faden and appears in his *The North American Atlas . . .* , No. [3]. The map is listed as Number 3 in the Faden Atlas in the Map Room of the New York Public Library, but it is listed as Number 4 in the copy of the Faden atlas in the Library of Congress.

SAYER, ROBERT, and JOHN BENNETT: *A Chart of the Gulf of St. Lawrence . . . [as charted between 1750 and 1765].* In *ibid.,* No. 4.

SMITH, HER'Y: *A View of Quebec from the Bason. Printed from the Drawing of Her'y Smith, Esq., by Francis Swain; P. C. Canot, sculp.* (London [1759]). Library of Congress Maps.

For useful modern maps, see: *A Historical Atlas of Canada* (Donald G. Kerr, ed., 1st edn., Toronto, 1961; 2nd edn., Ontario, 1966). Part II, section 3 contains maps of French Canada; Part III, Sections 1 and 2, maps of British Canada.

CONNECTICUT

A. BIBLIOGRAPHICAL AIDS

FLAGG, C. A.: "Reference List on Connecticut Local History," New York State Library, *Bulletin*, No. 53 (1900), 175-283.

HASSE, ADELAIDE R.: "Connecticut," in "Materials for a Bibliography of the Public Archives of the Thirteen Original States . . . ," American Historical Association, *Annual Report, 1906* (2 vols., Washington, D.C., 1908), II, 340-53.

TRUMBULL, JAMES H.: *List of Books Printed in Connecticut, 1709-1800* ([Hartford, Conn.], 1904).

ZEICHNER, OSCAR: "Bibliographical Essay," *Connecticut Years of Controversy*, pp. 359-82.

B. PRINTED SOURCE MATERIALS

1. *Government and related documents*

Acts and Laws of His Majesty's English Colony of Connecticut in New-England in America (4 vols., New London, Conn., 1750-69). The yearly publications of the *Acts and Laws* are also available for the years 1748 through 1776 on Readex cards.

"Correspondence of Connecticut with the British Government [1755-1757]," Connecticut Historical Society, *Collections*, I (1860), 257-332.

FITCH, THOMAS: *The Fitch Papers: Correspondence and Documents during Thomas Fitch's Governorship of the Colony of Connecticut, 1754-1766*, Connecticut Historical Society, *Collections*, XVII-XVIII (Albert C. Bates, ed., 2 vols., Hartford, Conn., 1918-20).

Heads of Inquiry Relative to the Present State and Condition of His Majesty's Colony of Connecticut, Signified by His Majesty's Secretary of State, in His Letter of the 5th July, 1773; With the Answers Thereto (New London, Conn., 1775). Reprinted in Vol. XIV of the *Records of the Colony of Connecticut*.

JOHNSON, WILLIAM SAMUEL: "Letters of William Samuel Johnson to the

Governors of Connecticut [1766-1771]" Massachusetts Historical Society, *Collections*, 5th ser., IX (1885), 211-490. Johnson's letters were written while acting as London agent for Connecticut.

LAW, JONATHAN: *The Law Papers: Correspondence and Documents during Jonathan Law's Governorship of the Colony of Connecticut, 1741-1750*, Connecticut Historical Society, *Collections*, X, XIII, XV (Albert C. Bates, ed., 3 vols., Hartford, Conn., 1907-14), *Vol. III: January 1747-October 1750*.

Petition of the General Assembly of Connecticut Respecting Susquehanna Matters ([n.p. 1774]); broadside.

PITKIN, WILLIAM: *The Pitkin Papers: Correspondence and Documents during William Pitkin's Governorship of the Colony of Connecticut, 1766-1769* . . . , Connecticut Historical Society, *Collections*, XIX (Albert C. Bates, ed., Hartford, Conn., 1921).

Report of the Commissioners Appointed by the General Assembly of This Colony to Treat with the Proprietaries of Pennsylvania Respecting the Boundaries of This Colony and That Province (Norwich, Conn., 1774).

TRUMBULL, JAMES HAMMOND, and C. J. HOADLY, eds.: *Public Records of the Colony of Connecticut (1636-1776)* (15 vols., Hartford, Conn., 1850-90).

TRUMBULL, JONATHAN: *Copy of a Letter to His Excellency Gen. Gage from the Hon. Jonathan Trumbull, Esq., Governor of His Majesty's Colony of Connecticut, in Behalf of the General Assembly of Said Colony* . . . ([Boston, 1775]). Among the Massachusetts Historical Society *Collections* there are the *Trumbull Papers*, embodied in Volumes IX and X of the Fifth Series and Volumes II and III of the Seventh Series. These papers, outside of the William Samuel Johnson correspondence, do not fall within the limits of this bibliography. Pertinent Trumbull correspondence, however, will be found in the Connecticut Historical Society *Collections*, Vol. XVI (1916), the *Wolcott Papers;* Vol. XVII (1918), the *Fitch Papers;* and Vol. XIX (1921), the *Pitkin Papers.*

WOLCOTT, ROGER: *The Wolcott Papers: Correspondence and Documents during Roger Wolcott's Governorship of the Colony of Connecticut, 1750-54* . . . , Connecticut Historical Society, *Collections*, XVI (Albert C. Bates, ed., Hartford, Conn., 1916).

2. *Non-official contemporary writings*

CLAP, THOMAS: *The Annals of History of Yale-College in New-Haven* . . . [1700-1766] (New Haven, Conn., 1766).

DEANE, SILAS: "Inside the American Revolution: A Silas Deane Diary Fragment, April 20 to October 25, 1775," Christopher Collier, ed., Connecticut Historical Society, *Bulletin*, XXIX (1964), 86-96A.

HUNTINGTON, JEDEDIAH: "Letters of Lieutenant [later Colonel and then General] Jedediah Huntington [of Connecticut, 1775-1776]," Massachusetts Historical Society, *Collections*, 5th ser., IX (1885), 491-518.

INGERSOLL, JARED: *Jared Ingersoll Papers, 1758-1764*, New Haven Colony Historical Society, *Papers*, IX (Franklin B. Dexter, ed., New Haven, Conn., 1918).

JOHNSON, WILLIAM SAMUEL. *Life and Correspondence of William Samuel Johnson* by E. Edward Beardsley (London & New York, 1874; 2nd edn., New York, 1886).

———: *The Superior Court Diary of William Samuel Johnson, 1772-1773 . . .*, American Legal Records, IV (John T. Farrell, ed., Washington, D.C., 1942).

SUSQUEHANNAH COMPANY: *The Susquehannah Company Papers* [1750-1772] (Julian Parks Boyd, ed., 4 vols., Wilkes-Barre, Pa., 1930-3; reissued w/added 5th vol., Ithaca, N.Y., 1963; volumes 6-12 anticipated).

TRUMBULL, JOHN: *The Autobiography of Colonel John Trumbull, Patriot-Artist, 1756-1843 . . .* (Theodore Sizer, ed., New Haven, Conn., 1953).

3. Contemporary pamphlets, tracts, and related documents

CHAMPION, JUDAH: *Christian and Civil Liberty and Freedom Considered and Recommended: A Sermon Delivered Before the General Assembly . . . May 9th, 1776 . . .*

[CHURCH, BENJAMIN]: *Liberty and Property Vindicated, and the St--pm-n Burnt: A Discourse Occasionally Made, on Burning the Effigy of the St--pm-n in New-London . . .* ([Hartford, Conn.], 1765). The stamp man was Jared Ingersoll.

FITCH, THOMAS: *Some Reasons that Influenced the Governor to Take and the Council to Administer the Oath Required by the Act of Parliament, Commonly Called the Stamp-Act . . .* (Hartford, Conn. [1766]). Governor Fitch offered a defence of his actions.

FROTHINGHAM, EBENEZER: *A Key to Unlock the Door That Leads in to Take a Fair View of the Religious Constitution Established by Law in the Colony of Connecticut . . .* ([Newport, R.I.], 1767).

GALE, BENJAMIN: *Doct. Gale's Letter to J. W. Esquire Containing a Narrative of the Principal Matters of a Public and Interesting Nature which Were Subjects of the Debates and Resolves of the General Assembly of the Colony of Connecticut, during Their Sessions in May, 1769* (Hartford, Conn., 1769). A reply to this letter was written by Eliphalet Dyer: *Remarks on Dr. Gale's Letter to J. W. Esq.* ([Hartford, Conn.], 1769), to which Gale replied with *Observations on a Pamphlet Entitled Remarks on Dr. Gale's Letter to J. W. Esq. . . .* (Hartford, Conn. [1769]). See also two letters from Gale to Jared Ingersoll (18 January 1765 and 8 February 1766) in *The Historical Magazine,* VI (1862), 138-9.

[————]: *The Present State of the Colony of Connecticut Considered* ([New Haven, Conn.], 1755). This pamphlet is a criticism of Thomas Clap's administration of Yale College and of his pamphlet *Religious Constitutions of Colleges.*

HART, LEVI: *Liberty Described and Recommended: In a Sermon Preached to the Corporation of Freemen in Farmington . . . September 20, 1774* (Hartford, Conn., 1775). The author urged the Connecticut Assembly to follow Rhode Island's example and pass legislation to prohibit the slave trade and free the Negroes in the colony.

JOHNSON, STEPHEN: *Integrity and Piety the Best Principles of a Good Administration of Government . . . A Sermon Preached before the General Assembly of the Colony of Connecticut . . .* (New London, Conn., 1770).

PERRY, JOSEPH: *A Sermon Preached Before the General Assembly of the Colony of Connecticut . . . Election May 11, 1775 . . .* (Hartford, Conn., 1775).

The Rights of the Governor and Company of the Colony of Connecticut to Claim and Hold Lands Within the Limits of their Charter, Lying West of the Province of New-York, Stated and Considered: In a Letter to J. H., Esquire . . . (Hartford, Conn., 1773).

SALTER, RICHARD: *A Sermon Preached before the General Assembly of the Colony of Connecticut . . . May 12, 1768* (New London, Conn., 1768).

The State of the Lands Said to Be Once Within the Bounds of the Charter of the Colony of Connecticut West of the Province of New-York Considered (New York, 1770).

TRUMBULL, BENJAMIN: *A Discourse Delivered at the Anniversary Meeting of the Freemen of the Town of New-Haven, April 12, 1773 . . .* (New Haven, Conn., 1773).

————: *A Plea in Vindication of the Connecticut Title to the Contested Lands Lying West of the Province of New-York: Addressed to the Public . . .* (1st & 2nd edns., New Haven, Conn., 1774).

4. Newspapers

The Connecticut Courant [The Connecticut Courant, and the Weekly Advertiser; The Connecticut Courant, and Hartford Weekly Intelligencer], b. 1764, Hartford. See the article by E. Wilder Spaulding: "The *Connecticut Courant:* A Representative Newspaper in the Eighteenth Century," *New England Quarterly,* III (1930), 443-63.

Connecticut Gazette, 1755-1768, New Haven.

Connecticut Gazette [*New London Gazette; The Connecticut Gazette and the Universal Intelligencer*], b. 1763, New London.

The Connecticut Journal [*Connecticut Journal, & New Haven Post-Boy*] b. 1767, New Haven.

The New-London Summary [*The New-London Summary, or the Weekly Advertiser*] 1758-1763, New London.

C. SECONDARY WORKS

1. General

ANDREWS, CHARLES MC LEAN: *Connecticut and the British Government*, Tercentenary Commission of . . . Connecticut, *Publications*, I (New Haven, Conn., 1933; rep. from *Fane's Reports on the Laws of Connecticut*, 1915).

DEMING, DOROTHY: *The Settlement of Connecticut Towns*, Tercentenary Commission of . . . Connecticut, *Publications*, VI (New Haven, Conn., 1933).

HOLLISTER, GIDEON HIRAM: *The History of Connecticut from the First Settlement of the Colony* (2nd edn., enl., 2 vols., Hartford, Conn., 1857).

HOOKER, ROLAND MATHER: *Boundaries of Connecticut*, Tercentenary Commission of . . . Connecticut, *Publication*, XI (New Haven, 1933).

JOHNSTON, ALEXANDER: *Connecticut: A Study of a Commonwealth Democracy, American Commonwealths*, X (Boston & New York, 1903).

MORROW, RISING LAKE: *Connecticut Influences in Western Massachusetts and Vermont*, Tercentenary Commission of . . . Connecticut, *Publications*, LVIII (New Haven, 1936).

PEASE, JOHN C., and JOHN M. NILES: *Gazetteer of the States of Connecticut and Rhode-Island* . . . (Hartford, Conn., 1819).

PETERS, SAMUEL: *A General History of Connecticut from Its First Settlement* . . . (London, 1781; New Haven, Conn., 1829). To be used with care.

PURCELL, R. J.: *Connecticut in Transition, 1775-1818* (Washington, D.C. & London, 1918).

ROSENBERRY, LOIS KIMBALL MATHEWS: *Migrations from Connecticut Prior to 1800*, Tercentenary Commission of . . . Connecticut, *Publications*, XXVIII (New Haven, 1934).

TRUMBULL, BENJAMIN: *A Complete History of Connecticut, Civil and Ecclesiastical, from the Emigration of Its First Planters from England* . . . (New Haven, Conn., 1818).

ZEICHNER, OSCAR: *Connecticut's Years of Controversy, 1750-1776* (Chapel Hill, N.C., c. 1949).

2. Local

ANDREWS, CHARLES MC LEAN: "The River Towns of Connecticut: A Study of Wethersfield, Hartford and Windsor," Johns Hopkins University, *Studies in Historical and Political Science*, 7th ser. (Baltimore, Md., 1889).

ATWATER, EDWARD E., ed.: *History of the City of New Haven* . . . (New York, 1887).

BLAKELY, QUINCY: *Farmington, One of the Mother Towns of Connecticut*, Tercentenary Commission of . . . Connecticut, *Publications*, XXXVIII (New Haven, 1935).

CAULKINS, FRANCES M.: *History of New London, Connecticut* . . . (Hartford, Conn., 1852).

———: *History of Norwich, Connecticut* . . . (Norwich, Conn., 1845).

DEMING, DOROTHY: *The Settlement of Litchfield County*, Tercentenary Commission of . . . Connecticut, *Publications*, VII (New Haven, Conn., 1933).

LARNED, ELLEN D.: *History of Windham County, Connecticut* (2 vols., Worcester, Mass., 1874-80).

OSTERWEIS, ROLLIN GUSTAV: *Three Centuries of New Haven, 1638-1938* (New Haven, Conn., 1953).

TRUMBULL, JAMES HAMMOND: *The Memorial History of Hartford County, Connecticut, 1633-1884* (2 vols., Boston, 1886).

3. Political

BAILEY, EDITH ANNA: "Influences toward Radicalism in Connecticut, 1754-1755," Smith College, *Studies in History*, V (1919-20), 175-252. A discussion of the Connecticut radicals whom the author sees as practically synonymous with the Susquehannah Company and the influence of both on political developments in Connecticut.

BOWEN, CLARENCE WINTHROP: *The Boundary Disputes of Connecticut* (Boston, 1882).

BOYD, JULIAN P.: "Connecticut's Experiment in Expansion: The Susquehannah Company, 1753-1803," *Journal of Economic and Business History*, IV (1931-2), 38-69; see also Tercentenary Commission of . . . Connecticut, *Publications*, XXXIV (New Haven, Conn., 1935).

GILBERT, GEORGE A.: "The Connecticut Loyalists," *American Historical Review*, IV (1898-9), 273-91.

GIPSON, LAWRENCE HENRY: *Connecticut Taxation, 1750-1775*, Tercentenary Commission of . . . Connecticut, *Publications*, X (New Haven, 1933), and "Connecticut Taxation and Parliamentary Aid Preceding the Revolutionary War," *American Historical Review*, XXXVI (1930-1), 721-39.

GRANT, CHARLES S.: *Democracy in the Connecticut Frontier Town of Kent,* Columbia University, *Studies in History, Economics, and Public Law,* No. 601 (New York, 1961).

HOOKER, ROLAND MATHER: *The Spanish Ship Case: A Troublesome Episode for Connecticut, 1752-1758,* Tercentenary Commission of . . . Connecticut, *Publications,* XXV (New Haven, 1934).

JONES, FREDERICK ROBERTSON: "History of Taxation in Connecticut, 1636-1776," Johns Hopkins University, *Studies in Historical and Political Science,* 14th ser. (1896), 345-418.

PECK, EPAPHRODITUS: *Loyalists of Connecticut,* Tercentenary Commision of . . . Connecticut, *Publications,* XXXI (New Haven, Conn., 1934).

SCOTT, KENNETH: *Counterfeiting in Colonial Connecticut* [1699-1776], *Numismatic Notes and Monographs,* No. 140 (New York, 1957).

SIEBERT, WILBUR H.: *The Refugee Loyalists of Connecticut,* Royal Society of Canada, *Transactions,* 3rd ser., X (1916), 75-92.

4. Economic

GRANT, CHARLES S.: "Land Speculation and the Settlement of Kent [in Litchfield County], *New England Quarterly,* XXVIII (1955) 51-71.

HOOKER, ROLAND MATHER: *The Colonial Trade of Connecticut,* Tercentenary Commission of . . . Connecticut, *Publications,* L (New Haven, 1936).

KEITH, HERBERT C., and CHARLES RUFUS HARTE: *The Early Iron Industry of Connecticut* (New Haven, 1935).

MARTIN, MARGARET E.: "Merchants and Trade of the Connecticut River Valley, 1750-1820," Smith College, *Studies in History,* XXIV (1939), 1-284.

OLSON, ALBERT LAVERNE: *Agricultural Economy and the Population in Eighteenth-Century Connecticut,* Tercentenary Commission of . . . Connecticut, *Publications,* XL (New Haven, 1935).

5. Social

BALDWIN, ALICE MARY: *The Clergy of Connecticut in Revolutionary Days,* Tercentenary Commission of . . . Connecticut, *Publications,* LVI (New Haven, 1936).

BATES, ALBERT CARLOS: "Fighting the Revolution with Printer's Ink in Connecticut: The Official Printing of That Colony from Lexington to the Declaration," New Haven Colony Historical Society, *Papers,* IX (1918), 129-60.

BEARDSLEY, E. EDWARD: *The History of the Episcopal Church in Connecticut . . .* (2 vols., New York, 1868-9).

CAPEN, EDWARD WARREN: *The Historical Development of the Poor Law in Connecticut,* Columbia University, *Studies in History, Economics, and Public Law,* No. 57 (London & New York, 1905).

COWIE, ALEXANDER: *Educational Problems at Yale College in the Eighteenth Century*, Tercentenary Commission of . . . Connecticut, *Publications*, LV (New Haven, 1936).

DEXTER, FRANKLIN BOWDITCH: *Biographical Sketches of the Graduates of Yale College with Annals of the College History, 1701-1792* (4 vols., New York, 1885-1907), and *Sketch of the History of Yale University* (New York, 1887).

GIPSON, LAWRENCE HENRY: "The Criminal Codes of Connecticut," American Institute of Criminal Law and Criminology, *Journal*, VI (1915), 177-89.

GREENE, MARIA LOUISE: *The Development of Religious Liberty in Connecticut* (Boston & New York, 1905).

JARVIS, LUCY CUSHING, ed.: *Sketches of Church Life in Colonial Connecticut: Being the Story of the Transplanting of the Church of England into Forty-Two Parishes of Connecticut* . . . (New Haven, Conn., 1902).

MITCHELL, MARY H.: *The Great Awakening and Other Revivals in the Religious Life of Connecticut*, Tercentenary Commission of . . . Connecticut, *Publications*, XXVI (New Haven, Conn., 1934).

——: "Slavery in Connecticut and Especially in New Haven," New Haven Colony Historical Society, *Papers*, X (1951), 286-312.

MORSE, JARVIS MEANS: *Connecticut Newspapers in the Eighteenth Century*, Tercentenary Commission of . . . Connecticut, *Publications*, XXXVI (New Haven, 1935).

O'NEIL, MAUD: "A Struggle for Religious Liberty: An Analysis of the Work of the S.P.G. in Connecticut," *Historical Magazine of the Protestant Episcopal Church*, XX (1951), 173-89.

PARKER, EDWIN P.: "The Congregationalist Separates of the Eighteenth Century in Connecticut," New Haven Colony Historical Society, *Papers*, VIII (1914), 151-61.

REICHENBACH, KARL H.: "The Connecticut Clergy and the Stamp Act," *Historical Essays*, University of Michigan, *Publications: History and Political Science*, XI (1937), 141-58.

SEYMOUR, ORIGEN STORRS: *The Beginnings of the Episcopal Church in Connecticut*, Tercentenary Commission of . . . Connecticut, *Publications*, XXX (New Haven, 1934).

SKLAR, ROBERT: "The Great Awakening and Colonial Politics: Connecticut's Revolution in the Minds of Men," Connecticut Historical Society, *Bulletin*, XXVIII (1963), 81-95.

STEINER, BERNARD CHRISTIAN: *The History of Education in Connecticut* (Washington, D.C., 1893).

TUCKER, LOUIS LEONARD: "The Church of England and Religious Liberty at Pre-Revolutionary Yale," *William and Mary Quarterly*, XVII (1960), 314-28.

WEAVER, GLENN: "Anglican-Congregationalist Tensions in Pre-Revolutionary Connecticut," *Historical Magazine of the Protestant Episcopal Church*, XXVI (1957), 269-85.

6. Biographical

ARNOLD, BENEDICT. *The Life of Benedict Arnold: His Patriotism and His Treason* by Isaac Newton Arnold (Chicago, 1880); *Benedict Arnold: The Proud Warrior* by Charles Coleman Sellers (New York, 1930); and *Traitorous Hero: The Life and Fortunes of Benedict Arnold* by Willard Mosher Wallace (New York, 1954).

CLAP, THOMAS. *Puritan Protagonist: President Thomas Clap of Yale College* by Louis L. Tucker (Chapel Hill, N.C., 1962). Also by Tucker, "President Thomas Clap and the Rise of Yale College, 1740-66," *Historian*, XIX (1956-7), 66-81, and "President Thomas Clap of Yale College: Another 'Founding Father' of American Science," *Isis*, LII (1961), 55-77.

DEANE, SILAS. *Silas Deane: A Connecticut Leader in the American Revolution* by George L. Clark (London & New York, 1913).

HALE, NATHAN. *Nathan Hale, 1776: Biography and Memorials* by Henry Phelps Johnston (rev. & enl., New Haven, Conn., 1914).

INGERSOLL, JARED. *See* Empire: Secondary Works for this citation.

JOHNSON, WILLIAM SAMUEL. *William Samuel Johnson: A Maker of the Constitution* by George C. Groce, Jr. (New York, 1937).

PUTNAM, ISRAEL. *An Essay on the Life of the Honourable Major General Israel Putnam . . .* by David Humphreys (Boston, 1818; 3rd edn., New York, 1848).

STILES, EZRA. *The Gentle Puritan: A Life of Ezra Stiles, 1727-1795* by Edmund S. Morgan (New Haven, Conn., 1962).

TRUMBULL, JONATHAN. *Life of Jonathan Trumbull, Sen., Governor of Connecticut* by Issac William Stuart (Boston, 1859); *Jonathan Trumbull: Governor of Connecticut, 1769-1784* by Jonathan Trumbull (Boston, 1919); and *Jonathan Trumbull: Connecticut's Merchant Magistrate* by Glenn Weaver (Hartford, Conn., 1956).

WILLIAMS, ELISHA. "Elisha Williams: Minister, Soldier, President of Yale" by Francis Parsons, New Haven Colony Historical Society, *Papers*, VII (1908), 188-217.

D. MAPS

KITCHIN, THOMAS: *A Map of the Colonies of Connecticut and Rhode Island, Divided into Counties and Townships.* In the *London Magazine*, XXVII (1758), opp. p. 168.

A Map of Connecticut and Rhode Island with Long Island Sound, Etc. In the *Gentleman's Magazine*, XLVI (1776), opp. p. 525.

A New and Accurate Map of Connecticut and Rhode Island from the
Best Authorities. In the Universal Magazine, LXVI (1780), opp.
p. 169.

ROMANS, BERNARD: Map of the State of Connecticut with Parts of New
York, New Jersey (Norwich, Conn., 1777), Connecticut State
Library.

DELAWARE   (the three lower counties on the Delaware)

A. BIBLIOGRAPHICAL AIDS

ECKMAN, JEANNETTE, ANTHONY HIGGINS, and WILLIAM H. CONNER, eds.:
Delaware: A Guide to the First State (New York, 1955).

HASSE, ADELAIDE R.: "Delaware, 1701-1789," in "Materials for a Bibliog-
raphy of the Public Archives of the Thirteen Original States.
...," American Historical Association, Annual Report, 1906, (2 vols.,
Washington, D.C., 1908), II, 444-5.

RYDEN, GEORGE H., comp.: Bibliography of Delaware History ([Newark,
Del., 1927]). Mimeographed.

B. PRINTED SOURCE MATERIALS

1. Government and related documents

Delaware Archives: Military (5 vols., Wilmington, Del., 1911-16).

HANCOCK, HAROLD, ed.: "The Kent County Loyalists, II: Documents,"
Delaware History, VI (1954-5), 92-139; prints the "Book of the
Proceedings and Transactions of the Committee of Correspond-
ence for Kent County."

Minutes [Votes and Proceedings] of the House of Representatives of the
Government of the Counties of New-Castle, Kent and Sussex,
upon Delaware . . . 1766 (Wilmington, Del., 1762, 1770; rep.,
Dover, Del., 1930, 1931).

Proceedings of the Convention of the Delaware State Held at New-
Castle on Tuesday the Twenty-Seventh of August, 1776 (Wilmington, Del.; rep., Dover, Del., 1927).

READ, GEORGE, ed.: Laws of the State of Delaware from . . . 1700 to 1816
(4 vols., Newcastle, Del., 1797-1816), Vols. I and II; see also
Laws of the Government of New-Castle, Kent and Sussex, upon
Delaware . . . (Philadelphia, 1752).

*Votes and Proceedings of the House of Representatives of . . . Delaware
. . . 1765* (Wilmington, 1770; rep., 1931). Printed but not published were the *Votes and Proceedings of the House of Representatives of . . . Dalaware,* for 1764, 1766, 1767, 1770, 1772,
1773, and 1774; these were printed in Wilmington and are available on Readex cards.

2. Non-official contemporary writings

READ, GEORGE. *Life and Correspondence of George Read, a Signer of
the Declaration of Independence . . .* by William Thompson Read
(Philadelphia, 1870).

RODNEY, CAESAR: *Letters to and from Caesar Rodney, 1756-1784 . . .*
(George Herbert Ryden, ed., Philadelphia, 1933). Other letters
are to be found in "Letters to and from Caesar Rodney," Harold
B. Hancock, ed., *Delaware History,* XII (1966), 54-76, 147-68.

C. SECONDARY WORKS

1. General

CONRAD, HENRY C.: *History of the State of Delaware from the Earliest
Settlements to the Year 1907* (Wilmington, Del., 1908).

GIPSON, LAWRENCE HENRY: "An Anomalous American Colony," *Pennsylvania History,* XXVII (1960), 144-64.

POWELL, WALTER A.: *A History of Delaware* (Boston, 1928).

REED, H. CLAY, ed.: *Delaware: A History of the First State* (3 vols., New
York, 1947).

SCHARF, JOHN THOMAS, *et al.: History of Delaware, 1609-1888* (2 vols.,
Philadelphia, 1888).

WOOTTEN, (MRS.) BAYARD, and ANTHONY HIGGINS: *New Castle, Delaware,
1651-1939* (Boston, 1939).

2. Political

DAUGHERTY, MARTIN M.: *Early Colonial Taxation in Delaware* (Wilmington, Del., 1938).

HANCOCK, HAROLD BELL: *The Delaware Loyalists,* Historical Society of
Delaware, *Papers,* n. ser., No. 3 (Wilmington, Del., 1940). See
also Hancock's articles: "Kent County Loyalists," *Delaware History,* VI (1954-5), 3-24, and "The New Castle County Loyalists,"
ibid., IV (1950-1), 315-53.

HAYES, J. CARROLL: "The Delaware Curve: The Story of the Pennsylvania-Delaware Circular Boundary," *Pennsylvania Magazine of History and Biography*, XLVII (1923), 238-58.

LUNT, DUDLEY: "The Bounds of Delaware," *Delaware History*, II (1947), 1-40.

RODNEY, RICHARD S.: *Colonial Finances in Delaware* (Wilmington, Del., 1928).

3. Economic

HANNA, MARY ALICE: "Trade of the Delaware District before the Revolution," Smith College, *Studies in History*, II (1917), No. 4.

TYLER, DAVID B.: "Shipbuilding in Delaware," *Delaware History*, VII (1956-7), 207-16.

WELSH, PETER C.: "The Brandywine Mills: A Chronicle of an Industry, 1762-1816," *Delaware History*, VII (1956), 17-36.

————: "Merchants, Millers and Ocean Ships: The Components of an Early American Industrial Town," *Delaware History*, VII (1956-1957), 319-36. The town under discussion is Wilmington, Delaware.

4. Social

BEARDSLEE, JOHN WALTER: "The Church in Delaware and Pennsylvania," *Tercentenary Studies, 1928: Reformed Church in America: A Record of Beginnings* . . . (New York, 1928).

JOHNSON, ALICE A.: "The Beginnings of Quakerism in Delaware," *Friends in Wilmington, 1738-1938* (Wilmington, Del., 1938).

PURCELL, RICHARD J.: "Irish Settlers in Early Delaware," *Pennsylvania History*, XIV (1947), 94-107.

5. Biographical

DICKINSON, JOHN. See Pennsylvania: Biographical.

HOLT, RYVES. "Ryves Holt of Lewes, Delaware, 1696-1763," by Daniel F. Wolcott, *Delaware History*, VIII (1958-9), 3-50.

ROBINSON, THOMAS. "Thomas Robinson: Delaware's Most Prominent Loyalist" by Harold Hancock, *ibid.*, IV (1950-1), 1-36.

6. Military and naval

DE VALINGER, LEON, JR.: *Colonial Military Organization in Delaware, 1638-1776* (Wilmington, Del., 1938).

MERVINE, WILLIAM M.: "Pirates and Privateers in the Delaware Bay and River," *Pennsylvania Magazine of History and Biography*, XXXII (1908), 459-70.

D. MAPS

FISHER, JOSHUA: *A Chart of Delaware Bay and River, Containing a Full and Exact Description of the Shores, Creeks, Harbours, Soundings, Shoals, Sands, and Bearings of the Most Considerable Landmarks from the Capes to Philadelphia* . . . (London, 1776). This map, which was engraved by William Faden, is to be found in Faden's *North American Atlas,* . . . (London, 1777), No. 26; and is analyzed by Lawrence C. Wroth in the *Pennsylvania Magazine of History and Biography,* LXXIV (1950), 90-109.

For more inclusive maps containing good delineations of Delaware, see Lewis Evans: *A Map of Pensilvania, New Jersey, New York, and the Three Delaware Counties,* fully cited under Pennsylvania, and Thomas Kitchin: *A Map of Maryland with the Delaware Counties and the Southern Part of New Jersey,* fully cited under Maryland.

THE FLORIDAS

A. BIBLIOGRAPHICAL AIDS

ARNADE, CHARLES: "A Guide to Spanish Florida Source Material," *Florida Historical Quarterly,* XXXV (1956-7), 320-5.
WROTH, LAWRENCE C.: "Source Materials of Florida History in the John Carter Brown Library of Brown University," *ibid.,* XX (1941), 3-46.

B. PRINTED SOURCE MATERIALS

1. Government and related documents

BOYD, MARK F., ed.: "From a Remote Frontier [Letters and Documents Pertaining to San Marcos de Apalache, 1763-1769, during the British Occupation of Florida]," *Florida Historical Quarterly,* XIX (1940-1)-XXI (1942-3), *passim.*
CHESTER, PETER: "The Reply of Peter Chester, Governor of West Florida, to Complaints Made Against His Administration," James A. Padgett, ed., *Louisiana Historical Quarterly,* XXII (1939), 31-46.
"A French Report on St. Augustine in the 1770's," Lee Kennett, ed. & trans., *Florida Historical Quarterly,* XLIV (1965-6), 133-5.

"Minutes of the . . . Session of the Assembly of West Florida . . . ,"
James A. Padgett, ed., *Louisiana Historical Quarterly*, XXII
(1939)-XXIII (1940), *passim*.

SIEBERT, WILBUR HENRY: *Loyalists in East Florida, 1774 to 1785: The
Most Important Documents Pertaining thereto . . .*, Florida State
Historical Society, *Publications*, No. 9 (2 vols., Deland, Fla.,
1929).

2. Non-official contemporary writings

[WALKER, FOWLER]: *The Case of Mr. John Gordon with Respect to the
Title to Certain Lands in East Florida, Purchased of his Catholic
Majesty's Subjects . . .* (London, 1772). A copy of this rare volume
is in the John Carter Brown Library.

ROMANS, BERNARD: *A Concise Natural History of East and West Florida:
Containing an Account of the Natural Produce of All the Southern
Part of British America . . .* (New York, 1775).

[STORK, WILLIAM]: *An Account of East Florida with Remarks on Its
Future Importance to Trade and Commerce* (London [1766]).
This work went thru several editions with title variations and with
the addition of John Bartram's Florida journal.

C. SECONDARY WORKS

1. General

BARRS, BURTON: *East Florida in the American Revolution* (Jacksonville,
Fla., 1932).

BRINTON, DANIEL GARRISON: *Notes on the Floridian Peninsula: Its Literary
History, Indian Tribes and Antiquities* (Philadelphia, 1859).

CHATELAIN, VERNE ELMO: *The Defenses of Spanish Florida, 1565 to 1763*,
Carnegie Institute of Washington, *Publications*, No. 511 (Washington, D.C., 1941).

DARBY, WILLIAM: *Memoir on the Geography and Natural and Civil History of Florida . . .* (Philadelphia, 1821).

FORBES, JAMES GRANT: *Sketches, Historical and Topographical, of the
Floridas, More Particularly of East Florida* (New York, 1821).

HOWARD, CLINTON N.: *The British Development of West Florida, 1763-
1769*, University of California, *Publications in History*, XXXIV
(Berkeley, Calif. & Los Angeles, 1947).

JOHNSON, CECIL: *British West Florida, 1763-1783, Yale Historical Publications: Miscellany*, XLII (London & New Haven, Conn., 1943).

MOWAT, CHARLES L.: *East Florida as a British Province, 1763-1784*, University of California, *Publications in History*, XXXII (Berkeley, Calif. & Los Angeles, 1943; rep., Gainesville, Fla., 1964).

PENNINGTON, EDGAR LEGARE: "East Florida and the American Revolution, 1775-1778," *Florida Historical Quarterly*, IX (1930), 24-46.

2. *Local*

DEWHURST, WILLIAM WHITWELL: *History of St. Augustine, Florida* . . . (New York, 1881).

FAIRBANKS, GEORGE R.: *The History and Antiquities of the City of St. Augustine, Florida* . . . (New York, 1858).

GONZALES, (MRS.) S. J.: "Pensacola: Its Early History," *Florida Historical Quarterly*, II (1909-10), 9-25.

GRIFFEN, WILLIAM B.: "Spanish Pensacola, 1700-1763," *ibid.*, XXXVII (1958-9), 242-61.

HAMILTON, PETER JOSEPH: *Colonial Mobile: An Historical Study* . . . (1st edn., Boston, 1897; rev. & enl. edn., Boston & New York, 1910).

HOWARD, CLINTON N.: "Colonial Pensacola: The British Period," *Florida Historical Quarterly*, XIX (1940-1), 109-27, 246-69, 368-401.

JOHNSON, CECIL: "Pensacola in the British Period: Summary and Significance," *ibid.*, XXXVII (1958-9), 263-80.

SIEBERT, WILBUR H.: "The Port of St. Augustine during the British Regime," *ibid.*, XXIV (1945-6), 247-65, XXV (1946-7), 76-93.

3. *Political*

CARTER, CLARENCE E.: "Some Aspects of British Administration in West Florida," *Mississippi Valley Historical Review*, I (1914-15), 364-75. Relating to the northern boundary and the settlement along the Mississippi River.

HOWARD, CLINTON N.: "The Interval of Military Government in West Florida," *Louisiana Historical Quarterly*, XXII (1939), 18-30, and "The Military Occupation of British West Florida, 1763," *Florida Historical Quarterly*, XVII (1938-9), 181-99. This article gives a description of British troops occupying the area in 1763; the two articles together provide a discussion of the government of West Florida during the years 1763-66 while the Treaty of Paris was being put into effect.

KERR, WILFRED B.: "The Stamp Act and the Floridas, 1765-1766," *Mississippi Valley Historical Review*, XXI (1934-5), 436-70.

SIEBERT, WILBUR H.: "The Departure of the Spaniards and Other Groups from East Florida, 1763-1764," *Florida Historical Quarterly*, XIX (1940-1), 145-54; and "East Florida, as a Refuge of Southern Loyalists, 1774-1785," American Antiquarian Society, *Proceedings*,

n. ser., XXXVII (1928), 226-46; "How the Spaniards Evacuated Pensacola in 1763," *Florida Historical Quarterly*, XI (1932), 48-57; see also "The Loyalists in West Florida and the Natchez District," *Mississippi Valley Historical Review*, II (1915-16), 465-83.

TE PASKE, JOHN JAY: *The Governorship of Spanish Florida, 1700-1763* (Durham, N.C., 1964).

4. Economic

HOWARD, CLINTON N.: "Some Economic Aspects of British West Florida, 1763-1768," *Journal of Southern History*, VI (1940), 201-21.

TE PASKE, JOHN JAY: "Economic Problems of Florida Governors, 1700-1763," *Florida Historical Quarterly*, XXXVII (1958-9), 42-52. Useful for background material.

5. Social

BEESON, KENNETH H., JR.: "Janas in British East Florida," *Florida Historical Quarterly*, XLIV (1965-6), 121-32. Deals with Minorcan settlers and establishment of New Smyrna.

BOHNENBERGER, CARL: "The Settlement of Charlotia (Rolles Town), 1765," *ibid.*, IV (1925-6), 43-9. Denys Rolle's attempt to establish an English settlement in Florida.

DUNKLE, JOHN R.: "Population Change as an Element in the Historical Geography of St. Augustine," *ibid.*, XXXVII (1958-9), 3-32.

GANNON, MICHAEL V.: *The Cross in the Sand: The Early Catholic Church in Florida, 1513-1870* (Gainesville, Fla., 1965).

PANAGOPOULOS, E. P.: "The Background of the Greek Settlers in the New Smyrna Colony," *Florida Historical Quarterly*, XXXV (1956-7), 95-115.

REA, ROBERT R.: "A Naval Visitor in British West Florida," *ibid.*, XL (1961-2), 142-53. The visit and report of Lt. John Blankett of the Royal Navy, 1764-5.

ROSELLI, BRUNO: *The Italians in Colonial Florida, 1513-1821: A Repertory of Italian Families . . .* (Fla., 1940).

SIEBERT, WILBUR H.: "Slavery and White Servitude in East Florida, 1726 to 1776," *Florida Historical Quarterly*, X (1931-2), 3-23.

6. Biographical

CHESTER, PETER. "Peter Chester: Third Governor of the Province of British West Florida under British Dominion, 1770-1781" by Mrs. Dunbar Rowland, Mississippi Historical Society, *Publications*, V (1925), 1-183.

ELLIS, JOHN. "The King's Agent for British West Florida" by Robert Rea, *Alabama Review*, XVI (1963), 141-53.

JOHNSTONE, GEORGE. "Governor Johnstone in West Florida" by Clinton Newton Howard, *Florida Historical Quarterly*, XVII (1938-9), 281-303. Relates to Johnstone's administration in West Florida, 1764-7.

ROLLE, DENYS. "Denys Rolle and Rollestown" by Carita Doggett-Corsi, *ibid.*, VII (1928), 115-34.

ROMANS, BERNARD. *Notes on the Life and Work of Bernard Romans* by P. Lee Phillips, Florida State Historical Society, *Publications*, No. 2 (Deland, Fla., 1924).

STRACHAN, CHARLES. "Charles Strachan in Mobile: The Frontier Ordeal of a Scottish Factor, 1764-68" by James D. Born, Jr., *Alabama Historical Quarterly*, XXVII (1965), 23-42.

TURNBULL, ANDREW. *Dr. Andrew Turnbull and the New Smyrna Colony of Florida* by Carita Doggett-Corsi ([Florida], 1919).

D. MAPS

BOWEN, EMANUEL, sculp.: *A Draught of West Florida from Cape St. Blaze to the River Ibberville with Part of the River Mississippi* ([London], 1766).

Carte de la Coste de la Floride depuis la Baye de la Mobile jusqu'aux Cayes de St. Martin. In Bellin: *Let Petit Atlas Maritime . . .* , I:4.

Harbour of St. Augustine. In Bowen: *A Complete or Distinct View of the Known World* (London, 1752), No. 66.

JEFFERYS, THOMAS: *The Coast of West Florida and Louisiana. The Peninsula and Gulf of Florida or Channel of Bahama with the Bahama Islands* [1775]. In Jefferys: *The American Atlas . . .* , No. 25.

———: *East Florida from Surveys Made since the Last Peace. . . .* In William Stork: *A Description of East Florida* (3rd edn., London, 1769), frontispiece. 1st edn. had the title *An Account of East Florida.*

———: *Florida from the Latest Authorities.* In his *A General Topography of North America and the West Indies* (London, 1768), No. 65.

———, sculp.: *Plan of the Harbour and Settlement of Pensacola* ([London, 1763]). In *ibid.*, No. 68a.

———: *St. Augustine: The Capital of East Florida.* In William Stork: *A Description of East Florida* (3rd edn., London, 1769), opp. p. 7.

KITCHEN, THOMAS: *A Plan of Mobile*. In Philip Pittman: *The Present State of the European Settlements on the Mississippi* . . . (London, 1770), opp. p. 96.

Map of the New Governments of East and West Florida, 1763. In the *Gentleman's Magazine*, XXXIII (1763), 552.

A New and Accurate Map of East and West Florida Drawn from the Best Authorities. In the *London Magazine*, XXXIV (1765), opp. p. 120.

A Perspective View of Pensacola. In the *Universal Magazine*, XXXIV (1764), 36.

ROMANS, BERNARD: *Chart Containing Part of East Florida, the Whole Coast of West Florida with All the Soundings, &c. All the Mouths of the Mississippi* . . . ([New York, 1775]).

————: *Chart Containing the Peninsula of Florida, the Bahama Islands, the North Side of the Island of Cuba, the Old Streight of Bahama, and All the Islands, Keys, Rocks, &c. in These Seas* ([New York, 1775]).

[————]: *Map of West Florida from Pensacola to the Mouth of the Iberville River with a View to Shew the Proper Spot for a Settlement on the Mississippi*. John Lodge was the sculptor of this map which appeared in the *Gentleman's Magazine*, XLII (1772), opp. p. 64.

————: *A Plan of Mobile Bar [&] Plan of the Harbour of Pensacola*. In J. Whittle and R. H. Laurie: *The West Indian Atlas*, No. 45.

GEORGIA

A. BIBLIOGRAPHICAL AIDS

COLEMAN, KENNETH: "Bibliography," *The American Revolution in Georgia*, pp. 328-40.

HASSE, ADELAIDE R., comp.: "Georgia, 1732-1789," in "Materials for a Bibliography of the Public Archives of the Thirteen Original States . . . ," *Annual Report, 1906* (2 vols., Washington, D.C., 1908), II, 550-8.

JACK, T. H.: "Historiography in Georgia," Georgia Historical Association, *Proceedings for 1917* ([Atlanta, Ga.], 1921).

REESE, T. R.: "Bibliography," *Colonial Georgia* . . . , pp. 154-67.

THORNTON, E. M.: . . . *List of Books and Pamphlets Relating to Georgia and Georgians* (Atlanta, Ga., 1928).

B. PRINTED SOURCE MATERIALS

1. *Government and related documents*

CANDLER, ALLEN D., ed.: *The Colonial Records of the State of Georgia* (26 vols., Atlanta, 1904-13). This series includes the *Statutes Enacted by the Royal Legislature of Georgia* . . . (3 vols., 1910-11), *Journal of the Upper House of Assembly* . . . (2 vols., 1907-8), *Journal of the Commons House of Assembly* . . . (3 vols., 1907), *Proceedings of the President and Assistants* . . . (1906), *Proceedings and Minutes of the Governors and Council* . . . (6 vols., 1906-1907), and *Journal of the Earl of Egmont* . . . (1908).

————: *The Revolutionary Records of the State of Georgia* . . . (3 vols., Atlanta, Ga., 1908).

"The Commissions of Georgia to Benjamin Franklin to Act as Colonial Agent [1768, 1770, 1773]," *Georgia Historical Quarterly*, II (1918), 150-64.

FLEMING, BERRY, comp.: *Autobiography of a Colony: The First Half-Century of Augusta, Georgia* (Athens, Ga., c. 1957).

GEORGIA HISTORICAL SOCIETY: *Collections* (12 vols.+, Savannah, Ga., 1840-1957+). Among the *Collections* those most useful for the period under consideration are: Volumes I and II, a number of contemporary publications concerned with the beginnings of Georgia as a colony; Volume III, letters of Governor James Wright to the Earl of Dartmouth, 1773-1782; Volume V, the proceedings of the Council of Safety; and Volume VI, the letters of James Habersham, 1756-1775.

JONES, C. C., ed.: *Acts Passed by the General Assembly of the Colony of Georgia, 1755 to 1774* (Wormsloe, Ga., 1881).

SURRENCY, ERWIN C., ed.: "Directions for Holding Court in Colonial Georgia," *American Journal of Legal History*, II (1958), 321-55.

Votes of the . . . General Assembly [of Georgia . . . (1755-1764)] (4 vols., issued for the 4 sessions [Charleston, S.C. & Savannah, Ga.], 1756-64).

WHITE, GEORGE, ed.: *Historical Collections of Georgia* (New York, 1854).

2. *Non-official contemporary writings*

ARREDONDO, ANTONIO DE: *Demostracion Historiographica del Derecho que Tiene el Rey Catolico á el Territorio que oy Posee el Rey Britanico con el Nombre de Nueva Georgia en las Provincias y Continente de la Florida* . . . (Havanna, 1742). This work, which clarifies the Anglo-Spanish contest over the South Carolina-Georgia coast region, has been reprinted as *Arredondo's Historical Proof of Spain's Title to Georgia: A Contribution to the History of One of the Spanish Borderlands* (Herbert E. Bolton, ed., Berkeley, Calif., 1925).

RASBERRY, THOMAS: "The Letter Book of Thomas Rasberry, 1758-1761," Lilla M. Hawes, ed., *Georgia Historical Quarterly*, XL (1956)-XLII (1958), *passim*.

TAILFER, PATRICK, *et al.*: *A True and Historical Narrative of the Colony of Georgia* (Clarence L. Ver Steeg, ed., Athens, Ga., 1960).

WHITEFIELD, GEORGE: *A Letter to His Excellency Governor Wright Giving an Account of the Steps Taken Relative to the Converting the Georgia Orphanage House into a College* . . . (Charleston, S.C., 1767; London, 1768).

[ZUBLY, JOHN JOACHIM]: *Calm and Respectful Thoughts on the Negative of the Crown on a Speaker Chosen and Presented by the Representatives of the People* . . . ([Savannah, Ga., 1772]).

3. Newspapers

Georgia Gazette, 1763-1776, Savannah.

C. SECONDARY WORKS

1. General

ABBOTT, WILLIAM WRIGHT: "A Cursory View of Eighteenth-Century Georgia," *South Atlantic Quarterly*, LXI (1962), 339-44.

BOLTON, HERBERT E., and MARY ROSS: *The Debatable Land: A Sketch of the Anglo-Spanish Contest for the Georgia Country* (Berkeley, Calif., 1925). Of an earlier period, but brings out Spain's claims to Georgia.

CALLAWAY, JAMES ETHERIDGE: *The Early Settlement of Georgia* [1732-1834] (Athens, Ga., 1948).

COLEMAN, KENNETH: *The American Revolution in Georgia 1763-1789* (Athens, Ga., 1958).

COULTER, E. MERTON: *Georgia: A Short History* (Chapel Hill, N.C., 1933; rev. & enl. edn., under title *A Short History of Georgia*, 1947).

CRANE, VERNER WINSLOW: "The Origins of Georgia," *Georgia Historical Quarterly*, XIV (1930), 93-110.

HEWAT, ALEXANDER: *see* under South Carolina.

JONES, CHARLES C.: *The History of Georgia* (2 vols., Boston & New York, 1883). See also his "The English Colonization of Georgia, 1733-

1752," *Narrative and Critical History of America* (Justin Winsor, ed., 8 vols., Boston & New York, 1884-9), V: 357-406.

LEE, F. D., and J. L. AGNEW: *Historical Record of the City of Savannah* (Savannah, Ga., 1869).

LEWIS, BESSIE MARY: "Darien: A Symbol of Defiance and Achievement," *Georgia Historical Quarterly*, XX (1936), 185-98.

MC CAIN, JAMES ROSS: *Georgia as a Proprietary Province: The Execution of a Trust* (Boston, 1917).

MC CALL, HUGH: *The History of Georgia: Containing Brief Sketches of the Most Remarkable Events . . .* (2 vols., Savannah, Ga., 1811-16).

SAYE, ALBERT BERRY: *New Viewpoints on Georgia History* (Athens, Ga., 1943).

STEVENS, WILLIAM BACON: *History of Georgia from Its First Discovery by Europeans to the Adoption of the Present Constitution in 1798* (2 vols., New York, 1847; [Philadelphia], 1859).

2. Political

ABBOTT, WILLIAM WRIGHT: *The Royal Governors of Georgia, 1754-1775* (Chapel Hill, N.C., 1959).

DANIEL, MARJORIE LOUISE: *The Revolutionary Movement in Georgia, 1763-1777* (Chicago, 1937).

DUNN, RICHARD S.: "The Trustees of Georgia and the House of Commons, 1732-1752," *William and Mary Quarterly*, 3rd ser., XI (1954), 551-65.

ELLEFSON, C. ASHLEY: "Loyalists and Patriots in Georgia during the American Revolution," *Historian*, XXIV (1961-2), 347-56.

———: "The Stamp Act in Georgia," *Georgia Historical Quarterly*, XLVI (1962), 1-19.

FLIPPIN, PERCY SCOTT: "The Royal Government in Georgia, 1752-1776," *Georgia Historical Quarterly*, IX (1925), 187-245; X (1926), 1-25.

GREENE, JACK P.: "The Georgia Commons House of Assembly and the Power of Appointment to Executive Offices, 1765-1775," *ibid.*, XLVI (1962), 151-61.

HEATH, MILTON SYDNEY: *Constructive Liberalism: The Role of the State in Economic Development in Georgia to 1860* (Cambridge, Mass., 1954).

REESE, TREVOR RICHARD: *Colonial Georgia: A Study in British Imperial Policy in the Eighteenth Century* (Athens, Ga., 1963).

SAYE, ALBERT BERRY: *A Constitutional History of Georgia, 1732-1945* (Athens, Ga., 1948).

WARE, ETHEL K.: *A Constitutional History of Georgia*, Columbia University, *Studies in History, Economics, and Public Law*, No. 528 (New York, 1947). The first three chapters pertain to the period prior to 1776.

3. Economic

BONNER, JAMES C.: *A History of Georgia Agriculture, 1732-1860* (Athens, Ga., 1964).

FANT, H. B.: "Financing the Colonization of Georgia," *Georgia Historical Quarterly*, XX (1936), 1-29.

HAMER, MARGUERITE B.: "The Foundation and Failure of the Silk Industry in Provincial Georgia," *North Carolina Historical Review*, XII (1935), 125-48.

HEATH, WILLIAM ESTILL: "The Early Colonial Money System of Georgia," *Georgia Historical Quarterly*, XIX (1935), 145-160.

JONES, CHARLES COLCOCK: *The Dead Towns of Georgia*, Georgia Historical Society, *Collections*, IV (Savannah, Ga., 1878). Deals with several towns which flourished during this period and later declined.

MCKINISTRY, MARY THOMAS: "Silk Culture in the Colony of Georgia," *Georgia Historical Quarterly*, XIV (1930), 225-35.

NEWTON, HESTER WALTON: "The Agricultural Activities of the Salzburgers in Colonial Georgia," *ibid.*, XVIII (1934), 248-63.

POTTER, DAVID M., JR.: "The Rise of the Plantation System in Georgia," *ibid.*, XVI (1932), 114-35.

STRICKLAND, REBA C.: "The Mercantile System as Applied to Georgia," *ibid.*, XXII (1938), 160-8.

4. Social

BRANTLEY, R. L.: "The Salzburgers in Georgia," *Georgia Historical Quarterly*, XIV (1930), 214-24.

CORRY, JOHN PITTS: "Education in Colonial Georgia," *ibid.*, XVI (1932), 136-45.

———: "Racial Elements in Colonial Georgia," *ibid.*, XX (1936), 30-40.

COULTER, E. MERTON: "The Acadians in Georgia," *ibid.*, XLVII (1963), 68-75.

———: "A Century of a Georgia Plantation," *Mississippi Valley Historical Review*, XVI (1929-30), 334-46.

———: "When John Wesley Preached in Georgia," *Georgia Historical Quarterly*, IX (1925), 317-51.

CRANE, VERNER W.: *The Promotion Literature of Georgia* (Cambridge, Mass., 1925). See also his article "The Philanthropists and the Genesis of Georgia," *American Historical Review*, XXVII (1921-2), 63-9.

FANT, H. B.: "The Labor Policy of the Trustees for Establishing the Colony of Georgia in America," *Georgia Historical Quarterly*, XVI (1932), 1-16, and "The Prohibition Policy of the Trustees for Establishing the Colony of Georgia in America," *ibid.*, XVII (1933), 286-92.

FLANDERS, RALPH BETTS: *Plantation Slavery in Georgia* (Chapel Hill, N.C., 1933).

GORDON, G. ARTHUR: "The Arrival of the Scotch Highlanders at Darien," *Georgia Historical Quarterly*, XX (1936), 199-209.

GREEN, E. R. R.: "Queensborough Township: Scotch-Irish Emigration and the Expansion of Georgia, 1763-1776," *William and Mary Quarterly*, 3rd ser., XVII (1960), 183-99.

HOFER, J. M.: "The Georgia Salzburgers," *Georgia Historical Quarterly*, XVIII (1934), 99-117.

LAWRENCE, JAMES B.: "Religious Education of the Negro in the Colony of Georgia," *ibid.*, XIV (1930), 41-57.

MC CAUL, ROBERT L.: "Education in Georgia during the Period of Royal Government, 1752-1776 . . . ," *ibid.*, XL (1956), 103-12, 248-59.

MAC DONELL, ALEXANDER R.: "The Settlement of the Scotch Highlanders at Darien," *ibid.*, XX (1936), 250-62.

MC MURTRIE, DOUGLAS C.: "Pioneer Printing in Georgia," *ibid.*, XVI (1932), 77-113.

MALONE, HENRY THOMPSON: *The Episcopal Church in Georgia, 1733-1957* (Atlanta, Ga., 1960).

MARTIN, JOSEPHINE D.: "The Society of Midway," *Georgia Historical Quarterly*, XI (1927), 321-9.

NEWTON, HESTER WALTON: "The Industrial and Social Influences of the Salzburgers in Colonial Georgia," *ibid.*, XVIII (1934), 335-53.

ROBERTS, R. A.: "The Birth of an American State, Georgia: An Effort of Philanthropy and Protestant Propaganda," Royal Historical Society, *Transactions*, 4th ser., VI (1923), 22-49.

RUBINCAM, MILTON: "Historical Background of the Salzburger Emigration to Georgia," *Georgia Historical Quarterly*, XXXV (1951), 99-115.

SAYE, ALBERT BERRY: "The Genesis of Georgia: Merchants as Well as Ministers," *ibid.*, XXIV (1940), 191-206.

——: "Was Georgia a Debtor Colony?" *ibid.*, XXIV (1940), 323-41.

STACY, JAMES: *History of the Midway Congregational Church, Liberty County, Georgia* (Newman, Ga., 1899; rev., 1903).

STRICKLAND, REBA C.: *Religion and the State in Georgia in the Eighteenth Century*, Columbia University, *Studies in History, Economics, and Public Law*, No. 460 (London & New York, 1939).

STROBEL, PHILIP A.: *The Salzburgers and Their Descendants: Being the History of a Colony of German (Lutheran) Protestants who Emigrated to Georgia . . .* (Baltimore, Md., 1855).

SURRENCY, ERWIN C.: "Whitefield, Habersham, and the Bethesda Orphanage, 1739-75," *Georgia Historical Quarterly*, XXXIV (1950), 87-105.

TANKERSLEY, ALLEN P.: "Midway District: A Study of Puritanism in Colonial Georgia," *ibid.*, XXXII (1948), 149-57.

TAYLOR, PAUL S.: "Colonizing Georgia, 1732-1752: A Statistical Note," *William and Mary Quarterly*, 3rd ser., XXII (1965), 119-27.

WAX, DAROLD D.: "Georgia and the Negro before the American Revolution," *Georgia Historical Quarterly*, LI (1967), 63-77.

5. Biographical

MONTGOMERY, HORACE, ed.: *Georgians in Profile: Historical Essays in Honor of Ellis Merton Coulter* (Athens, Ga., 1958). Includes the following essays: "John Percival, 1st Earl of Egmont" by Ruth and Albert B. Saye (pp. 1-16); "Henry Ellis" by William W. Abbott (pp. 17-39); "James Wright" by Kenneth Coleman (pp. 40-60); "Anthony Stokes" by Alexander A. Lawrence (pp. 61-88); and "Benjamin Hawkins" by Merritt B. Pound (pp. 89-101).

HABERSHAM, JAMES. "James Habersham and Georgia Loyalism 1764-1775" by C. Ashley Ellefson, *Georgia Historical Quarterly*, XLIV (1960), 359-80.

HABERSHAM, JOSEPH. "Joseph Habersham in the Revolutionary War" by John Mebane, *ibid.*, XLVII (1963), 76-83.

JOHNSTON, JAMES. *James Johnston: Georgia's First Printer* by Alexander A. Lawrence (Savannah, Ga., 1956).

MUSGROVE, MARY. "Mary Musgrove, 'Queen of the Creeks': A Chapter of Early Georgia Troubles" by E. Merton Coulter, *Georgia Historical Quarterly*, XI (1927), 1-30.

STEPHENS, WILLIAM. "William Stephens" by Natalie F. Bocock, *ibid.*, XVII (1933), 243-58.

WESLEY, JOHN. "John Wesley's Georgia Ministry" by Edgar Lagare Pennington, *Church History*, VIII (1939), 231-54.

WHITEFIELD, GEORGE. "George Whitefield Two Hundred and Fifty Years after His First American Visit: An Interpretation" by Jenning B. Sanders, *Georgia Historical Quarterly*, XLVIII (1964), 64-73.

WORMSLOE. *Wormsloe: Two Centuries of a Georgia Family* by E. Merton Coulter (Athens, Ga., 1955).

ZINZENDORF, NICHOLAS LEWIS, COUNT. *Life of Nicholas Lewis, Count Zinzendorf: Bishop and Ordinary of the Church of the United Brethern* (Samuel Jackson, trans., London, 1838).

ZOUBERBUHLER, BARTHOLOMEW. "The Reverend Bartholomew Zouberbuhler" by Edgar Legare Pennington, *Georgia Historical Quarterly*, XVIII (1934), 354-63.

D. MAPS

BOWEN, EMANUEL: *A New Map of Georgia with Part of Carolina, Florida and Louisiana*. In John Harris: *Navigantium Atque Itinerantium Bibliotheca: Or A Complete Collection of Voyages and Travels* (London, 1764), II: opp. p. 323.

A New and Accurate Map of the Province of Georgia in North America.
In the *Universal Magazine,* LXIV (1779), opp. p. 168.
See also: Thomas Kitchin's *A New Map of North & South Carolina &
Georgia,* fully cited under Chapter IV, D: Maps.

HUDSON BAY TERRITORY

A. PRINTED SOURCE MATERIALS

The Case of the Hudson's Bay Company ([London, 1748]). Relative to
the Company's exclusive right of trade.
*Charters, Statutes, Orders in Council, &c. Relating to the Hudson's Bay
Company* (London, 1931).
DOBBS, ARTHUR: *An Account of the Countries Adjoining to Hudson's
Bay* . . . (London, 1744; rep., New York, 1966).
————: *Short Narrative and Justification of the Proceedings of the Com-
mittee Appointed by the Adventurers to Prosecute the Discovery
of the Passage to the Western Ocean of America* (London, 1749).
[————]: *Short View of the Countries and Trade Carried on by the Com-
pany in Hudson's Bay: Shewing the Prejudice of That Exclusive
Trade and Benefit which Will Accrue to Great Britain by Opening
and Extending that Trade* . . . (London, 1749).
[DRAGE, THEODORE SWAINE]: *An Account of a Voyage for the Discovery
of a North-West Passage by Hudson's Streights to the Western
and Southern Ocean of America: Performed in the Year 1746 and
1747, in the Ship California* . . . (2 vols., London, 1748; rep., New
York [1967]).
ELLIS, HENRY: *Considerations of the Great Advantages which Would Arise
from Discovery of the Northwest Passage* . . . (London, 1750).
————: *A Voyage to Hudson's-Bay by the Dobbs Galley and California
in the Years 1746 and 1747: For Discovering a North West Passage* . . . (London, 1748; rep., New York, 1966).
HEARNE, SAMUEL: *A Journey from Prince of Wales's Fort in Hudson's Bay
to the Northern Ocean in the Years 1769* . . . [*1772*], J. B. Tyrell,
ed., Champlain Society, *Publications,* VI (n. edn., Toronto, 1911).
Also, *The Journals of Samuel Hearne and Philip Turnor* [*1774-92*],
J. B. Tyrell, ed., Champlain Society, *Publications,* XXI (Toronto,
1934).
HENDAY, ANTHONY: "The York Factory to the Blackfeet Country: The
Journal of Anthony Hendry [Henday], 1754-1755," L. J. Burpee,
ed., Royal Society of Canada, *Proceedings,* 3rd ser., I (1907), sec.
I: 307-60.

ISHAM, JAMES: *James Isham's Observations on Hudson's Bay, 1743, and Notes and Observations on a Book Entitled "A Voyage to Hudson's Bay in the Dobbs Galley [by Henry Ellis], 1749,"* E. E. Rich, ed., Hudson's Bay Record Society, *Publications*, XII (London, 1949).

MIDDLETON, CHRISTOPHER: *A Vindication of the Conduct of Captain Christopher Middleton in a Late Voyage on Board His Majesty's Ship Furnace for Discovering a North-West Passage to the Western American Ocean. In Answer to Certain Objections and Aspersions of Arthur Dobbs, Esq.* . . . (London, 1743; rep., New York, 1966). This pamphlet came as a reply to verbal accusations made by Dobbs before the Admiralty. For a reply, see Dobbs' *Remarks upon Capt. Middleton's Defence* . . . (London, 1744).

Report of the Committee [of the House of Commons] Appointed to Inquire into the State . . . *of the Countries Adjoining to Hudson's Bay and of the Trade Carried on There* (London, 1749).

Reports from Committees of the House of Commons Reprinted by Order of the House, Vol. II, *Miscellaneous Subjects, 1738-1765* (London, 1803).

RICH, E. E., *et al.*, eds.: *Cumberland House Journals and Indian Journal, 1775-82. First Series: 1775-79*, Hudson's Bay Record Society, *Publications*, XIV (London, 1951).

ROBSON, JOSEPH: *An Account of Six Years Residence in Hudson's-Bay from 1733 to 1736 and 1744 to 1747* . . . *Containing a Variety of Facts, Observations, and Discoveries* . . . (London, 1752; rep., New York, 1966).

A Short State of the Countries and Trade of North America Claimed by the Hudson's Bay Company under Pretense of a Charter for Ever . . . *Shewing the Illegality of the Said Grant* . . . (London, 1749).

A Short View of the Countries and Trade Carried on by the Company in Hudson's Bay: Shewing the Prejudice of That Exclusive Trade, and Benefit which will Accrue to Great Britain by Opening and Extending That Trade, Etc. ([London, 1748]).

B. SECONDARY WORKS

1. General

BRYCE, GEORGE: *The Remarkable History of the Hudson's Bay Company* . . . (London & Toronto, 1900).

GLOVER, R.: "The Difficulties of the Hudson's Bay Company's Penetration of the West," *Canadian Historical Review*, XXIX (1948), 240-54.

LAUT, AGNES C.: *The 'Adventure of England' on Hudson Bay: A Chronicle of the Fur-Trade in the North*, Chronicles of Canada Series, XVII (Toronto, 1914).

MAC KAY, DOUGLAS: *The Honourable Company: A History of the Hudson's Bay Company* (Indianapolis, Ind. & New York, 1936).

NEATBY, LESLIE H.: *In Quest of the North West Passage* (London, 1958).

PINKERTON, ROBERT EUGENE: *Hudson's Bay Company* (New York, c. 1931).

RICH, E. E.: *The History of the Hudson's Bay Company, 1670-1870*, Hudson's Bay Record Society, *Publications*, XXI-XXII (2 vols., London, 1958-9).

WILLIAMS, GLYNDWR: *The British Search for the Northwest Passage in the Eighteenth Century*, Royal Commonwealth Society, *Imperial Studies*, No. 24 (London, 1962).

WILLSON, BECKLES: *The Great Company, 1667-1871: Being a History of the Honourable Company of Merchants Adventurers Trading into Hudson's Bay* (2 vols., London, 1900).

2. *Biographical*

DOBBS, ARTHUR, and JOSEPH ROBSON. "Arthur Dobbs and Joseph Robson: New Light on the Relationship between Two Early Critics of the Hudson's Bay Company" by Glyndwr Williams, *Canadian Historical Review*, XL (1959), 132-6.

HEARNE, SAMUEL. *Samuel Hearne and the Northwest Passage* by Gordon Speck (Caldwell, Idaho, 1963).

C. MAPS

KITCHIN, THOMAS: *A Particular Map of Baffin and Hudson's Bay.* In Kitchin: *A General Atlas* . . . (London, 1777), No. 30 (inset).

MITCHELL, JOHN: *A New Map of Hudson's Bay and Labrador.* This is an inset on the famous Mitchell map, *A Map of . . . North America* . . . [1755].

POWNALL, THOMAS: *A Particular Map of Baffin's and Hudson's Bay, 1777.* In William Faden: *The North American Atlas* (London, 1777); inset in Nos. 1-2, which is Pownall's *A New and Correct Map of North America.*

MARYLAND

A. BIBLIOGRAPHICAL AIDS

GIDDENS, PAUL H.: "Bibliography on Maryland during the Time of Governor Horatio Sharpe, 1753-1769," *Maryland Historical Magazine*, XXXI (1936), 6-16.

HASSE, ADELAIDE R.: "Maryland, 1632-1789," in "Materials for a Bibliography of the Public Archives of the Thirteen Original States," American Historical Association, *Annual Report, 1906* (2 vols., Washington, D.C., 1908), II, 448-65. See also the bibliography in Charles Albro Barker's *The Background of the Revolution in Maryland*, pp. 392-9. For Maryland publications see the annotated bibliography in Lawrence C. Wroth's *A History of Printing in Colonial Maryland, 1686-1776.*

B. PRINTED SOURCE MATERIALS

1. *Government and related documents*

BACON, THOMAS, ed.: *Laws of Maryland at Large: With Proper Indexes* . . . (Annapolis, Md., 1765). This collection was supplemented by *Acts of Assembly to Compleat Bacon's Laws to This Time* (Annapolis, Md., 1768).

BISSET, JAMES, comp.: *Abridgment and Collection of the Acts of Assembly of the Province of Maryland at Present in Force* . . . (Philadelphia, 1759).

BROWNE, WILLIAM HAND, *et al.*, eds.: *Maryland Archives* (70 vols.+, Baltimore, Md., 1883-1964+). Included in this series are the *Proceedings of the Council* (1732-70), Vols. XXVIII, XXXI, and XXXII; the *Proceedings and Acts of the General Assembly* (1748-1774), Vols. XLVI, L, LII, LV, LVI, LVIII, LIX, LXI-LXIV (originally published as *Votes and Proceedings of the Lower House* . . . at Annapolis, Md. and now available on Readex microcards); the *Correspondence of Governor Horatio Sharpe* (1753-71), Vols. VI, IX, and XIV; *Journal of the Convention* (1775); and *Journal and Correspondence of the Council of Safety* (1775-76), Vols. XI and XII.

Council Proceedings from 10th of May 1756 to the 12th Nov. 1764 (Annapolis, Md., 1766). Some additional material of the Council is to be found in "Commission Book No. 82," *Maryland Historical Magazine*, XXVI (1931)-XXVII (1932), *passim*. The Commission Book contains various miscellaneous entries of the Council between the years 1733 and 1773.

EDEN, ROBERT: "Correspondence of Governor Eden [1769-1777]," *ibid.*, II (1907), 1-13, 97-110, 227-44, 293-309.

GARTH, CHARLES: "Stamp Act Papers," *ibid.*, VI (1911), 282-305.

HANSON, ALEXANDER C., ed.: *Laws of Maryland Made since 1763* . . . (Annapolis, Md., 1787).

HARTSOOK, ELIZABETH, and GUST SKORDAS, eds.: *Land Office and Preroga-*

tive Court Records of Colonial Maryland, Maryland Hall of Records Commission, *Publications,* No. 4 (Annapolis, Md., 1946).

KILTY, WILLIAM, ed.: *The Laws of Maryland . . . [1692-1799]* (2 vols., Annapolis, Md., 1799-1800).

MAXCY, VIRGIL, ed.: *Laws of Maryland: With the Charter, the Bill of Rights . . . [1704-1809]* (3 vols., Baltimore, Md., 1811).

The Proceedings of the Committee Appointed to Examine into the Importation of Goods per the Brigantine Good Intent . . . (Annapolis, Md., 1770). The pamphlet is reprinted in the *Maryland Historical Magazine,* III (1908), *passim,* where it is attributed to Stephen West. It is a minority report of a committee investigating the importation of goods in violation of the Non-Importation Agreement.

Proceedings of the Conventions of the Province of Maryland Held at the City of Annapolis . . . (5 nos., Annapolis, Md. [1775-6]).

SHARPE, HORATIO: "Sharpe's Confidential Report on Maryland, 1765," Aubrey C. Land, ed., *Maryland Historical Magazine,* XLIV (1949), 123-9. See also "The Familiar Letters of Governor Horatio Sharpe [1758-84]," Aubrey C. Land, ed., *ibid.,* LXI (1966), 189-210.

TREASURY OFFICE OF GREAT BRITAIN: "Papers Relating to Officers of the Customs in North America," *ibid.,* XXVII (1932), 231-9. Transcripts from the Public Record Office of customs administration in Maryland, 1770-6.

2. Non-official contemporary writings

Annapolis (in Maryland) June 22, 1769, We . . . the Merchants, Traders, Freeholders, Mechanics, and Other Inhabitants of the Province of Maryland . . . Will Strictly and Faithfully Conform to the Following Resolutions . . . ([Annapolis, Md., 1769]). This broadside presenting the non-importation agreement was signed by Robert Lloyd and forty-two others.

BOUCHER, JONATHAN: *A View of the Causes and Consequences of the American Revolution: In Thirteen Discourses Preached in North America between the Years 1763 and 1775 . . .* (London, 1797). See also *Reminiscences of an American Loyalist, 1738-1789: Being the Autobiography of Jonathan Boucher . . .* (Jonathan Bouchier, ed., Boston & New York, 1925). For correspondence, see Worthington Chauncey Ford's edition of *Letters of Jonathan Boucher to George Washington* (Brooklyn, N.Y., 1899) and "Letters of Rev. Jonathan Boucher," *Maryland Historical Magazine,* VII (1912)-VIII (1913), *passim.*

CARROLL, CHARLES: "Extracts from Account and Letter Books of Dr. Charles Carroll of Annapolis," *ibid.,* XVIII (1923)-XXVI (1931), *passim,* and "Extracts from the Carroll Papers," *ibid.,* X (1915)-

XVI (1921), *passim*. See also *The Life of Charles Carroll of Carrollton, 1737-1832: With His Correspondence and Public Papers* by Kate M. Rowland (2 vols., London & New York, 1898), and *Correspondence of "First Citizen"—Charles Carroll of Carrollton, and "Antilon"—Daniel Dulany, Jr., 1773: With a History of Governor Eden's Administration in Maryland, 1769-1776* (Elihu S. Riley, ed., Baltimore, Md., 1902). Charles Carroll of Annapolis was the father of Charles Carroll of Carrollton. Both were leading Roman Catholics.

DULANY, DANIEL: "Extracts from the Dulany Papers," *Maryland Historical Magazine*, XVI (1921), 43-50. For more material by Dulany, see "Maryland Gossip in 1755," *Pennsylvania Magazine of History and Biography*, III (1879), 144-9; and "Military and Political Affairs in the Middle Colonies in 1755," *ibid.*, III (1879), 11-31. These papers are those of Daniel Dulany, the younger.

EDDIS, WILLIAM: *Letters from America, Historical and Descriptive, Comprising Occurrences from 1769 to 1777, Inclusive* (London, 1792).

HAMILTON, ALEXANDER: "The Letterbooks of Alexander Hamilton, Piscataway Factor," Richard K. McMaster and David C. Skaggs, eds., *Maryland Historical Magazine*, LVI (1966), 146-66; 305-38.

LLOYD, EDWARD: "A Contemporary View of the Acadian Arrival in Maryland, 1755 [in a Letter]," William D. Hoyt, Jr., ed., *William and Mary Quarterly*, 3rd ser., V (1948), 571-5.

LOVE, DAVID: "Letters from the Reverend David Love to Horatio Sharpe, 1774-1779," James High, ed., *Historical Magazine of the Protestant Episcopal Church*, XIX(1950), 355-68.

"Maryland in 1773," *Maryland Historical Magazine*, II (1907), 354-62.

MASON, CHARLES, and JEREMIAH DIXON: "Mason and Dixon's Line [a Letter from Mason and Dixon to Hugh Hammersley, Esq., January 29, 1768]," *ibid.*, II (1907), 315-18.

"Resistance to the Stamp Act [Documents from the P.R.O.]," *ibid.*, IV (1909), 134-9.

WHITE, FRANK F., JR.: "A List of Convicts Transported to Maryland," *ibid.*, XLIII (1948), 55-60.

3. Newspapers

Maryland Gazette, Annapolis. See David D. Skaggs; "Editorial Policies of the *Maryland Gazette*, 1765-1783," *Maryland Historical Magazine*, LIX (1964), 341-9.

Maryland Journal [*Maryland Journal and the Baltimore Advertiser*], b. 1773, Baltimore.

C. SECONDARY WORKS

1. General

ANDREWS, MATTHEW PAGE: *The Founding of Maryland* (Baltimore, Md., 1933).

———: *History of Maryland: Province and State* (Garden City, N.Y., 1929).

ARCHER, GEORGE W.: *The Dismemberment of Maryland: An Historical and Critical Essay* . . . (Baltimore, Md., 1890).

BARKER, CHARLES ALBRO: *The Background of the Revolution in Maryland, Yale Historical Publications: Miscellany*, XXXVIII (London & New Haven, Conn., 1940).

COPE, THOMAS D., and H. W. ROBINSON: "When the Maryland-Pennsylvania Boundary Survey Changed from a Political and Legal Struggle into a Scientific and Technological Project," American Philosophical Society, *Proceedings*, XCVIII (1954), 432-41.

MERENESS, NEWTON DENNISON: *Maryland as a Proprietary Province* (New York, 1901).

SCHARF, JOHN THOMAS: *History of Maryland from the Earliest Period to the Present Day* (3 vols., Baltimore, 1879).

———: *History of Western Maryland* . . . (2 vols., Philadelphia, 1882).

STEINER, BERNARD C.: "Western Maryland in the Revolution," Johns Hopkins University, *Studies in Historical and Political Science*, 20th ser. (1902), 2-57.

2. Local

KLAPTHOR, MARGARET BROWN: *History of Charles County, Maryland* . . . (La Plata, Md., 1958).

OWENS, HAMILTON: *Baltimore on the Chesapeake* (Garden City, N. Y., 1941).

SCHARF, JOHN THOMAS: *Chronicles of Baltimore: Being a Complete History of "Baltimore Town" and Baltimore City* . . . (Baltimore, Md., 1874).

3. Political

BARKER, CHARLES A.: "The Revolutionary Impulse in Maryland," *Maryland Historical Magazine*, XXXVI (1941), 125-38.

ELLEFSON, C. ASHLEY: "The Writ of *Audita Querela* in Eighteenth Century Maryland," *ibid.*, LIX (1964), 369-79.

GIDDENS, PAUL H.: "Maryland and the Stamp Act Controversy," *ibid.*, XXVII (1932), 79-98.

HIGH, JAMES: "A Facet of Sovereignty: The Proprietary Governor and the Maryland Charter," *ibid.*, LV (1960), 67-81. Discusses the gradual limitation of the governor's power by the Assembly.

KLINGELHOFER, HERBERT E.: "The Cautious Revolution: Maryland and the Movement toward Independence, 1774-1776," *ibid.*, LX (1965), 261-313.

MC MAHON, JOHN V. L.: *An Historical View of the Government of Maryland from Its Colonization* . . . (Baltimore, Md., 1831).

MATHEWS, EDWARD B.: *see* under Pennsylvania.

OWINGS, DONNELL MAC CLURE: *His Lordship's Patronage: Offices of Profit in Colonial Maryland* (Baltimore, Md., 1953).

RILEY, ELIHU SAMUEL: *A History of the General Assembly of Maryland, 1635-1904* (Baltimore, Md., 1905).

SILVER, JOHN ARCHER: "The Provisional Government of Maryland, 1774-1777," Johns Hopkins University, *Studies in Historical and Political Science*, 13th ser. (1895), 481-537.

SIOUSSAT, ST. GEORGE L.: "The English Statutes in Maryland," *ibid.*, 21st ser. (1903), 465-568. Although this article deals with a controversy which occurred in the 1720's, the last chapter relates to the Revolutionary period.

STEIN, CHARLES F., JR.: *The Maryland Ground Rent System* (Baltimore, Md., 1952). A brief pamphlet.

TANSILL, CHARLES C.: *see* under Pennsylvania.

4. Economic

BARKER, CHARLES A.: "Property Rights in the Provincial System of Maryland: Proprietary Revenues," *Journal of Southern History*, II (1936), 211-32.

BEHRENS, KATHRYN L.: "Paper Money in Maryland, 1727-1789," Johns Hopkins University, *Studies in Historical and Political Science*, 41st ser. (1923), 1-98.

CRAVEN, AVERY O.: *see* under Virginia.

GIDDENS, PAUL H.: "Land Policies and Administration in Colonial Maryland, 1753-1769," *Maryland Historical Magazine*, XXVIII (1933), 142-71.

———: "Trade and Industry in Colonial Maryland, 1753-1769," *Journal of Economic and Business History*, XLII (1931-2), 512-38.

GOULD, CLARENCE P.: "The Land System in Maryland, 1720-1765," Johns Hopkins University, *Studies in Historical and Political Science*, 31st ser. (1913), 1-106, and "Money and Transportation in Maryland, 1720-65," *ibid.*, 33rd ser. (1915), 1-176.

HEMPHILL, JOHN M., II: "Freight Rates in the Maryland Tobacco Trade,

1705-1762," *Maryland Historical Magazine,* LIV (1959), 36-58, 153-87.

JOHNSON, KEACH: "The Baltimore Company Seeks English Subsidies for the Colonial Iron Industry," *ibid.,* XLVI (1951), 27-43, and "The Baltimore Company Seeks English Markets: A Study of the Anglo-American Iron Trade, 1731-1755," *William and Mary Quarterly,* 3rd ser., XVI (1959), 37-60.

LAND, AUBREY C.: "Economic Base and Social Structure: The Northern Chesapeake in the Eighteenth Century," *Journal of Economic History,* XXV (1965), 639-54.

MIDDLETON, ARTHUR PIERCE: "The Chesapeake Convoy System, 1662-1763," *William and Mary Quarterly,* 3rd ser., III (1946), 182-207.

————: *Tobacco Coast: A Maritime History of Chesapeake Bay in the Colonial Era* (Newport News, Va., 1953).

PRICE, JACOB M.: "The Economic Growth of the Chesapeake and the European Market, 1697-1775," *Journal of Economic History,* XXIV (1964), 496-511.

WHITELY, WILLIAM G.: "The Principio Company: A Historical Sketch of the First Iron-works in Maryland," *Pennsylvania Magazine of History and Biography,* XI (1897), 63-8, 190-8, 288-95.

WYCKOFF, VERTREES J.: *Tobacco Regulation in Colonial Maryland,* Johns Hopkins University, *Studies in Historical and Political Science,* n. ser., Extra Vol., XXII (Baltimore, Md., 1936).

5. Social

BARKER, CHARLES A.: "Maryland before the Revolution: Society and Thought," *American Historical Review,* XLVI (1940-1), 1-20.

BRACKETT, JEFFREY RICHARDSON: *The Negro in Maryland: A Study of the Institution of Slavery,* Johns Hopkins University, *Studies in Historical and Political Science,* Extra Vol., VI (Baltimore, Md., 1889).

CARROLL, KENNETH L.: "Maryland Quakers and Slavery," *Maryland Historical Magazine,* XLV (1950), 215-25.

CUNZ, DIETER: *The Maryland Germans: A History* (Princeton, N. J., 1948). Part I, 1640-1790, specifically pages 47-154 discusses German settlements, everyday life, and participation in the American Revolution.

ERVIN, SPENCER: "The Established Church of Colonial Maryland," *Historical Magazine of the Protestant Episcopal Church,* XXIV (1955), 232-92.

GOVE, PHILIP BABCOCK: "An Oxford Convict in Maryland," *Maryland Historical Magazine,* XXXVII (1942), 193-8. A discussion of a letter by one David Benfield who was transported to Maryland in punishment for crimes.

HENIGHAUSEN, LOUIS P.: "Early German Settlements in Western Maryland,"

Society for the History of Germans in Maryland, *Annual Report,* VI (1892), 11-25. The period covered is between 1733 and 1763.

HIGH, JAMES: "The Origins of Maryland's Middle Class in the Colonial Aristocratic Pattern," *Maryland Historical Magazine,* LVII (1962), 334-45.

MC CORMAC, EUGENE IRVING: "White Servitude in Maryland, 1634-1820," Johns Hopkins University, *Studies in Historical and Political Science,* 22nd ser. (1904), 113-224.

RIGHTMYER, NELSON: "The Anglican Church in Maryland: Factors Contributing to the American Revolution [1632-1775]," *Church History,* XIX (1950), 187-98, and "The Character of the Anglican Clergy of Colonial Maryland, 1675-1789," *Maryland Historical Magazine,* XLIV (1949), 229-50, which discusses accusations levelled against Maryland clergymen and concludes that aspersions were unfair.

————: *Maryland's Established Church* (Baltimore, Md., 1956).

SOLLERS, BASIL: "The Acadians (French Neutrals) Transported to Maryland," *Maryland Historical Magazine,* III (1908), 1-21.

WERLINE, ALBERT WARWICK: *Problems of Church and State in Maryland during the Seventeenth and Eighteenth Centuries* (South Lancaster, Mass. [1948]).

WROTH, LAWRENCE C.: *A History of Printing in Colonial Maryland, 1686-1776* (Baltimore, Md., 1922).

6. Biographical

MC GRATH, FRANCIS SIMS: *Pillars of Maryland* (Richmond, Va. [1950]). Biographical sketches of famous individuals including Daniel Dulany and Jonathan Boucher.

ALEXANDER, ROBERT. *Robert Alexander: Maryland Loyalist* by Janet Bassett Johnson (London & New York, 1942).

BOUCHER, JONATHAN. "Jonathan Boucher: Champion of the Minority" by Robert G. Walker, *William and Mary Quarterly,* 3rd ser., II (1945), 3-14. Strangely enough, there has been practically no work done on this important person.

CARROLL, CHARLES. *Charles Carroll of Carrollton* by Ellen Hart Smith (Cambridge, Mass., 1942). See also the article by R. Bruce Harley: "Dr. Charles Carroll: Land Speculator, 1730-1755," *Maryland Historical Magazine,* XLVI (1951), 93-107. Here again are studies of both son and father.

CHASE, SAMUEL. "Samuel Chase and the Annapolis Paper War" by Neil Strawser, *ibid.,* LVII (1962) 177-94, and "Sam Chase, 'Disturber'" by Francis F. Beirne, *ibid.,* LVII (1962), 78-89.

CHASE, THOMAS. "The Reverend Thomas Chase [1703-79]: Pugnacious Parson" by Rosamond Randall Beirne in *ibid.,* LIX (1964), 1-14.

CRESAP, THOMAS. *Thomas Cresap: Maryland Frontiersman* by Kenneth P. Bailey (Boston, 1944).

DULANY, DANIEL, FATHER AND SON. *The Dulanys of Maryland: A Biographical Study of Daniel Dulany, the Elder, and Daniel Dulany, the Younger* by Aubrey C. Land (Baltimore, Md., 1955). See also Land's "A Land Speculator in the Opening of Western Maryland," *Maryland Historical Magazine*, XLVIII (1953), 191-203, and the article by Richard Henry Spencer: "Hon. Daniel Dulany, 1685-1753," *ibid.*, *XIII* (1918), 20-8. These last two articles refer to Dulany, the Elder.

EDDIS, WILLIAM. "William Eddis: What the Sources Say" by George H. Williams, *ibid.*, LX (1965), 121-31.

EDEN, ROBERT. "Portrait of a Colonial Governor: Robert Eden" by Rosamond Randall Beirne, *ibid.*, XLV (1950), 153-75, 294-311.

SHARPE, HORATIO. *A Colonial Governor in Maryland: Horatio Sharpe and His Times, 1753-1773* by Matilda R. Edgar (London & New York, 1912), and the article by Paul H. Giddens: "Governor Horatio Sharpe and His Maryland Government," *Maryland Historical Magazine*, XXXII (1937), 156-74, and that by James High, "The Earl of Loudon [Loudoun] and Horatio Sharpe, 1757 and 1758," *ibid.*, XLV (1950), 14-32. See also the unpublished doctoral dissertation by High: "Reluctant Loyalist: Governor Horatio Sharpe of Maryland, 1753-1769," UCLA, 1951.

7. Military and naval

GIDDENS, PAUL H.: "The French and Indian War in Maryland, 1753 to 1756," *Maryland Historical Magazine*, XXX (1935), 281-310.

SCHLESINGER, ARTHUR M.: "Maryland's Share in the Last Intercolonial War," *ibid.*, VII (1912), 119-49, 243-68.

D. MAPS

The Boundary Lines between the Provinces of Maryland and Pennsylvania: Including the Three Lower Counties of Newcastle, Kent, and Sussex . . . as Defined by the Agreement of 1732, the Decree of Lord Chancellor Hardwicke, and the Agreement of 1760. In State of Maryland. Message of the Governor, Transmitting the Reports of the Joint Commissioners and of Col. Graham (Washington, D. C., 1850). This is based upon the Mason and Dixon survey.

KITCHIN, THOMAS: *A Map of Maryland with the Delaware Counties and the Southern Part of New Jersey, etc.* ([London, 1757]). In the *London Magazine*, XXVI (1757), opp. p. 376.

A New and Accurate Chart of the Bay of Chesapeake, with the Shoals, Channels, Islands, Etc. as Far as the Navigable Part of the Rivers Potomack, Patapsco, and North-east . . . (London, 1776). Library of Congress Maps.

Two other maps contain good depictions of Maryland. For full data on these maps, see the citations under Virginia: Emanuel Bowen: *A New and Accurate Map of Virginia and Maryland,* and Joshua Fry and Peter Jefferson: *A Map of the Most Inhabited Part of Virginia, Containing the Whole Province of Maryland* . . .

For additional information see: Edward B. Mathews's *Bibliography and Cartography of Maryland* . . . , *Maryland Geological Survey,* I, pt. 4 (Baltimore, Md., 1897), 332-401.

MASSACHUSETTS BAY

A. BIBLIOGRAPHICAL AIDS

BOSTON PUBLIC LIBRARY: *The Massachusetts Bay Colony and Boston: A Selected List of Works* . . . (Boston, 1930).

COLBURN, JEREMIAH: *Bibliography of the Local History of Massachusetts* (Boston, 1871).

FLAGG, CHARLES A.: *Guide to Massachusetts Local History* (Salem, Mass. [1907]).

FORD, WORTHINGTON CHAUNCEY: "Bibliography of the Massachusetts House Journals, 1715-1776," Colonial Society of Massachusetts, *Publications,* IV (1910), 201-289.

——, and ALBERT MATTHEWS: "Bibliography of the Laws of Massachusetts Bay, 1641-1776," *ibid.,* 291-480.

HALL, D. B.: "Reference List on Maine Local History," New York State Library, *Bulletin,* No. 63 (1901), 775-917.

HART, ALBERT BUSHNELL, ed.: "Select Bibliographies," *Commonwealth History of Massachusetts,* II and III, passim.

HASSE, ADELAIDE R.: "Massachusetts, 1620-1789," in "Materials for a Bibliography of the Public Archives of the Thirteen Original States . . . ," American Historical Association, *Annual Report, 1906* (2 vols., Washington, D. C., 1908), II, 292-323.

HISTORICAL RECORDS SURVEY: *Proclamations of Massachusetts Issued by Governors and Other Authorities, 1620-1936* (2 vols., Boston, 1937).

HUSTON, A. J.: *A Check List of Maine Local Histories* . . . (Portland, Me., 1915).

WILLIAMSON, JOSEPH: *A Bibliography of the State of Maine: From the Earliest Period to 1891* (2 vols., Portland, Me., 1896).

B. PRINTED SOURCE MATERIALS

1. Government and related documents

Acts and Laws Passed by the Great and General Court or Assembly of His Majesty's Province of the Massachusetts-Bay in New England . . . (published yearly, Boston, 1748-74).

The Acts and Resolves, Public and Private, of . . . Massachusetts-Bay: To which Are Prefixed the Charters of the Province . . . (21 vols., Boston, 1869-1922).

BARRINGTON, WILLIAM WILDMAN BARRINGTON, 2ND VISCOUNT, and FRANCIS BERNARD: *The Barrington-Bernard Correspondence and Illustrative Matter, 1760-1770: Drawn from the "Papers of Sir Francis Bernard" (Sometime Governor of Massachusetts-Bay), Harvard Historical Studies*, XVII (Edward Channing and Archibald Cary Coolidge, eds., Cambridge, Mass., 1912). In addition, see *Copies of Letters from Governor Bernard, &c., to the Earl of Hillsborough* ([Boston, 1769]), and *Letters to the Ministry from Governor Bernard, General Gage, and Commodore Hood: And also Memorials to the Lords of the Treasury from the Commissioners of the Customs* . . . (Boston, 1769; rep., London [1769]). A reply to these letters came with the publication of *An Appeal to the World: Or a Vindication of the Town of Boston from Many False and Malicious Aspersions Contain'd in Certain Letters and Memorials* . . . (Boston, 1769; London, 1770). This pamphlet was the work of a committee although Samuel Adams apparently did most of the writing.

[BOLLAN, WILLIAM]: *The Petition of Mr. Bollan, Agent for the Council of the Province of Massachusetts-Bay to the King in Council, Dated January 26, 1774: In Order Briefly to Shew . . . the Importance of Perfect Harmony between Great Britain and the Colonies* . . . (London, 1774). See also: *The Petitions of Mr. Bollan, Agent for the Council of the Province of Massachusetts Bay Lately Presented to the Two Houses of Parliament* . . . (London, 1774).

BOSTON: *Records Relating to the Early History of Boston* (39 vols., Boston, 1876-1909; vols. 1-22 were issued under the title *Reports of the Record Commission of the City of Boston* [1876-90]). Volumes 3, 5, 14, 16-21, 23, 24, 28-30 contain material germane to the period.

———: *The Votes and Proceedings of the Freeholders and Other Inhabitants of the Town of Boston, in Town Meeting Assembled According to Law* . . . (Boston, 1772, 1773).

BRADFORD, ALDEN, ed.: *Speeches of the Governors of Massachusetts from 1765 to 1775 and the Answers of the House of Representatives* . . . (Boston, 1818).

A Conference between the Commissaries of Massachusetts-Bay and the Commissaries of New-York at New-Haven in the Colony of Connecticut, 1767 (Boston, 1768).

Extract of a Letter from the House of Representatives of the Massachusetts-Bay, to Their Agent Dennys De Berdt, Esq.: With Some Remarks (London, 1770).

HUTCHINSON, THOMAS: *The Case of the Provinces of Massachusetts-Bay and New-York Respecting the Boundary Line between the Two Provinces* (Boston, 1764).

————, ed.: *Collection of Original Papers Relative to the History of the Colony of Massachusetts-Bay* (Boston, 1769; rep., 2 vols., Albany, N. Y., 1865).

————: *The Speeches of His Excellency Governor Hutchinson, to the General Assembly of the Massachusetts-Bay* . . . (Boston, 1773).

Journal of the Honourable House of Representatives of His Majesty's Province of the Massachusetts-Bay in New England . . . (published yearly, Boston, 1748-76). The yearly publications are available on Readex. Also available are the current publications of reproductions of the original journals under the editorship of Malcolm Freiberg with the title *Journals of the House of Representatives of Massachusetts* (37 vols.+, Boston 1919-1965+). The *Journals* presently cover the period 1715 thru 1761.

LINCOLN, WILLIAM, ed.: *Journals of Each Provincial Congress of Massachusetts in 1774 and 1775 . . . and Other Documents* (Boston, 1838).

MATTHEWS, ALBERT, ed.: "Documents Relating to the Last Meetings of the Massachusetts Royal Council, 1774-1776," Colonial Society of Massachusetts, *Publications*, XXXII (*Transactions*, *1933-1937*), 460-504.

Petition and Representation of the House of Representatives of Massachusetts-Bay to the King and His Majesty's Ministers, 20th January, 1768 . . . With Letters to Lord Shelburne, Rockingham, Camden, Chatham, and to D. De Berdt, Agent for the Province: Also a Letter from Lord Shelburne to Governor Bernard, September 17, 1767 ([Boston, 1768]).

QUINCY, JOSIAH, JR., and SAMUEL M. QUINCY, comp. & ed.: *Reports of Cases Argued and Adjudged in the Superior Court of Judicature of the Province of Massachusetts Bay, between 1761 and 1772: Appendix by Horace Gray, Jr.* (Boston, 1865).

SEYBOLT, ROBERT FRANCIS, comp.: *The Town Officials of Colonial Boston, 1634-1775* (Cambridge, Mass., 1939). A chronological arrangement of the names of Boston officials.

SHIRLEY, WILLIAM: *Correspondence of William Shirley, Governor of Massachusetts and Military Commander in America, 1731-1760* (Charles Henry Lincoln, ed., 2 vols., New York, 1912).

WHITMORE, WILLIAM H.: *The Massachusetts Civil List for the Colonial and Provincial Periods, 1630-1774: Being a List of the Names and Dates of Appointment for All the Civil Officers Constituted by Authority of the Charters or the Local Government* (Albany, N. Y., 1870).

WOLKINS, GEORGE G., ed.: "The Boston Customs District in 1768," Massachusetts Historical Society, *Proceedings*, LVIII (1924-5), 418-45.

2. Non-official contemporary writings

ADAMS, JOHN: *The Adams Papers*, First, Second and Third Series. Series I: *Diary and Autobiography of John Adams* (L. H. Butterfield, et al., eds., 4 vols., Cambridge, Mass., 1961) and *Diaries-Supplement to Diary and Autobiography of John Adams* (L. H. Butterfield, ed., Cambridge, Mass., 1966). Series II: *Adams Family Correspondence* (L. H. Butterfield, Wendell D. Garrett, and Marjorie E. Sprague, eds., 2 vols., Cambridge, Mass., 1963). Series III: *Legal Papers of John Adams* (L. Kinvin Wroth and Hiller B. Zobel, eds., 3 vols., Cambridge, Mass., 1965). In addition to these excellent editions of the writings of Adams, there is the earlier collection of *Works* . . . edited by Charles Francis Adams (10 vols., Boston, 1850-60), and *The Selected Writings of John and John Quincy Adams* (Adrienne Koch and William Peden, eds., New York, 1946). For Adams's correspondence, see the two works edited by Charles Francis Adams: *Letters of John Adams Addressed to His Wife* (Boston, 1841), and *Familiar Letters of John Adams and His Wife Abigail Adams during the Revolution* . . . (New York, 1876). Another collection of letters is that edited by Lester J. Cappon, *The Adams-Jefferson Letters: The Complete Correspondence between Thomas Jefferson and Abigail and John Adams* (2 vols., Chapel Hill, N. C., 1959). While these letters were written many years after the American Revolution, some of them do throw light on events of the period here under consideration.

ADAMS, RANDOLPH G., ed.: "New Light on the Boston Massacre," American Antiquarian Society, *Proceedings*, n. ser., XLVII (1937), 259-354. Contains letters from Preston and Hutchinson to General Gage.

ADAMS, SAMUEL: *The Writings of Samuel Adams* (Harry Alonzo Cushing, ed., 4 vols., New York, 1904-8). Also of use is *The Life and Public Services of Samuel Adams* . . . by William V. Wells (3 vols., Boston, 1865), which presents much original material.

ALMY, WILLIAM: "Letter of William Almy to Elisha Story [re: the Stamp Act riot in Boston, 1765]," Edward Gray, ed., Massachusetts Historical Society, *Proceedings*, LV (1921-2), 234-7.

ANDREWS, JOHN: *Letters of John Andrews, Esq., of Boston, 1772-1776* . . . (Winthrop Sargent, ed., Cambridge, Mass., 1866).

BARKER, JOHN: *The British in Boston: Being the Diary of Lieutenant John Barker of the King's Own Regiment from November 15, 1774 to May 31, 1776* (notes by Elizabeth Ellery Dana, Cambridge, Mass., 1924).

BOLLAN, WILLIAM: *The Petition of Mr. Bollan, Agent for the Council of the Province of Massachusetts-Bay, to the King in Council, Dated January 26, 1774* . . . (London, 1774), and "Bollan on Writs of Assistance," George G. Wolkins, ed., Massachusetts Historical Society, *Proceedings*, LIX (1925-6), 414-21.

BOYLE, JOHN: "Boyle's Journal of Occurrences in Boston, 1759-1778," *New England Historical and Genealogical Register*, LXXXIV (1930)-LXXXV (1931), *passim*. Boyle was a Boston printer and his journal provides a helpful narrative of events.

BROWNE, WILLIAM: "Letters of William Browne, American Loyalist," Sidney W. Jackman, ed., *Essex Institute Historical Collections*, XCVI (1960), 1-46. These letters, covering the period 1778-81, are important as indications of the character of a leading Massachusetts Bay Loyalist.

COOPER, SAMUEL: "Letters of Samuel Cooper to Thomas Pownall, 1769-1777," Frederick Tuckerman, ed., *American Historical Review*, VIII (1902-3), 301-30.

CURWEN, SAMUEL: *Journal and Letters of the Late Samuel Curwen . . . an American Refugee in England, from 1775 to 1784* (George A. Ward, ed., Boston & New York, 1842).

DE BERDT, DENNYS: "Letters of Dennys De Berdt, 1757-1770," Colonial Society of Massachusetts, *Publications*, XIII (*Transactions, 1910-1911*), 293-461.

DICKERSON, OLIVER M., ed.: *Boston under Military Rule, 1768-1769: As Revealed in a "Journal of the Times"* (Boston, 1936). Articles from the *New York Journal* and *Boston Evening-Post*.

"Early Coastwise and Foreign Shipping of Salem: A Record of the Entrances and Clearances of the Port of Salem, 1750-1769," Essex Institute, *Historical Collections*, LXII (1926)-LXIII (1927), *passim*.

EDWARDS, JONATHAN: *The Works of President Edwards* (E. Williams and E. Parsons, eds., 8 vols., Leeds, Eng., 1806-11; n. edn., 1817); also a collection under the same title, edited by Isaiah Thomas (8 vols., Worcester, Mass., 1808-9). Sereno E. Dwight edited *The Works of President Edwards: With a Memoir of His Life* (10 vols., New York, 1830); there is also available *The Works of Jonathan Edwards, A.M.: With an Essay on His Genius and Writings by Henry Rogers and a Memoir by Sereno E. Dwight* (Edward Hickman, ed., rev. edn., 2 vols., London, 1840). The latest collection is presently being edited by Iain H. Murray: *The Select Works of Jonathan Edwards: With an Account of His Life* (1 vol. +, London, 1958 +); moreover, the Yale University Press has begun issuing an edition under the editorship of Paul Ramsey: *The Works of Jonathan Edwards* ... (1 vol. +, New Haven, Conn, 1957 +). See, finally, Thomas H. Johnson's *The Printed Writings of Jonathan Edwards, 1703-1758: A Bibliography* (Princeton, N. J., 1940).

FARNSWORTH, AMOS: *Diary Kept by Lieut. Amos Farnsworth of Groton Mass., during a Part of the Revolutionary War, Apr. 1775-May 1779* ... (Samuel A. Green, ed., Cambridge, Mass., 1898).

GOELET, FRANCIS: "Extracts from Capt. Francis Goelet's Journal, Relative to Boston, Salem, and Marblehead, &c., 1746-1750," *New England Historical and Genealogical Register,* XXIV (1870), 50-63.

GREEN, S. A., ed.: "Minutes of the Tea Meetings in 1773, and Other Papers Relating to the Town of Boston," Massachusetts Historical Society, *Proceedings,* 1st ser., XX (1882-3), 10-17.

HARRISON, JOSEPH: "Joseph Harrison and the *Liberty* Incident," D. H. Watson, ed., *William and Mary Quarterly,* 3rd ser., XX (1963), 585-95. Harrison, the Boston customs official, who brought charges against John Hancock in June 1768, explains his behavior to Rockingham.

HASKELL, CALEB: *Caleb Haskell's Diary, May 5, 1775-May 30, 1776. A Revolutionary Soldier's Record before Boston and with Arnold's Expedition* (Newburyport, Mass., 1881). Haskell was first a fifer and then a private in a militia company from Newburyport.

HUTCHINSON, THOMAS: *The Diary and Letters of His Excellency Thomas Hutchinson* ... (Peter Orlando Hutchinson, ed., 2 vols., London, 1883-6).

————: *The History of the Colony and Province of Massachusetts-Bay* (2 vols., Boston, 1764-7; 3rd vol., John Hutchinson, ed., 1828; n. edn., 3 vols., Lawrence Shaw Mayo, ed., Cambridge, Mass., 1936). The Mayo edition of Hutchinson's *History* should be used in conjunction with Catherine Barton Mayo's *Additions* to Thomas Hutchinson's *"History of Massachusetts Bay"* (Worcester, Mass., 1949; rep. from the American Antiquarian Society, *Proceedings,* n. ser., LIX [1949], 11-74). For additional information, see L. S. Mayo's "Thomas Hutchinson and His 'History of Massachusetts-Bay,'" American Antiquarian Society, *Proceedings,* n. ser., XLI (1931), 321-39. See also the complementary volumes by George Richards Minot: *Continuation of the History of the Province of Massachusetts, from the year 1748 [to 1765]* (2 vols., Boston, 1798-1803).

LLOYD, HENRY: "The Boston Riot of 1765," Business Historical Society, *Bulletin,* VII (1933), 12-13. Prints material found in Lloyd's letter-book; he was a merchant in Boston.

MASSACHUSETTS HISTORICAL SOCIETY, *Collections* (79 vols. +, Boston, 1792-1941 +). The *Collections* contain a wealth of source material scattered throughout the various volumes. Some volumes containing specifically pertinent materials are included in the following list: *Aspinall Papers*, 4th ser., IX-X; *The Bowdoin and Temple Papers*, 6th ser., IX, and 7th ser., VI; *Warren-Adams Letters Being Chiefly a Correspondence Among John Adams, Samuel Adams, and James Warren* . . . , *1743-1777*, LXXII; *Jasper Mauduit: Agent in London* . . . , LXXIV; Worthington Chauncey Ford, ed.: *Broadsides, Ballads, & Printed in Massachusetts, 1639-1800*, LXXV.

MAUDUIT, ISRAEL: *A Short View of the History of the Colony of Massachusett's Bay: With Respect to their Charters and Constitution* (London, 1769; 2nd edn., w/add., 1774); this later was enlarged and appeared as *A Short View of the New England Colonies: With Respect to Their Charters and Constitutions* . . . (4th edn., w/add., London, 1776).

MAYHEW, JONATHAN. *Memoir of the Life and Writings of Rev. Jonathan Mayhew* . . . by Alden Bradford (Boston, 1938). See also "Thomas Hollis and Jonathan Mayhew: Their Correspondence, 1759-1766," Bernhard Knollenberg, ed., Massachusetts Historical Society, *Proceedings*, LXIX (1947-50), 102-93.

MERRITT, ELIZABETH, ed.: "The Lexington Alarm, April 19, 1775: Messages Sent to the Southward after the Battle," *Maryland Historical Magazine*, XLI (1946), 89-114.

Orations Delivered at the Request of the Inhabitants of the Town of Boston to Commemorate the Evening of the Fifth of March, 1770 . . . (Boston, 1785; 2nd edn., Boston, 1807).

OTIS, JAMES: "Some Political Writings of James Otis," Charles F. Mullett, ed., University of Missouri, *Studies: A Quarterly of Research*, IV (1929), 257-432; "Letters of James Otis, 1764-1765," Massachusetts Historical Society, *Proceedings*, XLIII (1910), 202-7 and "Letter from James Otis, 1768," *ibid.*, pp. 492-3.

Papers Relating to Public Events in Massachusetts Preceding the American Revolution (Philadelphia, 1856).

PARKMAN, EBENEZER: "The Diary of Ebenezer Parkman," Francis G. Walett, ed., American Antiquarian Society, *Proceedings*, n. ser., LXXIII (1963)–LXXVI (1966) +, *passim*, covering the years 1747-1755. Parkman was a minister at Westborough, Mass. from 1724 to 1782; his diary provides an excellent illumination of the life of a country parson and a glimpse of the history of the area in which he lived.

PAXTON, CHARLES: "The Letters of Charles Paxton," George G. Wolkins, ed., Massachusetts Historical Society, *Proceedings*, LVI (1922-3), 343-52.

PRESTON, THOMAS: "[Documents Relating to] Captain Thomas Preston and the Boston Massacre," Albert Matthews, ed., Colonial Society of Massachusetts, *Publications*, VII (*Transactions*, 1902), 2-22.

QUINCY, JOSIAH: "Journal of Josiah Quincy, Junior, 1773," M. A. De Wolfe

Howe, ed., Massachusetts Historical Society, *Proceedings*, XLIX (1915-16), 424-81, and "Journal of Josiah Quincy, Jun., during His Voyage and Residence in England from September 28th, 1774, to March 2d, 1775," *ibid.*, L (1916-17), 433-70. See also *Memoirs of the Life of Josiah Quincy, Jun., of Massachusetts* . . . by Josiah Quincy, III (Boston, 1825; 2nd edn., Eliza Susan Quincy, ed., Boston, 1874).

ROWE, JOHN: *Letters and Diary of John Rowe, Boston Merchant, 1759-1762, 1764-1779* (Anne Rowe Cunningham, ed., Boston, 1903).

SEYBOLT, ROBERT FRANCIS, ed.: "Trade Agreements in Colonial Boston," *New England Quarterly*, II (1929), 307-9.

TYLER, J. E., ed.: "An Account of Lexington in the Rockingham Mss. at Sheffield," *William and Mary Quarterly*, 3rd ser., X (1953), 99-107. Prints two letters to the Marquess of Rockingham from an unidentified person at Boston describing the battles of Lexington and Concord.

UPTON, L. F. S., ed.: "Proceedings of Ye Body Respecting the Tea," *ibid.*, 3rd ser., XXII (1965), 287-300.

3. *Contemporary pamphlets, tracts, and related materials: Chronologically arranged*

1 7 4 9

A Letter to the Freeholders and Qualified Voters: Relating to the Ensuing Election . . . (Boston, 1749).

1 7 5 4

[COOPER, SAMUEL]: *The Crisis: Scire Volunt, Secreta Domus Atque Inde Timeri* ([Boston], 1754). Reprinted with a longer title in London, 1766. This pamphlet criticized as unconstitutional the Massachusetts Excise Bill to raise money to help finance the Great War for the Empire. One edition contains a supplement praising the Governor for opposing the bill and pleading with the people to vote against it.

A Letter from a Gentleman to His Friend: Upon the Excise-Bill now under Consideration ([Boston, 1754]).

MAYHEW, JONATHAN: *A Sermon Preach'd in the Audience of His Excellency William Shirley, Esq. . . . , the Honourable His Majesty's Council, and the Honourable House of Representatives of the Province* . . . (Boston, 1754).

RUSTICUS, pseud.: *The Good of the Community Impartially Considered in a Letter to a Merchant in Boston, in Answer to One Received*

Respecting the Excise-Bill . . . By a True Friend of Liberty (Boston, 1754). Signed Rusticus, Salem, July 15, 1754.

WATERHOUSE, SAMUEL: *The Monster of Monsters: A True and Faithful Narrative of a Most Remarkable Phaenomenon Lately Seen in this Metropolis . . .* ([Boston, 1754]). This pamphlet was a response to the Massachusetts Excise Bill and was ordered burned by the common hangman under orders of the General Court. See also Daniel Fowle's *A Total Eclipse of Liberty: Being a True and Faithful Account of the Arraignment, and Examination of Daniel Fowle . . . Barely on Suspicion of His Being Concern'd in Printing and Publishing a Pamphlet, Entitled "The Monster of Monsters . . ."* (Boston, 1755).

1 7 6 1

STEVENS, BENJAMIN: *A Sermon Preached at Boston before the Great and General Court or Assembly of the Province . . .* (Boston, 1761).

1 7 6 2

SEWALL, JOSEPH: *A Serman Preached . . . September 16, 1762 before the Great and General Court of the Province of the Massachusetts-Bay in New-England: On the Joyful News of the Reduction of Havannah . . .* (Boston, 1762).

1 7 6 5

ELIOT, ANDREW: *A Sermon Preached Before His Excellency Francis Bernard, Esq., Governor; the Honorable His Majesty's Council and the Honorable House of Representatives of the Province . . . May 29th 1765 . . .* (Boston, 1765).

Liberty, Property, and No Excise: A Poem Compos'd . . . on the 14th of August, 1765 ([Boston], 1765).

1 7 6 6

BARNARD, EDWARD: *A Sermon Preached before His Excellency Francis Bernard, Esq., Governor and Commander in Chief, the Honourable His Majesty's Council, and the Honourable House of Representatives, of the Province . . . May 28th 1766 . . .* (Boston, 1766). Barnard was pastor of the First Church in Haverhill.

PATTEN, WILLIAM: *A Discourse Delivered at Hallifax [sic] in the County of Plymouth, July 24th 1766, on the day of Thanksgiving . . . for the Repeal of the Stamp-Act* (Boston, 1766).

1 7 6 7

BRIDGE, EBENEZER: *A Sermon Preached before His Excellency Francis Bernard, Esq., Governor; His Honor Thomas Hutchinson, Esq., Lieutenant Governor; the Honorable His Majesty's Council, and the Honorable House of Representatives of the Province . . . May 27th, 1767* . . . (Boston, 1767).

1 7 6 8

HOLLIS, THOMAS, comp.: *The True Sentiments of America: Contained in a Collection of Letters Sent from the House of Representatives of the Province of Massachusetts Bay to Several Persons of High Rank in This Kingdom* . . . (London, 1768). R. G. Adams in his *Ideas* (p. 204) attributes this work to Samuel Adams.

SHUTE, DANIEL: *A Sermon Preached before His Excellency Francis Bernard, Esq., Governor; His Honor Thomas Hutchinson, Esq., Lieutenant-Governor; the Honorable His Majesty's Council, and the Honorable House of Representatives of the Province . . . May 25, 1768* . . . (Boston, 1768).

1 7 6 9

[MEIN, JOHN]: *A State of the Importation from Great-Britain into the Port of Boston from the Beginning of January 1769, to August 17th, 1769* . . . (Boston, 1769).

Observations on Several Acts of Parliament . . . And also, on the Conduct of the Officers of the Customs since Those Acts Were Passed . . . Published by the Merchants of Boston (Boston, 1769; London, 1770). Boston merchants felt oppressed by duties and bonds on imports and exports and by the unrestricted power of the customs officials.

Truth Triumphant: Or in Defence of the Church of England, against the Second Solemn League and Covenant . . . (New York [1769]).

1 7 7 0

An Account of a Late Military Massacre at Boston: Or the Consequences of Quartering Troops in a Populace Town. Boston, March 12, 1770 ([New York, 1770]).

[BOWDOIN, JAMES, et al.]: *A Short Narrative of the Horrid Massacre in Boston Perpetrated in the Evening of the Fifth Day of March, 1770* . . . (Boston, 1770). According to this pamphlet, the shooting was deliberate, and the massacre was the logical outcome of a standing army. See also: *Additional Observations to A Short Narrative* . . . ([London], 1770).

CHAUNCY, CHARLES: *Trust in God, the Duty of a People in a Day of Trouble: A Sermon Preached May 30th 1770* . . . (Boston, 1770).

COOKE, SAMUEL: *A Sermon Preached at Cambridge in the Audience of his Honor Thomas Hutchinson, Esq. . . . His Majesty's Council, and the Honorable House of Representatives of the Province . . . May 30th 1770* . . . (Boston, 1770). See J. W. Thornton's *The Pulpit of the American Revolution* . . . (Boston & New York, 1860), 147-86.

A Fair Account of the Late Unhappy Disturbance At Boston in New England . . . With an Appendix Containing Some Affidavits and other Evidences Relating to the Affair . . . (London, 1770). A defence of the British troops in the Boston Massacre, accusing the citizens of provoking the attack.

HARRISON, JOSEPH: "Joseph Harrison and the *Liberty* Incident," D. H. Watson, ed., *William and Mary Quarterly*, 3rd ser., XX (1963), 585-95.

HODGSON, JOHN: *The Trial of William Wems . . . [and others], Soldiers in His Majesty's 29th Regiment of Foot, for the Murder of Crispus Attucks . . . [and others] on Monday-Evening, the 5th of March, 1770* . . . (Boston, 1770).

LATHROP, JOHN: *Innocent Blood Crying to God from the Streets of Boston: A Sermon Occasioned by the Horrid Murder . . . of the Fifth of March, 1770* . . . (London 1770; Boston, 1771).

[MEIN, JOHN]: *A State of the Importations from Great-Britain into the Port of Boston from the Beginning of January, 1770: Also an Account of All the Goods That Have Been Reshipped . . . for Great Britain since January 1769* . . . (Boston, 1770). One hundred fifty copies of this pamphlet were distributed in Philadelphia. The pamphlet indicated widespread violation of the non-importation agreement by Boston merchants.

1 7 7 1

[BACKUS, ISAAC]: *A Letter to a Gentleman in the Massachusetts General Assembly Concerning Taxes to Support Religious Worship* ([Boston], 1771). Signed "A Countryman."

LOVELL, JAMES: *An Oration Delivered April 2d, 1771 at the Request of the Inhabitants of the Town of Boston: To Commemorate the Bloody Tragedy of the Fifth of March, 1770* (Boston, 1771). The oration is reprinted in *Orations Delivered at the Request of the Inhabitants of the Town of Boston to Commemorate the Evening of the Fifth of March, 1770* . . . (2nd edn., Boston, 1807), pp. 3-11.

A Ministerial Catechise Suitable to Be Learned by All Modern Provincial Governors, Pensioners, Place-Men, &c., Dedicated to T[homas] H[utchinson], Esq. (Boston, 1771).

TUCKER, JOHN: *A Sermon Preached at Cambridge before his Excellency*

Thomas Hutchinson, Esq., Governor; His Honor Andrew Oliver, Esq., Lieutenant-Governor; the Honorable His Majesty's Council, and the Honorable House of Representatives . . . May 29th 1771 . . . (Boston, 1771).

1 7 7 2

[ALLEN, JAMES]: *The Poem which the Committee of the Town of Boston Had Voted [Unanimously] to Be Published* . . . (Boston, 1772). The poem, which refers to the Boston Massacre, was initially suppressed owing to doubts of Allen's patriotism, but it was later published by his friends with extracts from his "Retrospect."

Americans! Bear in Remembrance the Horrid Massacre! Perpetrated in King-Street, Boston, New-England, on the Evening of March the Fifth, 1770 ([Boston, 1772]).

PARSONS, MOSES: *A Sermon Preached at Cambridge before His Excellency Thomas Hutchinson, Esq., Governor; His Honor Andrew Oliver, Esq., Lieutenant-Governor; the Honorable His Majesty's Council, and the Honorable House of Representatives of the Province . . . May 27th 1772* . . . (Boston, 1772).

WARREN, JOSEPH: *An Oration Delivered March 5th, 1772 at the Request of the Inhabitants of the Town of Boston to Commemorate the Bloody Tragedy of the Fifth of March, 1770* . . . (1st & 2nd edns. Boston, 1772). Printed in *Orations Delivered at the Request of the Inhabitants of the Town of Boston to Commemorate the Evening of the Fifth of March 1770* . . . (2nd edn., Boston, 1807), pp. 13-25.

1 7 7 3

BARNARD, EDWARD: *A Sermon Preached before the Annual Convention of Ministers of the Massachusetts-Bay in Boston, May 27th, 1773* (Boston, 1773).

CHURCH, BENJAMIN: *An Oration Delivered March Fifth, 1773 . . . to Commemorate the Bloody Tragedy of the Fifth of March, 1770* (1st-4th edns., Boston, 1773). This is reprinted in *Orations Delivered at the Request of the Inhabitants of the Town of Boston to Commemorate the Evening of the Fifth of March, 1770* . . . (2nd edn., Boston, 1807), pp. 27-38.

Friends! Brethren! Countrymen! That Worst of All Plagues, the Detestable Tea Shipped for this Port by the East India Company Is now Arrived in this Harbour . . . ([Boston, 1773]). A broadside.

HOWARD, SIMEON: *A Sermon Preached to the Ancient and Honorable Artillery-Company in Boston, New-England, June 7th, 1773 . . .* (Boston, 1773).

HUTCHINSON, THOMAS, *et al.: Copy of Letters Sent to Great-Britain by His Excellency Thomas Hutchinson, the Hon. Andrew Oliver, and*

Several Other Persons Born and Educated among Us . . . (Boston, 1773). A number of editions of these famous letters were printed, one with the title *The Representations of Governor Hutchinson* . . . and another with the title *The Letters of Governor Hutchinson* . . . ; one edition was edited by Israel Mauduit. The letters are reprinted in *Franklin before the Privy Council . . . to Advocate the Removal of Hutchinson and Oliver* (Philadelphia, 1859), pp. 17-51.

The Tradesmen's Protest against the Proceedings of the Merchants Relative to the New Importations of Tea . . . ([Boston, 1773]). A broadside.

TURNER, CHARLES: *A Sermon Preached before His Excellency Thomas Hutchinson, Esq., Governor; the Honorable His Majesty's Council, and the Honorable House of Representatives of the Province* . . . *May 26th 1773* . . . (Boston, 1773).

1774

A Brief Review of the Rise, Progress, Services, and Sufferings of New-England, Especially the Province of Massachusetts-Bay . . . (Norwich, Conn., 1774).

[CHAUNCEY, CHARLES]: *A Letter to a Friend: Giving a Concise but Just Representation of the Hardships and Sufferings the Town of Boston Is Exposed to* . . . *in Consequence of the Late Act of the British-Parliament* . . . (Boston, 1774).

A Faithful Account of the Whole of the Transactions Relating to the, Late Affair of Honour between J. Temple and W. Whately, Esqrs. . . . (London, 1774). Relating to the Hutchinson-Oliver letters which were secretly transmitted by Franklin to the House of Representatives of Massachusetts.

[FRANKLIN, BENJAMIN]: *A True State of the Proceedings in the Parliament of Great Britain and in the Province of Massachusetts Bay Relative to the Giving and Granting the Money of the People of that Province and of all America in the House of Commons in Which They Are not Represented* (London & Philadelphia, 1774). While generally attributed to Arthur Lee, P. E. Du Simitière in his contemporary diary notes that it was "wrote by Dr. Franklin."

Gentlemen: The Evils Which We Have Long Foreseen Are Now Come Upon This Town and Province . . . *Signed by Order and in Behalf of the Committee of Correspondence for Boston. Boston, June 8, 1774* ([Boston, 1774]). It is a statement concerning the Boston Port Bill.

HANCOCK, JOHN: *An Oration Delivered March 5, 1774 at the Request of the Inhabitants of the Town of Boston: To Commemorate the Bloody Tragedy of the Fifth of March 1770* (Boston, 1774). This pamphlet, attributed to various authors, although delivered by

Hancock, was probably the work of several Boston patriots. Other editions were published in Newport, New Haven, and Philadelphia in 1774 and 1775.

HITCHCOCK, GAD: *A Sermon Preached Before His Excellency Thomas Gage, Esq., Governor; the Honorable His Majesty's Council, and the Honorable House of Representatives of the Province . . . May 25th 1774 . . .* (Boston, 1774).

HOLLY, ISRAEL: *God Brings about His Holy and Wise Purpose or Decree . . . In a Sermon Preached at Suffield, December 27, 1773 . . .* (Hartford, Conn., 1774). The author deemed the destruction of the tea at Boston necessary because the Tea Act infringed on English liberty. As the colonies tried to decide whether they should submit or resist, Holly suggested that they seek God's guidance.

[PRESCOTT, ROBERT]: *A Letter from a Veteran: To the Officers of the [British] Army Encamped at Boston* ([New York], 1774). Prescott was a captain who served with the 15th Foot.

QUINCY, JOSIAH, JR.: *Observations on the Act of Parliament Commonly Called the Boston Port-Bill: With Thoughts on Civil Society and Standing Armies* (Boston, Philadelphia & London, 1774). Quincy's pamphlet provides an incisive commentary on the Boston Port Bill.

[The Wonder of Wonders or] The Wonderful Appearance of an Angel, Devil, and Ghost to a Gentleman in the Town of Boston . . . To Whom in Some Measure May be Attributed the Distresses that Have of Late Fallen upon That Unhappy Metropolis . . . (Boston & New York, 1774). The title in brackets was added when printed.

1 7 7 5

ADAMS, ZABDIEL: *The Grounds of Confidence and Success in War Represented: A Sermon Preached . . . January 2d, 1775 . . .* (Boston, 1775).

A BLOODY Butchery by the British Troops: Or the Runaway Fight of the Regulars being the Particulars of the Victorious Battle Fought at and near Concord . . . (Salem, Mass. [1775]). This is a broadside about the battle of Concord.

BOLTON, THOMAS: *An Oration Delivered March Fifteenth, 1775 at the Request of a Number of the Inhabitants of the Town of Boston . . .* ([Boston], 1775). This speech attacking the patriot leaders in Boston satirizes the Boston Massacre orations, especially Warren's of March 6th, 1775.

A Circumstantial Account of an Attack that Happened on the 19th of April, 1775, on his Majesty's Troops by a Number of the People of the Province of Massachusetts' Bay (Boston, 1775). A broadside presenting the battle of Lexington as seen by a Britisher.

CLARKE, JOHN: *An Impartial and Authentic Narrative of the Battle Fought on the 17th of June, 1775 between His Britannic Majesty's Troops and the American Provincial Army on Bunker's Hill* . . . (London, 1775).

FISH, ELISHA: *A Discourse Delivered at Worcester, March 28th, 1775 at the Desire of the Convention of Committees for the County of Worcester* (Worcester, Mass., 1775).

GORDON, WILLIAM: *A Discourse Preached December 15th, 1774, Being the Day Recommended by the Provincial Congress; and Afterwards at the Boston Lecture* (Boston, 1775). Gordon also preached another sermon with almost the same title on the same day which was reprinted in J. W. Thornton's *The Pulpit of the American Revolution* . . . (Boston & New York, 1860), 187-226.

———: *A Sermon Preached before the Honorable House of Representatives on the Day [19 July 1775] Intended for the Choice of Counsellors, Agreeable to the Advice of the Continental Congress* (Watertown, Mass., 1775).

LANGDON, SAMUEL: *Government Corrupted by Vice and Recovered by Righteousness: A Sermon Preached Before the Honorable Congress of the Colony of the Massachusetts-Bay* . . . (Watertown, Mass., 1775); reprinted in J. W. Thornton's *The Pulpit and the American Revolution* . . . (Boston & New York, 1860), pp. 227-58. Strongly criticized the tyranny of the mother country.

A Narrative of the Excursion and Ravages of the King's Troops under the Command of General Gage on the Nineteenth of April, 1775 . . . (Worcester, Mass. [1775]).

NOBLE, OLIVER: *Some Strictures upon the Sacred Story Recorded in the Book of Esther, Showing the Power and Oppression of State Ministers . . . in a Discourse delivered . . . March 8th, 1775: In Commemoration of the Massacre at Boston* . . . (Newburyport, Mass., 1775).

WEBSTER, SAMUEL: *Rabshakeh's Proposals Considered: In a Sermon Delivered at Groton, February 21, 1775* . . . (Boston, 1775).

1 7 7 6

ANTI-STAMP FIRE SOCIETY: *Rules and Orders of the Anti-Stamp Fire Society: Instituted at Boston, 1763* (Boston, 1776).

CLARK, JONAS: *The Fate of Blood-Thirsty Oppressors and God's Tender Care of His Distressed People: A Sermon Preached at Lexington, April 19th, 1776, to Commemorate the Murder, Bloodshed, and Commencement of Hostilities between Great-Britain and America* . . . (Boston, 1776). Clark was pastor of the church in Lexington.

[DAVIS, TIMOTHY]: *A Letter from a Friend to Some of His Intimate Friends: On the Subject of Paying Taxes, &c.* (Watertown, Mass., 1776).

FITCH, ELIJAH: *A Discourse, The Substance of Which Was Delivered at Hopkinton . . . Following the Precipatate Flight of the British Troops from Boston* (Boston, 1776).

JOHNSTONE, GEORGE: *Governor Johnstone's Speech on the Question of Recommitting the Address Declaring the Colony of Massachusetts Bay in Rebellion . . .* (London [1776]).

THACHER, PETER: *An Oration Delivered at Watertown, March 5, 1776: To Commemorate the Bloody Massacre at Boston Perpetrated March 5, 1770 . . .* (Watertown, Mass., 1776). Printed in *Orations Delivered at the Request of the Inhabitants of the Town of Boston to Commemorate the Evening of the Fifth of March, 1770 . . .* (2nd edn., Boston, 1807), pp. 71-82.

[WARREN, MERCY OTIS]: *The Blockheads or the Affrighted Officers: A Farce* (Boston, 1776). The play satirizes Burgoyne's farce, *The Blockade.*

WEST, SAMUEL: *A Sermon Preached before the Honorable Council and the Honorable House of Representatives, of the Colony . . .* (Boston, 1776). Reprinted in J. W. Thornton: *The Pulpit in the American Revolution . . .* (Boston & New York, 1860), 259-322.

4. Newspapers

Boston Chronicle, 1767-1770, Boston.

Boston Evening-Post, e. 1775, Boston.

Boston Gazette [Boston Gazette, or, Weekly Journal; Boston Gazette, or, Weekly Advertiser; Boston Gazette, or Country Journal], Boston.

Boston News-Letter [Boston Weekly News-Letter; Boston News-Letter; Boston News-Letter and New England Chronicle; Massachusetts Gazette, and the New England Chronicle; The Massachusetts Gazette. And Boston News Letter], e. 1776. Boston.

Boston Post-Boy [The Boston Weekly Advertiser; Green & Russell's Boston Post-Boy & Advertiser; The Boston Post-Boy & Advertiser], e. 1775, Boston.

The Censor, 1771-1772, Boston.

Essex Gazette, 1768-1775, Salem.

The Essex Journal [The Essex Journal & Merrimack Packet: Or, the Massachusetts and New-Hampshire General Advertiser; The Essex Journal: Or, the Massachusetts and New Hampshire General Advertiser; The Essex Journal or New Hampshire Packet], 1773-1777, Newburyport.

The Massachusetts Spy [The Massachusetts Spy. Or, Thomas's Boston Journal], 1770-1775, Boston.

The New England Chronicle, b. 1776, Boston.

The Royal American Magazine; or Universal Repository of Instruction and Amusement, 1774-1775, Boston.

C. SECONDARY WORKS

1. General

BARRY, JOHN STETSON: *The History of Massachusetts* (3 vols., Boston, 1855-7).

BRADFORD, ALDEN: *History of Massachusetts . . . [1764-1820]* (3 vols., Boston, 1822-9).

HART, ALBERT BUSHNELL, ed.: *Commonwealth History of Massachusetts: Colony, Province and State* (5 vols., New York, 1927-30). A cooperative undertaking.

HOLLAND, JOSIAH GILBERT: *History of Western Massachusetts . . .* (2 vols., Springfield, Mass., 1855).

SMITH, MARION JAQUES: *A History of Maine: From Wilderness to Statehood [1497-1820]* (Portland, Me., 1949).

TAYLOR, ROBERT J.: *Western Massachusetts in the Revolution* (Providence, R.I., 1954).

2. Local

BYNNER, EDWIN L.: "Topography and Landmarks of [the Boston of] the Provincial Period," *Memorial History of Boston . . .* , II, 491-532.

COOK, SHERWIN LAWRENCE: "Boston: The Eighteenth Century Town," *Commonwealth History of Massachusetts*, II: 222-56.

DEWEY, CHESTER, et al.: *A History of the County of Berkshire, Massachusetts . . .* (Pittsfield, Mass., 1829).

FELT, JOSEPH BARLOW: *Annals of Salem: From Its First Settlement* (Salem, Mass., 1827).

HUDSON, ALFRED SERENO: *The History of Sudbury, Massachusetts, 1638-1889* (Boston, 1889).

LINCOLN, WILLIAM: *History of Worcester, Massachusetts . . . [to 1836]* (2 vols. in 1, Worcester, Mass., 1837; 1862).

MACY, OBED: *The History of Nantucket . . . with the Rise and Progress of the Whale Fishery . . .* (Boston, 1835).

MARVIN, ABIJAH PERKINS: *History of the Town of Lancaster, Massachusetts . . . 1643-1879* (Lancaster, Mass., 1879).

PHILLIPS, JAMES DUNCAN: *Salem in the Eighteenth Century* (Boston & New York, 1937).

QUINCY, JOSIAH: *A Municipal History of the Town and City of Boston during Two Centuries . . . [1630-1830]* (Boston, 1852).

SHAW, CHARLES H.: *A Topographical and Historical Description of Boston . . .* (Boston, 1817).

SHURTLEFF, NATHANIEL B.: *A Topographical and Historical Description of Boston* (Boston, 1871).

SNOW, CALEB H.: *A History of Boston, the Metropolis of Massachusetts . . .* (Boston, 1825).

STARBUCK, ALEXANDER: *The History of Nantucket County, Island, and Town . . .* (Boston, 1924).

WHITEHILL, WALTER MUIR: *Boston: A Topographical History* (Cambridge, Mass., 1959).

WINSOR, JUSTIN, ed.: *Memorial History of Boston: Including Suffolk County, Massachusetts, 1630-1880* (4 vols., Boston, 1880-1).

3. Political

BARNES, VIOLA F.: "Massachusetts in Ferment (1756-1763)," *Commonwealth History of Massachusetts*, II: 488-513.

BILLIAS, GEORGE A.: "Pox and Politics in Marblehead, 1773-4," *Essex Institute Historical Collections*, XCII (1956), 43-58. A Study on the "Smallpox War" occasioned by the erection of a hospital on that island and its use as an inoculation center.

BOYER, PAUL S.: "Borrowed Rhetoric: The Massachusetts Excise Controversy of 1754," *William and Mary Quarterly*, 3rd ser., XXI (1964), 328-51.

BRADBURY, FRANK E.: "Laws and Courts of Massachusetts Bay Colony," Bostonian Society, *Publications*, X (1913), 129-59.

BRALEY, ABNER L.: "Provincial Government of Massachusetts [1774-1780]," *Commonwealth History of Massachusetts*, III: 64-86.

BRENNAN, ELLEN E.: *Plural Office-Holding in Massachusetts, 1760-1780 . . .* (Chapel Hill, N.C., 1945).

BROWN, ROBERT E.: *Middle-Class Democracy and the Revolution in Massachusetts, 1691-1780* (Ithaca, N.Y., 1955). See in conjunction with this book, the article by John Cary, "Statistical Method and the Brown Thesis on Colonial Democracy," *William and Mary Quarterly*, 3rd ser., XX (1963), 251-64; and Robert E. Brown's rebuttal, *ibid.*, pp. 265-76.

COLE, MARTIN LAWRENCE: "The Rise of the Legislative Assembly in Provincial Massachusetts," *Abstracts in History*, IV, University of Iowa, *Studies in the Social Sciences*, XI (1941), 91-102.

CUSHING, HARRY ALONZO: *History of the Transition from Provincial to Commonwealth Government in Massachusetts* (New York, 1896).

DICKERSON, OLIVER M.: "The Commissioners of Customs and the 'Boston Massacre,'" *New England Quarterly*, XXVII (1954), 307-25.

———: "Opinion of Attorney General Jonathan Sewall of Massachusetts in the Case of the *Lydia*," *William and Mary Quarterly*, 3rd ser., IV (1947), 499-504.

EDMONDS, JOHN HENRY: "Massachusetts and Independency (1629-1780)," *Commonwealth History of Massachusetts,* III: 87-119.

ELLIS, GEORGE: "The Royal Governors of Massachusetts . . . ," *Memorial History of Boston . . . ,* II, 27-92.

FIORE, JORDAN D.: "The Temple-Bernard Affair: A Royal Custom House Scandal in Essex County," *Essex Institute Historical Collections,* XC (1954), 58-83. Account of feud raging in 1760's caused by Bernard's interference in customs affairs.

GIPSON, LAWRENCE HENRY: "Aspects of the Beginning of the American Revolution in Massachusetts Bay, 1760-1762," American Antiquarian Society, *Proceedings,* LXVII (1957), 11-32.

———: "Massachusetts Bay and American Colonial Union, 1754," *ibid.,* LXXI (1961), 63-92.

GRINNELL, F. W.: "The [Massachusetts] Bench and Bar in Colony and Province (1630-1776)," *Commonwealth History of Massachusetts,* II: 156-91.

HANDLIN, OSCAR, and MARY FLUG HANDLIN: *Commonwealth: A Study of the Role of Government in the American Economy: Massachusetts, 1774-1871* (New York, 1947).

HASKINS, GEORGE LEE: *Law and Authority in Early Massachusetts: A Study in Tradition and Design* (New York, 1960). This stresses the relationship of Massachusetts law to English law.

HUBBARD, CLIFFORD CHESLEY: "Controversies over British Control (1753-1765)," *Commonwealth History of Massachusetts,* II: 455-87.

KING, JOSEPH EDWARD: "Judicial Flotsam in Massachusetts-Bay, 1760-1765," *New England Quarterly,* XXVII (1954), 366-81. On colonial grievances regarding the vice-admiralty courts.

LABAREE, BENJAMIN W.: *The Boston Tea Party* (New York, 1964).

LORING, JAMES SPEAR: *The Hundred Boston Orators Appointed by the Municipal Authorities [of Boston] and Other Public Bodies from 1770 to 1852 . . .* (Boston, 1852; 4th edn., 1855). This work contains biographical sketches of the orators and excerpts from letters and other sources.

MATTHEWS, ALBERT: "The Solemn League and Covenant, 1774," Colonial Society of Massachusetts, *Publications,* XVIII (*Transactions, 1915-1916*), 103-22.

MAYO, LAWRENCE S.: "The Spirit of Massachusetts (1775)," *Commonwealth History of Massachusetts,* II: 534-61.

MILLER, JOHN C.: "The Massachusetts Convention, 1768," *New England Quarterly,* VII (1934), 445-74.

MUNROE, JAMES PHINNEY: "Last Chance for the Empire (1774)," *Commonwealth History of Massachusetts,* II: 514-533.

MORIARTY, G. ANDREWS: "The Royal Governors and the General Court (1717-1773)," *ibid.,* II: 122-55.

NEWCOMER, LEE NATHANIEL: "Yankee Rebels of Inland Massachusetts," *William and Mary Quarterly*, 3rd ser., IX (1952), 156-65.

POLE, J. R.: "Suffrage and Representation in Massachusetts: A Statistical Note," *ibid.*, 3rd ser., XIV (1957), 560-92.

POPE, FRANKLIN LEONARD: *The Western Boundary of Massachusetts: A Study of Indian and Colonial History* (Pittsfield, Mass., 1886).

PORTER, EDWARD G.: "The Beginning of the Revolution [in Boston]," *Memorial History of Boston . . .*, III: 1-66.

SCHUTZ, JOHN A.: "Imperialism in Massachusetts during the Governorship of William Shirley, 1741-1756," *Huntington Library Quarterly*, XXIII (1959-60), 217-36.

SIEBERT, WILBUR H.: "The Exodus of Loyalists from Penobscot and the Loyalist Settlements at Passamaquoddy," New Brunswick Historical Society, *Collections*, IX (1914), 485-529, and "The Exodus of the Loyalists from Penobscot to Passamaquoddy," Ohio State University, *Bulletin*, XVIII (1914).

SOSIN, JACK M.: "The Massachusetts Act of 1774: Coercive or Preventive?" *Huntington Library Quarterly*, XXVI (1962-3), 235-52.

STARK, JAMES H.: *The Loyalists of Massachusetts and the Other Side of the American Revolution* (Boston, 1910).

SYRETT, DAVID: "Town-Meeting Politics in Massachusetts, 1776-1786," *William and Mary Quarterly*, 3rd ser., XXI (1964), 352-66.

WALETT, FRANCIS G.: "The Massachusetts Council, 1766-1774: The Transformation of a Conservative Institution," *ibid.*, 3rd ser., VI (1949), 605-27.

WASHBURN, EMORY: *Sketches of the Judicial History of Massachusetts . . . [1630-1775]* (Boston, 1840).

WEBSTER, M. P.: "The Suffolk Resolves," *New England Magazine*, n. ser., XXVII (1902), 353-72.

WOLKINS, GEORGE G.: "The Seizure of John Hancock's Sloop *Liberty*," Massachusetts Historical Society, *Proceedings*, LV (1921-2), 239-284, with numerous supporting documents.

4. Economic

ANDREWS, CHARLES MC LEAN: "The Boston Merchants and the Non-Importation Movement," Colonial Society of Massachusetts, *Publications*, XIX (*Transactions, 1916-1917*), 159-259.

BAXTER, WILLIAM T.: *The House of Hancock: Business in Boston, 1724-1775, Harvard Studies in Business History*, X (Cambridge, Mass., 1945).

DAVIS, ANDREW MC FARLAND: *Currency and Banking in the Province of the Massachusetts Bay*, American Economic Association, *Publications*, 3rd ser., I (2 vols., New York, c. 1901). See also his "Provincial Banks: Land and Silver," Colonial Society of Massachusetts, *Publications,* III (*Transactions, 1895-1897*), 2-40.

DEWEY, DAVIS RICH: "[Massachusetts] Finance and Paper Money (1692-1775)," *Commonwealth History of Massachusetts,* II: 192-221.

DOUGLAS, CHARLES H. J.: *The Financial History of Massachusetts from the Organization of the Massachusetts Bay Colony to the American Revolution,* Columbia University, *Studies in History, Economics, and Public Law,* No. 4 (New York, 1892).

FELT, JOSEPH B.: *An Historical Account of Massachusetts Currency* (Boston, 1839).

HENRETTA, JAMES A.: "Economic Development and Social Structure in Colonial Boston," *William and Mary Quarterly,* 3rd ser., XXII (1965), 75-92.

LABAREE, BENJAMIN W.: *Patriots and Partisans: The Merchants of Newburyport, 1764-1815, Harvard Historical Studies,* LXXIII (Cambridge, Mass., 1962).

LAWSON, MURRAY G.: "The Boston Merchant Fleet of 1753," *American Neptune,* IX (1949), 207-15, and "The Routes of Boston's Trade, 1752-1765," Colonial Society of Massachusetts, *Publications,* XXXVIII (*Transactions, 1947-51*), 81-120.

USHER, A. P.: "Colonial Business and Transportation [Massachusetts, 1714-1776]," *Commonwealth History of Massachusetts,* II: 386-418.

5. Social

BLAKE, JOHN BALLARD: *Public Health in the Town of Boston, 1630-1822, Harvard Historical Studies,* LXXII (Cambridge, Mass., 1959).

CRUMB, LAWRENCE N.: "The Anglican Church in Colonial Maine," *Historical Magazine of the Protestant Episcopal Church,* XXXIII (1964), 251-60.

DICKERSON, OLIVER M.: "British Control of American Newspapers on the Eve of the Revolution: Boston, 1765-75," *New England Quarterly,* XXIV (1951), 453-68.

DUNIWAY, CLYDE AUGUSTUS: *The Development of Freedom of the Press in Massachusetts, Harvard Historical Studies,* XII (Cambridge, Mass., & London, 1906); Chapters VII and VIII are relevant.

EZELL, JOHN S.: "When Massachusetts Played the Lottery," *New England Quarterly,* XXII, (1949), 316-35.

FORBES, ALLYN BAILEY: "Social Life in Town and Country [in Massachusetts] (1689-1763)," *Commonwealth History of Massachusetts,* II: 257-90.

GODDARD, DELANO O.: "The [Boston] Press and Literature of the Provincial Period, 1692-1770," *Memorial History of Boston . . . ,* II: 387-436; and "The Pulpit, Press, and Literature of the Revolution," *ibid.,* III: 119-48.

HOOKER, RICHARD JAMES: "The Mayhew Controversy," *Church History,* V (1936), 239-55. A discussion of Mayhew's leadership of New England Congregationalists in anti-Episcopalian agitations.

LONGLEY, R. S.: "Mob Activities in Revolutionary Massachusetts," *New England Quarterly,* VI (1933), 98-130.

MC KENZIE, ALEXANDER: "The Religious History of the Provincial Period [of Boston]," *Memorial History of Boston . . . ,* II: 187-248.

MEYER, JACOB CONRAD: *Church and State in Massachusetts from 1740 to 1833: A Chapter in the History of the Development of Individual Freedom* (Cleveland, O., 1930).

MILLER, JOHN C.: "Religion, Finance, and Democracy in Massachusetts," *New England Quarterly,* VI (1933), 29-58.

MORISON, SAMUEL ELIOT: *Three Centuries of Harvard, 1636-1936* (Cambridge, Mass., 1936).

MOTT, FRANK LUTHER: "The Newspaper Coverage of Lexington and Concord," *New England Quarterly,* XVII (1944), 489-505.

POIRIER, PASCAL: "Des Acadiens Déportés à Boston en 1755," Royal Society of Canada, *Proceedings,* 3rd ser., II (1908), 125-80.

SCHLESINGER, ARTHUR M.: "Propaganda of the Boston Newspaper Press, 1767-1770," Colonial Society of Massachusetts, *Publications,* XXXII (*Transactions, 1933-37*), 396-416.

SCUDDER, HORACE E.: "Life in Boston in Its Provincial Period," *Memorial History of Boston . . . ,* II: 437-90; and "Life in Boston in the Revolutionary Period," *ibid.,* III, 149-88.

SEYBOLT, ROBERT FRANCIS: *The Private Schools of Colonial Boston* (Cambridge, Mass., 1935), and *The Public Schools of Colonial Boston, 1635-1775* (Cambridge, Mass., 1935).

SEXTON, JOHN E.: "Massachusetts' Religious Policy with the Indians under Governor Bernard, 1760-1769," *Catholic Historical Review,* XXIV (1938), 310-28.

SILVER, ROLLO GABRIEL: "Publishing in Boston, 1726-1757: The Accounts of Daniel Henchman," American Antiquarian Society, *Proceedings,* LXVI (1956), 17-36.

SMITH, CHARLES C.: "The French Protestants in Boston . . . ," *Memorial History of Boston . . . ,* II: 249-68.

STIMSON, FREDERIC J.: "Massachusetts Literature in the Eighteenth Century," *Commonwealth History of Massachusetts,* II: 291-322.

WATKINS, WALTER KENDALL: "Tarring and Feathering in Boston in 1770," *Old-Time New England,* XX (1929), 30-43.

6. Biographical

JONES, E. ALFRED: *The Loyalists of Massachusetts: Their Memorials, Petitions, and Claims* (Boston & London, 1930). Despite the title, the volume is composed almost entirely of biographical sketches.

ADAMS, ABIGAIL. *Abigail Adams* by Janet Whitney (Boston, 1947).

ADAMS, JOHN. For general biographies, see: Gilbert Chinard's *Honest John Adams* (Boston, 1933) and the now standard work by Page Smith: *John Adams, 1735-1826* (2 vols., Garden City, N.Y., 1962). For more specific studies, see: Catherine Drinker Bowen's *John Adams and the American Revolution* (Boston, 1950); Correa Moylan Walsh's *Political Science of John Adams: A Study in the Theory of Mixed Government and the Bicameral System* (London & New York, 1945); and John R. Howe, Jr's. *The Changing Political Thought of John Adams* (Princeton, N.J., 1966). See also the article by Bernard Bailyn: "Butterfield's Adams: Notes for a Sketch," *William and Mary Quarterly*, 3rd ser., XIX (1962), 328-52, and the one by R. B. Ripley: "Adams, Burke, and Eighteenth Century Conservatism," *Political Science Quarterly*, LXXX (1965), 216-35.

ADAMS, SAMUEL. *Samuel Adams, Promoter of the American Revolution: A Study in Psychology and Politics* by Ralph Volney Harlow (New York, 1923), and *Sam Adams: Pioneer in Propaganda* by John C. Miller (Boston, 1936). See also the articles by Edwin C. Kepler: "Samuel Adams, Master Propagandist," *PR: The Quarterly Review of Public Relations*, III (1958), 1-7, and by Bernhard Knollenberg: "Did Samuel Adams Provoke the Boston Tea Party and the Clash at Lexington?" American Antiquarian Society, *Proceedings*, n. ser., LXX (1960), 493-503.

ALLEN, JOHN. "New England's Tom Paine: John Allen and the Spirit of Liberty" by John M. Bumsted and Charles E. Clark, *William and Mary Quarterly*, 3rd ser., XXI (1964), 561-70.

BERNARD, FRANCIS. "Governor Bernard's Undoing: An Earlier Hutchinson Letters Affair" by Francis G. Walett, *New England Quarterly*, XXXVII (1965), 217-26.

BOWDOIN, JAMES. *The Life and Services of James Bowdoin* by Robert C. Winthrop (2nd. edn., Boston, 1876). See also the articles by Francis G. Walett: "James Bowdoin, Patriot Propagandist," *New England Quarterly*, XXIII (1950), 320-38, and "James Bowdoin, Massachusetts Patriot and Statesman," Bostonian Society, *Proceedings*, (1950), 27-47.

BYLES, MATHER. *The Famous Mather Byles: The Noted Boston Tory Preacher, Poet, and Wit, 1707-1788* by Arthur W. H. Eaton (Boston, 1914).

CHAUNCY, CHARLES. *Charles Chauncy: Colonial Liberal, 1705-1787* by Harold Ernest Bernhard (Chicago, 1948).

EDES, BENJAMIN. "Benjamin Edes, Trumpeter of Sedition" by Rollo G. Silver, Bibliographical Society of America, *Papers*, XLVII (1953), 248-68.

EDWARDS, JONATHAN. There are book length biographies by Alexander

V. G. Allen: *Jonathan Edwards* (Boston, 1891); by Perry Miller: *Jonathan Edwards* (New York, 1949); and by Ola Winslow: *Jonathan Edwards, 1703-1758: A Biography* (New York, 1940). Also of interest are the articles by Gerhard T. Alexis: "Jonathan Edwards and the Theocratic Ideal," *Church History*, XXXV (1966), 328-43; Frederic I. Carpenter: "The Radicalism of Jonathan Edwards," *New England Quarterly*, IV (1931), 629-44; Vincent Tomas: "The Modernity of Jonathan Edwards," *ibid.*, XXV (1952), 60-84; and Perry Miller's "Jonathan Edwards and the Great Awakening," *America in Crisis: Fourteen Crucial Episodes in American History* (Daniel Aaron, ed., New York, 1952), pp. 3-19.

HANCOCK, EBENEZER. "A Colonial Bankrupt: Ebenezer Hancock, 1741-1819" by W. T. Baxter, Business Historical Society, *Bulletin*, XXV (1951), 115-24. Ebenezer was a brother to John Hancock.

HANCOCK, JOHN. *John Hancock: The Picturesque Patriot* by Lorenzo Sears (Boston, 1912), and *John Hancock: Patriot in Purple* by Herbert Sanford Allan (New York, 1948). See also: James Truslow Adams's "Portrait of an Empty Barrel," *Harper's Magazine*, CLXI (1930), 425-34, in which the weaknesses of Hancock are stressed; and Oliver M. Dickerson's "John Hancock: Notorious Smuggler or Near Victim of British Revenue Racketeers?" *Mississippi Valley Historical Review*, XXXII (1945-6), 517-40.

HANCOCK, THOMAS. "Thomas Hancock: Colonial Merchant" by Edward Edelman, *Journal of Economic and Business History*, I (1928-9), 77-104.

HAWLEY, JOSEPH. *Joseph Hawley: Colonial Radical* by E. Francis Brown (New York, 1931). See also Brown's "The Law Career of Major Joseph Hawley," *New England Quarterly*, IV (1931), 482-508.

HUTCHINSON, THOMAS. To date there is but one book-length biography of Hutchinson available: James Kendall Hosmer's *The Life of Thomas Hutchinson: Royal Governor of the Province of Massachusetts Bay* (Boston, 1896). In view of Hutchinson's importance, it is strange that he has not been the subject of more major work. There have been published, however, a number of worthwhile articles on him, three of which were written by Malcolm Freiberg: "Thomas Hutchinson: The First Fifty Years (1711-1761)," *William and Mary Quarterly*, 3rd ser., XV (1958) 35-55; "Thomas Hutchinson and the Province Currency," *New England Quarterly*, XXX (1957), 190-208; and "How to Become a Colonial Governor: Thomas Hutchinson of Massachusetts," *Review of Politics*, XXI (1959), 646-56. Also of interest are the articles by L. H. Gipson: "Thomas Hutchinson and the Framing of the Albany Plan of Union, 1764," *Pennsylvania Magazine of History and Biography*, LXXIV (1959), 5-35; Richard M. Gummere's "Thomas Hutchinson and Samuel Adams: A Controversy in the Classical Tradition," Boston Public

Library, *Quarterly*, X (1958), 119-29; Edmund S. Morgan's "Thomas Hutchinson and the Stamp Act," *New England Quarterly*, XXI (1948), 459-92; and finally, the biographical sketch by Clifford K. Shipton in *Sibley's Harvard Graduates, Volume VIII: 1726-1730* (Boston, 1951), pp. 149-217.

MACKINTOSH, EBENEZER. "Ebenezer Mackintosh: Stamp Act Rioter and Patriot" by George P. Anderson, Colonial Society of Massachusetts, *Publications*, XXVI (*Transactions, 1924-1926*), 15-64; and also by Anderson, "A Note on Ebenezer Mackintosh," *ibid.*, pp. 348-61.

MALCOM, DANIEL. "Daniel Malcom and Writs of Assistance" by George G. Wolkins, Massachusetts Historical Society, *Proceedings*, LVIII (1924-5), 5-84.

MALCOM, JOHN. "Tar and Feathers: The Adventures of Captain John Malcom" by Frank W. C. Hersey, Colonial Society of Massachusetts, *Publications*, XXXIV (*Transactions, 1937-1942*), 429-73.

MAUDUIT, ISRAEL. "Israel Mauduit" by Robert J. Taylor, *New England Quarterly*, XXIV (1951), 208-30. Although a native of Great Britain, Mauduit's chief interests were bound up with those of Massachusetts Bay.

MAYHEW, JONATHAN. *Called Unto Liberty: a Life of Jonathan Mayhew, 1720-1766* by Charles W. Akers (Cambridge, Mass., 1964); and his article "The Making of a Religious Liberal: Jonathan Mayhew and the Great Awakening," New England Social Studies, *Bulletin*, XI (1954), 18-25. See also Clinton Rossiter's "The Life and Mind of Jonathan Mayhew," *William and Mary Quarterly*, 3rd ser., VII (1950), 531-58, and "Jonathan Mayhew" in his *Seedtime of the Republic* . . . (New York, 1953), pp. 227-46.

MEIN, JOHN. "John Mein: Scourge of Patriots" by John E. Alden, Colonial Society of Massachusetts, *Publications*, XXXIV (*Transactions, 1937-1942*), 571-99.

OTIS, JAMES. *The Life of James Otis of Massachusetts; Containing also Notices of Some Contemporary Characters and Events from the Year 1760 to 1775* by William Tudor (Boston, 1823). See also the biographical sketch by Clifford K. Shipton in *Sibley's Harvard Graduates, Volume XI: 1741-1745* (Boston, 1960), pp. 247-87, and the article by Ellen Elizabeth Brennan: "James Otis: Recreant and Patriot," *New England Quarterly*, XII (1939), 691-725 and that by Joseph R. Frese: "James Otis and Writs of Assistance," *ibid.*, XXX (1957), 496-508.

PEPPERRELL, WILLIAM. *The Life of Sir William Pepperrell, Bart.* . . . by Usher Parsons (Boston, 1855; 2nd edn., London & Boston, 1856) and *Messrs. William Pepperrell: Merchants at Piscataqua* by Byron Fairchild (Ithaca, N.Y., 1954).

POWNALL, THOMAS. *Thomas Pownall, M.P., F.R.S.: Governor of Massachusetts* . . . by Charles A. W. Pownall (London, 1908), and

Thomas Pownall, British Defender of American Liberty: A Study of Anglo-American Relations in the Eighteenth Century by John A. Schutz (Glendale, Calif., 1951). See also the article by Caroline Robbins: "An Active and Intelligent Antiquary: Governor Thomas Pownall," *Pennsylvania History*, XXVI (1959), 1-20.

REVERE, PAUL. *Paul Revere and the World He Lived in* by Esther Forbes (Boston, 1942).

SHIRLEY, WILLIAM. *William Shirley: King's Governor of Massachusetts* by John A. Schutz (Chapel Hill, N.C., 1961), and George Arthur Wood's *William Shirley, Governor of Massachusetts 1741-1756: A History*, Columbia University, *Studies in History, Economics, and Public Law*, No. 209 (2 vols., London & New York, 1920).

THOMPSON, BENJAMIN. *Memoir of Sir Benjamin Thompson, Count Rumford* . . . by George Edward Ellis (Boston [1871]).

WARREN, JOSEPH. *Joseph Warren: Physician, Politician, Patriot* by John Cary (Urbana, Ill., 1961), and the older *Life and Times of Joseph Warren* by Richard Frothingham (Boston, 1865).

WARREN, MERCY. *Mercy Warren* by Alice Brown (New York, 1896).

7. Military

ALDEN, JOHN RICHARD: "Why the March to Concord?" *American Historical Review*, XLIX (1943-4), 446-54.

COBURN, FRANK WARREN: *Fiction and Truth about the Battle on Lexington Common, April 19, 1775* (Lexington, Mass., 1918), and *Battle of April 19, 1775, in Lexington, Concord* . . . (1st edn., Lexington, Mass., 1912; 2nd edn., rev., 1922).

FRENCH, ALLEN: *The Day of Concord and Lexington: The Nineteenth of April, 1775* (Boston, 1925), and *General Gage's Informers: New Material upon Lexington and Concord* . . . (Ann Arbor, Mich., 1932). See also his "The Nineteenth of April, 1775," *Commonwealth History of Massachusetts*, II: 562-89.

FROTHINGHAM, RICHARD: *History of the Siege of Boston, and of the Battles of Lexington, Concord, and Bunker Hill* (3rd edn., Boston, 1872).

FROTHINGHAM, THOMAS G.: "Bunker Hill and the Siege of Boston (1775-1776)," *Commonwealth History of Massachusetts*, III: 1-29.

HALE, EDWARD E.: "The Siege of Boston," *Memorial History of Boston* . . . , III, 67-118.

HIGGINSON, THOMAS WENTWORTH: "[Boston and the] French and Indian Wars," *ibid.*, III, 93-130.

HOWE, OCTAVIUS, T.: "Massachusetts on the Seas in the War of the Revolution (1775-1783)," *Commonwealth History of Massachusetts*, III: 30-63.

KIDDER, FREDERIC: *History of the Boston Massacre: Consisting of the Nar-*

rative of the Town, the Trial of the Soldiers, etc. (Albany, N.Y., 1870).

MURDOCK, HAROLD: *Nineteenth of April, 1775* (Boston & New York, 1923).

NEWCOMER, LEE NATHANIEL: *The Embattled Farmers: A Massachusetts Countryside in the American Revolution* (New York, 1953).

PLIMPTON, GEORGE A.: "[Massachusetts and the] French and Indian Wars (1741-1763)," *Commonwealth History of Massachusetts*, II: 419-54.

D. MAPS

Most of the maps for the period 1748-1776 that present Massachusetts Bay are to be found listed in the general section on those maps depicting New England. See Chapter IV, D.

ARMSTRONG, M.: *Thirty Miles round Boston, 1775*. In the *Scots Magazine*, XXXVI (1775), p. 440.

BOWEN, EMANUEL: *A Draught of Boston Harbour*. In Bowen: *A Complete Atlas or Distinct View of the Known World . . .* (London, 1752), No. 66.

DE COSTA, J.: *A Plan of the Town and Harbour of Boston and the Country Adjacent with the Road from Boston to Concord Shewing the Place of the Late Engagement between the King's Troops and the Provincials . . .* (London, 1775).

A Map of 100 Miles round Boston. In the *Gentleman's Magazine*, XLV (1775), opp. p. 293.

A New and Accurate Plan of the Town of Boston in New England [and] A New Plan of Boston Harbor from an Actual Survey. In the *Universal Magazine*, LIV (1774), opp. p. 225.

A New Survey of the Harbour of Boston in New England, Done by Order of the Principal Officers and Commissioners of His Majesty's Navy. In *The English Pilot* (Dublin [1767]), 4th Book, btwn. pp. 22-3.

A New and Accurate Map of the Colony of Massachusetts Bay in North America from a Late Survey. In the *Universal Magazine*, LXVI (1780), opp. p. 281.

A Plan of the Town and Chart of the Harbour of Boston Exhibiting a View of the Islands, Castle, Forts, and Entrances into the Said Harbour. In the *Gentleman's Magazine*, XLV (1775), opp. p. 41.

PRICE, WILLIAM: *A New Plan of ye Great Town of Boston, New England in America; with the Many Additional Buildings & New Streets to the Year 1769* (Boston [1769]). This map is known as the "Bonner Map."

REVERE, PAUL: *A View of Part of the Town of Boston in New England and the British Ships of War Landing Their Troops, 1768.* In the *Magazine of American History,* XV (1886), 12.

NEW HAMPSHIRE

A. BIBLIOGRAPHICAL AIDS

HAMMOND, OTIS G.: *Check List of New Hampshire Local History* (Concord, N.H., 1925).

HASSE, ADELAIDE R.: "New Hampshire, 1629-1789," in "Materials for a Bibliography of the Public Archives of the Thirteen Original States . . . ," American Historical Association, *Annual Report, 1906* (2 vols., Washington, D.C., 1908), II, 259-78.

B. PRINTED SOURCE MATERIALS

1. Government and related documents

ADAMS, NATHANIEL, ed.: *Annals of Portsmouth: Comprising a Period of Two Hundred Years from the First Settlement of the Town . . .* (Portsmouth, N.H., 1825).

BATCHELLOR, ALBERT S., HENRY HARRISON METCALF, and E. BEAN, eds.: *Laws of the New Hampshire Including Public and Private Acts and Resolves and the Royal Commissions and Instructions: With Historical and Descriptive Notes* (10 vols., Manchester, Concord, & Bristol, N.H., 1904-22).

Concord Town Records, 1732-1820 (Concord, N.H., 1894).

Provincial Papers, Documents and Records Relating to the Province of New Hampshire . . . 1623-[1776] (Nathaniel Bouton, ed., 7 vols., Nashua, N.H., 1867-73). Volumes V-VII, covering the years 1738-1776, are relevant. They include: (1) "Records of the Council"; (2) "Records of the House of Representatives"; (3) "Journal of the General Assembly," including the Council acting in its legislative capacity; (4) "Governors' Messages"; (5) "Indian Hostilities"; (6) "Revolutionary Proceedings"; (7) "Provincial Congresses"; (8) "Miscellaneous Papers," all of which are arranged chronologically and are therefore intermixed. The series is of the greatest importance. Volume X of these papers also presents numerous documents relating to the boundary controversy with New York from 1749 to 1790 when Congress passed an act to admit Vermont to the status of a state in the Union which received President Washington's signature on February 18, 1791. With respect to documents bearing on local history, see Volume IX, "Town Papers: Documents and Records Relating to Towns in New Hampshire."

Two Reports on the Matter of Complaint of Mr. Livius against Governor Wentworth (London, 1773). This pamphlet prints reports of the Board of Trade and has to do with claims of Livius to New Hampshire lands. In this connection see *The Memorial of Peter Livius . . . to the Lords Commissioners for Trade and Plantations . . .* ([London], 1773).

2. Non-official contemporary materials

BELKNAP, JEREMY: *A Sermon in Military Duty, Preached at Dover, November 10, 1772, before His Excellency John Wentworth, Esq., LL.D. Governor . . .* (Salem, Mass., 1773).

MOORE, JACOB BAILEY, and JOHN FARMER, eds.: *Collections, Topographical, Historical, and Biographical, Relating Principally to New-Hampshire* (3 vols., Concord, N.H., 1822-4).

NEW HAMPSHIRE HISTORICAL SOCIETY, *Collections* (15 vols., Concord, N.H., 1824-1939). Some of the volumes contain important materials bearing upon the period under examination. See, for example, Volume III, 282-92, for letters by the Wentworths. Volume VII, 1-344, contains the "Records of the Committee of Safety" beginning with May 19, 1775, and Volumes XIII through XV comprise the *Letters and Papers of Major-General John Sullivan, Continental Army*.

PATTEN, MATTHEW: *The Diary of Matthew Patten of Bedford, N.H.: From Seventeen Hundred Fifty-Four to Seventeen Hundred Eighty-Eight* (Concord, N.H., 1903).

Portsmouth. "[Three Documents on the Covenant of the Committee of Correspondence of Portsmouth]," Charles Deane, ed., Massachusetts Historical Society, *Proceedings*, 2nd ser., II (1885-6), 481-6.

3. Newspapers

New Hampshire Gazette and Historical Chronicle [New Hampshire Gazette: New Hampshire Gazette. Or, State Journal and General Advertiser], b. 1756, Portsmouth.

Portsmouth Mercury, and Weekly Advertiser, 1765-1767, Portsmouth.

C. SECONDARY WORKS

1. General

BARSTOW, GEORGE: *The History of New Hampshire . . . [1614-1819]* (Concord, N.H., 1842).

BELKNAP, JEREMY: *The History of New-Hampshire: Comprehending the*

Events of One Complete Century and Seventy-Five Years . . . (3 vols., Boston, 1813). See in conjunction with this work Sidney Kaplan: "*The History of New Hampshire:* Jeremy Belknap as Literary Craftsman," *William and Mary Quarterly,* 3rd ser., XXI (1964), 18-39.

FRY, WILLIAM HENRY: *New Hampshire as a Royal Province,* Columbia University, *Studies in History, Economics, and Public Law,* No. 29 (London & New York, 1908).

GOODING, ALFRED: *Portsmouth in the Eighteenth Century* (Portsmouth, N.H., n.d.).

POWERS, GRANT: *Historical Sketches of the Discovery, Settlement, and Progress of Events in the Coos Country and Vicinity Principally Included between the Years 1754 and 1785* (Haverhill, N.H., 1841; rep., 1880).

UPTON, RICHARD FRANCIS: *Revolutionary New Hamsphire: An Account of the Social and Political Forces Underlying the Transition from Royal Province to American Commonwealth* (Hanover, N.H., 1936).

2. Political

DANIELL, JERE R.: "Politics in New Hampshire under Governor Benning Wenthworth, 1741-1767," *William and Mary Quarterly,* 3rd ser., XXIII (1966), 76-105.

HAMMOND, OTIS GRANT: *Tories of New Hampshire in the War of the Revolution* (Concord, N.H., 1917).

SCOTT, KENNETH: "Counterfeiting in Colonial New Hamsphire [1685-1774]," *Historical New Hampshire,* XIII (1957), 3-38, and "Tory Associators of Portsmouth," *William and Mary Quarterly,* 3rd ser., XVII (1960), 507-15. The article includes the occupations, offices, and relations to the governor of the fifty-nine men who in January 1775 pledged their support to Governor Wentworth.

SIEBERT, WILBUR H.: *Loyalist Refugees of New Hampshire,* Ohio State University, *Bulletin,* XXI (Columbus, O., 1916).

3. Economic

ANDERSON, GEORGE P.: "Land Grants Made in New Hampshire by Governor Benning Wentworth to Boston Men," Colonial Society of Massachusetts, *Publications,* XXV (*Transactions, 1922-1924*), 33-8.

ANDREWS, HENRY N., JR.: "The Royal Pines of New Hampshire [1623-1938]," *Appalachia,* XXVII (1948), 186-98.

4. Social

KINNEY, CHARLES B., JR.: *Church and State: The Struggle for Separation in New Hampshire, 1630-1900* (New York, 1955).

5. Biographical

WENTWORTH, JOHN. *John Wentworth: Governor of New Hampshire, 1767-1775* by Lawrence Shaw Mayo (Cambridge, Mass., 1921) and *The Loyal Wentworths . . .* by Allen Fea (London, 1928). See also John Wentworth's *The Wentworth Genealogy: English and American* (3 vols., Boston, 1878).

6. Military

PAGE, ELWIN L.: "The King's Powder, 1774," *New England Quarterly*, XVIII (1945), 83-92. An account of the removal of British powder from Fort William and Mary in New Hampshire.

D. MAPS

BLANCHARD, JOSEPH, and SAMUEL LANGDON: *An Accurate Map of His Majesty's Province of New-Hampshire in New England Taken from Actual Surveys of All the Inhabited Part . . . [and] the Theatre of This War in That Part of the World* ([London, 1761]). In Jefferys: *A General Topography of North America and the West Indies . . .* (London, 1768), Nos. 30-1.

CONDOR, T., sculp.: *New Hampshire, Vermont, Etc.* In William Gordon: *The History of the Rise, Progress, and Establishment of the Independence of the United States of America* (4 vols., London, 1788), II, opp. p. 584. The edition published in New York in 1801 is without the map that accompanied the earlier edition.

LANGDON, SAMUEL: *An Accurate Map of His Majesty's Province of New Hampshire in New England & All the Adjacent Country Northward to the River St. Lawrence & Eastward to Penobscot Bay. Containing the Principal Places which Relate to the Present War . . .* (1756). This is map No. 9 in the William Faden Collection of Maps in the Map Division of the Library of Congress. It shows many differences between the Blanchard and Langdon map.

NEW JERSEY

A. BIBLIOGRAPHICAL AIDS

BURR, NELSON ROLLIN: *A Narrative and Descriptive Bibliography of New Jersey, New Jersey Historical Series*, XXI (Princeton, N.J., 1964).

HASSE, ADELAIDE R.: "New Jersey, 1664-1789," in "Materials for a Bibli-

ography of the Public Archives of the Thirteen Original States,"
American Historical Association, *Annual Report, 1906* (2 vols.,
Washington, D.C., 1908), II, 390-406.

STEVENS, HENRY: *An Analytical Index to the Colonial Documents of New
Jersey in the State Paper Offices of England,* New Jersey Historical
Society, *Collections,* V (William A. Whitehead, ed., New York,
1858). The volume also contains references to other manuscripts
and to printed works relating to New Jersey.

B. PRINTED SOURCE MATERIALS

1. Government and related documents

ALLINSON, SAMUEL, ed.: *Acts of the General Assembly of the Province of
New Jersey* . . . [1702-1776] (Burlington, N.J., 1776).

. . . *At a General Assembly of the Colony of New Jersey* . . . (published
yearly, Philadelphia, 1748-58); see also *Votes and Proceedings.*

*A Brief of the Claims on the Part of the Province of New Jersey and of
the Proof Offered in Support of It* . . . *for Settling the Boundary
Line between the Said Province of New-Jersey and the Province
of New-York* . . . ([New York, 1769]).

Laws of the State of New Jersey [1703-1798] (New Brunswick, N.J.,
1800).

*Minutes of the Provincial Congress and the Council of Safety of the
State of New Jersey, [1774-1776]* (Trenton, N.J., 1879).

PHILLIPS, HENRY, JR., ed.: *A Catalogue of the New Jersey Bills of Credit,
Comprising Their Amounts, Denominations and the Names of the
Persons Appointed to Sign Them from 1723 to 1786* (Philadelphia,
1863).

"Proceedings of the Committees of Freehold and Shrewsbury in Mon-
mouth Co. on the Opening of the Revolution," New Jersey Historical Society, *Proceedings,* I (1845-6), 184-97.

*The Votes and Proceedings of the General Assembly of the Province of
New-Jersey* . . . (published yearly, Philadelphia, Burlington &
Woodbridge, N.J., 1748-71; becomes *Votes of Assembly* for the
years 1774 and 1775).

WEISS, HARRY BISCHOFF, and GRACE M. ZEIGLER, comps.: *Some Legislation
Affecting Rural Life in Colonial New Jersey* (Trenton, N.J.,
1957).

WHITEHEAD, WILLIAM A., et al., eds.: *Documents Relating to the Colonial,
Revolutionary, and Post-Revolutionary History of the State of
New Jersey* (36 vols., Newark, N.J., 1880-1941). These volumes
were published as *The Archives of the State of New Jersey.* The
most important papers, concerned with the years 1748-1776, relate

to the administrations of Governor Jonathan Belcher (1746-1757), 1st ser., VII-VIII; President of the Council John Reading (1757-1758), Governors Francis Bernard (1758-1760), Thomas Boone (1760-1761), Josiah Hardy (1701-1762), and William Franklin (1762-1776), 1st ser., IX-X. Supplementing these papers are the *Journals of the Governor and Council* (1748-1775), 1st ser., XVI-XVIII. There are also *Newspaper Extracts* (1740-1776), 1st ser., XII, XIX, XX, XXIV-XXIX, and XXXI.

2. Non-official contemporary writings

BARBER, JOHN W., and HENRY HOWE: *Historical Collections of the State of New Jersey* . . . (New Haven, Conn. & Newark, N.J., 1844; the work was reissued under the title *Historical Collections of New Jersey* . . . , New Haven, 1868).

BOUDINOT, ELIAS: *Journal: Or Historical Recollections of American Events during the Revolutionary War, etc.* (Philadelphia, 1894).

COLLIN, NICHOLAS: *The Journal and Biography of [the Rev.] Nicholas Collin, 1746-1831* . . . (Amandus Johnson, trans., Philadelphia, 1936).

FRANKLIN, WILLIAM: "Letters from William Franklin to William Strahan," Charles Henry Hart, ed., *Pennsylvania Magazine of History and Biography*, XXXV (1911), 415-62, and "Three Letters from William Franklin to His Father, June and October, 1767, and May, 1769," New Jersey Historical Society, *Proceedings*, I (1845-6), 102-9.

JONES, EDWARD ALFRED, ed.: *The Loyalists of New Jersey: Their Memorials, Petitions, Claims, Etc., from English Records*, New Jersey Historical Society, *Collections*, X (Newark, N.J., 1927).

LIVINGSTON, WILLIAM. *A Memoir of the Life of William Livingston* . . . *with Extracts from His Correspondence and Notices of Various Members of His Family* by Theodore Sedgwick, Jr. (New York, 1833).

The Memorial of the Council of Proprietors of the Eastern Division of New Jersey, to His Excellency, Jonathan Belcher . . . *Governor of the Province of New Jersey, November 20, 1753: With Documents Annexed* . . . ([New York, 1755]). Relating to the New Jersey claims in the land controversy with New York.

The Plea and Answer of the Right Honourable William Earl of Stirling and Others, Proprietors of East New-Jersey, to John Hunt's Bill in Chancery (New York, 1770).

READ, CHARLES. *Ploughs and Politicks: Charles Read of New Jersey and His Notes on Agriculture, 1715-1774* by Carl R. Woodward, Rutgers University, *Studies in History*, No. 2 (New Brunswick, N.J., 1941).

SHERWOOD, JOSEPH. "Letters of Joseph Sherwood, Agent for the Province of New Jersey in Great Britain from 1761-1766," New Jersey Historical Society, *Proceedings*, V (1850-1), 133-53.

SMITH, SAMUEL: *The History of the Colony of Nova-Caesaria or New-Jersey: Containing an Account . . . to the Year 1721 with Some Particulars since and a Short View of Its Present State . . .* (Burlington, N.J., 1765; rep., Trenton, N.J., 1877).

THOMPSON, THOMAS: *A Letter from New Jersey in America: Giving Some Account and Description of That Province* (London, 1756). This "letter," which was written by an Anglican clergyman serving in New Jersey between 1745 and 1751 is also reprinted under the title "A Letter from New Jersey: Monmouth County in the Mid-Eighteenth Century," Fred Shelley, ed., New Jersey Historical Society, *Proceedings*, LXXIV (1956), 293-303.

WITHERSPOON, JOHN: *John Witherspoon Comes to America: A Documentary Account Based Largely on New Materials* (Lyman H. Butterfield, ed., Princeton, N.J., 1953).

C. SECONDARY WORKS

1. General

BILL, ALFRED HOYT: *New Jersey and the Revolutionary War, New Jersey Historical Series*, XI (Princeton, N.J., 1964).

FISHER, EDGAR JACOB: *New Jersey as a Royal Province, 1738-1776*, Columbia University, *Studies in History, Economics, and Public Law*, No. 107 (London & New York, 1911).

GORDON, THOMAS F.: *The History of New Jersey: From Its Discovery by Europeans to the Adoption of the Federal Constitution* (Trenton, N.J., 1834).

KULL, IRVING STODDARD, ed.: *New Jersey: A History* (4 vols., New York, 1930).

LEE, FRANCIS BAZLEY: *New Jersey as a Colony and as a State: One of the Original Thirteen* (4 vols., New York, 1902).

LUNDIN, LEONARD: *Cockpit of the Revolution: The War for Independence in New Jersey, Princeton History of New Jersey*, II (London & Princeton, N.J., 1940).

MC CORMICK, RICHARD P.: *New Jersey from Colony to State, 1609-1789, New Jersey Historical Series*, I (Princeton, N.J., 1964).

MULFORD, ISAAC S.: *A Civil and Political History of New Jersey: Embracing a Compendious History of the State . . .* (Philadelphia, 1851).

MYERS, WILLIAM S., ed.: *The Story of New Jersey* (5 vols., New York, 1945).

2. Local

CLAYTON, W. WOODFORD: *History of Bergen and Passaic Counties, New Jersey* . . . (Philadelphia, 1882).

HESTON, ALFRED M., ed.: *South Jersey: A History, 1664-1924* (4 vols., Chicago & New York, 1924).

SICKLER, JOSEPH S.: *The History of Salem County, New Jersey* . . . (Salem, N.J. [1937]).

URQUHART, F. J.: *A History of the City of Newark, New Jersey* . . . (3 vols., New York, 1913).

WALKER, EDWIN ROBERT, et al.: *A History of Trenton, 1679-1929* . . . (2 vols., Princeton, N.J., 1929).

WESTERVELT, FRANCIS A., ed: *History of Bergen County, New Jersey, 1630-1923* (3 vols., Chicago & New York, 1923).

3. Political

CHROUST, ANTON-HERMANN: "The Lawyers of New Jersey and the Stamp Act, *American Journal of Legal History*, VI (1962), 286-97.

CONNOLLY, JAMES C.: "Quit-Rents in Colonial New Jersey as a Contributing Cause for the American Revolution," New Jersey Historical Society, *Proceedings*, n. ser., VII (1922), 13-21; and "The Stamp Act and New Jersey's Opposition to It," *ibid.*, IX (1924), 137-50.

FIELD, RICHARD S.: *The Provincial Courts of New Jersey* . . . , New Jersey Historical Society, *Collections*, III (New York, 1849).

KEESEY, RUTH M.: "Loyalism in Bergen County, New Jersey," *William and Mary Quarterly*, 3rd ser., XVIII (1961), 558-76.

KEMMERER, DONALD L.: *Path to Freedom: The Struggle for Self-Government in Colonial New Jersey, 1703-1776, Princeton History of New Jersey*, III (London & Princeton, N.J., 1940).

LILLY, EDWARD P.: *see* under New York.

MC CORMICK, RICHARD P.: *The History of Voting in New Jersey: A Study of the Development of Election Machinery, 1664-1911*, Rutgers University, *Studies in History*, No. 8 (New Brunswick, N.J., 1953).

SCOTT, KENNETH: "Counterfeiting in Colonial New Jersey [1752-76]," New Jersey Historical Society, *Proceedings*, LXXV (1957), 170-9.

WHITEHEAD, WILLIAM A.: "Northern Boundary Line: The Circumstances Leading to the Establishment, in 1769, of the Northern Boundary Line between New Jersey and New York," New Jersey Historical Society, *Proceedings*, VIII (1856-9), 157-86.

4. Economic

BOYER, CHARLES SHIMER: *Early Forges and Furnaces in New Jersey* (London & Philadelphia, 1931).

FISHER, EDGAR J.: *Colonial Land Conflicts in New Jersey*, Hudson County Historical Society, *Papers*, No. 6 (1908). Part IV, covering the years 1747 through 1757, is most relevant.

KEMMERER, DONALD L.: "The Colonial Loan-Office System in New Jersey," *Journal of Political Economy*, XLVII (1939), 867-74.

———: "A History of Paper Money in Colonial New Jersey, 1668-1775," New Jersey Historical Society, *Proceedings*, LXXIV (1956), 107-44.

PARKER, R. W.: "Taxes and Money in New Jersey Before the Revolution," New Jersey Historical Society, *Proceedings*, 2nd ser., VII, 143-57.

POMFRET, JOHN E.: *The New Jersey Proprietors and Their Lands, 1664-1776, New Jersey Historical Series*, IX (Princeton, N.J., 1964).

RAMSAY, HOBART C.: "New Jersey, Pioneer of American Industry," New Jersey Historical Society, *Proceedings*, LXXII (1954), 1-8.

SCOTT, KENNETH: "The Great Epidemic of Coining in the Jersies [1747-1751]," New Jersey Historical Society, *Proceedings*, LXXV (1957), 112-27.

WOODWARD, CARL R.: *The Development of Agriculture in New Jersey, 1640-1880: A Monographic Study in Agricultural History* (New Brunswick, N.J., 1927), and "Agricultural Legislation in Colonial New Jersey," *Agricultural History*, III (1929), 15-28.

5. Social

BURR, NELSON ROLLIN: *The Anglican Church in New Jersey [1664-1800]*, Church Historical Society, *Publications*, No. 40 (Philadelphia [1954]).

———: *Education in New Jersey, 1630-1871. Princeton History of New Jersey*, IV (Princeton, N.J., 1942).

JAMISON, WALLACE N.: *Religion in New Jersey: A Brief History, New Jersey Historical Series*, XIII (Princeton, N.J., 1964), Chapter II: "Diversity Takes Root (1702-1776)" is relevant.

LANE, WHEATON J.: *From Indian Trail to Iron Horse: Travel and Transportation in New Jersey, 1620-1860, Princeton History of New Jersey*, I (Princeton, N.J., 1939).

POMFRET, JOHN E.: "West New Jersey: A Quaker Society, 1675-1775," *William and Mary Quarterly*, 3rd ser., VIII (1951), 493-519.

WEISS, HARRY B.: *Life in Early New Jersey, New Jersey Historical Series*, XXVI (Princeton, N.J., 1964).

WERTENBAKER, THOMAS J.: *Princeton, 1746-1896* (Princeton, N.J., 1946).

WOODY, THOMAS: *Quaker Education in the Colony and State of New Jersey: A Source-Book* (Philadelphia, 1923). A secondary account interspersed with source materials.

6. Biographical

BOUDINOT, ELIAS. *Elias Boudinot: Patriot and Statesman, 1740-1821* by George Adams Boyd (Princeton, N.J., 1952).

CHANDLER, THOMAS BRADBURY. "Thomas Bradbury Chandler: Anglican Humanitarian in Colonial New Jersey" by Samuel Clyde Mc-Culloch, *British Humanitarianism: Essays Honoring Frank J. Klingberg* . . . (Samuel Clyde McCulloch, ed., Philadelphia, c. 1950), pp. 100-23.

FRANKLIN, WILLIAM. "A Biographical Sketch of William Franklin, Governor from 1763 to 1776" by William A. Whitehead, New Jersey Historical Society, *Proceedings*, III (1848-9), 139-59, and Catherine Fennelly's "William Franklin of New Jersey," *William and Mary Quarterly*, 3rd ser., VI (1949), 361-82.

READ, CHARLES. *Ploughs and Politicks: Charles Read of New Jersey* . . . by C. R. Woodward, Rutgers University, *Studies in History*, No. 2 (New Brunswick, N.J., 1941). It contains a biography in addition to Read's notes and papers.

STIRLING, WILLIAM ALEXANDER, EARL OF. *The Life of William Alexander, Earl of Stirling, Major General in the Army of the United States during the Revolution: With Selections from His Correspondence* by William Alexander Duer, New Jersey Historical Society, *Collections*, II (New York, 1847).

———. *Memorials of the Earl of Stirling and of the House of Alexander* by Charles Rogers (2 vols., Edinburgh, 1877).

WITHERSPOON, JOHN. *President Witherspoon: A Biography* by Varnum Lansing Collins (2 vols., Princeton, N.J., 1925).

WOOLMAN, JOHN. *John Woolman, American Quaker* by Janet Whitney (Boston, 1942).

7. Military

ANDERSON, JOHN R.: "Militia Law in Colonial New Jersey: The Beginnings, 1775-1776," New Jersey Historical Society, *Proceedings*, LXXVI (1958), 280-96.

SHY, JOHN: "Quartering His Majesty's Forces in New Jersey," *ibid.*, LXXVIII (1960), 82-94.

D. MAPS

FADEN, WILLIAM: *The Province of New Jersey Divided into East and West, Commonly Called the Jerseys* ([London], 1777). In Faden: *The North American Atlas*, No. 22; also in Jefferys: *The American Atlas*, No. 20½.

Maps Illustrating Mr. [William A.] Whitehead's Paper of the Northern Boundary of New Jersey. In the New Jersey Historical Society, *Proceedings,* VIII (1856-9), opp. p. 157.

Good delineations of New Jersey are also to be found on several more inclusive maps such as Emanuel Bowen's *A New and Accurate Map of New Jersey, Pensilvania, New York, and New England . . .* ; the Holland map of *The Provinces of New York and New Jersey with Part of Pensilvania . . .* ; and *Virginia, Maryland, Pensilvania, East and West New Jersey,* all fully cited under Chapter IV, D.

NEW YORK

A. BIBLIOGRAPHICAL AIDS

BROWN, KARL: *A Guide to the Reference Collections of the New York Public Library* (New York, 1941).

FLAGG, CHARLES A., and JUDSON T. JENNINGS: "Bibliography of New York Colonial History," New York State Library, *Bulletin,* No. 56, "Bibliography," No. 24 ([Albany, N.Y.], 1901).

GOSNELL, C. F., and EDNA L. JACOBSON: "History in the [New York] State Library," *New York History,* XXVII (1946), 531-3; XXIX (1948), 232-34.

GREENE, EVARTS B., and RICHARD B. MORRIS: *A Guide to the Principal Sources for Early American History (1600-1800) in the City of New York* (2nd edn., rev. by R. B. Morris, New York, 1953).

HASSE, ADELAIDE R.: "New York State, 1614-1775," in "Materials for a Bibliography of the Public Archives of the Thirteen Original States . . . ," American Historical Association, *Annual Report, 1906* (2 vols., Washington, D.C., 1908), II, 354-85.

HILL, ROBERT W.: "Resources on Colonial History in the New York Public Library," *New York History,* XL (1959), 387-413.

State Papers of Vermont, Vol. I: Index to the Papers of the Surveyors-General . . . (Rutland, Vt., 1918). The present state of Vermont was part of New York during the colonial period.

An excellent but dated bibliography of New York City is the one prepared by Victor H. Paltsits for Volume VI of Stoke's *The Iconography of Manhattan Island, 1498-1909 . . . ,* to be cited.

B. PRINTED SOURCE MATERIALS

1. Government and related documents

An Argument Delivered on the Part of New-York at the Hearing before
His Majesty's Commissioners . . . to Settle and Determine the
Boundary Line between the Colonies of New-York and New-Jer-
sey ([New York], 1769). The statement was signed by John Morin
Scott, James Duane, and Benjamin Kissom.

The Burghers of New Amsterdam and the Freemen of New York, 1675-
1866, New York Historical Society, Collections, XVIII (New
York, 1886). Contains the roll of freemen of New York City.

Calendar of Council Minutes, 1668-1783, Berthold Frenow, ed., New
York Library, History Bulletin, No. 6 (Albany, N.Y., 1902).

COLDEN, CADWALLADER: The Colden Letter Books, New York Historical
Society, Collections, IX-X (2 vols., New York, 1877-8). Also, The
Letters and Papers of Cadwallader Colden, 1711-1775, ibid., L-
LVI, LXVII-LXVIII (9 vols., New York, 1918-37).

HOUGH, CHARLES MERRILL, ed.: Reports of Cases in the Vice-Admiralty of
the Province of New York and in the Court of Admiralty of the
State of New York, 1715-1788 . . . (New Haven, Conn., 1925).
Important respecting cases involving the violation of the trade
and navigation acts.

Journal of the Legislative Council of the Colony of New York . . . [1691-
1775] (2 vols., Albany, N.Y., 1861).

Journal of the Proceedings of the Commissaries of the Colony of New-
York, at a Congress with the Commissaries of the Massachusetts-
Bay: Relating to the Establishment of a Partition Line of
Jurisdiction between the Two Provinces (New York [1767]).

Journal of the Votes and Proceedings of the General Assembly of the
Colony of New-York . . . [1691-1776] (3 vols., Albany, N.Y. &
New York, 1764-1820). Also available on Readex cards are yearly
issues of the Journal for most of the years from 1748 to 1775.

LINCOLN, CHARLES Z., WILLIAM H. JOHNSON, and A. JUDD NORTHROP, eds.:
The Colonial Laws of New York from . . . 1664 to the Revolution
(5 vols., Albany, N.Y., 1894-6).

MORRIS, RICHARD B., ed.: Select Cases of the Mayor's Court of New York
City, 1674-1784, American Legal Records, Vol. 2 (Washington,
D.C., 1935).

MUNSELL, JOEL: The Annals of Albany (10 vols., Albany, N.Y., 1850-9).

NEW YORK CITY: Laws, Statutes, Ordinances, and Constitutions Ordained,
Made, and Established by the Mayor, Recorder, Aldermen, and
Assistants of the City of New York . . . (New York, 1749).

NYE, MARY G., ed.: *New York Land Patents, 1688-1786, Covering Land now Included in the State of Vermont . . . , State Papers of Vermont,* VII ([Montpelier, Vt., 1947]).

O'CALLAGHAN, EDMUND BAILEY, ed.: *The Documentary History of the State of New York* (4 vols., Albany, N.Y., 1850-1).

————: *Documents Relative to the Colonial History of the State of New York* (15 vols., Albany, N.Y., 1853-87). This series and the one cited above contain much valuable information bearing upon the history of the Province of New York.

OSGOOD, HERBERT L., *et al.,* eds.: *Minutes of the Common Council of the City of New York, 1675-1776* (8 vols., New York, 1905).

Revolutionary [and Miscellaneous] Papers, New York Historical Society, *Collections,* XI-XIII (3 vols., New York, 1879-81). Most of the materials in these volumes are post 1776, although some of the papers of Charles Thomson relating to the Continental Congress are useful.

SLADE, WILLIAM, ed.: *Vermont State Papers: Being a Collection of Records and Documents . . .* (Middlebury, Vt., 1823). The lands contained within the bounds of the later state of Vermont were earlier, as already stated, legally a part of the Province of New York by decision of the King in Council.

SMITH, WILLIAM, JR., and WILLIAM LIVINGSTON, eds.: *Laws of New-York . . . [1691-1762]* (2 vols., New York, 1752-62).

A State of the Right of the Colony of New York . . . so Far as Concerns the Late Encroachments under the Government of New-Hampshire . . . (New York, 1773). This was written primarily by James Duane, most of whose property claims lay in the disputed area, and was published by the General Assembly of New York. See also the supplementary volume, *A Narrative of the Proceedings Subsequent to the Royal Adjudication Concerning the Lands to the Westward of Connecticut River . . .* (New York, 1773).

"Territorial Rights of New York: The N[ew] H[ampshire] Grants, Etc.," New York Historical Society, *Collections,* III (New York, 1871), pp. 1-144. Prints James Duane's "State of the Evidence and Argument in Support of the Territorial Rights and Jurisdiction of New York against the Government of New Hampshire . . . and against the Commonwealth of Massachusetts." This was a brief for the case to be heard in federal court in 1784, but was never used; the case was settled out of court in 1786.

Two Reports of a Committee of His Majesty's Council for the Province of New-York Relating to the Controverted Line between That Province and New-Jersey . . . (New York, 1754).

VAN SCHAACK, PETER, ed.: *Laws of New-York from the Year 1691 to 1773 Inclusive . . .* (2 vols., New York, 1774).

VERMONT HISTORICAL SOCIETY, *Collections* (2 vols., Montpelier, Vt., 1870-

71). Contains valuable materials relating to the New York-New Hampshire land dispute during the years 1765-1777.

WALTON, E. P., ed.: *Records of the Council of Safety and Governor and Council of the State of Vermont, 1775-1836* (8 vols., Montpelier, Vt., 1873-80), Vol. I.

2. Non-official contemporary writings

ALLEN, ETHAN: *A Brief Narrative of the Proceedings of the Government of New-York Relative to their Obtaining the Jurisdiction of that Large District of Land to the Westward from Connecticut River* . . . (Hartford, Conn. [1774]).

BARBER, JOHN W., and HENRY HOWE: *Historical Collections of the State of New York* . . . (New York, 1841).

BEAUCHAMP, WILLIAM MARTIN, ed.: *Moravian Journals Relating to Central New York, 1745-66* (Syracuse, N.Y., 1916).

CORWIN, EDWARD T., ed.: *Ecclesiastical Records [of the] State of New York* (7 vols., Albany, N.Y., 1901-16).

GRANT, ANNE MAC VICAR: *Memoirs of an American Lady: with Sketches of Manners and Scenery in America as They Existed Previous to the Revolution* (2 vols., London, 1808; 1 vol., New York, 1809; rep., Albany, N.Y., 1876). Largely concerned with upper New York.

HAMILTON, ALEXANDER: *The Works of Alexander Hamilton: Containing His Correspondence, and His Political and Official Writings* . . . (John C. Hamilton, ed., 7 vols., New York, 1850-1), I-II. Another collection of *Works* was edited by Henry Cabot Lodge (9 vols., New York, 1885-6; 12 vols., 1904). For the best collection, however, see *The Papers of Alexander Hamilton* (Harold C. Syrett and Jacob E. Cooke, eds., 11 vols. +, London & New York, 1961-5), Vol. I: 1768-1778.

HILDEBURN, CHARLES R., ed.: "Notes on the Stamp Act in New York and Virginia," *Pennsylvania Magazine of History and Biography*, II (1878), 296-302.

JOHNSON, SAMUEL. *Life and Correspondence of Samuel Johnson, D.D.* . . . by E. Edward Beardsley (2nd edn., New York, 1874).

JONES, THOMAS: *History of New York during the Revolutionary War and of the Leading Events in the Other Colonies at That Period* (Edward Floyd De Lancey, ed., 2 vols., New York, 1879). Jones was a justice of the Supreme Court of New York and a noted Loyalist. See in conjunction with his work, Henry P. Johnston: *Observations on Judge Jones' Loyalist History of the American Revolution: How Far Is It an Authority?* (New York, 1880).

LIVINGSTON, WILLIAM: *A Brief Consideration of New York with Respect to Its Natural Advantages* . . . , *Heartman's Historical Series*, No.

39 (Earl Gregg Swem, ed., Metuchen, N.J., 1925). This is a reprint of an article that appeared in the *Independent Reflector* in
1753.

——, *et al*: *The Independent Reflector: Or Weekly Essays on Sundry
Important Subjects More Particularly Adopted to the Province of
New York, by William Livingston and Others* (Milton M. Klein,
ed., Cambridge, Mass., 1963).

"Old New York and Trinity Church," New York Historical Society,
Collections, III (New York, 1871), pp. 145-408. Happenings in
New York City as reported in the newspapers, 1730-90.

OSGOOD, HERBERT L., ed.: "The Society of Dissenters Founded at New
York in 1769," *American Historical Review*, VI (1900-1), 498-
507. Minutes of meetings held in New York City in February and
March 1769 in which leading Presbyterians and Baptists attempted to form a Society of Dissenters.

*Papers of the Lloyd Family of the Manor of Queens Village, Lloyd's
Neck, Long Island, New York, 1654-1826,* New York Historical
Society, *Collections,* LIX-LX (2 vols., New York, 1927). Volume
II is most useful, covering the years from 1752 to 1826.

SEABURY, SAMUEL: *Life and Correspondence of the Right Rev. Samuel
Seabury, D.D. . . .* by E. Edward Beardsley, (2nd edn., Boston,
1881), and "The Seabury Minutes of the New York Clergy Conventions of 1766 and 1767," Walter Herbert Stow, ed., *Historical
Magazine of the Protestant Episcopal Church,* X (1941), 124-62.

SMITH, WILLIAM: *The History of the Province of New-York from the
First Discovery to the Year MDCCXXXII: To Which Is Annexed
a Description of the Country . . .* (London, 1757; 2nd edn., Philadelphia, 1792). Smith dedicated his work "To the Right Honourable George, Earl of Halifax, Viscount Sunbury, First Lord
Commissioner of Trade and Plantations, &c." The book was
based primarily upon available governmental and official records,
but the author acknowledged Colden's *History of the Five
Nations.* The *History* was reissued in 1814 with a continuation
which has been attributed to John Van Ness Yates. Before his
death in 1793, Smith completed a manuscript continuing the
history from 1732 to 1762, which was edited by his son, William
(the historian of Canada). It was published with the subtitle
"Continuation of the History of New-York" as Volume IV of the
New York Historical Society, *Collections* (New York, 1826).
When the Society decided to reissue the original volume of the
History, that volume was designated Volume IV of the *Collections*
and the continuation was Volume V (2 vols., New York, 1829).
See in conjunction with this work, Cadwallader Colden's "Letters
on Smith's History of New York," New York Historical Society,

Collections, I (New York, 1868), 177-235. The letters were written between 1759 and 1766.

————: *Historical Memoirs, from 16 March 1763 to 9 July 1776, of William Smith, Historian of the Province of New York . . .* (William H. W. Sabine, ed., New York, 1956). It may be pointed out that the "Historical Memoirs" in the New York Historical Society extend to 1783. A Smith diary covering the years 1784-93, and therefore beyond the period here under consideration, is presently being published by the Champlain Society.

————: "William Smith Jr.'s Alternative to the American Revolution," *William and Mary Quarterly,* 3rd ser., XXII (1965), 105-18. Prints a manuscript, "Thoughts upon the Dispute between Great Britain and Her Colonies."

STOKES, ISAAC NEWTON PHELPS: *The Iconography of Manhattan Island, 1498-1909: Compiled from Original Sources and Illustrated by . . . Reproductions of Important Maps, Plans, Views and Documents* (6 vols., New York, 1915-28). A very valuable source series.

SULLIVAN, JAMES. *Life of James Sullivan: With Selections from His Writings* by Thomas C. Amory (2 vols., Boston, 1859).

SWEAT, WILLIAM: "Captain William Sweat's Personal Diary of the Expedition against Ticonderoga, May 2-November 7, 1758," Paul O. Blanchette, ed., *Essex Institute Historical Collections,* XCIII (1957), 36-57. The expedition was begun from Salisbury, Mass.

VAN SCHAACK, PETER. *Life of Peter Van Schaack, LL.D.: Embracing Selections from His Correspondence and Other Writings . . .* by Henry Cruger Van Schaack (New York, 1842).

WATTS, JOHN: *Letter Book of John Watts, Merchant and Councillor of New York, January 1, 1762-December 22, 1765,* New York Historical Society, *Collections,* LXI (Dorothy C. Barck, ed., New York, 1928). Contains primarily business communications but is interspersed with useful observations on the New York economic and political situation and on British colonial policy.

WHITE, PHILIP L., ed.: *The Beekman Mercantile Papers, 1746-1799* (3 vols., New York, 1956). The commercial correspondence of the Beekman family.

3. Contemporary pamphlets, tracts, and related materials: Chronologically arranged

1750

A Letter from a Gentleman in New-York to his Friend in Brunswick ([New York, 1750]). A broadside.

1 7 6 4

YOUNG, THOMAS: *Some Reflections on the Disputes between New-York, New-Hampshire, and Col. John Henry Lydius of Albany . . . To These Reflections Are Added Some Rules of Law Fit to Be Observed in Purchasing Land &c.* (New Haven, Conn., 1764).

1 7 6 5

Liberty, Property, and no Stamps: A Serious Address to the Inhabitants of New York . . . (New York, 1765). Signed "Britannus Americanus" and dated 17 December 1765.

The Memorial of the Merchants of the City of New-York . . . to the Honourable the Knights, Citizens, and Burgesses, in Parliament Assembled: Read in the General Assembly of Said Colony, the 20th of April, 1764 (New York, 1765). Points out the dangers of the Sugar Act to Northern trade.

To the Freemen and Freeholders of the City of New-York ([New York, 1766]). A protest against sending the stamped paper back to England.

A Petition to His Majesty, King George the Third: To the King's Most Excellent Majesty, the Humble Petition of the Several Subscribers hereto Your Majesty's most Loyal Subjects . . . ([Hartford, Conn., 1766]). One of nineteen petitions of settlers on lands in what is now Vermont asking for relief from the claims of New York.

1 7 6 7

The Conduct of Cadwallader Colden, Esquire, Late Lieutenant Governor of New York: Relating to the Judges' Commissions, Appeals to the King, and the Stamp-Duty ([London & New York], 1767). Reprinted in New York Historical Society, *Collections,* X (New York, 1877), 429-467. The New York Assembly was unsuccessful in determining the author of this pamphlet.

The Commercial Conduct of the Province of New-York Considered, and the True Interest of That Colony Attempted to Be Shewn . . . (New York, 1767). Signed, "By a Linen Draper."

1 7 6 8

PHILANTHROPOS, pseud.: *A Few Observations on the Conduct of the General Assembly of New-York for Some Years Past: Addressed to the Freemen and Freeholders of the City and Province* ([New York], 1768).

1 7 6 9

A Citizen's Address to the Public . . . (New York, 1769). See also the reply: *An Answer to the Citizen's Address to the Public* . . . (New York, 1769). Both publications are broadsides, the first favouring the grant of public funds for the support of troops used against the rioters, tenants of the great estates, signed "A Citizen," and the second, opposing the grant, signed "A Plebian."

LIVINGSTON, ROBERT R.: *The Address of Mr. Justice Livingston to the House of Assembly in Support of His Right to a Seat* ([New York, 1769]). The author defends the necessity of three branches of government and challenges the arbitrary right of the Assembly to refuse to seat duly-elected members. Livingston's pamphlet drew the reply of "A Citizen": *Observations on Mr. Livingston's Address* . . . ([New York, 1769]).

[MAC DOUGALL, ALEXANDER]: *To the Betrayed Inhabitants of the City and Colony of New-York* . . . (New York, 1769). The broadside, criticizing the assembly for appropriating money for troops, is signed "A Son of Liberty." Lieutenant-Governor Cadwallader Colden issued a broadside offering £100 reward for the author or authors of this pamphlet. McDougall subsequently published the following broadside, dated 20th December 1770, to defend himself of the charge of having written *To the Betrayed Inhabitants* . . . : *To the Freeholders and Freemen of the City and Colony of New-York* . . . ([New York, 1770]).

To the Public: As It Is Generally Imagined, the Assembly will (contrary to the known sentiments of their constituents) Grant Supplies to the Troops . . . ([New York, 1769]). A broadside signed "A Freeholder" and dated 28th December 1769.

To the Public: The Spirit of the Times Renders It Necessary for the Inhabitants of This Colony to Convene . . . *to Avert [the] Destructive Consequences of the* . . . . *[General Assembly's Voting] Supplies to the Troops* . . . ([New York, 1769]). A broadside signed "Legion." Lieutenant Governor Colden issued a broadside offering £50 reward for the author or authors of this publication.

Union, Activity and Freedom: Or Division, Supineness and Slavery . . . ([New York, 1769]). A broadside signed "A Son of Liberty," describing the "dangerous consequences" of permitting a grant of funds for the troops.

1 7 7 0

The Dougliad. On Liberty: Humbly Inscribed to the Grand Jury for the City and County of New-York . . . ([New York, 1770]). This is a broadside calling for the punishment of Alexander McDougall.

LAELIUS, pseud.: *A Letter to the Celebrated Patriot of New York* . . .

([New York, 1770]). A broadside addressed to Alexander Mc-Dougall.

To the Public: Whoever Seriously Considers the Impoverished State of This City . . . ([New York, 1770]). A broadside signed "Brutus" and opposing a billeting act and accusing the regular soldiers of attempting to destroy the liberty pole.

SAWNEY, pseud.: *Paradise Regain'd: To all the Great and Glorious Patriots in New-York* . . . ([New York, 1770]). Satirizes Alexander McDougall's imprisonment.

The Speech of the Statue of the Right Hon. William Pitt, Earl of Chatham: To the Virtueous and Patriotick Citizens of New York . . . ([New York, 1770]). A broadside.

The Times: Mankind Is Highly Concerned to Support that, wherein Their Own Safety Is Concerned, and to Destroy Those Arts by which Their Ruin Is Consulted . . . ([New York, 1770]). On the payment of troops; signed "A Merchant."

1 7 7 3

THE ASSOCIATION OF THE SONS OF LIBERTY OF NEW YORK: *It Is Essential to the Freedom and Security of a Free People, That no Taxes be Imposed upon Them But by Their Own Consent, or Their Representatives* . . . *New-York, November 23, 1773* . . . (New York, 1773).

POPLICOLA, pseud.: *To the Worthy Inhabitants of the City of New-York: Every Good Citizen Will be Inclined from Duty, as Well as Interest, to Love his Country and be Zealous in Advancing its Welfare* . . . ([New York, 1773]). Presenting commercial arguments for the purchase of tea shipped by the East India Company. See also by "Poplicola": *To the Worthy Inhabitants of the City of New-York: No Subject is So Misunderstood . . . as Liberty* ([New York, 1773]). In opposition to the non-importation agreement and favoring the admission of the East India Company's shipment of tea. These pamphlets were the works of the Rev. Myles Cooper, President of King's College, and of John Vardille, a tutor in the college.

1 7 7 4

A Serious Address to the Inhabitants of the Colony of New-York: Containing a Full and Minute Survey of the Boston-Port Act . . . (New York, 1774). Signed "A Citizen of New-York," the pamphlet contains an appendix which includes the Port Act and a speech by Lord Camden on the Declaratory Act.

To the Inhabitants of New York . . . At a Time When Slavery Is Clanking Her Infernal Chains, and Tyranny Stands Ready with Goods and Ships to Enforce Obedience to Her Despotic and Cruel Mandates . . . ([New York, 1774]). Signed "Plain English."

[WILKINS, ISAAC]: *Short Advice to the Counties of New-York* . . . (New York, 1774). A loyalist pamphlet.

1775

BRUSH, CREAN: *Speech of a Member of the General Assembly of New-York at Their Session in 1775* (New York, 1775). The pamphlet is an attack on the Continental Congress.

No Standing Army in the British Colonies: Or an Address to the Inhabitants of the Colony of New-York against Unlawful Standing Armies (New York, 1775).

[SEABURY, SAMUEL]: *An Alarm to the Legislature of the Province of New-York Occasioned by the Present Political Disturbances in North America* . . . (New York, 1775). The last two pages of this article contain a list of pamphlets relating to the controversy between Great Britain and the Colonies. Also printed with the London edition of Chandler's *What Think Ye of the Congress Now?* It was reprinted in C. H. Vance's *Letters of a Westchester Farmer 1774-1775* . . . , Westchester County Historical Society, *Publications,* VIII (White Plains, N.Y., 1930).

To the Freeholders and Freemen of the City of New-York. Fellow Citizens . . . (New York, 1775). A broadside, signed "Americanus," which encouraged attendance at a meeting to discuss election of delegates to the Continental Congress.

1776

The Battle of Brooklyn: A Farce of Two Acts . . . (New York, 1776).

4. Newspapers

The New-York Chronicle, 1769-1770, New York.

The New-York Gazette [Weyman's] *[Weyman's New-York Gazette],* 1759-1767, New York.

The New York Gazette, and Weekly Mercury [The New-York Gazette; and the Weekly Mercury; The New-York Gazette: and the Weekly Mercury], b. 1768, New York. The changes in title as noted were very minor.

The New-York Gazette: Or, Weekly Post-Boy [Parker's New York Gazette, or the Weekly Post-Boy], e. 1773, New York.

The New-York Journal, or General Advertiser, 1766-1776, New York.

The New-York Mercury, 1752-1768, New York.

Rivington's New-York Gazetteer: Or, The Connecticut, New-Jersey, Hudson's River, and Quebec Weekly Advertiser, 1773-1775, New York.

C. SECONDARY WORKS

1. General

ABBOTT, WILBUR CORTEZ: *New York in the American Revolution* (London & New York, 1929).

ALLEN, IRA: *The Natural and Political History of the State of Vermont* . . . (London, 1798). As has been previously stressed, the area now comprising the state of Vermont was *legally* a part of New York during the period under consideration.

CROUSE, NELLIE M.: "The French in Colonial New York," *History of the State of New York* (Alexander C. Flick, ed., 10 vols., New York, 1933-7), II: 121-50.

DAY, RICHARD E.: "A Summary of the English Period," *ibid.*, III: 91-128.

ELLSWORTH, RICHARD C.: "The Settlement of the North Country [of New York]," *ibid.*, V: 177-215.

FLICK, ALEXANDER, ed.: *History of the State of New York* (10 vols., New York, 1933-7).

GREENE, EVARTS B.: "New York and the Old Empire," *History of the State of New York*, III: 129-44.

HALL, BENJAMIN H.: *History of Eastern Vermont from its Earliest Settlement to the Close of the Eighteenth Century* . . . (New York, 1858).

HALL, HILAND: *The History of Vermont from its Discovery to its Admission into the Union in 1791* (Albany, N.Y., 1868).

HIGGINS, RUTH L.: *Expansion in New York: With Especial Reference to the Eighteenth Century*, Ohio State University, *Contributions in History and Political Science*, No. 14 (Columbus, O., 1931).

JONES, MATT BUSHNELL: *Vermont in the Making, 1750-1777* (Cambridge, Mass., 1939).

ROBERTS, ELLIS HENRY: *New York: The Planting and the Growth of the Empire State*, American Commonwealths, VIII-IX (Boston & New York, 1904).

WATSON, JOHN F.: *Annals and Concurrences of New York, City and State, in the Olden Time* . . . (Philadelphia, 1846).

2. Local

BARCK, OSCAR THEODORE, JR.: *New York City during the War for Independence: With Special Reference to the Period of British Occupation* (London & New York, 1931).

BARNES, WILLIAM: *The Settlement and Early History of Albany* (Albany, N.Y., 1851; rep., 1864).

EDWARDS, GEORGE WILLIAM: *New York [City] as an Eighteenth Century Municipality, 1731-1776*, Columbia University, *Studies in History, Economics, and Public Law*, No. 178 (London & New York, 1917).

HAMILTON, EDWARD P.: *Lake Champlain and the Upper Hudson Valley* (Ticonderoga, N.Y., c. 1959).

HOWELL, G. R., and J. TENNEY, eds.: *Bi-Centennial History of Albany* (New York, 1886).

LAMB, MARTHA: *History of the City of New York: Its Origin, Rise, and Progress* (3 vols., Chicago & New York, 1877-96).

RUTTENBER, E. M.: *History of the County of Orange with a History of the Town and City of Newburgh* . . . (Newburgh, N.Y., 1875).

WEISE, ARTHUR J.: *The History of the City of Albany* (Albany, N.Y., 1884).

WERTENBAKER, THOMAS J.: *Father Knickerbocker Rebels: New York City during the Revolution* (London & New York, 1948).

WILSON, JAMES GRANT, ed.: *Memorial History of the City of New York and the Hudson River Valley* . . . (5 vols., New York, 1892-6).

ZERCHER, F. K.: "The Port of Oswego," *New York History*, XVI (1935), 308-17. An account of the growth of the Lake Erie port from 1653 to 1900.

3. Political

BECKER, CARL L.: *The History of Political Parties in the Province of New York, 1760-1776* (Madison, Wis., c. 1909; rep., 1960). See also his articles: "Growth of Revolutionary Parties and Methods in New York Province, 1765-1774," *American Historical Review*, VII (1901-1902), 56-76; "Nominations in Colonial New York," *ibid.*, VI (1900-1901), 260-75; and "The Nomination and Election of Delegates from New York to the First Continental Congress, 1774," *Political Science Quarterly*, XVIII (1903), 17-46.

BREWSTER, WILLIAM: *See* under Pennsylvania.

BURNETT, EDMUND C.: "New York in the Continental Congress," *History of the State of New York*, III: 291-324.

CHAMPAGNE, ROGER: "Family Politics versus Constitutional Principles: The New York Assembly Elections of 1768 and 1769," *William and Mary Quarterly*, 3rd ser., XX (1963), 57-79; "New York and the Intolerable Acts, 1774," New York Historical Society, *Quarterly*, XLV (1961), 195-207; "New York Politics and Independence, 1776," *ibid.*, XLVI (1962), 281-303; and "New York's Radicals and the Coming of Independence," *Journal of American History*, LI (1964), 21-40.

DAWSON, HENRY BARTON: *The Sons of Liberty in New York* . . . (Poughkeepsie, N.Y., 1859).

FLICK, ALEXANDER C.: *Loyalism in New York during the American Revolu-*

tion, Columbia University, *Studies in History, Economics, and Public Law,* No. 37 (London & New York, 1901); see also "How New York Won and Lost an Empire," *New York History,* XVIII (1937), 361-77; "The Provincial Congress and the Declaration of Independence," *History of the State of New York,* III: 255-90; and "The Loyalists," *ibid.,* III: 325-63.

FLICK, HUGH M.: "The Rise of the Revolutionary Committee System," *ibid.,* III: 209-54.

FOWLER, ROBERT LUDLOW: "Constitutional and Legal History of New-York in the Eighteenth Century," *Memorial History of the City of New-York and the Hudson River Valley . . . ,* II: 575-630.

FRIEDMAN, BERNARD: "The New York Assembly Elections of 1768 and 1769: The Description of Family Politics," *New York History,* XLVI (1965), 3-24.

GITTERMAN, JOHN M.: "George Clinton and his Contest with the Assembly, 1743-1753," *Memorial History of the City of New-York and the Hudson River Valley . . . ,* II: 259-86.

GOEBEL, JULIUS, JR.: "The Courts and the Law in Colonial New York," *History of the State of New York,* III: 1-43.

———, and T. RAYMOND NAUGHTON: *Law Enforcement in Colonial New York: A Study in Criminal Procedures (1664-1776)* (New York, 1944).

HANDLIN, OSCAR: "The Eastern Frontier of New York," *New York History,* XVIII (1937), 50-75. Relating to the Massachusetts-New York boundary dispute.

HARLOW, RALPH V.: "The Causes of the Revolution in New York," *History of the State of New York,* III: 165-208.

HUFELAND, OTTO: *Westchester County during the American Revolution, 1775-1783* (White Plains, N.Y., 1926).

KLEIN, MILTON M.: "Democracy and Politics in Colonial New York," *New York History,* XL (1957), 221-46; "Politics and Personalities in Colonial New York," *ibid.,* XLVII (1966), 3-16; and "Prelude to Revolution in New York: Jury Trials and Judicial Tenure," *William and Mary Quarterly,* 3rd ser., XVII (1960), 439-62.

LEDER, LAWRENCE H.: "The New York Elections of 1769: An Assault on Privilege," *Mississippi Valley Historical Review,* XLIX (1962-3), 675-82.

LEMISCH, L. JESSE: "New York's Petitions and Resolves of December 1765: Liberals vs. Radicals," New York Historical Society, *Quarterly,* XLIX (1965), 313-26.

LEVERMORE, CHARLES H.: "The Whigs of Colonial New York," *American Historical Review,* I (1895-6), 238-50.

LEVY, LEONARD W., and LAWRENCE H. LEDER: " 'Exotic Fruit': The Right against Compulsory Self-Incrimination in Colonial New York," *William and Mary Quarterly,* 3rd ser., XX (1963), 3-32.

LILLY, EDWARD P.: *The Colonial Agents of New York and New Jersey* (Washington, D.C., 1936).

LYND, STAUGHTON: "Who Should Rule at Home? Dutchess County, New York, in the American Revolution," *William and Mary Quarterly*, 3rd ser., XVIII (1961), 330-59.

MC ANEAR, BEVERLY: "The Albany Stamp Act Riots," *ibid.*, 3rd ser., IV (1947), 486-98; "Mr. Robert R. Livingston's Reasons against a Land Tax," *Journal of Political Economy*, XLVIII (1940), 63-90, and "The Place of the Freeman in Old New York," *New York History*, XXI (1940), 418-30.

MASON, BERNARD: *The Road to Independence: The Revolutionary Movement in New York, 1773-1777* (Lexington, Ky., 1966).

PELL, JOHN: "The Secession of Vermont," *History of the State of New York*, V: 1-28.

SEYBOLT, ROBERT FRANCIS: *The Colonial Citizen of New York City . . .* University of Wisconsin, *Studies in the Social Sciences and History*, No. 1 (Madison, Wis., 1918).

RODENBOUGH, THEOPHILUS T.: "New-York [City] during the Revolution . . . ," *Memorial History of the City of New-York and the Hudson River Valley . . . ,* III: 469-574.

SPENCER, CHARLES W.: "The Rise of the Assembly, 1691-1760," *History of the State of New York*, II: 151-200.

STEVENS, JOHN AUSTIN: "The Part of New-York [City] in the Stamp Act Troubles, 1761-1768," *Memorial History of the City of New-York and the Hudson River Valley . . .* , II: 325-90; "The Second Non-Importation Agreement and the [New York City] Committees of Correspondence and Observation, 1760-1775," *ibid.*, II: 391-444; and "Life in New-York [City] at the Close of the Colonial Period," *ibid.*, II: 445-68.

VARGA, NICHOLAS: "The New York Restraining Act: Its Passage and Some Effects, 1766-1768," *New York History*, XXXVII (1956), 233-58, and "Election Procedures and Practices in Colonial New York," *ibid.*, XL (1960), 249-77.

WERNER, EDGAR A.: *Civil List and Constitutional History of the Colony and State of New York* ([Albany, N.Y., 1855]).

4. Economic

HARRINGTON, VIRGINIA DRAPER: *The New York Merchant on the Eve of the Revolution*, Columbia University, *Studies in History, Economics, and Public Law*, No. 404 (London & New York, 1935); and "The Colonial Merchant's Ledger," *History of the State of New York*, II: 331-74.

HICKCOX, JOHN HOWARD: *A History of the Bills of Credit or Paper Money Issued by New York from 1709 to 1789 . . .* (Albany, N.Y., 1866).

MC KEE, SAMUEL, JR.: "The Economic Pattern of Colonial New York," *History of the State of New York*, II: 247-82; and "A Century of Labor," *ibid.*, II: 283-329.

NEU, IRENE D.: "The Iron Plantations of Colonial New York," *New York History*, XXXIII (1952), 3-24.

ROACH, GEORGE W.: "Colonial Highways in the Upper Hudson Valley," *ibid.*, XL (1959), 93-116.

SACHS, WILLIAM S.: "Interurban Correspondents and the Development of a National Economy before the Revolution: New York as a Case Study," *ibid.*, XXXVI (1955), 320-35.

5. Social

ALEXANDER, EDWARD PORTER: "The Provincial Aristocracy and the Land," *History of the State of New York*, III: 145-64.

BURR, NELSON R.: "The Episcopal Church and the Dutch in Colonial New York and New Jersey, 1664-1784," *Historical Magazine of the Protestant Episcopal Church*, XIX (1950), 90-111.

GRINSTEIN, HYMAN BOGOMOLNY: *The Rise of the Jewish Community in New York, 1654-1860* (Philadelphia, 1945).

HAAR, CHARLES M.: "White Indentured Servants in Colonial New York," *Americana*, XXXIV (1940), 370-92.

HAMILTON, MILTON W.: "The Library of Sir William Johnson," New York Historical Society, *Quarterly*, XL (1952), 208-51.

HAMLIN, PAUL M.: *Legal Education in Colonial New York* (New York, 1939).

KEMP, WILLIAM WEBB: *The Support of Schools in Colonial New York by the Society for the Propagation of the Gospel in Foreign Parts*, Columbia University Teachers College, *Contributions to Education*, No. 56 (New York, 1913).

KLINGBERG, FRANK JOSEPH: *Anglican Humanitarianism in Colonial New York* (Philadelphia, 1940).

KRAUS, MICHAEL: "Social Classes and Customs [in New York]," *History of the State of New York*, II: 375-412.

MC KEE, SAMUEL, JR.: *Labor in Colonial New York, 1664-1776*, Columbia University, *Studies in History, Economics, and Public Law*, No. 410 (London & New York, 1935).

MC MANUS, EDGAR J.: *A History of Negro Slavery in New York* (Syracuse, N.Y., 1966).

MARK, IRVING: *Agrarian Conflicts in Colonial New York, 1711-1775*, Columbia University, *Studies in History, Economics, and Public Law*, No. 469 (London & New York, 1940).

MORRIS, RICHARD B.: "Criminal Conspiracy and Early Labor Combinations in New York," *Political Science Quarterly*, LII (1937), 51-85.

SCHUYLER, MONTGOMERY: *The Patroons and Lords of Manors of the Hudson,* Order of Colonial Lords of Manors in America, *Publications,* No. 23 (New York, 1932).

SHEARER, AUGUSTUS H.: "The Church, the School, and the Press," *History of the State of New York,* III: 45-90.

6. Biographical

ALLEN, ETHAN. *Ethan Allen* by John Pell (Boston & New York, 1929). See also Darline Shapiro's "Ethan Allen: Philosopher-Theologian to a Generation of American Revolutionaries," *William and Mary Quarterly,* 3rd ser., XXI (1964), 236-55.

ALLEN, IRA. *Ira Allen: Founder of Vermont, 1751-1814* by James B. Wilbur (2 vols., Boston & New York, 1928).

Beekman Family. *The Beekmans of New York in Politics and Commerce, 1647-1877* by Philip L. White (New York, 1956). See also Bernard Bailyn's review article: "The Beekmans of New York: Trade, Politics, and Families . . . ," *William and Mary Quarterly,* 3rd ser., XIV (1957), 598-608.

COLDEN, CADWALLADER. *Cadwallader Colden: A Representative Eighteenth Century Official* by Alice Mapelsden Keys (New York, 1906). See also the article by F. L. Engleman: "Cadwallader Colden and the New York Stamp Act Riots," *William and Mary Quarterly,* 3rd ser., X (1953), 560-78, and that by Brooke Hindle: "A Colonial Governor's Family: The Coldens of Coldengham," New York Historical Society, *Quarterly,* XLV (1961), 233-50.

CHARLES, ROBERT. "Robert Charles: New York Agent, 1748-1770" by Nicholas Varga, *William and Mary Quarterly,* 3rd ser., XVIII (1961), 211-35.

DUANE, JAMES. *A Revolutionary Conservative: James Duane of New York* by Edward P. Alexander (New York, 1938).

GOMEZ, DANIEL. "Daniel Gomez: A Pioneer Merchant of Early New York" by Leon Huhner, American Jewish Historical Society, *Publications,* XLI (1951), 107-25.

HAMILTON, ALEXANDER. Among the biographies of Hamilton are the following: *Life of Alexander Hamilton* by John Church Hamilton (2 vols., New York, 1834-40); *The Life of Alexander Hamilton* by John Torrey Morse (2 vols., New York, 1876); *Alexander Hamilton* by Henry Cabot Lodge in *The American Statesman* series (New York, 1882); and lives by F. S. Oliver (London, 1906) and by Nathan Schachner (New York, 1946); even more recently has appeared *Alexander Hamilton: Portrait in Paradox* by John C. Miller (New York, 1959), and, most appropriate for the purpose of this bibliography, "Alexander Hamilton's Early Years in the American

Colonies" by Foster C. Nix, *William and Mary Quarterly*, 3rd ser., XXI (1964), 390-407.

JOHNSON, SAMUEL. *Samuel Johnson, President of King's College: His Career and Writings* . . . by Herbert and Carol Schneider (4 vols., New York, 1929). Volume I contains his autobiography and letters.

JOHNSON, WILLIAM. "Myths and Legends of Sir William Johnson" by Milton Wheaton Hamilton, *New York History*, XXXIV (1953), 3-29. See also under Indian Relations, Biographical.

KEMPE, JOHN TABOR. "The American Dream: John Tabor Kempe's Rise from Poverty to Riches" by Catherine Snell Crary, *William and Mary Quarterly*, 3rd ser., XIV (1957), 176-95.

KENNEDY, ARCHIBALD. "Captain Kennedy and the Stamp Act" by Neil R. Stout, *New York History*, XLV (1964), 44-58.

LIVINGSTON, ROBERT R. *Chancellor Robert R. Livingston of New York, 1746-1813* by George Dangerfield (New York, 1960).

LIVINGSTON, WILLIAM. *The New York Triumvirate: A Study of the Legal and Political Careers of William Livingston, John Morin Scott, William Smith, Jr.* by Dorothy Dillon, Columbia University, *Studies in History, Economics, and Public Law*, No. 548 (New York, 1949), and the article by Milton M. Klein: "The Rise of the New York Bar: The Legal Career of William Livingston," *William and Mary Quarterly*, 3rd ser., XV (1958), 334-58.

Livingston Family. *The Livingstons of Livingston Manor: Being the History of That Branch of the Scottish House of Callendar Which Settled in the English Province of New York* . . . by Edwin Brockholst Livingston (New York, 1910).

MC ADAM, JOHN LOUDON. "John Loudon McAdam in Revolutionary New York" by Robert H. Spiro, Jr., New York Historical Society, *Quarterly*, XL (1956), 28-54.

OSBORNE, DANVERS. "In Flocks, Like Ill-Boding Ravens: Being an Account of the Tragic End of Sir Danvers Osborne, Bart." by Wayne Andrews, *ibid.*, XXXV (1951), 405-7; and "Sir Danvers Osborne and Sir James Hardy, 1753-1761" by James Grant Wilson, *Memorial History of the City of New York and the Hudson River Valley*, II: 287-324.

RIVINGTON, JAMES. "The Tory and the Spy: The Double Life of James Rivington" by Catherine Snell Crary, *William and Mary Quarterly*, 3rd ser., XVI (1959), 61-72; "James Rivington, Tory Printer" by Leroy Hewlett, *Books in America's Past* (David Kaser, ed., Charlottesville, Va., 1966), 166-93; and "James Rivington, the Tory Printer: A Study of the Loyalist Pamphlets of the Revolution" by George H. Sargent, *American Collector*, II (1926), 336-41.

SCHUYLER, PHILIP. *Life of General Philip Schuyler, 1733-1804* by Bayard Tuckerman (New York, 1903), and Don R. Gerlach's *Philip Schuyler and the American Revolution in New York, 1733-1777*

(Lincoln, Neb., 1964). See also, Gerlach's "Philip Schuyler and 'The Road to Glory': A Question of Loyalty and Competence," New York Historical Society, *Quarterly*, XLIV (1965), 341-86.

SCOTT, JOHN MORIN. *See* under Livingston, William.

SEABURY, SAMUEL. *Samuel Seabury: Priest and Physician, Bishop of Connecticut* by Herbert Thomas (Hamden, Conn., 1963).

SEARS, ISAAC. " 'King' Sears, the Mob, and Freedom of the Press in New York, 1765-76" by Dwight L. Teeter, *Journalism Quarterly*, XLI (1964), 539-44.

SMITH, WILLIAM. "William Smith—The Historian" by Maturin L. Delafield, *Magazine of American History*, VI (1881), 418-39, and "William Smith, the Historian of New York" by Roger Andrew Wines, *New York History*, XL (1959), 3-17. See also under Livingston, William.

7. Military and naval

BUFFINGTON, WILLIAM H.: "The Colonial Wars and Their Results," *History of the State of New York*, II: 201-46.

CHAMPAGNE, ROGER: "The Military Association of the Sons of Liberty," New York Historical Society, *Quarterly*, XLI (1957), 338-50.

COOLIDGE, GUY CAMERON: "The French Occupation of the Champlain Valley, 1609-1759," Vermont Historical Society, *Proceedings*, n. ser., VI (1938), 143-313.

FISH, STUYVESANT: *The New York Privateers, 1756-1763* . . . (New York, 1945).

HAMILTON, MILTON W.: "Battle Report: General William Johnson's Letter to the Governors, Lake George, September 9-10, 1755," American Antiquarian Society, *Proceedings*, n. ser., LXXIV (1964), 19-36; and "Hero of Lake George: Johnson or Lyman?" *New England Quarterly*, XXXVI (1963), 371-82.

ISRAEL, FRED L.: "New York's Citizen Soldiers: The Militia and Their Armories," *New York History*, LIX (1961), 145-56.

THAYER, THEODORE: "The Army Contractors for the Niagara Campaign, 1755-1756," *William and Mary Quarterly*, 3rd ser., XIV (1957), 31-46.

D. MAPS

ANDREWS, P., sculp.: *A Plan of Fort Ontario*. In [John and] Ann Rocque: *A Set of Plans and Forts in America* . . . ([London], 1765), No. 8.

BARBER, J., sculp.: *The Country Twenty Five Miles round New York* . . . ([London], 1776).

BRASSIER, WILLIAM: *A Survey of Lake Champlain, Including Lake George, Crown Point and St. John. Surveyed by Order of Major-Gen. Sr. Jeffery Amherst* [1762]. In Jefferys: *The American Atlas* . . . (London, 1776), No. 18; and in *American Maps*, II: No. 24 and VI: No. 12.

A Chorographical Map of the Northern Department of North America. Drawn from the Latest and Most Accurate Observations. This map lays down the various grants made by the provinces of New Hampshire and New York in what is now the state of Vermont. In E. B. O'Callaghan: *Documentary History of the State of New York*, IV: opp. p. 331.

JOHNSON, GUY: *To His Excellency William Tryon, Esq., Captain General and Governor in Chief of the Province of New-York, etc.: This Map of the Country of the VI Nations Proper with Part of the Adjacent Colonies Is Humbly Inscribed.* . . . In E. B. O'Callaghan: *Documentary History of the State of New York*, IV: 661.

KITCHIN, THOMAS, engr.: *Communication between Albany and Oswego.* In Thomas Mante: *History of the Late War in North-America* . . . (London, 1772), p. 61.

———, engr.: *A Plan of Fort Edward and Its Environs on Hudsons River.* In *ibid.*, p. 34.

———: *A Map of the Eastern Part of the Province of New York with Part of New Jersey, etc.* ([London, 1756]). In the *London Magazine*, XXV (1756), p. 416.

LODGE, J., engr.: *Lake George, Etc.* In Thomas Mante: *History of the Late War in North America* . . . (London, 1772), opp. p. 33.

MAERSCHALCK, F., engr.: *A Plan of the City of New York from an Actual Survey, anno domini 1755* ([New York, 1755]). The map was done by the then city surveyor and engraved by G. Duyckinsk and is known by the name of the engraver. It appears as a frontispiece in [H. W. Dunshee]: *History of the Collegiate Reformed Church in the City of New York* . . . (New York, 1883).

A Map of the Country between Crown Point and Fort Edward. In the *Gentleman's Magazine*, XXIX (1759), 204.

Map of the French and English Grants on Lake Champlain. A modern map in O'Callaghan: *Documentary History of the State of New York*, I: opp. p. 368.

A Map of the Province of New York, with Part of Pensilvania and New England, from an Actual Survey by Captain Montresor, 1775 (London, 1775). In William Faden: *The North American Atlas* (London, 1777), No. 13; also in *American Maps*, I: No. 24, V: Nos. 17-18, and VI: Nos. 6-7.

MONTRÉSOR, JOHN: *A Plan of the City of New York and Its Environs to Greenwich on the North or Hudson River, and to Crown Point on the East or Sound River, Shewing the Several Streets, Public*

Buildings [Etc.] . . . ([London, 1766]). P. Andrews was the sculptor. In Jefferys: *A General Topography of North America and the West Indies* . . . , No. 35.

Outline of the Mohawk River and Wood Creek, Shewing the Relative Position of Fort Bull, Fort Williams, and the German Flats. A modern map in O'Callaghan: *Documentary History of the State of New York,* I: opp. p. 329.

A Particular Plan of Lake George: Surveyed in 1756 by Capt. Jackson (London, 1776). In Jefferys: *The American Atlas,* No. 18, an inset.

Plan of the City of Albany about the Year 1770: From the Original Survey by Robt. Yates. . . . In O'Callaghan: *Documentary History of the State of New York,* III: opp. p. 697.

A Plan of the City of Albany. In [John and] Ann Rocque: *A Set of Plans and Forts in America* . . . , No. 5.

A Plan of the City of New York (London, 1776). In Jefferys' *The American Atlas,* No. 17, inset.

RATZER, BERNARD, with THOMAS KITCHIN, sculp.: *Plan of the City of New York in North America, Surveyed 1766 and 1767. To His Excellency Sir Henry Moore, Bart., Captain General and Governor in Chief in and Over His Majesty's Province of New York, This Plan of the City of New York and Its Environs Is Most Humbly Dedicated* . . . ([London], 1776). In Faden: *The North American Atlas,* Nos. 20-1.

ROCQUE, JOHN, sculp.: *Plan of Fort Frederick at Albany.* In [John and] Ann Rocque: *A Set of Plans and Forts in America* . . . , No. 13.

————: *A Plan of the Fort at Saratoga.* In *ibid.,* No. 19.

SAUTHIER, CLAUDE JOSEPH: *A Chorographical Map of the Province of New York in North America Divided into Counties, Manors, Patents, and Townships* . . . (London, 1779). This map was dedicated to Governor William Tryon and is reprinted in O'Callaghan: *Documentary History of the State of New York,* I: opp. p. 526.

————: *A Topographical Map of Hudsons River . . . and the Country Adjacent, from Sandy Hook, New York and Bay to Fort Edward. Also the Communication with Canada by Lake George and Lake Champlain* . . . (London, 1777). The map was engraved by William Faden and appears in his *North American Atlas,* No. 15, as well as in Jefferys: *The American Atlas* . . . , No. 17a.

Topographical Map of the Country between the Mohawk River and Wood Creek, from an Actual Survey Taken in November 1758. . . . In O'Callaghan: *Documentary History of the State of New York,* IV: opp. p. 324. This map shows Fort Stanwix and the surrounding country.

Special note should be given to I. N. P. Stokes: *The Iconography of Manhattan Island* . . . (6 vols., New York, 1915-1928). This series contains a most unusual collection of reproduced maps, plans, views. etc.

NEWFOUNDLAND

Although not a part of North America, geographically, it is here treated, as is Cape Breton Island, as a part of the Continent. Labrador was attached to Newfoundland from 1763 to 1774.

A. BIBLIOGRAPHICAL AIDS

TROTTER, REGINALD GEORGE: "Bibliography," *The Cambridge History of the British Empire, VI: Canada and Newfoundland* (Cambridge, Eng., 1930), pp. 880-5.

B. PRINTED SOURCE MATERIALS

CHABERT, JOSEPH BERNARD, MARQUIS DE: *Voyage Fait par Ordre du Roi en 1750 et 1751, dans l'Amérique . . . de l'Île Royale & de l'Isle de Terre-Neuve, et Pour en Fixer les Principaux Points par des Observations Astronomiques* (Paris, 1753; rep., New York, 1966).

[DOUGLASS, WILLIAM]: *Considerations on the State of the British Fisheries in America and Their Consequence to Great Britain . . .* (London, 1745).

EARNSHAW, JAMES: *An Abstract of Various Penal and Other Statutes Relating to the Revenue of Customs . . . Together with the Laws . . . Relating to the Southern, Greenland, and Newfoundland Fisheries . . .* (2 vols., London, 1793-9).

In the Privy Council: In the Matter of the Boundary between the Dominion of Canada and the Colony of Newfoundland . . . (12 vols., London, 1928), Pt. 9, Vol. IV: *Documents Relating to the History of Newfoundland.*

MASSIE, JOSEPH: *An Historical Account of the Naval Power of France . . . with a State of English Fisheries in Newfoundland . . .* (London [1763]). First printed in 1712.

MILES, WILLIAM AUGUSTUS: *Remarks on an Act of Parliament . . . Intitled "An Act for the Encouragement of the Fisheries Carried on from Great Britain, Ireland, &c. to Newfoundland, &c. . . [with the] State of the Fishery in 1771* (London, 1779).

Official Copy of Orders from Governor Palliser for the Protection of the Fishery and Trade of Newfoundland on the Coast of Labrador (n.p., 1765).

Papers Relating to Newfoundland (London, 1793). This important body
of papers contains Board of Trade representations and other documents bearing upon them.

*Three Reports from the Select Committee [of the House of Commons]
on the State of the Trade of Newfoundland* [1696-1800], *The
Report of the House of Commons of 1793* (London, 1793).

WILLIAMS, GRIFFITH: *An Account of the Island of Newfoundland: With
the Nature of Its Trade and Method of Carrying on the Fishery
. . . To Which Is Annexed a Plan to Exclude the French from That
Trade . . .* ([London], 1765).

C. SECONDARY WORKS

1. General

HATTON, JOSEPH, and M. HARVEY: *Newfoundland: Its History, Its Present
Condition, and Its Prospects in the Future* (rev., cor. & enl. edn.,
Boston, 1883).

KERR, W. B.: "Newfoundland in the Period before the American Revolution," *Pennsylvania Magazine of History and Biography*, LXV
(1941), 56-78.

PAGE, F. R.: *A Concise History and Description of Newfoundland* (London, 1860).

PEDLEY, CHARLES: *History of Newfoundland . . . to 1860* (London, 1863).

PROWSE, DANIEL WOODLEY: *A History of Newfoundland from English,
Colonial, and Foreign Records* (London, 1895; 2nd edn., rev. &
cor., 1896).

ROGERS, J. D.: *Newfoundland, Historical Geography of the British Colonies* (Charles Lucas, ed., 7 vols. in 11, Oxford, 1898-1920), V, Pt.
IV.

ROTHNEY, G. O.: *Newfoundland: From International Fishery to Canadian
Province*, Canadian Historical Association, *Booklets*, No. 10 (Ottawa, 1959).

SMITH, F. E.: *The Story of Newfoundland.* (1st edn., London, 1901; n.
edn., 1920).

THOMPSON, FREDERIC F.: *The French Shore Problem in Newfoundland:
An Imperial Study* (Toronto, 1961).

2. Political

ANSPACH, LEWIS AMADEUS: *Summary of the Laws of Commerce and Navigation Adapted to the Present State, Government, and Trade of
the Island of Newfoundland* (London, 1809).

ISHAM, CHARLES: *The Fishery Question: its Origin, History, and Present Situation . . . , Questions of the Day*, XLI (New York, 1887).

REEVES, JOHN: *History of the Government of the Island of Newfoundland: With an Appendix Containing the Acts of Parliament Made Respecting the Trade and Fishery* (London, 1793; rep., New York, 1966).

3. Economic

INNIS, HAROLD A.: *The Cod Fisheries: The History of an International Economy* (New Haven, Conn., 1940; Toronto, 1954).

IRVINE, DALLAS D.: "The Newfoundland Fishery: A French Objective in the War of American Independence," *Canadian Historical Review*, XIII (1932), 268-84.

LOUNSBURY, RALPH GREENLEE: *The British Fishery at Newfoundland, 1634-1763, Yale Historical Publications: Miscellany*, XXVII (London & New Haven, Conn., 1934).

4. Social

CHRISTENSEN, RUTH M.: "The Establishment of S.P.G. Missions in Newfoundland, 1703-1783," *Historical Magazine of the Protestant Episcopal Church*, XX (1951), 207-29.

FAY, CHARLES RYLE: *Life and Labour in Newfoundland* (Toronto & Cambridge, Eng., 1956).

HOWLEY, MICHAEL FRANCIS: *Ecclesiastical History of Newfoundland* (Boston, 1881).

LANGTRY, JOHN: *History of the Church in Eastern Canada and Newfoundland, Colonial Church Histories* (London, 1892).

D. MAPS

BOWEN, EMANUEL: *A New & Accurate Map of the Islands of Newfoundland, Cape Breton, St. John, and Anticosta.* . . . In Bowen: *A Complete Atlas*, No. 63.

Carte des Isles de Miquelon et de St. Pierre et la Coste de Terre-Neuve Voisine. In Bellin: *Le Petit Atlas Maritime . . .* , I: No. 16.

Carte du Havre de Saint Jean dans l'Isle de Terre-Neuve. In Bellin: *Le Petit Atlas Maritime . . .* , I: No. 21.

COOK, JAMES: *Chart of Part of the South Coast of Newfoundland . . . from Surveys Made by Commodore Palliser* (London, 1766). In *The North American Pilot*, No. 9.

———: *A Chart of the Straights of Belleisle with Part of . . . Newfound-*

land and Labradore . . . from Actual Surveys . . . in 1766. In *ibid.,* No. 20.

————, and MICHAEL LANE: *A General Chart of the Island of Newfoundland with the Rocks and Soundings, Drawn from Surveys . . .* [*1775*]. In Jefferys: *The American Atlas,* No. 12.

GANDY, JOHN: *A Chart Shewing Part of the Seacoast of New Foundland from ye Bay of Bulls to Little Placentia.* In *The English Pilot,* p. 14.

GIBSON, JOHN, sculp.: *A New and Correct Map of the Isles of Newfoundland, Cape Breton, &c., with the Province of Nova Scotia.* In *The American Gazetteer* (London, 1762), Vol. III.

JEFFERYS, THOMAS: *A Chart of the Banks of Newfoundland, Drawn from a Great Number of . . . Surveys, Chiefly from Those of Chabert, Cook, and Fleurieu. . . .* In Jefferys: *The American Atlas . . . ,* No. 13.

KITCHIN, THOMAS: *A New Map of the Only Useful and Frequented Part of New Foundland.* In the *London Magazine,* XXXI (1762), opp. p. 408.

LANE, MICHAEL: *A Chart of Part of the Coast of Labrador from Cape Charles to Sandwich Bay.* [1770 and 1771]. In Faden: *The North American Atlas . . . ,* No. 2.

A New and Correct Chart of the Coast of New Foundland from Cape Raze to Cape Bonaviste, With Chebucto Harbour in Nova Scotia. In *The English Pilot,* p. 11.

NORTH CAROLINA

A. BIBLIOGRAPHICAL AIDS

BOYD, WILLIAM K., and J. G. DE ROULHAC HAMILTON: *A Syllabus of North Carolina History, 1584-1876* (Durham, N.C., 1913).

CRITTENDEN, CHARLES CHRISTOPHER, and DAN LACY, eds.: *The Historical Records of North Carolina: The County Records, North Carolina Historical Records Survey* (3 vols., Raleigh, N.C., 1938-9).

HASSE, ADELAIDE R.: "North Carolina, 1663-1789," in "Materials for a Bibliography of the Public Archives of the Thirteen Original States . . . ," American Historical Association, *Annual Report, 1906* (2 vols., Washington, D.C., 1908), II, 507-27.

JONES, HOUSTON GWYNNE: *For History's Sake: The Preservation and Publication of North Carolina History, 1663-1903* (Chapel Hill, N.C. [1966]).

LEFLER, HUGH TALMADGE: *A Guide to the Study and Reading of North Carolina History* (Chapel Hill, N.C., 1955).

MC MURTRIE, DOUGLAS C.: *Eighteenth Century North Carolina Imprints, 1749-1800* (Chapel Hill, N.C., 1938). Much of what appeared in this book had been published in the *North Carolina Historical Review* in 1936. See also William S. Powell's "Eighteenth-Century North Carolina Imprints: A Revision and Supplement to McMurtrie," *North Carolina Historical Review*, XXXV (1958), 50-73.

THORNTON, MARY L.: *Official Publications of the Colony and State of North Carolina, 1749-1939: A Bibliography* (Chapel Hill, N.C., 1954).

———: *A Bibliography of North Carolina, 1589-1956* (Chapel Hill, N.C., 1958).

B. PRINTED SOURCE MATERIALS

1. Government and related documents

Acts of Assembly of the Province of North Carolina (New Bern, N.C., 1765).

A Collection of All the Public Acts of Assembly of the Province of North-Carolina: Now in Force and Use . . . (New Bern, N.C., 1751; another issue, 1752). According to Evans, this was the first book published in North Carolina. Also, printed by the same printer, James Davis, is *A Collection of All the Acts of Assembly of the Province of North-Carolina, in Force and Use since the Revisal of the Laws in the Year 1751* . . . (New Bern, N.C., 1764).

A Complete Revisal of All the Acts of Assembly, of the Province of North-Carolina now in Force and Use . . . (New Bern, N.C., 1773).

The Journal of the House of Burgesses, of the Province of North Carolina [Sept. 26-Oct. 18] 1749 . . . (New Bern, N.C., 1749; rep., with an introduction by William S. Powell, Raleigh, N.C., 1949, 1958). The first known North Carolina imprint published by James Davis, reproduced in facsimile in celebration of the two hundreth anniversary of the establishment of the printing press in the colony.

The Journal of the Proceedings of the Provincial Congress of North-Carolina . . . (copies issued for the sessions of 1775 and 1776, New Bern, N.C., 1775-6 and reprinted at Raleigh in 1831).

SAUNDERS, WILLIAM L., WALTER CLARK, and STEPHEN B. WEEKS, eds.: *Colonial and State Records of North Carolina* (30 vols., Raleigh, Winston, Goldsboro, & Charlotte, N. C., 1886-1914). *The Colonial Records* comprise volumes I-X of the series and were edited by W. L.

Saunders; the last four volumes edited by Stephen B. Weeks form an *Index to the Colonial and State records of North Carolina, Covering Volumes I-XXV* (4 vols., Charlotte, Goldsboro, & Raleigh, N. C., 1909-14). Volumes IV-X cover the period 1734-1776.

2. Non-official contemporary writings

BOYD, WILLIAM K., ed.: *Some Eighteenth Century Tracts Concerning North Carolina* (Raleigh, N. C., 1927); reprinted from the *North Carolina Historical Review*, II (1925)-IV (1927), *passim*.

CORBITT, D. L., ed.: "Historical Notes [Letters to newspapers on Governor Tryon]," *North Carolina Historical Review*, III (1926), 477-505.

FRIES, ADELAIDE L., ed.: *Records of the Moravians in North Carolina* (6 vols., Raleigh, N. C., 1922-43).

HENDERSON, ARCHIBALD, ed.: "An Interesting Colonial Document," *Virginia Magazine of History and Biography*, XXVIII (1920), 54-7. Prints the purported Mecklenberg Declaration of Independence of 29 July 1774.

———, ed.: "The Origin of the Regulation in North Carolina," *American Historical Review*, XXI (1915-16), 320-32. Prints two documents relating to the Regulators.

HILL, J. H., ed.: *Reminiscences and Memoirs of North Carolina* (4 pts., Washington, D.C. & Columbus, O., 1883-4).

HUSBAND, HERMAN: *Some Remarks on Religion: With the Author's Experience in Pursuit thereof* . . . (Philadelphia, 1761; rep. in Boyd: *Some Eighteenth Century Tracts* . . . , pp. 193-246). The work has value for an understanding both of the author and the times.

[———]: *An Impartial Relation of the First Rise and Cause of the Recent Differences in Publick Affairs in the Province of North-Carolina and of the Past Tumults and Riots that Lately Happened in That Province* . . . (n. p., 1770). See also his supplementary volume, *A Continuation of the Impartial Relation* . . . (n. p., 1770) and *A Fan for Fanning and a Touch-stone to Tryon: Containing an Impartial Account of the Rise and Progress of the so Much Talked of Regulation in North-Carolina* (Boston, 1771), signed "Regulus."

Information Concerning the Province of North Carolina Addressed to Emmigrants from the Highlands and Western Isles of Scotland: By an Impartial Hand (Glasgow, 1773). Signed "Scotus Americanus."

IREDELL, JAMES. *Life and Correspondence of James Iredell* . . . by Griffith J. McRee (2 vols., New York, 1857-8; rep., 1 vol., 1949).

MICKLEJOHN, GEORGE: *On the Important Duty of Subjection to the Civil Powers: A Sermon Preached before* . . . *the Troops Raised to Quell the Late Insurrection* . . . (New Bern, N. C., 1768; rep. in Boyd's *Some Eighteenth Century Tracts* . . . , pp. 393-412). Reprinted as "A Sermon by Rev. George Micklejohn Preached before Governor

Tryon's Army at Hillsborough, September 25, 1768," R. D. W. Connor, ed., *North Carolina Booklet,* VIII (1908), 57-78.

PRICE, JONATHAN: *A Description of Occacock Inlet* . . . (Newbern, N. C., 1795). Reprinted in the *North Carolina Historical Review,* III (1926), 624-33, with D. L. Corbitt as editor.

TRYON, WILLIAM: "Tryon's 'Book' on North Carolina [1765]," William S. Powell, ed., *North Carolina Historical Review,* XXXIV (1957), 406-15.

WHEELER, JOHN H., ed.: *Historical Sketches of North Carolina from 1584 to 1851: Compiled from Original Records, Official Documents and Traditional Statements* . . . (Philadelphia, 1851).

3. Newspapers

The Cape Fear Mercury, 1769-1775, Wilmington.
The North-Carolina Gazette, 1751-1759, New Bern.
The North-Carolina Gazette, 1768-1778, New Bern.
The North-Carolina Gazette and Weekly Post-Boy [The North-Carolina Gazette], 1764-1766, Wilmington.
The North-Carolina Magazine: or, Universal Intelligencer, 1764-1768, New Bern.

For information regarding microfilmed newspapers, see H. G. Jones and Julius H. Avant, eds.: *North Carolina Newspapers on Microfilm: A Checklist of Early North Carolina Newspapers Available on Microfilm from the State Department of Archives and History* (3rd edn., Raleigh, N. C., 1965).

C. SECONDARY WORKS

1. General

ASHE, SAMUEL A'COURT: *History of North Carolina* (2 vols., Greensboro, N. C., 1908).

CONNOR, ROBERT D. W.: *History of North Carolina, Vol. I: The Colonial and Revolutionary Periods, 1584-1783* (Chicago & New York, 1919).

COULTER, ELLIS MERTON: "The Granville District," *James Sprunt Historical Publications,* XIII (1913), 33-56. Account of the refusal of John Lord Carteret, Earl of Granville, to relinquish his land grant to the Crown.

CRITTENDEN, CHARLES CHRISTOPHER: "The Sea Coast in North Carolina History, 1763-1789," *North Carolina Historical Review,* VII (1930), 433-42.

FOOTE, WILLIAM HENRY: *Sketches of North Carolina: Historical and Biographical* . . . (New York, 1846).

HUNTER, C. L.: *Sketches of Western North Carolina, Historical and Biographical: Illustrating Principally the Revolutionary Period . . .* (Raleigh, N. C., 1877).

JONES, JOSEPH SEAWELL: *A Defense of the Revolutionary History of the State of North Carolina from the Aspersions of Mr. Jefferson* (Boston & Raleigh, N. C., 1834).

LEFLER, HUGH T., and ALBERT RAY NEWSOME: *North Carolina: The History of a Southern State* (Chapel Hill, N. C., 1954).

MARTIN, FRANÇOIS-XAVIER: *The History of North Carolina from the Earliest Period* (2 vols., New Orleans, La., 1829).

MERRENS, HARRY ROY: *Colonial North Carolina in the Eighteenth Century: a Study in Historical Geography* (Chapel Hill, N. C., 1964).

MOORE, JOHN W.: *History of North Carolina: From the Earliest Discoveries to the Present Time* (2 vols., Raleigh, N. C., 1880).

SIKES, ENOCH WALTER: "The Transition of North Carolina from Colony to Commonwealth," Johns Hopkins University, *Studies in Historical and Political Science*, 16th ser. (1898), 477-561.

STICK, DAVID: *Graveyard of the Atlantic: Shipwrecks of the North Carolina Coast* (Chapel Hill, N. C., 1952).

2. Local

BRAWLEY, JAMES S.: *The Rowan Story, 1753-1953: A Narrative History of Rowan County, North Carolina* (Salisbury, N. C., 1953).

DILL, ALONZO THOMAS, JR.: "Eighteenth Century New Bern: A History of the Town and Craven County, 1700-1800," *North Carolina Historical Review*, XXII (1945), XXIII (1946), passim.

LEE, E. LAWRENCE: *The Lower Cape Fear in Colonial Days* (Chapel Hill, N. C., 1965), and "Old Brunswick: The Story of a Colonial Town," *North Carolina Historical Review*, XXIX (1952), 230-45.

LEFLER, HUGH T., and PAUL WAGER, eds.: *Orange County, 1752-1952* (Chapel Hill, N. C., 1953).

SPRUNT, JAMES: *Chronicles of the Cape Fear River . . .* (Raleigh, N. C., 1914; 2nd edn., 1916).

STICK, DAVID: *The Outer Banks of North Carolina, 1584-1958* (Chapel Hill, N. C., 1958).

TURNER, JOSEPH KELLY, and JOHN LUTHER BRIDGES, JR.: *History of Edgecombe County, North Carolina* (Raleigh, N. C., 1920).

3. Political

BASSETT, JOHN: "The Regulators of North Carolina, 1765-71," American Historical Association, *Annual Report, 1894* (Washington, D. C., 1895), pp. 141-212.

BOYD, JULIAN P.: "The Sheriff in Colonial North Carolina," *North Carolina Historical Review*, V (1928), 151-80.

DE MOND, ROBERT O.: *The Loyalists in North Carolina during the Revolution* (Durham, N. C., 1940).

DILL, ALONZO THOMAS, JR.: *Governor Tryon and His Palace* (Chapel Hill, N. C. [1955]). Also by Dill: "Tryon's Palace: A Neglected Niche of North Carolina History," *North Carolina Historical Review*, XIX (1942), 119-67.

FORD, WORTHINGTON C.: "Dr. S. Millington Miller and the Mecklenburg Declaration," *American Historical Review*, XI (1905-6), 548-58.

FRIES, ADELAIDE L.: *The Mecklenburg Declaration of Independence: As Mentioned in Records of Wachovia* (Raleigh, N. C., 1907).

GRAHAM, GEORGE WASHINGTON: *The Mecklenburg Declaration of Independence, May 20, 1775, and Lives of Its Signers* (New York & Washington, D. C., 1905).

GREENE, JACK P.: "The North Carolina Lower House and the Power to Appoint Public Treasurers, 1711-1775," *North Carolina Historical Review*, XL (1963), 37-53.

HARRELL, ISAAC S.: "North Carolina Loyalists," *ibid.*, III (1926), 575-90.

HAYWOOD, C. ROBERT: "The Mind of North Carolina Opponents of the Stamp Act," *ibid.*, XXIX (1952), 317-43.

HENDERSON, ARCHIBALD: *Cradle of Liberty: Historical Essays Concerning the Mecklenburg Declaration of Independence, Mecklenburg County, North Carolina, May 20, 1775* (Charlotte, N. C., 1955).

HOYT, WILLIAM HENRY: *The Mecklenburg Declaration of Independence: A Study of Evidence Showing that the Alleged Early Declaration of Independence by Mecklenburg County, North Carolina, on May 20, 1775 Is Spurious* (London & New York, 1907). See also "The Mecklenberg Declaration Once More," *Magazine of History*, VI (1907), 135-54.

LEE, E. LAWRENCE: "Days of Defiance: Resistance to the Stamp Act in the Lower Cape Fear," *North Carolina Historical Review*, XLIII (1966), 186-202.

LONDON, LAWRENCE F.: "The Representation Controversy in Colonial North Carolina," *ibid.*, XI (1934), 255-70.

MC NITT, VIRGIL V.: *Chain of Error and the Mecklenburg Declarations of Independence: A New Study of Manuscripts: Their Use, Abuse, and Neglect* (New York & Palmer, Mass., 1960).

MOORE, JAMES HALL: *Defence of the Mecklenburg Declaration of Independence: An Exhaustive Review of and Answer to All Attacks on the Declaration* (Raleigh, N. C., 1908).

PARKER, CORALIE: *The History of Taxation in North Carolina during the Colonial Period, 1663-1776* (New York, 1928).

RAPER, CHARLES LEE: *North Carolina: A Study in English Colonial Government* (London & New York, 1904).

SALLEY, ALEXANDER SAMUEL, JR.: "The Mecklenburg Declaration: The Present Status of the Question," *American Historical Review,* XIII (1907-8), 16-43.

———: *The True Mecklenburg "Declaration of Independence"* (Columbia, S. C., 1905).

SCOTT, KENNETH: "Counterfeiting in Colonial North Carolina [1714-76]" *North Carolina Historical Review,* XXXIV (1957), 467-82.

SELLERS, CHARLES GRIER, JR.: "Making a Revolution: The North Carolina Whigs, 1765-1775," J. Carlyle Sitterson, ed., *Studies in Southern History in Memory of Albert Ray Newsome . . . , James Sprunt Studies in History and Political Science,* XXXIX (1957), 23-46.

SKAGGS, MARVIN L.: *North Carolina Boundary Disputes Involving Her Southern Line, James Sprunt Studies in History and Political Science,* XXV (Chapel Hill, N. C., 1941).

UBBELOHDE, CARL W., JR.: "The Vice-Admiralty Court of Royal North Carolina, 1729-1759," *North Carolina Historical Review,* XXXI (1954), 517-28.

WEIR, ROBERT M.: "North Carolina's Reaction to the Currency Act of 1764," *ibid.,* XL (1963), 183-99.

WHITAKER, BESSIE LEWIS: *The Provincial Council and Committees of Safety in North Carolina,* University of North Carolina: *James Sprunt Historical Monographs,* VIII (Chapel Hill, N. C., 1908).

4. Economic

CRITTENDEN, CHARLES CHRISTOPHER: *The Commerce of North Carolina, 1763-1789, Yale Historical Publications: Miscellany,* XXIX (New Haven, Conn., 1936). See also his articles: "Inland Navigation in North Carolina, 1763-1789," *North Carolina Historical Review,* VIII (1931), 145-54, and "Ships and Shipping in North Carolina, 1763-89," *ibid.,* VIII (1931), 1-13.

FRANKLIN, W. NEIL: "Agriculture in Colonial North Carolina," *North Carolina Historical Review,* III (1926), 539-74.

HAYWOOD, C. ROBERT: "The Mind of the North Carolina Advocates of Mercantilism," *ibid.,* XXXIII (1956), 139-65.

ROBERT, JOSEPH CLARKE: *see* under Virginia.

SELLERS, C. G., JR.: "Private Profits and British Colonial Policy: The Speculations of Henry McCulloh," *William and Mary Quarterly,* 3rd ser., VIII (1951), 535-51.

TILLEY, NANNIE MAY: "Industries of Colonial Granville County," *North Carolina Historical Review,* XIII (1936), 273-89.

WILLIAMS, JUSTIN: "English Mercantilism and Carolina Naval Stores, 1705-1776," *Journal of Southern History,* I (1935), 169-85.

5. Social

BALDWIN, ALICE M.: *see* under Virginia.

BASSETT, JOHN SPENCER: "Slavery and Servitude in the Colony of North Carolina," Johns Hopkins University, *Studies in Historical and Political Science*, 14th ser. (1896), 179-254. See also his "Some Phases of Early Plantation Life in North Carolina," *Trinity College Archive*, VI (1892), 98-103.

BLACKWELDER, RUTH: "Attitude of the North Carolina Moravians toward the American Revolution," *North Carolina Historical Review*, IX (1932), 1-21.

CLEWELL, JOHN HENRY: *History of Wachovia in North Carolina: The Unitas Fratrum or Moravian Church in North Carolina* . . . [1752-1902] (New York, 1902).

CLONTS, F. W.: "Travel and Transportation in Colonial North Carolina," *North Carolina Historical Review*, III (1926), 16-35.

CONKIN, PAUL: "The Church Establishment in North Carolina, 1765-1776," *ibid.*, XXXII (1955), 1-30.

CONNOR, R. D. W.: "The Genesis of Higher Education in North Carolina," *ibid.*, XXVIII (1951), 1-14.

CRITTENDEN, CHARLES CHRISTOPHER: "Means of Communication in North Carolina, 1763-1789," *ibid.*, VIII (1931), 373-83 and "Overland Travel and Transportation in North Carolina, 1763-1789," *ibid.*, pp. 239-57.

DUFFY, JOHN: "Eighteenth-Century Carolina Health Conditions," *Journal of Southern History*, XVIII (1952), 289-302.

ERVIN, SPENCER: "The Anglican Church in North Carolina," *Historical Magazine of the Protestant Episcopal Church*, XXV (1956), 102-61.

FRIES, ADELAIDE L.: "The Moravian Contribution to Colonial North Carolina," *North Carolina Historical Review*, VII (1930), 1-14.

GREEN, E. R. R.: "The Scotch-Irish and the Coming of the Revolution in North Carolina," *Irish Historical Studies*, VII (1950), 77-86.

HAYWOOD, MARSHALL DE LANCEY: "The Story of Queen's College or Liberty Hall in the Province of North Carolina," *North Carolina Booklet*, XI (1912), 169-175.

HOLDER, EDWARD M.: "Social Life of the Early Moravians in North Carolina," *North Carolina Historical Review*, XI (1934), 167-84.

HUDSON, ARTHUR PALMER: "Songs of the North Carolina Regulators," *William and Mary Quarterly*, 3rd ser., IV (1947), 470-85.

LEMMON, SARAH MC CULLOH: "The Genesis of the Protestant Episcopal Diocese of North Carolina, 1701-1823," *North Carolina Historical Review*, XXVIII (1951), 426-62.

MC MURTRIE, DOUGLAS C.: "The First Twelve Years of Printing in North Carolina, 1749-1760," *ibid.*, X (1933), 214-34.

MEYER, DUANE GILBERT: *The Highland Scots of North Carolina, 1732-1776* (Chapel Hill, N. C., 1961).

NOBLE, MARCUS CISCO STEPHENS: *A History of the Public Schools of North Carolina* (Chapel Hill, N. C., 1930).

OLIVER, DAVID D.: *The Society for the Propagation of the Gospel in the Province of North Carolina* (Raleigh, N. C., 1910).

PASCHAL, GEORGE WASHINGTON: *History of North Carolina Baptists* (Raleigh, N. C., 1930), I: 1663-1805.

RAMSAY, ROBERT W.: *Carolina Cradle: Settlement of the Northwest Carolina Frontier, 1747-1762* (Chapel Hill, N. C., 1964).

RAPER, CHARLES LEE: *The Church and Private Schools in North Carolina: A Historical Study* (Greensboro, N. C., 1898).

SMITH, CHARLES LEE: *The History of Education in North Carolina* (Washington, D.C., 1888).

TILLEY, NANNIE MAY: "The Settlement of Granville County," *North Carolina Historical Review*, XI (1934), 1-19.

6. Biographical

ASHE, SAMUEL A'COURT, STEPHEN B. WEEKS, and CHARLES L. VAN NOPPEN, eds.: *Biographical History of North Carolina from Colonial Times to the Present* (8 vols., Greensboro, N. C., 1905-17).

ALEXANDER, JOHN. "John Alexander, Anglican Missionary" by Thomas G. Parramore, *North Carolina Historical Review*, XLIII (1966), 305-15.

CALDWELL, DAVID. *A Sketch of the Life and Character of the Rev. David Caldwell, D.D. . . .* by Eli Washington Caruthers (Greensborough, N. C., 1842).

CASWELL, RICHARD. "The Training of Richard Caswell" by C. B. Alexander, *North Carolina Historical Review*, XXIII (1946), 13-31, and, also by Alexander, "Richard Caswell: Versatile Leader of the Revolution," *ibid.*, pp. 119-41.

DAVIDSON, WILLIAM LEE. *Piedmont Partisan: The Life and Times of Brigadier-General William Lee Davidson* by Chalmers Gaston Davidson (Davidson, N. C., 1951).

DAVIS, JAMES. "James Davis and the Beginning of the Newspaper in North Carolina [1751]" by Robert N. Elliott, Jr., *North Carolina Historical Review*, XLII (1965), 1-20.

DOBBS, ARTHUR. *Arthur Dobbs, Esquire, 1689-1765: Surveyor-General of Ireland, Prospector and Governor of North Carolina* by Desmond Clarke (Chapel Hill, N. C., 1957).

FEW, JAMES. "The First American Anarchist" by Arthur Dudley Vinton, *Magazine of American History with Notes and Queries*, XVI (1886), 443-5.

HUSBAND, HERMAN. *Herman Husband: A Story of His Life* . . . by Mary
Elinor Lazenby (Washington, D. C., 1940).

IREDELL, JAMES. See the article by Hampton L. Carson under James
Wilson (Pennsylvania).

MC CULLOH, HENRY. "Henry McCulloh: Progenitor of the Stamp Act" by
James High, *North Carolina Historical Review*, XXIX (1952), 24-
38, and "Henry McCulloch and Henry McCulloh" by John Cannon,
William and Mary Quarterly, 3rd ser., XV (1958), 71-3.

TRYON, WILLIAM. *Governor William Tryon and His Administration in the
Province of North Carolina, 1765-1771* . . . by Marshall De Lancey
Haywood (Raleigh, N. C., 1903).

WILLIAMSON, HUGH. *A Biographical Memoir of Hugh Williamson* . . . by
David Hosack (New York, 1820).

7. Military

COOKE, WILLIAM D.: "Battle of Alamance," *Revolutionary History of North
Carolina in Three Lectures* . . . (New York & Raleigh, N. C., 1853).

FRECH, LAURA PAGE: "The Wilmington Committee of Public Safety and
the Loyalist Rising of February, 1776," *North Carolina Historical
Review*, XLI (1964), 21-33

HAMER, P. M.: "Fort Loudoun in the Cherokee War, 1758-1761," *ibid.*, II
(1925), 442-58.

M'NEILLY, JAMES H.: "The Battle of the Alamance," *Confederate Veteran*,
XXIX (1921), 376-8.

SWAIN, DAVID L.: "The War of the Regulation," North Carolina University,
Magazine, IX (1859-60)-X (1860-1), *passim*.

WHEELER, E. MILTON: "Development and Organization of the North Carolina Militia," *North Carolina Historical Review*, XLI (1964), 307-
323.

D. MAPS

BAYLEY, I., engr.: *A Compleat Map of North Carolina from an Actual
Survey by Captain Collet, Governor of Fort Johnston* (London,
1770). Library of Congress Maps.

HYRNE, EDWARD: *A New and Exact Plan of Cape Fear River from the
Bar to Brunswick.* . . . In Jefferys: *A General Topography of North
America and the West Indies*, No. 63.

MACKAY, ARTHUR: *A Survey of the Coast about Cape Lookout in North
Carolina Taken the 29th of June, 1756* ([London, 1768]). In *ibid.*,
No. 58.

MOUZON, HENRY, *et al.*: *An Accurate Map of North and South Carolina
with Their Indian Frontiers . . . Mountains, Rivers, Swamps,*

Marshes, Bays, Creeks, Harbours, &c. . . . (London, 1775). In Jefferys: *The American Atlas,* Nos. 23-4; also in *American Maps,* I: No. 23, V: Nos. 25-6.

SAUTHIER, CLAUDE JOSEPH, sculp.: *A Plan of the Camp and Battle of Alamance, the 16th May 1771.* In Haywood's *Governor Tryon . . . ,* opp. p. 124.

THORNTON, JOHN, and WILLIAM FISHER: *A New Mapp of Carolina.* In *The English Pilot,* 4th Book, p. 26.

See also the Fry and Jefferson map cited under Virginia; Emanuel Bowen's *A New and Accurate Map of the Provinces of North and South Carolina, Georgia . . . ;* and Thomas Kitchin's *A New Map of North & South Carolina & Georgia,* cited under Chapter IV, D.

NOVA SCOTIA

A. BIBLIOGRAPHICAL AIDS

BREBNER, JOHN BARTLET: "Bibliography," *The Neutral Yankees of Nova Scotia . . . ,* pp. 367-75.

STEWART, SHEILA J., and D. C. MEDLEY: *A Catalogue of the [Thomas Beamish] Akins Collection of Books and Pamphlets,* Public Archives of Nova Scotia, *Publications,* No. 1 (Halifax, N. S., 1933).

B. PRINTED SOURCE MATERIALS

1. *Government and related documents*

"Acts of the Province of Nova Scotia, 1749-1753," Public Archives of Canada, *Report, 1913* (Arthur G. Doughty, ed., Ottawa, 1914), Appendix C.

AKINS, THOMAS BEAMISH, ed.: *Selections from the Public Documents of the Province of Nova Scotia [1714-68], Nova Scotia Archives,* Vol. I (Halifax, N. S., 1869).

BREBNER, JOHN BARTLET, ed.: "Nova Scotia's Remedy for the American Revolution," *Canadian Historical Review,* XV (1934), 171-81.

Extract from the Votes of the House of Assembly of the Province of Nova-Scotia Containing an Address, Petition, and Memorial to the King's Most Excellent Majesty . . . (Boston, 1775).

A Fair Representation of His Majesty's Right to Nova Scotia or Acadie briefly stated from the Memorials of the English Commissaries:

With an Answer to the Objections Contained in the French Memorials . . . (London, 1756). A defence by the English Commissioners against the French claims.

A Genuine Account of Nova Scotia . . . To Which is Added His Majesty's Proposals as an Encouragement to Those Who Are Willing to Settle There (London & Dublin, 1750).

HARVEY, D. C., ed.: "Governor Lawrence's Case Against an Assembly in Nova Scotia," *Canadian Historical Review*, XIII (1932), 184-94.

"Return of the Several Townships in the Province of Nova Scotia for the First Day of January, 1767," Nova Scotia Historical Society, *Collections*, VIII (1889-91), 45-71.

The Temporary Acts of the General Assemblies of His Majesty's Province of Nova Scotia [1750-1766] (Halifax, N. S., 1767; rev., 1784).

UNIACKE, RICHARD J., ed.: *Statutes at Large Passed in the Several General Assemblies Held in Nova Scotia from the First Assembly in 1758 to 1804, Inclusive* . . . (2 vols., Halifax, N. S., 1805-[24]).

2. *Non-official contemporary writings*

[JEFFERYS, THOMAS], ed.: *Remarks on the French Memorials Concerning the Limits of Acadia . . . To Which is Added An Answer to the Summary Discussion, etc.* . . . (London, 1756).

LE LOUTRE, JEAN LOUIS: "Une Autobiographie de l'abbé Le Loutre," Albert David, ed., *Nova Francia*, VI (1931), 1-34 and *The Career of the Abbé Le Loutre in Nova Scotia: With a Translation of His Autobiography* (John C. Webster, ed., Shediac, N. B., 1933).

OWEN, WILLIAM: "Narrative of American Voyages and Travels of Captain William Owen, R. N., and the Settlement of the Island of Campobello in the Bay of Fundy, 1766-1771," Victor Hugh Paltsits, ed., New York Public Library, *Bulletin*, XXXV (1931), *passim.*

PERKINS, SIMEON: *The Diary of Simeon Perkins, 1766-1780*, Champlain Society, *Publications*, XXIX (Harold A. Innis, ed., Toronto, 1948).

PICHON, THOMAS: *Lettres et Mémoires pour Servir à l'Histoire Naturelle, Civile, et Politique du Cap-Breton* . . . (The Hague, 1760; rep., New York, 1966); also published in an English translation (London, 1760). See also *Thomas Pichon, The Spy of Beauséjour . . . with Many Original Documents* by John Clarence Webster (Sackville, N. B., 1937). Alice Webster translated the documents contained in this volume.

SHORTT, ADAM, VICTOR KENNETH JOHNSTON, and GUSTAVE LANCTÔT, eds.: *Documents Relating to Currency, Exchange and Finance in Nova Scotia: With Prefatory Documents, 1675-1758* (Ottawa, 1933).

WEBSTER, JOHN CLARENCE, ed.: *Journals of Beauséjour: Diary of John Thomas [and] Journal of Louis de Courville* (Sackville, N. B., 1937).

WILLARD, ABIJAH: *Journal of Abijah Willard, 1755*, New Brunswick Historical Society, *Collections*, No. 13 (J. Clarence Webster, ed. [St. John,
N. B.], 1930). The journal was kept by Willard, a militia officer
from Lancaster, Mass., during the capture of Fort Beauséjour in
1755.

WINSLOW, JOHN: "Journal of Colonel John Winslow of the Provincial
Troops which Engaged in the Siege of Fort Beauséjour in the
Summer and Autumn of 1755," Nova Scotia Historical Society,
Collections, IV (1884), 113-246, and the continuation "The Journal
. . . While Engaged in Removing the Acadian French Inhabitants
from Grand Pré and Neighboring Settlements, in the Autumn of
the Year 1755," *ibid.*, III (1882-3), 71-196.

3. Contemporary pamphlets, tracts, and related materials

An Account of the Colony of Nova Scotia ([n. p., 1751]).

*An Account of the Present State of Nova-Scotia: In Two Letters to a
Noble Lord* . . . (London, 1756). The letters are signed respectively
"J. B." and "W. M."

[BOLLAN, WILLIAM]: *The Importance and Advantages of Cape Breton
Truly Stated and Impartially Considered* . . . (London, 1746; rep.,
New York, 1966).

[DAY, JOHN]: *An Essay on the Present State of the Province of Nova
Scotia: With Some Strictures on the Measures Pursued by Government from Its First Settlement by the English in the Year 1749*
([Halifax, N. S., 1774-5]). Signed a "Member of the Assembly," the
authorship is uncertain, but evidence points to Day.

*The Importance of Cape Breton Considered: In a Letter to a Member of
Parliament from an Inhabitant of New-England* (London, 1746).

*The Importance of Settling and Fortifying Nova Scotia: With an Account
of the Country* . . . (London, 1751).

4. Newspapers

Halifax Gazette, b. 1752, Halifax, N. S.

C. SECONDARY WORKS

1. General

BREBNER, JOHN BARTLET: *New England's Outpost: Acadia before the Conquest of Canada*, Columbia University, *Studies in History,
Economics, and Public Law*, No. 293 (London & New York, 1927),

and *The Neutral Yankees of Nova Scotia: A Marginal Colony during the Revolutionary Years* (New York, 1937).

EATON, ARTHUR W. H.: "Chapters in the History of Halifax, Nova Scotia," *Americana*, X (1915)-XV (1921), *passim*. See also his *The History of King's County, Nova Scotia, Heart of the Acadian Land . . . 1604-1910* (Salem, Mass., 1910).

GIPSON, LAWRENCE HENRY: "Acadia and the Beginnings of Modern British Imperialism," *Essays in Modern English History: In Honor of Wibur Cortez Abbott* (Cambridge, Mass., 1941), pp. 177-202.

HALIBURTON, THOMAS C.: *An Historical and Statistical Account of Nova Scotia . . .* (2 vols., Halifax, N. S., 1829).

MURDOCK, BEAMISH: *A History of Nova Scotia or Acadie* (3 vols., Halifax, N. S., 1865-7).

RICHARD, ÉDOUARD: *Acadie: Reconstitution d'un Chapitre Perdue de l'Histoire d'Amérique . . .* (2 vols., Boston & Quebec, 1916-18).

SMITH, PHILIP H.: *Acadia: A Lost Chapter in American History* (Pawling, N. Y., 1884). For a searching reply to Smith, see Francis Parkman's letter in the January 22, 1885 issue of *The Nation*.

STEWART, JOHN: *An Account of Prince Edward Island in the Gulph of St. Lawrence, North America . . .* (London, 1806; rep., New York, 1966).

WEAVER, EMILY P.: "Nova Scotia and New England during the Revolution," *American Historical Review*, X (1904-5), 52-71.

2. Political

ELLS, MARGARET: "Clearing the Decks for the Loyalists," Canadian Historical Association, *Report for 1933*, (Toronto, 1933), 43-58. On the government policy and land speculation in relation to the coming of Loyalists to Nova Scotia.

FERGUSSON, C. BRUCE: "The First Canadian Parliament," *Canadian Geographical Journal*, LVII (1958), 209-17.

INNIS, HAROLD A.: "Cape Breton and the French Régime," Royal Society of Canada, *Proceedings*, 3rd ser., XXIX (1935), 51-87.

KERR, WILFRED B.: "The Stamp Act in Nova Scotia," *New England Quarterly*, VI (1933), 552-66.

MAC NUTT, W. S.: "The Beginnings of Nova Scotian Politics, 1758-1766," *Canadian Historical Review*, XVI (1935), 41-53.

RAYMOND, W. O.: "Nova Scotia under English Rule: From the Capture of Port Royal to the Conquest of Canada, A.D., 1710-1760," Royal Society of Canada, *Proceedings*, 3rd ser., IV (1911), 55-84.

3. Economic

KERR, WILFRED B.: "The Merchants of Nova Scotia and the American Revolution," *Canadian Historical Review*, XIII (1932), 20-36.

SAWTELLE, WILLIAM A.: "Acadia: The Pre-Loyalist Migration and the Philadelphia Plantation," *Pennsylvania Magazine of History and Biography,* LI (1927), 244-85. Concerned with the migration of New Englanders to Nova Scotia, 1759-1763, also with land grants made to Benjamin Franklin and associates in Pennsylvania and of plans for colonizing them.

4. *Social*

ARMSTRONG, MAURICE W.: "Neutrality and Religion in Revolutionary Nova Scotia," *New England Quarterly,* XIX (1946), 50-62.

BELL, WINTHROP PICKARD: *The Foreign Protestants and the Settlement of Nova Scotia: The History of a Piece of Arrested British Colonial Policy in the Eighteenth Century* (Toronto, 1961).

BISHOP, OLGA BERNICE: "The First Printing Press in Canada, 1751-1800," *Books in America's Past: Essays Honoring Rudolph H. Gjelsness* (David Kaser, ed., Charlottesville, Va., 1966), 130-48. Recounts the establishment of the Halifax *Gazette,* including the projects of the printer who published it.

DOUGHTY, ARTHUR GEORGE: *The Acadian Exiles: A Chronicle of the Land of Evangeline* (Glasgow & Toronto, 1916).

EATON, ARTHUR W. H.: "The Settling of Colchester County, Nova Scotia, by New England Puritans and Ulster Scotsmen," Royal Society of Canada, *Transactions,* 3rd ser., VI (1912), 221-65. See also his article "Rhode Island Settlers on the French Lands in Nova Scotia in 1760 and 1761," *Americana,* X (1915), 1-43, 83-104, 179-97.

ELLS, MARGARET: "Settling Loyalists in Nova Scotia," Canadian Historical Association, *Report for 1934* (Toronto, 1934), 105-9.

GAUDET, PLACIDE: *Le Grand Derangement sur qui Retombe la Responsibilité de l'Expulsion des Acadiens* (Ottawa, 1922).

LAUVRIÈRE, ÉMILE: *La Tragédie d'un Peuple: Histoire du Peuple Acadien de ses Origines à nos Jours* (2 vols., Paris, 1924).

LE BLANC, DUDLEY J.: *The True Story of the Acadians* (Lafayette, La., 1932).

MARTIN, ERNEST: *Les Exiles Acadiens en France au XVIII Siècle et Leur Établissement en Poitou* (Paris, 1936).

MARTELL, J. S.: "The Second Expulsion of Acadians," *Dalhousie Review,* XIII (1933-4), 359-71. Discusses the second attempt to disperse the Acadians in 1759-61.

5. *Biographical*

LEGGE, FRANCIS. "Francis Legge, Governor of Loyalist Nova Scotia, 1773-1776" by Viola F. Barnes, *New England Quarterly,* IV (1931), 420-47.

MAC NUTT, ALEXANDER. "Colonel Alexander MacNutt and the Pre-Loyalist Settlements of Nova Scotia" by William O. Raymond, Royal Society of Canada, *Proceedings,* 3rd ser., V (1912), 23-115.

PICHON, THOMAS. "Le Judas de l'Acadie" by Albert David, *Ottawa University Review,* III (1933), 492-513; IV (1934), 22-35.

6. Military and naval

DOUGLAS, W. A. B.: "The Sea Militia of Nova Scotia, 1749-1755: A Comment on Naval Policy," *Canadian Historical Review,* XLVII (1966), 22-37.

DOWNEY, FAIRFAX: *Louisbourg: Key to a Continent* (Englewood Cliffs, N. J., 1965).

SMITH, CHARLES C.: "The Wars on the Seaboard: Acadia and Cape Breton," *Narrative and Critical History of America,* V: 407-19.

WEBSTER, JOHN CLARENCE: *The Forts of Chignecto: A Study of the Eighteenth Century Conflict between France and Great Britain in Acadia* (St. John, N. B., 1930).

D. MAPS

BELLIN, J. N.: *Map of the Island of Cape Breton.* In William Bollan: *The Importance and Advantages of Cape Breton. . . .*

Carte de l'Acadie et Pays Voisins. In Jacques Nicholas Bellin: *Le Petit Atlas Maritime . . . ,* I: No. 26.

JEFFERYS, THOMAS: *A Chart of the Harbour of Halifax in Nova Scotia . . . Survey'd by . . . Charles Morris, Chief Surveyor.* In Jefferys: *The American Atlas . . . ,* No. 14a.

———: *A Map Exhibiting a View of the English Rights, Relative to the Ancient Limits of Acadia, as Supported by Express & Incontestable Authorities in Opposition to That of Ye French.* In Jefferys: *A General Topography of North America and the West Indies,* No. 22a.

———: *A Map of the Island of St. John* [later called Prince Edward Island] *in the Gulf of St. Laurence . . . from the Late Survey of Captain Holland* [1775]. In Jefferys: *The American Atlas . . . ,* No. 11.

———: *A New Map of Nova Scotia and Cape Breton Island . . .* In *ibid.,* No. 14.

———: *A Plan of the City and Harbour of Louisbourg with the French Batteries that Defended It and Those of the English . . . in 1758.* In Thomas Jefferys: *The Natural and Civil History of the French Dominions* (London, 1760), opp. p. 124. *A Plan of the City and*

Fortification of Louisbourg from a Survey Made by Richard Gridley is an inset to this map.

KITCHIN, THOMAS: *Nova Scotia: Drawn from Surveys.* In the *London Magazine*, XVIII (1749), 181.

Map of Nova Scotia or Acadia: With the Islands of Cape Breton and St. John's, from Actual Surveys by Capt Montresor, 1768. In Faden: *The North American Atlas . . .* , Nos. 6-7; also in *American Maps*, V: Nos. 7-8.

A Map of the Southern Part of Nova Scotia and Its Fishing Banks. In *The English Pilot*, (Dublin, 1767), 4th Book, opp. p. 25. In this map is an inset, *A Plan of Halifax, Surveyed by Mr. Harris.*

MORRIS, CHARLES: *A Chart of the Harbour of Halifax in Nova Scotia, with Jebucto Bay and Cape Sanbrô . . . 1759.* In Jefferys: *A General Topography of North America and the West Indies*, No. 25.

Plan de la Baye de Chibouctou Nommée par les Anglois Halifax. In Bellin: *Le Petit Atlas Maritime . . .* , I: No. 28.

Plan du Port Royal dans l'Acadie, Appellé Aujourd'hui par les Anglois Annapolis Royal. In *ibid.*, I: 27.

A Plan of the City and Fortifications of Louisburg [and] *A Map of the Harbour of Louisburg.* In the *London Magazine*, XXVII (1758), opp. p. 384.

A Plan of the Island of Cape Breton Reduced from Capt. Holland's Survey . . . 1776. Library of Congress Maps.

Port de Louisbourg dans d'Isle Royale. In Bellin: *Le Petit Atlas Maritime . . .* I: Nos. 23.

SEALE, ———, sculp.: *Map of the Island of Cape Breton as Laid Down by Sieur. Bellin.* In William Bollan: *The Importance and Advantage of Cape Breton* (London, 1746).

See also Justin Winsor's "The Maps and Bounds of Acadia," *Narrative and Critical History of America*, V: 472-82.

PENNSYLVANIA

A. BIBLIOGRAPHICAL AIDS

BAUSMAN, L. M.: *A Bibliography of Lancaster County, Pennsylvania, 1745-1912* (Philadelphia [1917]).

BEERS, HENRY PUTNEY: *Pennsylvania Bibliographies* (Philadelphia, 1936). This material was originally printed in volumes II and III of *Pennsylvania History*.

BINING, ARTHUR CECIL: *Pennsylvania History: A Selected Bibliography of Secondary Works on Pennsylvania History* ([Harrisburg, Pa.], 1933). This was also printed in *Pennsylvania Library Notes* for 1933.

DUNAWAY, WAYLAND FULLER: "A Brief Bibliography of Pennsylvania History for High School Teachers," *Pennsylvania History,* I (1934), 38-46.

ELIOT, MARGARET SHERBURNE, and SYLVESTER K. STEVENS: *Guide to Depositories of Manuscript Collections in Pennsylvania,* Pennsylvania Historical Commission, *Bulletin,* No. 4 (Harrisburg, Pa., 1939).

HASSE, ADELAIDE R.: "Pennsylvania, 1681-1789," in "Materials for a Bibliography of the Public Archives of the Thirteen Original States," American Historical Association, *Annual Report, 1906* (2 vols., Washington, D.C., 1908), II, 412-65.

HECKMAN, OLIVER S.: *What to Read about Pennsylvania* (Harrisburg, Pa., 1942).

PENNSYLVANIA HISTORICAL AND MUSEUM COMMISSION: *Bibliography of Pennsylvania History* (Norman B. Wilkinson, comp., Sylvester K. Stevens and Donald H. Kent, eds., 2nd edn., Harrisburg, Pa., 1957). The commission is presently involved in the process of revising and updating this work. The first edition of this work was published as *Writings on Pennsylvania History: A Bibliography* (Arthur C. Bining, Robert L. Brunhouse, and Norman B. Wilkinson, eds., Harrisburg, Pa., 1946).

B. PRINTED SOURCE MATERIALS

1. Government and related documents

The Acts of Assembly of the Province of Pennsylvania, Carefully Compared with the Originals . . . (Philadelphia, 1775).

The Charters and Acts of Assembly of the Province of Pennsylvania . . . [1700-1759] (2 vols., Philadelphia, 1762).

Colonial Records: Minutes of the Provincial Council of Pennsylvania from the Organization to the Termination of the Proprietary Government (16 vols., Harrisburg, Pa., 1852-3). For an index, see Samuel Hazard: *General Index to the Colonial Records in 16 Volumes and to the Pennsylvania Archives in 12 Volumes* (Philadelphia, 1860).

HAZARD, SAMUEL, *et al.,* eds.: *Pennsylvania Archives: Selected and Arranged from Original Documents in the Office of the Secretary of the Commonwealth* . . . (138 vols. in 9 series, Harrisburg, Pa., & Philadelphia, 1852-1935). Attention is especially directed to the twelve volumes of the First Series which contain many miscellaneous documents of importance, to the Fourth Series in nine volumes concerned with the papers of the governors, and to the Eighth Series in eight volumes, bearing the title *Votes and Proceedings of the House of Representatives* which were originally printed between 1752 and 1776 at Philadelphia in six volumes, and are now available on Readex cards. For a guide and index, see Henry Howard Eddy: *Guide to the Published Archives of Pennsylvania Covering the 138 Volumes of Colonial Records and Pennsylvania Archives, Series I-IX* (Harrisburg, Pa., 1949).

————, ed.: *The Register of Pennsylvania, Devoted to the Preservation of Facts and Documents, and Every Kind of Useful Information Respecting the State of Pennsylvania* (16 vols., Philadelphia, 1828-1835).

MITCHELL, JAMES TYNDALE, and HENRY FLANDERS, eds.: *The Statutes at Large of Pennsylvania from 1682 to 1801* (17 vols. [Harrisburg, Pa.], 1896-1915).

2. *Non-official contemporary writings*

ALLEN, WILLIAM: "William Allen-Benjamin Chew Correspondence, 1763-1764," David A. Kimball and Miriam Quinn, eds., *Pennsylvania Magazine of History and Biography*, XC (1966), 202-26. Extracts from Allen's letter book are to be found in *The Burd Papers* (Lewis Burd Walker, ed., 2 vols., Pottsville, Pa., 1897-9).

BALCH, THOMAS W., ed.: *Letters and Papers Relating Chiefly to the Provincial History of Pennsylvania . . .* (Philadelphia, 1855).

BARKLY, GILBERT: "A British Spy in Philadelphia, 1775-1777," Geoffrey Seed, ed., *Pennsylvania Magazine of History and Biography*, LXXXV (1961), 3-37.

BARTRAM, JOHN and WILLIAM: *John and William Bartram's America: Selections from the Writings of the Philadelphia Naturalists* (Helen Gere Cruickshank, ed., New York, 1957). Also, *The Travels of William Bartram . . .* (Francis Harper, ed., New Haven, Conn., 1958).

BEATTY, CHARLES: *The Journal of Two Months Tour: With a View of Promoting Religion Among the Frontier Inhabitants of Pennsylvania . . . and Among the Indians . . .* (London, 1768). Although written for religious purposes, the pamphlet also gives a picture of life among the Delaware Indians. The author concludes that they were the descendants of the Ten Lost Tribes of Israel.

BENEZET, ANTHONY. *Memoirs of the Life of Anthony Benezet* by Roberts Vaux (Philadelphia, 1817).

BRADDOCK, EDWARD: *Major-General Edward Braddock's Orderly Books from February 26 to June 17, 1755 . . .* (Cumberland, Md., 1878).

BROWN, WALLACE, ed.: "Viewpoints of a Pennsylvania Loyalist," *Pennsylvania Magazine of History and Biography*, XCI (1967), 419-33. Prints the answers of a Pennsylvania merchant to a questionnaire apparently submitted to several American Loyalists; from the original in the Public Record Office.

BUTLER, AMOS W., ed.: "A Visit to Easton [1756]," *Indiana Magazine of History*, XXXII (1936), 265-74.

BUTLER, RICHARD: "The Journal of Richard Butler, 1775: Continental Congress's Envoy to the Western Indians," Edward G. Williams, ed., *Western Pennsylvania Historical Magazine*, XLVI (1963), 381-95; XLVII (1964), 31-46, 141-56.

CRÈVECOEUR, MICHEL-GUILLAUME JEAN DE: *Crèvecoeur's Eighteenth-Century Travels in Pennsylvania and New York* (Percy G. Adams, trans. & ed., Lexington, Ky., c. 1961). Also, another edition: *Journey into Northern Pennsylvania and the State of New York* (Clarissa Spencer Bostelmann, trans. & ed., Ann Arbor, Mich., c. 1964).

CUTHBERTSON, JOHN: "The Diary of John Cuthbertson, Missionary to the Covenanters of Colonial Pennsylvania," William L. Fisk, Jr., ed., *Pennsylvania Magazine of History and Biography*, LXXIII (1949), 441-58.

DICKINSON, JOHN: *The Writings of John Dickinson*, Historical Society of Pennsylvania, *Memoirs*, XIV (Paul Leicester Ford, ed., 1 vol., only pub., Philadelphia, 1895). See also "A Pennsylvania Farmer at the Court of King George: John Dickinson's London Letters, 1754-1756," H. Trevor Colbourn, ed., *Pennsylvania Magazine of History and Biography*, LXXXVI (1962), 241-86, 417-53, and "John Dickinson on Church and State," Richard J. Hooker, ed., *American Literature*, XVI (1944-5), 82-98.

DUNBAR, JOHN R., ed.: *The Paxton Papers* (The Hague, 1957).

FOULKE, SAMUEL: "The Pennsylvania Assembly in 1761-2: A Memorandum Kept by Samuel Foulke," Howard M. Jenkins, ed., *Pennsylvania Magazine of History and Biography*, VIII (1884), 407-13.

FRANKLIN, BENJAMIN: There have been several collections of Franklin's works published, including *The Works of Benjamin Franklin . . .* edited by Jared Sparks (10 vols., Boston, 1836-40; rep., 1844-56), an edition by John Bigelow (10 vols., London & New York, 1887-8), and Albert Henry Smyth's edition: *Writings of Benjamin Franklin* (10 vols., London & New York, 1905-7). The most recent and by far the best collection is that being sponsored by the American Philosophical Society and Yale University, Leonard Labaree, *et al.*, editors: *The Papers of Benjamin Franklin* (10 vols. +, New Haven, Conn., 1959-66 +). Labaree and his staff have also edited the *Autobiography* (New Haven, Conn., 1964), and the one-volume

Mr. Franklin: A Selection from His Personal Papers (New Haven, Conn., 1956). Among the mass of published material having to do with Franklin's writings are Verner W. Crane's edition of *Benjamin Franklin's Letters to the Press, 1758-1775* (Chapel Hill, N. C., c. 1950), and Carl Van Doren's edition of *Letters and Papers of Benjamin Franklin and Richard Jackson, 1753-1785*, American Philosophical Society, *Memoirs*, Vol. 24 (Philadelphia, 1947). For a useful bibliographic essay on Franklin's anonymously published writings, see Verner W. Crane: "Certain Writings of Benjamin Franklin on the British Empire and the American Colonies," Bibliographical Society of America, *Papers*, XXVII (1934), 1-27.

GIPSON, LAWRENCE HENRY, ed.: *Lewis Evans* . . . (Philadelphia, 1939). Evans's writings and maps are reproduced.

GRATZ, BERNARD and MICHAEL: *B. and M. Gratz, Merchants in Philadelphia, 1754-1798* . . . (William Vincent Byars, ed., Jefferson City, Mo., 1916).

GRAYDON, ALEXANDER: *Memoirs of a Life Chiefly Passed in Pennsylvania, within the Last Sixty Years* . . . (Harrisburg, Pa., 1811; rep., Edinburgh, 1822).

HALL, DAVID. For Hall's correspondence with William Strachan, see Chapter II, B. Hall published the *Pennsylvania Gazette*.

HAMILTON, CHARLES, ed.: *Braddock's Defeat: The Journal of Captain Robert Chalmley's Batman. The Journal of a British Officer [and] Halkett's Orderly Book* . . . (Norman, Okla., 1959).

HECKEWELDER, JOHN: *Thirty Thousand Miles with John Heckewelder* (Paul A. W. Wallace, ed., Pittsburgh, Pa., c. 1958).

LAWRENCE, THOMAS: "Correspondence between Thomas Lawrence, Provincial Councillor of Pennsylvania and Mayor of Philadelphia, and George and Robert Charles [of Leicesterfield, England], 1746-1752," *Pennsylvania Magazine of History and Biography*, VII (1883), 231-3.

MACKRABY, ALEXANDER: "Philadelphia Society Before the Revolution: Extracts from Letters of Alexander Mackraby to Sir Philip Francis," [from Memoirs of Sir Philip Francis, K.C.B.] *Pennsylvania Magazine of History and Biography*, XI (1887), 276-87, 491-4.

MARSHALL, CHRISTOPHER: *Extracts from the Diary of Christopher Marshall Kept in Philadelphia and Lancaster during the American Revolution, 1771-1781* (William Duane, ed., Philadelphia, 1839; Albany, N. Y., 1877).

MASON, WILLIAM SMITH, ed.: "Franklin and Galloway: Some Unpublished Letters," American Antiquarian Society, *Proceedings*, n. ser., XXIV 1925), 227-58.

MICHENER, EZRA, ed.: *A Retrospect of Early Quakerism: Being Extracts from the Records of Philadelphia Yearly Meeting and the Meetings Composing It* (Philadelphia, 1860).

MITTELBERGER, GOTTLIEB: *Gottlieb Mittelberger's Reise nach Pennsylvanien im Jahr 1750 und Rükreise nach Teutschland im Jahr 1754 . . .* (Stuttgart, 1756). This work was translated from the German by Carl T. Eben and published in Philadelphia in 1898, as *Gottlieb Mittelberger's Journey to Philadelphia in the Year 1750 and Return to Germany in the Year 1754*. It pictured the conditions of the German colonists in Pennsylvania.

MUHLENBERG, HENRY MELCHIOR: *The Journals of Henry Melchior Muhlenberg* (Theodore G. Tappert and John W. Doberstein, eds., 2 vols., Philadelphia, 1942-5).

Ohio Company. *The Ohio Company Papers, 1753-1817: Being Primarily Papers of the "Suffering Traders" of Pennsylvania* (Kenneth P. Bailey, ed., Arcata, Calif., 1947).

POWNALL, THOMAS: "Governor Pownall's Reasons for Declining the Government of Pennsylvania, 1758," *Pennsylvania Magazine of History and Biography*, XIII (1889), 441-6.

PRIME, ALFRED COXE, comp.: *The Arts and Crafts in Philadelphia, Maryland and South Carolina . . . Gleanings from [Contemporary] Newspapers* (Topsfield, Mass., 1929).

REED, JOSEPH. *Life and Correspondence of Joseph Reed . . .* by William B. Reed (2 vols., Philadelphia, 1847).

RUPP, I. DANIEL, comp.: *A Collection of Upwards of Thirty-Thousand Names of German, Swiss, Dutch, French, and Other Immigrants in Pennsylvania from 1727-1776 . . .* (2nd edn., rev. & enl., Philadelphia, 1876).

RUSH, BENJAMIN: *Letters of Benjamin Rush*, American Philosophical Society, *Memoirs*, XXX (Lyman H. Butterfield, ed., 2 vols. [Princeton, N. J.], 1951). Also, "Further Letters of Benjamin Rush," L. H. Butterfield, ed., *Pennsylvania Magazine of History and Biography*, LXVIII (1954), 2-44.

ST. CLAIR, ARTHUR: *The St. Clair Papers: The Life and Public Services of Arthur St. Clair . . . with His Correspondence and Other Papers* (William Henry Smith, ed., 2 vols., Cincinnati, O., 1882).

SARGENT, WINTHROP, ed.: *The History of an Expedition against Fort Du Quesne in 1755 under Major-General Edward Braddock . . .*, Historical Society of Pennsylvania, *Memoirs*, V (Philadelphia, 1856).

SMITH, WILLIAM: *The Works of William Smith, D.D., Late Provost of the College and Academy of Philadelphia . . .* (Hugh Maxwell and William Fry, eds., 2 vols., Philadelphia, 1803). See also the *Life and Correspondence of the Rev. William Smith, D.D. . . . With*

Copious Extracts from His Writings by Horace Wemyss Smith (2 vols., Philadelphia, 1880).

STEVENS, SYLVESTER K. [ed.]: *Pennsylvania: The Keystone State,* Vol. II: *Documents from Printed and Manuscript Sources, 1681-1955* (New York, 1956). Contains approximately 120 pages of excerpts from documents relating to Pennsylvania in this period under examination.

STRASSBURGER, RALPH BEAVER, comp.: *Pennsylvania German Pioneers: A Publication of the Original Lists of Arrivals in the Port of Philadelphia from 1727 to 1808,* Pennsylvania German Society, *Proceedings,* XLII-XLIV (William John Hinke, ed., 3 vols., Norristown, Pa., 1934).

THOMSON, CHARLES: *Causes of the Alienation of the Delaware and Shawanese Indians from the British Interest* (London, 1759; Philadelphia, 1867). See also the article, "Early Days of the Revolution in Philadelphia: Charles Thomson's Account of the Opposition to the Boston Port Bill," *Pennsylvania Magazine of History and Biography,* II (1878), 411-23.

WALSH, RICHARD, ed.: "Braddock on July 9, 1755," *Maryland Historical Magazine,* LX (1965), 421-7. Prints the letter of an unidentified eyewitness to the battle.

WATSON, JOHN: "Penn versus Baltimore: Journal of John Watson, Assistant Surveyor to the Commissioners of the Province of Pennsylvania, 1750," John W. Jordan, ed., *Pennsylvania Magazine of History and Biography,* XXXVIII (1914), 385-406.

WEISER, CONRAD: "Two Addresses of Conrad Weiser to the German Voters of Pennsylvania," *ibid.,* XXIII (1899), 516-21.

WHARTON, THOMAS: "Selections from the Letter-Books of Thomas Wharton of Philadelphia, 1773-1783," *ibid.,* XXXIII (1909), 319-39, 432-53; XXXIV (1910), 41-61.

Wilderness Chronicles of Northwestern Pennsylvania (Sylvester K. Stevens and Donald H. Kent, eds., Harrisburg, Pa., 1941).

WILLING, THOMAS: *Willing Letters and Papers: Edited, with a Biographical Essay of Thomas Willing of Philadelphia* (Thomas W. Balch, ed., Philadelphia, 1922).

3. Contemporary pamphlets, tracts, and related materials: Chronologically arranged

For a useful listing of contemporary titles, see Charles S. R. Hildeburn: *A Century of Printing: The Issues of the Press in Pennsylvania, 1685-1784* (2 vols., Philadelphia, 1885-6).

1 7 4 9

[FRANKLIN, BENJAMIN]: *Proposals Relating to the Education of the Youth in Pensilvania* (Philadelphia, 1749).

1 7 5 5

[SMITH, WILLIAM]: *A Brief State of the Province of Pennsylvania in Which the Conduct of Their Assemblies for Several Years Past Is Impartially Examined* . . . (London & Dublin, 1755). See also Smith's continuation: *A Brief View of the Condition of Pennsylvania for the Year 1755 . . . Being a Sequel to a Well-Known Pamphlet* . . . (London, 1756). The first of the two pamphlets was an attack on the Pennsylvania Quakers for their role in the Assembly.

1 7 5 9

[GALLOWAY, JOSEPH]: *A True and Impartial State of the Province of Pennsylvania: Containing an Exact Account of the Nature of Its Government, the Power of Its Proprietaries, and Their Governors . . . also the Rights and Privileges of the Assembly and People* . . . (Philadelphia, 1759). Evans attributes this work to Benjamin Franklin. As an answer to the two Smith pamphlets, *A Brief State* and *A Brief View,* it is dedicated to William Pitt.

1 7 6 0

[GALLOWAY, JOSEPH]: *A Letter to the People of Pennsylvania: Occasioned by the Assembly's Passing that Important Act, for Constituting the Judges of the Supream [sic] Courts and Common-Pleas during Good Behaviour* (Philadelphia, 1760).

1 7 6 4

BARTON, THOMAS: *The Conduct of the Paxton-Men Impartially Represented: With Some Remarks on the Narrative* . . . (Philadelphia, 1764). This pamphlet is reprinted along with twenty-seven others in John R. Dunbar's *The Paxton Papers* (The Hague, 1957), 265-98. All of the pamphlets deal with the Paxton Boys' massacre of the Conestoga Indians near Lancaster and the so-called Paxton Rebellion. For a reply, see: *An Answer to the Pamphlet Entitled the Conduct of the Paxton Men* . . . (Philadelphia, 1764); also reprinted in Dunbar, pp. 317-37. This pamphlet denounces the Paxton Men as murderers.

A Battle! a Battle! a Battle a Squirt: Where No Man is Kill'd and No Man is Hurt! . . . ([Philadelphia, 1764]). This poem related to the Paxton Boys and was reprinted in Dunbar: *The Paxton Papers,* pp. 173-82.

DICKINSON, JOHN: *A Speech Delivered in the House of Assembly of the Province of Pennsylvania, May 24th, 1764 . . . on Occasion of a Petition Drawn up by Order and then under Consideration of the House Praying His Majesty for a Change of Government of This Province* . . . (Philadelphia, 1764). See also *The May Be: Or Some Observations. Occasion'd by Reading a Speech Deliver'd in the House of Assembly the 24th of May* . . . (Philadelphia [1764]), and especially the reply by Joseph Galloway: *The Speech of Joseph Galloway, Esq., One of the Members for Philadelphia County: In Answer to the Speech of John Dickinson, Esq.* . . . (Philadelphia, 1764); to which John Dickinson responded in *A Reply to a Piece called the Speech of Joseph Galloway, Esquire* (Philadelphia, 1764; London, 1765). Galloway then published a broadside answering Dickinson's charge that his speech of May 24th was never spoken: *To the Public* . . . ([Philadelphia, 1764]).

Explanatory Remarks on the Assembly's Resolves Published in the Pennsylvania Gazette, No. 1840 (Philadelphia, 1764). This two-page publication deals with the movement in the province to substitute royal government for the proprietary form.

[FRANKLIN, BENJAMIN]: *A Narrative of the Late Massacres in Lancaster County of a Number of Indians . . . With Some Observations of the Same* (Philadelphia, 1764). This pamphlet has been reprinted in Albert H. Smyth's *The Writings of Benjamin Franklin,* IV: 289-314, and in Dunbar: *The Paxton Papers,* pp. 55-75.

————: *Remarks on a Late Protest against the Appointment of Mr. Franklin an Agent for This Province* ([Philadelphia, 1764]). For a reply, see: William Smith: *An Answer to Mr. Franklin's Remarks* . . . (Philadelphia, 1764).

A Petition to the King (Philadelphia, 1764). Requesting the revocation of the proprietary charter. For a reply, see: *To the King's Most Excellent Majesty in Council, the Representation and Petition of Your Majesty's Dutiful and Loyal Subjects, Freeholders and Inhabitants of the Province of Pennsylvania* . . . ([Philadelphia, 1764]). This broadside opposed the petition of the Assembly requesting a change in the form of government.

The Scribler: Being a Letter from a Gentleman in Town to his Friend in the Country Concerning the Present State of Public Affairs; With a Lapidary Character [of Dr. William Smith] ([Philadelphia], 1764).

SMITH, MATTHEW, and JAMES GIBSON: *A Declaration and Remonstrance of the Distressed and Bleeding Frontier Inhabitants of the Province of Pennsylvania . . . Shewing the Causes of Their Late Discontent . . .* (Philadelphia, 1764). Reprinted in Dunbar: *The Paxton Papers,* 99-110.

1 7 6 5

BIDDLE, JAMES: *To the Freeholders and Electors of the Province of Pennsylvania* ([Philadelphia, 1765]). An anti-Franklin election address, accusing him of having encouraged passage of the Stamp Act.

GALLOWAY, JOSEPH: *Advertisement, Philadelphia, December 20, 1765: To the Publick* (Philadelphia, 1765). In this broadside Galloway denied that he opposed the transaction of judicial business except on stamped paper.

[HUNT, ISAAC]: *A Humble Attempt at Scurrility: In Imitation of Those Great Masters of the Art . . .* ([Philadelphia], 1765). The pamphlet has also been attributed to Benjamin Franklin.

The Lamentation of Pennsylvania on Account of the Stamp-Act . . . ([Philadelphia, 1765]).

To the Freeholders and Other Electors of Assembly-Men for Pennsylvania ([Philadelphia, 1765]). Favoring Franklin's election.

To the Merchants and Manufacturers of Great-Britain: The Memorial of the Merchants and Traders of the City of Philadelphia ([Philadelphia, 1765]).

1 7 6 8

An Address to the Merchants, Freeholders and All Other the Inhabitants of the Province of Pennsylvania in Particular and of the Southern Colonies in General ([Philadelphia, 1768]). Signed "An Englishman," this pamphlet protests non-importation agreements; it also suggests the introduction of Anglican bishops into the colonies "so that New England Puritans would vent their spleen upon the ceremonies of the Church and not upon the political Government of England."

The Following Address Was Read at a Meeting of the Merchants . . . the 25th of April 1768 ([Philadelphia, 1768]). The broadside recommended that the non-importation agreement be renewed by the Philadelphia merchants.

Letter from a Gentleman in Virginia to a Merchant in Philadelphia, July 22, 1768 (Philadelphia, 1768). This broadside was answered by one signed Pacificus: *To the Public . . .* (Philadelphia [1768]). Both publications relate to the renewal of the non-importation agreement.

1 7 7 0

GODDARD, WILLIAM: *The Partnership: Or the History of the Rise and Progress of the Pennsylvania Chronicle* . . . (Philadelphia, 1770). This pamphlet discusses the conduct of Joseph Galloway, Thomas Wharton, and others who were in partnership with Goddard in publishing the *Pennsylvania Chronicle.*

MAC PHERSON, JOHN: *Letter to John Dickinson, Esq.* . . . (Philadelphia [1770]). Dated 13 November 1770.

The State of the Lands Said to be Once Within the Bounds of the Charter of the Colony of Connecticut West of the Province of New York Considered (New York, 1770).

1 7 7 3

[DICKINSON, JOHN]: *A Letter from the Country, to a Gentleman in Philadelphia* ([Philadelphia, 1773]). This broadside, signed "Rusticus," deals with the East India Company tea being shipped to Philadelphia.

REGULUS, pseud.: *To the Freemen of Pennsylvania* ([Philadelphia, 1773]). This is a broadside urging a limited opposition to landing of the the tea at Philadelphia.

SCAEVOLA, pseud.: *To the Commissioners Appointed by the East-India Company for the Sale of Tea in America* . . . *If you Refuse, no One Will Dare to Execute the Diabolical Commission* ([Philadelphia, 1773]). Broadside.

1 7 7 4

[DRINKER, JOHN]: *Observations on the Late Popular Measures, Offered to the Serious Considerations of the Sober Inhabitants of Pennsylvania* (Philadelphia, 1774). Signed "A Tradesman of Philadelphia." Evans attributes this pamphlet to John Brookes. It contains two essays, one dated August 5th and the other August 20th, 1774.

SMITH, WILLIAM: *An Examination of the Connecticut Claim to Lands in Pennsylvania: With an Appendix Containing Extracts and Copies Taken from Original Papers* (Philadelphia, 1774).

1 7 7 5

The Testimony of the People Called Quakers Given forth by a Meeting of the Representatives of Said People in Pennsylvania and New-Jersey . . . ([Philadelphia, 1775]). A broadside declaring the Quakers' opposition to any illegal or rebellious activities.

1 7 7 6

An Essay of a Frame of Government for Pennsylvania (Philadelphia, 1776). This pamphlet proposed a governmental system having three legislative bodies.

4. Newspapers

For information on the location and availability of Philadelphia newspapers, see the publication of the Pennsylvania Historical Commission: *A Checklist of Pennsylvania Newspapers, Vol I: Philadelphia County* (1 vol. only pub., Harrisburg, Pa., 1944).

Germantowner Zeitung [Pennsylvanische Berichte], 1762-1777, Philadelphia.

The Pennsylvania Chronicle, and Universal Advertiser, 1767-1774, Philadelphia.

The Pennsylvania Gazette, Philadelphia.

The Pennsylvania Journal and Weekly Advertiser, Philadelphia.

The Pennsylvania Magazine: or American Monthly Museum, 1775-1776, Philadelphia.

The Pennsylvania Packet [The Pennsylvania Packet and the General Advertiser; Dunlap's Pennsylvania Packet, or, the General Advertiser], b. 1771, Philadelphia.

Story & Humphrey's Pennsylvania Mercury [The Pennsylvania Mercury, and Universal Advertiser; Story & Humphrey's Pennsylvania Mercury, and Universal Advertiser], b. 1775, Philadelphia.

Der Wochentliche Philadelphische Staatsbote [Der Wochentliche Pennsylvanische Staatsbote; Henrich Millers Pennsylvanische Staatsbote], b. 1762, Philadelphia.

C. SECONDARY WORKS

1. General

BELL, WHITFIELD, JR.: "Carlisle to Pittsburgh: A Gateway to the West, 1750-1915," *Western Pennsylvania Historical Magazine*, XXXV (1952), 157-66.

BOLLES, ALBERT SIDNEY: *Pennsylvania, Province and State: A History from 1609 to 1790* (2 vols., New York & Philadelphia, 1899).

BRIDENBAUGH, CARL and JESSICA: *Rebels and Gentlemen: Philadelphia in the Age of Franklin* (New York, 1942).

BUCK, SOLON J., and ELIZABETH HAWTHORNE BUCK: *The Planting of Civilization in Western Pennsylvania* (Pittsburgh, Pa., 1939).

DONEHOO, GEORGE PATTERSON, ed.: *Pennsylvania: A History* (7 vols., Chicago & New York, 1926). Volumes I through IV contain the history while volumes V through VII deal with biographical sketches of prominent Pennsylvanians.

DUNAWAY, WAYLAND FULLER: *A History of Pennsylvania* (New York, 1935; 2nd edn., 1950).

FISHER, SYDNEY GEORGE: *Pennsylvania: Colony and Commonwealth* (Philadelphia, 1897). Chapters VII-XXII are relevant.

GIPSON, LAWRENCE H.: *Two Centuries Ago in Pennsylvania*, Wyoming [Pennsylvania] Commemorative Association, *Proceedings* (1941), 7-20.

JENKINS, HOWARD M., ed.: *Pennsylvania, Colonial and Federal: A History, 1608-1903* (3 vols., Philadelphia, 1903). Vol. I, 402-575 and Vol. II, 1-70 are relevant.

PROUD, ROBERT: *The History of Pennsylvania, in North America . . .* (2 vols., Philadelphia, 1797-8).

RUPP, ISRAEL DANIEL: *Early History of Western Pennsylvania, and of the West . . . [1754-1783]* (Harrisburg & Pittsburgh, Pa., 1846). Contains an appendix of letters and journals relative to the period.

STEVENS, SYLVESTER K.: *Pennsylvania: The Keystone State, Vol. I: History of Pennsylvania, 1616-1955* (New York, 1956).

WALLACE, PAUL A. W.: *Pennsylvania: Seed of a Nation* (New York, 1962).

WATSON, JOHN F.: *Annals of Philadelphia and Pennsylvania in the Olden Time . . .* (2 vols., Philadelphia, 1844; enl. by Willis P. Hazard, 3 vols., 1879).

2. Local

ALLINSON, EDWARD P., and BOIES PENROSE: *Philadelphia, 1681-1887: A History of Municipal Development*, Johns Hopkins University, *Studies in Historical and Political Science, Extra Vol. II* (Philadelphia, 1887).

BOMBERGER, CHRISTIAN M.: *A Short History of Westmoreland County: The First County West of the Appalachians* (Jeannette, Pa., c. 1941).

BURT, MAXWELL STRUTHERS: *Philadelphia: Holy Experiment* (Garden City, N. Y., 1945).

DIAMONDSTONE, JUDITH M.: "Philadelphia's Municipal Corporation, 1701-1776," *Pennsylvania Magazine of History and Biography*, XC (1966), 183-201.

ELLIS, FRANKLIN, ed.: *History of Fayette County, Pennsylvania: With Biographical Sketches of Many of Its Pioneers and Prominent Men* (Philadelphia, 1882).

HARVEY, OSCAR JEWELL: *A History of Wilkes-Barre, Luzerne County, Pennsylvania . . .* (6 vols., Wilkes-Barre, Pa., 1909-30).

LEVERING, JOSEPH MORTIMER: *A History of Bethlehem, Pennsylvania, 1741-1892* . . . (Bethlehem, Pa., 1903).

MINER, CHARLES: *History of Wyoming: In a Series of Letters* . . . (Philadelphia, 1845).

PLUMB, HENRY BLACKMAN: *History of Hanover Township . . . and also . . . of Wyoming Valley in Luzerne County, Pennsylvania* (Wilkes-Barre, Pa., 1885).

REYNOLDS, JOHN EARLE: *In French Creek Valley* (Meadville, Pa., 1938).

SCHARF, JOHN THOMAS, and THOMPSON WESTCOTT: *History of Philadelphia* [1609-1884] (3 vols., Philadelphia, 1884).

WATSON, JOHN F.: *Annals of Philadelphia: Being a Collection of Memoirs, Anecdotes, and Incidents* . . . (Philadelphia, 1830).

3. Political

BREWSTER, WILLIAM: *The Pennsylvania and New York Frontier: History of, from 1720 to the Close of the Revolution* (Philadelphia, 1954).

BRUNHOUSE, R. L.: "The Effect of the Townshend Acts in Pennsylvania," *Pennsylvania Magazine of History and Biography*, LIV (1930), 355-73.

CUMMINGS, HUBERTIS M.: *The Mason and Dixon Line: Story for a Bicentenary, 1763-1963* (Harrisburg, Pa., 1962).

DAVIDSON, ROBERT L. D.: *War Comes to Quaker Pennsylvania, 1682-1756* (New York, 1957).

FERGUSON, RUSSELL J.: *Early Western Pennsylvania Politics [1773-1823]* (Pittsburgh, Pa., 1938).

GILLINGHAM, HARROLD E.: *Counterfeiting in Colonial Pennsylvania, Numismatic Notes and Monographs*, No. 86 (New York, 1939).

GLEASON, J. PHILIP: "A Scurrilous Colonial Election and Franklin's Reputation," *William and Mary Quarterly*, 3rd ser., XVIII (1961), 68-84.

HAWKE, DAVID: *In the Midst of a Revolution* (Philadelphia, c. 1961). An examination of the technics of revolution in Pennsylvania.

HAYES, J. CARROLL: "Penn vs. Lord Baltimore: A Brief for the Penns in Re Mason and Dixon Line," *Pennsylvania History*, VIII (1941), 278-303.

HERSHBERGER, GUY F.: "The Pennsylvania Quaker Experiment in Politics, 1682-1756," *Mennonite Quarterly Review*, X (1936), 187-221.

KEITH, CHARLES PENROSE: *Provincial Councillors of Pennsylvania Who Held Office between 1733 and 1776* . . . (Philadelphia, 1883).

KETCHAM, RALPH L.: "Conscience, War, and Politics in Pennsylvania, 1755-1757," *William and Mary Quarterly*, 3rd ser., XX (1963), 416-39.

LEONARD, SISTER JOAN DE LOURDES: "Elections in Colonial Pennsylvania," *William and Mary Quarterly*, 3rd ser., XI (1954), 385-401.

LINCOLN, CHARLES H.: *The Revolutionary Movement in Pennsylvania, 1760-1776*, University of Pennsylvania, *Publications: Series in History,*

No. 1 (Philadelphia, 1901), and "Representation in the Pennsylvania Assembly Prior to the Revolution," *Pennsylvania Magazine of History and Biography*, XXIII (1899), 23-24.

MARTIN, ALFRED S.: "The King's Customs: Philadelphia, 1763-1774," *William and Mary Quarterly*, 3rd ser., V (1948), 201-16.

MATHEWS, EDWARD B., ed.: *Report on the Resurvey of the Maryland-Pennsylvania Boundary, Part of the Mason and Dixon Line* (Harrisburg, Pa., 1909).

NEWCOMB, BENJAMIN H.: "Effects of the Stamp Act on Colonial Pennsylvania Politics," *William and Mary Quarterly*, 3rd ser., XXIII (1966), 257-72.

POTTER, JOHN E.: "The Pennsylvania and Virginia Boundary Controversy," *Pennsylvania Magazine of History and Biography*, XXXVIII (1914), 407-26.

ROOT, WINFRED TREXLER: *The Relations of Pennsylvania with the British Government, 1696-1765* ([New York & Philadelphia], 1912).

SCHLESINGER, ARTHUR M.: "Politics, Propaganda, and the Philadelphia Press, 1767-1770," *Pennsylvania Magazine of History and Biography*, LX (1936), 309-22.

SCOTT, KENNETH: *Counterfeiting in Colonial Pennsylvania, Numismatic Notes and Monographs*, No. 132 (New York, 1955).

SHARPLESS, ISAAC: *A Quaker Experiment in Government* (2 vols., Philadelphia, 1898; another edition with the addition of the subtitle, *History of Quaker Government in Pennsylvania, 1682-1783*, 2 pts. in 1 vol., 1902).

SHEPHERD, WILLIAM ROBERT: *History of Proprietary Government in Pennsylvania*, Columbia University, *Studies in History, Economics, and Public Law*, No. 16 (New York, 1896).

SIEBERT, WILBUR H.: "The Loyalists of Pennsylvania," Ohio State University, *Bulletin*, XXIV (1920), No. 23.

SMITH, W. ROY: "Sectionalism in Pennsylvania during the Revolution," *Political Science Quarterly*, XXIV (1909), 208-35.

STONE, FREDERICK D.: "How the Landing of Tea was Opposed in Philadelphia by Colonel William Bradford and Others in 1773," *Pennsylvania Magazine of History and Biography*, XV (1891), 385-93.

TANSILL, CHARLES C.: *The Pennsylvania-Maryland Boundary Controversy* ([Washington, D.C.], 1915).

THAYER, THEODORE: *Pennsylvania Politics and the Growth of Democracy, 1740-1776* (Harrisburg, Pa., 1953), and "The Quaker Party of Pennsylvania, 1755-1765," *Pennsylvania Magazine of History and Biography*, LXXI (1947), 19-43.

TRASK, ROGER R.: "Pennsylvania and the Albany Congress, 1754," *Pennsylvania History*, XXVII (1960), 273-90.

WARDEN, G. B.: "The Proprietary Group in Pennsylvania, 1754-1764," *William and Mary Quarterly*, 3rd ser., XXI (1964), 367-89.

WOLFF, MABEL PAULINE: *The Colonial Agency of Pennsylvania, 1712-1757* (Philadelphia, 1933).

YOUNG, HENRY J.: "Agrarian Reactions to the Stamp Act in Pennsylvania," *Pennsylvania History*, XXXIV (1967), 25-30, and "Treason and Its Punishment in Revolutionary Pennsylvania," *Pennsylvania Magazine of History and Biography*, XC (1966), 287-313.

4. Economic

BERG, HARRY D.: "Merchants and Mercantile Life of Colonial Philadelphia, 1748-1763," *Abstracts in History*, V, University of Iowa, *Studies in the Social Sciences*, XI (1939-42), 91-101.

BEZANSON, ANNE, *et al.*: *Prices and Inflation during the American Revolution: Pennsylvania, 1770-1790* (Philadelphia, 1951), and *Prices in Colonial Pennsylvania* (Philadelphia, 1935).

BILLINGER, ROBERT D.: "Early Ironworks of Pennsylvania: The Durham Furnaces," *Industrial and Engineering Chemistry*, XXX (1938), 428-37.

BINING, ARTHUR CECIL: *Pennsylvania Iron Manufacture in the Eighteenth Century*, Pennsylvania Historical Commission, *Publications*, IV (Harrisburg, Pa., 1938). See also his articles: "The Iron Plantations of Early Pennsylvania," *Pennsylvania Magazine of History and Biography*, LVII (1933), 117-37 and "Early Ironmasters of Pennsylvania," *Pennsylvania History*, XVIII (1951), 93-103.

BRESSLER, LEO A.: "Agriculture Among the Germans in Pennsylvania during the Eighteenth Century," *Pennsylvania History*, XXII (1955), 103-33.

FACKENTHAL, BENJAMIN FRANKLIN, JR.: "The Durham Iron Works, Durham Township," Bucks County Historical Society, *Papers*, VII (1937), 59-94.

FLETCHER, STEVEN WHITCOMB: *Pennsylvania Agriculture and Country Life* [1640-1840] (2 vols., Harrisburg, Pa., 1950-5).

Forges and Furnaces in the Province of Pennsylvania, Pennsylvania Society of the Colonial Dames of America, *Publications*, III (Philadelphia, 1914).

GAGLIARDO, JOHN G.: "Germans and Agriculture in Colonial Pennsylvania," *Pennsylvania Magazine of History and Biography*, LXXXIII (1959), 192-218.

GILLINGHAM, HARROLD E.: *Marine Insurance in Philadelphia, 1721-1800: With a List of Brokers and Underwriters* . . . (Philadelphia, 1933).

JENSEN, ARTHUR L.: *The Maritime Commerce of Colonial Philadelphia* (Madison, Wis., 1963). See also his article "The Inspection of Exports in Colonial Pennsylvania," *Pennsylvania Magazine of History and Biography* LXXVIII (1954), 275-97.

JOHNSON, VICTOR L.: "Fair Traders and Smugglers in Philadelphia, 1754-

1763," *Pennsylvania Magazine of History and Biography,* LXXXIII (1959), 125-49.

LEMON, JAMES T.: "Household Consumption in Eighteenth-Century America and Its Relationship to Production and Trade: The Situation among Farmers in Southwestern Pennsylvania," *Agricultural History,* XLI (1967), 59-70.

MONTGOMERY, MORTON L.: "Early Furnaces and Forges of Berks County, Penna." *Pennsylvania Magazine of History and Biography,* VIII (1884), 56-81.

PARKER, PETER J.: "The Philadelphia Printer: A Study of an Eighteenth-Century Businessman," *Business History Review,* XV (1966), 24-46.

SOLIS-COHEN, BERTHA: "Philadelphia's Expeditions to Labrador [1753-54]," *Pennsylvania History,* XIX (1952), 148-62.

STRADLEY, LEIGHTON P.: *Early Financial and Economic History of Pennsylvania* (Chicago & New York, 1942).

SWANK, JAMES M.: *Introduction to a History of Ironmaking and Coal Mining in Pennsylvania* (Philadelphia, 1878).

THURMAN, LAWRENCE S.: "An Account Book of Baynton, Wharton, and Morgan at Fort Pitt, 1765-1767," *Western Pennsylvania Historical Magazine,* XXIX (1946), 141-6.

TOLLES, FREDERICK B.: "Benjamin Franklin's Business Mentors: The Philadelphia Quaker Merchants," *William and Mary Quarterly,* 3rd ser., IV (1947), 60-9.

WAX, DAROLD D.: "The Demand for Slave Labor in Colonial Pennsylvania," *Pennsylvania History,* XXXIV (1967), 331-45; "Negro Imports into Pennsylvania, 1720-1766," *ibid.,* XXXII (1965), 254-87; and "Quaker Merchants and the Slave Trade in Colonial Pennsylvania," *Pennsylvania Magazine of History and Biography,* LXXXVI (1962), 143-59.

5. Social

CHEYNEY, EDWARD POTTS: *The History of the University of Pennsylvania, 1740-1940* (Philadelphia, 1940).

CUMMINGS, HUBERTIS M.: "The Paxton Killings [1763]," *Journal of Presbyterian History,* XLIV (1966), 219-43.

DIFFENDERFFER, FRANK RIED: *The German Immigration into Pennsylvania through the Port of Philadelphia from 1700 to 1775* (Lancaster, Pa., 1900); reprinted from the Pennsylvania German Society, *Proceedings,* Vol. X.

DUNAWAY, WAYLAND FULLER: *The Scotch-Irish of Colonial Pennsylvania* (Chapel Hill., N.C., 1944), and "Pennsylvania as an Early Distributing Center of Population," *Pennsylvania Magazine of History and Biography,* LV (1931), 134-69.

FITZROY, HERBERT W. K.: "The Punishment of Crime in Provincial Pennsylvania," *Pennsylvania Magazine of History and Biography*, LX (1936), 242-69.

GEISER, KARL FREDERICK: *Redemptioners and Indentured Servants in the Colony and Commonwealth of Pennsylvania* (New Haven, Conn., 1901).

GILBERT, RUSSELL WIEDER: *A Picture of the Pennsylvania Germans, Pennsylvania History Studies*, No. 1 (rev. edn., Gettysburg, Pa., 1958).

GIPSON, LAWRENCE HENRY: "The Criminal Codes of Pennsylvania . . . ," American Institute of Criminal Law and Criminology, *Journal*, VI (1915-16), 323-44; and "Crime and Its Punishment in Provincial Pennsylvania: A Phase of the Social History of the Commonwealth," *Pennsylvania History*, II (1935), 3-16.

GOLLIN, GILLIAN LINDT: *Moravians in Two Worlds* (New York, 1967).

GRAHAM, ROBERT EARLE: "The Taverns of Colonial Philadelphia," American Philosophical Society, *Transactions*, n. ser., XLIII (1953), 318-25.

HARLAN, ROBERT D.: "David Hall's Bookshop and Its British Sources of Supply," *Books in America's Past: Essays Honoring Rudolph H. Gjelsness* (David Kaser, ed., Charlottesville, Va., 1966), pp. 2-23.

HERRICK, CHESSMAN ABIAH: *White Servitude in Pennsylvania: Indentured and Redemption Labor in Colony and Commonwealth* (Philadelphia, 1926).

HERSHBERGER, GUY FRANKLIN: "Pacifism and the State in Colonial Pennsylvania," *Church History*, VIII (1939), 54-75.

HINKE, WILLIAM J.: "German Reformed Church Records in Pennsylvania [1725-1947]," National Genealogical Society, *Quarterly*, XXXVII (1949), 33-8.

JORDAN, JOHN W.: "Moravian Immigration to Pennsylvania, 1734-1767: With Some Account of Transport Vessels," Moravian Historical Society, *Transactions*, V (1895-9), 51-90.

KLEES, FREDERICK: *The Pennsylvania Dutch* (New York, 1950).

KLETT, GUY S.: *Presbyterians in Colonial Pennsylvania* (Philadelphia, 1937) and *The Scotch-Irish in Pennsylvania* (Gettysburg, Pa., 1948).

KLINGBERG, FRANK J.: "The African Immigrant in Colonial Pennsylvania and Delaware," *Historical Magazine of the Protestant Episcopal Church*, XI (1942), 126-53.

KNAUSS, JAMES OWEN: *Social Conditions among the Pennsylvania Germans in the Eighteenth Century: As Revealed in the German Newspapers Published in America* (Lancaster, Pa., 1922); reprinted from the Pennsylvania German Society, *Proceedings*, Vol. XXIX.

KRIEBEL, HOWARD WIEGNER: *The Schwenkfelders in Pennsylvania: A Historical Sketch* (Lancaster, Pa., 1904); reprinted from the Pennsylvania German Society, *Proceedings*, Vol. XIII.

LEDET, WILTON PAUL: "Acadian Exiles in Pennsylvania," *Pennsylvania History*, IX (1942), 118-28.

MARIE BLANCHE, SISTER: "The Catholic Church in Colonial Pennsylvania," *Pennsylvania History*, III (1936), 240-58.

PENNINGTON, EDWARD LEGARE: "The Anglican Clergy of Pennsylvania in the American Revolution," *Pennsylvania Magazine of History and Biography*, LXIII (1939), 401-31.

REED, WILLIAM B.: "The Acadian Exiles, or French Neutrals in Pennsylvania," Historical Society of Pennsylvania, *Memoirs*, VI (1858), 285-316.

ROTHERMUND, DIETMAR: *The Layman's Progress: Religious and Political Experience in Colonial Pennsylvania, 1740-1770* (Philadelphia, 1961), and the articles: "The German Problem of Colonial Pennsylvania," *Pennsylvania Magazine of History and Biography*, LXXXIV (1960), 3-21, and "Political Factions and the Great Awakening," *Pennsylvania History*, XXVI (1959), 317-31. This article deals primarily with the pre-1748 period but is useful for background material.

SACHSE, JULIUS FRIEDRICH: *The German Sectarians of Pennsylvania, 1708-1800: A Critical and Legendary History of the Ephrata Cloister and the Dunkers* (2 vols., Philadelphia, 1899-1900).

SCHANTZ, FRANKLIN J. F.: *The Domestic Life and Characteristics of the Pennsylvania-German Pioneer* (Lancaster, Pa., 1900); reprinted from the Pennsylvania German Society, *Proceedings*, Vol. X.

SMITH, C. HENRY: *The Mennonite Immigration to Pennsylvania in the Eighteenth Century* (Norristown, Pa., 1929); reprinted from the Pennsylvania German Society, *Proceedings*, Vol. XXXV.

STOUDT, JOHN JOSEPH: "The German Press in Pennsylvania and the American Revolution," *Pennsylvania Magazine of History and Biography*, LIX (1935), 74-90.

STRAUB, JEAN S.: "Teaching in the Friends' Latin School of Philadelphia in the Eighteenth Century," *Pennsylvania Magazine of History and Biography*, XCI (1967), 434-56.

TOLLES, FREDERICK B.: *Meeting House and Counting House: The Quaker Merchants of Colonial Philadelphia, 1682-1763* (Chapel Hill, N.C., 1948).

TURNER, EDWARD RAYMOND: *The Negro in Pennsylvania: Slavery-Servitude-Freedom, 1639-1861* (Washington, D.C., 1911).

WALLACE, PAUL A. W.: "The John Heckewelder Papers," *Pennsylvania History*, XXVII (1960), 249-62.

WINDHAUSEN, JOHN D.: "Quaker Pacifism and the Image of Isaac Norris, II," *ibid.*, XXXIV (1967), 346-60.

WOLF, EDWIN, JR., and MAXWELL WHITEMAN: *The History of the Jews in Philadelphia* (Philadelphia, 1957).

WOLF, GEORGE D.: "The Politics of Fair Play [1769-84]," *Pennsylvania His-*

tory, XXXII (1965), 8-24. Refers to the settlement of the community of Fair Play established along the Susquehanna River by 150 families.

6. Biographical

BARTRAM, JOHN and WILLIAM. *Memorial of John Bartram and Humphrey Marshall: With Notices of Their Botanical Contemporaries* by William Darlington (Philadelphia, 1849); *John and William Bartram . . .* by Ernest Earnest (Philadelphia, 1940); and *William Bartram [1739-1823] Interpreter of the American Landscape* by Nathan B. Fagin (Baltimore, Md., 1933).

BENEZET, ANTHONY. *Friend Anthony Benezet* by George S. Brooke (London & Philadelphia, 1937). Includes a large collection of Benezet's letters.

BEISSEL, JOHANN CONRAD. *Johann Conrad Beissel: Mystic and Martinet, 1690-1786* by Walter C. Klein (Philadelphia, 1942).

BRYAN, GEORGE. *George Bryan and the Constitution of Pennsylvania, 1731-1791* by Burton A. Konkle (Philadelphia, 1922).

BURD, JAMES. *James Burd: Frontier Defender, 1726-1793* by Lily Lee Nixon (Philadelphia, 1941).

CHEW, BENJAMIN. *Benjamin Chew, 1722-1810 . . .* by Burton A. Konkle (Philadelphia, 1932).

DENNY, WILLIAM. "Governor Denny and the Quartering Act of 1756" by John J. Zimmerman, *Pennsylvania Magazine of History and Biography*, XCI (1967), 266-81.

DICKINSON, JOHN. Despite Dickinson's prominence in Pennsylvania politics and the Revolutionary movement, there have been, relatively few worthwhile studies of him. At present, there are two book-length studies, including the dated biography by Charles J. Stillé: *The Life and Times of John Dickinson, 1732-1808*, Historical Society of Pennsylvania, *Memoirs*, XIII (Philadelphia, 1891), and the study of David L. Jacobson: *John Dickinson and the Revolution in Pennsylvania, 1764-1776*, University of California, *Publications in History*, Vol. 78 (Berkeley, Calif. & Los Angeles, 1965). There is also the biographical sketch by Isaac Sharpless in his *Political Leaders of Provincial Pennsylvania* (New York, 1919), pp. 224-43. In recent years several articles have appeared of which the most valuable is undoubtedly H. Trevor Colbourn's "The Historical Perspective of John Dickinson," *Early Dickinsoniana: The Boyd Lee Spahr Lectures in Americana, 1957-1961* (Carlisle, Pa., 1961), pp. 3-37. See also Colburn's "John Dickinson, Historical Revolutionary," *Pennsylvania Magazine of History and Biography*, LXXXIII (1959), 271-92; David L. Jacobson: "John Dickinson's

Fight against Royal Government, 1764," *William and Mary Quarterly*, 3rd ser., XIX (1962), 64-85; and Bernhard Knollenberg: "John Dickinson vs. John Adams, 1774-1776," American Philosophical Society, *Proceedings*, CVII (1963), 138-44. Two unpublished doctoral dissertations that might be consulted are David L. Jacobson's "John Dickinson and Joseph Galloway, 1764-1776: A Study in Contrasts," Princeton University, 1959; and John H. Powell's "John Dickinson, Penman of the American Revolution, 1732-1767," University of Iowa, 1938; for an abstract of the latter see: *Abstracts in History*, IV, University of Iowa, *Studies in the Social Sciences*, XI: No. 393 (Iowa City, Iowa, 1941), pp. 103-16.

DUCHÉ, JACOB. "Rev. Jacob Duché, the First Chaplain of Congress" by Edward Duffield Neill, *Pennsylvania Magazine of History and Biography*, II (1878), 58-73.

FRANKLIN, BENJAMIN. Over the years, Franklin has remained one of the most popular subjects for writers on this period. It would not be feasible to cite here all the materials that have been published concerning this man, but some of the more significant items follow: Older biographical sketches include James Parton's *Life and Times of Benjamin Franklin* (2 vols., Boston & New York, 1864), and Sydney George Fisher's *The True Benjamin Franklin* (Philadelphia, 1899; reissued as *Benjamin Franklin*, London & Philadelphia, 1927). Later biographies include *Benjamin Franklin* by Carl Van Doren (New York, 1938), an outstanding biography; *Benjamin Franklin: A Biographical Sketch* by Carl Becker (Ithaca, N.Y., 1946); and, most recent, Ralph L. Ketcham's *Benjamin Franklin* (New York, 1965).

More numerous are the works dealing with some particular aspect of Franklin's life. Two recent writers deal with his relationship to colonial politics; William S. Hanna: *Benjamin Franklin and Pennsylvania Politics* (Stanford, Calif., 1964), and Paul W. Conner: *Poor Richard's Politicks: Benjamin Franklin and His New American Order* (New York, 1965). For a consideration of Franklin's relationship to other spheres of public life, see Gerald Stourzh's *Benjamin Franklin and American Foreign Policy* (Chicago, 1954); Ruth Lapham Butler's *Doctor Franklin: Postmaster General* (Garden City, N.Y., 1928); and J. Bennett Nolan's *General Benjamin Franklin: The Military Career of a Philosopher* (London & Philadelphia, 1936), the last dealing with Franklin's activities during the Great War for the Empire. Verner W. Crane sought in his *Benjamin Franklin and a Rising People* (Boston, 1954) to typify American history using Franklin as an example. See also Crane's *Benjamin Franklin: Englishman and American* (Baltimore, Md. & Providence, R.I., 1936), which is more concerned with the philosophical aspects of Franklin. Three recent books also emphasize that aspect of the man—Bruce I. Granger: *Benjamin Franklin: An American Man of Letters* (Ithaca, N.Y., 1964), and two books by Alfred Owen Aldridge: *Benjamin Franklin: Philosopher and Man* (Philadelphia, 1965) and *Benjamin Franklin and Nature's God* (Durham, N.C., 1967).

In addition to the great number of books available, there is a profusion of articles that shed light upon various aspects of Franklin's life and career, a few of the more significant follow. Several worthwhile articles relating to Franklin's political conduct include James H. Hutson's "Benjamin Franklin and the Parliamentary Grant for 1758," *William and Mary Quarterly*, XXIII (1966), 575-95; Verner W. Crane's "Benjamin Franklin and the Stamp Act," Colonial Society of Massachusetts, *Publications*, XXXII (*Transactions, 1933-1937*), 56-77; William Renwick Riddell's "Benjamin Franklin and Colonial Money," *Pennsylvania Magazine of History and Biography*, LIV (1930), 52-64; and John J. Zimmerman's "Benjamin Franklin and the Quaker Party, 1755-1756," *William and Mary Quarterly*, 3rd ser., XVIII (1960), 291-313. For essays on political theory, one should consult Clinton Rossiter's "The Political Theory of Benjamin Franklin," *Pennsylvania Magazine of History and Biography*, LXXVI (1952), 259-93; Gerald Stourzh's "Reason and Power in Benjamin Franklin's Political Thought," *American Political Science Review*, XLVII (1953), 1092-1115; and Max Savelle's "Benjamin Franklin and American Liberalism," *Western Humanities Review*, XVIII (1964), 197-209. Other articles which are well worth consulting are Glenn Weaver's "Benjamin Franklin and the Pennsylvania Germans," *William and Mary Quarterly*, 3rd ser., XIV (1957), 536-59; John J. Zimmerman's "Benjamin Franklin and the *Pennsylvania Chronicle*," *Pennsylvania Magazine of History and Biography*, LXXXI (1957), 351-364; Ralph L. Ketcham's "Benjamin Franklin and William Smith: New Light on an Old Philadelphia Quarrel," *Pennsylvania Magazine of History and Biography*, LXXXVIII (1964), 142-63; and Leonard W. Labaree's "In Search of 'B. Franklin,'" *William and Mary Quarterly*, 3rd ser., XVI (1959), 188-97. For two rather recent bibliographies of works on Franklin, see the American Philosophical Society, *Library Bulletin* for 1955, *Studies on Benjamin Franklin: The Two Hundred and Fiftieth Anniversary of His Birth, Jan. 17, 1956*, and "Benjamin Franklin," *Bibliography of Pennsylvania History* (Norman B. Wilkinson, comp., and S. K. Stevens, ed., Harrisburg, 1957).

FRASER, JOHN. "John Fraser: Western Pennsylvania Frontiersman" by Howard Glenn Clark, *Western Pennsylvania Historical Magazine*, XXXIX (1956), 35-43, 109-24.

GALLOWAY, JOSEPH. "Joseph Galloway, the Loyalist Politician" by Ernest H. Baldwin, *Pennsylvania Magazine of History and Biography*, XXVI (1902), 161-91, 289-321, 417-42. See also the following doctoral dissertations: "Joseph Galloway: Loyalist" by Oliver C. Kuntzleman, Temple University, 1941; and "Joseph Galloway: His Life and Times" by Raymond C. Werner, Iowa State University, 1927.

GRUBER, JOHANN ADAM. "Johann Adam Gruber, Pennsylvania-German Prophet and Poet" by Donald F. Durnbaugh, *Pennsylvania Magazine of History and Biography*, LXXXIII (1959), 382-408.

HECKEWELDER, JOHN. "The Influence of John Heckewelder, Moravian Missionary, on the Lives of Western Pennsylvania Indians and Settlers" by Philip H. Lantz, *Western Pennsylvania Historical Magazine*, XXXVIII (1955), 21-32.

MARSHALL, HUMPHREY, *see* under Bartram, John.

MIFFLIN, THOMAS. *Thomas Mifflin and the Politics of the American Revolution* by Kenneth R. Rossman ([Chapel Hill, N.C., 1952]).

MONTOUR, MADAME. "Madame Montour" by John P. Penny, Jr., *Western Pennsylvania Historical Magazine*, XIII (1930), 55-8.

MORGAN, JOHN. *John Morgan: Continental Doctor* by Whitfield J. Bell, Jr. (Philadelphia, 1965).

MORRIS, ROBERT. *Robert Morris: Patriot and Financier* by Ellis Paxson Oberholtzer (London & New York, 1903).

MUHLENBERG, HENRY MELCHIOR. *Life and Times of Henry Melchior Muhlenberg* by William J. Mann (2nd edn., Philadelphia, 1888).

MUHLENBERG, PETER. *The Fighting Parson of the American Revolution: A Biography of General Peter Muhlenberg . . .* by Edward W. Hocker (Philadelphia, 1936).

PEMBERTON, ISRAEL. *Israel Pemberton, King of the Quakers* by Theodore Thayer (Philadelphia, 1943).

PEMBERTON, JAMES. "James Pemberton" by Isaac Sharpless, *Political Leaders of Provincial Pennsylvania* (New York, 1919), pp. 200-23.

Penn Family. *The Penns of Pennsylvania and England* by Arthur Pound (New York, 1932).

PETERS, RICHARD. *Richard Peters: Provincial Secretary and Cleric, 1704-1776* by Hubertis Cummings (Philadelphia, 1944).

REED, JOSEPH. *Joseph Reed: A Moderate in the American Revolution* by John F. Roche, Columbia University, *Studies in the Social Sciences*, No. 595 (New York, 1957). See also Roche's article: "Was Joseph Reed Disloyal?" *William and Mary Quarterly*, 3rd ser., VII (1951), 406-17, and William B. Reed's *Life and Correspondence of Joseph Reed*, already listed.

RITTENHOUSE, DAVID. *David Rittenhouse: Astronomer-Patriot, 1732-1796* by Edward Ford (Philadelphia, 1946) and *David Rittenhouse* by Brooke Hindle (Princeton, N.J., 1964). See also Hindle's article co-authored with his wife, Helen: "David Rittenhouse and the Illusion of Reversible Relief," *Isis,* L (1959), 135-40.

RUSH, BENJAMIN. *Benjamin Rush, Physician and Citizen, 1746-1818* by Nathan G. Goodman (Philadelphia, 1934), and *Revolutionary Doctor: Benjamin Rush, 1746-1813* by Carl Binger (New York, 1966). For a discussion of Rush's educational contributions, see: *Benjamin Rush and His Services to American Education* by Harry S. Good (Berne, Ind., c. 1918). Also of value are the articles: "The Reputation of Benjamin Rush" by Lyman H. Butterfield, *Pennsylvania History,* XVII (1950), 3-22; Iminder Gwynneth: "An Exhibit of the Life and Works of Benjamin Rush, M.D.," History of Medicine, *Bulletin,* XIX (1946), 96-112; "Benjamin Rush, M.D., 1746-1813, the American Sydenham" by John E. Kieffer, *Pennsylvania Health,* I (1940), 19-25; and "A Physician Philanthropist in the Eighteenth Century: Benjamin Rush, 1746-1813," *Social Service Review,* II (1928), 274-304.

RUSH, JACOB. "Hon. Jacob Rush of the Pennsylvania Judiciary" by Louis Richards, *Pennsylvania Magazine of History and Biography,* XXXIX (1915), 53-68.

SAUER, CHRISTOPHER. "Christopher Sauer, Pensylvania-German Printer: His Youth in Germany and Later Relationships with Europe" by Donald F. Durnbaugh, *Pennsylvania Magazine of History and Biography,* LXXXII (1958), 316-40.

SMITH, WILLIAM. *William Smith, Educator and Churchman, 1727-1803* by Albert Frank Gegenheimer (Philadelphia, 1943) and the article "Provost Smith and the Quest for Funds" by Bertha Sprague Fox, *Pennsylvania History,* II (1935), 225-38. See also Ketcham's article under Franklin, Benjamin.

THOMSON, CHARLES. *The Life of Charles Thomson: Secretary of the Continental Congress* . . . by Lewis R. Harley (Philadelphia, 1900). See also John J. Zimmerman's article: "Charles Thomson: 'The Sam Adams of Philadelphia,'" *Mississippi Valley Historical Review,* XLV (1958), 464-80.

WAYNE, ANTHONY. *Anthony Wayne: A Trouble Shooter of the American Revolution* by Harry Emerson Wildes (New York, 1941).

WEISER, CONRAD. *Conrad Weiser, 1696-1760: Friend of Colonist and Mohawk* by Paul A. W. Wallace (London & Philadelphia, 1945); *The Life of Conrad Weiser as It Relates to His Services as Official Interpreter between New York and Pennsylvania* . . . by William M. Beauchamp (Syracuse, N.Y., 1925); *Conrad Weiser, Pennsylvania Peacemaker* by Arthur D. Graeff (Allentown, Pa., 1943); and "Conrad Weiser, an Early Lutheran Patriot" by Henry M. M. Richards, Lebanon County Historical Society, *Papers,* IX (1928-9), 163-85.

WILSON, JAMES. *James Wilson: Founding Father, 1742-1798* by Charles
Page Smith (Chapel Hill, N.C., 1956). See also the articles: "James
Wilson and James Iredell: A Parallel and a Contrast" by Hampton
L. Carson, *Pennsylvania Magazine of History and Biography*, XLV
(1921), 1-33, which may also be found in American Bar Associa-
tion, *Journal*, VII (1921), 123-31, and "James Wilson and the
Philosophy of Freedom in the American Revolution" by William
C. Smith, American Catholic Historical Society of Philadelphia,
Records, LI (1939), 65-71.

7. Military

ALBERT, GEORGE DALLAS: *Report of the Commission to Locate the Site of
the Frontier Forts of Pennsylvania, Vol. II: The Frontier Forts
of Western Pennsylvania* (Harrisburg, Pa., 1896).

ANDERSON, NILES: *The Battle of Bushy Run* (Harrisburg, Pa., 1966).

DAVIS, N. DARNELL: "British Newspaper Accounts of Braddock's Defeat,"
Pennsylvania Magazine of History and Biography, XXIII (1899),
310-28.

HUNTER, WILLIAM A.: *Forts on the Pennsylvania Frontier, 1753-1758*
(Harrisburg, Pa., 1960).

JAMES, ALFRED PROCTER, and CHARLES MORSE STOTZ: *Drums in the Forest*
([Pittsburgh, Pa., 1958]).

LACOCK, JOHN KENNEDY: "Braddock Road," *Pennsylvania Magazine of
History and Biography*, XXXVIII (1914), 1-38.

MC CARDELL, LEE: *Ill-Starred General: Braddock of the Coldstream Guards*
(New York, 1958).

NESS, GEORGE T., JR.: "The Braddock Campaign, 1755 . . . ," *Military Engineer*, LI (1959), 18-23, 111-17, 211-13.

O'MEARA, WALTER: *Guns at the Forks* (Englewood, N.J., 1965).

PARGELLIS, STANLEY M.: "Braddock's Defeat," *American Historical Review*,
XLI (1935-6), 253-69.

SHEA, JOHN GILMARY DAWSON: *Relations Diverses sur la Bataille du Malan-
gueulé gagné le 9 Juillet 1755 par les François sous M. Le Beaujeu
. . . sur les Anglois sous M. Braddock . . .* (New York, 1860).

WALLACE, PAUL A. W.: " 'Blunder Camp': A Note on the Braddock Road,"
Pennsylvania Magazine of History and Biography, LXXXVII
(1963), 21-30.

WEBSTER, ELEANOR M.: "Insurrection at Fort Loudon in 1765: Rebellion
or Preservation of Peace?" *Western Pennsylvania Historical Magazine*, XLVII (1964), 125-39.

D. MAPS

EVANS, LEWIS: *A Map of Pensilvania, New-Jersey, New-York, and the Three Delaware Counties* ([Philadelphia, 1749]). The sculptor for this map was L. Herbert; it is to be found in *Pennsylvania Archives*, 3rd series, Appendix I-X.

FADEN, WILLIAM, engr.: *Plan of the City and Environs of Philadelphia Surveyed by N. Scull and G. Heap. 1777.* In Jefferys: *The American Atlas . . .* , No. 20. It will be noted that while this atlas was published in 1776, the map was engraved by Faden in 1777. Jefferys died in 1771 and Faden took over the enterprise of publishing the atlas and doubtless for prestige reasons referred to the atlas as Jefferys'. Further, some of the maps may well have been produced earlier by Jefferys.

The First Fort Pitt, 1758. In *Pennsylvania Archives* XII (1856), 430.

HEAP, GEORGE: *An East Prospect of the City of Philadelphia: Taken by George Heap, from the Jersey Shore, under the Direction of Nicholas Scull.* In Jefferys: *A General Topography of North America and the West Indies*, No. 44.

HOWELL, READING: *A Map of the State of Pennsylvania* (Philadelphia, 1792). In *Pennsylvania Archives*, 3rd series, Appendix, I-X. Although the map falls beyond the limits of the period, it is very useful to the student of the late provincial years in its illustration of the development of counties, roads, and settled areas.

HUTCHINS, THOMAS: *Plan of Fort Machault, Called Fort Venango, 1759.* The Public Archives of Canada has the original sketch. In S. K. Stevens and D. H. Kent: *Wilderness Chronicles of Northwestern Pennsylvania*, opp. p. 166.

————: *Plan of the Battle near Bushy-Run, Gained by Col. Bouquet on the 5th and 6th of Aug. 1763.* In Jefferys: *A General Topography of North America and the West Indies*, No. 53.

JEFFERYS, THOMAS, sculp.: *A Map of the Province of Pennsylvania Intended Chiefly to Illustrate the Account of the Several Indian Purchases Made by the Proprietors of the Said Province, the Claims Made by the Indians. . . .* In Charles Thomson: *An Enquiry into the Causes of the Alienation of the Delaware and Shawanese Indians from the British Interest* (London, 1759; Philadelphia, 1867).

KITCHEN, THOMAS: *A Map of the Province of Pensilvania* ([London], 1756). In the *London Magazine*, XXV (1756), opp. p. 599.

————: *Plan of Fort Pitt or Pittsbourg.* In Thomas Mante: *The History of the Late War in North America . . .* (London, 1772), opp. p. 158.

A *Map of the Country round Philadelphia Including Part of New Jersey, New York, Staten Island & Long Island*. In the *Gentleman's Magazine*, XLVI (1776), opp. p. 396.

A *Map of Part of the Province of Pennsylvania and of the Counties of Newcastle, Kent, and Sussex on Delaware: Shewing the Temporary Limits of the Jurisdiction of Pennsylvania and Maryland Fixed According to an Order of His Majesty in Council, Dated the 25th Day of May in the Year 1738. Surveyed in the Year 1739*. In *Report of the Resurvey of the Maryland-Pennsylvania Boundary: Part of Mason and Dixon Line* . . . , opp. p. 166.

[Map Showing the Boundary Conflict between Connecticut and Pennsylvania]. This purely outline map carries no title; it was prepared for the Proprietors of Pennsylvania about 1755. In Boyd: *The Susquehannah Company Papers*, I: opp. p. 8.

MYNDE, J., sculp.: *A Map of That Part of America where a Degree of Latitude Was Measured for the Royal Society by Cha: Mason & Jere: Dixon, 1768*. In *Philosophical Transactions*, LVIII (London, 1769), p. 325.

A *Plan of the Boundary Lines between the Province of Maryland and the Three Lower Counties on Delaware with Part of the Parallel of Latitude Which Is the Boundary between the Province of Maryland and Pennsylvania*. This is a facsimile of the original Mason and Dixon map as ratified November 9, 1768 by the authorized representatives of the two provinces. In *Report on the Resurvey of the Maryland-Pennsylvania Boundary: Part of the Mason and Dixon Line*. . . . The folded map is an end-piece, not to be confused with the map cited on p. 166 of the *Report*.

Plan of the City of Philadelphia, the Capital of Pennsylvania, from an Actual Survey by Benjamin Eastburn, Surveyor General, 1776. In Jefferys: *The American Atlas* . . . , No. 20a.

REED, JOHN: *Map of the City and Liberties of Philadelphia, with the Catalogue of Purchases* ([Philadelphia, 1774]). James Smithers was the sculptor of this map which appeared in Reed: *An Explanation of the City and Liberties of Philadelphia* (Philadelphia, 1774); the work is available on Readex microprint cards.

ROCQUE, JOHN: *Fort Bedford*. In [John and] Ann Rocque: *A Set of Plans and Forts in America* . . . , No. 14.

————: *Plan of the Retrench'd Camp at Fort Ligonier*. In *ibid.*, No. 20.

SCULL, NICHOLAS: *To the Honourable Thomas Penn and Richard Penn* . . . *This Map of the Improved Part of the Province of Pennsylvania Is Humbly Dedicated* . . . *1758*. Reprinted in *Pennsylvania Archives*, 3rd ser., Appendix I-X.

————, and GEORGE HEAP: *A Map of Philadelphia and Parts Adjacent*. In the *Gentleman's Magazine*, XXIII (1753), 373.

————, and ————: *A Plan of the City and Environs of Philadelphia*

(Philadelphia, 1777). William Faden engraved this map which appeared in Faden: *The North American Atlas* . . . , No. 25.

SCULL, WILLIAM: *A Map of Pennsylvania Exhibiting not only the improved Parts of the Province but also Its Extensive Frontiers: Laid down from Actual Surveys, and Chiefly from the Late Map of W. Scull, Published in 1770.* . . . In Jefferys: *The American Atlas* . . . , No. 20.

[STOBO, ROBERT]: *Plan of Fort Le Quesne [Duquesne], Built by the French at the Fork of the Ohio and Monongahela in 1754* ([London, 1768]). In Jefferys: *A General Topography of North America and the West Indies,* No. 45; also in *American Maps,* V: No. 24.

WALL, J. SUTTON: *Outline Map of Virginia Claims in Southwestern Pennsylvania* . . . *[1754-99].* In *Pennsylvania Archives,* 3rd ser., III: 482.

WALLACE, PAUL A. W.: *Indian Paths of Pennsylvania* (Harrisburg, Pa., 1964). This volume provides descriptions and modern sketch maps of Indian and trader paths in the state, including the path followed by Washington to Fort Le Boeuf.

RHODE ISLAND

A. BIBLIOGRAPHICAL AIDS

ALDEN, JOHN ELIOT, ed.: *Rhode Island Imprints, 1727-1800* (New York, 1949).

BARTLETT, JOHN RUSSELL: *Bibliography of Rhode Island: A Catalogue of Books and Other Publications Relating to the State of Rhode Island* . . . (Providence, R.I., 1864).

BRIGHAM, CLARENCE SAUNDERS: *Bibliography of Rhode Island History* ([Boston & Syracuse, N.Y.], 1902).

————: *List of Books upon Rhode Island History, Rhode Island Educational Circulars: Historical Series,* I (Providence, R.I., 1908).

HASSE, ADELAIDE R.: "Rhode Island, 1638-1789," in "Materials for a Bibliography of the Public Archives of the Thirteen Original States . . . ," American Historical Association, *Annual Report, 1906* (2 vols., Washington, D.C., 1908), II, 327-37.

"Index to the Providence Town Papers . . . 1642-1790," Record Commissioners, *Fourth Report . . . Relative to the Early Town Records* . . . (1895), 1-188. See also: "Index to the Providence Town Papers . . . 1639 to 1823," which appeared in the *Fifth Report* (1897), 1-136.

LOVEJOY, DAVID S.: "Bibliography," *Rhode Island Politics and the American Revolution, 1760-1776,* pp. 221-36.

B. PRINTED SOURCE MATERIALS

1. Government and related documents

Acts and Laws of His Majesty's Colony of Rhode-Island and Providence
Plantations, in America (Newport, R.I., 1752), covering the period
1745 to 1752.

Acts and Laws of the English Colony of Rhode Island and Providence-
Plantations . . . Made and passed since the Revision in June 1767
([Newport, R.I.], 1772).

. . . At the General Assembly of the Governor and Company of the English Colony of Rhode-Island, and Providence-Plantations in New-
England, in America . . . (published yearly, Newport, R.I., 1751-
1776).

BARTLETT, JOHN RUSSELL, ed.: Census of the Inhabitants of the Colony of
Rhode Island and Providence Plantations, Taken by Order of the
General Assembly, in the Year 1774 . . . (Providence, R.I., 1858).

———, ed.: Records of the Colony of Rhode Island and the Providence
Plantations in New England (10 vols., Providence, R.I., 1856-65).
Volumes V-VII are relevant to the period.

Early Records of the Town of Providence (Horatio Rogers, et al., eds.,
21 vols., Providence, R.I., 1892-1915).

KIMBALL, GERTRUDE SELWYN, ed.: The Correspondence of the Colonial
Governors of Rhode Island, 1723-1775 (2 vols., Boston & New
York, 1902-3).

Rhode Island: Acts and Resolves, 1747-1776 [Binder's title], (Facsimile,
9 vols., Providence, n.d.).

SMITH, JOSEPH JENCKS, ed.: Civil and Military List of Rhode Island, 1647-
1800: A List of All Officers Elected by the General Assembly . . .
to 1800 (Providence, R.I., 1900).

TOWLE, DOROTHY S., ed: The Records of the Vice-Admiralty Courts of
Rhode Island, 1716-1752, American Legal Records, III (Washing-
ton, D.C., 1936). The introduction was written by Charles M.
Andrews.

WARD, SAMUEL: Correspondence of Governor Samuel Ward, May 1775-
March 1776 (Bernhard Knollenberg, ed., Providence, R.I., 1952).
Contains an introductory biographical sketch by the editor.

2. Non-official contemporary writings

BARTLETT, JOHN RUSSELL: A History of the Destruction of His Britannic
Majesty's Schooner Gaspee in Naragansett Bay on the 10th June

1772, *Accompanied by the Correspondence Connected Therewith* . . . (Providence, R.I., 1861).

BRYANT, SAMUEL W., ed.: "HMS *Gaspee*: The Court-Martial [1772]," *Rhode Island History*, XXV (1966), 65-72. Includes minutes of the court martial proceedings.

[CHAMPLIN, ROBERT]: *A Rhode Island Slaver: Trade Book of the Sloop Adventure, 1773-1774* . . . (Verner W. Crane, ed., Providence, R.I., 1922).

Commerce of Rhode Island, 1726-1800, Massachusetts Historical Society, *Collections*, 7th ser., IX-X (Worthington Chauncey Ford, *et al.*, eds., 2 vols., Boston, 1914-15).

A Discourse Addressed to the Sons of Liberty: At a Solemn Assembly near Liberty-Tree in Providence, February 14, 1766 (Providence [1766]). Signed "Pro Patria." The author asserted that the colonists were being victimized by the English merchants and statesmen.

[DOWNER, SILAS]: *A Discourse Delivered in Providence in the Colony of Rhode Island, upon the 25th Day of July 1768: At the Dedication of the Tree of Liberty* . . . (Providence, R.I., 1768). The pamphlet also includes a description of the ceremonies following the discourse.

MASON, GEORGE CHAMPLIN, ed.: *Annals of Trinity Church, Newport, Rhode Island, 1698-1821* (2 vols., Newport, R.I., 1890).

ROELKER, WILLIAM G., and CLARKSON A. COLLINS, III, comps.: "The Patrol of Narragansett Bay (1774-1776) by H.M.S. *Rose*, Captain James Wallace," *Rhode Island History*, VII-IX (1948-50), *passim*. Discusses the colonists' problems with the British Navy.

STAPLES, WILLIAM R., comp.: *The Documentary History of the Destruction of the Gaspee* (Providence, R.I., 1845).

3. Newspapers

The Newport Mercury [The Newport Mercury, or the Weekly Advertiser], b. 1758, Newport.

The Providence Gazette; and Country Journal, b. 1762, Providence.

C. SECONDARY WORKS

1. General

ARNOLD, SAMUEL GREENE: *History of the State of Rhode Island and Providence Plantations* (2 vols., London & New York, 1859-60).

BATES, FRANK GREENE: *Rhode Island and the Formation of the Union*,

Columbia University, *Studies in History, Economics, and Public Law*, No. 27 (London & New York, 1898).

BICKNELL, THOMAS WILLIAMS: *The History of the State of Rhode Island and Providence Plantations* (3 vols., New York, 1920). Vols. II and III contain pertinent material.

FIELD, EDWARD, ed.: *State of Rhode Island and Providence Plantations at the End of the Century: A History* . . . (3 vols., Boston & Syracuse, New York, 1902).

PEASE, JOHN C.: *see* under Connecticut.

PRESTON, HOWARD WILLIS: *Rhode Island's Historic Background*, Rhode Island State Bureau of Information, *Historical Publication*, No. 3 (Providence, R.I., 1930).

TANNER, EARL C.: *Rhode Island: a Brief History* (Providence, R.I., 1954).

2. *Local*

DENISON, FREDERIC: *Westerly, Rhode Island and Its Witnesses* . . . *[1626-1876]* (Providence, R.I., 1878).

DORR, HENRY C.: *Planting and Growth of Providence* . . . , *Rhode Island Historical Tracts*, 1st ser., No. 15 (Providence, R.I., 1882).

GREENE, WELCOME ARNOLD: *The Providence Plantations for Two Hundred and Fifty Years: An Historical Review of the Foundation, Rise, and Progress of the City* . . . (Providence, R.I., 1886).

KIMBALL, GERTRUDE SELWYN: *Providence in Colonial Times* (Boston & New York, 1912).

PETERSON, EDWARD: *History of Rhode Island* (New York, 1853). This is concerned only with Newport and the island of Rhode Island.

PORTER, ELISHA R., JR.: *The Early History of Narragansett: With an Appendix of Original Documents* . . . , Rhode Island Historical Society, *Collections*, III (Providence, R.I., 1835).

STAPLES, WILLIAM R.: *Annals of the Town of Providence* . . . , Rhode Island Historical Society, *Collections*, V (Providence, R.I., 1843).

THOMPSON, CHARLES O. F.: *Sketches of Old Bristol* (Providence, R.I., 1942).

3. *Political*

CREECH, MARGARET: *Three Centuries of Poor Law Administration: A Study of Legislation in Rhode Island*, Social Service Monographs, No. 24 (Chicago, 1936).

FOSTER, WILLIAM EATON: "Town Government in Rhode Island," Johns Hopkins University, *Studies in Historical and Political Science*, 4th ser. (1886), 69-104.

LESLIE, WILLIAM R.: "The *Gaspee* Affair: A Study of Its Constitutional

Significance," *Mississippi Valley Historical Review,* XXXIX (1952-1953), 233-56.

LOVEJOY, DAVID SHERMAN: *Rhode Island Politics and the American Revolution, 1760-1776,* Brown University, *Studies,* XXIII (Providence, R.I., 1958).

RIDER, SIDNEY S.: *An Inquiry Concerning the Origin of the Clause in the Laws of Rhode Island (1719-1783) Disfranchising Roman Catholics, Rhode Island Historical Tracts,* 2nd ser., No. 1 (Providence, R.I., 1889).

STAPLES, WILLIAM R.: *Rhode Island in the Continental Congress . . . 1765-1790* (Reuben Aldridge Guild, ed., Providence, R.I., 1870).

THOMPSON, MACK E.: "The Ward-Hopkins Controversy and the American Revolution in Rhode Island: An Interpretation," *William and Mary Quarterly,* 3rd ser., XVI (1959), 363-75. The author refutes the claim that Rhode Island's northern agrarian radicals led the colony into the Revolution.

WIENER, FREDERICK BERNAYS: "Notes on the Rhode Island Admiralty, 1727-1790," *Harvard Law Review,* XLVI (1932-3), 44-90. Included is an appendix of source materials, pages 73-90.

WULSIN, EUGENE: "The Political Consequences of the Burning of the *Gaspee,*" *Rhode Island History,* III (1944), 1-11, 55-64.

4. *Economic*

COLEMAN, PETER J.: "The Insolvent Debtor in Rhode Island, 1745-1828," *William and Mary Quarterly,* 3rd ser., XXII (1965), 413-34.

CRAWFORD, WALTER FREEMAN: "The Commerce of Rhode Island with the Southern Colonies in the Eighteenth Century," Rhode Island Historical Society, *Collections,* XIV (1921), 99-110, 124-30.

MAYER, KURT BERND: *Economic Development and Population Growth in Rhode Island, 1636-1950* (Providence, R.I., 1953). Pages 13-26 are relevant to the period.

POTTER, ELISHA R., and SIDNEY S. RIDER: *Some Account of the Bills of Credit or Paper Money of Rhode Island 1710 to 1786, Rhode Island Historical Tracts,* No. 8 (Providence, R.I., 1880).

STOKES, HOWARD KEMBLE: *The Finances and Administration of Providence,* Johns Hopkins University, *Studies in Historical and Political Science,* Extra Vol., XXV (Baltimore, Md., 1903).

WIENER, FREDERICK BERNAYS: "The Rhode Island Merchants and the Sugar Act," *New England Quarterly,* III (1930), 464-500.

5. *Social*

ADELMAN, DAVID C.: "Strangers: Civil Rights of Jews in the Colony of Rhode Island," *Rhode Island History,* XIII (1954), 65-77.

BRIDENBAUGH, CARL: "Colonial Newport as a Summer Resort," Rhode Island Historical Society, *Collections*, XXVI (1933), 1-23. For lists of prominent southern planters who summered in Newport, see also his "Charlestonians at Newport, 1767-1775," *South Carolina Historical and Genealogical Magazine*, XLI (1940), 43-7.

BRONSON, WALTER COCHRANE: *The History of Brown University, 1764-1914* (Providence, R.I., 1914).

CHANNING, EDWARD: "The Narragansett Planters: A Study of Causes," Johns Hopkins University, *Studies in Historical and Political Science*, 4th ser. (1886), 105-27. Chiefly valuable for its background.

JOHNSTON, W. D.: "Slavery in Rhode Island, 1775-1776," *Papers from the Historical Seminary of Brown University* (J. Franklin Jameson, ed., Providence, R.I., 1895), No. 5.

KOHLER, MAX J.: "The Jews in Newport," American Jewish Historical Society, *Publications*, VI (1897), 61-80.

MILLER, WILLIAM DAVIS: "The Narragansett Planters," American Antiquarian Society, *Proceedings*, n. ser., XLIII (1933), 49-115. Pages 105-15, containing a discussion of the causes of decline, are relevant to the period.

STINESS, JOHN H.: *A Century of Lotteries in Rhode Island, 1744-1844*, *Rhode Island Historical Tracts*, 2nd ser., No. 3 (Providence, R.I., 1896).

UPDIKE, WILKINS: *A History of the Episcopal Church in Narragansett, Rhode Island* . . . (1st edn., New York, 1847; 2nd edn., rev. & enl. by David Goodwin, 3 vols., Boston, 1907). Contains some original materials.

WEEDEN, WILLIAM B.: *Early Rhode Island: A Social History of the People* (New York, 1910).

6. Biographical

Brown Family. *The Browns of Providence Plantations: Colonial Years* by James Blaine Hedges (Cambridge, Mass., 1952).

ELLERY, WILLIAM. *Life of William Ellery* by Edward T. Channing, *Library of American Biography*, VI (Boston, 1836).

GODDARD, WILLIAM. *William Goddard, Newspaperman* by Ward L. Miner (Durham, N.C., 1962).

GREENE, NATHANAEL. *The Life of Nathanael Green, Major-General in the Army of the Revolution* by George Washington Greene (3 vols., New York, 1867-71).

HOPKINS, STEPHEN. *Stephen Hopkins: A Rhode Island Statesman* . . . by William E. Foster, *Rhode Island Historical Tracts*, No. 19 (2 vols., Providence, R.I., 1884).

LOPEZ, AARON. "Aaron Lopez: Colonial Merchant of Newport" by Bruce M. Bigelow, *New England Quarterly*, IV (1931), 757-76.

MARCHANT, HENRY. "Henry Marchant and the *Mistress of the World*" by David S. Lovejoy, *William and Mary Quarterly*, 3rd ser., XII (1955), 375-98.

PARTRIDGE, RICHARD. "Richard Partridge: Colonial Agent" by Marguerite Appleton, *New England Quarterly*, V (1932), 293-309.

Wanton Family. *History of the Wanton Family of Newport, Rhode Island* by John Russell Bartlett, *Rhode Island Historical Tracts*, No. 3 (Providence, R.I., 1878).

WARD, SAMUEL. *A Life of Samuel Ward* by William Gammell, *Library of American Biography*, IX (Boston, 1864).

D. MAPS

BLASKOWITZ, CHARLES: *A Topographical Chart of the Bay of Narragansett in the Province of New England, with All the Isles Contained Therein, among which Rhode Island and Connocticut [sic] Have Been Particularly Surveyed* ([London], 1777). In Faden: *The North American Atlas . . .* , No. 10.

FADEN, WILLIAM: *A Plan of the Town of Newport in Rhode Island Surveyed by Charles Blaskowitz*. In Faden: *The North American Atlas . . .* , No. 11.

KITCHIN, THOMAS: *A Map of the Colony of Rhode Island: With the Adjacent Parts of Connecticut, Massachusetts Bay, &c.* ([London, 1778]). In the *London Magazine*, XLVII (1778), opp. p. 513.

A Map of Connecticut and Rhode Island: With Long Island Sound, Etc. In the *Gentleman's Magazine*, XLVI (1776), opp. p. 525.

SOUTH CAROLINA

A. BIBLIOGRAPHICAL AIDS

EASTERBY, J. H.: *Guide to the Study and Reading of South Carolina History: A General Classified Bibliography, South Carolina Bibliographies*, No. 2 (Columbia, S.C., 1950).

HASSE, ADELAIDE R.: "South Carolina, 1664-1789," in "Materials for a Bibliography of the Public Archives of the Thirteen Original

States . . . ," American Historical Association, *Annual Report, 1906* (2 vols., Washington, D.C., 1908), II, 532-47.

LEE, CHARLES E., and RUTH S. GREENE: "A Guide to South Carolina Council Journals, 1761-1775," *South Carolina Historical Magazine*, LXVIII (1967), 1-13.

———, and ———: "A Guide to the Commons House Journals of the South Carolina General Assembly, 1721-1775," *ibid.*, 165-83.

———, and ———: "A Guide to the Upper House Journals of the South Carolina General Assembly, 1721-1775," *ibid.*, LXVII (1966), 187-202.

List of Publications of the South Carolina Archives Department (Columbia, S.C., 1957).

WHITNEY, EDSON L.: "Bibliography of the Colonial History of South Carolina," American Historical Association, *Annual Report, 1894* (Washington, D.C., 1895), pp. 563-66.

For a good up-to-date bibliography in a secondary work, see M. Eugene Sirmans's "Bibliographical Essay," *Colonial South Carolina* . . . , pp. 361-376.

B. PRINTED SOURCE MATERIALS

1. *Government and related documents*

COOPER, T., and DAVID JAMES MAC CORD, eds.: *The Statutes at Large of South Carolina* [1682-1838] (10 vols., Columbia, S.C., 1836-41).

EASTERBY, J. H., ed.: *The Journal of the Commons House of Assembly of South Carolina, South Carolina Colonial Records* (9 vols. +, Columbia, S.C., 1951-62 +).

Extracts from the Journals of the Provincial Congress of South-Carolina . . . (Charlestown, 1775-6).

GARTH, CHARLES: "Correspondence of Charles Garth," Joseph Barnwell, ed., *South Carolina Historical and Genealogical Magazine*, XXVIII (1927)-XXXIII (1932), *passim*. See also, "Hon. Charles Garth, M.P.: The Last Colonial Agent of South Carolina in England and Some of His Work," Joseph W. Barnwell [ed.], *ibid.*, XXVI (1925), 67-92.

GREGORIE, ANNE KING, and J. NELSON FRIERSON, eds.: *Records of the Court of Chancery of South Carolina, 1671-1779, American Legal Records*, VI (Washington, D.C., 1950).

GRIMKÉ, JOHN FAUCHERAUD: *The Public Laws of the State of South Carolina* . . . (Philadelphia, 1790).

HEMPHILL, WILLIAM E., and WYLMA ANNE WATES, eds.: *Extracts from the*

Journals of the Provincial Congresses of South Carolina, 1775-1776,
State Records of South Carolina (Columbia, S.C., 1960). The
Extracts are available on Readex cards.

WESTON, P. C. J., ed.: *Documents Connected with the History of South
Carolina* . . . (London, 1856).

2. Non-official contemporary writings

CARROLL, BARTHOLOMEW RIVERS, ed.: *Historical Collections of South Carolina: Embracing Many Rare and Valuable Pamphlets and Other
Documents* . . . (2 vols., New York, 1836).

"Charleston in 1774 as Described by an English Traveler," *South Carolina Historical and Genealogical Magazine,* XLVII (1946), 179-
80.

DRAYTON, JOHN and WILLIAM HENRY: *Memoirs of the American Revolution
from Its Commencement to the Year 1776, Inclusive: As Relating
to the State of South-Carolina* . . . (2 vols., Charleston, S.C., 1821).

GADSDEN, CHRISTOPHER: *The Writings of Christopher Gadsden, 1746-1805*
(Richard Walsh, ed., Columbia, S.C., 1967).

GARDEN, ALEXANDER: "Correspondence between Alexander Garden, M.D.
and the Royal Society of Arts [1757-60]," Joseph I. Waring, ed.,
South Carolina Historical Magazine, LXIV (1963), 16-22, 86-94.

GIBBES, ROBERT WILSON, ed.: *Documentary History of the American Revolution Consisting of Letters and Papers Relating to the Contest
for Liberty Chiefly in South Carolina* . . . (3 vols., New York,
1855-7).

GLEN, JAMES: *A Description of South Carolina* (London, 1761); see also
Milligan-Johnston, George.

INNES, ALEXANDER: "Charlestown Loyalism in 1775: The Secret Reports
of Alexander Innes," B. D. Bargar, ed., *South Carolina Historical
Magazine,* LXIII (1962), 125-36.

IZARD, RALPH: *Correspondence of Mr. Ralph Izard of South Carolina* . . .
[1774-1804] (Anne Izard Deas, ed., New York, 1844).

LAURENS, HENRY: *Correspondence of Henry Laurens of South Carolina*
. . . (Frank Moore, ed., New York, 1861). See also "Correspondence
of Henry Laurens," Joseph W. Barnwell, ed., *South Carolina Historical and Genealogical Magazine,* XXVIII (1927)-XXXI (1930),
passim.

LOPEZ, MOSES: "Charles Town in 1764," Thomas J. Tobias, ed., *South
Carolina Historical Magazine,* LXVII (1966), 63-74. Letters written
by Portuguese-speaking Lopez of his business activities while in
Charleston.

MANIGAULT, PETER: "Peter Manigault's Letters," Mabel L. Webber, ed.,
South Carolina Historical and Genealogical Magazine, XXXI
(1930)-XXXIII (1932), *passim.*

MIDDLETON, ARTHUR: "Correspondence of Hon. Arthur Middleton, Signer of the Declaration of Independence," Joseph W. Barnwell, ed., *ibid.*, XXVI (1925)-XXVII (1926), *passim.*

MILLIGAN-JOHNSTON, GEORGE: *A Short Description of the Province of South Carolina* . . . (London, 1770). This and Governor Glen's description have been reprinted by Chapman James Milling in a volume carrying the title *Colonial South Carolina: Two Contemporary Descriptions, South Caroliniana: Sesquicentennial Series*, No. 1 (Columbia, S.C., 1951).

RAMSAY, DAVID: *The History of the Revolution of South Carolina: From a British Province to an Independent State* (2 vols., Trenton, N.J., 1785), and *The History of South Carolina from Its First Settlement in 1670 to the Year 1808* (2 vols., Charleston, S.C., 1809).

RAMSAY, MARTHA LAURENS. *Memoirs of the Life of Martha Laurens Ramsay* . . . *Containing Extracts from Her Diary, Letters, and Other Private Papers* . . . by David Ramsay (Philadelphia, 1811; rep., London, 1815).

"South Carolina's Colonial Constitution: Two Proposals for Reform," Jack P. Greene, ed., *South Carolina Historical Magazine*, LXII (1961), 72-81. Prints two papers, one by Edmund Atkin and one giving the objections of the Board of Trade on the South Carolina constitutional alteration.

TENNENT, WILLIAM: "Writings of the Reverend William Tennent, 1740-1777," Newton B. Jones, ed., *ibid.*, LXI (1960), 129-45, 189-209.

WOODMASON, CHARLES: *The Carolina Backcountry on the Eve of the Revolution: The Journal and Other Writings of Charles Woodmason, Anglican Itinerant* (Richard J. Hooker, ed., Chapel Hill, N.C., 1953).

3. Contemporary pamphlets, tracts, and related materials

[CROKATT, JAMES], ed.: *Further Observations Intended for Improving the Culture and Curing of Indigo* . . . *in South Carolina* (London, 1747).

DRAYTON, WILLIAM HENRY: *A Charge on the Rise of the American Empire Delivered* . . . *to the Grand Jury for the District of Charlestown* (Charleston, S.C., 1776).

[LAURENS, HENRY]: *Extracts from the Proceedings of the Court of Vice-Admiralty in Charlestown, South-Carolina in the Cause, George Roupell, Esq., v. the Ship Ann and Goods* . . . (Philadelphia, 1768; Charleston, S.C., 1769). Egerton Leigh replied with *The Man Unmasked: Or the World Undeceived in the Author of a Late Pamphlet Intitled "Extracts . . ."* (Charleston, 1769). The second edition of the *Extracts* . . . contains an appendix which constitutes a reply to Leigh's *The Man Unmasked.* . . .

[LEIGH, EGERTON]: *Considerations on Certain Political Transactions of the Province of South Carolina: Containing a View of the Colony Legislatures . . . With Observations Shewing Their Resemblance to the British Model* (London, 1774). William Henry Drayton penned the following reply to Leigh's pamphlet: *An Answer to "Considerations . . ."* (London, 1774).

PHILODEMUS, pseud.: *Conciliatory Hints . . . Submitted to the Consideration of the Citizens of the Commonwealth of South-Carolina* (Charleston, S.C., 1774).

PHILOPATRIOS, pseud.: *Observations on Two Campaigns Against the Cherokee Indians in 1760 and 1761* (Charleston, S.C., 1762). See also: *Some Observations on the Two Campaigns Against the Cherokee Indians in 1760 and 1761: In a Second Letter from Philopatrios* (Charleston, S.C., 1762).

A Representation of Facts Relative to the Conduct of Daniel Moore, Esquire, Collector of His Majesty's Customs at Charles-Town . . . (Charleston, S.C., 1767). This is a printing of a letter from the South Carolina Committee of Correspondence to colonial agent Charles Garth.

4. Newspapers

The South Carolina Gazette, e. 1775, Charleston. See Hennig Cohen's *"The South Carolina Gazette,"* 1732-1775 (Columbia, S.C., 1953) for a history of the paper.

The South Carolina Gazette: and Country Journal [South-Carolina Gazetteer and Country Journal], 1765-1775, Charleston.

The South-Carolina Weekly Gazette [The South Carolina and American General Gazette], b. 1758, Charleston.

C. SECONDARY WORKS

1. General

DRAYTON, JOHN: *A View of South-Carolina as Respects Her Natural and Civil Concerns* (Charleston, S.C., 1802).

HEWAT, ALEXANDER: *An Historical Account of the Rise and Progress of the Colonies of South Carolina and Georgia* (2 vols., London, 1779). The first history of South Carolina published.

MC CRADY, EDWARD: *The History of South Carolina under the Royal Government, 1719-1776* (London & New York, 1899).

MERIWETHER, ROBERT L.: *The Expansion of South Carolina, 1729-1765* (Kingsport, Tenn., 1940). Deals largely with period 1748-1765.

SMITH, HENRY A. M.: "The Ashley River: Its Seats and Settlements," *South Carolina Historical and Genealogical Magazine*, XX (1919), 3-51, 75-122. A description of various large land-holdings along the Ashley River, including a map opposite page 3. For the completion of this account see Smith: "The Upper Ashley and the Mutations of Families," *ibid.*, 151-98, with a map opposite page 151.

SMITH, WILLIAM ROY: *South Carolina as a Royal Province, 1719-1776* (London & New York, 1903).

WALLACE, DAVID DUNCAN: *South Carolina: A Short History, 1520-1948* (Chapel Hill, N.C., 1951). See also his *The History of South Carolina* (4 vols., New York, 1934). Volume II covers the period 1720-1776.

2. Political

ANDREANO, RALPH LOUIS, and HERBERT D. WERNER: "Charleston Loyalists: A Statistical Note," *South Carolina Historical Magazine*, LX (1959), 164-8.

BROWN, RICHARD MAXWELL: *The South Carolina Regulators* (Cambridge, Mass., 1963).

GREENE, JACK P.: "Bridge to Revolution: The Wilkes Fund Controversy in South Carolina, 1769-1775," *Journal of Southern History*, XXIX (1963), 19-52.

——: "The Gadsden Election Controversy and the Revolutionary Movement in South Carolina," *Mississippi Valley Historical Review*, XLVI (1958-9), 469-92.

——: "The South Carolina Quartering Dispute, 1757-1758," *South Carolina Historical Magazine*, LX (1959), 193-204.

LEVETT, ELLA PETTIT: "Loyalism in Charleston, 1761-1784," South Carolina Historical Association, *Proceedings*, VI (1935), 3-17.

RYAN, FRANK W., JR.: "The Role of South Carolina in the First Continental Congress," *South Carolina Historical Magazine*, LX (1959), 147-53.

SALLEY, ALEXANDER S., JR.: *Delegates to the Continental Congress from South Carolina, 1774-1789* . . . , South Carolina Historical Commission, *Bulletin*, No. 9 (Columbia, S.C., 1927).

SCHAPER, WILLIAM A.: "Sectionalism and Representation in South Carolina," American Historical Association, *Annual Report, 1900* (2 vols., Washington, D.C., 1901), I: 237-463.

SIRMANS, M. EUGENE: *Colonial South Carolina: A Political History, 1663-1763* (Chapel Hill, N.C. [1966]). See also his article, "The South Carolina Royal Council, 1720-1763," *William and Mary Quarterly*, 3rd ser., XVIII (1961), 373-92.

WALLACE, DAVID DUNCAN: *Constitutional History of South Carolina from 1725 to 1775* (Abbeville, S.C., 1899).

WALSH, RICHARD: *Charleston's Sons of Liberty: A Study of the Artisans, 1763-1789* (Columbia, S.C., 1959); see also his "The Charleston Mechanics: A Brief Study, 1760-1776," *South Carolina Historical Magazine*, LX (1959), 123-44.

WHITNEY, EDSON L.: "The Government of the Colony of South Carolina," Johns Hopkins University, *Studies in Historical and Political Science*, 13th ser. (1895), 9-121.

3. Economic

GAYLE, CHARLES JOSEPH: "The Nature and Volume of Exports from Charleston, 1724-1774," South Carolina Historical Association, *Proceedings*, VIII (1937), 25-33.

HAYWOOD, C. ROBERT: "Mercantilism and South Carolina Agriculture, 1700-1763," *South Carolina Historical Magazine*, LX (1959), 15-27.

HIGGINS, W. ROBERT: "Charles Town Merchants and Factors Dealing in the External Negro Trade, 1735-1775," *ibid.*, LXV (1964), 205-17.

MINCHINTON, WALTER E.: "Richard Champion, Nicholas Pocock, and the Carolina Trade [1768]," *South Carolina Historical Magazine*, LXV (1964), 87-97.

SALLEY, A. S., JR.: *The Introduction of Rice Culture into South Carolina*, Historical Commission of South Carolina, *Bulletin*, No. 6 (Columbia, 1919).

SELLERS, LEILA: *Charleston Business on the Eve of the Revolution* (Chapel Hill, N.C., 1934).

TAYLOR, GEORGE ROGERS: "Wholesale Commodity Prices at Charleston, South Carolina, 1732-1791," *Journal of Economic and Business History*, IV (1932), 356-77.

4. Social

BOWES, FREDERICK PATTEN: *The Culture of Early Charleston* (Chapel Hill, N.C., 1942).

DONNAN, ELIZABETH: "The Slave Trade into South Carolina before the Revolution," *American Historical Review*, XXXIII (1927-8), 804-828.

DUFFY, JOHN: "Eighteenth Century Carolina Health Conditions," *Journal of Southern History*, XVIII (1952), 289-302. Includes examples from both North and South Carolina.

HAMER, MARGUERITE B.: "A Century before Manumission: Sidelights on Slavery in Mid-Eighteenth Century South Carolina," *North Carolina Historical Review*, XVII (1940), 232-6. Brief account of the treatment of Negro slaves in the 1750's.

————: "The Fate of the Exiled Acadians in South Carolina," *Journal of Southern History*, IV (1938), 199-208.

HIRSCH, ARTHUR HENRY: *The Huguenots of Colonial South Carolina* (Durham, N.C., 1928). Discusses the contributions of the French Huguenots to the social, political, and religious development of South Carolina.

HUDNUT, RUTH ALLISON, and HAYES BAKER-CROTHERS: "Acadian Transients in South Carolina," *American Historical Review*, XLIII (1937-8), 500-13.

KLINGBERG, FRANK J.: *An Appraisal of the Negro in Colonial South Carolina: A Study in Americanization* (Washington, D.C., 1941).

LEIDING, HARRIETTE K.: *Charleston, Historic and Romantic* (Philadelphia, 1931).

MADDEN, RICHARD C.: "Catholics in Colonial South Carolina," American Catholic Historical Society of Philadelphia, *Records*, LXXIII (1962), 10-44.

SIRMANS, M. EUGENE: "Charleston Two Hundred Years Ago," Emery University, *Quarterly*, XIX (1963), 129-36. A description of Charleston social life in 1763.

SMITH, WARREN B.: *White Servitude in Colonial South Carolina* (Columbia, S.C., 1961).

TOWNSEND, LEAH: *South Carolina Baptists, 1670-1805* (Florence, S.C., 1935).

VOIGT, GILBERT PAUL: "Religious Conditions among German Speaking Settlers in South Carolina, 1732-1774," *South Carolina Historical Magazine*, LVI (1955), 59-66.

WILLIAMS, GEORGE W.: *St. Michaels, Charleston, 1751-1951* (Columbus, S.C., 1951).

5. *Biographical*

Bull Family. "Politicians and Planters: The Bull Family of Colonial South Carolina" by M. Eugene Sirmans, South Carolina Historical Association, *Proceedings, 1962*, pp. 32-41.

Calhoun Family. "The Calhoun Family in South Carolina" by Alexander Samuel Salley, Jr., *South Carolina Historical and Genealogical Magazine*, VII (1906), 81-96, 153-69.

DRAYTON, WILLIAM. "The Enigma of William Drayton" by Charles L. Mowat, *Florida Historical Quarterly*, XXII (1943-4), 3-33.

DRAYTON, WILLIAM HENRY. *William Henry Drayton and the American Revolution* by William M. Dabney and Marion Dargan (Albuquerque, N.M., 1962). See also, Dabney's "Drayton and Laurens in the Continental Congress," *South Carolina Historical Magazine*, LX (1959), 74-82.

GADSDEN, CHRISTOPHER. "Christopher Gadsden and the Stamp Act" by Robert H. Woody, South Carolina Historical Association, *Proceeding*, IX (1939), 7-9.

GARTH, CHARLES. "Charles Garth [agent for South Carolina]" by Sir Lewis Namier, *English Historical Review*, LIV (1939), 443-70, 632-52.

LAURENS, HENRY. *The Life of Henry Laurens: With a Sketch of the Life of Lieutenant-Colonel John Laurens* by David Duncan Wallace (London & New York, 1915). See also Dabney's article under Drayton, William Henry.

LAWTON, WILLIAM. "Captain William Lawton: 18th Century Planter of Edisto" by Thomas O. Lawton, Jr., *South Carolina Historical Magazine*, LX (1959), 86-93.

Leigh Family. "The Leighs in South Carolina" by H. Hale Bellot, Royal Historical Society, *Transactions*, 5th ser., VI (1956), 161-87.

MOORE, ALFRED, and JAMES IREDELL. *Alfred Moore and James Iredell: Revolutionary Patriots . . .* by Junius Davis (Raleigh, N.C., 1889).

PINCKNEY, ELIZABETH LUCAS. *Eliza Pinckney* by Harriott Horry R. Ravenel (New York, c. 1909).

RUTLEDGE, JOHN. *Mr. Rutledge of South Carolina* by Richard H. Barry (New York, 1942).

6. Military

FOOTE, WILLIAM A.: "The South Carolina Independents," *South Carolina Historical Magazine*, LXII (1961), 195-9. Discusses the companies of troops stationed in South Carolina for that colony's defence, 1720-64.

D. MAPS

The Bar and Harbour of Charleston [From actual Surveys by Henry Mouzon and others] (London, 1775). In Faden: *The North American Atlas . . .*, Nos. 29-30.

Charlestown: An Exact Plan of Charlestown Bar and Harbor from an Actual Survey with the Attack of Fort Sullivan on the 28th June 1776 by His Majesty's Squadron . . . (London, 1791).

An Exact Prospect of Charlestown, the Metropolis of the Province of South Carolina. In the *London Magazine*, XXXI (1762), opp. p. 296; also in *American Maps*, II: No. 2a.

JEFFERYS, THOMAS, eng.: *A Map of South Carolina and a Part of Georgia Containing the Whole Sea Coast, All the Islands . . .*

Composed from Surveys Taken by the Hon. William Bull, Capt. Gascoigne, Hugh Bryan, and the Author William de Brahm (London, 1758; rep., 1780). In Jefferys: *A General Topography of North America and the West Indies,* Nos. 59-62; also in Faden: *The North American Atlas* . . . , Nos. 32-3; and *American Maps,* V; Nos. 288-9.

——, and WILLIAM FADEN, engrs.: *A Plan of the River and Sound of Dawfoskee in South Carolina, Surveyed by Captain John Gascoigne* ([London, 1773]).

MOUZON, HENRY, et al.: *An Accurate Map of North and South Carolina with Their Indian Frontiers . . . Mountains, Rivers, Swamps . . . Harbours, Etc. . . . from Actual Surveys, 1775.* In Jefferys: *The American Atlas* . . . , Nos. 23-4. As an insert there is also the *Bar and Harbour of Charlestown.*

A Plan of Port Royal in South Carolina: Survey'd by Capn. John Gascoigne (London [1773]).

A Sketch of the Cherokee Country. In Mante: *History of the Late War in North America,* opp. p. 286.

South Carolina in the Regulator Period. In Richard Maxwell Brown: *The South Carolina Regulators,* facing p. 1; a second map *Location of Regulator Residences,* faces p. 113. These are both modern maps.

THORNTON, JOHN, and WILLIAM FISHER: *A New Mapp of Carolina.* In the *English Pilot,* 4th Book (Dublin, 1767), p. 26.

See also the Emanuel Bowen map, *A New and Accurate Map . . . of North & South Carolina, Georgia* . . . , and Kitchin's *A New Map of North & South Carolina & Georgia* cited in full under Chapter IV, D.

VIRGINIA

A. BIBLIOGRAPHICAL AIDS

BEAR, JAMES A., JR., and MARY CAPERTON: *A Checklist of Virginia Almanacs, 1732-1850* (Charlottesville, Va., 1962).

BOYD, JULIAN P.: "A New Guide to the Indispensable Sources of Virginia History," *William and Mary Quarterly,* 3rd ser., XV (1958), 3-13.

CARSON, JANE: *Travelers in Tidewater Virginia, 1700-1800: A Bibliography* (Williamsburg, Va., 1965).

HASSE, ADELAIDE R.: "Virginia, 1606-1798," in "Materials for a Bibliography of the Public Archives of the Thirteen Original States . . . ," American Historical Association, *Annual Report, 1906* (2 vols., Washington, D.C., 1908), II, 468-94.

SWEM, EARL GREGG: "A Bibliography of Virginia," Virginia State Library, *Bulletins,* VIII, X, XI, XII, XVII ([Richmond, Va.], 1915-32).

————: *Virginia Historical Index . . .* (2 vols., Roanoke, Va., 1934-36). This is the best modern guide to the printed sources of a single state.

B. PRINTED SOURCE MATERIALS

1. *Government and related documents*

The Acts of Assembly, now in Force, in the Colony of Virginia . . . (2 vols., Williamsburg, Va., 1752-69).

DINWIDDIE, ROBERT: *The Official Records of Robert Dinwiddie, Lieutenant Governor of the Colony of Virginia, 1751-1758* (Robert A. Brock, ed., 2 vols., Richmond, Va., 1883-4).

GREENE, JACK P., ed.: "The Case of the Pistole Fee: The Report of a Hearing on the Pistole Fee Dispute before the Privy Council, June 18, 1764," *Virginia Magazine of History and Biography,* LXVI (1958), 399-422.

HARWELL, RICHARD BARKSDALE, ed.: *Proceedings of the County Committees, 1774-1776: The Committees of Safety of Westmoreland and Fincastle,* Virginia State Library, *Publications,* No. 1 (Richmond, Va., 1956).

HENING, WILLIAM WALLER, ed.: *The Statutes at Large: Being a Collection of All the Laws of Virginia from . . . 1619* (13 vols., Richmond, Va., 1809-23).

KENNEDY, JOHN PENDLETON, and HENRY READ MCILWAINE, eds.: *Journals of the House of Burgesses of Virginia . . .* (13 vols., Richmond, 1905-15). The *Journals* are also available on Readex cards in the individual issues published yearly, except for the years 1765-1771.

MCILWAINE, HENRY READ, ed.: *Legislative Journals of the Council of Colonial Virginia* (3 vols., Richmond, 1918-19).

————, WILMER L. HALL, and BENJAMIN I. HILLMAN, eds.: *Executive Journals of the Council of Colonial Virginia* [1680-1775] (6 vols., Richmond, Va., 1925-66).

The Proceedings of the Convention of Delegates for the Counties and Corporations in the Colony of Virginia, Held at Richmond Town . . . [1775] (Richmond, Va., 1816). There are numerous copies of contemporary publications of journals, proceedings, and ordinances of the Convention contained in Evans's *American Bibliography.*

"Proceedings of the Virginia Committee of Correspondence, 1759-70," *Virginia Magazine of History and Biography*, X (1902-3)-XIII (1904-5), *passim.*

"Virginia Legislative Documents [Papers] [1764-1776]," *Virginia Magazine of History and Biography*, IX (1901-2)-XVIII (1910-11), *passim.*

2. Non-official contemporary writings

ALLASON, WILLIAM: "The Letters of William Allason, Merchant of Falmouth, Virginia," Richmond College, *Historical Papers*, II (1917), 118-75. Valuable to illustrate the activities of British merchants in America and the economic situation at the time.

BEVERLY, ROBERT: " 'A Sorrowful Spectator of These Tumultuous Times': Robert Beverly Describes the Coming of the Revolution," Robert M. Calhoon, ed., *Virginia Magazine of History and Biography*, LXXIII (1965), 41-55.

CARSON, JANE, ed.: *"We Were There": Descriptions of Williamsburg, 1699-1859 Compiled from Contemporary Sources and Arranged Chronologically* (Williamsburg, Va., c. 1965).

CARTER, LANDON: *The Diary of Colonel Landon Carter of Sabine Hall, 1752-1778*, Virginia Historical Society, *Documents*, IV-V (Jack P. Greene, ed., 2 vols., Charlottesville, Va., 1965). This compilation includes Carter's private journal of the House of Burgesses and diaries for most of the years between 1752 and 1778.

CARTER, ROBERT WORMELEY: "The Daybook of Robert Wormeley Carter of Sabine Hall, 1766," Louis Morton, ed., *Virginia Magazine of History and Biography*, LXVIII (1960), 301-16. Useful for the picture it provides of the everyday life of a Virginia planter.

CHALKLEY, LYMAN, ed.: *Chronicles of the Scotch-Irish Settlement in Virginia: Extracted from the Original Court Records of Augusta County, 1745-1800* (3 vols., Rosslyn Va., 1912-13).

CHRIST CHURCH: *The Vestry Book of Christ Church Parish, Middlesex County, Virginia, 1663-1767* . . . (C. G. Chamberlayne, ed., Richmond, Va., 1927).

CRESSWELL, NICHOLAS: *The Journal of Nicholas Cresswell, 1774-1777* (L. MacVeagh, ed., New York, 1924).

FITHIAN, PHILIP VICKERS: *Philip Vickers Fithian. Journal and Letters, 1767-1774, Student at Princeton College, 1770-72, Tutor at Nomini Hall in Virginia, 1773-74* (John Rogers Williams, ed., 2 vols., Princeton, N. J., 1900-34). See also *Journal and Letters of Philip Vickers Fithian, 1773-1774: A Plantation Tutor of the Old Dominion* (Hunter Dickinson Farish, ed., 1st edn., Williamsburg, Va., 1900; n. edn., 1957); also available is "Journal of Philip Fithian; Kept at Nomini Hall, Virginia, 1773-1774," John Rogers Williams, ed., *American Historical Review*, V (1899-1900), 290-319.

HARROWER, JOHN: *The Journal of John Harrower: An Indentured Servant in the Colony of Virginia, 1773-1776* (Edward Miles Riley, ed., New York, 1963). See also the "Diary of John Harrower, 1773-1776," *American Historical Review*, VI (1900-1), 65-107. Useful for its picture of the life of an indentured servant.

HENRY, PATRICK. *Patrick Henry: Life, Correspondence and Speeches* by William Wirt Henry (3 vols., New York, 1891).

HONYMAN, ROBERT: *Colonial Panorama, 1775: Dr. Robert Honyman's Journal for March and April* (Philip Padelford, ed., San Marino, Calif., 1939). Honyman was a Scot who settled in Virginia.

JARRATT, DEVEREUX: "The Autobiography of the Reverend Devereux Jarratt, 1732-1763," Douglass Adair, ed., *William and Mary Quarterly*, 3rd ser., IX (1952), 346-93. On the author's boyhood and Anglican ministry in Virginia.

JEFFERSON, THOMAS: There are available three collections, each entitled *The Writings of Thomas Jefferson* . . .: H. A. Washington edited one collection (9 vols., Philadelphia, 1869-71), and two later editions, one by Paul Leicester Ford (10 vols., London & New York, 1892-99) and one by Andrew A. Lipscomb and Albert Ellery Bergh (20 vols. in 10, Washington, D.C., 1905). By far the best collection, however, is that presently underway at Princeton University being edited by Julian P. Boyd, *et al: The Papers of Thomas Jefferson* (17 vols. +, Princeton, N.J., 1950-65 +). See also Gilbert Chinard, ed.: *The Commonplace Book of Thomas Jefferson: A Repertory of His Ideas on Government,* Johns Hopkins University, *Studies in Romance Literatures and Languages, Extra Vol.,* II (Baltimore, Md. & Paris, 1926). Another useful work is the *Catalogue of the Library of Thomas Jefferson,* E. Millicent Sowerby, ed. (5 vols., Washington, D.C., 1952-9), indicating Jefferson's intellectual range.

LEE, ARTHUR. *Life of Arthur Lee, LL.D. . . . With His Diplomatic and Literary Correspondence and His Papers* . . . by Richard Henry Lee (2 vols., Boston, 1829). This work is important for the correspondence between Lee and American Revolutionary leaders.

LEE, RICHARD HENRY: *The Letters of Richard Henry Lee* (James Curtis Ballagh, ed., 2 vols., New York, 1911-14), I: 1762-1778. See also *Memoir of the Life of Richard Henry Lee, and His Correspondence* . . . by Richard H. Lee (2 vols., Philadelphia, 1825).

LEE, WILLIAM: *Letters of William Lee* . . . (Worthington Chauncey Ford, ed., 3 vols., Brooklyn, N. Y., 1891).

MC ANEAR, BEVERLY, ed.: "The Income of the Royal Governors of Virginia [1759-1763]," *Journal of Southern History*, XVI (1950), 196-211. Letters of Amherst, Fauquier, and Calcraft on the governors' pay.

MASON, GEORGE. *The Life of George Mason, 1725-1792 . . . Including His*

Speeches, Public Papers, and Correspondence . . . by Kate Rowland (2 vols., London & New York, 1892).

MAZZEI, FILIPPO: *Memoirs of the Life and Peregrinations of the Florentine, Philip Mazzei, 1730-1816* (Howard R. Marraro, trans., New York, 1942). Mazzei came to Virginia in 1773 and was an active supporter of the revolution.

MERCER, GEORGE: "Colonel George Mercer's Papers," J. E. Tyler, ed., *Virginia Magazine of History and Biography*, LX (1952), 405-20, relating to Mercer's examination in the House of Commons as the distributor of stamps for Virginia. For Mercer see also Trans-Appalachian West.

MUMFORD, ROBERT: "Robert Mumford's *The Candidates*," Jay B. Hubbell and Douglass Adair, eds., *William and Mary Quarterly*, 3rd ser., V (1948), 217-25. Prints the text of *The Candidates: Or the Humours of a Virginia Election. A Comedy in Three Acts*.

NORTON, JOHN: *John Norton and Sons, Merchants of London and Virginia: Being the Papers from Their Counting House for the Years 1750 to 1795* (Frances Norton Mason, ed., Richmond, Va., 1937).

PENDLETON, EDMUND: *The Letters and Papers of Edmund Pendleton*, Virginia Historical Society, *Documents*, VII-VIII (David John Mays, ed., 2 vols., Charlottesville, Va., 1967). Also available is "Unpublished Letters of Edmund Pendleton," Massachusetts Historical Society, *Proceedings*, XIX (1905), 107-67.

WASHINGTON, GEORGE: For the best collection of Washington's writings see John C. Fitzpatrick, ed.: *The Writings of George Washington: From the Original Manuscript Sources, 1745-1799* (39 vols., Washington, D.C., 1931-44). Volumes 38 and 39 are a general index by D. M. Matteson. In addition to this collection, there are also the earlier editions, by Jared Sparks (12 vols., Boston, 1834-7) and by Worthington Chauncey Ford (14 vols., London & New York, 1889-1893). For Washington's journals, see the contemporary *The Journal of Major George Washington, Sent by the Hon. Robert Dinwiddie, Esq. . . . to the Commandant of the French Forces in Ohio* . . . (London & Williamsburg, Va., 1754) and J. M. Toner's edition of *The Daily Journal of Major George Washington in 1751-1752: Kept While on Tour from Virginia to the Island of Barbadoes* . . . (Albany, N. Y., 1892). John C. Fitzpatrick edited, in addition to the *Writings*, *The Diaries of George Washington, 1748-1799* (4 vols., Boston & New York, 1925). For Washington's correspondence, see: C. W. Butterfield, ed.: *The Washington-Crawford Letters* . . . [1767-1781] (Cincinnati, O., 1877), dealing with Washington's interests in western lands; Stanislaus Murray Hamilton, ed.: *Letters to Washington and Accompanying Papers* [1755-1775] (5 vols., Boston & New York, 1898-1902); and "Letters of George Washington to Lord Dunmore," *William and Mary Quarterly*, 2nd ser., XX (1940), 161-6, which prints four letters, 1772-1774. Other materials available include Peter Brock, ed.: "Colonel Washington and the Quaker Conscientious Objectors," *Quaker History*, LIII (1964), 12-26; John R. Alden, ed.: "Washington and the Pittsburgh Route, 1768," *American Historical Review*, XLIV (1938-9), 849-51; and "Washington and the Potomac: Manuscripts of the Minnesota Historical Society, 1769-1796," *ibid.*, XXVIII (1922-3), 497-519, 705-22; and two items dealing with Washington and the Ohio region: Archer B. Hulbert, ed.: "Washington's 'Tour to the Ohio' and Articles of the 'Mississippi Company,' " Ohio Archaeological and Historical Society, *Publications*, XVII (1908), 431-88, and Hugh Cleland's *George Washington in the Ohio Valley* (Pittsburgh, Pa., 1955), which consists primarily of reprinted documents and extracts relating to Washington's western experiences.

WAYLES, JOHN: "John Wayles Rates His Neighbors," John M. Hemphill, II, ed., *Virginia Magazine of History and Biography*, LXVI (1958), 302-6.

3. *Contemporary pamphlets, tracts, and related materials*

BLAND, RICHARD: *A Letter to the Clergy of Virginia in which the Conduct of the General Assembly is Vindicated* . . . (Williamsburg, Va., 1760), in defence of the Virginia Twopenny Act. This was followed by *The Colonel Dismounted or the Rector Vindicated: In a Letter Addressed to His Reverence: Containing a Dissertation Upon the Constitution of the Colony* . . . (n. p., 1764). Signed "Common Sense," this pamphlet ridicules the Rev. John Camm. Although mainly concerned with the Twopenny Act and the Parson's Cause, it also contains a strong defence of colonial self-government. Camm replied with the pamphlet *Critical Remarks on a Letter Ascribed to Common Sense Containing an Attempt to Prove that the Said Letter Is an Imposition on Common Sense* . . . (Williamsburg, Va., 1765). Bland's greatest effort was his memorable *An Inquiry into the Rights of the British Colonies, intended as an Answer to "The Regulations lately made Concerning the Colonies, and the Taxes Imposed upon Them Considered," in a Letter Addressed to the Author of that Pamphlet* (Williamsburg, Va. [1766]).

[BRAXTON, CARTER]: *An Address to the Convention of the Colony and Ancient Dominion of Virginia: On the Subject of Government in General and Recommending a Particular Form to Their Considera-tion* . . . (Philadelphia, 1776).

[CAMM, JOHN]: *A Single and Distinct View of the Act Vulgarly Entitled Three-Penny [Twopenny] Act: Containing an Account of Its*

Beneficial and Wholesome Effect in York-Hampton Parish . . .
(Annapolis, Md., 1763). For a reply, see Landon Carter's *The
Rector Detected: Being a Just Defence of the Two-Penny Act
against the Artful Misrepresentations of the Reverend John Camm
. . .* (Williamsburg, Va., 1764), to which Camm replied with *A
Review of the Rector Detected: Or the Colonel Reconnoitered
. . .* (Williamsburg, Va., 1764).

CARTER, LANDON: *A Letter to the Right Reverend Father in God, the Lord
B——p of L——n . . . on the Subject of the Act of Assembly
Passed in the Year 1758 . . .* (Williamsburg, Va., 1759; London,
1760). A copy of the letter of the Bishop of London was attached
to the "Report of the Lords Commissioners for His Majesty's
Disallowance of Several Acts Passed in Virginia . . ." and may be
found in W. S. Perry's *Historical Collections Relating to the American Colonial Church,* I: 461-3.

DAVIES, SAMUEL: *The Curse of Cowardice: A Sermon Preached to the
Militia of Hanover County in Virginia at a General Muster, May 8,
1758 . . .* (Woodbridge, N. J., 1759).

——: *Virginia's Danger and Remedy: Two Discourses, Occasioned by
the Severe Drought in Sundry Parts of the Country, and the Defeat
of General Braddock* (Williamsburg, Va., 1756).

JEFFERSON, THOMAS: *A Summary View of the Rights of British America
set forth in Some Resolutions for the Inspection of the Present
Delegates of the People of Virginia Now in Convention . . .*
(Williamsburg, Va. [1774]).

[RANDOLPH, JOHN]: *Considerations on the Present State of Virginia*
([Williamsburg, Va.], 1774), and the reply by Robert Carter
Nicholas also published anonymously: *Considerations on the
Present State of Virginia Examined* ([Williamsburg, Va.], 1774).
Both of these pamphlets can be found in Earl Gregg Swem's
*Considerations on the Present State of Virginia . . . Virginia and
the Revolution—Two Pamphlets, 1774, Heartman's Historical
Series,* No. 32 (New York, 1919).

4. Newspapers

The Virginia Gazette. There were three newspapers published at
Williamsburg under this title. The first was a revival in 1751 by
William Hunter of the paper founded by William Parks in 1736,
subsequently published by Dixon and Hunter; the second, founded
in 1766 by William Rind, was later published by Clementina Rind
and then by John Pinkney; and the third, established in 1775, was
published by Alexander Purdie. See the exceedingly useful guide
by Lester J. Cappon and Stella F. Duff: *Virginia Gazette Index,*

1736-1780 (2 vols., Williamsburg, Va., 1950). Because items were frequently reprinted from various newspapers, this index is useful in the study of other colonies.

The Virginia Gazette, or, the Norfolk Intelligencer, 1774-1775, Norfolk, Va.

C. SECONDARY WORKS

1. *General*

ABERNETHY, THOMAS PERKINS: *Three Virginia Frontiers* (University, La., 1940). Dealing with the three stages of frontier in Virginia: the Tidewater, the Piedmont, and the Transmontane.

BURK, JOHN D.: *The History of Virginia: From Its First Settlement to the Present Day [1775]* (4 vols., Petersburg, Va., 1804-16).

CAMPBELL, CHARLES: *History of the Colony and the Ancient Dominion of Virginia* (Philadelphia, 1860).

ECKENRODE, HAMILTON J.: *The Revolution in Virginia* (Boston & New York, 1916).

FISHWICK, MARSHALL: *Virginia: A New Look at the Old Dominion* (New York, 1959).

FOOTE, WILLIAM HENRY: *Sketches of Virginia: Historical and Biographical* (Philadelphia, 1850; 2nd ser., 1855). Places special emphasis on church history.

HART, FREEMAN H.: *The Valley of Virginia in the American Revolution, 1763-1789* (Chapel Hill, N. C., 1942).

KEGLEY, FREDERICK BITTLE: *Kegley's Virginia Frontier . . . The Roanoke of Colonial Days, 1740-1783* (Roanoke, Va., 1938).

KERCHEVAL, SAMUEL: *A History of the Valley of Virginia* (Winchester, Va., 1833; 3rd edn., rev., Woodstock, Va., 1902; 4th edn., rev. & ext., Strasburg, Va., 1925).

KOONTZ, LOUIS K.: "Virginia Frontier, 1754-1763," Johns Hopkins University, *Studies in Historical and Political Science*, 43rd ser. (1925), 185-370. Appendix II contains source materials.

LINGLEY, CHARLES RAMSDELL: *The Transition in Virginia from Colony to Commonwealth,* Columbia University, *Studies in History, Economics, and Public Law*, No. 96 (New York, 1910).

MAPP, ALF J., JR.: *The Virginia Experiment: The Old Dominion's Role in the Making of America (1607-1789)* (Richmond, Va., 1957).

MORTON, ROBERT L.: *Colonial Virginia* (2 vols., Chapel Hill, N. C. & London, 1960). Volume II extends to 1763.

RUTMAN, DARRETT B., ed.: *The Old Dominion: Essays for Thomas Perkins Abernethy* (Charlottesville, Va., 1964). Among the essays the following have bearing upon the period under review. "Virginia and the Cherokees: Indian Policy from Spotswood to Dinwiddie" by W. S. Robinson; "The Rise and Decline of the Virginia Aristocracy in the Eighteenth Century: The Nelsons" by E. G. Evans; "Two men on a Tax: Richard Henry Lee, Archibald Ritchie, and the Stamp Act" by J. C. Matthews; "Letters from Norfolk: Scottish Merchants View the Revolutionary Crisis" by W. M. Dabney; and "Weights, Measures, and Mercantilism: the Inspection of Exports in Virginia, 1742-1820" by Newton B. Jones.

2. Local

CAMPBELL, THOMAS ELLIOTT: *Colonial Caroline: A History of Caroline County, Virginia [1655-1781]* (Richmond, Va., 1954).

PENDLETON, WILLIAM CECIL: *History of Tazewell County and Southeast Virginia, 1748-1920* (Richmond, Va., 1920).

PEYTON, JOHN LEWIS: *History of Augusta County, Virginia* (Staunton, Va., 1882).

SUMMERS, LEWIS PRESTON: *The Annals of Southwest Virginia, 1769-1800* (Abingdon, Va., 1929).

WERTENBAKER, THOMAS J.: *Norfolk: Historic Southern Port* (Durham, N. C., 1931).

3. Political

ALVORD, CLARENCE WALWORTH: "Virginia and the West: An Interpretation," *Mississippi Valley Historical Review,* III (1916-17), 19-38. Discusses the attempts to establish Virginia claims in the west, 1750-1770.

BRIDENBAUGH, CARL: *Seat of Empire: The Political Role of Eighteenth-Century Williamsburg, Williamsburg in America Series,* I (Williamsburg, Va., 1950; n. edn., 1958).

BROWN, ROBERT E. and B. KATHERINE: *Virginia, 1705-1786: Democracy or Aristocracy?* (East Lansing, Mich., 1964).

CHANDLER, JULIAN A. C.: "The History of Suffrage in Virginia," Johns Hopkins University, *Studies in Historical and Political Science,* 19th ser. (1901), 271-346.

CHITWOOD, OLIVER PERRY: "Justice in Colonial Virginia," *ibid.,* 23rd ser. (1905), 399-522.

CHUMBLEY, GEORGE LEWIS: *Colonial Justice in Virginia: The Development of Judical System* . . . (Richmond, Va., 1938).

DUFF, STELLA F.: "The Case against the King: *The Virginia Gazettes* Indict George III," *William and Mary Quarterly,* 3rd ser., VI (1949), 383-97.

FERGUSON, ISABEL: "County Court in Virginia, 1700-1830," *North Carolina*

Historical Review, VIII (1931), 14-40. Relating to the influence of the county courts.

FLIPPIN, PERCY SCOTT: *The Royal Government in Virginia*, Columbia University, *Studies in History, Economics, and Public Law*, No. 194 (London & New York, 1919).

GREENE, JACK P.: "Foundations of Political Power in the Virginia House of Burgesses, 1720-1776," *William and Mary Quarterly*, 3rd ser., XVI (1959), 485-506, and "The Attempt to Separate the Offices of Speaker and Treasurer in Virginia, 1758-1766," *Virginia Magazine of History and Biography*, LXXI (1963), 11-18.

GRIFFITH, LUCILLE: *Virginia House of Burgesses, 1750-1774* (Northport, Ala., 1963).

GRIGSBY, HUGH B.: *The Virginia Convention of 1776* . . . (Richmond, Va., 1855).

MILLER, ELMER I.: *The Legislature of the Province of Virginia: Its Internal Development*, Columbia University, *Studies in History, Economics, and Public Law*, No. 76 (London & New York, 1907); a detailed study of the machinery of legislation. See also Miller's article: "The Virginia Committee of Correspondence . . . ," *William and Mary Quarterly*, 1st ser., XXII (1913), 1-20.

MINCHINTON, WALTER E.: "The Stamp Act Crisis: Bristol and Virginia," *Virginia Magazine of History and Biography*, LXXIII (1965), 145-155.

MORISON, SAMUEL ELIOT: "Prelude to Independence: The Virginia Resolutions of May 15, 1776," *William and Mary Quarterly*, 3rd ser., VIII (1951), 483-92.

PORTER, ALBERT OGDEN: *County Government in Virginia: A Legislative History, 1607-1904*, Columbia University, *Studies in History, Economics, and Public Law*, No. 526 (New York, 1947). This study shows the evolution of local government in Virginia.

POTTER, JOHN E.: *see* under Pennsylvania

RANKIN, HUGH F.: *Criminal Trial Proceedings in the General Court of Colonial Virginia* (Williamsburg, Va., c. 1965). See also his article of the same title, *Virginia Magazine of History and Biography*, LXXII (1964), 50-74; and "The General Court of Colonial Virginia: Its Jurisdiction and Personnel," *ibid.*, LXX (1962), 142-53.

SCOTT, ARTHUR P.: "Constitutional Aspects of the 'Parsons' Cause,'" *Political Science Quarterly*, XXXI (1916), 558-77.

SMITH, GLENN CURTIS: "The Affair of the Pistole Fee: Virginia, 1752-55," *Virginia Magazine of History and Biography*, XLVIII (1940), 209-21, and "The Parsons' Cause, 1755-65," *Tyler's Quarterly Historical and Genealogical Magazine*, XXI (1940), 140-71, 291-306.

SYDNOR, CHARLES S.: *Political Leadership in Eighteenth-Century Virginia* (Oxford, Eng., 1951), and *Gentlemen Freeholders: Political Practices in Washington's Virginia* (Chapel Hill, N. C., 1952).

TATE, THAD W.: "The Coming of the Revolution in Virginia: Britain's Challenge to Virginia's Ruling Class, 1763-1776," *William and Mary Quarterly*, 3rd ser., XIX (1962), 323-43.

VOORHIS, MANNING C.: "Crown versus Council in the Virginia Land Policy," *ibid.*, III (1946), 499-514.

WERTENBAKER, THOMAS J.: *Give Me Liberty: The Struggle for Self-Government in Virginia* (Philadelphia, 1958).

4. Economic

BROCK, ROBERT ALONZO: "A Succinct Account of Tobacco in Virginia," *Tenth Census of the United States*, III (1883), 806-819.

BRUCE, KATHLEEN: *Virginia Iron Manufacture in the Slave Era* (London & New York, 1930), and her article "Slave Labor in the Virginia Iron Industry," *William and Mary Quarterly*, 2nd ser., VI (1926), 289-302.

COULTER, CALVIN B.: "The Import Trade of Colonial Virginia," *William and Mary Quarterly*, 3rd ser., II (1945), 296-314.

CRAVEN, AVERY O.: *Soil Exhaustion as a Factor in the Agricultural History of Virginia and Maryland, 1606-1860*, University of Illinois, *Studies in the Social Sciences*, XIII, No. 1 (Urbana, Ill., 1926).

ERNST, JOSEPH A.: "Genesis of the Currency Act of 1764: Virginia Paper Money and the Protection of British Investments," *William and Mary Quarterly*, 3rd ser., XXII (1965), 33-74.

EVANS, EMORY: "Planter Indebtedness and the Coming of the Revolution in Virginia," *ibid.*, XIX (1962), 511-33.

FLIPPEN, PERCY SCOTT: "The Financial Administration of the Colony of Virginia," Johns Hopkins University, *Studies in Historical and Political Science*, 33rd ser. (1915), 177-271.

GIPSON, LAWRENCE HENRY: "Virginia Planter Debts before the American Revolution," *Virginia Magazine of History and Biography*, LXIX (1961), 259-77.

HARRELL, ISAAC SAMUEL: *Loyalism in Virginia: Chapters in the Economic History of the Revolution* (Durham, N. C., 1926), and his article "Some Neglected Phases of the Revolution in Virginia," *William and Mary Quarterly*, 2nd ser., V (1925), 159-70.

HARRISON, FAIRFAX: *Virginia Land Grants: A Study of Conveyancing in Relation to Colonial Politics* (Richmond, Va., 1925).

HUNTLEY, FRANCIS CARROLL: "The Seaborne Trade of Virginia in Mid-Eighteenth Century: Port Hampton [1752]," *Virginia Magazine of History and Biography*, LIX (1951), 297-308.

MALONE, MILES S.: "Falmouth and the Shenandoah: Trade before the Revolution," *American Historical Review*, XL (1934-5), 693-703; a description of the contents of the Allason manuscripts in the

Virginia State Library, with suggestions for the study of socio-economic conditions in the Shenandoah, 1750-1800.

MIDDLETON, ARTHUR PIERCE: *see* under Maryland.

NEWMAN, ERIC P.: *Coinage for Colonial Virginia, Numismatic Notes and Monographs,* No. 135 (New York, 1956). Covers the period from 1636 to 1774.

PRICE, JACOB M.: "The Beginnings of Tobacco Manufacture in Virginia," *Virginia Magazine of History and Biography,* LXIV (1956), 3-29. See also his articles cited under Great Britain and under Maryland, Secondary Works.

RIPLEY, WILLIAM ZEBINA: *Financial History of Virginia, 1609-1776* (New York, 1893).

ROSENBLATT, SAMUEL M.: "Merchant-Planter Relations in the Tobacco Consignment Trade: John Norton and Robert Carter Nicholas," *Virginia Magazine of History and Biography,* LXXII (1964), 454-70; and "The Significance of Credit in the Tobacco Consignment Trade: A Study of John Norton and Sons, 1768-1775," *William and Mary Quarterly,* 3rd ser., XIX (1962), 383-99.

SEILER, WILLIAM H.: "Land Processioning in Colonial Virginia [1661-1785]," *ibid.,* VI (1949), 416-36.

SNOW, SINCLAIR: "Naval Stores in Colonial Virginia," *Virginia Magazine of History and Biography,* LXXII (1964), 75-93.

SOLTOW, JAMES H.: *The Economic Role of Williamsburg* (Williamsburg, Va., c. 1965). See also his article "The Role of Williamsburg in the Virginia Economy, 1750-1775," *William and Mary Quarterly,* 3rd ser., XV (1958), 467-82.

THOMSON, ROBERT P.: "The Tobacco Export of the Upper James River Naval District, 1773-75," *William and Mary Quarterly,* 3rd ser., XVIII (1961), 393-407. See also his "The Merchant in Virginia, 1700-1775," unpublished doctoral dissertation, University of Wisconsin, 1955.

5. Social

ALTFATHER, ALTON B.: "Early Presbyterianism in Virginia," Presbyterian Historical Society, *Journal,* XIII (1929), 267-81.

BALDWIN, ALICE M.: "Sowers of Sedition: The Political Theories of Some of the New Light Presbyterian Clergy of Virginia and North Carolina," *William and Mary Quarterly,* 3rd ser., V (1948), 52-76.

BALLAGH, JAMES CURTIS: *A History of Slavery in Virginia,* John Hopkins University, *Studies in Historical and Political Science, Extra Vol.,* XXIV (Baltimore, Md., 1902). See also his "White Servitude in the Colony of Virginia: A Study of the System of Indentured Labor in the American Colonies," *ibid.,* 13th ser. (1895), 265-357.

BRYDON, G. MAC LAREN: *Virginia's Mother Church and the Political Con-*

ditions under Which It Grew (2 vols., Richmond, Va., 1947-52),
Vol. II: *The Story of the Anglican Church and the Development
of Religion in Virginia, 1727-1814.* See also his article: "New Light
upon the History of the Church in Colonial Virginia," *Historical
Magazine of the Protestant Episcopal Church,* X (1941), 69-103.

CARSON, JANE: *Colonial Virginians at Play* (Williamsburg, Va., c. 1965).

EATON, CLEMENT: "A Mirror of the Southern Colonial Lawyer: The Fee
Books of Patrick Henry, Thomas Jefferson, and Waightstill Avery,"
William and Mary Quarterly, 3rd ser., VIII (1951), 520-34.

ECKENRODE, HAMILTON JAMES: *Separation of Church and State in Virginia:
A Study in the Development of the Revolution* (Richmond, Va.,
1910).

ERVIN, SPENCER: "The Establishment, Government, and Functioning of
the Church in Colonial Virginia," *Historical Magazine of the Protestant Episcopal Church,* XXVI (1957), 65-110.

GEWEHR, WESLEY MARSH: *The Great Awakening in Virginia, 1740-1790*
(Durham, N. C., 1930).

GOODWIN, EDWARD LEWIS: *The Colonial Church in Virginia . . . with Brief
Biographical Sketches of the Colonial Clergy of Virginia* (London,
1927).

HENDERSON, PATRICK: "Smallpox and Patriotism: The Norfolk Riots, 1768-
1769," *Virginia Magazine of History and Biography* LXXIII (1965),
413-24.

JAMES, CHARLES FENTON: *Documentary History of the Struggle for Religious Liberty in Virginia* (Lynchburg, Va., 1900).

JERNEGAN, MARCUS W.: "The Development of Poor Relief in Colonial
Virginia," *Social Service Review,* III (1929), 1-19.

MC ILWAINE, HENRY READ: "The Struggle of Protestant Dissenters for Religious Toleration in Virginia," Johns Hopkins University, *Studies
in Historical and Political Science,* 12th ser. (1894), 175-235.

MILLARD, CLIFFORD: "The Acadians in Virginia," *Virginia Magazine of
History and Biography,* XL (1932), 241-58.

MORGAN, EDMUND S.: *Virginians at Home: Family Life in the Eighteenth
Century, Williamsburg in America Series,* No. 2 (Williamsburg,
Va., c. 1952).

NOËL HUME, IVOR: *1775: Another Part of the Field* (New York, 1966). A
description of various aspects of daily life in colonial Virginia.

PILCHER, GEORGE W.: "The Pamphlet War on the Proposed Virginia
Anglican Episcopate, 1767-1775," *Historical Magazine of the
Protestant Episcopal Church,* XXX (1961), 266-79, and "Virginia
Newspapers and the Dispute over the Proposed Colonial
Episcopate, 1771-1772," *Historian,* XXIII (1960-1), 98-113.

PINCHBECK, RAYMOND B.: *The Virginia Negro Artisan and Tradesman*
(Richmond, Va., 1926).

RUSSELL, JOHN HENDERSON: "The Free Negro in Virginia, 1619-1865," Johns

Hopkins University, *Studies in Historical and Political Science,* 31st ser. (1913), 349-542.

SCOTT, ROBERT F.: "Colonial Presbyterianism in the Valley of Virginia, 1727-1775," Presbyterian Historical Society, *Journal,* XXXV (1957), 71-92, 171-92.

SEILER, WILLIAM H.: "The Anglican Parish Vestry in Colonial Virginia," *Journal of Southern History,* XXII (1956), 310-37.

SEMPLE, ROBERT BAYLOR: *A History of the Rise and Progress of the Baptists in Virginia* (rev. by G. W. Beale, Richmond, Va., 1894).

SQUIRES, WILLIAM HENRY TAPPEY: *The Presbyterian Church in the Colony of Virginia, 1562-1788* ([Richmond, Va., 1938]).

SWEET, WILLIAM WARREN: *Virginia Methodism: A History [1744-1952]* (Richmond, Va. [1955]).

TALPALAR, MORRIS: *The Sociology of Colonial Virginia* (New York, 1960). An account of the social milieu in colonial Virginia with special emphasis on the aristocracy.

TATE, THAD W.: *The Negro in Eighteenth-Century Williamsburg* (Williamsburg, Va., c. 1965).

WAYLAND, JOHN WALTER: *The German Element of the Shenandoah Valley of Virginia* (Charlottesville, Va., 1907).

WERTENBAKER, THOMAS J.: *Patrician and Plebian in Virginia: Or the Origin and Development of the Social Classes of the Old Dominion* (Charlottesville, Va., 1910), and *The Planters of Colonial Virginia* (Princeton, N.J., 1922).

WRIGHT, LOUIS B.: *The First Gentlemen of Virginia: Intellectual Qualities of the Early Colonial Ruling Class* (San Marino, Calif., 1940).

WUST, KLAUS G.: "German Mystics and Sabbatarians in Virginia, 1700-1764," *Virginia Magazine of History and Biography,* LXXII (1964), 330-47.

YOUNG, CHESTER RAYMOND: "The Stress of War upon the Civilian Population of Virginia, 1739-1760," *West Virginia History,* XXVII (1966), 251-77.

6. Biographical

BRUCE, PHILIP ALEXANDER: *The Virginia Plutarch* (2 vols., Chapel Hill, N.C., 1929), Vol. I: *The Colonial and Revolutionary Eras* includes sketches of Patrick Henry (pp. 173-94), Thomas Jefferson (pp. 195-211), George Mason (pp. 212-28), Richard Henry Lee (pp. 229-50), George Rogers Clark (pp. 269-86), and two sketches of George Washington (pp. 155-72 and 251-68).

ALLASON, WILLIAM. "A Scottish Merchant in Falmouth in the Eighteenth Century" by Edith E. B. Thomson, *Virginia Magazine of History and Biography,* XXXIX (1931), 108-17, 230-8.

BLAND, RICHARD. "Richard Bland: The Whig in America" by Clinton Rossiter, *William and Mary Quarterly*, 3rd ser., X (1953), 33-79, and "Richard Bland," in Rossiter's *Seedtime of the Republic* . . . (New York, c. 1953), pp. 247-80.

CARTER, LANDON. "Landon Carter and the Pistole Fee Dispute" by Jack P. Greene, *William and Mary Quarterly*, XIV (1957), 66-9.

CARTER, ROBERT. *Robert Carter of Nomini Hall: A Virginia Tobacco Planter of the Eighteenth Century* by Louis Morton (Williamsburg, Va., 1941).

CARTER, ROBERT WORMELEY. "Robert Wormeley Carter of Sabine Hall; Notes on the Life of a Virginia Planter" by Louis Morton, *Journal of Southern History*, XII (1946), 345-65.

DAVIES, SAMUEL. "Samuel Davies and Religious Toleration in Virginia [1748-1759]" by George William Pilcher, *Historian*, XXVIII (1965), 48-71. See also Pilcher's "Samuel Davies and the Instruction of Negroes in Virginia," *Virginia Magazine of History and Biography*, LXXIV (1966), 293-300.

DINWIDDIE, ROBERT. *Robert Dinwiddie: His Career in American Colonial Government and Westward Expansion* by Louis Knott Koontz, *Old Northwest Historical Series*, III (Glendale, Calif., 1941).

DUNMORE, JOHN MURRAY, 4TH EARL OF. "Lord Dunmore and the Pennsylvania-Virginia Boundary Dispute" by Percy B. Caley, *Western Pennsylvania Historical Magazine*, XXII (1939), 87-100.

FITHIAN, PHILIP VICKERS. "Philip Vickers Fithian: Northern Tutor on a Southern Plantation" by Franklin Parker, *Journal of the West*, IV (1965), 56-62.

GATES, HORATIO. *Horatio Gates: Defender of American Liberties* by Samuel White Patterson (New York, 1941), as a resident of Virginia.

HENRY, PATRICK. *Patrick Henry: The Voice of Freedom* by Jacob Axelrad (New York, 1947), and *Patrick Henry: Patriot in the Making* by Robert Douthat Meade (Philadelphia, 1957). See also "Judge Edmund Winston's Memoir of Patrick Henry," Robert Douthat Meade, ed., *Virginia Magazine of History and Biography*, LXIX (1961), 28-41; "The Enigma of Patrick Henry" by Bernard Mayo in his *Myths and Men* . . . (Athens, Ga., 1959), pp. 1-23; and the early biography by William Wirt: *Sketches of the Life and Character of Patrick Henry* (Philadelphia, 1817; 15th edn., 1859).

INNES, JAMES. *James Innes and His Brothers of the F.H.C.* by Jane Carson (Williamsburg, Va., c. 1965).

JEFFERSON, THOMAS. For the most useable biographies of Jefferson concerned with this period, see Gilbert Chinard's *Thomas Jefferson: The Apostle of Americanism* (Boston, 1929; 2nd edn., Ann Arbor, Mich., 1957), of which the first two sections are relevant; Marie Kimball's *Jefferson: The Road to Glory, 1743 to 1776* (New York, 1943); Nathan Schachner's *Thomas Jefferson: A Biography*

(2 vols., New York, c. 1951), Vol. I; and especially *Jefferson and His Time, Vol. I: Jefferson the Virginian* by Dumas Malone (Boston, 1948); other volumes of this important life by Malone are concerned with the post-American Revolution period. See also the article by H. Trevor Colbourn: "Thomas Jefferson's Use of the Past," *William and Mary Quarterly*, 3rd ser., XV (1958), 56-70, and that by Bernard Mayo: "The Strange Case of Thomas Jefferson," *Myths and Men* . . . (Athens, Ga., 1959), pp. 49-71.

LEE, ARTHUR. *A Vindication of Arthur Lee, LL.D., F.S.R.* . . . *1770-1781* by Charles Henry Lee (Richmond, Va., 1894).

Lee Family. *The Lees of Virginia: Biography of a Family* by Burton Jesse Hendrick (Boston, 1935).

MADISON, JAMES. *James Madison, Vol. I: The Virginia Revolutionist, 1751-1780* by Irving Brant (Indianapolis, Ind. & New York, c. 1941); other volumes of this life fall into the national period. Among other lives see *History of the Life and Times of James Madison* by William C. Rives (3 vols., Boston, 1859-70), Vol. I; *The Life of James Madison* by Gailland Hunt (New York, 1902); and *James Madison* by Sydney H. Gay (Boston & New York, 1885), a volume in the *American Statesmen* series. For the influence of Princeton on Madison see *Madison's "Advice to My Country"* by Adrienne Koch (Princton, N.J., 1966).

MADISON, THE REV. JAMES. "The Reverend James Madison in Williamsburg and London, 1768-1771," Charles Crowe, *West Virginia History*, XXV (1964), 270-8.

MASON, GEORGE. *George Mason: Constitutionalist* by Helen D. Hill (Cambridge, Mass., 1938); the recent biography by Robert Allen Rutland: *George Mason: Reluctant Statesman, Williamsburg in America Series*, IV (New York, c. 1961); and Herbert Laurence Ganter's "The Machiavellianism of George Mason," *William and Mary Quarterly*, 2nd ser., XVII (1937), 239-64.

NORTON, JOHN. "Who was John Norton? A Note on the Historical Character of Some Eighteenth-Century London Virginia Firms" by Jacob M. Price, *William and Mary Quarterly*, 3rd ser., XIX (1962), 400-7.

PENDLETON, EDMUND. *Edmund Pendleton, 1721-1803: A Biography* by David J. Mays (2 vols., Cambridge, Mass., 1952).

SAVAGE, NATHANIEL LITTLETON. "A Typical Virginia Business Man of the Revolutionary Era: Nathaniel Littleton Savage and His Account Book" by Susie M. Ames, *Journal of Economic and Business History*, III (1931), 407-23.

WALKER, THOMAS. "Dr. Thomas Walker and the Loyal Land Company of Virginia" by Archibald Henderson, American Antiquarian Society, *Proceedings*, n. ser., XLI (1931), 77-178.

WASHINGTON, GEORGE. The available biographies of Washington range from the contemporary work of David Ramsay: *The Life of George Washington* . . . (New York, 1807), to such late nineteenth-century works as Henry Cabot Lodge's *George Washington* (2 vols., Boston & New York, 1889) and Paul Leicester Ford's *The True George Washington* (Philadelphia, 1896; 10th edn., 1903). More recent studies include Rupert Hughes: *George Washington* . . . (3 vols., New York, 1926-30) and John C. Fitzpatrick: *George Washington Himself: A Common Sense Biography* . . . (Indianapolis, Ind., 1933). The most useful studies are the very recent works of Douglas Southall Freeman: *George Washington: A Biography* (7 vols., Vol. VII by John A. Carroll and Mary Wells Ashworth, New York, 1948-57), a great and detailed biography; Bernhard Knollenberg: *George Washington: The Virginia Period, 1732-1775* (Durham, N.C., 1964); and the biography by James Thomas Flexner: *George Washington: The Forge of Experience, 1732-1775* (Boston, 1965). A number of more specialized studies treating Washington are available, including Charles H. Ambler's *George Washington and the West* (Chapel Hill, N.C., 1936); Knollenberg's *Washington and the Revolution. A Reappraisal: Gates, Conway and the Continental Congress* (New York, 1940); and Esmond Wright's brief volume, *Washington and the American Revolution* (New York, c. 1957). Two works which deal with Washington's character are Nathaniel Wright Stephenson and Waldo Hilary Dunn: *George Washington* (2 vols., London & New York, 1940), *Vol. I: 1732-1777;* and Howard Swiggett: *The Great Man: George Washington as a Human Being* (Garden City, N.Y., 1953). Also of value is Bernard Mayo's sketch: "George Washington," *Georgia Review,* XIII (1959), 135-50; his "Washington: 'Freedom Myth' and 'More than Man,'" *Myths and Men* . . . (Athens, Ga., 1959), pp. 25-48; and the sketch by Samuel Eliot Morison: "The Young Washington," *By Land and by Sea: Essays and Addresses* (New York, 1953), pp. 161-80.

7. Military

DOWNES, RANDOLPH C.: "Dunmore's War: An Interpretation," *Mississippi Valley Historical Review,* XXI (1934-5), 311-30. A consideration of the role of English settlers in bringing on the war with the Indians.

MOOMAW, W. HUGH: "The British Leave Colonial Virginia," *Virginia Magazine of History and Biography,* LXVI (1958), 147-60. Relates to the flight of the royal authorities in 1775 and attempts to regain Virginia in 1776.

NORKUS, NELLIE: "Virginia's Role in the Capture of Fort Duquesne, 1758," *Western Pennsylvania Historical Magazine,* XLV (1962), 291- 308.

D. MAPS

BOWEN, EMANUEL: *A New and Accurate Map of Virginia & Maryland Laid down from Surveys and Regulated by Astron'l Observations.* In Bowen: *A Complete or Distinct View of the Known World,* No. 59.

FRY, JOSHUA, and PETER JEFFERSON: *A Map of the Most Inhabited Part of Virginia Containing the Whole Province of Maryland with Part of Pensilvania, New Jersey and North Carolina [1751]* (revised by J. Dalrymple, London, 1755). Engraved by Thomas Jefferys, it appears as Nos. 54-7 in his *A General Topography of North America and the West Indies.*

MOLL, HERMAN: *Virginia and Maryland.* In Moll: *Atlas Minor* ([London, 1736]).

A New and Accurate Map of the Province of Virginia in North America. In the *Universal Magazine,* LXV (1779), opp. p. 281.

SWEM, EARL GREGG: *Maps Relating to Virginia in the Virginia State Library and Other Departments of the Commonwealth with the 17th and 18th Century Atlas—Maps in the Library of Congress,* Virginia State Library, *Bulletin,* VII (Richmond, Va., 1914).

THE TRANS-APPALACHIAN WEST AND THE GREAT LAKES REGION

A. BIBLIOGRAPHICAL AIDS

DONNOLLY, JOSEPH P.: *A Tentative Bibliography for the Colonial Fur Trade in the American Colonies: 1608-1800* (St. Louis, Mo., 1947).

VAIL, R. W. G., ed.: *The View of the Old Frontier* (Philadelphia, 1949). This volume surveys the literature on the frontier (1542-1800).

B. PRINTED SOURCE MATERIALS

1. Government and related documents

ALVORD, CLARENCE W., and CLARENCE E. CARTER, eds: *The Critical Period, 1763-1765,* Illinois State Historical Library, *Collections,* X: *British Series,* I (Springfield, Ill., 1915). This volume prints a large number of French sources relating to the Illinois country. The only one of these demanding separate listing is "The Journal of M. Dabbadie, 1763-1764," chapter 4.

———: *The New Regime, 1765-1767*, Illinois State Historical Library, *Collections*, XI: *British Series*, II (Springfield, Ill., 1916).

———: *Trade and Politics, 1767-1769*, Illinois State Historical Library, *Collections*, XVI: *British Series*, III (Springfield, Ill., 1921).

CARTER, CLARENCE E., ed.: "Documents Relating to the Mississippi Land Company, 1763-1769," *American Historical Review*, XVI (1910-1911), 311-19. Contains documents from the Earl of Chatham's Papers, Public Record Office, London.

CRANE, VERNER W., ed.: "Hints Relative to the Division and Government of the Conquered and Newly Acquired Countries in America," *Mississippi Valley Historical Review*, VIII (1921-2), 367-73. This document, which is among the Board of Trade Papers in the Public Record Office, looks to a new western policy and is one of the key documents leading to the proclamation of October 7, 1763.

CRUZAT, HELOISE H., ed. and trans.: "Records of the Superior Council of Louisiana . . . ," *Louisiana Historical Quarterly*, XX (1937)-XXVI (1943), *passim*. This series of records covers the years 1748 to 1763 of French control of Louisiana.

HOUCK, LOUIS, ed.: *The Spanish Régime in Missouri: A Collection of Papers and Documents Relating to Upper Louisiana Principally within the Present Limits of Missouri during the Dominion of Spain* . . . (2 vols., Chicago, 1909).

KINNAIRD, LAWRENCE, ed.: *Spain in the Mississippi Valley, 1765-1794, Part I: The Revolutionary Period, 1765-1781*, American Historical Association, *Annual Report, 1945* (4 vols., Washington, D.C., 1949), Vol. II.

PEASE, THEODORE C., ed.: *Anglo-French Boundary Disputes in the West, 1749-1763*, Illinois State Historical Library, *Collections*, XXVII: *French Series*, II (Springfield, Ill., 1936).

———, and ERNESTINE JENISON, eds.: *Illinois on the Eve of the Seven Years' War, 1747-1755*, Illinois State Historical Library, *Collections*, XXIX: *French Series*, III (Springfield, Ill., 1940). Includes French documents with translations.

ROWLAND, DUNBAR, ed.: *Mississippi Provincial Archives . . . English Dominion . . . 1763-1781* (Nashville, Tenn., 1911).

———, ed.: *Mississippi Provincial Archives, French Dominion . . . [1701-1763]* (Jackson, Miss., 1927).

THWAITES, REUBEN GOLD, ed.: "The British Regime in Wisconsin," Wisconsin State Historical Society, *Collections*, XVIII (Madison, Wis., 1908), pp. 223-468. Contains much documentary material pertaining to Indian affairs.

————: *The French Regime in Wisconsin . . . 1634-1760*, Wisconsin State Historical Society, *Collections*, XVI-XVIII (3 vols., Madison, Wis., 1902-8). Volume XVIII, to p. 222 covers the French period from 1743 to 1760.

————, and LOUISE PHELPS KELLOGG, eds.: *Documentary History of Dunmore's War, 1774: Compiled from the Draper Manuscripts . . .* (Madison, Wis., 1905).

2. *Non-official contemporary writings*

BOSSU, JEAN BERNARD: *Travels in the Interior of North America, 1751-1762, American Exploration and Travel Series,* No. 35 (Seymour Feiler, ed. & trans., Norman, Okla., 1962). This work was first published in French (2 vols., Paris, 1768) and subsequently published in an English translation by John R. Forster (2 vols., London, 1771).

BOUGAINVILLE, LOUIS ANTOINE, COMTE DE: *Adventure in the Wilderness: The American Journals of Louis Antoine de Bougainville, 1756-1760, American Exploration and Travel Series,* No. 42 (Edward P. Hamilton, ed. & trans., Norman, Okla., 1964).

CÉLERON DE BLAINVILLE, PIERRE JOSEPH: "Céleron's Journal," A. A. Lambing, ed., *Ohio Archaeological and Historical Quarterly,* XXIX (1920), 335-96; also, "Céleron's Journal [1749]," A. A. Lambing ed., *American Catholic Historical Researches,* II (1885)-III (1886) *passim.*

CLARK, GEORGE ROGERS: *George Rogers Clark Papers, 1771-1781,* Illinois State Historical Library, *Collections,* VIII: *Virginia Series,* III (James Alton James, ed., Springfield, Ill., 1912).

CRAIG, NEVILLE B., ed.: *The Olden Time: A Monthly Publication Devoted to the Preservation of Documents and Other Authentic Information in Relation to the Early Explorations and the Settlement and Improvement of the Country around the Head of the Ohio . . .* (2 vols., Pittsburgh, Pa., 1846-8; rep., Cincinnati, O., 1876). A most useful collection of documents.

GIST, CHRISTOPHER: *Christopher Gist's Journals: With Historical Geographical, and Ethnological Notes and Biographies of His Contemporaries* (William M. Darlington, ed., Pittsburgh, Pa., 1893). The journals cover the years 1751-54 when Gist was in the Ohio Valley.

GORDON, HARRY: "Journal of Captain Harry Gordon's Journey from Pittsburg down the Ohio and the Mississippi to New Orleans, Mobile, and Pensacola, 1766," *Travels in the American Colonies* (Newton D. Mereness, ed., New York, 1916), pp. 455-89.

HAZARD, SAMUEL: *Scheme for the Settlement of a New Colony to the Westward of Pennsylvania . . .* (n.p., 1755).

HENRY, ALEXANDER: *Travels and Adventures in Canada and the Indian Territories between the Years 1760 and 1776* (2 pts., New York, 1809; n. edn., James Bain, ed., Toronto, 1901).

HUTCHINS, THOMAS: *A Topographical Description of Virginia, Pennsylvania, Maryland, and North Carolina, Comprehending the Rivers Ohio . . . Illinois, Mississippi . . . Containing Mr. Patrick Kennedy's Journal up the Illinois River . . .* (London, 1778).

JOHNSTON, JOSIAH STODDARD, ed.: *First Explorations of Kentucky: Doctor Thomas Walker's Journal of an Exploration of Kentucky in 1750 . . . ; Also Colonel Christopher Gist's Journal of a Tour through Ohio and Kentucky in 1751 . . .* , Filson Club, *Publication*, No. 13 (Louisville, Ky., 1898).

KENNY, JAMES: "James Kenny's 'Journal to the Westward,' 1758-9," John W. Jordan, ed., *Pennsylvania Magazine of History and Biography*, XXXVII (1913), 395-449; and "Journal of James Kenny, 1761-1763," *ibid.*, pp. 1-47, 152-201.

MERCER, GEORGE: *George Mercer Papers Relating to the Ohio Company of Virginia* (Lois Mulkearn, ed., Pittsburgh, Pa., 1954).

MORRIS, THOMAS: "Journal of Captain Thomas Morris of His Majesty's XVII Regiment of Infantry, Detroit, September 25, 1764," *Early Western Travels, 1748-1846 . . .* (Reuben Gold Thwaites, ed., 32 vols., Cleveland, O., 1904), I: 293-328.

PRATZ, LE PAGE DU, trans.: *The History of Louisiana, or of the Western Parts of Virginia and Carolina: Containing a Description of the Countries that Lye on Both Sides of the River Mississipi [sic] . . .* (originally pub. in French, 1758; trans., 2 vols., London, 1763).

ROBERTSON, JAMES A., ed.: "A Projected Settlement of English-Speaking Catholics from Maryland in Spanish Louisiana, 1767, 1768," *American Historical Review*, XVI (1911-12), 319-27.

ROGERS, ROBERT: *Diary of the Siege of Detroit in the War with Pontiac: Also a Narrative of the Principal Events of the Siege . . . and Other Authentick Documents . . .* (Franklin B. Hough, ed., Albany, N.Y., 1860). See also *Journals of Major Robert Rogers: Containing an Account of the Several Excursions He Made under the Generals who Commanded upon the Continent of North America during the Late War . . .* (London, 1765; Franklin B. Hough, ed., Albany, N.Y., 1883); "Rogers' Michilimackinac Journal [1766-1767]," William L. Clements, ed., American Antiquarian Society, *Proceedings*, n. ser., XXVIII (1918), 224-73; "Journal of Robert Rogers, the Ranger, on His Expedition for Receiving the Capitulation of the Western French Posts [1760-1]," Victor Hugo Paltsits, ed., New York Public Library, *Bulletin*, XXXVII (1933), 261-76; and finally, *Reminiscences of the French War: Containing Rogers' Expeditions with the New England Rangers under His Command . . .* (Caleb Stark, ed., Concord, N.H., 1831).

SHEA, JOHN GILMARY, ed.: *Discovery and Exploration of the Mississippi Valley: With the Original Narratives* . . . (Redfield, N.Y., 1852).

THWAITES, REUBEN GOLD, ed.: *The Jesuit Relations and Allied Documents: Travels and Explorations of the Jesuit Missionaries in New France, 1610–1791* . . . (73 vols., Cleveland, O., 1896–1901). A vast storehouse of information respecting the Indians and the land.

———, and LOUISE PHELPS KELLOGG, eds.: *The Revolution on the Upper Ohio, 1775–1777: Compiled from the Draper Manuscripts . . . , Draper Series,* II (Madison, Wis., 1908).

WILLIAMS, SAMUEL COLE, ed.: *Early Travels in the Tennessee Country, 1540–1800* . . . (Johnson City, Tenn., 1828).

3. Contemporary pamphlets, tracts, and related materials

The Expediency of Securing Our American Colonies by Settling the Country Adjoining the River Mississippi, and the Country upon the Ohio Considered (Edinburgh, 1763).

An Impartial Enquiry into the Right of the French King to the Territory West of the Great River Mississippi in North America . . . (London [1762]).

PITTMAN, PHILIP: *The Present State of the European Settlements on the Mississippi: With a Geographical Description of that River* . . . (London, 1770). Written from first-hand knowledge by a man who surveyed and explored much of the area.

Report of the Lords Commissioners for Trade and Plantations on the Petition of the Honourable Thomas Walpole, Benjamin Franklin, John Sargent, and Samuel Wharton . . . for a Grant of Lands on the River Ohio in North America for the Purpose of Erecting a New Government: With Remarks and Observations (London, 1772). The *Report* was written by Lord Hillsborough and the *Remarks and Observations* by Samuel Wharton.

WALPOLE, THOMAS: *To the King's Most Excellent Majesty in Council: The Memorial of the Honourable Thomas Walpole, in Behalf of Himself and [others]* . . . ([London, 1774]); this concerns the famous Walpole Company.

[WHARTON, SAMUEL]: *The Advantages of a Settlement Upon the Ohio in North America* (London, 1763 [i.e., 1773]).

[———]: *Considerations on the Agreement of the Lords Commissioners of His Majesty's Treasury with the Honourable Thomas Walpole and His Associates for Lands upon the River Ohio in North America: In a Letter to a Member of Parliament* (London, 1774).

[———]: *Facts and Observations Respecting the Country Granted to His Majesty by the Six Nations of Indians* . . . (London, 1775).

[———] *Plain Facts: Being an Examination into the Rights of the Indian Nations of America to Their Respective Countries and a Vindica-*

tion of the Grant from the Six United Nations of Indians ... (Philadelphia, 1781). Authorship has also been attributed to Franklin and Benezet.

[————]: [*Statement of the Petitioners in the Case of the Walpole Company*] ([London, 1771]). No title pages of this rare pamphlet are extant; the exact title is unknown.

[————]: *View of the Title to Indiana, a Tract of Country on the River Ohio: Containing Indian Conferences at Johnson-Hall, in May, 1765; the Deed of the Six Nations to the Proprietors of Indiana ...* (Philadelphia, 1776).

C. SECONDARY WORKS

1. General

ABERNETHY, THOMAS PERKINS: *From Frontier to Plantation in Tennessee: A Study in Frontier Democracy* (Chapel Hill, N.C., 1932).

ALDEN, JOHN R.: *Pioneer America* (New York, 1966). Gives a clear picture of the frontier in British North America and the United States to 1865.

ALVORD, CLARENCE W.: *The Centennial History of Illinois, Vol. I: The Illinois Country, 1673-1818* (Springfield, Ill., 1920).

BAILEY, KENNETH P.: *The Ohio Company of Virginia and the Westward Movement, 1748-1792: A Chapter in the History of the Colonial Frontier* (Glendale, Calif., 1939).

BELTING, NATALIA MAREE: *Kaskaskia under the French Regime*, University of Illinois, *Studies in the Social Sciences*, XXIX (Urbana, Ill., 1948; rep. 1966).

BILLINGTON, RAY A.: *America's Frontier Heritage* (New York, 1966).

————, and JAMES BLAINE HEDGES: *Westward Expansion: A History of the American Frontier [1492-1896]* (1st edn., New York, 1949; 2nd edn., 1960).

BODLEY, TEMPLE: *Our First Great West: In Revolutionary War, Diplomacy and Politics ...*, Filson Club, *Publications* No. 36 (Louisville, Ky., 1938).

BREBNER, JOHN BARTLET: *The Explorers of North America, 1492-1806* (London & New York, 1933), pp. 1-428.

BUCK, S. J. and ELIZABETH H.: *See* under Pennsylvania, Secondary Works.

BURPEE, LAWRENCE J.: *The Search for the Western Sea: The Story of the Exploration of North-Western America* (Toronto, 1908; rev. edn., 2 vols., 1935). See also "Western Exploration, 1763-1841," *Canada and Its Provinces ...*, IV: 639-92.

CALDWELL, NORMAN W.: *The French in the Mississippi Valley, 1740-1750.*

University of Illinois, *Studies in the Social Sciences,* XXVI (Urbana, Ill., 1941; rep., J. F. McDermott, ed., 1965).

CALEY, PERCY B.: "Lord Dunmore and the Pennsylvania-Virginia Boundary Dispute," *Western Pennsylvania Historical Magazine,* XXII (1939), 87-100.

CARTER, CLARENCE E.: *Great Britain and the Illinois Country, 1763-1774* (Washington, D.C., 1910).

CARUSO, JOHN ANTHONY: *The Appalachian Frontier: America's First Surge Westward* (Indianapolis, Ind., 1959).

DURRIE, DANIEL STEELE: *The Early Outposts of Wisconsin* (Madison, Wis., 1872).

GALBREATH, C. B.: "Expedition of Céleron," *Ohio Archeological and Historical Quarterly,* XXIX (1920), 331-4.

GAYARRE, CHARLES E. A.: *Histoire de la Louisiane* (2 vols., New Orleans, La., 1846-7). Also published in English: *The History of Louisiana* ... (4 vols, New York, 1854-66; 4th edn., New Orleans, La., 1903).

HANNA, CHARLES AUGUSTUS: *The Wilderness Trail: Or the Ventures and Adventures of the Pennsylvania Traders* ... (2 vols., London & New York, 1911).

HENDERSON, ARCHIBALD: *The Star of Empire: Phases of the Westward Movement in the Old Southwest* (Durham, N.C., 1919); *The Conquest of the Old Southwest: The Romantic Story of the Early Pioneers into Virginia, the Carolinas, Tennessee, and Kentucky, 1740-1790* (New York, c. 1920); and "Dr. Thomas Walker and the Loyal Land Company of Virginia," American Antiquarian Society, *Proceedings,* n. ser., XLI (1931), 77-178.

HOUCK, LOUIS: *A History of Missouri* ... (3 vols., Chicago, 1908). Important for its treatment of early Indian trade.

JAMES, ALFRED P.: *The Ohio Company: Its Inner History* (Pittsburgh, Pa., 1959); see also his article "The First English-Speaking Trans-Appalachian Frontier," *Mississippi Valley Historical Review,* XVII (1930-1), 55-71.

LAUVRIÈRE, ÉMILE: *Histoire de la Louisiane Française, 1673-1939,* Louisiana State University, *Romance Languages Series,* No. 3 (University, La., 1940).

LEACH, DOUGLAS EDWARD: *The Northern Colonial Frontier, 1607-1763* (New York, 1966).

LESTER, WILLIAM STEWART: *The Transylvania Colony* (Spencer, Ind., 1935).

LOGAN, JOHN H.: *A History of the Upper Country of South Carolina* ... (Charleston, S.C., 1859).

MC DERMOTT, JOHN FRANCIS: *The French in the Mississippi Valley* (Urbana, Ill., 1965).

MARSHALL, PETER: "Lord Hillsborough, Samuel Wharton and the Ohio

Grant, 1769-1775," *English Historical Review*, LXXX (1965), 717-39.

MOOD, FULMER: "Studies in the History of American Settled Areas and Frontier Lines: Settled Areas and Frontier Lines, 1625-1790," *Agricultural History*, XXVI (1952), 16-34.

PARKINS, ALMON ERNEST: *The Historical Geography of Detroit, Michigan Historical Publications: University Series*, III (Lansing, Mich., 1918).

PHELPS, DAWSON A.: "The Vaudreuil Expedition, 1752," *William and Mary Quarterly*, 3rd ser., XV (1958), 483-93.

PHILBRICK, FRANCIS S.: *The Rise of the West, 1754-1830* (New York, 1966).

RAMSAY, ROBERT W.: *Carolina Cradle: Settlement of the Northwest Carolina Frontier, 1747-1762* (Chapel Hill, N.C., 1964).

SCHLARMAN, JOSEPH H.: *From Quebec to New Orleans: The Story of the French in America* (Belleville, Ill., 1929).

SEVERANCE, FRANK H.: *An Old Frontier of France: The Niagara Region and Adjacent Lakes under French Control*, Buffalo Historical Society, *Publications*, XX-XXI (2 vols., New York, 1917).

THWAITES, REUBEN GOLD: *France in America, 1497-1763, The American Nation: A History*, VII (London & New York, 1907).

VEECH, JAMES: *The Monongahela of Old: Or Historical Sketches of South-Western Pennsylvania to the Year 1800* (Pittsburgh, Pa., 1892).

WILLIAMS, SAMUEL COLE: *Dawn of Tennessee Valley and Tennessee History* (Johnson City, Tenn., 1937).

———: *History of the Lost State of Franklin* (Johnson City, Tenn., 1924; rev. edn., New York, 1933).

WINSOR, JUSTIN: *The Mississippi Basin: The Struggle in America between England and France, 1697-1763* (London, 1895). See also "Cartography of Louisiana and the Mississippi Basin under the French Domination," *Narrative and Critical History of America*, V: 79-86.

2. Political

ABERNETHY, THOMAS PERKINS: *Western Lands and the American Revolution*, University of Virginia Institute for Research in the Social Sciences, *Monograph*, No. 25 (London & New York, 1937).

ALDEN, GEORGE HENRY: "New Governments West of the Alleghenies before 1780," University of Wisconsin, *Bulletin*, II (1897), 1-74.

ALVORD, CLARENCE W.: *Mississippi Valley in British Politics: A Study of the Trade, Land Speculation, and Experiments in Imperialism Culminating in the American Revolution* (2 vols., Cleveland, O., 1917). See also his articles: "The British Ministry and the Treaty of Fort Stanwix," Wisconsin Historical Society, *Proceedings*, LVI (1909), 165-83, and "The Genesis of the Proclamation of 1763,"

Michigan Historical Society, *Collections,* XXXVI (1907), 20-52. For a revision of this latter article, see R. A. Humphreys' "Lord Shelburne and the Proclamation of 1763," *English Historical Review,* XLIX (1934), 241-264.

BOBB, BERNARD E.: *The Viceregency of Antonio Mariá Bucareli in New Spain, 1771-1779* (Austin, Tex., 1962).

BUFFINGTON, ARTHUR H.: "The Policy of Albany and the English Westward Expansion," *Mississippi Valley Historical Review,* VIII (1921-2), 327-66.

FULLERTON, JAMES N.: "Squatters and Titles to Land in Early Western Pennsylvania . . . ," *Western Pennsylvania Historical Magazine,* VI (1923), 165-76.

HURT, N. FRANKLIN: "Growth of Local Action during British Military Rule at Detroit, 1760-1774," *Michigan History,* XL (1956), 451-64.

KELLOGG, LOUISE PHELPS: *The French Regime in Wisconsin and the Northwest, Wisconsin Historical Series,* I (Madison, Wis., 1925), and her companion volume, *The British Regime in Wisconsin and the Northwest, ibid.,* II (Madison, Wis., 1935).

METZGER, CHARLES: "An Appraisal of Shelburne's Western Policy," *Mid-America,* XIX (1937), 169-81.

PEASE, THEODORE C.: "The Mississippi Boundary of 1763: A Reappraisal of Responsibility," *American Historical Review,* XL (1934-5), 278-86.

PHILLIPS, PAUL C.: "Vincennes in Its Relation to French Colonial Policy," *Indiana Magazine of History,* XVII (1921), 311-37.

———: *The West in the Diplomacy of the American Revolution,* University of Illinois, *Studies in the Social Sciences,* II (Urbana, Ill., 1913; rep., 1966).

PRIESTLEY, HERBERT INGRAM: *France Overseas through the Old Regime: A Study of European Expansion* (London & New York, 1939).

RIDDELL, WILLIAM RENWICK: *Michigan under British Rule: Law and Law Courts, 1760-1796* (Lansing, Mich., 1926).

RUSSELL, NELSON VANCE: *The British Régime in Michigan and the Old Northwest, 1760-1796* (Northfield, Minn. [1939]).

SOSIN, JACK M.: *Whitehall and the Wilderness: The Middle West in British Colonial Policy, 1760-1775* (Lincoln, Neb., 1961). See also Sosin's unpublished doctoral dissertation: "The North American Interior in British Colonial Policy, 1760-1775 . . . ," Indiana University, 1958. In addition, see his articles dealing with the West: "The Yorke-Camden Opinion and American Land Speculators," *Pennsylvania Magazine of History and Biography,* LXXXV (1961), 38-49, and "The French Settlements in British Policy for the North American Interior, 1760-1774," *Canadian Historical Review,* XXXIX (1958), 185-208.

3. Economic

ADAIR, E. R.: "Anglo-French Rivalry in the Fur Trade during the 18th Century," *Culture*, VIII (1947), 434-55.

BAILEY, KENNETH P.: *The Ohio Company of Virginia and the Westward Movement, 1748-1792: A Chapter in the History of the Colonial Frontier* (Glendale, Calif., 1939).

COOK, ROY BIRD: *Washington's Western Lands* (Strasburg, Va., 1930).

JOHNSON, IDA AMANDA: *The Michigan Fur Trade, Michigan Historical Publications: University Series*, V, pt. 1 (Lansing, Mich., 1919).

LEWIS, GEORGE E.: *The Indiana Company, 1763-1798: A Study in Eighteenth Century Frontier Land Speculation and Business Venture*, Old Northwest Historical Series, IV (Glendale, Calif., 1941).

LEYLAND, HERBERT T.: *The Ohio Company: A Colonial Corporation*, Historical and Philosophical Society of Ohio, *Publications*, XVI (Cincinnati, O., 1921).

LIVERMORE, SHAW: *Early American Land Companies: Their Influence on Corporate Development* (London & New York, 1939).

MULKEARN, LOIS: "The English Eye the French in North America," *Pennsylvania History*, XXI (1954), 316-37. This article discusses English and French trade competition on the American frontier before 1754.

MUNRO, WILLIAM BENNETT: "The Coureurs-de-Bois," Massachusetts Historical Society, *Proceedings*, LVII (1923-4), 192-205.

PHILLIPS, PAUL C.: *The Fur Trade* (2 vols., Norman, Okla., 1961). Volume I is relevant to the period under review.

REID, MARJORIE G.: "The Quebec Fur-Traders and Western Policy, 1763-1774," *Canadian Historical Review*, VI (1925), 15-32.

ROWLAND, KATE MASON: "The Ohio Company," *William and Mary Quarterly*, I (1892-3), 197-203. Includes list of the papers of John, James, and George Mercer.

SAKOLSKI, AARON MORTON: *The Great American Land Bubble: The Amazing Story of Land-Grabbing, Speculations, and Booms from Colonial Days to the Present Time* (London & New York, 1932).

SAUM, LEWIS O.: *The Fur Trader and the Indian* (Seattle, Wash., 1965). This work examines Indian life and the business dealings between them and the early traders.

STEVENS, WAYNE E.: *The Northwest Fur Trade, 1763-1800*, University of Illinois, *Studies in the Social Sciences*, XIV (Urbana, Ill., 1928).

SURREY, NANCY MARIA (MILLER): *The Commerce of Louisiana during the French Regime, 1699-1763*, Columbia University, *Studies in History, Economics, and Public Law*, No. 167 (London & New York, 1916).

THOMAS, CHARLES M.: "Successful and Unsuccessful Merchants in the

Illinois Country," Illinois State Historical Society, *Journal,* XXX
(1938), 429-40.

VIRTUE, GEORGE OLIEN: *British Land Policy and the American Revolution:
A Belated Lecture in Economic History,* University of Nebraska,
Studies, n. ser., XI (Lincoln, Neb., 1955).

WELLS, GORDON M., comp.: "British Land Grants: William Wilton Map,
1774," *Journal of Mississippi History,* XXVIII (1966), 152-60.

WILSON, SAMUEL M.: *The Ohio Company of Virginia, 1748-1798* (Lexington, Ky., 1926).

4. Social

BRYCE, CHARLES C.: "The Backwoodsman Era in Western Pennsylvania,"
Western Pennsylvania Historical Magazine, XXIV (1941), 23-35.

DELANGLEZ, JEAN: *The French Jesuits in Lower Louisiana, 1700-1763,*
Catholic University of America, *Studies in American Church History,* XXI (Washington, D.C., 1935).

VOGEL, CLAUDE L.: *The Capuchins in French Louisiana (1722-1766), Fran-
ciscan Studies,* No. 8 (New York [1928]).

WRIGHT, J. E., and DORIS S. CORBETT: *Pioneer Life in Western Pennsylvania*
([Pittsburgh, Pa., 1940]).

5. Biographical

BOONE, DANIEL. *Daniel Boone* by Reuben Gold Thwaites (New York,
1902), and *Daniel Boone and the Wilderness Road* by H. Adding-
ton Bruce (New York, 1910). See also the following articles:
"Daniel Boone and the American Pioneer" by Archibald Henderson, *Century Magazine,* C (1920), 708-13; a second one by Henderson cited below under Richard Henderson; and "The Daniel
Boone Myth" by Clarence W. Alvord, Illinois State Historical Society, *Journal,* XIX (1926), 16-30.

BOUQUET, HENRY. "Henry Bouquet: Professional Soldier" by E. Douglas
Branch, *Pennsylvania Magazine of History and Biography,* LXII
(1938), 41-51.

CLARK, GEORGE ROGERS. *The Life of George Rogers Clark* by James Alton
James (Chicago, 1928).

CÉLORON, DE BLAINVILLE, PIERRE-JOSEPH. *La Famille Céloron de Blainville*
by Pierre Georges Roy (Quebec, 1909); and the George A. Woods
article: "Céloron de Blainville and French Expansion in the Ohio
Valley," *Mississippi Valley Historical Review,* IX (1922-3), 302-19.

CROGHAN, GEORGE. *George Croghan and the Westward Movement, 1741-
1782* by Albert T. Volwiler, *Early Western Journals,* III (Cleveland, O., 1926), and Nicholas B. Wainwright's *George Croghan:
Wilderness Diplomat* (Chapel Hill, N.C., c. 1959).

DUNMORE, JOHN MURRAY, 4TH EARL OF. "Lord Dunmore and the West: A Re-evaluation" by Richard Curry, *West Virginia History*, XIX (1957-8), 231-43, and a second article by Curry: "Lord Dunmore: Tool of Land Jobbers or Realistic Champion of Colonial 'Rights'?: An Inquiry," *ibid.*, XXIV (1963), 289-95.

GIST, CHRISTOPHER. "Christopher Gist and Settlement on the Monongahela, 1752-1754" by David B. Trimble, *Virginia Magazine of History and Biography*, LXIII (1955), 15-27.

HENDERSON, RICHARD. "Richard Henderson and the Occupation of Kentucky, 1775" by Archibald Henderson, *Mississippi Valley Historical Review*, I (1914-15), 341-63; also, Henderson's "The Creative Forces in American Expansion: Henderson and Boone," *American Historical Review*, XX (1914-15), 86-107.

MC MILLAN, JOHN. *John McMillan: The Apostle of Presbyterianism in the West, 1752-1833* by Dwight Raymond Guthrie ([Pittsburgh, Pa., 1952]). Included in this study are McMillan's journal, expense account and autobiography.

MERCER, GEORGE. *George Mercer of the Ohio Company: A Study in Frustration* by Alfred Procter James (Pittsburgh, Pa., 1963). See also his article of the same title in *Western Pennsylvania Historical Magazine*, XLVI (1963), 1-43, 141-83.

MORGAN, GEORGE. *George Morgan: Colony Builder* by Max Savelle (New York, 1932).

PATTEN, JOHN. *Map Maker & Indian Traders: An Account of John Patten, Trader, Arctic Explorer, and Map Maker . . .* by Howard N. Eavenson (Pittsburgh, Pa., 1949). This work also includes biographies of Charles Swaine and Theodorus Swaine Drage.

ROGERS, ROBERT. *Robert Rogers of the Rangers* by John R. Cuneo (New York, 1959).

STOBO, ROBERT. *The Most Extraordinary Adventures of Major Robert Stobo* by Robert C. Alberts (Boston, 1965). See also Alberts's article: "The Expedition of Captain Robert Stobo [1754]," *Western Pennsylvania Historical Magazine*, XLVII (1964), 177-97.

6. Military and naval

LOESCHER, BURT GARFIELD: *The History of Rogers Rangers . . .* (San Francisco, 1946).

MC COY, RAYMOND: *The Massacre of Old Fort Mackinac (Michilimackinac): A Tragedy of the American Frontier . . .* ([Bay City, Mich., 1939]).

RUSSELL, NELSON VANCE: "Transportation and Naval Defense in the Old Northwest during the British Régime, 1760-96," *University of Michigan Historical Essays*, University of Michigan, *Publications: History and Political Science*, XI (A.E.R. Boak, ed., Ann Arbor, Mich., 1937), 113-39.

D. MAPS

BOWEN, EMANUEL: *A New and Accurate Map of Louisiana with Part of Florida and Canada and the Adjacent Countries: Drawn from Surveys, Assisted by the Most Approved English & French Maps & Charts.* In Bowen: *A Complete or Distinct View of the Known World,* No. 57.

BROWN, LLOYD ARNOLD: *Early Maps of the Ohio Valley: A Selection of Maps, Plans, and Views Made by Indians and Colonials from 1673 to 1783* (Pittsburgh, Pa., c. 1959).

Carte de la Louisiane. Dressée et Gravée par Chambon. In Georges Marie Butel-Dumont: *Mémoires Historiques sur la Louisiane* (Paris, 1753), I:2.

Cours du Fleuve Saint Louis [the Mississippi] depuis ses Embouchures jusqu'à la Rivière d'Iberville. . . . In Bellin: *Le Petit Atlas Maritime . . . ,* I:43.

GIBSON, JOHN, sculp.: *Map of the Western Parts of the Colony of Virginia as Far as the Mississippi [1754].* In *The Journal of Major Washington Sent by the Hon. Robert Dinwiddie To the Commandant of the French Forces on the Ohio* (London, 1754).

JEFFERYS, THOMAS: *Course of the River Mississippi from Balise to Fort Chartres; Taken on an Expedition to the Illinois . . . 1765, by Lieut. Ross . . . Improved from the Surveys of the River Made by the French . . . 1775.* In Jefferys: *The American Atlas . . . ,* No. 26.

————: *Plan of New Orleans, the Capital of Louisiana, with the Disposition of Its Quarters and Canals . . .* ([London], 1759). In Jefferys: *The Natural and Civil History of the French Dominions in North and South America,* Pt. I: opp. p. 148.

KITCHIN, THOMAS, sculp.: *Draught of the R. Iberville Being a Short Communication from the Sea to the First English Settlements on the Mississippi.* In Philip Pittman: *The Present State of the European Settlements on the Mississippi* (London, 1770), opp. p. 26.

————: *Louisiana, as Formerly Claimed by France, now Containing Part of British America to the East & Spanish America to the West of the Mississippi.* In the *London Magazine,* XXXIV (1765), opp. p. 276.

La Louisiane en 1744. In Marcel Trudel: *Collection de Cartes Anciennes et Modernes pour Servir à l'étude de l'Histoire de l'Amérique et du Canada* (Quebec, 1948), p. 6.

La Louisiane et Pays Voisins. In Bellin: *Le Petit Atlas Maritime . . . ,* I: No. 40.

LERY, CHAUSSEGROS DE: *Carte de la Belle Rivière [1740].* In S. K. Stevens and D. H. Kent: *Wilderness Chronicles of Northwestern Pennsylvania,* opp. p. 12. Lery made this survey in 1740.

A Map of the Country from the Western Lakes to the Eastern Part of the Center Colonies of North America, 1765. British War Office Maps, in *ibid.,* frontispiece (not a very satisfactory reproduction).

Plan de la Nouvelle Orleans. In Bellin: *Le Petit Atlas Martime* . . . , I: No. 45.

ROSS, JOHN: *Course of the River Mississippi* . . . *1765.* In Kitchin: *A General Atlas* . . . , No. 33. This illustrates the British approach to the eastern bank of the Mississippi by way of the Iberville River.

————: *Course of the River Mississippi from the Balise to Fort Chartres, Taken on an Expedition to the Illinois in the Latter End of the Year 1765* . . . (London, 1775). In *American Maps,* II: No. 30, Library of Congress.

INDIAN RELATIONS

A. BIBLIOGRAPHICAL AIDS

BISSELL, BENJAMIN HEZEKIAH: *The American Indian in the English Literature of the Eighteenth Century,* Yale University, *Studies in English,* LXVIII (New Haven, 1925).

DE PUY, HENRY F.: *A Bibliography of the English Colonial Treaties with the American Indians: Including a Synopsis of Each Treaty* (New York, 1917).

FIELD, THOMAS WARREN: *An Essay toward an Indian Bibliography* . . . (New York, 1873).

HODGE, FREDERICK WEBB, ed.: *Handbook of American Indians North of Mexico,* Smithsonian Institution: Bureau of American Ethnology, *Bulletin,* No. 30 (2 vols., Washington, 1907-10). This provides both a subject and author list.

UNITED STATES AMERICAN BUREAU OF ETHNOLOGY: *List of Publications of the Bureau of American Ethnology: With Index to Authors and Titles* (Washington, D.C., 1937; rev. edn., 1962).

B. PRINTED SOURCE MATERIALS

1. *Government and related documents*

ATKIN, EDMOND: *Indians of the Southern Colonial Frontier: The Edmond Atkin Report and Plan of 1755* (Wilbur R. Jacobs, ed., Columbia, S.C., 1954).

BOYD, JULIAN P., and CARL VAN DOREN, eds.: *Indian Treaties Printed by Benjamin Franklin, 1736-1762* (Philadelphia, 1938).

COVINGTON, JAMES W., ed.: *The British Meet the Seminoles: Negotiations between British Authorities in East Florida and the Indians, 1763-68*, Florida State Museum, *Contributions: Social Sciences*, No. 7 ([Gainesville, Fla., 1961]).

GLADWIN, HENRY: "The Gladwin Manuscripts," Charles Moore, ed., *Michigan Pioneer and Historical Collections*, XXVII (1896), 605-80.

GRANT, LODOVICK: "Historical Relation of Facts Delivered by Lodovick Grant, Indian Trader, to His Excellency the Governor of South Carolina," *South Carolina Historical and Genealogical Magazine*, X (1909), 54-68. This material was taken from the Charleston Probate Court Book, 1754-1758.

JOHNSON, WILLIAM: *The Papers of Sir William Johnson* . . . (James Sullivan, Alexander C. Flick, Almon W. Lauber, and Milton W. Hamilton, eds., 14 vols., Albany, N.Y., 1921-65). A great collection of papers covering the period 1738-1774, with a general index in Volume 14. Many Johnson papers relating to Indian affairs are not included since they had already been embodied in E. B. O'Callaghan's *Documentary History of the State of New York*, Volumes II and IV, and in his *Documents Relating to the Colonial History of the State of New York*, Volumes VI, VII, VIII, and X. The three series therefore must be used together in dealing with the record of Johnson's activities as Superintendent of Indian Affairs for the Northern District.

MC DOWELL, WILLIAM L., JR., ed.: *Documents Relating to Indian Affairs, May 21, 1750-August 7, 1754, Colonial Records of South Carolina, Ser. 2: The Indian Books* (Columbia, S.C., 1958).

Minutes of Conferences, Held at Fort Pitt in April and May 1768 under the Direction of George Crogan, Esquire, Deputy Agent for Indian Affairs, with the Chiefs and Warriors of the Ohio and Other Western Indians (Philadelphia, 1769).

STUART, JOHN, and JAMES GRANT: "Observations of Superintendent John Stuart and Governor James Grant of East Florida on the Proposed Plan of 1764 for the Future Management of Indian Affairs," Clarence E. Carter, ed., *American Historical Review*, XX (1914-15), 815-31.

"The Treaty of Logg's Town, 1752: Commission, Instructions, Etc.; Journal of Virginia Commissioners and Text of Treaty," *Virginia Magazine of History and Biography*, XIII (1905-6), 143-74. In addition to this treaty, others have also been reprinted: "A Treaty between Virginia and the Catawbas and Cherokees, &c.: The Treaties of 1768 and 1770," *ibid.*, pp. 20-36, 139-41; and "Treaty with the Cherokees at Lochabor, S.C., 1770," *ibid.*, IX (1901-2), 360-4.

2. Non-official contemporary writings

ADAIR, JAMES: *The History of the American Indians: Particularly Those Nations Adjoining to the Mississippi, East and West Florida, Georgia, South and North Carolina, and Virginia* (London, 1775; n. edn., Samuel Cole Williams, ed., Johnson City, Tenn., 1930).

BEAUCHAMP, CHEVALIER DE: "Journal of Beauchamp's Journey from Mobile to the Choctaws, 1746," *Travels in the American Colonies* (Newton D. Mereness, ed., New York, 1916), pp. 255-97.

BOUQUET, HENRY: *The Papers of Col. Henry Bouquet* (Sylvester K. Stevens and Donald H. Kent, eds., 19 vols., Harrisburg, Pa., 1940-3). Contains transcripts from the British Museum published in mimeographed form by the Pennsylvania Historical Commission. Thus far one volume has been printed under the editorship of Stevens, Kent, and Autumn L. Leonard (1951). See also: "Indian Captives Released by Colonel Bouquet [1764-65]," William S. Ewing, ed., *Western Pennsylvania Historical Magazine*, XXXIX (1956), 187-203, and "The Orderly Book of Colonel Henry Bouquet's Expedition Against the Ohio Indians, 1764," Edward G. Williams, ed., *ibid.*, XLII (1959), 9-33.

BURTON, M. AGNES, ed.: *Journal of Pontiac's Conspiracy, 1763* . . . (R. Clyde Ford, trans. [Detroit, Mich.], 1912). The translation of a French manuscript which has been attributed to Robert Navarre.

COLDEN, CADWALLADER: *The History of the Five Nations Depending on the Province of New York in America* (New York, 1727; rev. edn., w/2nd part, London, 1747). A third part not previously published continues his Indian history from 1707 through 1720 in *The Letters and Papers of Cadwallader Colden, Vol. IX: Additional Letters and Papers 1749-1775 and Some of Colden's Writings*, New York Historical Society, *Collections*, LXVIII (New York, 1937), 357-434. The work was reprinted in New York in 1866 with annotations by John Gilmary Shea. Colden's continuation (the 1747 edn.) was edited and reprinted by Thomas Osborne under the title *The History of the Five Indian Nations of Canada* . . . (London, 1747; 3rd edn., 1755; n. edn., 2 vols., New York, 1902). The early history of the Five Nations as stressed by Colden is important for an understanding of the Confederation after 1748.

CROGHAN, GEORGE: "A Selection of Letters and Journals Relating to Tours into the Western Country, November 16, 1750-November 1765," *Early Western Travels, 1748-1846* . . . (Reuben Gold Thwaites, ed., 32 vols., Cleveland, O., 1904-7), I: 45-173. Portions of the journals have been published in a number of other places, including "George Croghan's Journal, 1759-1763: From the Original in the Cadwalader Collection of the Historical Society of Pennsylvania," Nicholas B. Wainwright, ed., *Pennsylvania Magazine of*

History and Biography, LXXI (1947), 303-444. Another section of the journal is printed as "George Croghan's Journals, February 28, 1765, to October 8, 1765," *The New Régime, 1765-1767*, Illinois State Historical Library, *Collections*, XI: *British Series*, II (Clarence W. Alvord and Clarence E. Carter, eds., Springfield, Ill., 1916), Chapter 1; and still another portion has been published: *George Croghan's Journal of His Trip to Detroit in 1767: With His Correspondence Relating Thereto* . . . (Howard H. Peckham, ed., Ann Arbor, Mich. & London, 1939). Croghan's chief importance is in his Indian relations as Deputy Superintendent for the Northern District.

GORRELL, JAMES: "Lieutenant James Gorrell's Journal [1761-3]," Wisconsin State Historical Society, . . . *Collections*, I (1855), 24-48; the journal is also to be found in *The Papers of Sir William Johnson*, X: 697-714.

HECKEWELDER, JOHN: *An Account of the History, Manners, and Customs of the Indian Nations who once Inhabited Pennsylvania and the Neighboring States*, American Philosophical Society, *Transactions*, I (1819-43), 3-347.

HOPKINS, SAMUEL: *An Abridgement of Mr. Hopkins' Historical Memoirs Relating to the . . . Indians; Or a Brief Account of the Methods Used and Pains Taken for Civilizing and Propagating the Gospel among that Heathenish Tribe* . . . (Philadelphia, 1757). Contains a letter on Indian affairs by Conrad Weiser.

JOHNSON, WILLIAM. *The Life and Times of Sir William Johnson, Bart.* by William L. Stone (2 vols., Albany, N.Y., 1865). Included in this work is Johnson's diary.

KENNEDY, ARCHIBALD: *The Importance of Gaining and Preserving the Friendship of the Indians to the British Interest Considered* (New York, 1751; London, 1752). The author recommended a colonial confederation for mutual defence and for developing friendly relations with the Indians.

LONG, JOHN: "Voyages and Travels of an Indian Interpreter and Trader, Describing the Manners and Customs of the North American Indians . . . April 10, 1768-Spring 1782," *Early Western Travels, 1748-1846* . . . (Reuben Gold Thwaites, ed., 32 vols., Cleveland, O., 1904-7), II.

LOUDON, ARCHIBALD, comp.: *A Selection of Some of the Most Interesting Narratives of Outrages Committed by the Indians in Their Wars with the White People* . . . (2 vols., Carlisle, Pa., 1808-11; rep., Harrisburg, Pa., 1888).

LOVE, WILLIAM DELOSS: *Samuel Occom and the Christian Indians of New England* (Boston, c. 1899).

MONTAULT DE MONBERAUT, HENRY: *Mémoire Justificatif: Indian Diplomacy in British West Florida, 1763-1765*, Southern Historical Pub-

lications, No. 3 (Milo B. Howard, Jr., and Robert R. Rea, trans., University, Ala., 1965).

POST, CHRISTIAN FREDERICK: "Two Journals of Western Tours [relating to Pennsylvania Indian affairs]," *Early Western Travels, 1748-1846* . . . (Reuben Gold Thwaites, ed., 32 vols., Cleveland, O., 1904-7), I: 175-291. Post's first journal was originally published in Thomson's *An Enquiry into the Causes of the Alienation of the Delaware and Shawanese Indians* . . . which is cited below. His second account, *The Second Journal of Christian Frederick Post on a Message from the Governor of Pensilvania to the Indians on the Ohio*, was published in London in 1759.

POWNALL, THOMAS: *Proposals for Securing the Friendship of the Five Nations* (New York, 1756).

[SMITH, WILLIAM]: *An Historical Account of the Expedition against the Ohio Indians in the Year 1764: Under the Command of Henry Bouquet, Esq.* . . . (Philadelphia, 1765). This work was reprinted with a slightly revised title as No. 1 in the *Ohio Valley Historical Series* (Cincinnati, O., 1868).

TAITT, DAVID: "Journal of David Taitt's Travels from Pensacola, West Florida, to and through the Country of the Upper and the Lower Creeks, 1772," *Travels in the American Colonies* (Newton D. Mereness, ed., New York, 1916), pp. 491-565.

[THOMSON, CHARLES]: *An Enquiry into the Causes of the Alienation of the Delaware and Shawanese Indians from the British Interest and into the Measures Taken for Recovering Their Friendship* . . . *Together with the Remarkable Journal of Christian Frederic Post* . . . (London, 1759). Reprinted as *Causes of the Alienation of the Delaware and Shawanese Indians from the British Interest* (Philadelphia, 1867).

THWAITES, REUBEN GOLD: See under Trans-Appalachian West, B: 1.

TIMBERLAKE, HENRY: *The Memoirs of Lieut. Henry Timberlake* . . . (London, 1765; rep. under title *Lieut. Henry Timberlake's Memoirs, 1756-1765*, Samuel Cole Williams, ed., Johnson City, Tenn., 1927).

TRENT, WILLIAM: *Journal of Captain William Trent from Logstown to Pickawillany, A.D. 1752* . . . (Alfred T. Goodman, ed., Cincinnati, O., 1871).

WEISER, CONRAD: "Journal of a Tour to the Ohio, August 11-October 2, 1748," *Early Western Travels, 1748-1846* . . . (Reuben Gold Thwaites, ed., 32 vols., Cleveland, O., 1904-7), I: 15-44, relating to Weiser's activities as Indian interpreter.

WILLIAMSON, PETER: *The Travels of Peter Williamson Among the Different Nations and Tribes of Savage Indians in America with an Account of their Principles* . . . *with Every Thing Remarkable Concerning Their Manners, Customs* . . . (Edinburgh, 1768).

WRAXALL, PETER: *An Abridgement of the Indian Affairs* . . . *Transacted in the Colony of New York . . . [1678-1751], Harvard Historical Studies,* XXII (Charles Howard McIlwain, ed., Cambridge, Mass. & London, 1915).

C. SECONDARY WORKS

1. General

Note: From the extensive literature relating to the American Indians only those works are listed that have a direct relationship to British imperial affairs 1748-1776.

BAUMAN, ROBERT F.: "Claims vs. Realities: The Anglo-Iroquois Partnership," *Northwest Ohio Quarterly,* XXXII (1960), 87-101. Provides a background sketch of the Iroquois.

BROWN, DOUGLAS SUMMERS: *The Catawba Indians: The People of the River* (Columbia, S.C., 1966). A discussion of the Catawba-Iroquois hostility which was continued through most of the colonial period.

CORKRAN, DAVID H.: *The Cherokee Frontiers: Conflict and Survival, 1740-62* (Norman, Okla., 1962).

CORRY, JOHN PITTS: *Indian Affairs in Georgia, 1732-1756* (Philadelphia, 1936).

DEBO, ANGIE: *The Rise and Fall of the Choctaw Republic* (Norman, Okla., 1934). Of limited use, concerned primarily with the post-Civil War era.

DOWNES, RANDOLPH C.: *Council Fires on the Upper Ohio: A Narrative of Indian Affairs in the Upper Ohio Valley until 1795* ([Pittsburgh, Pa.], 1940).

ESHLEMAN, H. FRANK: *Lancaster County [Pa.] Indians: Annals of the Susquehannocks and Other Indian Tribes of the Susquehanna Territory . . . [to 1763]* (Lancaster, Pa., 1909).

HARRISON, WILLIAM HENRY: *A Discourse on the Aborigines of the Valley of the Ohio . . . ,* Historical and Philosophical Society of Ohio, *Transactions,* I (1838), 217-67. Reprinted in *Fergus Historical Series,* No. 26 (Chicago, 1883).

HULBERT, ARCHER BUTLER: *Red Men's Roads: The Indian Thoroughfares of the Central West* (Columbus, O., 1900).

JENNINGS, FRANCIS P.: "The Delaware Interregnum," *Pennsylvania Magazine of History and Biography,* LXXXIX (1965), 174-98. The article deals with the Delaware Indians during the period 1729-1752.

KINIETZ, W. VERNON: *The Indians of the Western Great Lakes, 1615-1760* (Ann Arbor, Mich., 1940; rep., 1965).

LYDEKKER, JOHN WOLFE: *The Faithful Mohawks* (Cambridge, Eng., 1938). A study of the Mohawks in the eighteenth century.

MATHEWS, ALFRED: "Indian Occupation of the Ohio," *Magazine of Western History*, I (1884-5), 41-9.

MAURAULT, JOSEPH PIERRE ANSELME: *Historie des Abenakis depuis 1605 jusqu' à nos jours* ([Sorel]), 1866; rep., New York [1967]).

MILLING, CHAPMAN JAMES: *Red Carolinians* (Chapel Hill, N.C., 1940). This relates to Indian tribes of the southeast areas of what is now the United States.

MORGAN, EDMUND S.: "The American Indian: Incorrigible Individualist," *Mirror of the Indian* . . . (Providence, R.I., 1958), pp. 5-19.

MORGAN, LEWIS HENRY: *League of the Ho-dé-no-sau-nee or Iroquois* (New York & Rochester, N.Y., 1851; n. edn., Herbert M. Lloyd, ed., 2 vols., New York, 1901).

RIGHTS, DOUGLAS L.: *The American Indian in North Carolina* (Durham, N.C., 1947; 2nd edn., Winston-Salem, N.C., 1957).

SCHOOLCRAFT, HENRY ROWE: *The American Indians: Their History, Condition and Prospects: From Original Notes and Manuscripts* . . . (n. edn., rev. by George H. Derby, Buffalo, N.Y., 1851). See also his *Information Respecting the History, Condition and Prospects of the Indian Tribes of the United States* . . . (6 vols., Philadelphia, 1853-7). These works are of great repute.

STANLEY, GEORGE F. S.: "The Six Nations and the American Revolution," *Ontario History*, LVI (1964), 217-32.

SWANTON, JOHN R.: *Early History of the Creek Indians and Their Neighbors*, Smithsonian Institution, Bureau of American Ethnology, *Bulletin*, No. 73 (Washington, D.C., 1962). See also: *Indian Tribes of the Lower Mississippi Valley and Adjacent Coast of the Gulf of Mexico*, ibid., No. 43 (Washington, D.C., 1911).

TUCKER, SARA JULIA, and WAYNE C. TEMPLE: *Indian Villages of the Illinois Country*, Illinois State Museum, *Scientific Papers*, II (2 vols., Springfield, Ill., 1942-58). The first volume, by Tucker, is an atlas.

UHLER, SHERMAN P.: *Pennsylvania's Indian Relations to 1754* (Allentown, Pa., 1951).

WALLACE, PAUL A. W.: *Indians in Pennsylvania* (Harrisburg, Pa., 1961).

WILCOX, FRANK N.: *Ohio Indian Trails* (Cleveland, O., 1933).

2. Government policy and the Indians

ALDEN, JOHN RICHARD: "The Albany Congress and the Creation of the Indian Superintendencies," *Mississippi Valley Historical Review*, XXVII (1940-1), 193-210.

BILLINGTON, RAY ALLEN: "The Fort Stanwix Treaty of 1768," *New York History*, XXV (1944), 182-94.

CARTER, CLARENCE E.: "British Policy towards the American Indians in the South [1763-8]," *English Historical Review,* XXXIII (1918), 37-56.

CORKRAN, DAVID H.: "The Unpleasantness at Stecoe," *North Carolina Historical Review,* XXXII (1955), 358-75.

DEVORSEY, LOUIS, JR.: *The Indian Boundary in the Southern Colonies, 1763-1775* (Chapel Hill, N.C., 1966), and his "The Virginia Cherokee Boundary of 1771," East Tennessee Historical Society, *Publications,* No. 33 (1961), 17-31.

EVERETT, EDWARD G.: "Pennsylvania's Indian Diplomacy, 1747-1753," *Western Pennsylvania Historical Magazine,* XLIV (1961), 241-56.

FARRAND, MAX: "The Indian Boundary Line," *American Historical Review,* X(1904-5), 782-91.

GOLD, ROBERT L.: "The East Florida Indians under Spanish and English Control, 1763-1765," *Florida Historical Quarterly,* XLIV (1965-6), 105-20.

JACOBS, WILBUR R.: *Diplomacy and Indian Gifts: Anglo-French Rivalry along the Ohio and Northwest Frontiers, 1748-1763* (London & Stanford, Calif., 1950), and *Wilderness Politics and Indian Gifts: The Northern Colonial Frontier, 1748-1763* (Lincoln, Neb., 1966). See also Jacobs's articles: "Presents to the Indians along the French Frontiers in the Old Northwest, 1748-1763," *Indiana Magazine of History,* XLIV (1948), 245-56; "Presents to Indians as a Factor in the Conspiracy of Pontiac [1760-63]," *Michigan History,* XXXIII (1949), 314-22; and "Edmond Atkin's Plan for Imperial Indian Control," *Journal of Southern History,* XIX (1953), 311-20.

JAMES, JAMES ALTON: "Indian Diplomacy and the Opening of the Revolution in the West," Wisconsin Historical Society, *Proceedings,* LVI (1909), 125-42.

MOHR, WALTER H.: *Federal Indian Relations, 1774-1788* (London & Philadelphia, 1933).

PARKER, ARTHUR: *The Constitution of the Five Nations,* New York State Museum, *Bulletin,* No. 184 (Albany, N.Y., 1916).

SAHLI, JOHN R.: "The Growth of British Influence Among the Seneca to 1768," *Western Pennsylvania Historical Magazine,* XLIX (1966), 127-39.

SCOTT, DUNCAN C.: "Indian Affairs, 1763-1841," *Canada and Its Provinces* . . . , IV: 695-725.

SHAW, HELEN L.: *British Administration of the Southern Indians, 1756-1783* . . . ([Lancaster, Pa., 1931]).

SIEBERT, WILBUR H.: "The Loyalists and the Six Nation Indians in the Niagara Peninsula," Royal Society of Canada, *Transactions,* 3rd ser., IX (1915), 79-128.

SOSIN, JACK M.: "The British Indian Department and Dunmore's War," *Virginia Magazine of History and Biography,* LXXIV (1966), 34-50.

3. Economic

ADAMS, JOHN ARTHUR: "The Indian Trader of the Upper Ohio Valley," *Western Pennsylvania Historical Magazine*, XVII (1934), 163-74. Deals with the years 1725-76.

FANT, H. B.: "The Indian Trade Policy of the Trustees for Establishing the Colony of Georgia in America," *Georgia Historical Quarterly*, XV (1931), 207-22.

FRANKLIN, W. NEIL: "Pennsylvania-Virginia Rivalry for the Indian Trade of the Ohio Valley," *Mississippi Valley Historical Review*, XX (1933-4), 463-80, and "Virginia and the Cherokee Indian Trade, 1673-1752," East Tennessee Historical Society, *Publications*, IV (1932), 3-21.

KING, JAMES C.: "Indian Credit as a Source of Friction in the Colonial Fur trade," *Western Pennsylvania Historical Magazine*, XLIX (1966), 57-66.

SOWTER, T. W. E.: "Indian Trade, Travel, and Transportation," Ontario Provincial Museum, *Annual Archeological Report* (1916), 26-39.

TURNER, FREDERICK JACKSON: *The Character and Influence of the Indian Trade in Wisconsin . . .*, Johns Hopkins University, *Studies in Historical and Political Science*, 9th ser. (Baltimore, Md., 1891).

4. Social

GOLD, ROBERT L.: "The Settlement of the Pensacola Indians in New Spain, 1763-1770," *Hispanic American Historical Review*, XLV (1965), 567-76.

GRAY, ELMA E., and LESLIE ROBB GRAY: *Wilderness Christians: The Moravian Mission to the Delaware Indians* (Ithaca, N.Y., 1956).

KELLAWAY, WILLIAM: *The New England Company, 1649-1776: Missionary Society to the American Indians* (London, 1961; New York, 1962).

KLINGBERG, FRANK J.: "The Efforts of S.P.G. to Christianize the Mosquito Indians, 1742-1785," *Historical Magazine of the Protestant Episcopal Church*, IX (1940), 305-21. The area of the Mosquito Coast or shore in Central America was held by the British during the period that concerns this series. Another article by Klingberg which provides useful background is "The Noble Savage as Seen by the Missionary of the Society for the Propagation of the Gospel in Colonial New York, 1702-1750," *ibid.*, VIII (1939), 128-65.

LAUBER, ALMON WHEELER: *Indian Slavery in Colonial Times Within the Present Limits of the United States*, Columbia University, *Studies in History, Economics, and Public Law*, No. 134 (New York, 1913).

ROBINSON, W. STITT, JR.: "Indian Education and Missions in Colonial Virginia," *Journal of Southern History*, XVIII (1952), 152-68. See also his "The Legal Status of the Indian in Colonial Virginia," *Virginia Magazine of History and Biography*, LXI (1953), 247-59.

5. Biographical

CROGHAN, GEORGE. See under Trans-Appalachian West.

GIST, CHRISTOPHER. "Christopher Gist and the Indian Service in Virginia, 1757-1759" by David B. Trimble, *Virginia Magazine of History and Biography*, LXIV (1956), 143-65.

JOHNSON, WILLIAM. *Johnson of the Mohawks: A Biography* . . . by Arthur Pound and Richard E. Day (New York, 1930); *Mohawk Baronet: Sir William Johnson of New York* by James Thomas Flexner (New York, 1959); and "Sir William Johnson and the Society for the Propagation of the Gospel, 1749-1774" by Frank J. Klingberg, *Historical Magazine of the Protestant Episcopal Church*, VIII (1939), 4-37. See Johnson also under New York.

MC GILLIVRAY, ALEXANDER. *McGillivray of the Creeks* by John Walton Caughey (Norman, Okla., 1938).

PONTIAC. *Pontiac and the Indian Uprising* by Howard H. Peckham (Princeton, N.J., 1947).

STUART, JOHN. *John Stuart and the Southern Colonial Frontier: A Study of Indian Relations, War, Trade, and Land Problems in the Southern Wilderness, 1754-1775* by John Richard Alden, University of Michigan, *Publications: History and Political Science*, XV (Ann Arbor, Mich. & London, 1944).

TEEDYUSCUNG. *King of the Delawares: Teedyuscung, 1700-1763* by Anthony F. C. Wallace (Philadelphia, 1949).

6. Military

GRANT, CHARLES S.: "Pontiac's Rebellion and the British Troop Moves of 1763," *Mississippi Valley Historical Review*, XL (1953-4), 75-88.

HAMER, P. M.: "Anglo-French Rivalry in the Cherokee Country, 1754-1757," *North Carolina Historical Review*, II (1925), 303-22.

HUNT, GEORGE T.: *The Wars of the Iroquois: A Study in Intertribal Trade Relations* (Madison, Wis. [1940]).

JACOBS, WILBUR R.: "Was the Pontiac Uprising a Conspiracy?" Ohio State Archaeological and Historical Society, *Quarterly*, LIX (1950), 26-37.

MAHON, JOHN K.: "Anglo-American Methods of Indian Warfare, 1676-1794," *Mississippi Valley Historical Review*, XLV (1958-9), 254-75.

MARGAIS, T. G.: "Pontiac's War," *Canada and Its Provinces* . . . , III: 53-70.

PARKMAN, FRANCIS: *History of the Conspiracy of Pontiac and the War of the North American Tribes against the English Colonies after the Conquest of Canada* (Boston, 1851). See in conjunction with this work Howard H. Peckham's "Sources and Revisions of Parkman's *Pontiac*," Bibliographical Society of America, *Papers*, XXXVII (1943), 293-307.

REEVE, J. C.: "Henry Bouquet: His Indian Campaigns," *Ohio Archeological and Historical Quarterly*, XXVI (1917), 489-506.

D. MAPS

BOARD OF TRADE: *Map of the British Colonies in the Year 1765*. This map lays down a tentative boundary between the British colonies and the Indian country. Starting with the Indian settlement at Owegé in northern Pennsylvania, it extended to the southern part of East Florida and continued along the western coast of East Florida and then north to the Gulf of Mexico to the Mississippi River. This large map in facsimile was reprinted for the *Pennsylvania Archives*, 3rd ser., Appendix I-X. Another Board of Trade map, with a long representation dated 7 March 1768, was designed to lay down a boundary between the western Indians and the more northern British settlements. It is printed in O'Callaghan: *Colonial Documents Relative to the History of the State of New-York*, VIII: opp. p. 30.

BROWN, LLOYD ARNOLD: *Early Maps of the Ohio Valley: A Selection of Maps, Plans, and Views Made by Indians and Colonials from 1673 to 1783* (Pittsburgh, Pa., 1959). Depends heavily on the map collection in Darlington Memorial Library, University of Pittsburgh.

CORKRAN, DAVID H.: *The Cherokee Country, 1740-62*. In Corkran's *The Cherokee Frontier: Conflict and Survival, 1740-1762* (Norman, Okla. [1962]), p. 7; and *The Southern Indian Country, 1740-1762, Showing the Approximate Location of Various Important Tribes*. In *ibid.*, p. 57.

HUTCHINS, THOMAS: *A Map of the Country on the Ohio & Muskingum Rivers Shewing the Situation of the Indian Towns with Respect to the Army under the Command of Colonel Bouquet*. In William Smith: *An Historical Account of the Expedition against the Ohio Indians in the Year 1764*, frontispiece.

JOHNSON, GUY: *Map of the Frontiers of the Northern Colonies with the Boundary Line Established between Them and the Indians at a Treaty Held by S[ir] Will. Johnson at Fort Stanwix in Nov. 1768. Corrected and Improved from Evans's Map*. In O'Callaghan: *Documentary History of the State of New York*, I: opp. p. 376.

LODGE, JOHN, sculp.: *A Map of the American Indian Nations Adjoining to the Mississippi, West & East Florida, Georgia, S. & N. Carolina,*

Virginia, &c. In James Adair: *The History of the American Indians,* p. 286.

Part of the Pursell Map [with the location of various southern Indian tribes] Prepared not Later Than 1770 in the Interest of British Indian Trade by John Stuart, H. M. Sup't. of Indian Affairs. This map is to be found as a plate in the Smithsonian Institute: Bureau of Ethnology, *Bulletin,* No. 73 (Washington, D.C.).

TIMBERLAKE, HENRY: *A Draught of the Cherokee Country on the West Side of Twenty Four Mountains. . . .* In Jefferys: *A General Topography of North America and the West Indies,* No. 64.

CHAPTER VI

The West Indies and
Other Atlantic Possessions

*BRITISH WEST INDIES, THE BAHAMAS,
THE BERMUDAS, BRITISH HONDURAS,
AND THE FALKLAND ISLANDS*

A. BIBLIOGRAPHICAL AIDS

BAKER, E. C.: *A Guide to Records in the Leeward Islands* (Oxford, Eng., 1965).

BELL, HERBERT C., *et al.*: *Guide to the British West Indian Archive Materials in London and in the Islands* . . . Carnegie Institution of Washington, *Publications*, No. 372 (Washington, D.C., 1926). See also the supplementary material by Richard Pares: "Public Records in the British West Indian Islands," Institute of Historical Research, *Bulletin*, VII (1930), 149-57.

CHANDLER, MICHAEL JOHN: *A Guide to Records in Barbados* (Oxford, Eng., 1965).

COLE, GEORGE WATSON: *Bermuda in Periodical Literature With Occasional References to Other Works: A Bibliography* ([Brookline, Mass.], 1907).

CUNDALL, FRANK: *Bibliography of the West Indies (Excluding Jamaica)* (Kingston, 1909).

———: *Bibliotheca Jamaicensis: Some Account of the Principal Works in Jamaica in the Library of the Institute [of Jamaica]* . . . (Kingston, 1895; rep., 1902; supplement, 1908).

———: "List of Works in the New York Public Library Relating to the West Indies," New York Public Library, *Bulletin*, XVI (1912), *passim.*

GOVEIA, ELSA V.: *A Study on the Historiography of the British West Indies to the End of the Nineteenth Century*, Instituto Panamericano de Geografia e Historia, *Publicaciones*, No. 186 (Mexico, 1956).

MALCOLM, HARCOURT G.: *Historical Documents Relating to the Bahama Islands* . . . (Nassau, 1910).

———: *List of Documents Relating to the Bahama Islands in the British Museum and the [Public] Record Office, London* (Nassau, 1910).

RAGATZ, LOWELL JOSEPH: *A Guide for the Study of British Caribbean History, 1763-1834: Including the Abolition and Emancipation Movements*, American Historical Association, *Annual Report, 1930* (4 vols., Washington, 1932), III.

———: *A Guide to the Official Correspondence of the Governors of the British West India Colonies with the Secretary of State, 1763-1833* (London, 1927).

———: *A Check-List of House of Commons Sessional Papers Relating to the British West Indies and to the West India Slave Trade and Slavery, 1763-1834* (London, 1927), and the supplementary work, *A Check-List of House of Lords Sessional Papers Relating to the British West Indies and to the West Indian Slave Trade and Slavery, 1763-1834* (London, 1931).

———: *The West Indian Approach to the Study of American Colonial History* . . . (London, 1935).

WILLIAMS, ERIC E.: *British Historians and the West Indies* (New York, 1967).

B. PRINTED SOURCE MATERIALS

1. *Government and related documents*

The Bahamas

Acts of Assembly of the Bahama Islands [1729-1813] (3 vols., Nassau, 1806-14).

House of Assembly Journal . . . *[1728-1786]* (5 vols., Nassau, 1910-12).

MALCOLM, HARCOURT G., ed.: *Historical Documents Relating to the Bahama Islands* (Nassau, 1910).

Votes of the Honourable House of Assembly of the Bahama Islands (4 vols., Nassau, 1910-11).

The Bermudas

Ancient Journals of the House of Assembly of Bermuda from 1691 to 1785 (4 vols., London, 1906).

GRAY, REGINALD, ed.: *Acts of the Legislature of the Islands of Bermuda, 1690 to 1883* . . . (2 vols., London, 1884).

HUXLEY, DAVID BRUCE, ed.: *Public Acts of the Legislature of the Islands of Bermuda, 1620-1952: Together with Statutory Instruments in Force thereunder* (5 vols. [Hamilton], 1953).

British Honduras

BURDON, JOHN ALDER, ed.: *Archives of British Honduras: Being Extracts and Précis from Records* . . . (3 vols., London, 1931-5), Vol. I.

The British West Indies

Antigua. Laws of the Island of Antigua: Consisting of the Acts of the Leeward Islands . . . [1690-1798] *and the Acts of Antigua* [1688-1845] (4 vols., London, 1805-46).

Barbados. RICHARD HALL, comp.: *Acts Passed in the Island of Barbados: From 1643-1762* . . . (London, 1764); *Laws of Barbados* [1646-1863] (2 vols., London, 1855-64); Samuel Moore, ed.: *The Public Acts in Force: Passed by the Legislature of Barbados* . . . [1762-1800] (London, 1801). An abridgement of the acts.

Dominica. Laws of the Colony of Dominica . . . *[to] 1818* (Roseau, 1818); *Laws of the Island of Dominica from 1763 to 1841* . . . (2 vols., Dominica, 1858-60); *Regulations for Opening the Island of Dominica as a Free Port Approved by the Merchants of the West Indian and North American Committees* . . . ([London, 1766]).

Grenada. The Laws of Grenada and the Grenadines from the Year 1766 to the Year 1852 (Grenada, 1852), and *The Laws of Grenada from the Year 1763 to the Year 1805* . . . (George Smith, ed., London, 1808).

Jamaica. Acts of Assembly Passed in the Island of Jamaica, from 1681 to 1754 Inclusive (2 pts., London, 1756); *Acts of Assembly Passed in the Island of Jamaica from 1770 to 1783 Inclusive* (Kingston, 1784); *Acts of Assembly Passed in the Island of J. from the Year 1681 to the Year 1769 Inclusive* (2 vols., Kingston, 1787); *The Journals of the Assembly of Jamaica* . . . *1663-[1826]* (15 vols., Jamaica, 1811-29); *The Laws of Jamaica: Comprehending All the Acts in Force Passed between* . . . *[1681-1792]* (3 vols., St. Jago de la Vega, 1792-3). Volume III is an abridgement of the first two volumes.

Montserrat. Montserrat Code of Laws from 1668 to 1788 (London, 1790).

Nevis. HUGGINS, H. C., ed.: *Laws of Nevis from 1681 to 1861 Inclusive* . . . (London, 1862).

St. Christopher. Acts of Assembly Passed in the Island of St. Christopher from the Year 1711-1769 (2 pts., St. Christopher, 1769). *Laws of the Island of St. Christopher* . . . *[1711-1791]* (St. Christopher, 1791).

St. Vincent. Laws of . . . St. Vincent and Its Dependencies from the First Establishment of a Legislature to . . . 1809 (Bridgworth, 1811); Charles Shepard: *The Colonial Practice of Saint Vincent: Containing an Abstract of the Court Acts, and the Rules of the Several Courts in the Island . . .* (London, 1822).

Tobago. Acts of the Legislature of the Island of Tobago from 1768 to 1775 Inclusive (London, 1776).

2. Non-official contemporary writings

Authentic Papers Relative to the Expedition against the Charibbs and the Sale of Lands in the Island of St. Vincent (London, 1773).

BECKFORD, WILLIAM: *A Descriptive Account of the Island of Jamaica: With Remarks upon the Cultivation of Sugar-Cane . . . also Observations and Reflections . . . [on Slavery and the Slave-Trade]* (2 vols., London, 1790). See also Beckford's *Remarks upon the Situation of Negroes in Jamaica Impartially Made from a Local Experience of Nearly Thirteen Years in That Island* (London, 1788).

[BUTEL-DUMONT, GEORGE MARIE]: *Histoire et Commerce des Antilles Angloises où l'on Trouve l'État Actuel de Leur Population & Quelques Détails sur le Commerce de Contrebande des Anglois avec des Espagnols dans le Nouveau Monde . . .* ([Paris], 1758).

EDWARDS, BRYAN: *The History, Civil and Commercial, of the British Colonies in the West Indies* (3 vols., London, 1793-1801; 5th edn., 6 vols., 1818-19).

ELLETSON, ROGER HOPE: "Roger Hope Elletson's Letter Book," H. P. Jacobs, ed., *Jamaican Historical Review*, II (1949-53), *passim*. This does contain some official correspondence.

FOWLER, JOHN: *A Summary Account of the Present Flourishing State of the Respectable Colony of Tobago . . .* (London, 1774).

[FRERE, GEORGE]: *A Short History of Barbados from Its First Discovery and Settlement to the End of the Year 1767* (London, 1768). A reply to this work was written by Sir John Gay Alleyne and published anonymously: *Remarks on a Book Entitled "A Short History of Barbados" . . .* (London, 1768; Barbados, 1770).

GARDINER, RICHARD: *An Account of the Expedition to the West Indies against Martinico, Guadeloupe, and Other [of] the Leeward Islands Subject to the French King, 1759* (London, 1759; 3rd edn., Birmingham, Eng., 1762).

GUTIERREZ DE RUBALCAVA, DON JOSEPH: *Tratado historico, politico y legal de el comercio de las Indias Occidentales . . .* (Cadiz [1750]).

HUGHES, GRIFFITH: *The Natural History of Barbados . . .* (London, 1750).

KLINGBERG, FRANK J., ed.: *Codrington Chronicle: An Experiment in Anglican Altruism on a Barbados Plantation, 1710-1834*, University of

California, *Publications in History*, XXXVII (Berkeley, Calif. & Los Angeles, 1949).

[LESLIE, CHARLES]: *A New and Exact Account of Jamaica: Wherein the Antient and Present State of That Colony, Its Importance to Great Britain . . . Are Described . . .* (Edinburgh, 1739; 3rd edn., w/add., 1740).

[LONG, EDWARD]: *The History of Jamaica or General Survey of the Antient and Modern State of That Island . . .* (3 vols., London, 1774).

MC KINNEN, DANIEL: *A Tour through the British West Indies in the Years 1802 and 1803 Giving a Particular Account of the Bahama Islands* (London, 1804).

A Narrative of the Proceedings upon Complaint Against Governor Melville (London, 1770).

Papers Relative to Codrington College, Barbados, 1709-1826 (London, 1828).

RAGATZ, LOWELL JOSEPH, ed.: *Statistics for the Study of British Caribbean Economic History, 1763-1833* (London [1928]).

RAMSAY, JAMES: *An Essay on the Treatment and Conversion of African Slaves in the British Sugar Colonies* (London, 1784).

[RAYNAL, GUILLAUME THOMAS FRANÇOIS]: *Histoire philosophique et politique des Établissemens et du Commerce des Européens dans les deux Indes* (6 vols., Amsterdam, 1770; 1st Eng. edn., J. Justamond, trans., 4 vols., London, 1776).

TUCKER, ST. GEORGE: "Randolph and Tucker Letters," (Mrs.) George P. Coleman, ed., *Virginia Magazine of History and Biography*, XLII (1934), 211-21. Included is the draft of a letter intended for Richard Rush, written on October 27, 1813, in which Tucker gives a brief biographic sketch of himself. These letters relate to the Bermudas.

TULLIDEPH, WALTER: "Letters from a Sugar Plantation in Antigua, 1739-1758," Richard B. Sheridan, ed., *Agricultural History*, XXXI (1957), 3-23.

YOUNG, WILLIAM, comp.: *The West India Commonplace Book: Compiled from Parliamentary and Official Documents Shewing the Interest of Great Britain in Its Sugar Colonies &c. &c.* (London, 1807).

3. Contemporary pamphlets, tracts, and related materials: Chronologically arranged

The Importance of Jamaica to Great-Britain Consider'd: With Some Account of That Island from Its Discovery to This Time . . . (London [1744]).

The Alarm Bell: Or Considerations on the Present Dangerous State of the Sugar Colonies . . . (London, 1749).

[MARTIN, SAMUEL]: *An Essay upon Plantership* . . . (2nd edn., Antigua, 1750; 4th edn., Antigua & London, 1765; 7th edn., Antigua, 1785). The first editions were published under the pseudonym Agricola Ante-Gonianus.

MASSIE, JOSEPH: *A State of the British Sugar-Colony Trade* . . . (London, 1759). Massie discussed in this pamphlet the decline of trade, French competition, and planter profits.

[CAMPBELL, JOHN]: *Candid and Impartial Considerations on the Nature of the Sugar Trade, the Comparative Importance of the British and French Islands in the West Indies: With the Value and Consequences of St. Lucia and Grenada Truly Stated* (London, 1763). This work provided a brief history of the sugar trade and urged development of the newly acquired islands.

[YOUNG, ARTHUR and WILLIAM]: *Considerations Which May Tend to Promote the Settlement of the New West-India Colonies by Encouraging Individuals to Embark in the Undertaking* . . . (London, 1764; 2nd edn., same year, w/rev. title).

[DICKINSON, JOHN]: *An Address to the Committee of Correspondence in Barbados: Occasioned by a Late Letter from Them to Their Agent in London. By a North American* (Philadelphia, 1766; printed in *Writings of John Dickinson*, Pennsylvania Historical Society, *Memoirs*, XIV [Philadelphia, 1894], pp. 247-76). This pamphlet provoked the following replies: the pamphlet by Kenneth Morrison, published anonymously, *An Essay Towards the Vindication of the Committee of Correspondence in Barbados from the Aspersions and Calumnies Thrown upon Them in an Anonymous Piece* . . . (Barbados, 1766); *Candid Observations on Two Pamphlets Lately Published, Viz. "An Address to the Committee of Correspondence in Barbados . . ." and "An Essay Towards the Vindication of the Committee of Correspondence . . .": By a Native of Barbados* . . . (Barbados, 1766); and *A Letter to the North American on Occasion of His Address to the Committee of Correspondence in Barbados: By a Native of the Island* (Barbados, 1766).

The Privileges of the Island of Jamaica Vindicated: With an Impartial Narrative of the Late Dispute between the Governor and House of Representatives upon the Case of Mr. Olyphant, a Member of That House (London, 1766).

A Letter to the Right Honourable the Earl of H[ills]b[orough]h, Secretary of State for the Colonies, on the Present Situation of Affairs in the Island of Grenada (London, 1769). See also *"Audi Alteram Partem": Or a Counter-Letter to the Right Hon. the Earl of H[i]ll-[sborou]gh on the Late and Present State of Affairs in the Island of G[re]n[ad]a* (London, 1770).

A Plan for the Abolition of Slavery in the West Indies (London, 1772).

Considerations on the Imposition of 4½ per cent Collected on Grenada

*and the Southern Charibbee Islands by Virtue of His Majesty's
Letters Patent under Pretence of the Prerogative Royal without
Grant of Parliament* (London, 1774; rep., 1900).

GLOVER, RICHARD: *The Evidence Delivered on the Petition Presented by
the West-India Planters and Merchants to the Hon. House of
Commons as It was Introduced at the Bar and Summ'd up by Mr.
Glover on Thursday the 16th of March 1775* ([London, 1775]).
This pamphlet, which went through several editions and title
variations, was concerned with the question of the commercial
relations of the West Indies with the Thirteen Colonies.

4. Newspapers

As Professor Ragatz has pointed out in his *A Guide for the Study of
British Caribbean History, 1763-1834* (pp. 391 and 401), there are in
existence no complete files for any of the West Indies newspapers,
and indeed, files for most of the papers are no where near complete.
Single copies are occasionally found in the correspondence of the
governors with the Secretaries of State in the Public Record Office as
well as in various libraries in Great Britain and in the United States.
The American Antiquarian Society has formed the best collection of these
papers, while the most comprehensive collections are in the Institute of
Jamaica at Kingston and in the Public Library in Port-au-Spain, Trinidad.
Some of the available publications are quite useful in providing price
quotations on American and European goods as well as reporting events
in the various islands.

Affiches Américaines, 1774-1775, Port au Prince, Dominica.
Antigua Gazette, b. [1753], St. Johns, Antigua.
The Antigua Mercury or St. Johns Weekly Advertiser, b. [1767], St. Johns,
   Antigua.
The Barbadoes Gazette, Bridgetown, Barbados.
*The Barbadoes Mercury [The Barbados Mercury and Bridgetown Ga-
   zette]*, b. 1762. Bridgetown, Barbados.
The Charibbean Register or Ancient and Original Dominica Gazette, b.
   [1770], Roseau, Dominica.
The Charibbean and General Gazette: Or the St. Christopher Chronicle,
   b. 1769, Basseterre, St. Christopher.
*The Cornwall Chronicle or County Gazette [The Cornwall Chronicle
   and General Advertiser]*, b. 1773, Montego Bay, Jamaica.
The Freeport Gazette: Or the Dominica Advertiser, b. 1765, Roseau,
   Dominica.
The Free-Port Gazette: Or the Dominica Chronicle, b. 1770, Roseau,
   Dominica.
Gazette de S. Dominique [Avis Divers et Petites Affiches Américaines]

(the same title but not the same paper which was published in 1774 at Port au Prince), b. 1764, Cap Français, Dominica.

The Jamaica Gazette, b. [1775], Kingston, Jamaica.

The Kingston Journal, b. 1756, Kingston, Jamaica.

The Kingston Journal and Jamaica Universal Museum, b. 1776, Kingston, Jamaica.

The Royal Danish American Gazette, b. [1770], Christiansted, St. Croix.

The Royal Grenada Gazette, b. 1765, St. George's, Grenada.

The St. Christopher Gazette, Basseterre, St. Christopher.

The St. Jago de la Vega Gazette, b. 1755, St. Jago de la Vega, Jamaica.

The St. Jago Intelligencer, 1756-[1768], St. Jago de la Vega, Jamaica.

C. SECONDARY WORKS

1. General

The Bahamas

CRATON, MICHAEL: *A History of the Bahamas* (London, 1962).

The Bermudas

GODET, THEODORE L.: *Bermuda: Its History, Geology, Climate, Products, Agriculture, Commerce and Government . . .* (London, 1860).

HAYWARD, WALTER BROWNELL: *Bermuda Past and Present: A Descriptive and Historical Account of the Somers Islands* (London [1923]).

KERR, WILFRED B.: *Bermuda and the American Revolution, 1760-1783* (Princeton, N.J., 1936).

OGILVY, JOHN: *An Account of Bermuda: Past and Present* (Hamilton, Bermuda, 1883).

WILKINSON, HENRY C.: *Bermuda in the Old Empire: A History of the Island . . . 1684-1784* (London & New York, 1950).

WILLIAMS, WILLIAM FRITH: *An Historical and Statistical Account of the Bermudas from Their Discovery to the Present Time* (London, 1848).

The British West Indies and British Honduras

ATWOOD, THOMAS: *The History of the Island of Dominica: Containing a Description of Its Situation . . .* (London, 1791).

BREEN, HENRY: *St. Lucia: Historical, Statistical, and Descriptive* (London, 1844).

BRIDGES, GEORGE WILSON: *The Annals of Jamaica* (1st edn., 2 vols., London, 1827; 2nd edn., 1828).

BURN, W. L.: *The British West Indies* (London, 1951).

BURNS, ALAN CUTHBERT: *History of the British West Indies* (London, 1954; 2nd edn., rev., New York, 1965).

COKE, THOMAS: *A History of the West Indies* . . . (3 vols., Liverpool, Eng., & London, 1808-11).

CAIGER, STEPHEN LANGRISH: *British Honduras, Past and Present* (London, 1951), pp. 11-100.

GARDNER, WILLIAM JAMES: *A History of Jamaica from Its Discovery* . . . (London, 1873; n. edn., 1909).

MAKINSON, DAVID H.: *Barbados: A Study of North-American-West-Indian Relations, 1739-1789* (The Hague, 1964).

OLIVER, VERE LANGFORD: *The History of the Island of Antigua . . . from the First Settlement in 1635* . . . (3 vols., London, 1894-9).

PARES, RICHARD: *War and Trade in the West Indies, 1739-1763* (Oxford, Eng., 1936).

PARRY, J. H., and P. M. SHERLOCK: *A Short History of the West Indies* (London & New York, 1956). A general volume with only a limited amount of immediately germane material.

PITMAN, FRANK WESLEY: *The Development of the British West Indies, 1700-1763, Yale Historical Publications: Studies,* IV (London & New Haven, Conn., 1917).

POYER, JOHN: *The History of Barbados . . . [1605-1801]* (London, 1808).

SCHOMBURGK, ROBERT HERMANN: *The History of Barbados: Comprising a Geographical and Statistical Description of the Island* . . . (London, 1848).

SHEPHARD, CHARLES: *An Historical Account of Saint Vincent* (London, 1831).

SOUTHEY, THOMAS: *Chronological History of the West Indies* (3 vols., London, 1827).

WOODCOCK, HENRY ILES: *The History of Tobago* (Ayr, Scotland, 1867).

2. Political

HIGHAM, C. S. S.: "The General Assembly of the Leeward Islands, Part II," *English Historical Review,* XLI (1926), 366-88; deals with the 1760's and 70's.

HUMPHREYS, ROBERT ARTHUR: *The Diplomatic History of British Honduras, 1683-1901* (London, 1961); pp. 1-9 are relevant.

[MALCOLM, HARCOURT]: *A History of the Bahama House of Assembly: Written and Presented to the House by Mr. Speaker* (Nassau, 1921).

PARRY, J. H.: "The Patent Offices in the British West Indies," *English Historical Review,* LXIX (1954), 200-25. Relating to the appointment of senior colonial officials for West Indian service.

PENSON, LILLIAN MARGERY: *Colonial Agents of the British West Indies:*

A Study in Colonial Administration Mainly in the Eighteenth Century (London, 1924).

SPURDLE, F. G.: Early West Indian Government: Showing the Progress of Government in Barbados, Jamaica, and the Leeward Islands, 1660-1783 (New York, 1963).

VERRILL, A. E.: "Relation between Bermuda and the American Colonies during the Revolutionary War," Connecticut Academy of Arts and Sciences, Transactions, XIII (1907), 47-64.

3. Economic

ARMYTAGE, FRANCES: The Free Port System in the British West Indies: A Study in Commercial Policy, 1766-1822 (London, 1953).

BARRETT, WARD: "Caribbean Sugar-Production Standards in the Seventeenth and Eighteenth Centuries," Merchants and Scholars: Essays in the History of Exploration and Trade (John Parker, ed., Minneapolis, Minn., 1965), pp. 145-71.

BELL, HERBRT C.: "West India Trade before the American Revolution," American Historical Review, XXII (1916-17), 272-87.

DAVIES, K. G.: "The Origins of the Commission System in the West India Trade," Royal Historical Society, Transactions, 5th ser., II (1952), 89-107.

DEERR, NOËL: The History of Sugar (2 vols., London, 1949-50). Relevant material is scattered topically throughout the work.

GORDON, WILLIAM E.: "Imperial Policy Decisions in the Economic History of Jamaica, 1664-1934," Social and Economic Studies, VI (1957), 1-28.

GOULD, CLARENCE P.: "Trade between the Windward Isles and the Continental Colonies of the French Empire, 1683-1763," Mississippi Valley Historical Review, XXV (1938-9), 473-90.

"Historical Account of the Land Tenure Systems in the Caribbean," Caribbean Economic Review, I (1949), 133-52.

PARES, RICHARD: A West-India Fortune (London, 1950), a history of the Pinney family of Nevis, and Merchants and Planters, Economic History Review: Supplements, No. 4 (New York, 1960), an analysis of the merchants as agents of the planters, showing the merchant power to take the initiative on deciding what crops were to be grown. See in addition Pares's article, "A London West-India Merchant House, 1740-1769," Essays Presented to Sir Lewis Namier (Richard Pares and A. J. P. Taylor, eds., London & New York, 1956), pp. 75-107.

PENSON, LILLIAN M.: "The London West India Interest in the Eighteenth Century," English Historical Review, XXXVI (1921), 373-92. Relating to the West India planters living in London.

PHILLIPS, ULRICH B.: "A Jamaica Slave Plantation," American Historical Review, XIX (1913-14), 543-58.

RAGATZ, LOWELL JOSEPH: *The Old Plantation System in the British Caribbean* (London [1926]); and his article "Absentee Landlordism in the British Caribbean, 1750-1833," *Agricultural History,* V (1931), 7-24.

SHERIDAN, RICHARD B.: "The Molasses Act and the Market Strategy of the British Sugar Planters," *Journal of Economic History,* XVII (1957), 62-83.

————: "The Wealth of Jamaica in the Eighteenth Century," *Economic History Review,* 2nd ser., XVIII (1965), 292-311.

STARKEY, OTIS PAUL: *The Economic Geography of Barbados: A Study of the Relationships between Environmental Variations and Economic Development* (New York, 1939).

WHITSON, AGNES M.: "The Outlook of the Continental American Colonies on the British West Indies, 1760-1775," *Political Science Quarterly,* XLV (1930), 56-86.

4. Social

BENNETT, J. HARRY: *Bondsmen and Bishops: Slavery and Apprenticeship on the Codrington Plantations of Barbados, 1710-1838,* University of California, *Publications in History,* LXII (Berkeley, Calif. & Los Angeles, 1958).

BUCHNER, J. H.: *The Moravians in Jamaica: History of the United Brethren's Church to the Negroes . . . 1754-1854* (London, 1854).

DALLAS, ROBERT CHARLES: *History of the Maroons from Their Origin to the Establishment of Their Chief Tribe at Sierre Leone . . .* (2 vols., London, 1803). This deals with the free Negroes of Jamaica, called Maroons.

GOVEIA, ELSA V.: *Slave Society in the British Leeward Islands at the End of the Eighteenth Century* (New Haven, Conn., 1965).

HARCOURT-SMITH, SIMON: "The Maroons of Jamaica," *History Today,* XVI (1966), 21-8. A very brief survey of the Maroons over four centuries.

PITMAN, FRANK WESLEY: "Slavery on West India Plantations in the Eighteenth Century," *Journal of Negro History,* XI (1926), 584-668.

RAGATZ, LOWELL JOSEPH: *The Fall of the Planter Class in the British Caribbean, 1763-1833: A Study in Social and Economic History* (London & New York, 1928). The first part of this work, dealing with the old plantation system, is germane to the period.

SHERIDAN, RICHARD B.: "The Rise of a Colonial Gentry: A Case Study of Antigua, 1730-1775," *Economic History Review,* 2nd ser., XIII (1960-1), 342-57.

SMITH, ROBERT WORTHINGTON: "The Legal Status of Jamaican Slaves before the Anti-Slavery Movement," *Journal of Negro History,* XXX (1945), 293-303.

5. Biographical

MARTIN, SAMUEL. "Samuel Martin: Innovating Sugar Planter of Antigua, 1750-1776" by Richard B. Sheridan, *Agricultural History*, XXXIV (1960), 126-39.

6. Military and naval

HART, FRANCIS RUSSELL: *The Siege of Havana, 1762* (Boston & New York, 1931).

PARES, RICHARD: *War and Trade in the West Indies, 1739-1763* (Oxford, 1936); this was followed by his *Colonial Blockade and Neutral Rights, 1739-1763* (Oxford, 1938), which is also primarily concerned with hostilities in the West Indies.

POCOCK, TOM: "The Capture of Havana, 1762," *History Today*, XII (1962), 580-6.

SMELSER, MARSHALL: "Insular Campaign of 1759: Guadeloupe," *American Neptune*, VII (1947), 21-34, and "The Insular Campaign of 1759: Martinique," *ibid.*, VI (1946), 290-300.

D. MAPS

There are several collections of maps depicting the Bahamas, Bermudas, and West Indies islands, including *The English Pilot, the Fourth Book: Describing the West-India Navigation from Hudson's Bay to the River Amazones* . . . (London, 1758; another edn., 1770; Dublin edn., 1767). This work was used for many years and went thru numerous editions and alterations. Two works by Thomas Jefferys that should be consulted are *A General Topography of North America and the West Indies* . . . (London, 1768), which contains 109 maps, and *The West India Atlas or a Compendius Description of the West Indies* . . . (London, 1775) which contains forty maps. For additional information on the availability of maps see Lowell Joseph Ragatz: *A List of West Indian Maps and Plans and Illustrations Relative to the West Indies Contained in the Gentleman's Magazine, 1731-1833* (London [1934]).

The Bahamas

Carte des Isles Lucayes. In Bellin: *Le Petit Atlas Maritime.* . . . I: No. 49.

JEFFERYS, THOMAS: *The Coast of West Florida and Louisiana [&] The Peninsula and Gulf of Florida or Channel of Bahama with the Bahama Islands* (London, 1775). In Faden: *The North American Atlas* . . . , No. 34, and in Jefferys: *The American Atlas* . . . , No. 25.

A Map of the Isle of Cuba with the Bahama Islands, Gulf of Florida, and the Windward Passage. In Jefferys: *A General Topography of North America and the West Indies* . . . , No. 79.

THORNTON, SAMUEL: *A New Chart of the Bahama Islands and the Windward Passage.* In *The English Pilot* . . . (Dublin, 1767), p. 49.

The Bermudas

BOWEN, EMANUEL: *A New & Accurate Map of Bermudas or Sommer's Islands.* In Bowen: *A Complete Atlas* . . . , No. 64.

Carte des Îsles Bermudes ou de Sommer. In Bellin: *Le Petit Atlas Maritime* . . . , I: No. 48.

JEFFERYS, THOMAS: *The Bermudas or Sumer's Islands from a Survey by C. Lempriere.* In Jefferys: *A West India Atlas* . . . , Plate F.

MOLL, HERMAN: *The Island of Bermudas, Divided into Tribes, with the Castles, Forts, Etc.* In Moll: *Atlas Minor* (London [1732]).

British Honduras

BONNE, M.: *Partie Méridionale de l'Ancien Méxique* . . . . In *Atlas de Toutes Parties Connues du Globe Terreste* (Geneva, 1780), No. 27.

JEFFERYS, THOMAS: *The Bay of Honduras [and the adjacent country].* In Jefferys: *The American Atlas* . . . , No. 27.

————: *Ruatan or Rattan, Surveyed by Lieutenant Henry Barnsley.* . . . In Jefferys: *A West India Atlas* . . . , Plate II.

The West Indies: General

BELL, A., engr.: *An Accurate Map of the West Indies.* In the *Scots Magazine*, II (1762), 557.

BELLIN, JACQUES NICOLAS: *Déscription Géographique des Isles Antilles Possedées par les Anglois* . . . ([Paris], 1758). This book contains 15 maps and 7 views.

BOWEN, EMANUEL: *An Accurate Map of the West Indies Drawn from the Best Authorities, Assisted by the Most Approved Modern Maps and Charts and Regulated by Astronomical Observations.* In Bowen: *A Complete or Distinct View of the Known World*, No. 55.

DUNN, SAMUEL: *A Compleat Map of the West Indies, Containing the Coasts of Florida, Louisiana, New Spain, and Terra Firma, With All the Islands* (London, 1774). In *The American Military Pocket Atlas*, No. 2.

GIBSON, JOHN, sculp.: *An Accurate Map of the West Indies with the Adjacent Coast.* In the *Gentleman's Magazine*, XXXII (1762), 50.

JEFFREYS, THOMAS: *A Map of the Caribbee Islands, Shewing Which Belong to England, France, Spain, Dutch & Danes: Collected from the Best Authorities.* In the *Gentleman's Magazine*, XXVI (1756),

368; on a much larger scale see Jeffreys: *A General Topography of North America and the West Indies* . . . , Nos. 70-1.

KITCHIN, THOMAS: *An Accurate Map of the Caribby Islands, with the Crowns, Etc. to Which They Severally Belong.* In the *London Magazine*, XXVIII (1759), 120.

———: *A New and Correct Map of American Islands now Called the West Indies, with the Whole Coast of the Neighboring Continent.* In *ibid.*, XXXI (1762), opp. p. 464.

Les Petites Antilles ou Les Isles du Vent. In Bellin: *Le Petit Atlas Maritime* . . . , I: No. 79. This map depicts the entire West Indies area. Plate 80, *Partie des Isles Antilles, I. Partie*, depicts St. Lucia, St. Vincent, and Grenada, and Plate 81, *Suite des Isles Antilles, II. Partie*, depicts Guadaloupe, Dominica, and Martinque.

A New and Correct Chart of the Trading Part of the West Indies. In *The English Pilot* . . . (London, 1758), p. 58.

ROCHETTE, L. S. DE LA: *A General Chart of the West Indian Islands with the Adjacent Coasts of the Spanish Continent* . . . [1796]. In Jefferys: *The American Atlas* . . . , No. 26*. It must be noted that William Faden, who took over Jeffery's map-making business upon the death of the latter in 1771, inserted this map in 1796 or thereafter, but continued to publish the *Atlas* as of 1776 before the Thirteen Colonies declared their independence.

SEALE, ROBERT W., sculp.: *A New and Accurate Map of the West Indies and the Adjacent Parts of North and South America.* In the *Universal Magazine*, XVII (1775), 241.

SPEER, JOSEPH SMITH: *Chart of the West Indies* ([London], 1774). Thomas Bowen was the sculptor of this map. It is in *American Maps*, II: No. 33, Library of Congress Map Collection.

Antigua

Carte de l'Isle d'Antigue. . . . In Bellin: *Le Petit Atlas Maritime* . . . , I: No. 85.

BOWEN, EMANUEL: *A New and Accurate Map of the Island of Antigua.* In Bowen: *A Complete Atlas*, No. 67.

JEFFERYS, THOMAS: *Antigua: Surveyed by Robert Baker.* . . . In Jefferys: *West India Atlas* . . . , Plate V. *English Harbour* is an inset on this plate.

A Map of the Island of Antigua. In Jefferys: *A General Topography of North America and the West Indies* . . . , No. 93.

Barbados

BOWEN, EMANUEL: *An Accurate Map of the Island of Barbados.* In Bowen: *A Complete Atlas* . . . , No. 69.

JEFFERYS, THOMAS: *Barbadoes Surveyed by William Mayo.* In Jefferys: *The West India Atlas . . .* , Plate X. This map also appeared in Whittle and Laurie's *The West India Atlas . . .* , No. 26.

MOLL, HERMAN: *A New Map of the Island of Barbadoes.* In [John Old-mixon]: *The British Empire in America . . .* (2nd edn., 2 vols., London, 1741), II, frontispiece.

A Plan of Bridgetown in the Island of Barbadoes. In the *Gentleman's Magazine*, XXXVI (1766), 425.

Dominica

BOWEN, THOMAS: *A Map of the Island of Dominica, Taken from an Actual Survey: Also Part of Martinico & Guadeloupe Shewing Their True Bearing & Distances from Each Other.* In the *Gentleman's Magazine*, XLVIII (1778), opp. p. 603.

JEFFERYS, THOMAS: *Dominica.* In Jefferys: *A General Topography of North America and the West Indies . . .* , No. 99.

————: *Dominica from an Actual Survey Completed in the Year 1773.* In Jefferys: *A West India Atlas . . .* , Plate VII.

Grenada

Carte de l'Isle de la Grenade. In Bellin: *Le Petit Atlas Maritime . . .* , I: No. 101.

DE CAYLUS, M.: *Plan of the Town and Fort of Grenada.* In Jefferys: *The Natural and Civil History of the French Dominion in North and South America*, Pt. II: opp. p. 146, and in his *A General Topography of North America and the West Indies . . .* , No. 103. It also appeared in the *London Magazine*, XXXI (1762), 640.

JEFFERYS, THOMAS: *Grenada Divided into Its Parishes, Surveyed by Order of His Excellency Governor Scott.* In Jefferys: *A West India Atlas . . .* , Plate XIII; for this map see also *Plan de l'Isle de la Grenade. Fait par Ordre de son Excellence Mr. George Scott, 1763.* In Jefferys: *A General Topography of North America and the West Indies*, No. 104.

Guadeloupe

(Among the islands captured by Britain and returned to France in 1763)

JEFFERYS, THOMAS: *A Map of the Island of Guadeloupe, Drawn from an Accurate Survey by Lieut. Archibald Campbell.* In Jefferys: *A General Topography of North America and the West Indies . . .* , No. 94.

————: *Guadeloupe: Done from Actual Surveys and Observations of the*

English, whilst the Island Was in Their Possession. . . . In Jefferys: *A West India Atlas* . . . , Plate VI.

LE ROUGE, GEORGE LOUIS: *La Guadeloupe* ([Paris, 1753]). In Le Rouge: *Atlas Amériquain Septentrional,* No. 24.

A Map of Guadeloupe, One of the Caribby Islands in the West Indies Subject to France ([London, 1759]). In the *London Magazine,* XXVIII (1759), opp. p. 144.

A New and Accurate Map of the Isles of Guadeloupe, Marie-Galante, Etc. from the Best Authorities. In the *Gentleman's Magazine,* XXIX (1759), 276.

Jamaica

BOWEN, EMANUEL: *A New and Accurate Map of the Island of Jamaica.* In Bowen: *A Complete Atlas or Distinct View of the Known World,* No. 66.

JEFFERYS, THOMAS: *Jamaica from the Latest Surveys Improved. . . .* In Jefferys: *A West India Atlas* . . . , Plate I, with *The Harbours of Kingston and Port Royal* as an insert.

KITCHIN, THOMAS: *A New Map of the Island of Jamaica Divided into Its Parishes.* In the *London Magazine,* XXXII (1763), opp. p. 348.

A Map of the Island of Jamaica. In the *Gentleman's Magazine,* XXXII (1762), 416.

Martinique

(Among the islands captured by Britain but returned to France in 1763)

BELL, A., sculp.: *A Map of Martinico from the Latest and Best Authorities.* In the *Scots Magazine,* XXI (1759), 92.

DE CAYLUS, M.: *Plan of the Town and Citadel of Fort Royal, the Capital of Martinico: With the Bay of Cul de Sac Royal.* In Jefferys: *A General Topography of North America and the West Indies,* No. 101.

JEFFERYS, THOMAS: *Martinico, Done from Actual Surveys and Observations Made by English Engineers Whilst the Island Was in Their Possession.* In Jefferys: *A West India Atlas* . . . , Plate VIII.

———: *Martinico, One of the Caribbee Islands, in the West Indies: Subject to the French. According to the Observations of Mr. Hovel* ([London, 1768]). In Jefferys: *A General Topography of North America and the West Indies,* No. 100.

A New and Accurate Map of the Island of Martinico, 1763. In John Entick: *A History of the Late War* . . . , V: opp. p. 257.

Nevis

Carte de l'Isle de Nieves. In Bellin: *Le Petit Atlas Maritime . . .* , I: No. 84.

JEFFERYS, THOMAS: *Nevis.* In Jefferys: *A West India Atlas . . .* , Plate IV, inset.

St. Christopher

BOWEN, EMANUEL: *An Accurate Map of St. Christopher, Vulgarly Called St. Kitts.* In Bowen: *A Complete Atlas,* No. 64.

Carte de l'Isle de St. Christophe. In Bellin: *Le Petit Atlas Maritime . . .* , I: No. 83.

JEFFERYS, THOMAS: *St. Christopher: Surveyed by Anthony Ravell.* In Jefferys: *A General Topography of North America and the West Indies,* No. 92.

MOLL, HERMAN: *The Island of St. Christopher's.* In [John Oldmixon]: *The British Empire in America* (2nd edn., 2 vols., London, 1741), II: between pp. 258-9; with inserts of the island of "Antego."

St. Lucia

Carte de l'Isle de Sainte Lucie. In Bellin: *Le Petit Atlas Maritime . . .* , I: No. 95.

JEFFERYS, THOMAS, engr.: *Plan of the West Coast of the Island of Saint Lucia. This Island Was Taken by a Squadron of Ships Commanded by the Honourable Captain Augustus Hervey.* In Mante: *History of the Late War in North-America . . .* , opp. p. 387.

————: *St Lucia, Done from Surveys and Observations Made by the English whilst in Their Possession.* In Jefferys: *A West India Atlas . . .* , Plate IX; with *Plan of the Carenage* as an inset.

St. Vincent

Carte de l'Isle de Saint Vincent. In Bellin: *Le Petit Atlas Maritime . . .* , I: No. 99.

JEFFERYS, THOMAS: *St. Vincent from an Actual Survey Made in the Year 1773, after the Treaty with the Caribs.* In Jefferys: *A West India Atlas . . .* , Plate XI.

Tobago

BOWEN, THOMAS: *A Map of the Island of Tobago.* In the *Gentleman's Magazine,* XLVIII (1778), opp. supplement for 1778.

BYRES, JOHN: *Plan of the Island of Tobago, Laid Down by Actual Survey*

. . . *1776*. I. Bayley was the sculptor for this map. In *American Maps*, I: No. 21, Library of Congress.

JEFFERYS, THOMAS: *Tobago* ([London], 1765). In Jefferys: *A General Topography of North America and the West Indies*, No. 105.

————: *Tobago from Actual Surveys and Observations*. In Jefferys: *A West India Atlas . . .* , Plate XIV; with *Man of War Bay* as an inset.

THE FALKLAND ISLANDS

A. PRINTED SOURCE MATERIALS AND SECONDARY WORKS

[BOUGAINVILLE, L. A. DE]: *Voyage Autour du Monde par la Frégate du Roi La Boudeuse et la Flûte L'Étoile . . .* (Paris, 1771). This includes the French occupation of East Falkland.

British Diplomatic Instructions, 1689-1789, Vol. VIII: France, Part IV, 1745-1789, L. G. Wickham Legg, ed., *Camden Third Series*, XLIX (1934), 114-22. Relating to the Falklands.

BYRON, JOHN: "An Account of a Voyage Round the World [1764-6]." In John Hawkesworth: *An Account of the Voyages Undertaken . . . for Making Discoveries in the Southern Hemisphere* (3 vols., London, 1773), I: 1-139, for the British occupation of West Falkland in 1764.

CORNEY, BOLTON GLANVILLE: *The Quest and Occupation of Tahaiti . . . ,* Hakluyt Society, *Works*, XXXII, XXXVI, XLIII (3 vols., London, 1913-19). Corney prints the instructions for the occupation of the Falklands, XXXVI: 432-7, 441-5.

GOEBEL, JULIUS, JR.: *The Struggle for the Falkland Islands: A Study in Legal and Diplomatic History* (New Haven, Conn., 1927).

HARLOW, VINCENT T.: *The Founding of the Second British Empire, 1763-1793* (2 vols., London & New York, 1952, 1964), I, 22-32.

HEADLAM, CECIL: "International Relations in the Colonial Sphere," *The Cambridge History of the British Empire, Vol. I: The Old Empire . . . to 1783*, pp. 685-716.

[JOHNSON, SAMUEL]: *Thoughts on the Late Transactions Respecting Falkland's Islands* (1st & 2nd edns., London, 1771; rep., Leigh-on-Sea, 1948).

Papers Relating to the Late Negociations with Spain and the Taking of Falkland's Island from the English (London [1771]).

PENROSE, BERNARD: *An Account of the Last Expedition to Port Egmont in Falkland's Islands in the Year 1772 . . .* (London, 1775).

It should also be noted that useful material is to be found in G. B. Hertz's *British Imperialism in the Eighteenth Century,* Chapter IV, and D. A. Winstanley's *Lord Chatham and the Whig Opposition* which contains an account of the negotiations between Great Britain, France, and Spain over the Falklands.

B. MAPS

A Chart Magellania with Falkland's Islands. This is an insert in *A Chart of the Straits of Magellan. Inlarged from the Chart Published at Madrid in 1769, by Don Juan de la Cruz Cano y Olmedilla . . . and Imprinted from Observations and Survey of Captains Byron, Wallis, and Carteret, Compared with Those of Monsieur de Bougainville.* In Jefferys: *The America Atlas . . . ,* No. 30.

GIBSON, JOHN: *A Chart of Falkland's Islands* (Paris, 1764). Map Division, Library of Congress.

JEFFERYS, THOMAS: *Hawkins's Maiden-Land Called afterwards Falkland's Islands.* In Jeffreys: *The American Atlas . . . ,* No. 31.

LODGE, JOHN, sculp.: *A Map of Falklands Islands in the Latitude of 51° 22' South, Longitude 64° 30' West: From the Latest Observations.* In the *Gentleman's Magazine,* XL (1770), 480.

CHAPTER VII

India

A. BIBLIOGRAPHICAL AIDS

Bibliography of Bengal Records, 1632-1858: List of English Records Relating to the Company's Administration in Bengal which Can Be Consulted in Print . . . (2nd edn., Calcutta, 1925).

Bibliography of Bengal Records, 1756-1858: List of Records of the Government of Bengal . . . ([Calcutta], 1924).

Calendar of Records of the Select Committee at Fort William in Bengal Preserved in the Bengal Secretariat Record Room (Calcutta, 1915).

CRANE, ROBERT I.: *The History of India: Its Study and Interpretation,* Service Center for Teachers of History, *Publications,* No. 17 (Washington, D.C. [1958]).

DIGHE, VASHANATH GOVIND: *Descriptive Catalogue of the Secret and Political Department Series, 1755-1820* (Bombay, 1954).

DODWELL, HENRY HERBERT: "Bibliography," *The Cambridge History of India, Vol. V: British India, 1497-1858* (Cambridge, Eng., 1929), 609-53.

———: *Calendar of the Madras Despatches, 1744-1755* (Madras, 1920).

———: *Report on the Madras Records* (Madras [1916]).

FOSTER, WILLIAM: *Guide to the Indian Office Records, 1600-1858* (London, 1919).

HILL, SAMUEL CHARLES: *Catalogue of the Home Miscellaneous Series of the India Office Records* (London, 1927).

———: *Catalogue of the Orme Manuscripts* (London, 1916). This volume, which is Vol. II, pt. 1 of *Catalogue of Manuscripts in European Languages,* relates to the 231 manuscripts concerning India left by Robert Orme (1728-1801).

KINDERSLEY, ARTHUR F.: *A Handbook of the Bombay Government Records* (Bombay, 1921).

LEWIN, PERCY EVANS: *Subject Catalogue of the Library of the Royal Empire*

Society (formerly the Royal Colonial Institute), Vol. IV . . . Indian Empire (London, 1937).

PARGELLIS, STANLEY, and D. J. MEDLEY, eds.: "Chapter XVI: India," *Bibliography of British History: The Eighteenth Century, 1714-1789* (Oxford, Eng., 1951), 495-505.

PHILIPS, CYRIL HENRY: *Handbook of Oriental History . . .* , Royal Historical Society, *Guides and Handbooks,* No. 6 (London, 1951).

B. PRINTED SOURCE MATERIALS

1. A note on French documents and source materials relating to India, 1748-1776.

Among the most important French documents are those published by the Société de l'histoire de l'Inde française. Three that bear upon the period 1748-1776 are (1) *Acts de l'état civil, Volume II: 1736-1761;* (2) *Correspondance du Conseil Supérieur de Pondichéry et de la Compaignie, Vol. V: 1755-1759* (Alfred Martineau, ed., Paris, 1920); and (3) *Correspondance du Conseil Supérieur de Pondichéry avec le Conseil de Chandernagar, Vol. III: 1747-1757* (Alfred Martineau, ed., Paris, 1919).

Among the French leaders in India who bore the chief responsibility for protecting French interests there during the period were the Comte d'Aché, commander of the French fleet, Charles Castelnau de Bussy, Joseph François Dupleix, Charles Robert Godeheu, the Comte de Lally, Jean Law, and Duval de Leyrit. Each of these men wrote either memoirs, letters, or dispatches involving the contest with the British which later appeared in print. D'Aché left to the historian *Lettres de d'Aché à Lally* (Paris, 1766); *Mémoire pour d'Aché* (Paris, 1766); and his dispatches embodied in Mouffle d'Angerville's *La vie privée de Louis XV, ou Principaux événements et anecdotes de son regne* (n. edn., London, 1781). For Bussy there exists *Mémoires, Lettres . . .* (Paris, 1764); *Mémoire pour Bussy expositif de ses créances sur la Compagnie des Inde* (Paris, 1764); *Mémoire pour Bussy au sujet du mémoire que Lally vient de Répandre dans le Public* (Paris, 1766); and *Mémoire pour Bussy contre la Compagnie* (Paris, 1767). For Dupleix there are the *Mémoire le Sieur D. contre la compagnie des Indes: Avec les pièces justificatives* (2 pts., Paris, 1759); *Mémoire pour la Famille de Dupleix* (Paris, 1751); *Mémoire pour Dupleix contre la Compagnie des Indes* (Paris, 1763); *Mémoire pour la Compagnie des Indes contre Dupleix* (Paris, 1763); *Reponse de Dupleix à la Lettre de Godehue* [Paris], 1763); and the modern *Dupleix and His Letters (1742-1754)* (Virginia McLean Thompson, ed., New York, 1933), which presents significant extracts from letters, with connecting comment to reconstruct events as seen through Dupleix's eyes. The student might also consult C. R. Godeheu's *Lettre à M. Dupleix: Mémoire à consulter*

(Paris, 1760). Finally, there are Tibulle Hamont's *Un Essai d'Empire Français dans l'Inde au 18ᵉ Siècle: Dupleix d'Apres sa Correspondance Inédite* (Paris, 1881) and Marquis de Nazalle's *Dupleix et la Defénse de Pondichéry* . . . (Paris, 1908), containing many Dupleix documents. For Godeheu see *Lettre de Godeheu à Dupleix* (Paris, 1760), and *Réfutation des faits imputés à Godeheu* (Paris, 1764). For Lally there are the *Mémoire pour Lally contre le Procureur-Général* (3 pts., Paris, 1766), and *Plaidoyer du Comte de Lally-Tollendal, curateur à la Mémoire du feu Comte de Lally, son père* (Rouen, 1780). For Jean Law there is his *Mémoire sur Quelques affaires de l'empire Mogul, 1756-1761* (Alfred Martineau, ed., Paris, 1913). Finally, for Leyrit these are *Lettres de Leyrit à Lally* (Paris, 1766). The importance of most of these documents lies in the efforts of the writers to explain why misfortune followed their efforts to serve and save the Compagnie des Indes in the subcontinent. Two other French works, made up largely of source material, are recommended: Elis Honoré Julien Vinson's *Les Français dans l'Inde . . . Extraits du journal d'Anendarangappoullé [Ananda Range Pillai] . . . Traduits* . . . (Paris, 1894), and Jean B. J. Gentil's *Mémoires sur l'Indoustan ou Empire Mogul* . . . (Paris, 1822).

2. A selection of government and company documents

AITCHISON, CHARLES UMPHERSTON, ed.: *A Collection of Treaties, Engagements, and Sunnuds Relating to India and Neighbouring Countries* (7 vols., London, 1862-5; another edn., rev. & cont'd. by A.C. Talbot, 8 vols., 1876-8). There are also two other editions with continuation, one of eleven volumes published at Calcutta in 1892 and one of thirteen volumes published in 1909.

Calendar of Persian Correspondence: Being Letters Referring Mainly to Affairs in Bengal which Passed between Some of the Company's Servants and Indian Rulers and Notables (5 vols., Calcutta, 1911-1930), covering the period 1759-1780.

Charters Granted to the East-India Company from 1601: also the Treaties and Grants Made with, or Obtained from, the Princes and Powers in India from the Year 1756 to 1772 ([London, 1773]).

DATTA, K. K., et al., eds.: *Fort William-India House Correspondence and Other Contemporary Papers Relating Thereto* (5 vols. +, Delhi, 1949-62 +).

FIRMINGER, WALTER K., ed.: *Proceedings of the Select Committee at Fort William in Bengal, 1758* (Calcutta, 1914).

———: *Records of the Government of Bengal* . . . (12 vols., Calcutta, 1919-24).

[FORREST, GEORGE WILLIAM], ed.: *Bengal and Madras Papers, 1746-1785* (2 vols., Calcutta, n.d.).

———, ed.: *Selections from the Letters, Despatches, and Other State*

Papers Preserved in the Bombay Secretariat: Home Series (2 vols.,
Bombay, 1887), and also *Marátha Series* (Vol. 1, Bombay, 1885).
These collections contain the most important documents relative
to the administration of the Bombay presidency in the eighteenth
century.

――――, ed.: *Selections from the Letters, Despatches, and Other State
Papers Preserved in the Foreign Department of the Government of
India, 1772-1785* (3 vols., Calcutta, 1890).

――――, ed.: *Selections from the State Papers of the Governors-General of
India* (4 vols., London, 1910-26). Vols. I and II deal with Warren
Hastings.

HILL, SAMUEL CHARLES, ed.: *Bengal in 1756-1757 . . . , Indian Records Series*
(3 vols., London, 1905). This has been termed the most important
printed selection of material relating to Bengal for these years.

JONES, MARY EVELYN MONCKTON: *Warren Hastings in Bengal, 1772-1774,
Oxford Historical and Literary Studies*, IX (Oxford, Eng., 1918).
The primary value of this work is in the large body of "hitherto
unpublished documents" it contains.

LONG, JAMES, ed.: *Selections from Unpublished Records of the Government for the Years 1748 to 1767 Inclusive: Relating Mainly to the
Social Condition of Bengal . . .* (Vol. I, London, 1869). The selections deal primarily with the Company and English merchants.

MUIR, RAMSAY, ed.: *The Making of British India, 1756-1858 . . .*, University
of Manchester, *Publications: Historical Series*, XXVIII (Manchester, Eng., 1915). Excerpts from source materials.

MUKHOPADHYAYA, PANCHANANADASA, ed.: *Indian Constitutional Documents, 1600-1918* (2nd edn., 2 vols., Calcutta, 1918).

*The Origin and Authentic Narrative of the Present Maratha War and
Also the Late Rohilla War in 1773 and 1774 . . . To Which is Added
the Proceedings of the Military Store-Keeper's Office in Bengal*
(London, 1781).

Press Lists of Ancient Records in Fort St. George from 1670-1800 (35
vols., Madras, 1891 +).

PRINSEP, CHARLES CAMPBELL, ed.: *Record of Services of the Honourable
East India Company's Civil Servants in the Madras Presidency
from 1741-1858* (London, 1885).

*Proceedings of the Governor and Council of Fort William Respecting
the Administration of Justice Amongst the Natives of Bengal*
([London], 1774). This was republished in 1775 by John Almon.

Records of Fort St. George. . . . Most of the documents in five series of
over 200 volumes are eighteenth century, and consist of consulta-
tive, country correspondence, diaries, consultation books, sundry
books, and letters. Published at Madras from 1908 on.

*Reports of the Committee of Secrecy Appointed by the House of Commons
. . . to Enquire into the State of the East India Company* (London,

1772; n. edn., 1773). These reports are printed as Nos. 20-9, vols. 32-3, House of Commons *Reports*, II and III, *Parliamentary Papers . . . 1731-1800* and are available on Readex Microprint cards edited by Edgar L. Erickson.

Reports of the Select Committee of the House of Commons (London, 1772-3). These reports are printed as Nos. 15-19, House of Commons, *Reports*, II. *Parliamentary Papers . . . 1731-1800*; also on Readex cards.

RUSSELL, FRANCIS, comp.: *A Collection of Statutes Concerning the Incorporation, Trade, and Commerce of the East India Company, the Government of the British Possessions in India . . .* (1st edn., London, 1786; 2nd edn., 1794).

SHAW, JOHN, ed.: *Charters Relating to the East India Company from 1600 to 1761 . . .* (Madras, 1887).

[VANSITTART, HENRY], ed.: *Original Papers Relative to the Disturbances in Bengal: Containing Every Material Transaction from 1759 to 1764* (2 vols., London, 1765).

WHEELER, JAMES TALBOYS: *Madras in the Olden Time: Being a History of the Presidency . . . Compiled from Official Records* (3 vols., Madras, 1861-2).

WILSON, CHARLES ROBERT, ed.: *Old Fort William in Bengal: A Selection of Official Documents Dealing with Its History, Indian Record Series* (2 vols., London, 1906).

3. Non-official contemporary writings

CAMBRIDGE, RICHARD OWEN: *An Account of the War in India between the English and French on the Coast of Coromandel from the Year 1750 to the Year 1760 . . .* (London, 1761; 2nd edn., 1762).

CARACCIOLI, CHARLES: *The Life of Robert Lord Clive, Baron Plassey: Wherein Are Delineated His Military Talents in the Field, His Maxims of Government in the Cabinet . . .* (4 vols., London, 1775-7). An important work quoting many documents, but to be used with great care as it was designed primarily to destroy Clive's reputation.

DOW, ALEXANDER: *The History of Hindostan* (3 vols., London, 1768-72; Eng. trans. from the Persian of Muhammad Kāsim Ibn Hindū Shāh's *Astrābādī*).

FRANCIS, PHILIP. *Memoirs of Sir Philip Francis, K. C. B.: With Correspondence and Journals* by Joseph Parkes and Herman Merivale (2 vols., London, 1867). To be used with care.

GROSE, JOHN HENRY: *A Voyage to the East-Indies: With Observations* (London, 1757; 2nd edn., cont'd to 1764, 2 vols., 1766; n. edn., 4 vols., 1772). A survey of the governments and customs of India with some notice of the trade.

HASTINGS, WARREN. *Memoirs of the Life of the Right Hon. Warren Hastings, First Governor-General of Bengal* by George Robert Gleig (3 vols., London, 1841). See also "The Benares Diary of Warren Hastings," C. Collin Davies, ed., *Camden Miscellany*, 3rd ser., XVIII (1948), 1-40; *Warren Hastings' Letters to Sir John Macpherson* (H. H. Dodwell, ed., London, 1927); and *Mr. Hastings's Review of the State of Bengal* (London, 1786; another edition the same year bore the title *Memoirs Relative to the State of India* . . .).

HOLWELL, JOHN ZEPHANIAH: *India Tracts* (2nd edn., London 1764; 3rd edn., w/add., 1774).

————: *Interesting Historical Events Relative to the Provinces of Bengal and the Empire of Indostan* . . . (London, 1765; 2nd edn., 2 vols., 1766-71).

IMPEY, ELIJAH BARWELL: *Memoirs of Sir Elijah Impey* . . . *with Anecdotes of Warren Hastings, Sir Philip Francis,* . . . *and Other Contemporaries* . . . (London, 1846).

IVES, EDWARD: *A Voyage from England to India in the Year 1754 and an Historical Narrative of the Operations of the Squadron and Army in India* . . . *Also a Journey from Persia to England* . . . (London, 1773).

JOSHI, M. P., ed.: *Selections from the Peshwa Daftor, New Series, I: Expansion of Maratha Power (1701-1761)* (Bombay, 1957).

[MACPHERSON, JAMES]: *The History and Management of the East India Company from Its Origin in 1600 to the Present Times* (London, 1779).

MACPHERSON, WILLIAM CHARLES, ed.: *Soldiering in India, 1764-1787: Extracts from Journals and Letters Left by Lt. Colonel Allan Macpherson and Lt. Colonel John Macpherson, of the East India Company's Service* (Edinburgh & London, 1928).

[MOIR, JOHN]: *Transactions in India: From the Commencement of the French War in Seventeen Hundred and Fifty-Six to the Conclusion of the Late Peace in Seventeen Hundred and Eighty-Three* (n.p., 1786).

A Narrative of the Transactions of the British Squadrons in the East Indies during the Late War: Comprehending a Particular Account of the Loss of Madras . . . *By an Officer who Serv'd in Those Squadrons* (London, 1751).

[ORME, ROBERT]: *A History of the Military Transactions of the British Nation in Indostan from the Year 1745* . . . (2 vols., London, 1763-78; 4th edn., 3 vols., 1803). This work remains the principal account of the Coromandel and Bengal wars.

————: *Historical Fragments of the Mogul Empire, of the Morattoes, and of the British Concerns in Indostan from the Year MDCLIX* . . . (n.p., 1782; another ed., London, 1805). To the *Historical*

Fragments is prefixed a life of Orme (1728-1801), who after some sixteen years in India became the historiographer for the Company.

PILLAI, ANANDA RANGA: *The Private Diary of Ananda Ranga Pillai, Dubash to Joseph François Dupleix . . . Governor of Pondichery: A Record of Matters Political, Historical, Social, and Personal from 1736 to 1761 . . .* (J. Frederick Price, K. Rangachari, and Henry H. Dodwell, eds., 12 vols., Madras, 1904-28).

PUNDIT, KASI RAJA: *An Account of the Last Battle of Panipat and of the Events Leading up to It* (H. G. Rawlinson, ed., Oxford, Eng., 1926). The account was translated from the Persian in 1791.

STRACHEY, HENRY: *A Narrative of the Mutiny of the Officers of the Army in Bengal in [1766] . . .* (London, 1773).

[TOUR, MAISTRE DE LA]: *The History of Ayder Ali Khan, Nabob-Bahader, or New Memoirs Concerning the East Indies: With Historical Notes* (2 vols., Dublin, 1774).

[WATTS, WILLIAM]: *Memoirs of the Revolution in Bengal, Anno Dom. 1757: By Which Meer Jaffeir Was Raised to the Government of That Province together with Those of Bahar and Orixa* (London, 1760). This work has also been attributed to John Campbell.

4. Contemporary pamphlets, tracts, and related materials: Chronologically arranged

A Letter to a Proprietor of the East India Company ([London, 1749]). On the loss and ransom of Madras.

A Collection of Letters Relating to the East India Company and to a Free Trade: Dedicated to Robert Nugent, Esq. . . . (London, 1754). The pamphlet presents an opposition to the company's trade monopoly with India and China.

Some Thoughts on the Present State of Our Trade to India. By a Merchant of London (London, 1754). This pamphlet also presents a brief criticism of the East India Company monopoly.

Some Thoughts Relating to Trade in General and to the East India Trade in Particular (London, 1754). Signed A. Z.

HOLWELL, JOHN ZEPHANIAH: *A Genuine Narrative of the Deplorable Deaths of the English Gentlemen and Others Who Were Suffocated in the Black Hole in Fort William at Calcutta . . .* (London, 1758). See in connection with this work J. H. Little's "The Black Hole: The Question of Holwell's Veracity," *Bengal: Past and Present*, XI (Calcutta, 1915), 75-104.

A Complete History of the War in India from 1749 to . . . 1761 with an Accurate Detail of Colonel Clive's Military Transactions . . . (London, 1761).

SCRAFTON, LUKE: *Reflections on the Government . . . of Indostan: With a Short Sketch of the History of Bengal from 1739 to 1756; and an*

Account of the English Affairs to 1758 (London, 1763; another edn., 1770).

CLIVE of PLASSEY, ROBERT CLIVE, BARON: *A Letter to the Proprietors of the East India Stock* . . . (London, 1764; another edn., w/add., 1773), in defense of his conduct in India. For a reply, see the pamphlet of John Dunning, Lord Ashburton: *A Letter to the Proprietors of East-India Stock on the Subject of Lord Clive's Jaghire: Occasioned by His Lordship's Letter on That Subject* (London, 1764).

A Vindication of Mr. Holwell's Character from the Aspersions thrown out in an Anonymous Pamphlet . . . (London, 1764).

JOHNSTONE, JOHN: *A Letter to the Proprietors of East-India Stock* (London, 1766).

VANSITTART, HENRY: *A Narrative of the Transactions in Bengal from* . . . *1760 to 1764: During the Government of H. Vansittart* . . . (3 vols., London, 1766). Vansittart was answered by Luke Scrafton in *Observations on Mr. Vansittart's Narrative* (London [1767]); this work was in turn answered by John Zephaniah Holwell: *An Address* . . . *to L. Scrafton, Esq. in Reply to His Pamphlet Intitled Observations on Mr. Vansittart's Narrative* . . . (London, 1767).

A Caution to the Directors of the East India Company with Regard to Their Making the Midsummer Dividend of Five per cent without Due Attention to a Late Act of Parliament and a By-Law of Their Own (London, 1767).

A Letter to the Proprietors of East India Stock upon the Question to Be Ballotted for on Tuesday the 23d Day of March for Granting to Lord Clive Three Thousand Pounds (London, 1767).

VANSITTART, HENRY: *A Letter to the Proprietors of East-India Stock* . . . *Occasioned by a Late Anonymous Pamphlet* . . . (London, 1767).

YOUNG, ARTHUR: *A Letter to Lord Clive on the Great Benefits which May Result to the Publick from Patriotically Expending a Small Part of a Large Private Fortune* . . . (London, 1767).

State of the East India Company's Affairs: With a View to the Intended Bill for Regulating the Dividend, December, 1767 (London, 1768).

An Essay on the East India Trade and Its Importance to This Kingdom with A Comparative View of the Dutch, French, and English East Indies Companies (London, 1770). An attempt to estimate the increase of wealth produced by the Company's activities, using that as an argument against government restriction of the Company.

The Importance of the British Dominion in India Compared with That in America (London, 1770).

[JOHNSTONE, GEORGE]: *Thoughts on Our Acquisitions in the East Indies, Particularly Respecting Bengal* (London, 1771). This pamphlet presents the views of a prominent member of the East India Company in London; he had also been Governor of West Florida.

Observations on the Present State of the East India Company and on the Measures to Be Pursued for Ensuring Its Permanency and Augmenting Its Commerce (London, 1771). This pamphlet has been attributed to Alexander Dalrymple.

CLIVE of PLASSEY, ROBERT CLIVE, BARON: *Lord Clive's Speech in the House of Commons, 30th March 1772, on the Motion Made for Leave to Bring in a Bill for the Better Regulation of the Affairs of the East India Company* . . . (London [1772]).

[DALRYMPLE, ALEXANDER]: *An Enquiry into the Rights of the East India Company of Making War and Peace and of Possessing Their Territorial Acquisitions without the Participation or Inspection of the British Government* (London, 1772).

[———]: *A General View of the East-India Company Written in January 1769: To Which Are Added Some Observations on the Present State of Their Affairs* (London, 1772).

[———]: *The Measures to Be Pursued in India for Ensuring the Permanency and Augmenting the Commerce of the Company Further Considered* . . . (London, 1772). This pamphlet has also been attributed to John Scott.

HOOLE, JOHN: *The Present State of the English East-India Company Affairs, Comprehending the Accounts Delivered . . . by the Court of Directors to the Treasury which Were Laid before the Committee of Secrecy* . . . (London, 1772).

KEIR, ARCHIBALD: *Thoughts on the Affairs of Bengal* (London, 1772).

A Letter to the Right Honourable Lord North on the East-India Bill now Depending in Parliament (London, 1772).

The Origin and Cause of the Continuance of the Disorders in Our East India Affairs . . . (London, 1772).

A Plan for the Government of the Provinces of Bengal: Addressed to the Directors of the East India Company ([London, 1772]).

VERELST, HARRY: *A View of the Rise, Progress, and Present State of the English Government in Bengal: Including a Reply to the Misrepresentations of Mr. Bolts and Other Writers* (London, 1772). Earlier in 1772 William Bolts published Volume I of *Considerations* completed in 1775. Verelst's membership in both the Fort William Council and the Select Committee gives this *View* a semi-official standing.

General Remarks on the System of Government in India: With Further Considerations on the Present State of the Company at Home and Abroad . . . (London, 1773). This work was supposedly authored by a Captain Smith who commanded a regiment under Clive in India.

A Letter to the Right Honourable Lord North . . . on the Present Proceedings Concerning the East-India Company (London, 1773). Signed B.A.

POWNALL, THOMAS: *The Right, Interest and Duty of Government as Concerned in the Affairs of the East Indies* (London, 1773).

An Account of the Proceedings at the India House with Respect to the Regulations Proposed to Be Made Bye Laws by a Committee of Proprietors . . . (London, 1774).

BOLTS, WILLIAM: *Considerations on India Affairs* . . . (3 vols., London, 1772-1775), Volumes II and III. See Harry Verelst, under 1772 above, for a reply to Volume I of Bolt's work.

The Trial of Joseph Fowke, Frances Fowke, Maha Rajah Nundocomar, and Roy Rada Churn for a Conspiracy against Warren Hastings, Esq. . . . (London, 1776).

C. SECONDARY WORKS

1. General

AUBER, PETER: *History of the Rise and Progress of British Power in India* . . . (2nd edn., 2 vols., London, 1846).

BEVERIDGE, HENRY: *A Comprehensive History of India: Civil, Military and Social* . . . (3 vols., London, 1858-62). See especially volumes I and II.

BOSE, NEMAI SADHAN: *The Indian Awakening and Bengal* (Calcutta, 1960).

BUCHANAN, FRANCIS HAMILTON: *The History, Antiquities, Topography, and Statistics of Eastern India* . . . (3 vols., London, 1838).

DATTA, KALIKINKAR: *Studies in the History of the Bengal Subah, 1740–70* (Calcutta, 1936).

DATTA, RAMESACHANDRA: *History of India under Early British Rule* (2nd edn., London, 1906).

DODWELL, HENRY HERBERT, ed.: *The Cambridge History of India, Vol. V: British India, 1497-1858* (Cambridge, Eng., 1929). The contributors of chapters covering the period 1748-1776, are Dodwell: Chap. VII, "Clive in Bengal, 1756-70"; Chap. VIII, "The Seven Years' War"; Chap. IX, "Bengal, 1760-72"; Chap. XV, "The Carnatic, 1761-84"; Chap. XXXII, "The Development of Sovereignty in British India"; and "Bibliographies"; Lt. Col. C. E. Luard: Chap. XIV, "The First Conflict of the Company with the Marathas, 1761-82"; Alfred Martineau: Chap. VI, "Dupleix and Bussy"; and P. E. Roberts: Chap. X, "The East India Company and the State, 1772-86"; Chap. XI, "The Early Reforms of Warren Hastings in Bengal"; Chap. XII, "External Relations and the Rohilla War"; and Chap. XIII, "Hastings and his Colleagues."

———: *Dupleix and Clive: The Beginning of Empire* (London, 1920).

DUFF, JAMES GRANT: *A History of the Mahrattas* (3 vols., London, 1826; rev. by Stephen Meredyth Edwardes, 2 vols., 1921).

ELLIOT, HENRY MIERS, and JOHN DOWSON, eds.: *The History of India: As Told by Its Own Historians* (8 vols., London, 1867-77), Vol. VIII.

ELPHINSTONE, MOUNTSTUART: *The Rise of the British Power in the East* . . . (Sir Edward Colebrooke, ed., London, 1887).

GLEIG, GEORGE ROBERT: *The History of the British Empire in India* (4 vols., London, 1830-5).

GRIFFITHS, PERCIVAL JOSEPH: *The British Impact on India* (London, 1952).

HAMILTON, CHARLES: *An Historical Relation of the Origin, Progress, and Final Dissolution of the Government of the Rohilla Afgans* . . . (London, 1787).

HAMONT, TIBULLE: *La fin d'un Empire français aux Indes sous Louis XV: Lally-Tollendal, d'après des documents inédits* . . . (Paris, 1887).

HOUGH, WILLIAM: *Political and Military Events in British India from the Years 1756 to 1849* (2 vols., London, 1853).

KINCAID, CHARLES AUGUSTUS, and RAO BAHADUR D. B. PARASNIS: *A History of the Maratha People* (3 vols., London, 1918-25). This history was written for Indians and embodies the results of the nineteenth-century scholarship.

KOSAMBI, DAMODAR DHARMANAND: *An Introduction to the Study of Indian History* (Bombay, c. 1956).

LYALL, ALFRED COMYN: *The Rise and Expansion of the British Dominion in India* . . . (1st edn., London, 1893; 5th edn., 1910).

MAJUMDAR, R. C., H. C. RAYCHAUDHURI, and KALIKINKAR DATTA: *An Advanced History of India* (London, 1948).

MALLESON, GEORGE BRUCE: *History of the French in India* . . . *[1674-1761]* (London, 1868).

———: *Final French Struggles in India and on the Indian Seas* . . . (London, 1878).

MILL, JAMES: *The History of British India* (3 vols., London, 1817; 5th edn., Horace Hayman Wilson, ed., 10 vols., 1858).

MORELAND, W. H., and ATUL CHANDRA CHATTERJEE: *A Short History of India* (1st edn., London, 1936; 3rd edn., 1953).

RAWLINSON, H. G.: *The British Achievement in India: A Survey* (London, 1948).

SARKAR, YADUNATH: *Fall of the Mughal Empire* [1739-88] (4 vols., Calcutta, 1932-50), and *Bihar and Orissa during the Fall of the Mughal Empire* . . . (Patna, India, 1932).

SEN, SIBA PADA: *The French in India: First Establishment and Struggle* (Calcutta, 1947), and *The French in India, 1763-1816* (Calcutta, c. 1958).

SMITH, VINCENT A.: *The Oxford History of India* . . . [to 1911] (Oxford, Eng., 1911; 2nd edn., rev. & cont'd. to 1921 by S. M. Edwardes, 1921).

SPEAR, PERCIVAL: *India: A Modern History*, University of Michigan, *History of the Modern World* (Ann Arbor, Mich., 1961).

STANHOPE, PHILIP HENRY STANHOPE, 5TH EARL OF: *The Rise of Our Indian Empire . . . Being the History of British India from Its Origin till the Peace of 1783: Extracted from Lord Mahon's History of England* (London, 1838).

THORNTON, EDWARD: *The History of the British Empire in India* (6 vols., London, 1841-5).

2. Political

AUBER, PETER: *An Analysis of the Constitution of the East-India Company and of the Laws Passed by Parliament for the Government of Their Affairs . . .* (London, 1826).

BANERJEE, D. N.: *Early Administrative System of the East India Company in Bengal, Vol. I: 1765-1774* (1 vol. only pub., London & Madras, 1943).

———: *Early Land Revenue System in Bengal and Bihar, Vol. I: 1765-1772* (Calcutta & London, 1936; no more pub.).

BEVERIDGE, HENRY: *The Trial of Maharaja Nanda Kumar: A Narrative of a Judicial Murder* (Calcutta, 1886).

FAWCETT, CHARLES GORDON HILL: *The First Century of British Justice in India . . .* (London & Oxford, Eng., 1934).

FURBER, HOLDEN: *Bombay Presidency in the Mid-Eighteenth Century* (London, 1965).

HASTINGS, G. W.: *Vindication of Warren Hastings* (Oxford, Eng., 1909).

ILBERT, COURTENAY: *The Government of India: A Brief Historical Survey of Parliamentary Legislation Relating to India* (Oxford, Eng., 1922).

KAYE, JOHN WILLIAM: *The Administration of the East India Company: A History of Indian Progress* (1st & 2nd edns., London, 1853).

KEITH, A. BERRIEDALE: *A Constitutional History of India, 1600-1935* (London, 1936).

MAJUMDAR, N.: *Justice and Police in Bengal, 1765–1793: A Study of the Nizamat in Decline* (Calcutta, 1960).

MARSHALL, P. J.: *The Impeachment of Warren Hastings, Oxford Historical Series*, 2nd ser. (London, 1965).

MARTINEAU, HARRIET: *British Rule in India: A Historical Sketch* (London, 1857).

MASANI, R. P.: *Britain in India: An Account of British Rule in the Indian Subcontinent* (New York, 1960).

MASON, PHILIP (using pseud. Philip Woodruff): *The Men Who Ruled India* (2 vols., London, 1953; 1 vol., New York, 1954).

MISRA, BANKEY BIHARI: *The Central Administration of the East India Company, 1773-1834* (Manchester, Eng., 1959).

MUSTAFA, SAYID GHULAM: *Cross in the Subcontinent: A Brief Political and Constitutional Survey of British Rule in India* (Karachi, 1960).

RAMSBOTHAM, RICHARD B.: *Studies in the Land Revenue History of Bengal, 1769-1787* (London & New York, 1926).

SARKAR, YADUNATHA: *Mughal Administration* (3rd edn., rev. & enl., Calcutta, 1935).

SEN, SAILENDRA NATH: *Anglo-Maratha Relations during the Administration of Warren Hastings, 1772-1785* (Calcutta, 1961).

STEPHEN, JAMES FITZJAMES: *The Story of Nuncomar and the Impeachment of Sir Elijah Impey* (2 vols., London, 1885).

SUTHERLAND, LUCY S: *The East India Company in Eighteenth-Century Politics* (Oxford, Eng., 1952). See also her articles: "The East India Company and the Peace of Paris," *English Historical Review*, LXII (1947), 179-90, and "New Evidence on the Nandakuma Trial," *ibid.*, LXXII (1957), 438-65.

THOMPSON, EDWARD JOHN, and GEOFFREY THEODORE GARRATT: *Rise and Fulfillment of British Rule in India* (London, 1934).

WEBER, HENRY: *The Compagnie Française des Indies (1604-1875)* (Paris, 1904).

WHEELER, JAMES TALBOYS: *India under British Rule: From the Foundation of the East India Company* (London, 1886).

3. Economic

BANERJEA, PRAMATHANATH: *Indian Finance in the Days of the Company* (London, 1928).

DALGLIESH, WILBERT HAROLD: *The Perpetual Company of the Indies in the Days of Dupleix: Its Administration and Organization for the Handling of Indian Commerce, 1722-1754* (Philadelphia, 1933).

DATTA, K. K.: "India's Trade with Europe and America in the Eighteenth Century," *Journal of the Economic and Social History of the Orient*, II (1959), 313-23.

DATTA, RAMESACHANDRA: *The Economic History of British India: A Record of Agriculture, Trade and Manufacturing, Industries, Finance, Administration* . . . [1757-1837] (London, 1902).

DIGBY, WILLIAM: *"Prosperous" British India: A Revelation from Official Records* (London, 1901).

DUTT, ROMESH CHUNDER: *The Economic History of India under Early British Rule: From the Rise of British Power in 1757 to . . . 1837* (Edinburgh, 1902; 7th edn., London, 1950).

FAWCETT, CHARLES: *The English Factories in India* (4 vols., Oxford, Eng., 1936-55).

FOSTER, WILLIAM: *The East India House: Its History and Association* (London, c. 1924), and *John Company* . . . (London, c. 1924).

FURBER, HOLDEN: *John Company at Work: A Study of European Expansion in India in the Late Eighteenth Century, Harvard Historical Studies.* LV (Cambridge, Mass., 1948).

GRANT, ROBERT: *A Sketch of the History of the East India Company: From Its First Formation to the Passing of the Regulating Act of 1773* ... (London, 1813).

HILL, SAMUEL CHARLES: *Three Frenchmen in Bengal: Or the Commercial Ruin of the French Settlements in 1757* (London, 1903). The three Frenchmen were Pierre Rènault, Jean Law, and Jacques Ignace Courtin.

KRISHNA, BAL: *Commercial Relations between India and England, 1601 to 1757* (London, 1924).

MACPHERSON, DAVID: *The History of the European Commerce with India* ... (London, 1812).

MOTTRAM, RALPH H.: *Traders' Dream: The Romance of the East India Company* (London & New York, 1939).

ROBINSON, FREDERICK P.: *The Trade of the East India Company from 1709 to 1813* ... (Cambridge, Eng., 1912).

SARKAR, YADUNATHA: *Economics of British India* (4th edn., Calcutta, 1917).

THOMAS, PARAKUNNEL JOSEPH: *Mercantilism and the East India Trade: An Early Phase of the Protection v. Free Trade Controversy* (London, 1926).

WILBUR, MARGUERITE EYER: *The East India Company and the British Empire in the Far East* (New York, 1945; reiss., Stanford, Calif., c. 1951).

WILLSON, HENRY BECKLES: *Ledger and Sword: Or the Honourable Company of Merchants of England Trading to the East Indies, 1599-1874* (2 vols., London, 1903).

4. Social

BEARCE, GEORGE D.: "Intellectual and Cultural Characteristics of India in a Changing Era, 1740-1800," *Journal of Asian Studies*, XXV (1965), 3-17.

BUCHANAN, FRANCIS HAMILTON: *A Journey from Madras through the Countries of Mysore, Canara, and Malabar* ... (3 vols., London, 1807).

CHATTERTON, EYRE: *A History of the Church of England in India since the Early days of the East India Company* (London, 1924).

DATTA, RAMESACHANDRA: *The Peasantry of Bengal: a View of Their Conditions under the Hindu* ... *Mahomedan, and* ... *English Rule* (Calcutta, 1874).

DODWELL, HENRY HERBERT: *The Nabobs of Madras* (London, 1926).

HUNTER, WILLIAM WILSON: *The Annals of Rural Bengal* ... (3 vols., Edinburgh & London, 1868-72). A description of native society, 1765-1790; vols. II & III deal with Orissa.

KINCAID, DENNIS: *British Social Life in India, 1608-1937* (London, 1938).

RAWLINSON, HUGH GEORGE: *A Concise History of the Indian People* (3rd impression, rev., London, 1946).

SARKAR, YADUNATHA: *India through the Ages: A Survey of the Growth of Indian Life and Thought* (Calcutta, 1928).

SPEAR, PERCIVAL: *The Nabobs: A Study of the Social Life of the English in Eighteenth Century India* (London, 1932).

SRINIVASACHARI, M. A.: "The Historical Material in the Private Diary of Ananda Ranga Pillai, 1736-1761," *Journal of Indian History*, VIII (1929)-IX (1930), *passim*.

5. *Biographical*

BOLTS, WILLIAM. *William Bolts: A Dutch Adventurer under John Company* by Norman Leslie Hallward (Cambridge, Eng., 1920).

CLIVE OF PLASSEY, ROBERT CLIVE, BARON. For a contemporary biography of Clive, see Charles Caraccioli's *The Life of Robert Lord Clive, Baron of Plassey* . . . , cited in full under section B:3. Several older works are: Sir John Malcolm's *The Life of Robert, Lord Clive: Collected from the Family Papers* . . . (3 vols., London, 1836), in connection with which see Macaulay's review of the work in Volume XIX of the *Traveller's Library;* Alexander John Arbuthnot's *Lord Clive: The Foundation of British Rule in India, Builders of Britain,* V (London, 1889); and George Bruce Malleson's *Lord Clive and the Establishment of the English in India, Rulers of India,* VII (Oxford, Eng., 1895). The more recent studies include: Sir George W. Forrest's *The Life of Lord Clive* . . . (2 vols., London, 1918); Reginald A. A. Gatty's *Robert Clive and the Founding of British India* (London & New York, 1927); Thomas A. Rennard's *Life and Times of Robert Clive, 1725-1774, Makers of History,* No. 7 (Exeter, Eng., 1935); Sir George Duff-Sutherland Dunbar's *Clive, Great Lives,* No. 73 (London, 1936); and Alfred Mervyn Davies's *Clive of Plassey: A Biography* (London, 1939). See also the noted essays by Lord Macaulay included in *Macaulay's Essays on Lord Clive & Warren Hastings* (John Lord, ed., London [1931]) and published separately as *Lord Clive and Warren Hastings* . . . (intro. by H. K. Prescot, Glasgow & London [1934]).

DUPLEIX, JOSEPH FRANÇOIS. *Dupleix, ses plans politiques: Sa disgrace. Étude d'Histoire Coloniale* by Prosper Cultru (Paris, 1901); *Dupleix, ses dernières luttes dans l'Inde* . . . *extrait des Annales le l'Extrême Orient et de l'Afrique* by Castonnet des Fosses (Paris, 1889); and *Dupleix* by George Bruce Malleson (London, 1890).

GRANT, CHARLES. *Charles Grant and British Rule in India* by Ainslie T. Embree (London & New York, 1962).

HASTINGS, WARREN. There are several older studies dealing with Hastings including: Lionel J. Trotter's *Warren Hastings: A Biography* (London, 1878; reiss. [1910]); Sir Alfred C. Lyall's *Warren Hastings* (London & New York, 1889); Sir John Strachey's *Hastings and the Rohilla War* (Oxford, Eng., 1892); George Bruce Malleson's *Life of Warren Hastings* (London, 1894); and Charles Allen Lawson's *The Private Life of Warren Hastings, First Governor of India* . . . (London, 1895). See also the essays by Lord Macaulay on Lord Clive and Warren Hastings listed under Clive. More recent works include Sophia Weitzman's *Warren Hastings and Philip Francis,* University of Manchester, *Publications: Historical Series,* No. 56 (Manchester, Eng., 1929); Alfred Mervyn Davies's *Warren Hastings, Maker of British India* . . . (London, 1935); and Keith Feiling's *Warren Hastings* (London & New York, 1954). See also the article by P. E. Roberts: "Warren Hastings and His Accusers," *Journal of Indian History,* III (1924), 91-134. Finally, see the work by M. E. Monckton Jones, *Warren Hastings in Bengal* . . . , cited under section B: 2.

LALLY, THOMAS ARTHUR, COMTE DE. *The Career of Count Lally* . . . by George Bruce Malleson (Calcutta, 1865).

LAWRENCE, STRINGER. *Stringer Lawrence, the Father of the Indian Army* by John Biddulph (London, 1901).

NADIR SHAH. *Nadir Shah in India* by Yadunatha Sarkar (Patna, India, 1925).

6. Military and naval

AUSTEN, HAROLD CHOMLEY MANSFIELD: *Sea Fights and Corsairs of the Indian Ocean: Being the Naval History of Mauritius from 1715 to 1810* (Port Louis, Mauritius, 1934).

BROOME, ARTHUR: *History of the Rise and Progress of the Bengal Army* (Vol. I only pub., Calcutta, 1851).

FORTESCUE, JOHN WILLIAM: *A History of the British Army* (13 vols., London, 1910-30), II: Books 8 and 10 and III: Book 11.

GOPAL, RAM: *How the British Occupied Bengal: A Corrected Account of the 1756-1765 Events* (New York, 1963).

JHA, SRI ADITYA PRASAD: "The First Mutiny in the Bengal Army, 1764," Bihar Research Society, *Journal* (1956).

LOW, CHARLES RATHBONE: *History of the Indian Navy (1613-1863)* (2 vols., London, 1877).

MALLESON, GEORGE BRUCE: *The Decisive Battles of India: From 1746 to 1849 Inclusive* (London, 1883).

ROACH, JOHN: "The 39th Regiment of Foot and the East India Company, 1754-1757," John Rylands Library, *Bulletin,* XLI (1958-9), 102-38.

ROSE, JOHN HOLLAND: "Influence of Sea Power on Indian History, 1746-

1802," *Journal of Indian History,* III (1924-6), 188-204. Reprinted in his *The Indecisiveness of Modern War and Other Essays* (London, 1927), pp. 81-97.

TOY, SIDNEY: *The Strongholds of India* (Melbourne, Australia, 1957).

WILSON, WILLIAM JOHN: *History of the Madras Army* (3 vols., Madras, 1882-9).

D. MAPS

For aid in determining what cartographic materials exist for India, see *A Catalogue of Maps, Plans, &c. of India and Burma and Other Parts of Asia* . . . (London, 1891).

ANVILLE, JEAN BAPTISTE BOURGUINON D': *[The] Coromandel [Coast, India].* This map is No. 27 in a collection of 48 d'Anville maps bound together without title ([Paris, 1771]). Map Division, New York Public Library.

———: *Carte de l'Inde. Dressée pour la Compagnie des Indes,* 1752. In *ibid.,* Nos. 25-6. There is an inset on this plate: *Entrée du Gange et son Cours en remontant jusqu'à Ugli.* The inset also appears as No. 41 in volume III of Bellin's *Le Petit Atlas Maritime.*

ARROWSMITH, AARON: . . . *Map of India, Compiled from Various Interesting and Valuable Materials* . . . (London, 1804).

———: *Atlas of South India* (London, 1822).

Coste de Coromandel et les Pays de Tonda, Mandalum et Tanjaor. In Bellin: *Le Petit Atlas Maritime* . . . , III: No. 38.

HUGHES, W.: *Sketch Map of India Illustrating the History* . . . *to the Battle of Plassey.* In Henry Beveridge: *A Compendius History of India.* . . , I: frontispiece.

India: Showing Distribution of the Principal European Factories in 1756. In Julian S. Corbett: *England in the Seven Years' War* . . . , I: opp. p. 341.

Indostan, the Deccan, and the Carnatic with two insets: *Calcutta, 1757* and *Madras, 1758.* In Fortescue: *A History of the British Army,* II: at end of volume.

JEFFERYS, THOMAS: *The East Indies: Drawn from the Latest Discoveries.* In the *Gentleman's Magazine,* XVIII (1748), 251.

A Map of the Mouths of the Ganges in the Bay of Bengal Shewing the English Settlements Lately Destroyd by the Nabob of That Province. In *ibid.,* XXVII (1757), 308.

The Moguls Empire Divided into Its Principal Governments. In *ibid.,* XXXVII (1767), 99.

Plan de Bombay et ses Environs. In Bellin: *Le Petit Atlas Maritime* . . . , III: No. 25.

Plan de Madras à la Coste de Coromandel. In *ibid.,* III: No. 37.

Plan de la Ville de Pondicheri. In *ibid.,* III: No. 35.

RENNELL, JAMES: *A Bengal Atlas: Containing Maps of the Theatre of War and Commerce on That Side of Hindoostan* . . . (London, 1781). This work contains 21 maps and plans.

————: *Map of Bengal, Behar, Oude, Allahabad, and Part of Agra and Delhi* (London, 1776; reiss. 1786, 1794, 1824). This map was the standard map of India for many years. Rennell was the greatest of the early cartographers of India.

Suite de la Carte de l'Indoustan . . . . In Bellin: *Le Petit Atlas Maritime* . . . , III: No. 22.

CHAPTER VIII

Africa, Gibraltar, and Minorca

AFRICA

A. BIBLIOGRAPHICAL AIDS

WORK, MONROE NATHAN, comp.: *A Bibliography of the Negro in Africa and America* (New York, 1928; rep. 1965). This is a standard reference work for the subject.

CONOVER, HELEN FIELD: *The British Empire in Africa: Selected References* (4 vols., Washington, D.C., 1942-3).

B. PRINTED SOURCE MATERIALS

ADANSON, MICHEL: *A Voyage to Senegal, the Isle of Goree, and the River Gambia: Translated from the French with Notes by an English Gentleman who Resided Some Time in That Country* (London, 1759).

[BENEZET, ANTHONY]: *A Short Account of That Part of Africa Inhabited by the Negroes; with Respect to the Fertility of the Country; the Good Disposition of Many of the Natives, and the Manner in Which the Slave Trade is Carried on* . . . (Philadelphia, 1762; 3rd edn., London, 1768).

———: *Some Historical Account of Guinea; Its Situation, Produce, and the General Disposition of Its Inhabitants; With an Inquiry into the Rise and Progress of the Slave Trade, Its Nature and Lamentable Effects* . . . (Philadelphia, 1771; n. edn., London, 1772).

Considerations and Remarks on the Present State of the Trade to Africa; With Some Account of the British Settlements in That Country . . . *By a Gentleman Who Resided upwards of Fifteen Years in That Country* (London, 1771).

[DEMARIN, JOHN PETER]: *A Treatise upon the Trade from Great Britain to Africa: Humbly Recommended to the Attention of the Government* (London, 1772).

Detection of the Proceedings and Practices of the Directors of the Royal African Company of England . . . [1672-1748] (London, 1749).

DONNAN, ELIZABETH, ed.: *Documents Illustrative of the History of the Slave Trade to America* (4 vols., Washington, D. C., 1930-5). Volume II carries the subtitle *The Eighteenth Century.*

DU BOIS, W. E. B., *et al.*: *Encyclopedia of the Negro: Preparatory Volume with Reference Lists and Reports* (New York, 1945; rev. & enl. edn., 1946).

GRACE, EDWARD: *Letters of a West African Trader: Edward Grace, 1767-70* (T. S. Ashton, ed., London, 1950).

HIPPISLEY, JOHN: *Essays: I. On the Populousness of Africa; II. On the Trade at the Forts on the Gold Coast; III. On the Necessity of Erecting a Fort at Cape Appolonia . . .* (London, 1764).

LE VAILLANT, FRANÇOIS: *Travels from the Cape of Good Hope into the Interior Parts of Africa* (London, 1790) and *New Travels into the Interior Parts of Africa* (London, 1796).

MOOR, FRANCIS: *Travels into the Inland Parts of Africa . . .* (2 pts., London, 1738).

O'CONNOR, MR.: *Considerations on the Trade to Africa . . .* (London, 1749).

OWEN, NICHOLAS: *Journal of a Slave Dealer: "A View of Some Remarkable Axcedents [sic] in the Life of Nics. Owen on the Coast of Africa and America from the Year 1746 to the Year 1757"* (Eveline C. Martin, ed., London, 1930).

[POSTLETHWAYT, MALACHY]: *The African Trade: The Pillar & Support of the British Plantation Trade in America* (London, 1745).

———: *In Honour to the Administration: The Importance of the African Expedition Considered with Copies of the Memorials . . .* (London, 1758).

———: *The National and Private Advantages of the African Trade Considered* (London, 1746; 2nd edn., 1772).

The Present State of the British and French Trade to Africa and America Consider'd and Compar'd: With Some Propositions in Favour of the Trade of Great Britain (London, 1745). Sabin suggests that John Ashley may have been the author.

[ROBERTS, JOHN]: *Considerations on the Present Peace as Far as It Is Relative to the Colonies and the African Trade* (London, 1763). Captain Roberts was Governor of Cape Coast Castle.

———: *Cursory Observations on the African Trade . . . Submitted to the Consideration of Parliament* ([London, 1778]).

———: *Extracts from an Account of the State of the British Forts on the Gold Coast of Africa . . . to Which Are Added Observations . . .* (n.p., 1778).

SMITH, WILLIAM: *A New Voyage to Guinea* (London [1744]).

SNELGRAVE, WILLIAM: *A New Account of Guinea and the Slave Trade . . .* (London, 1754). A defence of the slave trade, first published in 1734.

A Treatise upon the Trade from Great Britain to Africa: Humbly Recommended to the Attention of Parliament. By an African Merchant (London, 1772). The "treatise" is an argument for government support of the African trade.

WINTERBOTTOM, THOMAS: *An Account of the Native Africans in the Neighborhood of Sierra Leone* (London, 1803).

C. SECONDARY WORKS

BANDINEL, JAMES: *Some Account of the Trade in Slaves from Africa as Connected with Europe and America* (London, 1842).

BURNS, ALAN CUTHBERT: *History of Nigeria* (1st edn., London, 1929; 5th edn., c. 1955).

CLARIDGE, WILLIAM WALTON: *A History of the Gold Coast and Ashanti: From the Earliest Times to . . . [1900]* (2 vols., London, 1915). Volume I, part 3 describes the rise of Ashanti and the relations of the British factories for this period.

CLARKSON, THOMAS: *The History of the . . . Abolition of the Slave Trade by the British Parliament* (2 vols., London, 1808; 3 vols., New York, 1836).

DALZELL, ARCHIBALD: *The History of Dahomy, an Inland Kingdom of Africa: Compiled from Authentic Memoirs with an Introduction and Notes* (London, 1793).

DAVIES, KENNETH GORDON: *The Royal African Company* (London & New York, 1957).

ELLIS, ALFRED BURDON: *History of the Gold Coast of West Africa* (London, 1893).

FAGE, J. D.: *An Introduction to the History of West Africa* (Cambridge, Eng., 1955).

GALLACHER, J.: "Economic Relations in Africa and the Far East, Part I," *The New Cambridge Modern History* (J. O. Lindsay, ed., Cambridge, Eng., 1957), VII: 566-79.

GEORGE, KATHERINE: "The Civilized West Looks at Primitive Africa: 1400-1800: A Study in Ethnocentrism," *Isis*, XLIX (1958), 62-72.

GRAY, JOHN MILNER: *A History of the Gambia . . .* (Cambridge, Eng., 1940).

HERBERTSON, ANDREW JOHN, and O. J. R. HOWARTH: *Oxford Survey of the British Empire, Vol. III: Africa* (Oxford, Eng., 1914).

HYDE, FRANCIS E., BRADBURY B. PARKINSON, and SHEILA MARRINER: "The

Nature and Profitability of the Liverpool Slave Trade [1768-1788]," *Economic History Review*, 2nd ser., V (1952-3), 368-77.

LUCAS, CHARLES PRESTWOOD: *A Historical Geography of the British Colonies, Vol. III: West Africa* (2nd edn., Oxford, Eng., 1900).

MARTIN, EVELINE C.: *The British West African Settlements, 1750-1821: A Study in Local Administration*, Royal Colonial Institute, *Imperial Studies*, No. 2 (London & New York, 1927). See also by the same writer: "The English Establishments on the Gold Coast in the Second Half of the Eighteenth Century," Royal Historical Society, *Transactions*, 4th series, V (1922), 167-208, and "The English Slave Trade and the African Settlements," *The Cambridge History of the British Empire, Vol. I: The Old Empire . . . to 1783* pp. 437-59.

MASON, GEORGE C.: "The African Slave Trade in Colonial Times," *American Historical Record* . . . , I (1872), 311-19, 338-45.

MEREDITH, HENRY: *An Account of the Gold Coast of Africa: With a Brief History of the African Company* (London, 1812). Meredith stressed the advantages of the Gold Coast as a source of supply for sugar, coffee, cotton, indigo, etc.

PARK, MUNGO: *Travels in the Interior Districts of Africa: Perform'd Under the Direction and Patronage of the African Association in the Years 1795, 1796, and 1797* . . . (Bryan Edwards, ed., London, 1799).

REINDORF, C. C.: *History of the Gold Coast and Asiante: Based on Traditions and Historical Facts . . . [1500-1860]* (Basel, Switzerland, 1895).

SHERIDAN, R. B.: "The Commercial and Financial Organization of the British Slave Trade, 1750-1807," *Economic History Review*, 2nd ser., XI (1958-9), 249-63.

SYPHER, WYLIE: *Guinea's Captive Kings: British Anti-Slavery Literature of the XVIIIth Century* (Chapel Hill, N. C., 1942).

WARD, W. E. F.: *A History of Ghana* (2nd edn., rev., London, 1958; 1st edn., published under the title *A History of the Gold Coast*, 1948).

ZOOK, GEORGE FREDERICK: *The Company of Royal Adventurers Trading into Africa* (Lancaster, Pa., 1919); rep. from the *Journal of Negro History*, IV (1919), pp. 134-231.

D. MAPS

ANVILLE, JEAN BAPTISTE BOURGUINON D': *Carte Particulière de la Côte Occidentale de l'Afrique . . . 1751*. In a collection of 48 d'Anville maps bound together without title. Paris, 1771, Nos. 32-3. Map Division, New York Public Library.

BELLIN, JACQUES NICOLAS: *Carte Réduite Des Costes Occidentales d'Afrique Depuis l'Equateur jusqu'au Vingtieme Degré de Latitude Méridionale Comprenant les Isles de St. Thomé et du Prince, Les Costes d'Angole, de Congo, de Loango* . . . ([Paris], 1754). In *Hydrographie Française* . . . , No. 89. A second edition, corrected, was published in Paris in 1765.

Carte de l'Entrée de la Rivière de Sanaga ou Senegal. In Bellin: *Le Petit Atlas Maritime* . . . , III: No. 95.

Carte de la Rivière de Gambra ou Gambie . . . . In *ibid.*, III: No. 101.

Carte du Golfe de Benin et Partie de la Côte de Guinée . . . . In *ibid.*, III: No. 107.

Coste de Guinée Depuis le Cap Apollonia jusqu'à la Rivière de Valta ou la Coste d'Or. In *ibid.*, III: No. 106.

Costes du Senegal depuis le Cap Blanc jusqu'à la Rivière de Gambie. In *ibid.*, III: No. 95.

KITCHIN, THOMAS: *Africa According to M. D'Anville, with Several Additions & Improvements* . . . . In Kitchin: *A General Atlas* . . . , Nos. 26 and 27. An inset on this plate is entitled, *Particular Chart of the Gold Coast wherein are Distinguished all the European Forts and Factories.*

A New and Correct Map of the Coast of Africa . . . *1746.* In Malachy Postlethwayt: *The National and Private Advantages of the African Trade Considered* . . . (London, 1746).

NORRIS, ROBERT, *et al.*: *The African Pilot* (London, 1801; another edn., 1816).

Plan de l'Isle de Goré Avec ses Fortifications. In Bellin: *Le Petit Atlas Maritime* . . . , III: No. 99.

SAYER, R.: *Africa* (London, 1772). Library of Congress Maps.

GIBRALTAR, MINORCA, AND THE MEDITERRANEAN AREA

A. PRINTED SOURCE MATERIALS AND SECONDARY WORKS

ABBOTT, WILBUR C.: *An Introduction to the Documents Relating to the International Status of Gibraltar, 1704-1934* (New York, 1934).

ANDERSON, M. S.: "Great Britain and the Barbary States in the Eighteenth Century," London University Institute of Historical Research, *Bulletin*, XXIX (1956), 87-107.

ARMSTRONG, JOHN: *The History of the Island of Minorca* (London, 1752; 2nd edn., 1756).

CARRINGTON, C. E.: *Gibraltar, Chatham House Memoranda*, Royal Institute of International Affairs (London, 1956; reiss., w/add., 1958).

CONN, STETSON: *Gibraltar in British Diplomacy in the Eighteenth Century*, *Yale Historical Publications: Miscellany*, XLI (New Haven, Conn.,

GARRATT, GEOFFREY THEODORE: *Gibraltar and the Mediterranean* (London & New York, 1939). There are three chapters dealing with the eighteenth century.

Gibraltar a Bulwark of Great Britain . . . with Proposals for Erecting a Civil Magistracy There and for Lessening [the expense] . . . in Maintaining That Garrison . . . By a Gentleman of the Navy (2nd edn., London, 1725). Early but excellent for background material.

LOPEZ DE AYALÁ, IGNACIO: *Historia de Gibraltar . . .* (2 pts., Madrid, 1782; trans. & cont'd by James Bell: *The History of Gibraltar*, London, 1845).

MARSHALL, F. H.: "A Greek Community in Minorca," *Slavonic and East European Review*, XI (1932-3), 100-7.

MONK, WINSTON FRANCIS: *Britain in the Western Mediterranean* (London & New York, 1953).

RICHMOND, HERBERT WILLIAM, ed.: *Papers Relating to the Loss of Minorca in 1756*, Navy Records Society, *Publications*, XLII (London, 1913).

The Royal Charter for Establishing a Civil Government at Gibraltar to Which Is Prefixed a Prefatory Discourse Recapitulating the Benefits which Have Been Proposed Therefrom (London, 1742). Dated the tenth of May 1740.

[SINCLAIR, JOHN]: *The Propriety of Retaining Gibraltar Impartially Considered* (London, 1783).

[STEPHENS, FREDERICK G.]: *A History of Gibraltar and Its Sieges* (London, 1870).

The Trial of the Honourable John Byng at a Court Martial . . . (Dublin & London, 1757).

TUNSTALL, BRIAN: *Admiral Byng and the Loss of Minorca* (London, 1928).

B. MAPS

Gibraltar

GIBSON, JOHN, sculp.: *Plan of Gibraltar*. In the *Gentleman's Magazine*, XXXII (1762), opp. p. 104.

Plan de Gibraltar. In Bellin: *Le Petit Atlas Maritime . . .*, IV: No. 60.

Minorca

BOWEN, EMANUEL: *Minorca, Taken from an Original Drawing of an Actual Survey of the Island: With Some Improvements by Eman. Bowen . . . [1756]*. Library of Congress Maps.

A Correct Map of the Island of Minorca, 1752. In John Armstrong: *The History of the Island of Minorca* (London, 1756), frontispiece.

Isle de Minorque. In Bellin: *Le Petit Atlas Maritime . . .*, IV: No. 66.

A New and Accurate Map of the Island of Minorca with the Town and

Harbour of Mahon, & St. Philips Castle & Fortifications. In Entick: *The History of the Late War* . . . , I: opp. p. 332.

Plan de la Ville et du Fort Saint-Philippe dans L'Isle de Minorque: Assiézée le 8 Mai par l'Armée Française . . . . In Richard Waddington: *Louis XV et le Renversement des Alliances: Préliminaires de la Guerre de Sept Ans, 1754-1756* (Paris, 1896), opp. p. 460.

Plan du Port et Ville de Mahon avec ses Forts. In Bellin: *Le Petit Atlas Maritime* . . . , IV: No. 67.

CHAPTER IX

Geographical Aids

A. BIBLIOGRAPHY

BOWLES, CARINGTON: *New and Enlarged Catalogue of Useful and Accurate Maps, Charts, and Plans* (London [1786]).

BRITISH MUSEUM: *Catalogue of the Manuscript Maps, Charts, and Plans, and of the Topographical Drawings in the British Museum* (3 vols., London, 1844-61).

BROWN, LLOYD A.: *The Story of Maps* (Boston, 1949).

BRUZEN DEL LA MARTINIÈRE, ANTOINE AUGUSTIN: *Le Grand Dictionaire Géographique, Historique et Critique* . . . (2nd edn., 6 vols., Paris, 1768).

CHUBB, THOMAS: *The Printed Maps in the Atlases of Great Britain and Ireland: A Bibliography, 1579-1870* (London, 1927).

DOUGLAS, ROBERT KENNAWAY: *Catalogue of the Printed Maps, Plans, and Charts in the British Museum* (2 vols., London, 1885).

FORDHAM, HERBERT GEORGE: *Hand-List of Catalogues and Works of Reference Relating to Carto-Bibliography and Kindred Subjects for Great Britain and Ireland, 1720 to 1927* (Cambridge, Eng., 1928).

GOUGH, RICHARD: *British Topography: Or, An Historical Account of What Has Been Done for Illustrating the Topographical Antiquities of Great Britain and Ireland* (2 vols., London, 1780). This gives an exhaustive description, among other things, of maps.

HOLMDEN, H. R.: *Catalogue of Maps, Plans and Charts in the Map Room of the Dominion [of Canada] Archives* (Ottawa, 1912).

INDIA OFFICE: *A Catalogue of . . . Maps . . . of the Indian Surveys* (London, 1878).

MUSEUM BOOK STORE: *A Catalogue of Maps of America from the Middle of the Sixteeth to the Middle of the Nineteenth Centuries* (London, 1924). Most of these maps are now in the Huntington Library at San Marino, California.

PARGELLIS, STANLEY, and D. J. MEDLEY: "Maps," *Bibliography of British History: The Eighteenth Century, 1714-1789* (Oxford, Eng., 1951), pp. 370-4.

PHILLIPS, PHILIP LEE: *A List of Geographical Atlases in the Library of Congress* (4 vols., Washington, D.C., 1909-20).

———: *A List of Maps of America in the Library of Congress* (Washington, D.C., 1901).

TOOLEY, R. V.: *Maps and Map-Makers* (London, 1949; 2nd edn., rev., c. 1952, 1962).

B. ATLASES AND COLLECTIONS OF MAPS

ADAMS, RANDOLPH GREENFIELD: *British Headquarters Maps and Sketches* . . . [relating to the War for American Independence] (Ann Arbor, Mich., 1928).

ANVILLE, JEAN BAPTISTE BOURGUIGNON D': *Atlas Général* (Paris, 1727 to 1780 editions), and *Atlas de Toutes les Parties Connues du Globe Terrestre* . . . (Paris, 1798).

BELLIN, JACQUES NICOLAS: *Atlas Maritime* (Paris, 1751); *Description Géographique des Antilles* (Paris, 1758); *Hydrographie Française,* covering the period 1737-1776, in various editions, one of which in two volumes is limited to maps drawn between the years 1756 and 1765; *Mémoirs sur Cartes des Côtes de l'Amérique* (Paris, 1755); and *Petit Atlas Maritime* (5 vols., Paris, 1764), with 581 maps.

BOWEN, EMANUEL: *A Complete System of Geography: Being a Description of . . . the Known World* (2 vols., London, 1747), and *A Complete Atlas or Distinct View of the Known World* . . . (London, 1752).

———, and THOMAS KITCHIN: *The Larger English Atlas* (London, 1755), and their *Royal English Atlas* (London, 1762; 1778). The maps, as the title of each atlas implies, relate to England.

CARY, JOHN: *Cary's New Universal Atlas Containing Distinct Maps of All the Principal States and Kingdoms Throughout the World* (London, 1808; 2nd edn., 1819). Contain 60 maps.

CUMMING, WILLIAM P.: *The Southeast in Early Maps* . . . (Princeton, N.J., 1958).

DES BARRES, JOSEPH FREDERICK WALSH: *The Atlantic Neptune: Published for the Use of the Royal Navy of Great Britain* (London, 1774-84).

HALLEY, EDMOND: *Atlas Maritimus et Commercialis . . . Describing All the Coasts, Ports, Harbours, and Noted Rivers* (London, 1728). The collection, which contains many excellent maps, is apparently based on the work of such map-makers as John Harris, John Senex, and Henry Wilson.

HULBERT, A. B.: *The Crown Collection of Photographs of American Maps*

(Ser. I, 5 vols., Cleveland, O. [1904-08]; Ser. II, 5 vols., [Harrow, Eng., 1909-12]; Ser. III [1914-16]). Series I and II consists of maps in the British Museum while Series III contains maps in the Public Record Office.

————: *Historic Highways of America* (16 vols., Cleveland, O., 1902-05). Vols. I-VI are pertinent.

HUTCHINS, THOMAS: *The Courses of the Ohio River. Taken by Lt. T. Hutchins, anno 1766 and . . . Maps*, Beverly W. Bond, Jr., ed., Ohio Historical and Philosophical Society, *Publications* (Cincinnati, O., 1942); *An Historical Narrative and Topographical Description of Louisiana and West Florida . . .* (Philadelphia, 1784); and *A Topographical Description of Virginia, Pennsylvania, Maryland, and North Carolina . . .* (London, 1778).

INGLIS, HARRY R. G., JOHN MATHIESON, and CHARLES B. B. WATSON: *The Early Maps of Scotland . . .* (Edinburgh, 1934; 2nd edn., 1936).

JEFFERYS, THOMAS: *The American Atlas: Or, A Geographical Description of the Whole Continent of America . . .* (London, 1776; 1778); *A Description of the Spanish Islands and Settlements on the Coast of the East Indies . . .* (London, 1762); *A General Topography of North America and the West Indies* (London, 1768); and *The Natural and Civil History of the French Dominions in North and South America . . . Illustrated with Maps and Plans . . . Collected from the Best Authorities . . .* (London, 1760, 1761).

KARPINSKI, LOUIS CHARLES: *Manuscript Maps Printed Prior to 1800, Relating to America . . .* (n.p. [1927]); a collection of 986 map facsimiles to be found in many of the larger American libraries. See also his "Cartographical Collections in America," *Imago Mundi*, Part I (Berlin, 1935).

KITCHIN, THOMAS: *Geographia Scotiae: Being New and Correct Maps of all . . . Scotland* (London, 1749).

LEWIS, SAMUEL: *A Topographical Dictionary of England . . .* (London, 1831; 5th edn., 1844), with a portfolio of maps; *A Topographical Dictionary of Ireland . . .* (London, 1847); and *A Topographical Dictionary of Scotland . . .* (London, 1846).

LOWERY, WOODBURY: *The Lowery Collection: A Descriptive List of Maps of the Spanish Possessions Within the Present Limits of the United States, 1502-1820* (P. L. Phillips, ed., Washington, D.C., 1912).

MOLL, HERMANN: *The World Described: Or, A New and Correct Sett [sic] of Maps, 1709-20* (London, 1709-1758).

A New Geographical Dictionary (2 vols., London, 1759-60).

MORRIS, ROBERT, WILLIAM WOODVILLE, et al.: *The African Pilot* (London, 1801; 1816).

RENNELL, JAMES: *A Bengal Atlas: Containing Maps of the Theatre of War and Commerce on that Side of Hindoostan. Compiled from Original Surveys* (London, 1781).

ROCQUE [JOHN and] ANN: *A Set of Plans and Forts in America Reduced from Actual Surveys, 1765* ([London], 1765). Contains 30 maps and plans.

SALMON, THOMAS: *A New Geographical and Historical Grammar* (London, 1754).

———, et al.: *A New Universal Atlas Exhibiting All the Empires, Kingdoms, States . . . in the Whole World: Being a Complete Collection of the Most Approved Maps Extant* . . . (London, 1795; numerous edns. to 1805).

WHITTLE, J., and R. H. LAURIE: *The Complete East India Pilot* . . . (London, 1800; another edn., 1816).

WINSOR, JUSTIN: *The Kohl Collection (now in the Library of Congress) of Maps Relating to America* (Washington, D.C., 1904); Winsor's *Narrative and Critical History of America* also contains much valuable cartographical material.

Index

Since the table of contents includes a detailed analysis of the volume's divisions, the index is confined to a single list of authors and selected topics not referred to in the table of contents. A page number preceded by an asterisk indicates an author, editor, compiler or translator.

LAWRENCE HENRY GIPSON is Research Professor of History, Emeritus, at Lehigh University. After receiving a bachelor of arts degree from the University of Idaho, he entered Oxford as the first Rhodes Scholar from the state of Idaho; there he gained a degree in the Oxford Honours School of Modern History. He was later a Bulkley Fellow in the graduate school at Yale, where his doctoral dissertation, *Jared Ingersoll: A Study of American Loyalism in Relation to British Colonial Government*, received the Porter Prize as the best work in literary form presented by a student in any division of the university during the preceding year; it was also awarded the Justin Winsor Prize by the American Historical Association. Since then he has written and published many works relating to colonial history (including fourteen volumes of his *magnum opus*—Volume XV, a guide to manuscripts relating to the British Empire, 1748–1776, is in preparation). During the academic year 1951–2 he occupied the Harmsworth Chair in American History at Oxford; he also has been a member of the board of editors of the *American Historical Review*, was a founder of the Conference on Early American History, and is a past president of both the Conference on British Studies and the Pennsylvania Historical Association. He was the Honorary Consultant in American Colonial History to the Library of Congress for the period 1965 through 1967. Many prizes and honours have come to him as a result of his writing, including the Loubat, Bancroft, and Pulitzer prizes and, most recently, his election as Honorary Fellow of Lincoln College, Oxford University.

A NOTE ON THE TYPE

THE TEXT of this book is set in Caledonia, a typeface designed by W(ILLIAM) A(DDISON) DWIGGINS for the Mergenthaler Linotype Company in 1939. Dwiggins chose to call his new typeface Caledonia, the Roman name for Scotland, because it was inspired by the Scotch types cast about 1833 by Alexander Wilson & Son, Glasgow type founders. However, there is a calligraphic quality about this face that is totally lacking in the Wilson types. Dwiggins referred to an even earlier typeface for this "liveliness of action"— one cut around 1790 by William Martin for the printer William Bulmer. Caledonia has more weight than the Martin letters, and the bottom finishing strokes (serifs) of the letters are cut straight across, without brackets, to make sharp angles with the upright stems, thus giving a "modern face" appearance.

W. A. Dwiggins (1880–1956) was born in Martinsville, Ohio, and studied art in Chicago. In 1904 he moved to Hingham, Massachusetts, where he built a solid reputation as a designer of advertisements and as a calligrapher. He began an association with the Mergenthaler Linotype Company in 1929 and over the next twenty-seven years designed a number of book types for that firm. Of especial interest are the Metro series, Electra, Caledonia, Eldorado, and Falcon. In 1930, Dwiggins first became interested in marionettes, and through the years made many important contributions to the art of puppetry and the design of marionettes.

Composed, printed, and bound by
The Haddon Craftsmen, Inc., Scranton, Pa.
Typography and binding design by
W. A. DWIGGINS